FICTIONING

For Plastique Fantastique

FICTIONING

The Myth-Functions of
Contemporary Art and Philosophy

David Burrows and Simon O'Sullivan

EDINBURGH
University Press

Edinburgh University Press is one of the leading university presses in the UK. We publish academic books and journals in our selected subject areas across the humanities and social sciences, combining cutting-edge scholarship with high editorial and production values to produce academic works of lasting importance. For more information visit our website: edinburghuniversitypress.com

Edinburgh University Press Ltd
The Tun – Holyrood Road, 12(2f) Jackson's Entry, Edinburgh EH8 8PJ

Typeset in Warnock Pro
by Biblichor Ltd, Edinburgh

A CIP record for this book is available from the British Library

ISBN 978 1 4744 3239 9 (hardback)
ISBN 978 1 4744 3241 2 (webready PDF)
ISBN 978 1 4744 3240 5 (paperback)
ISBN 978 1 4744 3242 9 (epub)

Contents

List of Figures

Acknowledgements

THANKS TO Jon K. Shaw for his careful and attentive reading of a draft of the book and his many helpful suggestions; to Lucy R. Sames for help with picture research; to Tim Clark for his thorough copy-editing; and to Carol Macdonald for her faith in us and support for this project. Thanks are also due to Mark Harris and Gary Genosko for comments at an early stage of our research. Martin Holbraad provided invaluable perspectives on anthropological material and myth as well as the diagram of perspectivism in Chapter 10.

Many of the artworks, texts and pieces of music addressed in our book have been discussed in the Undergraduate Fine Art Media Reading Group at the Slade School of Fine Art, UCL. The contributions and insights of individuals attending the group have been important for shaping questions about the material attended to in this book. Similarly, the students attending the 'Fictioning: From Control to Myth-Science' course on the Undergraduate BA Art History and BA Fine Art and Art History programmes in the Department of Visual Cultures at Goldsmiths College have provided important insights for the development of our concepts and perspectives on fictioning.

Versions of some of the material in the book have been presented at various conferences and panels or as lectures, and we want to take this opportunity to thank all those who offered invitations, hosted us and interrogated our project at different stages.

We are also grateful to the artists and writers, and to their galleries, publishers, management and estates, who have given permission for the reproduction of the images.

Finally, as well as friends and colleagues – too many to name here – this book has also drawn more particularly on our collaboration Plastique Fantastique, and we owe a great debt to all who have participated in this performance fiction. In particular, thanks are due to our collaborators Alex Marzeta, Vanessa Page, Mark Jackson,

Motsonian, Harriet Skully, Lawrence Leaman, Simon Davenport, Joe Murray, Stuart Tait, Ana Benelloch, Samudradaka and Aryapala.

Parts of Chapter 1 appeared in Simon O'Sullivan, 'Myth-Science and the Fictioning of Reality', *Paragrana*, 25.2 (2016): 80–93; and Simon O'Sullivan, 'Memories of a Deleuzian: To Think is Always to Follow the Witches Flight', *A Thousand Plateaus and Philosophy*, ed. H. Somers-Hall, J. Bell and J. Williams, Edinburgh: Edinburgh University Press, 2016, pp. 172–89. Parts of Chapter 2 appeared in Simon O'Sullivan, 'Deleuze Against Control: from Fictioning to Myth-Science', *Theory, Culture and Society*, 33.7–8 (2016): 1–16. An earlier version of Chapter 4 appeared as David Burrows, 'Obliteration Through Self-Love', *Black Mirror I: Embodiment*, ed. J. Noble, D. Shepard, J. Bransford, R. Ansell and M. Cos, Somerset: Fulgur, 2016, pp. 136–57. An earlier version of Chapter 5 appeared as Simon O'Sullivan, 'Myth-Science as Residual Culture and Magical Thinking', *Postmedieval*, 9.4 (2018). Parts of Chapters 7 and 12 appeared in Simon O'Sullivan, 'Fictioning the Landscape: Robert Smithson and Ruins in Reverse', *Take On Art Magazine*, 3.2 (2017): 60–3; and Simon O'Sullivan, 'Fictioning the Landscape', *Journal of Aesthetics and Phenomenology*, 5.1 (2018): 53–65. Parts of Chapter 8 appeared in Simon O'Sullivan, 'Mythopoesis or Fiction as Mode of Existence: Three Case Studies from Contemporary Art', *Visual Culture in Britain*, 18.2 (2017): 292–311. Parts of Chapter 9 appeared in Simon O'Sullivan, 'Mythopoesis, Scenes and Performance Fictions: Two Case Studies (Crass and Thee Temple ov Psychick Youth)', *Parasol: Journal for the Centre of Experimental Ontology*, 2 (2017): 94–106. Parts of Chapter 16 appeared in Simon O'Sullivan, 'From Science Fiction to Science Fictioning: SF's Traction on the Real', *Foundation: The International Review Of Science Fiction*, 46.1 (2017): 74–84. Parts of Chapter 17 appeared in Simon O'Sullivan, 'Non-Philosophy and Art Practice (or, Fiction as Method)', *Fiction as Method*, ed. J. K. Shaw and T. Reeves-Evisson, Berlin: Sternberg, 2017, pp. 277–324. Parts of of Chapter 18 appeared in Simon O'Sullivan, 'Accelerationism, Prometheanism and Mythotechnesis', *Aesthetics After Finitude*, ed. B. Brits, P. Gibson and A. Ireland, Melbourne: re.press, 2017, pp. 171–89. An earlier version of Chapter 19 appeared as David Burrows, 'The Subject Who Fell To Earth', *The Psychopathologies of Cognitive Capitalism: Part Three*, ed. W. Niedich, Berlin: Archive Books, 2017, pp. 431–51. Parts of Chapter 21 appeared in Simon O'Sullivan, 'From Financial Fictions to Mythotechnesis', *Futures and Fictions*, ed. A. Hameed, H. Gunkel and S. O'Sullivan, London: Repeater, 2017, pp. 318–46.

All of the above have been substantially re-worked in collaboration for the present volume.

Introduction

What the artist seeks ... is the fiction reality will sooner or later imitate.

Robert Smithson, *The Collected Writings*

Fictioning

Our book defines and maps out a set of practices and theories of mythopoesis, myth-science and mythotechnesis (and the related terms of performance fictioning, science fictioning and machine fictioning). These are what we call the myth-functions of contemporary art and philosophy. We do not address our three myth-functions as exclusive of each other, for they seem to us to overlap in many of the examples we gather together in this volume. Mythopoesis is proposed as productive of worlds, people and communities to come, often drawing upon residual and emergent cultures. Myth-science functions by producing alternate perspectives and models, revealing habits of thought concerning physical, historical and social realities as yet more myth. Lastly, mythotechnesis concerns the ways in which technology enters into discourse and life, through projections of the existing and future influence of machines. We are also interested, especially as our book progresses, in a related theme: how these practices and theories are often engaged in speculations concerning future human and non-human modes of existence, particularly in relation to the potential of the body or what might be better called embodiment.

As implied above and, of course, foregrounded by the main title of our book, our key concept in this critical survey is *fictioning*. This is a concept – and mode of operation – common to mythopoesis, myth-science and mythotechnesis, each of which *fiction* reality in different ways. By using the term fiction as a verb we refer to the writing, imaging, performing or other material instantiation of worlds or social bodies that mark out trajectories different to those engendered by the dominant organisations of life currently in existence. Or, to put this another way, we are interested in exploring those fictions that involve potential realities to come – as our epigraph from the artist Robert Smithson suggests – as well as the more general idea of fiction as intervention in, and augmentation of, existing reality. In this, we are also concerned with how fictioning can take on a critical power when it is set against, or foregrounded within, a given reality.

We should say from the outset that the term fictioning is not our own invention and we develop and expand a concept that is found, though not widely used, in continental philosophy. Jeffrey A. Bell, for example, articulates fiction as a verb in his book *Philosophy at the Edge of Chaos: Gilles Deleuze and the Philosophy of Difference* (2006), when addressing Nietzsche's rejection of Plato's caution regarding poetry. Bell suggests that Plato is disturbed by the fictioning essence of poetry, for such invention should belong only to the Gods:

> The fictioning of the 'ideas', in other words, occurs in the supersensuous realm 'above heaven'. For Nietzsche, on the other hand, the fictioning occurs in the sensuous realm of life, and it is only as a consequence of life that the notion of the supersensuous 'ideas' comes about (i.e. are 'fictioned'). (Bell 2006: 77)

We quote Bell here firstly to point to a definition of fictioning as invention in the realm of life (a technology of immanence as it were), and secondly to show how fictioning is a troublesome mode (at least for Plato) in so far as it destabilises order (not least that between gods and mortal humans).

This theme of fictioning as disruptive of order is also discussed by Max Statkiewicz in *Rhapsody of Philosophy: Dialogues with Plato in Contemporary Thought* (2009). Statkiewicz quotes the philosopher Philippe Lacoue-Labarthe, who suggests that Plato is aware that discourse would have no 'fictioning power' if it did not have the capacity to dramatise, but that this power of fictioning is also a problem in Plato's ideal society, the Republic (Statkiewicz 2009: 50). Statkiewicz notes that Plato is wary of mimesis and play, for unlike narration, such simulation (the acting out of something, the copying of a member of another class, the impersonation of someone else) threatens the social order (51). In this it becomes clear that it is not exactly mimesis and play that are the problem, but that narration or simple diegesis can become contaminated by mimesis and play (53). More than this, Statkiewicz points out that Plato's Socrates is himself a mixture of modes – a rhapsodic philosophical character – being, at different times, a narrator, a fabricator and playful (53). Indeed, Statkiewicz asserts that mimesis or play can be found in all literary productions, even 'pure narrative' (54). Although we are not interested in mimesis as such, we find Statkiewicz's observations insightful here, since play (as performance) is an important theme that we return to throughout our investigation of fictioning practices.

Following this account of Plato's thinking about fictioning, Statkiewicz goes on to address Heidegger's critique of Plato's opposition of philosophy and poetry in order to further interrogate the problem. He explains that Heidegger's concern for poetry as a mode of unconcealment informs the German philosopher's notion that being has 'in the last analysis a fictioning, poetic essence' (57). In fact, for Heidegger, all reasoning involves fictioning, which is reason enough (for Statkiewicz at least) to account for Heidegger's valorisation of poetry.

Statkiewicz goes on to attend to a further figure, Gilles Deleuze, and his thoughts concerning absolute simulacra (without referent) which put 'into question the very notion of copy and model', noting that Deleuze would allow simulacra to escape Plato's cavern or resist elevation, or to even 'search for "another cave beyond, always another in which to hide"' (109). Following Deleuze, Statkiewicz himself suggests that:

> Instead of thinking of philosophy and poetry or mimesis as facing each other, we should rather consider there to be two kinds of the theater of philosophy: the representational (Aristotelian, neoclassical) and the fantastic (Nietzsche's 'Dionysian Machine'). It is the latter that Deleuze regards as the essence of modern art, striving to become 'a veritable *theatre* of metamorphoses and permutations'. (110)

In Statkiewicz's quoting of Deleuze, then, we find a further definition of fictioning, as 'a veritable *theatre* of metamorphoses and permutations', one that involves a collapsing of any hierarchical distinction between art and philosophy. This is one further theme of our book.

If the problem of fictioning – this tension between modes of narration and play, and between modes that would be identified as producing truth or unconcealment and fiction or simulacra – has long been explored in philosophy, then today we also find it increasingly addressed in the practices of, and commentary on, contemporary art. An interrogation of this more contemporary instantiation of an old problem is found in Carrie Lambert-Beatty's article 'Make-Believe: Parafiction and Plausibility' (2009), which attends to contemporary art practices concerned with deception and dissimulation (often with the intention of exploring possibilities for art as activism or political critique, as with *The Yes Men* or *The Atlas Group*). While Lambert-Beatty uses the term parafiction rather than fictioning, it is clear that she has identified something important about contemporary fictioning practices in art. To quote from the beginning of her article:

> Fiction or fictiveness has emerged as an important category in recent art. But, like a paramedic as opposed to a medical doctor, a parafiction is related to but not quite

a member of the category of fiction as established in literary and dramatic art. It remains a bit outside. It does not perform its procedures in the hygienic clinics of literature, but has one foot in the field of the real. Unlike historical fiction's fact-based but imagined worlds, in parafiction real and/or imaginary personages and stories intersect with the world as it is being lived. Post-simulacral, parafictional strategies are oriented less toward the disappearance of the real than toward the pragmatics of trust. Simply put, with various degrees of success, for various durations, and for various purposes, these fictions are experienced as fact. (Lambert-Beatty 2009: 54)

Here we would agree with Lambert-Beatty and add that fictioning has efficacy – that it only has a power – when involving or addressing life or reality and, most importantly, through a play of fiction *as* life and reality.

Such a blurring between fact (or truth) and fiction is troubling for many, precisely because the orders of reality and representation are seen to be elided by fictioning, sometimes with problematic results. Dana A. Williams (2016), who writes about cultural practices that explore *blackness* and other aspects of diasporic experience, views fictioning in just such negative terms and as potentially supporting a (sometimes unknowing) racial myth-making; the problem for Williams is that fictioning can result from 'conditioning' rather than attending to 'historicity' (836). To develop her critique, Williams draws and comments upon Wole Soyinka's book *Of Africa* (2012), in which fictioning, as a political act, is described as having the potential to fuel a cycle of repetition, sustaining oppressive narratives and organisations (2016: 836). Soyinka warns that 'first-comers in the stakes of power after colonialism . . . actualize power, then fictionalize a people' (2012: 52). We do not take this caution lightly and note that in a chapter titled 'Fictioning the Fourth Dimension', Soyinka, while conceding that the motives to fictionalise can be positive, is distrustful of fictioning as it may lead towards a 'slide down the chute of emotionalism and drop into the ancient pit of self-gratification' (54). While we do not think historicity should dictate the forms that invention take, this important criticism of fictioning – as a mode that can perpetuate problematic myths – needs heeding and suggests to us that fictioning practices (or at least books addressing fictioning) which intend critical or radical ends need to guard against reiterating dominant or existing forms of fictions and myth.

We understand the dangers that Soyinka identifies, and it is true that a number of practices we examine (particularly in section one), though undermining dominant myths, potentially (and unknowingly) support problematic narratives too. We have attempted to identify and discuss this problem throughout the book (when and where we find it) but remain convinced (and hope to convince our readers too) that there exist fictioning practices engaged in experimenting with alternatives to oppressive narratives and organisations.

We find a definition of experimental fictioning offered by the contemporary artist John Russell, who recognises the problem of repetitive acts that sustain existing regimes whilst also insisting that fictioning can be productive of different realities or relations to come (Russell 2011a). In this, fictioning is identified with performative gestures or enunciations, an example being the moment when a judge declares an individual 'guilty' and the accused becomes a prisoner. The judge's enunciation does not physically change anything, but everything changes in terms of the accused's relations. This example is borrowed by Russell (2011a: 75) from a passage in Gilles Deleuze and Félix Guattari's *A Thousand Plateaus* (1988: 80–1) which comments on the notion of enunciations as statements marking roles or positions within a number of discursive regimes. This theory is itself borrowed from Michel Foucault, who asserts that new statements, though rare, can result from enunciations that mutate or traverse more than one structure or regime (Foucault 1972: 105–25). While we take on board Foucault's insistence on the rarity of new statements, we look for and address fictioning practices that generate precisely this, something different rather than more of the same.

Russell extends his analysis of fictioning by tracing a theoretical thread from J. L. Austin's notion of a performative utterance as a promise – as when the words 'I do' are said in a marriage ceremony – to Jacques Derrida's critical interpretation of this act as a reiteration of existing social conventions and relations, and, further, to Judith Butler's exploration of the performativity of gender (Russell 2011a: 73). For Russell, fictioning (as performative act) is generative of social identities and relations. In fact the latter might be said to rely on performative acts – this leads Russell to quote (and also to inscribe on a T-Shirt for a performance) the words of Foucault from *Power/Knowledge* (1980: 193):

> the possibility exists for fiction to function in truth, for a fictional discourse to induce the effects of truth, and for bringing it about that a true discourse engenders or manufactures that which does not as yet exist, that is, 'fictions it'. (Foucault quoted by Russell 2011a: 78)

Here we find an axiom for our book: we too declare the possibility of practices that engender that which does not yet exist, that, precisely, fictions it. It is towards such a productive notion of fictioning – beyond parody or simulation (which is where we might depart with some of the notions of fictioning mentioned above) – that we have written our book. The comments by Russell quoted above appear in an essay in an edited collection that was part of a series of publications on art writing.[1] Our own contributions to that series develop a concept and practice of *performance fictions*, which we defined as producing 'a zone of activity that once entered produces a shift in how relations are understood and formed' (Burrows 2011a: 6), and that describes a presentation and performance that 'speaks back to its producer – or simply goes beyond any straightforward intention' (O'Sullivan 2011: 72). We should also say that, unlike Russell, who is concerned that fictioning – like a stage play – needs to address the problem of making an ending (Russell 2011a: 83), we view such performance fictioning as a durational event or process, an ongoing practice that is without a set beginning or ending. A fictioning practice then, involves performing, diagramming or assembling new and different modes of existence through open-ended experimentation.

Mythopoesis/Myth-Science/Mythotechnesis

If fictioning is our key concept then the myth-functions we introduced above play a significant role in organising our material. Although historically structured to a certain extent – more on this sequencing below – our book can also be said to address the three myth-functions as different *technics of fictioning* evident in contemporary art and music as well as philosophical and fictional writing. In this, as implied above, we extend the notion of fictioning beyond invention through writing, discourse or performative acts to include visual material and sonic arrangements. Furthermore, as we indicated at the beginning of our introduction, to explore the technics of fictioning, we present mythopoesis, myth-science and mythotechnesis as relating to three specific fictioning modes: performance fictioning, science fictioning and machine fictioning.

In section one, we address mythopoesis as the generation of different worlds and communities that are the potential of, and alternatives to, existing worlds. This section also begins the interrogation of a central theme of the book: the fiction of the self. In this, we explore performance fictioning as engendering new subjectivities and collectivities – calling forth a people to come – through actions and performances, experiments with drugs and rituals, and the production of assemblages and writing of various kinds. Different pasts and futures are manifested and made coextensive through technics of *looping* and *nesting*, something that necessarily leads to the instantiation of layered narrative constructions and complex temporalities. It is in the second half of the section especially that we necessarily connect the summoning of a people with the idea that all times can be potentially manifested by (or through) different subjectivities, collectives, practices and journeys.

The chapters in this first section are, in the main, concerned with a particular historical sequence and a certain avant-garde take on art that is still apparent and in play in many contemporary practices. They are – as implied above – also concerned more often than not with European and Anglo-American – and, indeed, masculine – subjectivities (even when they interrogate these or introduce exceptions). This is also evident in our initial focus in this section on Gilles Deleuze and Félix Guattari alongside William Burroughs, all of whom provide some key conceptual resources for our exploration of mythopoesis. We might describe this particular configuration as 'countercultural' (or, more colloquially, as concerning the 'bachelors'). There is at times, a Romanticism at play in some of this material, alongside a longing or redemptive quality to some of the practices and conceptual resources we look to. More generally the complex temporalities mentioned above are produced by a turn to 'residual culture' (the term is from Raymond Williams) as a resource (alongside a concern with magical thinking).

Section two, on myth-science, is similarly concerned with the fictioning of different realities but specifically addresses a technics of producing *perspectives* and *models* as parallel or multiple worlds, often through modes we identify as a science fictioning (our key conceptual persona here is the musician and visionary Sun Ra, who lends this section its title). In such practices, loops between existing and potential perspectives (including alternate models of the world, different human cultures and animal species) are produced by diverse presentations and put to specific ends.

The first four chapters in this second section shift the focus towards different currents of twentieth and twenty-first century thought and practice, especially non-European and diasporic cultures (and the colonisation and decolonisation of history and thought), but also various feminist and anthropological practices that provide some necessary tools of analysis.[2] Our second section then, although partly concerned with different pasts (in relation to different futures), begins by turning away from some of the attitudes and orientations explored in section one. The latter half of the second section takes a further turn and explores the production of non-human and alien perspectives through addressing Science Fiction (and science fictioning) in more detail. This is a genre that we attend to as important to myth-science (and particularly afrofuturism) but that, in the latter half of section two, is explored through modelisations and worldings of different societies and realities.

Our third and final section, on mythotechnesis, approaches the fictioning of new modes of existence by specifically attending to future human-machine relations and assemblages through a consideration of the technics of *adaptation* and *cloning*, as well as through technologies of *coding, compression* and *layering*, and also *editing, scanning, time-stretching, copying* and *pasting*. We suggest that such technics produce a machine fictioning which explores the future development of analogue and digital technologies and also modes of embodiment and disembodiment. In this last section, key ideas are provided by Promethean thinkers such as Reza Negarestani, who are put in dialogue with those who would be critical of Prometheanism. We also draw on the work of N. Katherine Hayles, who we see as a primary theorist of human-machine adaptation.

Our writing in this section then addresses technological themes emerging more recently in art, music and philosophy (contexts that twentieth-century practitioners could only guess at). More generally we are concerned here with the different logics of our increasingly technologically mediated reality. At stake is the very idea of the future and how this is being produced, managed and, indeed, is increasingly operative in the present. In discussing this, the section also attends to non-conscious processes, and to cognition and embodiment as they relate to the development of technological environments, thus looping back to earlier chapters of the book concerning fictions of the self.

Metamodelisation

This emphasis on fictioning as operating through diverse technics – relating to the analogue and the digital, and to actual and potential or virtual realities – pertains more generally to a method which, following Félix Guattari, might be called meta-modelisation. Our book, we might say, performs its own fictioning, especially in its forcing of different encounters and fostering of various couplings (as such, it is itself – it seems to us – an example of theory as practice). Indeed, although there are certain theoretical resources that recur throughout, we have been keen to refuse any partisanship or single philosophical dogma. Our intention has been to produce a diagram – syncretic in character – of an expanded field of fictioning practices that embraces both the rhapsodic and the scientifically inflected.

In relation to this syncretic diagram, a key theoretical doubling becomes increasingly apparent towards the end of the book. On the one hand we are concerned with autonomy and autopoesis (as self-generation and Promethean invention), and on the other with the co-development of the human and the non-human (as multispecies sympoesis and human-machine ecologies). That is, we recognise that while a number of fictioning practices pursue human agency and human potential (when this includes ideas of Prometheanism *and* human becomings), others focus on the non-human or partial-human (when this moves from alien or biological systems to intelligent machines and, more generally, economies, objects and scenes). Each of these two 'takes' on our contemporary moment operates in our book (and we would contend, more generally, in the fields of art and philosophy concerned with the future) as foreground or background to the other. In fact, if we can make any claim to originality it is in bringing together these two key orientations or attitudes in a sustained meta-modelisation of the paradigm of the future of human and non-human life and intelligence.

In relation to this paradigm the book is necessarily composed of different methods and speeds, and operates on a variety of registers (to a certain extent it also changes in nature as it progresses). These shifts occur because the book is a collaboration – and more than just between the two of us: it attends to a whole host of different voices, a diversity of perspectives. In short, our book is a wild gathering of practices and theories that draws on many disciplines, bringing together philosophies and concepts that ordinarily never meet, or would not normally give each other the time of the day. This is not so much an approach that develops out of a position but a necessity that evolves out of addressing fictioning in all its guises.

Context

We want to end this introduction with a word or two about the wider context of our book. On the one hand, our discussion of fictioning attends to particular (art, music and philosophical) scenes that we are familiar with and, to a certain extent, part of. It is this that determines some of the choices we have made about who we read and, especially, which practices we look to – though we have attempted to see beyond our own interests and engage with unfamiliar practices and scenes too. In relation to this, it is one of our contentions that scenes (involving both human and non-human agents) produce difference (or allow something different to emerge from within existing reality). In this, our book's site of production is important, arriving as it does from a very particular space-time. To a large extent, we have researched the art and music that we write about through first-hand encounters – attending events, talks, exhibitions, performances and so on – as much as through documentation (all of which is acknowledged here), which has necessarily meant an engagement with galleries and venues in London. Even more important, in terms of any scene, is our collaborative art practice, Plastique Fantastique, in which many of the ideas presented here were either generated or tested.[3]

But, as we suggested towards the beginning of this introduction, our book is indicative of a renewed interest in fiction (and the future) evident across contemporary art (when this names a number of different practices) and the arts and critical humanities more generally. As such, the book's conceptual resources are often drawn from what might be called the 'speculative turn' in art and philosophy. We also draw on what might be termed the (post)humanities that employ interdisciplinary approaches to investigate the potential for new subjectivities, the decolonisation of thought, and multi-species and human-machine co-adaptations. In fact, we see an intimate connection here (which the book tracks) between certain art scenes and philosophy/theory scenes, both of which are concerned with fictioning worlds beyond a human-centred viewpoint.

Of course, fiction is a term that has increasing valence in wider political cultures, as indicated especially in the new terminology used to describe contemporary political reality: 'post-fact' and 'post-truth'. Reality is itself an increasingly relative term on this terrain, with ideas of perception management replacing any idea of truth. It is here that we would position the urgency of our own work – not simply as a critique of this new terrain, but as something that operates on the same level as these fictions, and engages with the strategies and tactics deployed by agencies engaging in managing and experimenting with perception and reality, particularly when this includes mass-media technologies. Ultimately then, our book might be seen as having a political and ethical charge, as well as an aesthetic one. It seeks both to map out alternatives to the dominant fictions of reality and to contribute to questions concerning the kinds of human, part-human and non-human bodies and societies to come.

Notes

1   The Art-Writing Series included *Performance Fictions* edited by David Burrows, who was also the series editor (2011b); *Barefoot in the Head* edited by Mark Beasley, Alun Rowlands and John Russell (2011); *Performing Knowledge* edited by Gavin Butt (2011); *Who Is This Who Is Coming?* edited by Maria Fusco (2011); and *Materiality of Theory* edited by Jonathan Lacey Dronsfield (2011).

2   In terms of this anthropological perspective we should note the resonances between our book's subtitle and Roland Barthes' *Mythologies*, but also point out that, in general, our book is not concerned with the demystification of myth or a critique of what Barthes calls the '*what-goes-without-saying*' (Barthes 1973: 11) but, rather, with the production of new myths.

3   We refer here to the performance fiction Plastique Fantastique, produced with Alex Marzeta, Vanessa Page, Mark Jackson and others. See www.plastiquefantastique.org.

I. MYTHOPOESIS TO PERFORMANCE FICTIONING

A. MYTHOPOESIS:
AGAINST CONTROL AND
THE FICTION OF THE SELF

1 Mythopoesis, Fabulous Images and Memories of a Sorcerer

... theres some thing in us it dont have no
name ... it aint us but yet its in us ...

Russell Hoban, *Riddley Walker*

What we're interested in, you see, are modes of individuation beyond
those of things, persons or subjects: the individuation, say, of a time of
day, of a region, a climate, a river or a wind, of an event. And maybe
it's a mistake to believe in the existence of things, persons, or subjects.

Gilles Deleuze, *Negotiations*

IN THIS FIRST chapter of section one we develop more fully our key concept of mythopoesis, which, as suggested in the introduction, broadly names the 'world-making' character of certain practices and presentations. We are concerned here with what we understand as Deleuze's development, notably in *Cinema 2* (1989), of key insights concerning such practices (though Deleuze does not himself directly use the term mythopoesis). In particular we are interested in his idea that certain films and novels 'are like the seeds of the people to come' (Deleuze 1989: 221). Or, to put this another way, we want to suggest that mythopoesis is a name for a summoning – or calling forth – of a people who are appropriate and adequate to those new and different worlds presented in art, films, performances, writing and other practices (a future-orientation which, paradoxically, in certain instances, might also involve a turn to the past).

After discussing the concept of mythopoesis, the chapter then turns to the writings of Félix Guattari and, specifically, his essay 'Genet Regained', in which Guattari develops his own parallel concept of 'fabulous images' in relation to Jean Genet. These images, found in literature *and* life, operate as 'points of subjectification'. Put simply, for Guattari, fiction is a resource in the production of different kinds of subjectivity and thus, again, of the different kinds of worlds that attend the latter (when a world is defined wholly or partially as a subjective production).

Guattari's account of fabulous images and the production of subjectivity is quite technical, involving as it does different levels of operation (which allows us to attempt a more analytic account of how mythopoesis might invent a people). It is also through Guattari's complex reflections concerning subjectivity that we might think about how performance fictioning is not merely performative – it does not just involve acting something out. Rather, such practices explore new percepts or a different sense of the world or new ways of existing together, through experimenting with embodiment and with desire, consciousness and the senses (including their potential and limitations). This is something we explore in more depth in Chapter 3 on literature and drugs, and in Chapter 4, which addresses myths of self-obliteration.

To develop this last idea of embodiment as a technology of mythopoesis and of performance fictioning involving the affective as well as the conceptual, this chapter concludes with a brief discussion of Deleuze and Guattari's collaborative work, *A Thousand Plateaus* (1988). This book both utilises fiction in its particular accounts of the individuation of worlds – as Deleuze tells us in the second of our epigraphs above – but also, it seems to us, has its own mythopoetic character in so far as it calls forth its own people. It is a work that demands its reader perform its content in this sense.

Mythopoesis (and the People to Come)

For us then, mythopoesis names a particular kind of address to the future. As Deleuze puts it, there are art practices and presentations that are not necessarily for an audience already in place – they are not for us as we already are – but for a 'people who are missing' (1997: 4). But who exactly are the people called forth by mythopoesis? One way of answering this is to refer to Russell Hoban's novel *Riddley Walker* (2012) – which is also the name of a future-past character we will return to in our fifth chapter. In the novel, Walker is told by the 'tel woman' Lorna that there is '*some thing in us*' that '*aint us*' (6). We find this brief statement cryptic, but also a compelling way to understand the process and agent of mythopoesis. In this, mythopoesis involves a disruption of a more dominant fiction of the self (a theme we will return to more fully in subsequent chapters). The concept of mythopoesis speaks to the multiplicity that would deterritorialise our usual identifications (or it speaks to the potential selves we also are), whilst addressing us as part of a wider collectivity – as potentially part of a community to come.

More than this, mythopoesis results from practice: we might call it the art (and/ or science) of calling forth the *something in us* that *aint us*. This necessarily involves the fictioning of other ways of thinking, speaking, enjoying, relating and existing. These other modes of being are engendered by images, sounds, writing and events, all of which may consist of, or be the product of, other performance fictions by other artists, musicians or writers. That is, performance fictions produce or invite other performance fictions. Something happens through mythopoesis that involves this kind of performing – whether by an individual or collective – of a people to come: art and writing are the catalyst not for judgement or education but for the articulation and actualisation of this missing people.

Mythopoesis names a *collective enunciation* in this sense, one that is for a people (even when there is only a single reader or participant), but also from a people (even when there is apparently only a single author or artist). It names a strange temporality (the temporality of avant-garde practices but also of those non-European films Deleuze writes about in *Cinema 2* (1989)). This temporality involves a particular kind of feedback loop in which *future-images* (of people and worlds) are manifested within the present, in order to call forth new times and relations from within what is perceived or said to exist.

We suggest that Deleuze develops the concept of an enunciation that calls forth a missing people and their potential worlds in relation to what he calls (following Henri Bergson) 'fabulation', or the 'story-telling function'. This concept is laid out in the last few pages of *Bergsonism*, where it is portrayed as a particular mechanism that produces an interval within society through which 'creative emotion' might arise (see Deleuze 1991: 106–12). Fabulation operates, in Deleuze's reading of Bergson, to create 'fictitious representations' that counter the more utilitarian principles of human society and, indeed, of an intelligence that is premised on this. Fabulation (myth or fictitious representation) then allows something non-human to arise for the human. It is a kind of performance, or, again, a mechanism, for the production of a different kind of affect. Another way of putting this is to say that fabulation involves resistance to the world as it is perceived or understood:

> Art is resistance: it resists death, slavery, infamy, shame. But a people can't worry about art. How is a people created, through what terrible sufferings? When a people's created, it's through its own resources, but in a way that links up with something in art . . . or links up art to what it lacked. Utopia isn't the right concept: it's more a question of 'fabulation' in which a people and art both share. (Deleuze 1995b: 174)

To a certain extent there is a romanticism to these claims; certainly it is not clear, today, how art might contribute to some of this resistance (against slavery for example). As implied above, Deleuze's ideas, at least here, are part of a particular avant-garde take on art, an avant-garde mythopoesis as it were. That said, the concept of fabulation, it seems to us, is important. As Deleuze remarks this is not the same as a utopia (especially when produced by a teleology), which can be thought of as a fiction that can work to defer the production of a new people (always the receding horizon, always the end of history), but something that has a more pronounced traction on reality in so far as it is partly involved in the actual invention of a people in the here and now. Mythopoesis does not promise another world (or offer an 'escape' from this one) – it is not a technology of transcendence in this sense. Rather, it helps set up further conditions – contours and coordination points – for the production of a different mode of being (and thus, again, a different world) from within already existing ones.

Elsewhere, Deleuze deploys the concept of fabulation more specifically in relation to this kind of political project, where it operates as a bridge between an author's subjectivity and the author's work, but also between the work and those it calls forth – as, for example, in 'Literature and Life' where he suggests that 'It is the task of the fabulating function to invent a people.' The context here is American literature and the production 'of a universal people composed of immigrants from all countries', 'a minor people, eternally minor, taken up in a becoming-revolutionary' (Deleuze 1997: 4).

Deleuze and Guattari first outline the concept of the *minor* in relation to literature in their book *Kafka: Towards a Minor Literature* (1986), but it seems to us that this particular concept can be explored in relation to other practices too. Certainly, Deleuze suggests in his later work, *Cinema 2*, that film – especially that which involves an imbrication of fact and fiction – has its own minor forms and, as such, can contribute to the envisioning of future collectivities (or, to say the same, posits a missing people):

> This acknowledgement of a people who are missing is not a renunciation of political cinema, but on the contrary the new basis on which it is founded, in the third world and for minorities. Art, and especially cinematographic art, must take part in this task: not that of addressing a people, which is presupposed as already there, but of contributing to the invention of a people. (Deleuze 1989: 217)

For Deleuze it is this that differentiates modern cinema from classical cinema, which, in contrast, is 'for a people already there' (216).[1]

It might be that we again find a romanticism (or, at least, a romanticising of minorities) in Deleuze's writing here, and even something of an Orientalism in the gathering up of immigrants in one concept – the minor – to pitch against another – the major. Does this make the concept of the minor no longer relevant today? Edward Said, a critic of Orientalism, comments on Deleuze and Guattari's writing, specifically on minor literature, and suggests that the concept is still of value:

I think that the concept, that Deleuze and Guattari mobilize in the whole business of minor literature, turns out to be a description of a much larger and more influential phenomenon than they suspected . . . it's not just a question of a minor literature it's really that the major literature is sort of unhousing itself in the process of its creation . . . So I think we have to change the landscape from a discussion of dominant to peripheral literatures. A series of assembled peripherals is really what we have, peripherals that work in an elaboration that is simply unceasing. I think what we have is a new perspective, and we're able to see all literatures working in that way instead of major versus minor, which is the theory. (Said 2003: 647–8)

Said's generous interpretation of Deleuze and Guattari's ideas develops the concept of minor literature and the minor in ways that we would like to take up. Certainly, it is the minor as an enunciation or assemblage that is always in a state of incompleteness that interests us. Mythopoesis, at least in its radical form, can be said to address such a minority. Towards the end of his life, Deleuze himself states that a minority is not a recognised type of community or group, suggesting, in terms that seem to echo Said's comments on minor and major literature, that:

A minority, on the other hand, has no model, it's a becoming, a process. One might say the majority is nobody. Everybody's caught, one way or another, in a minority becoming that would lead them into unknown paths if they opted to follow it through. (1995b: 173)

This quote is taken from 'Control and Becoming', an interview that we explore in more depth in the next chapter, in which Deleuze returns to the concept of the minor and talks about minorities in relation to revolutionary becomings. As implied above, minorities, for Deleuze, are not based on identity (as, for example, with class – at least when this is thought as stable), but on a common lack of identity. For Deleuze, a minority is not to do with number (it is not necessarily smaller), but to do with a model – the major – that it refuses, departs from or, more simply, cannot live up to.

But to return to the earlier formation of the concept of minor literature, the minor names a strategic operation – as in the becoming-minor of a major language. We find this idea in Deleuze and Guattari's *Kafka* book (1986) which foregrounds the affective character of language; a stuttering and stammering of the major – the undoing and remaking of sense.[2] We mention this as it aids us in thinking further about the strange temporality of mythopoesis we alluded to earlier. Mythopoesis, we might say, involves a kind of unmaking and making of sense. Like minor literature it involves a kind of performance of a rupture in a given signifying regime that points towards another regime to come. Which is to say that sense and affects may abound in mythopoesis but they are alien to majority forms of signification. Mythopoesis, like minor literature, is always already political in this sense – in so far as it forges 'the means for another consciousness and another sensibility' (Deleuze and Guattari 1986: 17).

So far we have outlined how we think mythopoesis, as a performance fictioning, might operate as a minor literature. Before moving on though we need to address more clearly how myth plays out in all of this (as minor myths or myths of the minor even). As we implied in our introduction, a future-oriented mythopoesis might, in fact, involve the utilisation of past myth, albeit in new and novel combinations (such myths will be precisely syncretic). As we shall see in later chapters of this first section – in relation to Raymond Williams' work on residual culture – past myths might produce a certain amount of resistance against the narratives of the dominant culture, although it will be crucial to demarcate those that have been 'incorporated' (which Williams calls 'archaic' and which in Deleuze's terms might be called major) from those which remain potentially resistant (more minor myths): the present is always already a complex temporal terrain and, as such, certain aspects of the past can be mobilised against the present.

Deleuze says something similar in *Cinema 2* about this productive utilisation (but also critique) of yesterday's myths in relation to the films of Glauber Rocha, where, he argues, 'it is not a matter of analysing myth in order to discover its archaic meaning or structure, but of connecting archaic myth to the state of the drives in an absolutely contemporary society, hunger, thirst, sexuality, power, death, worship'. He goes on to suggest that this work consists, precisely, in crossing the boundaries between the private and the political, again producing collective enunciations – of '*putting everything into a trance*, the people and its masters, and the camera itself' (Deleuze 1989: 219).

There is another possible imbrication of reality and fiction here when real historical figures operate as interlocutors (something we have already touched upon in our brief discussion of Lambert-Beatty's parafiction), creating 'the possibility of the author providing himself with "intercessors", that is, of taking real and fictional characters, but putting these very characters in the condition of "making up fiction", of "making legends", of "story-telling"' (222). As Deleuze goes on to say:

> The author takes a step towards his characters, but the characters take a step towards the author: double becoming. Story-telling is not an impersonal myth, but neither is it a personal fiction: it is a word in act, a speech-act through which the character continually crosses the boundary which would separate his private business from politics, and which *itself produces collective utterances*. (222)

Here, once again, we suggest that Deleuze's double becoming is a mythopoesis that breaks with a certain 'reality principle', and especially that which separates public and private realms (again, it is a collective enunciation). But it also names a certain kind of nesting of fictions, where characters themselves become story-tellers.[3] Once again mythopoesis involves a performative element in this way, or a sense that different fictions are often traversed by a kind of staging. We will return to this idea of the nesting of fictions later in this first section.

Fabulous Images (and the Production of Subjectivity)

In some of his own writings Guattari attends to the idea of fiction as a kind of bridge – or transversal connector – between different regimes of life. In fact, in many ways Guattari is more attuned to fiction's actual connections to everyday life than Deleuze, perhaps partly because of his involvement with therapeutic work (and the 'hands-on' production of subjectivity) or, more simply, his own connections to an outside (when this is understood both in a literal sense – the outside of any given institution – and as something more abstract or non-human). As he puts it in an interview from around the same time as the publication of *A Thousand Plateaus*:

> For me, a literary machine starts itself, or can start itself, when writing connects with other machines of desire . . . Writing begins to function in something else, as for example for the Beat generation in the relation with drugs; for Kerouac in the relation with travel, or with mountains, with yoga . . . Rhythms appear, a need, a desire to speak. Where is it possible for a writer to start this literary machine if it isn't precisely outside of writing and of the field of literature. (Guattari 1996: 208–9)

This statement concerning literary machines emphasises for us the importance of performances – or performance fictionings – which produce rhythms that, in turn, produce a new sense of things. In this way fiction has traction on reality – or crosses over to life. It is this that constitutes fictioning as an important kind of subjective technology.

In the essay titled 'Genet Regained' in *Schizoanalytic Cartography* (2013) Guattari offers a more detailed account of, and inflection on, the connection of poetics to politics and the production of a people (Guattari, like Deleuze, is attending to what might be called an avant-garde mythopoesis here).[4] In Genet's case, Guattari suggests, there is a 'subterranean process' – a kind of ur-processuality – that characterises, but is also prior to, the work and life of the author. It is this ground, Guattari argues, that provides a link between the two (which we suggest relates to our notion that fictioning – and in turn mythopoesis – is more than performative).

This understanding of an intimate connection between art and life suggests that the former should not be considered as simply a representation of the latter, nor, again, can it be defined as a utopian imaging. Supplementing Deleuze's use of the term fabulation, Guattari suggests that Genet offers not so much a 'derealising fabulation', but rather 'fabulous images' (amongst other things) that are involved in a particular 'image function' (Guattari 2013: 220). This function is part of a processual praxis (in our terms, a call for new performances) that ultimately opens the reader up to what Guattari calls 'new universes of reference' and, consequently, the production of a new subjectivity (225). We suggest that fabulous images are important for any mythopoetic enunciation of a people to come.

Guattari writes of Genet's fascination with the Black Panthers as an example of this image function: 'the ways of being and dressing of the Black Panthers, which almost overnight change the way black people as a whole perceive the colour of their skin or the texture of their hair for example' (222). Assertions of this kind are problematic (there is a larger and longer history to be attended to in terms of these transformations – if indeed the instantaneous transformations described by Genet and Guattari did take place as they suggest; such statements also belie a certain fetishisation of the exotic), but it does seem to us that Guattari has pinpointed something important about the power of the image – its potential to fiction a people – and its traction in and on reality. Guattari suggests that:

> one can legitimately broaden this expression to all the imaginary formations that, from this same perspective, acquire a particular – transversal – capacity to bridge times of life, existential levels as much as social segments, even – why not – cosmic stratifications. (220)

As well as operating to bridge different existential levels, the image function offers up a 'point of subjectification' (or what we might call a point of inspiration) around which a different kind of construction can begin to occur and, ultimately, attain consistency. Here fiction operates as the friction – the cohering mechanism – for a different subjectivity (and here we should note that subjectivity, for Guattari, is not necessarily tethered to the individual but extends to groups).

The first stage in this processuality – 'modular crystallisation' – involves the production of various images and names that collapse different universes of reference together (including a shuttling between signifier and signified, content and expression) (222–5). Guattari suggests that this is somewhat akin to what Freud writes about in his work on jokes and, crucially, on dreams (223). It is the work of displacement and condensation.

The second stage involves the production of 'fabulous images' themselves (225–7). These enlarge 'fields of virtuality', allowing 'singular modalities of expression to emerge by conjugating heterogeneous voices' (225). The fabulous images – points of conden-sation that become points of conjunction (achieving a certain density and complexity as well as an autonomy) – operate as experimental devices (might we call them probe-heads?) that themselves map out 'another real', which, as Guattari suggests, is 'correlative to another subjectivity' (225).[5]

The third and final moment is when these images themselves become 'existential operators' – or what Guattari calls 'synapses' – for new kinds of enunciation whose 'function is to produce a singular temporality, a specific way of discursivizing subjec-tivity' (229). This is when fiction – or fictioning – operates as what Guattari calls in 'On the Production of Subjectivity' a 'poetic-existential catalysis'. As he goes on to remark in that essay, this can be found 'in the midst of scriptural, vocal, musical or plastic discursivities' and is a process that engages both the producer and audience of a work, or the analyst and patient in the clinic (Guattari 1995: 19). In this commen-tary on the production of subjectivity then, ideas from his collaboration with Deleuze are developed towards a complex theory of aesthetic and ethical practice: Guattari's image function and, indeed, larger aesthetic paradigm, involve both maker and participant becoming an 'enunciative crystallisation' (19).

Memories of a Sorcerer

While the writings of Deleuze and Guattari provide key concepts for our development of mythopoesis, we suggest that it is with *A Thousand Plateaus* that they produce a mythopoetic work. Certainly, for Deleuze and Guattari, philosophy – alongside art – has its own future-orientation and calls forth its own people.[6] They write about this in their final collaboration *What is Philosophy?*, where they suggest that philosophy involves a 'creation of concepts' which 'in itself calls for a future form, for a new earth and people that do not yet exist' (Deleuze and Guattari 1994: 108). But it is in their previous collaborative *Capitalism and Schizophrenia* project, and especially the second volume, *A Thousand Plateaus*, that we find a philosophy replete with what we suggest are fabulous images and myths: wolves and wolf packs, a body without organs as an egg, nomads and war machines, a thinking Earth and sorcery and sorcerers.

A Thousand Plateaus abounds in references to fiction too, and literature in particu-lar is utilised as a resource as much as the history of philosophy. It is in fiction that Deleuze and Guattari find many kinds of individuation of the world taking place, and other, stranger modes of being are conjured into existence. All of this has been remarked on by other commentators, but it bears restating here: in reading *A Thousand Plateaus* one enters into a kind of becoming with it (providing one is open to that possibility).

The processes *A Thousand Plateaus* describes, and itself initiates, do not then proceed solely by reason, nor is the book itself about the human in what we might call its habitual form. *A Thousand Plateaus* is not for us as we are typically constituted (the human figure drawn in sand, as Foucault once had it), but for something we might become. Which is to say again, partly, that a book like *A Thousand Plateaus* is itself mythopoetic. As such, this would be a mythopoesis that, far from representing existing myths, functions by producing new constellations and compositions that allow new myths to cohere.

This character is nowhere more apparent than in the central Becoming plateau (Deleuze and Guattari 1988: 232–309), a section of *A Thousand Plateaus* which concerns itself specifically with a different individuation of the world (and of any entities within it):

> between substantial forms and determined subjects, *between the two*, there is not only a whole operation of demonic local transports but a natural play of haecceities, degrees, intensities, events, and accidents that compose individuations totally differ-ent from those of the well-formed subjects that receive them. (Deleuze and Guattari 1988: 253)

Although the Becoming plateau begins with sections on Bergson and Spinoza as the two philosophers who have gone furthest in this project of de- and re-individuating the world, it is the 'Memories of a Sorcerer' sections which, it seems to us, play the most important role in so far as these 'memories' foreground both a non-philosophical perspective and the more pragmatic idea of a transformation of both self and world (they also utilise a writer who appears several times in our own book: Carlos Castaneda).

The key resources in the first sorcerer section are not philosophical concepts per se, but literature – fiction – with its authors and their invented avatars: Virginia Woolf experiencing herself 'as a troop of monkeys, a school of fish'; alongside H. P. Lovecraft's Carter, who lives a series of 'human and non-human, vertebrate and invertebrate, conscious and mindless, animal and vegetable' becomings, leading to more extreme inorganic – molecular and cosmic – ones (239–40). In this plateau, it is Lovecraft as much as Spinoza who is the thinker of becoming (any philosophical principles are, in this sense, always doubled by these literary examples).

In relation to this use of fiction we might briefly note Deleuze and Guattari's comments in *What is Philosophy?* on the intrinsic interferences between the different planes of thought, and, in particular, between philosophy and art:[7]

> concepts and conceptual personae seem to leave a plane of immanence that would correspond to them, so as to slip among the functions and partial observers, or

among the sensations and aesthetic figures, on another plane . . . These slidings are
so subtle . . . that we find ourselves on complex planes that are difficult to qualify.
(Deleuze and Guattari 1994: 217)

Here, we introduce one more concept from Deleuze and Guattari that extends our
development of mythopoesis as performance fictioning. It seems to us that aesthetic
figures *as* conceptual personae involve producing a grey zone between concept and
affect, which is important for all kinds of becomings for the human. Indeed, we would
question any straightforward division of philosophy (as concerned with concept
production) and art (as concerned with affect) such as we find in *What is Philosophy?*
In many ways this seems to us a somewhat narrow theory of art.

In 'Memories of a Sorcerer II' Deleuze and Guattari suggest that the first principle
of becoming-animal – multiplicity and contagion – is invariably doubled by a second:
alliance with something more singular, the anomalous, understood as that which
borders the pack. Again, literary examples are crucial in helping to define this
principle: Captain Ahab's complex relation with the singular Moby Dick and
Josephine, the privileged mouse singer of Kafka's mouse society. In passing we would
point out that there may be a naturalism of a kind at work in Deleuze and Guattari's
thinking here, especially with the division of a social human from a non-social
animal. This is something we will return to explicitly in the second section of the
book. What is clear, however, is that for Deleuze and Guattari, literary fiction not
only allows readers to perform an escape from human habits and organisations,
but also seems to operate as a kind of manual, offering up case studies for a life
that might be lived differently.

In 'Memories of a Sorcerer III' becoming-animal is placed in a sequence, with
becoming-woman on the near side and becoming-molecular – ultimately, becoming-imperceptible – on the far side. Once again Lovecraft, this time alongside
Castaneda, is deployed (and here we note that the thinking of the 'becoming bachelors'
may not be appreciated by feminists who view Lovecraft as a misogynist), but Deleuze
and Guattari also point to Science Fiction in general as a genre that concerns becoming:
'science fiction has gone through a whole evolution taking it from animal, vegetable,
and mineral becomings to becomings of bacteria, viruses, molecules, and things
imperceptible' (248).

We might say then that in *A Thousand Plateaus*, and in the Becoming plateau in
particular, a programme is drawn out, again one of transformation, dependent on a
very precise ontology, but developed through aesthetic figures (as conceptual personae) that live through these transformations. This is not exactly a therapeutics, but
it is certainly a form of practical analysis, where this is also understood as involving
an ethico-aesthetics (or a form of molecular politics in Guattari's sense).

To conclude this first chapter then, both Deleuze and Guattari are attentive to the way in which certain works of fiction can have traction on reality beyond their status as literature. For both, fiction is a key technology in the calling forth of something different in and from the world. But *A Thousand Plateaus*, while it attends to this operation in writing *about* it (when this includes philosophy's own future-orientation), also performs it. The book is itself an example of the world-making it describes. It is partly this that gives the work its mythopoetic quality (and why many artists and art students respond so well to it): the book constitutes its own very particular worlds as well as the terms by which those worlds might be approached. *A Thousand Plateaus* is then both a collective enunciation and, it seems to us, *for* a people to come. Or, more simply, it *fictions* another world from within this one.

Notes

1   Deleuze has in mind Alain Resnais and Jean-Marie Straub but also, in relation to the deployment of fiction as a kind of political method, the films of Glauber Rocha (Deleuze 1989: 218–19).

2   In terms of the foregrounding of affect – the stuttering and stammering character of a minor literature – and the relation of this to art practice, see O'Sullivan 2006a: 69–97.

3   For a compelling and historical account of a left-orientated 'political mythopoesis', especially in relation to Wu Ming, see Thoburn 2016: 272–99. Thoburn draws attention to the way in which such a political mythopoesis can operate 'without or against a unified subjectivity' (282), but also, following Deleuze, demonstrates how real-life characters might be re-purposed in the service of myth.

4   Thanks to Theo Reeves-Evison for first pointing us towards Guattari's essay on Genet.

5   Deleuze and Guattari define probe-heads in *A Thousand Plateaus* as follows: 'Beyond the face lies an altogether different inhumanity: no longer that of the primitive head, but of "probe-heads"; here, cutting edges of deterritorialization become operative and lines of deterritorialization positive and absolute, forming strange new becomings, new polyvocalities' (Deleuze and Guattari 1988: 190–1). For a discussion of this concept in relation to art practice see O'Sullivan 2012: 189–92.

6   In fact, Deleuze and Guattari suggest that art and philosophy converge specifically at this point: 'the constitution of an earth and a people that are lacking as the correlate of creation' (1994: 108). This convergence relates to the way in which both these forms of thought – and the third great form, science – involve a confrontation with chaos and, indeed, the production of a certain consistency from out of this chaos. *What is Philosophy?* also closes with some cryptic remarks about how the brain's own submersion in chaos allows the extraction of forms of subjectivity (or even, perhaps, non-subjectivity?) that are wilder, untethered from the cogito. As they put it: 'there is extracted from chaos

the shadow of the "people to come" in the form that art, but also philosophy and science, summon forth: mass-people, world-people, brain-people, chaos-people' (218).

7 This is the second form of interference after a first, more straightforward one of either philosophy, science or art having a take, from its own perspective, on one of the others; as, for example, 'when a philosopher attempts to create the concept of a sensation' (Deleuze and Guattari 1994: 217).

2   Against Control: Nothing is True, Everything is Permitted

Our ability to resist control, or our submission to it, has to be assessed at the level of our every move. We need both creativity and a people.

Gilles Deleuze, 'Postscript on Control Societies'

To all the scribes and artists and practitioners of magic through whom these spirits have been manifested . . . NOTHING IS TRUE. EVERYTHING IS PERMITTED.

William Burroughs, *Cities of the Red Night*

HAVING LAID OUT some of the characteristics of mythopoesis as a fictioning of a people to come in our previous chapter we want now to discuss fictioning in relation to the specific context of societies shaped by capitalist production, mass media technologies and automation (especially as this dovetails with state bureaucracy and regulation). We do so through the work of two figures who propose concepts and fictioning practices as a means of resisting the fictions of capitalism and the state. The second of these is William Burroughs, who writes of societies or governments that maintain power through psychological control rather than physical force and violence (see, for example, Burroughs 2014). Before looking to Burroughs though, we want to turn back to Gilles Deleuze, and, specifically, his late writings on what he calls 'Control Societies' and, indeed, on the need for 'new weapons' to combat the logics and operating protocols of such societies (Deleuze 1995a: 178). We note here that although there are key differences between our two figures – not least that one is an artist, the other a philosopher – both, it seems to us, are concerned with excavating a kind of freedom, or opening up a different space-time, from within the world as it is perceived to be. The chapter then attempts a metamodelisation, at least of a kind: a laying of these two crucial figures side by side so as to further develop our understanding of fictioning.

In Part 1 of this Chapter our main resources are Deleuze's writings on control, but we also look again to *A Thousand Plateaus*, which, it seems to us, is a particularly valuable resource for thinking this new terrain and the possibilities opened up by it. In the second part, Burroughs operates for us as a more concrete example of fictioning, and thus works as a counterbalance to Deleuze's abstract theorising. We look at some key passages relating to Burroughs' method from the interviews (and other writings) gathered in *The Job* (2008). Burroughs' ideas on control are less straightforward than Deleuze's in so far as Burroughs both pitched his work against control but also, in some senses, wanted to maintain it (certainly he wanted a form of control that allowed him to experiment with his own life). There are other complex and paradoxical ideas to be found in *The Job*, for example – as we will see – in Burroughs' attitude to the Mayans, who were, for him, both an example of an extreme control society and yet, with their hieroglyphic language system, a possible resource in the fight against our own modern control systems.

The chapter ends by bringing Burroughs and Deleuze together (using the moment of their possible encounter at the infamous Schizo-Culture conference at Columbia University in 1975 as entry point), before offering two brief codas: one on a further important fictioning practitioner who was influenced by Burroughs; the other containing some caveats and further thoughts about control as it operates today and which, to a certain extent, take us away from Deleuze's own definitions.

PART I: Against control

Postscript on Societies of Control

Although written at the end of the last century, Deleuze's short polemical essay 'Postscript on Control Societies' (1995a) remains highly influential in terms of its diagnosis of our contemporary moment. We attend to this essay – and Deleuze's thoughts on control society more generally – not as a completely accurate prediction or depiction of contemporary life as it is today but partly as itself a Science Fiction written when the most radical social transformations wrought by digital and information technology have yet to take place (indeed, we make some suggestions as to how control might be changing in a coda to this chapter). In doing so, we read Deleuze's essay as a kind of fiction written to call forth a people who might resist the forms of communication and exchange that Deleuze sees as indicative of a new phase of capitalism and control.

It is also in the Postscript essay that we encounter a Deleuze more sober, and at times pessimistic, than when he co-wrote the *Capitalism and Schizophrenia* books.

The joy and affirmative tone of the collaborations with Guattari give way to a polemic that, if not a lament, certainly has something of the Frankfurt School diagnostic about it, especially in its attention to the way technology can transform society and how such advances, although at first ostensibly a positive move away from previous, harsher, regimes, have brought their own more insidious and intricate issues and problems. We would even say that the ominous and melancholic tone of the essay gives the Postscript its particular affective charge.

For Deleuze it is Burroughs who first identifies and names this new kind of society which is 'knocking on the door' of those disciplinary regimes analysed by Foucault (1975). Control societies are characterised by modulation rather than confinement: continuous monitoring and ongoing assessment replace discrete temporal segmentation; and, in terms of the proliferation of more dominant image worlds and narratives, there is the superseding of the analogical by the digital with the emergence of different kinds of cybernetic machine (leading to the computer). One gets the feeling that Deleuze's essay is a letter to the future; certainly the sense is that it will be the generations after his own that will have to fully attend to the various twists and turns, the feints and bluffs – or 'snakes' as Deleuze calls them – which, in some parts of the world, have replaced the more straightforward strategies of power of previous societies.

Here we note that the *dividual*, as presented by Deleuze, is an important concept for understanding how he conceives of the modulating operations of control societies. Deleuze uses the term to refer to the way in which people become connections between other connections; data-driven dividuals articulate and are articulated by a system of communication or exchange. In this, Deleuze makes an interesting and prophetic observation, suggesting that signatures and watchwords give way to code and passwords in control societies. This development is further commented on: 'Disciplinary man produced energy in discrete amounts, while control man undulates, moving among a continuous range of different orbits' (Deleuze 1995a: 180).[1] When Deleuze states that, for 'control man', surfing replaces all the old sports (180), he does not make this declaration with any enthusiasm.

Nevertheless, despite this pessimism, we find in the Postscript essay something else that does hark back to a book like *A Thousand Plateaus*: a call to look to what has been opened up by these 'new' developments – or, at least, to the possibilities of resistance that, for Deleuze, will always and everywhere accompany control. As he remarks towards the end of the essay, in a counterpoint to resignation and melancholic paralysis: 'It's not a question of worrying or hoping for the best, but of finding new weapons' (178).

War Machines

In the interview on 'Control and Becoming' (1995b) that accompanies the Postscript, Deleuze reflects further on what he sees as this new mode of capitalism, outlining four conceptual categories (the new weapons), three of which he and Guattari had attended to in *A Thousand Plateaus* – lines of flight, minorities, war machines – to which he adds a fourth, vacuoles of noncommunication. In relation to our task at hand, we have already acknowledged the importance of Deleuze's work on one of these categories – minorities and the minor – for our thinking. Lines of flight – as a movement that resists representation or signifying regimes – and vacuoles of noncommunication – manifested by a refusal to be productive of any representation or signification – seem less directly related to mythopoetic fictioning, serving only to break with or clear away existing economies of sense (rather than producing new mythopoetic works or fabulous images). However, in this, we understand that the two concepts play a part in the deterritorialising operations of the war machine, which seems to us to operate as a performance (and indeed a performance fictioning), or in Deleuze and Guattari's terms, as a movement in which reterritorialisation follows a deterritorialisation. Deleuze develops his concept of the war machine by

> finding a characterization of 'war machines' that's nothing to do with war but to do with a particular way of occupying, taking up, space-time, or inventing new space-times: revolutionary moments . . . artistic movements too, are war-machines in this sense. (Deleuze 1995b: 172)

The concept of the war machine then, involves a spatio-temporal aspect (the occupying of a different space-time) and an organisational aspect (the actual composition of the machine, with its own particular speeds and slownesses). Another way of putting this is to say that a war machine concerns both duration and composition. As such, and as Deleuze remarks, art movements – and we would we also add specific fictioning practices – can be thought of as war machines (172). Certainly, examples of this abound in contemporary art and culture, including: the video game *All New Gen* (1993), designed by VNS Matrix, that warns players that it is a zone with no moral code; the relentless dancing of groups of men and women from Chicago who developed the Footwork style in which feet move frenetically and at great speed, as if influenced by the editing and time-stretch tools that produced the music they move to; and Benedict Drew's Big Band, which produced a durational and impro-vised performance at the Whitechapel Gallery for his exhibition *The Trickle-Down Syndrome* (2017), or the artist's *Dyslexic Shanty* (2014), which makes a space for the development of a radical dyslexia (see Figure 2.1). All of these examples – which we

discuss in the last section of our book –
are zones of performance that fiction
dissonant collectivities. It is such
manifestations that dissent by affirming
something different that characterises
war machines.

Of interest too, though, is Deleuze's
suggestion that 'people don't take
enough account, for instance, of how
the PLO has had to invent a space-time
in the Arab world' (170). Deleuze's
appreciation of the Palestine Liberation
Organisation as a war machine suggests
to us that he valued the way the organisation produced a new or transformed
Arab culture, and indeed redefined
(fictioned) what it is to be an Arab and

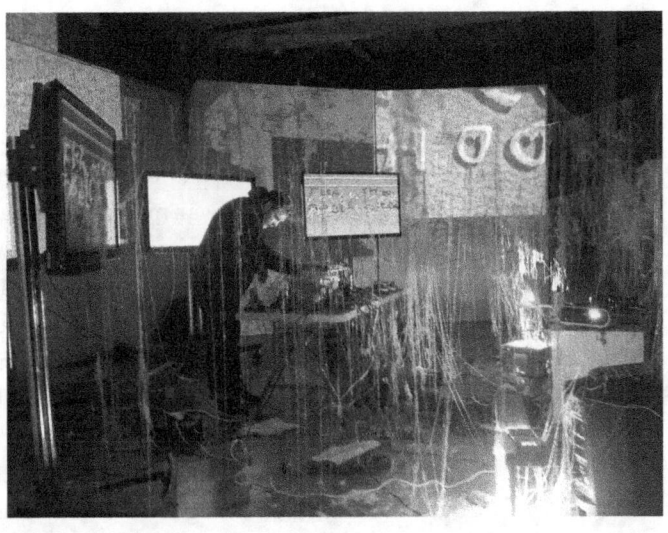

2.1 Benedict Drew, *Dyslexic Shanty*, 2014, performance at Chelsea
Space as part of *Bob Cobbing: Bill Jubobe* (courtesy of the artist and
Matt's Gallery, London).

a Palestinian (as a people to come). It seems to us that Burroughs' writing, as we
shall see, operates as a war machine in this sense in so far as it involves the mobilisation of different speeds and, indeed, constructs different space-times for avatars
and characters – conceptual personae and people to come – through mythopoetic
function.

In *A Thousand Plateaus* Deleuze and Guattari go into more detail about the
composition of these machines and their complex relation to both war and the state.
Indeed, they suggest that the state, although wary, often appropriates – or employs –
a radically exterior war machine (it does not have such machines of its own).[2] In
these moments war becomes the machine's object. However, it is always an uneasy
marriage in so far as a war machine, in its essence, involves something different: the
'drawing of a creative line of flight, the composition of a smooth space and . . . the
movement of people in that space' (Deleuze and Guattari 1988: 422). Any critique –
'against the state and against the worldwide axiomatic expressed by States'– is an
important but secondary effect of this prior creative impulse (422).

For Deleuze and Guattari, and in terms of actual composition, it is in fiction, with
Kleist's writing machine (and in particular *Penthesilea*), that we encounter the most
accurate and radical depiction of the different speeds and impersonal affects of the
war machine, involving as it does 'a succession of flights of madness and catatonic
freezes in which no subjective interiority remains' (356). In the war machine
everything is always already exterior, involving a different kind of rhythm – a different
composition of becomings – to the state machine and to those modes of being that

tend to accompany the latter. The war machine is also necessarily collective in character, involving decentralised bands or packs, 'groups of the rhizome type' that are 'formally distinct from all state apparatuses or their equivalents which are instead what structure centralized societies' (358). (We will be returning to this idea of collectivity towards the end of this first section.)

In the plateau on the war machine Deleuze and Guattari write about a nomad – or minor – science that is nourished by this machine (and involved in more hydraulic and non-hylomorphic models of matter), as well as a more general nomadology that opposes state knowledge.[3] Indeed, they go further, pitching the idea of a more nomadic form of thought against the dominant image of thought (or its state form). Once again Kleist, along with Nietzsche and Artaud, are the crucial figures of this stammering 'counterthought' that both destroys previous images but also connects with an exterior – or the forces of the outside (see Deleuze and Guattari 1988: 376–8).[4] Could this nomadic thought be characterised as a kind of fictioning of reality in so far as it invariably involves recourse to, and a mobilisation of, those images and narratives – fictions – overlooked and occluded by dominant state forms?

Belief in the World

> What we most lack is a belief in the world, we've quite lost the world, it's been taken from us. If you believe in the world you precipitate events, however inconspicuous, that elude control, you engender new space-times, however small their surface or volume. (Deleuze 1995b: 176)

What would it mean to believe in the world? It seems to us that it would be to believe that another world is indeed possible, besides the one of 'Capitalist Realism' as Mark Fisher puts it (2009). It might also be for some that to believe in the world is to maintain a kind of Spinozist faith in the potential of a body – understood in its most expanded (and compound) form; and thus, again following Spinoza, to maintain a belief in the potential of thought itself.

In those practices that present different images and narratives – and that 'engender different space-times' – we have a practical elaboration or manifestation of this belief. Indeed, when alternative and resistant strategies for life and living become stymied, creative and aesthetic practices can offer up other resources – alternative models or fictions – for a different mode of existence. As we suggested in the previous chapter, mythopoetic practices involve not exactly the production of another world – that, as Deleuze remarks, is the business of politics – but a kind of embodied preview of other places. As we also noted in the previous chapter, for Deleuze utopia is not quite the right word as it suggests something too far off, too far removed from the world as it is.[5] Mythopoetic fictioning is not an escape from, or panacea for, the existing conditions, but something sharper: the material exploration of other imaginary possibilities in the contemporary moment. Fictioning in this sense is a kind of weaponisation of fiction *per se*. In this, it is Burroughs (who we suggest is self-written, his own Science Fiction character) who may be seen as exemplary in the weaponisation of fiction against control. His axiom: *NOTHING IS TRUE. EVERYTHING IS PERMITTED.*[6]

PART 2: THE CUT-UP

Reality is a Recording

As Deleuze remarks in relation to the shift from disciplinary societies to control ones: 'Burroughs was the first to address this' (Deleuze 1995b: 174). All of Burroughs' writings might be said to concern – and be pitched against – control; the novels in particular evidence this in their mobilisation of other narratives and dissident image worlds. In so far as Burroughs figures as an actor within his fictions, which often give accounts of his own and his collaborators' lives, the writer can be said to be more than an author of Science Fiction; indeed the life led by Burroughs is an example of fiction as a mode of existence, in that he does more than simply write about resisting control. However, it is especially with the *Nova* trilogy – and the development of the cut-up technique – that his assault on control is made most manifest, at least in literary form. The cut-up technique involves the cutting, folding and splicing of text so as to undo sequencing and syntax, producing a different narrative or composition. Burroughs also experimented with this technique in other media, for example with tape recorders and what he called 'playback': the splicing together of different recordings before literally playing them back in order to fiction other realities from already existing ones. In what follows we look especially to *The Job*, which contains interviews (from a little after Burroughs completed the trilogy) that are themselves spliced together with other longer passages and, indeed, examples of cut-up text. *The Job* is, in this sense, an interesting example of writing that is both about Burroughs' method (an auto-reflection as it were), but also an example of it.

Cut-up to Playback

For Burroughs control operates predominantly through language – when this names particular sequences of words and images – and thus any practice that pitches itself against control needs to attack language in some way. As he remarks in the interview 'Journey through Time-Space':

> The word of course is one of the most powerful instruments of control as exercised by the newspaper and images as well, there are both words and images in news-papers . . . Now if you start cutting these up and rearranging them you are breaking down the control system. (Burroughs 2008: 33)

In this interview Burroughs is specifically reflecting on the development of his tech-nique of the 'cut-up and fold-in method' which, as he says, first occurred 'between *Naked Lunch* and *Nova Express*' (27). In particular he talks about the need to treat language as its own kind of material to be manipulated and, with that, the develop-ment of a 'precise science of words':

> The writer does not yet know what words are. He deals only with abstractions from the source point of words. The painter's ability to touch and handle his medium led to montage techniques sixty years ago. It is to be hoped that the extension of cut-up techniques will lead to more precise verbal experiments closing the gap and giving a whole new dimension to writing. These techniques can show the writer what words are and put him in tactile communication with his medium. (27)

The cut-up then foregrounds the matter of language – especially its affective char-acter – whilst at the same time introducing an element of chance, something outside of conscious control (or contrary to the typical control mind). The results of the process are, however, then carefully selected and edited by Burroughs: 'In cutting up you will get a point of intersection where the new material that you have intersects with what is already there in some very precise way, and then you start from there' (32). For Burroughs the point of the cut-up was not that it was purely random, but that it might produce surprising conjunctions and compatibilities that connected with, but also opened up, other avenues from an already existing reality and its accompanying narratives.

'Journey through Time-Space' is concerned with film and how this particular combination of word and image – again, a certain sequencing – might be cut in to and rearranged. As Burroughs suggests in his brief essay on 'Playback from Eden to Watergate' (that comes at the very beginning of *The Job*), reality is itself a kind of audio-visual script, and new cut-ups – recordings that have been spliced together – can then be 'played back' in order to interfere with more dominant narrative sequences. Indeed, playback – especially audio – was a kind of magical technology in this sense, a way of transforming a given 'reality': 'The basic operation of recording, pictures, more pictures, and playback can be carried out by anyone with a recorder and camera' which could then 'nullify the control system' (20). Burroughs offers up concrete instances of his use of playback to deliberately and successfully affect reality in this sense, such as when he caused the closure of a café he frequented. By recording negative sounds from the television and playing them back on the street opposite the café, Burroughs claims to have influenced potential customers to turn away from the establishment, destroying the business for reasons of 'outrageous and unprovoked discourtesy and poisonous cheesecake' (18).

The cut-up also played with temporality. As Burroughs remarks, it could allow a kind of prediction, or writing of the future:

> I would say that my most interesting experience with the earlier techniques was the realization that when you make cut-ups you do not get simply random juxtapositions of words, that they do mean something, and often these meanings refer to some future event. (28)

In so far as linear time involves a particular sequencing then the cut-up could also involve a re-engineering of the past: 'We think of the past as being there unchangeable. Actually the past is ours to shape and change as we will' (35). In relation to this attitude to the past in 'Journey through Time-Space' there is a long passage about the importance of the Mayan civilisation and its use of different calendars as forms of control (linked, as these are, to specific temporal sequencings): 'the priest could calculate into the future or the past exactly what the populace should be doing or hearing on a given date' (39).[7] Burroughs links this to certain command or control words than can activate certain behaviours. Indeed, throughout the interview he refers to the 'control mind', identifying the practices of Scientology as a particularly effective way of countering – or erasing – this 'reactive mind'. Control here is linked to the triggering of behaviour, but also, more generally, to certain logics connected to language: the 'either/or' and 'is' of Aristotelian logic (hence the importance, for Burroughs, of a figure like Alfred Korzybski and his 'general semantics' (48)).

In 'Journey through Time-Space' Burroughs is asked whether his '"new mythology" – this new framework of associations and images – can itself affect the awareness of the reader, and, in so doing, make him move about in space and time' (37). Burroughs responds:

> That would depend entirely on the reader, how open he is to new experience, and how able he is to move out of his own frame of reference. Of course most people are only able to give a very small fraction of their attention to what they read – to anything they're doing – because of the various compulsive preoccupations, and

with just a tenth of their attention on something they don't move very far. Others are able to apply much more attention. (37)

The cut-up, we might say, requires a new kind of reader-subject that is adequate and appropriate to it. Or, to say the same thing differently, it requires 'a new way of thinking' – and we suggest a fictioning of life (or a people to come) – that might be cultivated outside of control.

The New Way of Thinking

In the interview 'Prisoners of the Earth Come Out' Burroughs talks about the 'important difference between a hieroglyphic and syllabic language' (Burroughs 2008: 59). The latter is an instrument of control in so far as such a language system involves 'automatic relations to words themselves and enable[s] those who manipulate words to control thought on a mass scale' (59). In a longer passage Burroughs talks/writes about an academy in which a 'new way of thinking' against this linguistic control system might be inculcated. A place of training where 'We learn to stop words' (91).

The new way of thinking involves experimentation with a kind of pre or non-conscious mode of being in the world (that is, a 'non-control' consciousness):

> The new way of thinking has nothing to do with logical thought. It is no oceanic organismal subconscious body thinking. It is precisely delineated by what it is not. Not knowing what is and is not knowing we know not. Like a moving film the flow of thoughts seem to be continuous while actually the thoughts flow stop change and flow again. At the point where one flow stops there is a split second hiatus. The new way of thinking grows in the hiatus between thoughts. (91)

Burroughs continues a few lines later: 'The new way of thinking is the thinking you would do if you didn't have to think about any of the things you ordinarily think about if you had no work to do nothing to be afraid of no plans to make' (91). The new way of thinking is then different to our more usual concerns and especially our tendency to avoid being in the present moment (the way we tend to 'make plans'). This idea relates to some of the material we will come to write about later in this section, particularly on the fiction of the self, but also to material in the second and third sections on the kinds of thought enabled by human-machine co-adaptation. In fact, Burroughs also addresses the role of machines in relation to control in this interview, offering up, it seems to us, a crucial corrective not only to any straightforward accelerationist agenda that views technology in generally positive terms, but also to those who, following Deleuze's writing on control societies, would see information technology in generally negative and determinist terms. When asked by the interviewer, Daniel Odier, whether he believes in 'the frequently reiterated promises of a future humanity made better by the development of automation, or technology in general', Burroughs replies: 'Decidedly not. It depends on who is directing the technology' (67). It seems to us that this is in marked difference to the Deleuze of the Postscript. Burroughs also references cybernetics and Norbert Wiener: 'Wiener warned that the machine can think a thousand times quicker than we can and that it may well sweep its masters to disaster before they know what the machine is about' (70). We will be returning to Wiener in Chapter 21 but would note here that Burroughs' comments suggest he is wary of cybernetic machines, at least to some extent.

Burroughs' thinking concerning machines is, however, more complex and messy than this quotation might suggest. He is not interested in preserving the image of an unsullied human; a novel like *Nova Express*, for example, is concerned more with the possibilities and potentials of prosthesis and human-machine hybrids. Indeed, later in 'Prisoners of the Earth Come Out', Burroughs speculates on the 'new' humans that might be produced through science, noting that 'we're very near being able to make all sorts of alterations to the human body. They are now able to replace parts, like an old car when it runs down' (113). Again, Burroughs' take on the future, in which machine and human are libidinally inter-meshed, looks forward to the practices of mythotechnesis we will be looking at in section three.

In a further interview in *The Job* – 'A New Frog' – Burroughs also talks about sex more generally as a powerful counter to control. In response to a question about pornography and eroticism he suggests that:

> we don't know what eroticism is, we don't know what sex is, we don't know why its pleasurable, and the reason we don't know these things is that it's such a highly charged area no one can look at it . . . The idea of any scientific investigation throws people in to puritanical convulsions. (111)

Sexuality operates against two of the key operating principles of control: fear and shame, hence the importance for Burroughs of Wilhelm Reich and his experiments with liberating – and experimenting with – sexual energy. Reich's research addressed repression, the key aspects of this for Burroughs being the family and, more generally, heteronormativity. Burroughs own explorations – and, indeed, his explicit writing about sexuality and self-identification as queer – were thus pitched against these particular forms of control. While it might be a step too far to suggest that sexual pleasure and experimentation are themselves forms of writing or fictioning, they can certainly be seen as important to Burroughs' life praxis and, therefore, as an aspect of his fictioning of reality.

Fictioning Reality

In the 'Prisoners of the Earth Come Out' interview Burroughs makes reference to dreams: 'The dream is a spontaneous happening and therefore dangerous to a control system set up by the non-dreamers' (2008: 102). Dreams were themselves an important resource for his own work as well as evidencing a certain delirium that his writing also possessed (see Burroughs 1995). Following this comment on dreams there is a sequence that fictions or performs this other reality. To quote an indicative passage:

> Saharan blue where a thousand blue devils dance in the air like flowers of fire supine oppositionally pillaged inaccessible jackals howling across deserts of thyme stridently misinformed preparations communicated the question of pillaged consensus it is raining internalized concordance dawn rising like a flock of doves softly on the town shivering of Venetian blinds at four o'clock and the yellow blue awakening concentrates the sleep of love on orifices summer accessibility the skinny dogs internalized flowers of fire. (2008: 106)

Burroughs continues immediately after:

> Anything they can do you can do better. Pick up *The Concise Oxford Dictionary* mix your own linguistic virus concentrate fire burn and caldron bubble mix it black and mix it strong folks hereabouts have done you wrong return confluently the complement: e. (106)

And then, after this rhythmic address to the reader, there comes a delirious stream of signifiers: 'Fristic elite impacted lilitrophic imposture impotently flailing effluvial grout mud incumbent MN grume intervolving abrasively affricative incubus . . .' (106). Language, the very tool of control, through a kind of dream-delirium-channelling, is re-purposed by Burroughs into something that escapes its confines.

In the final interview of *The Job*, 'Academy 23', Burroughs turns to another of his key concerns: drugs. These are both used by control (as in the production and managing of addicts), but also operate counter to it (in so far as they can open up other space-times). We will be returning to this terrain in the next chapter, but note here that drugs are a technology – like language – which humans use and are used by. With regard to fictioning, it is psychedelics especially that can open up another reality from within this one.

In terms of the concepts introduced in the previous chapter, Burroughs' writing has a mythopoeic character: it calls forth its own kind of people, a people adequate and appropriate to the worlds it depicts. As a work of minor literature Burroughs' writing pitches itself against Oedipal configurations – or to go further, there is a queering of language – and, as such, it connects to an outside of the domestic and familial. Indeed, Burroughs specifically writes against the nation (which he sees as simply an extension of the family), but also *for* the new communities in formation:

> The Black Muslims are moving in that direction. So are the hippies. Other preferential units could be set up: all male communities, ESP communities, health communities, karate and judo communities, glider balloonist communities, yoga communities, Reichean communities, silence and sense withdrawal communities. Such communities would soon become international and break down national borders . . . (98–9)

This can involve 'intercessors' – 'real' people that enter into the fiction (Burroughs himself is fictioned as the character 'Old Bull Lee' in some of his writings). In this, and through other means, Burroughs' writing tracks a move from reality to fiction: 'you'll read something in a newspaper or see something in the street, pick up a character maybe from someone you see in the street, then you transform the character and change the setting' (31). He talks, for example, of writing a film script for the life of the mobster Dutch Schultz, where he 'cut up every page and suddenly got a lot of new ideas that were then incorporated into the structure of the narrative' (30).

In *The Job* this tracking works back the other way, with the idea that there can be a reciprocal movement of fiction back into reality (again, this is what playback entails). Indeed, Burroughs explicitly hopes 'that some of his readers will turn into his characters' (56) and, in fact, it seems to us that his novels in particular are crammed full of alternate points of subjectification. Similar to Guattari's own ideas about fabulous images (and his attraction to the exotic and non-Western other), Burroughs talks, for example, about how the Beat generation connected with Arabs on 'certain fundamental levels, on sex, habit, drugs. But more than that, they're coordinated with pop music, with a way of dressing, a way of life' (53). Indeed, fictioning is as much a way of life – a performance – as it is about a life.

Schizo-Culture and Performance Fictioning

Deleuze attended the infamous 'Schizo-Culture' conference at Columbia University in 1975 – an encounter between French desiring-thought and American counterculture – and may well have heard Burroughs' talk on 'The Limits of Control', which, along with Burroughs' other writings, influenced his own thesis on control societies. For Burroughs, although it's hard to identify precisely who or what is doing the controlling in Western societies, it is the corporate-controlled mass medias – which Guy Debord named as *The Society of the Spectacle* (1983) and that we recognise as kinds of fictioning machines – that he sees as especially culpable. Fiction – as spectacle – operates here as a strategy of control.

When applied to mass media, Burroughs' use of the cut-up technique can be seen as a use of fictioning against fiction or spectacle machines. In Deleuzian terms, it functions as a 'new weapon' – or war machine. Burroughs and his collaborator Brion Gysin (who Burroughs in fact credits as inventing the cut-up after accidently slicing through a newspaper in his studio) cut up newspaper headlines and other mass-produced material so as to present new fictions, but also so as to reveal the cut-up operations employed by newspapers and other media themselves. An example here is an untitled collage by the pair that addresses their fascination with the number 23 and places distressing headline next to distressing headline to make up a hyper-alarming front-page.

For Burroughs then, it is possible to undermine the operations of media control through transforming and disrupting existing media with further fictions or cut-ups. In *The Electronic Revolution*, first published in 1970, Burroughs argues that a weaponised fiction ('Illusion is a revolutionary weapon') can operate against the monopoly on producing reality, and urges fellow travellers of the counterculture to deploy cut-ups to make trouble – using recordings of riots to produce riots – and to cut 'the lines of association' or 'mutter lines' produced by the mass media (Burroughs 2005: 12–13).[8] Burroughs' example of a cut-up that might cut a mutter line: 'President Johnson burst into a swank apartment, held three girls at gunpoint, 26 miles north of Saigon yesterday' (14).

The cut-up then undermines what another attendee of the Schizo-Culture event, Jean-François Lyotard, once called the 'fantasies of realism' (1984: 74). Certainly, such fantasies for Lyotard are produced by a logical syntax and sequencing of both words and images (1984: 74). The effect of the cut-up is precisely to disrupt – and rear-range – this sequencing. In fact, in so far as grammar and syntax can produce linearity and temporal progression, the cut-up, especially as evidenced in Burroughs' novels, invents different durations – a stuttering of the realities offered up by capitalist cultures. Indeed, the breaks and jumps – but also the repetitions and layering – of the cut-up novels produce a very different kind of space-time (following Brion Gysin, might we even say that the cut-up is a form of space-time travel in this sense).

The cut-up produces different images – often startling – that appear to come from somewhere else (and that then speak back to their progenitor). This is a side-stepping of authorship (the mobilisation of chance – a contact with an outside to the subject – alongside processes of selection and editing) and the insertion of the writer into the more inhuman semiotic chain of the unconscious (when this is both signifying and asignifying). In this way one produces something that has not been wholly intended: a circumnavigation of the self that opens up a new world and a new kind of subject appropriate to that world. As we will see in Chapter 7, J. G. Ballard (himself a purveyor of mythopoesis) was interested in this approach, and once remarked that with the *Nova* trilogy Burroughs was producing a new mythography. Indeed, Burroughs himself refers to the later *Cities of the Red Night* trilogy as a 'mythography for the space age'.

Coda I: *Blood and Guts in High School*

As a first coda to this second chapter, we suggest there are many writers and artists influenced by Burroughs who might be said to write for a people to come. Such is the case with Kathy Acker, a writer on whom Burroughs had a profound effect. Acker's novel *Blood and Guts in High School* (1978) presents a splintered narrative in which multiple styles of writing accompany different and distinct voices. Indeed, the book is a collection of different perspectives with no single unified character or self-present author (as others have pointed out, Acker's novels are exemplary post-modern artefacts in this sense, staging as they do the 'death of the author'). The worlds imagined and imaged seem contemporary but also, in other ways, quite different: at times more brutal, at others more tender.

Acker's writing is often intimate, honest and confessional. It lays bare the desires and libidinal economy of a feminine subjectivity (at least of a kind). In fact, it seems to us that Acker is explicitly involved in a form of feminist myth-making. In this respect she foregrounds the importance of dreaming as an alternative to dominant/ typical image worlds, and writes compellingly about what she calls 'vision' and 'the vision world' as a further alternative to more dominant paradigms of sense-making and reason. This alternative paradigm is also pitched against the self:

> Once we have gotten a glimpse of the vision world (notice here how the conventional language obscures: WE as if somebodies are the centre of the activity SEE what is the centre of activity: pure VISION. Actually the VISION creates US. Is anything true?) Once we have gotten a glimpse of the vision world, we must be careful not to think the vision world is us. We must go farther and become crazier. (Acker 1984: 37)

Interspersed throughout the writing are Acker's drawings – often erotic – and especially her dream maps that themselves draw on pre-modern and non-Western styles

2.2 Kathy Acker, 'A Map of my Dreams' from *Blood and Guts in High School*, 1984 (© Grove Press and thanks to Matias Viegener).

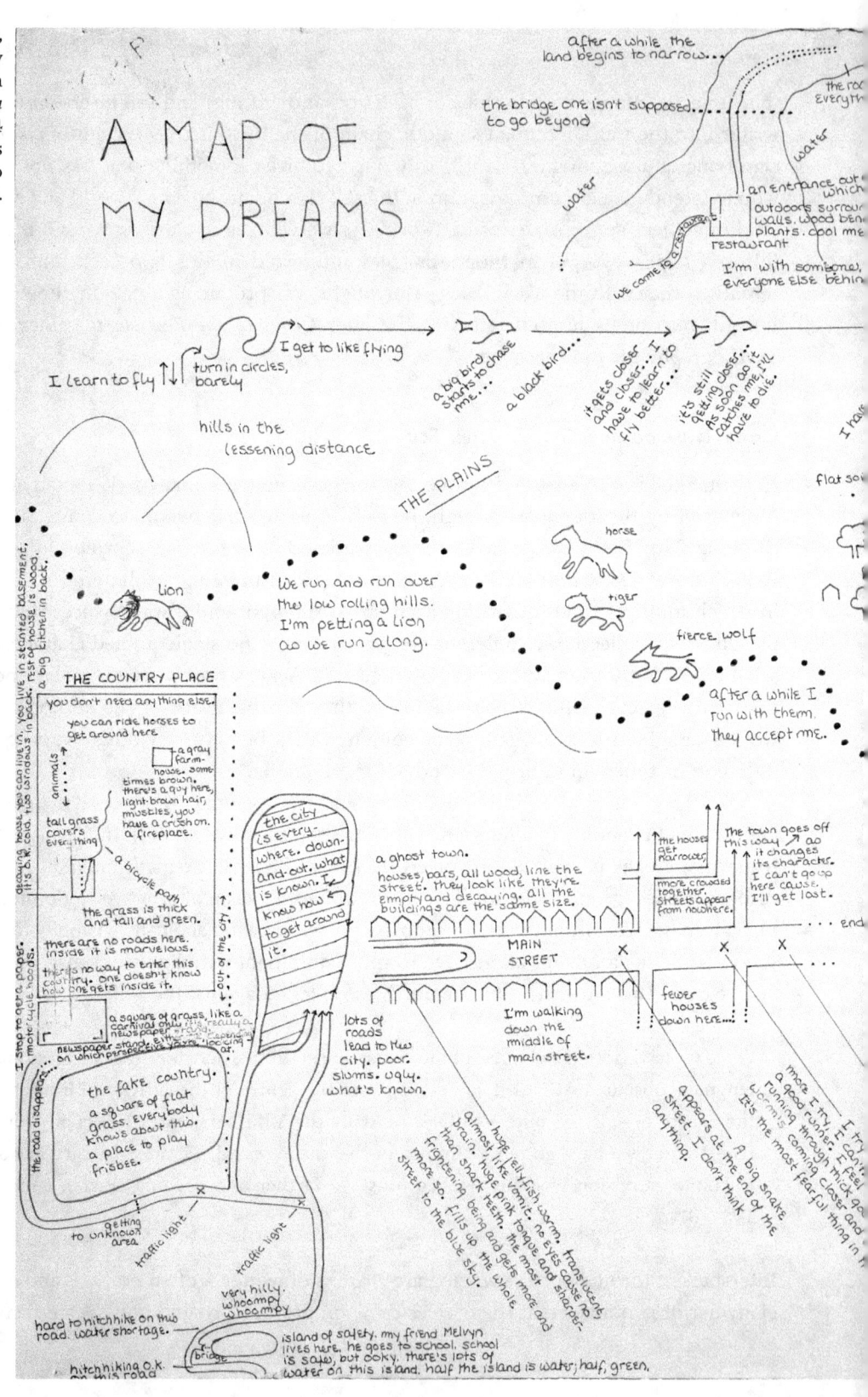

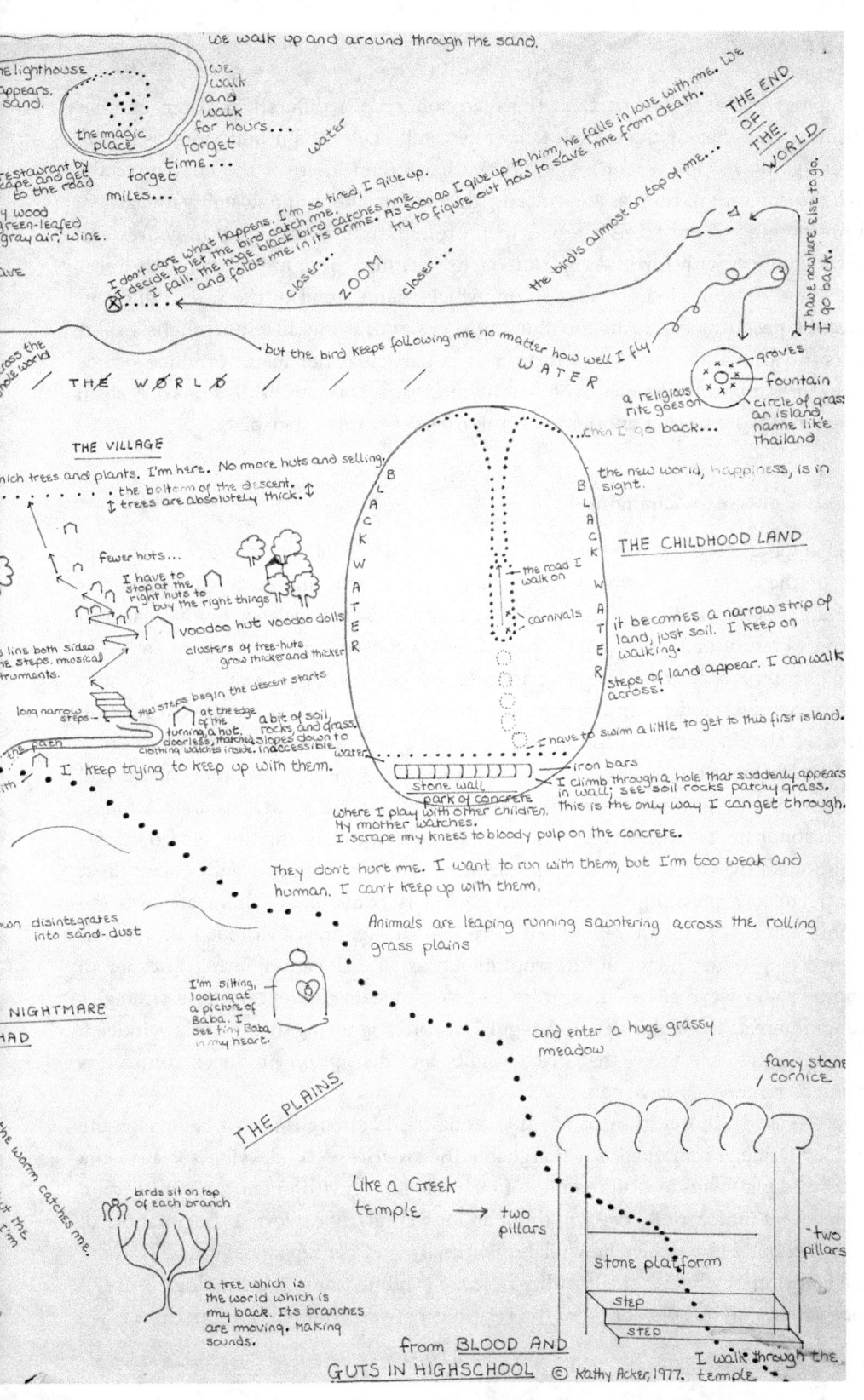

and hieroglyphs (see Figure 2.2). The maps offer up a different register, another non-linear way into myths (which makes us think of Acker's productions as a kind of avant-garde *mappa mundi*). On the one hand then, there is the content of the novel: the different narratives and tracking through of a feminine sexuality unleashed; but on the other hand there is a play with presentation, a mixing up of genres and experimentation with form. As in Burroughs' writing, there are breaks with linear sequencing, cause and effect, and so on, which then extend to the use of different forms of typesetting alongside the different styles of drawing. Like Burroughs' experiments in various media, Acker's texts, and in particular her maps, produce worlds that, by foregrounding the means of their manufacture, counter the illusions of realism and spectacle, presenting another world *written from* this other place.

Coda 2: Control is Changing

This chapter and the last have partly utilised Deleuzian concepts in order to diagram some of the operating protocols of an engaged (and avant-garde) mythopoetic/fictioning practice. But it is worth noting that a once-radical Deleuze has increasingly become a kind of orthodoxy within the Academy and, as such, it is our intention in future chapters to depart from this particular framework, or at least to put it under pressure by metamodelising Deleuze with further conceptual resources. In relation to this we should note that the nature of control societies is changing. There may now be a different relation between communication or profit and other modes and practices that foreground affect or produce discontinuous presentations. Certainly, today, capitalism produces many ambient (asignifying) information environments and products in which continuity of narrative is not maintained and where affect rather than any meaning or overcoded reality is consumed.[9] There are also the business models of Silicon Valley tech firms and the actions of various nation states designed to produce chaos and disruption, so as to dislocate or bring disorder to economies and ways of living in order to profit or gain influence. These strategies advance interests through risk and deregulation, often ignoring the rule of law. Indeed, might it be the case today that discontinuity and disruption produces control (as Burroughs might well have agreed).[10]

There is also the question of whether, today, it is enough just to believe in the world, as Deleuze remarked, since arguably the *creatives* who develop social media devices and platforms and all manner of technological environments and objects are also believers (at least of a certain kind), and are similarly exploring the potential of the human body to produce new relations. Finally, and perhaps most crucially, there is the question of whether the hostility Deleuze exhibits towards technology is useful or problematic in its conception of the relations between humans and machines. We will attend further to this in our section on mythotechnesis, but would suggest here that increasingly it might be less a question of unplugging from the networks – and attempting to claim some degree of autonomy – than of exploring and fictioning human-machine conjunctions – the path that Burroughs encourages.

This has implications for art practice, which might involve less a line of flight or vacuole of noncommunication (which, on this new terrain of fictioning, might be seen as too much of a retreat)[11] than a certain self-positioning – as an actor – in a larger field of interaction. In fact, as we shall see in later chapters, it is often the case that a multiplicity of actors or performances – human and non-human – are in play at any given time. If control is still a useful concept here, it perhaps names less an overarching logic than the proliferation of new fictions involved in short-term and strategic synchronisations and consistencies involving many kinds of agents (who themselves might operate on a new terrain of risk management and chaos, as in the case of financial derivatives). There are larger questions to consider here about resistance and where it might be located – and, indeed, about how relevant the term 'resistance' is when the very notion of disruption has become increasingly crucial to control. We will go on to explore some of this new terrain, but would note here that it is partly these changes to control that give the concept of fictioning developed throughout the book a particular traction and urgency in what is sometimes referred to as a post-fact and post-truth world.

Notes

1   In fact, it might be more accurate to say that different societies operate in different ways, and just as our own societies have perhaps moved beyond Deleuze's definitions (see the second coda to this chapter), others involve a combination of discipline and control, with the former playing the preeminent role in more repressive regimes, the latter in more 'democratic' ones. David Savat has convincingly argued that these two modes of power not only use the same 'writing machines' (databases), but that Deleuze's 'dividual' is itself a 'product' of the two modes of power in combination (treated as both form and flow, as it were) (Savat 2009).

2   Today, looking back at Deleuze and Guattari's notion of the war machine produced over forty years ago, we note that some of their pronouncements have been challenged by recent developments and scholarship, including Eyal Weizman's account of Israeli army officers employing Deleuze and Guattari's notion of smooth and striated space to develop their own war machines (2007: 200). In relation to contemporary populist politics, a case might also be made for Donald Trump's presidency as a war machine that attacks established political institutions and hierarchies.

3   It should be noted that Deleuze's use of the orientalist cliché of the desert nomad does not stand up to anthropological scrutiny. That said, Arun Saldanha has offered a defence

of what he terms Deleuze's use of available stereotypes so as to 'delineate in a visceral way, a novel conceptual sensibility otherwise difficult to name' (2017: 55). While Deleuze's romantic or Orientalist use of stereotypes is questionable, in this case he is said not to address nomads as such but produce 'the nomad-idea' (55).

4   For a discussion of Artaud in relation to this Deleuzian reading of him see Shaw 2016.

5   For more philosophical detail on this critique of utopia – as well as an intriguing footnote to the work of Ernst Bloch as a thinker of a more immanent concept of utopia – see Deleuze and Guattari 1994: 99–100.

6   This axiom – that comes at the end of the invocation at the beginning of *Cities of the Red Night* (1981) – is borrowed by Burroughs from the 1938 novel *Alamut* by Vladimir Bartol, about the eleventh-century figure Hassan-I-Sabbah, leader of the Ismailis.

7   Or, as Burroughs puts it in *The Soft Machine*:

> Because as soon as I walked out into the field I felt this terrible weight on me and there I was planting corn with them and everything I did and thought was already done and thought and there was this round of festivals where the priests put on lobster suits and danced around snapping their claws like castanets and nothing but maize maize maize – And I guess I would be there fructifying the maize God except for this one cat who was in Maya drag like me but I could see he was a foreigner too – He was very technical and a lovely fellow – he began drawing formulae on the floor and showed me how the priests operated their control racket 'It's like with the festivals and the fucking corn they know what everyone will see and hear and smell and taste and that's what thought is and these thought units are represented by symbols in their books and they rotate the symbols around and around the calendar' And as I looked at his formulas something began to crack up in my brain and I was free of the control beam and next thing we both got busted and sentenced to 'Death In Centipede' . . . (1968: 15)

8   Here, it is interesting to think of the alt-right and the Left and other agents posting rumours or 'fake news' on social media, to undermine liberal and capitalist media-machines, or of Donald Trump declaring that the established media produce fake news, to undermine the power of Fourth Estate. We will return to some of these concerns in the last section of the book.

9   For a discussion along these lines see Shaviro 2010.

10   See Klein 2007 and Bartlett 2017.

11   The Occupy movement could be said to have produced vacuoles of noncommunication that were ineffective in opposing capitalism. This led some to suggest that its emphasis on refusing representation and myth was a problem. In this, non-sense may be productive but can also be limiting (for an argument along these lines see Burrows 2015).

3   Overcoming the Fiction of the Self

'One day the masks will come off, and you will understand
all' – it came to pass, and I *was one of the masks.*

Philip K. Dick, *The Exegesis*

IN THIS CHAPTER and the next we want to focus on a key form of fiction that has been implicit (and sometimes explicit) in our discussions so far: the fiction of the self. With the term 'self' we refer to the consciousness we invariably have of ourselves as a single coherent and cohesive entity – our sense of our own self. In particular we will be discussing various case studies which both 'reveal' and obliterate this fiction, but which also offer up alternative models – other fictions – and/or foreground a form of embodied self-less experience. In Chapter 4 we look to performance art practices and turn to an idea of magical thinking. We also explore some aspects of neuroscience that specifically attend to our sense of self. In this chapter we begin our enquiry by looking to an area which is also more tangential to art practice: the use of drugs. Here we return to Burroughs but also look at works by Carlos Castaneda, Timothy Leary and Philip K. Dick. What interests us especially are the different ways in which these writers fiction their drug experiences, which is to say we are interested both in the use of drugs as a technology of transformation, but also in how this work is continued in their associated writings and the concomitant myths they produce.

All drugs involve an alteration in our body and thus our consciousness; put simply, they introduce something different into our experience. But it is with what are known as psychedelic drugs that the particular fiction of the self is revealed. In what follows, we consider three examples of psychedelic drug use from a specific moment – the 1960s – especially as this is combined with a certain kind of writing about these experiences which itself blurs the distinction between fiction and fact: writing which, precisely, fictions those experiences. Here mythopoesis involves a kind of experimental 'fiction science' (in so far as some sort of knowledge production is taking place), but also a kind of 'schizoanalysis', to use Deleuze and Guattari's term, when this names a programme (at least of sorts) for the transformation of the subject.

Yage and the Cut-up

Burroughs' is known for his addiction to heroin, and his writings are marked by his experiences with that drug. But he also experimented with other drugs, especially psychedelics and, perhaps most famously, yage – or ayahuasca – as recorded in an exchange of letters with Allen Ginsberg, published as *The Yage Letters* (Burroughs and Ginsberg 1963) (see Figure 3.1). Burroughs went looking for this 'drug of drugs', as he called it, in South America, having heard it could 'change fact'. He hoped that it might cure his heroin addiction but also, more generally, offer him another mode of being in the world. Indeed, when he eventually takes it and it has an effect beyond inducing vomiting, Burroughs writes of yage that it is precisely 'space time travel'

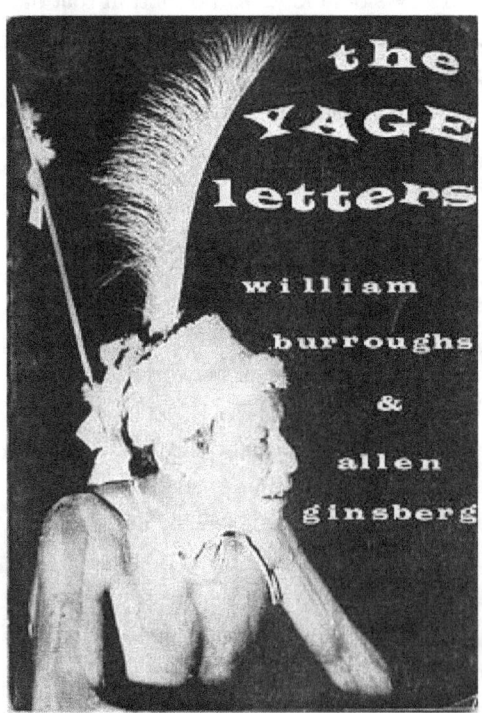

(Burroughs and Ginsberg 1963: 44). It puts him – and later Ginsberg, who repeats the journey and experiment seven years later – in touch with a more magical reality (Ginsberg himself encountered 'The Great Being'), whilst also revealing the edges of the dominant fiction of a single coherent and centred self.

Although yage does offer up a series of profound experiences and visions, crucially it is with writing that this disruption of the self and its reality is to be extended: it is the cut-up which is, eventually, the technology able to 'change fact'. When Ginsberg writes to Burroughs during his own travels, in a panic about losing his sense of self in the ego death brought on by yage, Burroughs responds with a cryptic injunction to Ginsberg to keep going and, specifically, to use the cut-up method to continue and consolidate the drug's work:

3.1 Cover of first edition of *The Yage Letters* by William S. Burroughs and Allen Ginsberg, San Francisco: City Lights, 1963 (reproduced with permission of City Lights Books).

Dear Allen:

There is no thing to fear. Vaya adelante. Look. Listen. Hear. Your AYUASKA consciousness is more valid than 'Normal consciousness'? Why return to? Why are you surprised to see me? You are following in my steps. I know thee way. And yes know the area better than you I think. Tried more than once to tell you to communicate what I know. 'You can not show to anyone what he has not seen.' Brion Gysin for Hassan Sabbah. Listen now? Take the enclosed copy of this letter. Cut along the lines. Rearrange putting section one by section three and section two by section four. Now read aloud and you will hear my voice. Whose voice? Listen. Cut and rearrange in any combination. Read aloud. I can not chose but hear. Don't think about it. Don't theorize. Try it. (59)

As we saw in Chapter 2, for Burroughs, the sequencing and syntax of language produces a particular kind of reality, or what he would come to call 'control'. The cut-up was then a method for cutting into this reality system, rearranging it, and thereby enabling the concomitant production of something different. In Burroughs' letter this is equated with the way drugs similarly produce altered states.

The Yage Letters are, however, a kind of fiction themselves, or at least not straight-forward reportage. Certainly Burroughs made the trip and took the drug, but, as the editor of the 'Redux' edition of the letters Oliver Harris makes clear, the various dates and sequence of letters do not make sense in any strictly linear manner, and there are writings included which are not directly connected to the trip, such as the compelling 'I Am Dying, Meester' script which ends up – reworked – in *The Naked Lunch* (1969). Burroughs' writing blurs the boundary between fact and fiction or, we might say, works to fiction Burroughs' journey and his drug experiences. But, in all this, *The Yage Letters* tells a story more appropriate and adequate to its subject matter: the enigmatic yage. In fact, Burroughs also wrote a more scientific article about yage and its effects, but it is certainly unclear whether this would be a more useful, accurate or pertinent account of the drug.

As a book then, *The Yage Letters* confuses any clearly demarcated genre. It is, to quote Harris again, 'a hybrid of the comic picaresque tradition, travel writing, the ethnobotanical field report, political satire, psychedelic literature and epistolary narrative' (2006: xi). There are other aspects that are also experimental: it is, of course, a collaboration – as much a work by Ginsberg as by Burroughs; but, more radically, there is a kind of folding of the one into the other, with each working as avatar and foil for the other. It contains a more basic play with form (the letter form itself, but also the irregular use of capital letters), and deploys other registers beyond the textual, as with Ginsberg's drawings of 'The Vomiter' (see Figure 3.2) and 'The Great Being'.[1]

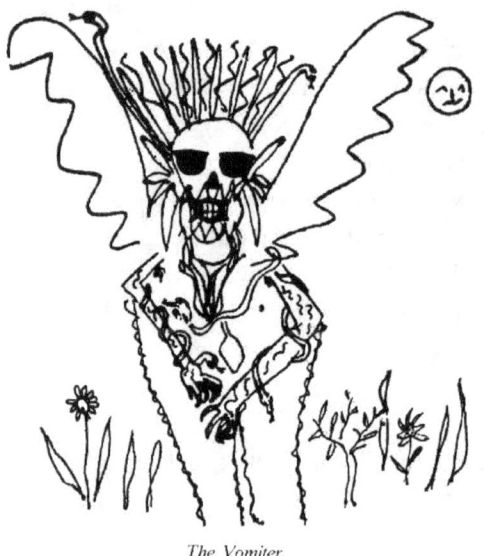

The Vomiter

3.2 'The Vomiter' from *The Yage Letters* by William S. Burroughs and Allen Ginsberg. ©1963, Allen Ginsberg LLC, used by permission of The Wylie Agency (UK) Limited.

The book, then, records a journey and quest (as we shall see, this is often a key characteristic of what we define as mytho-poetic practices), but before yage is found there is a sense that travel – what we might call Burroughs' nomadism – is also a way of sidestepping the fiction of the self (in so far as the latter tends to be solidified by habit), and, indeed, that writing might be its own kind of 'stationary voyage'. In relation to the particular archive we are exploring in this section of our own book – and especially to some of the fictions to come in Chapters 7 and 8 – there is, in part, a colonial explorer or adventurer attitude at work here, and in other of Burroughs' writings. Certainly he is as much denigrating as affirming of the people and places he visits. Although *The Yage Letters* operates as a critique of sorts of US expansion (and especially of the rubber and oil industries), it does contain, at least superficially, a colonial consciousness. But there is something radical at play here too, operating at the level of the production of subjectivity, as Burroughs' books cut up the forms by which a dominant Anglo-American imperialist subjectivity might recognise itself and be confirmed/affirmed in its existence.

According to Burroughs, one of the fabled characteristics of yage is that it produces visions of a city, and, indeed, *The Yage Letters* ends with Burroughs' compelling account of his own vision of a composite city (a collapsing of New York, Mexico City and others) in the 'I Am Dying, Meester' text mentioned above. This is how it begins:

> Panama clung to our bodies – Probably cut – Anything made this dream – It has consumed the customers of fossil orgasm – Ran into my old friend Jones – So badly off, forgotten, coughing in 1920 movie – Vaudeville voices hustle sick breath on bed service – Idiot Mambo spattered backwards – I nearly suffocated trying on the boy's breath – That's Panama – Nitrous flesh swept out by your voice and end of receiving set – Brain eating birds patrol the low frequency brain waves – Postcard waiting forgotten civilians 'and they are all on jellyfish, Meester – Panama photo town – Dead post card of junk'. (Burroughs and Ginsberg 1963: 65)

We are reminded of the psychogeographical experiments of the Situationists, albeit here it is a psychedelico/pharmico-geography, pushed and accelerated to the extreme. It is the portrayal of a city in which desire has been unleashed. In fact, with yage a strange combinatory logic seems to be at play – a kind of flattening of space-time – and, with that, the production of 'a place where the unknown past and the emergent future meet in a vibrating soundless hum' (46). Burroughs' writings involve a particular take on our spatio-temporal coordinates in this sense; causality and linear sequencing are seen as simply one more aspect of a moribund consensual reality.[2]

With *The Yage Letters* we have a form of fictioning that moves towards a kind of myth-production. Indeed, in Burroughs' letters we can see the beginnings of a new mythos which is more fully deployed in the cut-up *Nova Trilogy* and, later, in *The Cities of the Red Night* trilogy.[3] Such a mythopoesis operates against the anchoring fiction of dominant and consensual reality: the self. But this against is itself the side-effect of a more joyous affirmation of a different mode of being, one untethered from the self and its attendant logics, and which we might describe as an experimentation with that which the human might become.

Sorcerers and *Tales of Power*

Another work that is partly about psychedelic drugs (or, at least, informed by them) and the dissembling of the self – and which operates on the border between fiction and fact, dream and reality – is Carlos Castaneda's *Tales of Power*, the second in the series of books about the author's encounter – and subsequent training – with the Yaqui shaman and sorcerer don Juan. As with *The Yage Letters*, Castaneda's book is as much about the counterculture of the 1960s, and the exploration of altered states and other realities therein, as it is an anthropological or ethnobotanical study (though the first book in the series is certainly more akin to this kind of 'factual' field work). In fact, subsequent to the publication of the series it was discovered that Castaneda had invented (at least) a large proportion of the content of his books. Marcel de Lima has convincingly portrayed Castaneda's oeuvre as a form of 'ethnopoetics', in this sense of blurring the distinction between fiction and fact, but de Lima also points to the importance of using these different forms of representation in order to adequately account for the different realities that the books are about (de Lima 2014: 161–208). The very ambiguous status of *Tales of Power* is, we might say, part of its message. The book – and the whole sequence of novels about don Juan – might then be described as a kind of fictioning set against Western, rational and technoscientific paradigms of reality.

In the book Castaneda himself goes through a series of initiations in what don Juan calls the 'way of the warrior'. In the previous book in the series the use of peyote is a key method, but here it is a certain discipline (what don Juan calls a 'becoming impeccable') which allows for the shrinking of the ego and, with that, a 'side stepping' of any typical sense of self. In particular, this involves the halting of internal dialogue and description – the 'stopping of the world' as Castaneda puts it – and the concomitant 'seeing' of a deeper (or, at any rate, different) reality:

> 'I've told you that the internal dialogue is what grounds us', don Juan said. 'The world is such and such or so and so, only because we talk to ourselves about its being such and such or so and so.'
>
> Don Juan explained that the passageway into the world of sorcerers opens up after the warrior has learned to shut off the internal dialogue.
>
> 'To change our idea of the world is the crux of sorcery', he said. 'And stopping the internal dialogue is the only way to accomplish it'. (Castaneda 1974: 22)

The warrior is understood to move in a different space-time to that associated with a Western subject, hence the various miraculous feats of travel performed by don Juan and the startling coincidences that knock Castaneda off balance, precisely because they run contrary to his own description of reality and the laws by which it operates. Throughout these experiments and adventures Castaneda keeps a notebook as a way of maintaining a sense of self which is itself pinned to a propensity to interpret and explain through reason and rationality. *Tales of Power* is as much about this confrontation between two realities – the scientific and the magical – as it is a kind of instruction manual. As Deleuze and Guattari point out, the importance of Castaneda's books is in large part that they lay out a programme of transformation which operates irrespective of their status as fiction or fact (1984: 161–2).

In fact, the importance of Castaneda's writing for Deleuze and Guattari, and for some of their concepts that we have drawn upon to develop our ideas about aspects of a mythopoetic function, should not be underestimated. We saw in Chapter 1 how, in *A Thousand Plateaus*, Deleuze and Guattari turn directly to Castaneda's fictions (alongside others, including Burroughs) in order to develop their particular description of reality and, from that, their own experimental ethics or 'philosophy as a way of life', to borrow Pierre Hadot's phrase (see Hadot 1995). In particular, they develop their concepts of 'becoming-molecular' and 'becoming-imperceptible' from Castaneda's writings, and refer to key concepts from Castaneda such as the 'tonal' and 'nagual' (equivalents of phenomena and noumena, but, crucially, on a continuum); the ideas of the ally and of alliance with an outside; and the well-known concept of the rhizome. Indeed, in developing the key Deleuzo-Guattarian concept of multiplicity the pair look to Castaneda as much as Spinoza; and, as suggested in Chapter 1, central to the Becoming plateau are the 'Memories of a Sorcerer', the sorcerer here operating to blur the distinction between aesthetic figure and conceptual persona (the figure of don Juan in Castaneda's books).

The destabilising of perceived reality (and selfhood) through fiction is explored in many ways in Castaneda's works. This includes a focus on dreaming as a technology involving the production of a double (the self in the dream), which allows a shift in perspective on so-called reality (and on the sense of any 'real' self). We will be returning to the idea of perspective as important for producing realities – and to Castaneda – at the beginning of section two, but it is worth pointing out here that awareness and control of the dreaming body ('lucid dreaming') was a key technology throughout Castaneda's books. Lucid dreaming is also a phenomenon investigated by the neuroscience philosopher Thomas Metzinger, who we discuss in the next chapter and whose work on lucid dreaming features in the last chapter of our book. But Castaneda's interest in the dreaming body is very much less didactic than Metzinger's dream experiments, for Castaneda treats lucid dreams as something like a technology to explore different realities rather than to understand how our own reality is perceived. More generally, through our reading of Castaneda, we might note that dreams offer something different and unexpected, something that arrives from an elsewhere and surprises the subject. Dreams are of course unconscious in this sense, and as such might be understood as a key resource for mythopoesis (it is worth noting that Burroughs also kept a diary of his dreams as a resource for his writing; see Burroughs 1995). The same is true of visions in general – waking dreams – which, depending on one's point of view, involve either the superimposition of one reality on another or the revelation of a different reality. We have in mind especially an individual like William Blake, who engaged in a mythopoetic practice premised partly on his visions.

The Politics of Ecstasy

A third figure who can be positioned alongside Burroughs and Castaneda is Timothy Leary, who conducted his own pharmaceutical experiments with the synthetic psychedelic drug LSD, organised events including performances, and, notably, wrote about these experiences. His seminal text *The Politics of Ecstasy* (1970) is not a fiction, but it does involve a style of writing which moves between the scientific and poetic, and, in general, concerns itself with the fiction of the self. In terms of its 'scientific' aspect, Leary lists a number of 'sub-disciplines' which he thought would inevitably develop out of increasing experimentation with psychedelics. The list includes 'seven new sciences of psychedelic psychology' (Leary 1970: 279) alongside various art forms of the future:

1. Soletics – atomic-nuclear dramas
2. Genetics – evolutionary dramas

3. Som-aesthetics – bodily dramas
4. Aesthetics (erotics) – sensory dramas
5. Ascetics – intellectual dramas
6. Athletics (politics) – emotional dramas
7. Anaesthetics – escape dramas (281)

For Leary LSD offered a genuine mystical experience, altering the consciousness of its users and allowing the exploration of different space-times. Echoing Deleuze and Guattari's Bergsonian thesis about organic and inorganic 'memories' (that we alluded to in Chapter 1), Leary claimed that LSD puts the user in touch with past and future states of being, and, not least, with a 'cellular consciousness'. Like Burroughs, Leary saw the new forms of consciousness attendant on drugs as involving a refusal of control/ consensual reality and an associated and radical affirmation of self-determination (his key slogan was 'think for yourself and question authority').[4] He also presumed that this would necessarily involve people inventing their own mythologies and religions:[5]

Reader – Write Your Own

The inflexible, dogmatic teachings of our League for Spiritual Discovery (which naturally change every few weeks) hold that every human being is born divine and that the purpose of life is to rediscover your forgotten divinity.

Specifically, to relive, to regenerate, to re-enact all the classic spiritual dramas in your own seed style and to add a few flourishes of your own to the good old double-helical fleshy prayer wheel.

Thus we suggest that anyone who takes the Divine Plan seriously will inevitably spend some time and energy attending to the ancient tasks.

Start Your Own Religion

(Sorry, baby, no one else can do it for you) (299)

Visions, World-Making and *The Exegesis*

Philip K. Dick is well known for his tremendous productivity (he wrote a total of forty-four novels, including at one point four in a single year), and, perhaps unsurprisingly given this output, for his amphetamine use. But he also experimented with LSD and other psychedelics. This is not to say that his novels can simply be understood as drug writing – they contain, for example, many other references to myth-systems and dream-worlds – but it is true that for Dick writing and drug use were inextricably bound up with one another, both involving the production of altered states. His novels call into question what we have been calling consensual reality, and it is this that gives them both their paranoid edge and their resonance with Burroughs' accounts of control. But they also explore other realities and how these intersect with our familiar worlds – Dick was, after all, a Science Fiction writer in this sense. This exploration entailed a continuing questioning of the self and, ultimately, Dick's questioning of his own personal identity.

Nowhere is this more apparent than in what he came to call his 'Exegesis', only an edited selection of which has so far been published. *The Exegesis of Philip K. Dick* (2011) comprises the voluminous notes, essays and diagrams made after, and in response to, a series of revelatory experiences – but also a crisis – in February and March of 1974 (collectively titled by Dick '2-3-74'). The primary event in this sequence involved a young woman delivering a medical drug to Dick's house. When her necklace, representing the early Christian fish symbol (see Figure 3.3), caught the sun it 'activated' Dick's revelation or vision (at the time he was also on sodium pentothal for toothache). Dick's *Exegesis* involves his attempts to work out what had happened to him when, in this single moment (and then in subsequent episodes of what he called an 'anamnesis'), he was suddenly party to a vast non-human intelligence. Indeed, it is unclear to the reader – but also to Dick himself – whether this knowledge came from a distant past or a future to come, from outer space or God, or from himself (drug induced or as a result of neural atypicality).

The status of the *Exegesis* is then uncertain. At times, Dick dismissed the years of work he had put into it as a waste of time, concluding that his visions had simply been acid flashbacks. But some of the details are difficult to account for in these terms, such as the knowledge he gained of his son's life-threatening medical condition, which doctors subsequently confirmed. Is the *Exegesis* fact or fiction? The question, it seems to us, is not whether Dick was hallucinating or, on the contrary, accessing a deeper reality; rather, we would suggest that in the *Exegesis*, as in his writing more generally, Dick was constructing a world – a mythopoetic project – and, in doing so, working out who 'he' was or might become within that world, especially once all the typical coordination points (including his typical sense of self) had been removed.

The *Exegesis* also involves Dick reflecting on his own writings, which he comes to see as precursors to the

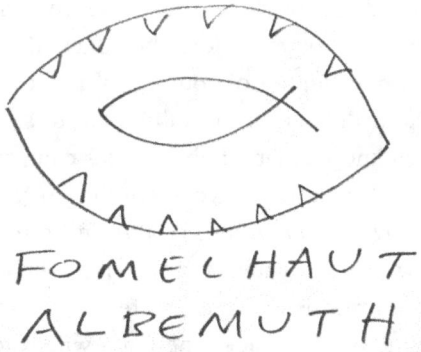

3.3 Philip K. Dick, diagram from the *Exegesis*, 2011 (used by permission of Houghton Mifflin Harcourt and Orion Books).

monumental event of 2-3-74 or, at least, as foreshadowing it, and as such giving him material with which to make sense of it. As he remarks in 1979: 'An overriding quiddity of the 2-3-74 experience is this: It's as if certain books of mine went *out* from me (*Unteleported Man, Ubik, Tears*, etc.) and then (years) later (or weeks) *came* back' (Dick 2011: 473). Dick continues a paragraph later:

> The explanation of 'who or what fed me back my books', in particular *Ubik* (in 3–74), is found in the contents of *Ubik* itself; i.e., the formulation of the information entity Ubik. Obviously I envisioned an entity which actually existed and therefore which responded *with* a feedback confirmation. (473)

His fictions were like experimental probes in this sense, writing a reality to come. Indeed, Dick's life, especially after 2-3-74, reads like one of his novels. We will be returning more directly to this idea of writing the future later, but it is worth emphasising again that Dick seems to be producing or fictioning a certain subjective and psychological reality – one that he can be said to inhabit – through his work. The novels that come after 2-3-74 likewise involved a continuing – we would say fictioning – enquiry, not least with *VALIS* (2001), the title of which stands for the 'Vast Active Living Intelligence System' which Dick had accessed (or that had accessed him). Which, we might ask, is the true account of his crisis: *VALIS* or the *Exegesis*?

As the editors suggest in their Introduction to the published *Exegesis*, the latter might be understood as a 'laboratory of interpretation' involving a 'long experiment of the mind regarding itself' (Dick 2011: xiii; xx). Certainly, there is a sense in reading it that Dick is involved in an interminable self-referential study, with interpretations nested in interpretations, fictions nested within fictions. The *Exegesis* constitutes its own dense world in this sense. In terms of the fiction of the self more specifically, Dick's writings explore the edges of the single consistent self – especially, again, in the questioning of consensual reality – and, with that, they involve the production and proliferation of multiple avatars. In this there is something of a psychosis (it is well known that amphetamines can bring on psychotic episodes).[6] In fact, in its style as well as some of its content the *Exegesis* can read like Daniel Paul Schreber's *Memoirs of my Nervous Illness* (2000). In both there is the same attention to detail, a certain puzzlement, often a melancholy, and, especially, a desire to interpret (a veritable interpretosis). Also characteristic of both is the idea that certain thoughts are felt to come from outside. These are wilder forms of thought untethered from the self and which do not obey any laws of connection, contiguity and causality. Indeed, like drug experiences, psychosis involves the production of difference from within the same, and, once again, the question of reality versus hallucination is paramount.

Dick was involved in these kinds of explorations and enquiries before 2-3-74, not just with drugs but also with technologies such as the *I-Ching*, which we might describe in this context as a technology of chance that allows access to something outside the self (Dick used the *I-Ching* to write *Man in a High Castle*). In fact, *VALIS* was partly based on the bardos and dreamtime of *The Tibetan Book of the Dead*, as well as on the Dogon myth-system. As with Burroughs and Castaneda, then, drugs were just one technology in the questioning of the self and its reality, and, as such, part of a tradition that reaches way back in time (we should note here that the past was a kind of living resource for Dick: one of the key phrases in *VALIS* and the *Exegesis* is precisely that 'time can be overcome').

In his afterword to the published *Exegesis*, Richard Doyle places Dick in what he calls a shamanic tradition, as part of the 'perennial philosophy' which Aldous Huxley wrote about (a tradition which, for Doyle, goes back to Blake, Coleridge, Julian of Norwich and Dionysius). For Doyle, the shaman is involved in practices intent on 'dissolving the ordinary self such that we might get a glimpse of reality' (Dick 2011: 899). This might be achieved by drugs or various other magical substances and potions, but also by other means, for example the repetitive beating of drums or other percussion. It is not entirely clear that writing was this kind of shamanic technology for Dick, but certainly the labour of writing the *Exegesis* involved him in attempting to construct meaning out of chaos, as a kind of world-making (and thus self-making) exercise. It is worth noting Dick's particular style of writing in relation to this. In the *Exegesis* it tends to the baroque, a veritable proliferation of frameworks, narratives, descriptions and diagrams (which, again, draws on many other sources – in fact an encyclopaedic archive). The book at times feels channelled (it is certainly written at a very particular speed). But, as the editors suggest, it has an aphoristic quality to it not unlike Nietzsche or, at times, Emil Cioran (certain phrases are incredibly condensed but also cryptic and revelatory).

Burroughs (2010) wrote that language is a virus and a parasite that has invaded its human hosts, and there is something of this evident in Dick's relationship with the signifier. Doyle also notes that Dick's account of a kind of 'info-world' – a universe teeming with information – is deeply prescient of our own networked present (and we would suggest this relates to the idea that everything is connected in some way too). Indeed, a characteristic of Dick's novels, pointed to above, is that they can exhibit paranoia and, at times, tend towards conspiracy theory. In this there are resonances with psychoanalysis, which reveals that there is always something else going on besides what we apparently know. But psychoanalysis offers a very particular kind of account of clinical analysis (for example, in terms of how the ego is involved in representations and identifications) which does not exactly dovetail with Dick's writing. It is schizoanalysis, developed by Deleuze and Guattari, that seems more relevant when discussing that writing – schizoanalysis being the name for experiments that dissemble and dissolve the self and other configurations and modes of organisation, but that also propose that an individual is composed of a diversity of different individuations, of other durations, both organic and inorganic, that can be explored through clinical and art practices.

If Dick's novels seem to us to have much in common with schizoanalysis, it is because they skirt close to chaos and the real, and towards breakdown (at least for their protagonists, who often do not know what is real and what is not), but also (or in order to) offer alternative fictions and models (this is what Guattari's other term for schizoanalysis – *metamodelisation* – gestures towards). For it is schizoanalysis that reveals that a sense of self can be made and unmade (which in turn effects subject constructions, subjectivity and identities and identifications). In using the phrase the fiction of the self as the title of the chapter we have this unmaking/making process in mind: the fiction of *a self* but also – through experimentation – alternative fictions of other possible and *multiple selves*. As we have seen, certain drugs can dislodge the fiction of *a self* – nudge our reality, show us the edges of our world – but they can also contribute to the opening up of a different reality and a different way of inhabiting it, even if, to follow Deleuze and Guattari once more, all drugs come with their own very real dangers.

Notes

1 The whole look of the original City Lights edition – with its cover image of a shaman, chosen by Burroughs (Figure 3.1) – also gives the book a certain affect or, to use a term we will deploy in subsequent chapters, a particular 'structure of feeling'.

2 In relation to this sequencing and reality effect it is worth referring back to some of the comments we made in Chapter 2 about Burroughs' interest in the audio-visual and in cutting up film: as well as securing and reinforcing a consensual reality, film can also offer another reality, or, indeed, blur the lines between fiction and reality. To take one example, Burroughs was involved in Conrad Rooks' *Chappaqua* (1967), itself a film about drugs and travel which operated as a kind of schizoanalytic therapy for its director. But this film also involved experiments with form and association, and foregrounded its own status as film (or as a fictional set-up). As Burroughs remarks in an untitled text about the film:

There is a hiatus between blocks of association, rents as it were in the fabric of reality through which we glimpse the old myths that were before the white man came, and will be after he is gone, a brief inglorious actor washed off the stage in the waters of silence. Rooks has brought to the screen the immediate experience of silent beauty conveyed in Peyote vision – older Gods waiting impassively at the end of the line. (Burroughs n.d.)

3   Ginsberg's life and poetry might also be understood as a form of mythopoesis – an example is him being crowned May King at the Prague revolution, and subsequently writing about it in his poem 'Kraj Majales (King of May)'. Ginsberg also performed his fictions, utilising mantra, chanting, and so forth.

4   We want to note here that Mark Fisher, up until his untimely death, was also working on the importance of developing a contemporary psychedelic consciousness as an antidote to 'capitalist realism'. This was part of a book project with the compelling title *Acid Communism*.

5   There are other counter-culture figures involved in this science of psychedelia and myth, for example Aldous Huxley and Ken Kesey. Both wrote about their drug experiences and, of course, also wrote fiction per se, and with Kesey and the 'Merry Pranksters' we have the performance fiction of the fabled Acid Test parties. In terms of peyote and mescaline use, two other key figures are worth mentioning in passing, one a fellow traveller, the other a precursor of sorts: Henri Michaux and Antonin Artaud, both of whom also wrote about their drug experiences in a style of writing that followed from the particular drugs they took. In an almost direct pre-parallel with Castaneda, Artaud claimed to have travelled to South America to visit the Tarahumara and take peyote. Like Burroughs, he was a heroin addict looking for a cure – in fact, for relief from the chronic pain he was in. It seems that rather than a cure, peyote fostered the invention of fictions and even new languages. As with Burroughs, Artaud's experiments with language called for a new kind of humanity – a 'people to come'. In the landscape of South America Artaud was also put in touch with other, older cultures. As he wrote in 'Here Lies':

> Here working the iron cymbals
> I take the low road of gouges
> in the esophagus of the right eye
> under the tomb of the rigid plexus
> which on the road sharply flexes
> to extricate the child by right.
> **nuyon kidi**
> **nuyon kadan**
> **nuyon kada**
> **tara dada i i**
> **ota papa**
> **ota strsakman**

tarma strapido

ota rapido

ota brutan

otargugido

ote krutan

For I was Inca but not king. (Artaud 1995: 201)

Michaux's experiments with mescaline were more clinical, but they also elicited a certain kind of writing which necessarily involved formal experimentation (as, for example, in the marginal notes to *Miserable Miracle*). Michaux himself, however, suggested that to really describe his experiences 'would require a picturesque style which I do not possess, made up of surprises, of nonsense, of sudden flashes, of bounds and rebounds, an unstable style, tobogganing and prankish' (2002: 6).

6   Dick's 1977 *A Scanner Darkly* might be seen as a more direct example of a fictioning of an episode of amphetamine psychosis.

4   Mirror Work: Self-Obliteration

The self, how empty! How prolific of incompleteness! . . . By self-effacement would seem reality.

Osman Spare, *The Book of Pleasure (Self-Love)*

THIS CHAPTER CONTINUES our discussion of the fiction of the self by attending to practices that produce self-obliteration. More specifically it addresses performances which fiction states beyond everyday, Western conceptions of space and time, and which as such counteract, or are critical of, the illusions produced by consciousness and the senses. From the perspective of the sciences, the fiction of a self is difficult to overcome, not least because human motor-sensory processes and the brain are 'wired' to produce a sense of selfhood. Indeed, selfhood is an evolutionary development that contributes greatly to the survival of the human species (and to its domination over other natures). In identifying art practices that fiction a *selfless experience* as the *after-effect* of arresting sensory processes, we propose that such practices provide valuable insight into the fiction of the self and, specifically, the relation of motor-sensory processes to selfhood. The practices in question are those of Austin Osman Spare, Robert Smithson and Yoyoi Kusama, all of which, we argue, engender depersonalised, embodied states – through rituals and disorientating processes and interventions within environments – and which might, as such, be pitched against (scientific) orientations that would dismiss embodiment as being constitutively unable to access, or provide insight into, the real.

There is no historical or geographical connection between Spare (who lived in London and died in 1956) and Smithson and Kusama (who are identified with New York's post-Second World War avant-garde); indeed, we are not concerned here with the perspective of historians attempting to trace historical influences or connections. Rather, we position these three together as each were involved in a particular kind of mythopoetic calling forth of a people attuned to the limits of selfhood, and, as such, they have some resonance with the interests of the practitioners writing on drugs addressed in the previous chapter. Furthermore, our interest in Spare, Kusama and Smithson focuses on the accounts of their art and practices to be found in their own writings – Spare's reflections on art, magic and life, published in the first quarter of the twentieth century; Kusama's autobiography *Infinity Nets* (2011); and Smithson's *Collected Writings* (1996a). These writings do not stake out an allegiance to any particular philosophical or religious tradition, but rather offer up accounts and myths of – and protocols for – self-obliteration.

Self-Love

Self-love is a practice developed by artist and occultist Austin Osman Spare, which he explains in detail in two books, *The Focus of Life* (2007a) and *The Book of Pleasure (Self-Love)* (2007b). Though one might suppose that such a practice must lead to vanity and egoism, Spare's writing is anything but a call for self-aggrandisement. Instead, Spare argues that self-love is a realisation of potential that entails understanding the self to be an illusion. Pleasure plays no small part in this. In *The Focus of Life*, published in 1921, the artist states that a will to pleasure is a function underlying all activity and that negation of self-love – the stifling of potential through the prohibition of desire – is a disease that leads to 'homicide' (2007a: 39). The reasoning behind such an extreme view relates to Spare's critique of the conscious 'I'. Captured by morality, this 'I' is without understanding of its embodiment[1] and unable to 'realize the living Self' (39).[2] Though it seems paradoxical, for Spare it is self-love which overcomes the limits of selfhood – the illusions of a thou and an I – by producing a sexuality unfettered by morality and rejecting any duality that divides the world so as to produce the illusion or consciousness of a self separate from other entities or life. At the end of 'Aphorism I' in *The Focus of Life* we are bid: 'Purge thyself of belief: live like a walking tree! Take no thought of good and evil. Become self-active causality by Unity of thine, I and Self. Reality exists not in consciousness of such: this phenomenal "I" is noumenal' (31).[3] In suggesting that selfhood, this phenomenal 'I', is in fact noumenal and cannot be fully registered through the perception of appearances, Spare is proposing that the senses deliver semblances – representations of the world – which prevent humans from understanding actual and embodied modes of life. This is of interest to us not least because Spare argues that a human cannot know or realise life through consciousness. This may accord with the scientific claim that reality involves much more than our senses can capture, but whereas scientists might seek to produce critical representations of consciousness and approximate reality through concepts, Spare's response to the problem is very different. He experiments with various modes of becoming a 'walking tree' through art and other practices, so as to produce more (or perhaps less) than a scientific, third-hand or objective account of the human and selfhood. That is, he develops self-love as the elision of selfhood through a number of practices that attend to, as well as disorientate, the body's senses and consciousness, producing artworks but also magical performances.

Spare's notion of the practice of magic involves a syncretic appropriation of esoteric and Eastern philosophies, similar to a number of syncretic art practices that appeared in Europe in the nineteenth and twentieth centuries. He defines such practice as 'the reduction of properties to simplicity, making them transmutable to utilize afresh by direction, bearing fruit many times' (2007b: 84). Here, magic is a method that breaks the attributes of forms down to their most rudimentary elements. This process is at the core of Spare's practice and, in pragmatic terms, involves methods that register the real through a state of vacuity. Such performances, through confounding or overwhelming the senses, embrace a void (a voiding of ego, selfhood and identity) which reveals the blind spots or limits of experience. In this, the body and its senses – as a technology that processes information and facilitates consciousness – becomes a measure or indexical instrument of a kind. In Spare's writing, the absence of self-consciousness is presented (or fictioned) as the embodiment of a negative state, the state of self-obliteration. A question might be raised here as to the nature of this state which is necessarily closed to selfhood and not accessible to self-consciousness – reason dictates this – and which, therefore, might be said to be inaccessible to experience. For this reason we emphasise that the fictioning of self-obliteration occurs through protocols for performances and writing, not just to present or register self-lessness but to provide a means for others to enter into self-obliteration, both by engaging with certain methods and accounts and through artworks that provide platforms or the means for experimentation.

Self-Illusion

Before discussing vacuity and self-obliteration in twentieth-century art practice, it is instructive to comment further on contemporary scientific and philosophical discourses which problematise selfhood and, in doing so, cast doubt on the notion that the body and its senses can engender knowledge of any significant kind. For example, the neuroscience philosopher Thomas Metzinger has asserted that 'a theory saying that a certain state of affairs is actually perceived by the senses' is 'folk epistemology' (2003: 499). To counter this naive epistemology, Metzinger explains that the senses engender a sense of self, which is a process not evident to experience:

> Ultimately subjective experience is a biological data format, a highly specific mode of presenting information about the world by letting it appear as if it were an Ego's

knowledge. But no such things as selves exist in the world. A biological organism, as such, is not a self. An Ego is not a self, either, but merely a form of representational content of a transparent self-model activated in the organism's brain (8).

Metzinger – interestingly, someone who has researched vipassana meditation – is one of the leading exponents of the neuroscientific account of the self as a kind of myth or illusion. For Metzinger, we experience life in and through our own particular 'ego tunnel': 'the content of our conscious experience is not only an internal construct but also an extremely selective way of representing information . . . What we see and hear and smell and taste, is only a small fraction of what actually exists out there' (6). Although consciousness is an important mechanism for human survival, Metzinger demonstrates that it invariably has limited access to 'the enormous wealth and richness of reality in all its unfathomable depth' (2009: 6). At the beginning of his book on *The Ego Tunnel*, Metzinger suggests that his key idea – that the senses produce a narrow or limited (tunnel-like) registration of reality – was developed, in part, from countercultural ideas of a 'reality tunnel' proposed by figures such as Robert Anton Wilson and Timothy Leary, although he is also keen to highlight the problems with this more popular account (8–9). As far as the counterculture's exploration of human consciousness goes, drugs were clearly important in revealing perception as a tunnel, but Metzinger's own approach tends towards the more scientific and involves laboratory experiments and the language and concepts of the sciences.

Important in Metzinger's account of the 'ego tunnel' is the idea of a 'phenomenally transparent self-model' (2003: 331). He explains this as a system in which motor-sensory processes produce a sense or representation of the boundaries of a body that, in turn, generate the sense of an interiority of selfhood within an environment perceived as an exterior. Importantly, as implied above, humans do not experience this model as a representational process, for the process is transparent (not apparent) to the system, activating a self-model that is felt to be '*ourselves, living in the world right now*'. This produces an illusion of 'direct contact with the contents of self-consciousness', for the fact is that self-experience is produced through a '*medium*' that is inaccessible to human experience (331). Metzinger names this self-experience a 'special form of darkness' (331), one that produces '*naive-realistic misunderstanding*' (332).

This insight is yet one more scientific blow to a human-centric worldview, and one which Spare, Kusama and Smithson – as we will see – might have had sympathy with. What they may have disagreed with, however, is Metzinger's idea that there is no way we can access or experience a greater reality outside our particular representations or models: for him, 'the whole idea of potentially being in touch with reality is a sort of romantic folklore' (2009: 9). Any knowledge we have is necessarily through representations – indeed, this, for Metzinger, is what knowledge is (his view on things is profoundly Kantian in this sense). As he remarks, in a statement that sums up his take on the matter: 'All evidence now points to the conclusion that phenomenal content is determined locally, not by the environment at all but by internal properties of the brain' (10).

If experience is limited, and self-consciousness limiting, what might be the alternatives to the darkness of selfhood? Metzinger proposes that, by way of the conceptual instruments of neuroscience and cognitive studies, a shift in perspective can be produced that he names *methodological nemocentricism* (2003: 628).[4] This entails producing a nemocentric reality model that:

> satisfies a sufficiently rich set of constraints for conscious experience, while at the same time not exemplifying phenomenal selfhood. It may be functionally egocentric but phenomenologically selfless. It would, while still being a functionally centred representational structure, not be accompanied by the phenomenal experience of being someone. (336)

We would add here that the 'it' of Metzinger's proposal is a new subject (a nemocentric people to come) that has knowledge of, if not freedom from, the mechanisms that produce selfhood: an imagined subject who's potential to be manifested in the here and now is explored (or, we would suggest, fictioned) by Metzinger through the conceptual instruments and laboratory experiments of cognitive science.[5] In this, the mediation of selfhood becomes apparent and a critical distance is opened up for this new subject through the concepts and practices of science, leaving 'folk' practices, including art, with an uncertain if not redundant status. It seems that if we wish to dispense with the myths of selfhood, then we have little choice but to accept the limitations of humans and become cognitive scientists (and perhaps abandon art).

Metzinger's nemocentric subject might think Spare naive, but one of the artist's criticisms of the sciences is worth noting. Spare thought scientific theories not only limited but also limiting. In *The Book of Pleasure (Self-Love)*, he makes it clear that he does not value morals or religion, nor any beliefs that employ words as a means to control or limit desire. This includes the sciences, which add only a 'dearly paid inch to our height: no more' (2007b: 61). Scientific knowledge is cast by Spare as yet more bondage (to concepts), a view that may be misguided and unjust in suggesting that science is limiting, but which raises important questions concerning mastery and the privileging of discourse in scientific perspectives.

We have some sympathy with Spare's critique. While we broadly accept the arguments of neuroscience, we continue to be interested in experience and embodiment, which may be thought of as an unvalued or diminished remainder of Metzinger's production of a nemocentric reality. How easy it might be to achieve a pure nemocentric reality is an interesting question too, for even a scientist, after giving the most rigorous of explanations concerning the illusions of selfhood, will find experience and embodiment hard to overcome or dispense with in life.[6] But perhaps it is not necessarily impossible, and – as we will see in the final section of our book – many have attempted to overcome what are perceived as the limitations of the body, including experience and embodiment, by transcending the world of flesh and desire through conceptual and technological instruments. As such, the question as to what is gained or lost by the transcendence of cognition over experience and embodiment becomes an important matter.

It is in relation to this that Spare's accounts of embodied states that register appearance as illusion – through approaching the body as a technology – seem to be significant, offering alternatives to scientifically informed methods that attend to the body, embodiment and experience as material for study. It is true, however, that conceiving of such a thing as a body is problematic or needs thought. Given that phenomenal and psychological processes produce a unity or image of the body, and that technology produces cyborgs, artificial life and intelligences with ever increasing complexity, the notion or definition of 'the body' and embodiment should be continually questioned as a construct. Furthermore, in Metzinger's account of the phenomenal-self-model, embodiment is said to engender phenomenal immediacy – the feeling of being in a body – and we have learnt from Metzinger that embodiment too is itself a highly mediated process not apparent to humans. As he states: 'the phenomenal experience of being an embodied self certainly cannot function as a successor of the Cartesian cogito in terms of providing a safe foundation for all knowledge. Phenomenal embodiment is not a reliable epistemic anchor in physical reality' (2003: 442). So, while Metzinger may accept that embodiment and experience can develop intelligence, embodiment and experience are themselves unreliable. This is why he turns to the conceptual instruments of the sciences and philosophy as a means to counter the errors of experience.

There remains the question, however, as to whether human intelligence can be separated from embodiment. We also think the body and perception are ripe for experimentation, which may produce knowledge of a kind. As we saw in the last chapter, changing or adding to the chemical composition of a human body, and even changing the location or environment in which that body is situated, can alter states of consciousness and transform experiences of space, time and selfhood. In discussing the practices of Spare and others, then, our concern is not so much with defining what the body is as with exploring what its motor-sensory processes as a medium can do or produce. That is, our interest here is in whether such practices can engender new perspectives beyond the limits of selfhood; whether it is possible to register selfless experience as an embodied state (as collapse or interruption). Not least because mastery and belief would be suspended in such instances of self-obliteration, making precariousness and discontinuity a focus of life.

Neither-Neither

The Book of Pleasure (Self-Love), published in 1913, makes a bold claim: self-love dissolves conceptions of self and other and opens up a path to a state Spare calls *Kia*, producing an unmodified 'I' which is neither male nor female, neither hermaphrodite nor eunuch (2007b: 65). Spare is cautious (and perhaps sounds a little contradictory) when writing about *Kia*, which is his name for something eternal which has no name, which 'burns up belief', and which he claims to be the 'archetype of self' enslaved by mortality (65). Spare seeks freedom through self-love, but a freedom of a strange kind: freedom from concepts and beliefs, as already discussed, but also an absolute freedom registered when the ego is able to receive *Kia* without preconceived notions. An objection might be raised here as to how a state or reality might be identified at all, and given the name *Kia*, if it is beyond (or escapes) concepts and belief? It is hard to accept that Spare's notion of *Kia* does not involve a concept or two, for all discourse and sense made from perception relies on concepts. What we think he is suggesting, however, is that self-obliteration is an episode registered through certain practices or in specific instances; it is a condition (or experience) that is passed through and remembered, reflected upon, identified and imagined or imaged afterwards. Only then are concepts and language called upon to register the *Kia*-event, even if they invariably fall short of the task.

In embracing freedom, as we have noted above, Spare declares that duality must be rejected as a limit and illusion. When you are conscious of a butterfly that flits across the sky, he asks, how could you be conscious of something that is not you? How can you and the butterfly not be one and the same? (70). Consciousness of 'Thee' and 'Me' is an unwelcome 'torturer' (70) producing self-deception. How can one love (or hate) another if there is no other? Only self-love is possible. While the implications of Spare's statements on duality can be questioned – in particular that you and the butterfly are the same thing – his critique can be read in more complex ways, as pointing to the fact that the conscious 'I' registers or produces the appearance of the butterfly as separate and other. Furthermore, as the butterfly flits through the air, the conscious 'I' fails to register that a desire to fly from one place to another may be shared by both human and butterfly. Spare refuses to divide the world, not just because appearances are untrustworthy, but also because, as far as he is concerned, division and classification – which might be thought of as a scientific approach but also as an everyday mode of attending to the world – are products of consciousness.

A question emerges here as to where this refusal of identity might leave Spare himself? In eschewing identification he adopts a process he names as the *Neither-Neither* principle, which can be understood as a negation of negation[7] in which all duality is refused and everything is embraced as equal (and thus as a voiding of self). In other words, the rejection of duality is the basis for Spare's presentation or fictioning of the figure (or myth) of an unmodified 'I'. Of this process he writes: 'all these conditions I transcend by a "Neither" principle, yet although a "Neither" is vague, the fact of conceiving it proves its palpability, and again implies a different "Neither"' (73). Spare suggests that through this principle he is able to pass beyond concepts and embrace a state which is not balanced by another. In this, he suggests, 'The "I" principle has reached the "Does not matter–need not be" state, and is not related to form' (73).

To achieve such a state, Spare promotes what he calls 'The Death Posture', or perceiving light without shadow, a negative or death state in which self-consciousness sleeps and from which an awakening (rebirth or return) is possible, revealing duality as fiction (74–5). He describes the posture as 'expressing' the condition of yawning, which a person performs by sighing (taking in and expelling air) and smiling while lying on their back. Alternatively, and in preparation for the smiling yawn, Spare suggests extending the neck and standing on tiptoe while clasping the hands behind the back, breathing rapidly until giddiness and exhaustion overtake the body. One more practice he proposes for realising the *Neither-Neither* principle involves using a mirror: he instructs us to gaze into a mirror until our focus becomes blurred and the features reflected in the glass are no longer recognisable, then to close our eyes and concentrate on the light flickering behind the eyelids (see Figure 4.1) (74).

All these practices produce results which are explicable or understandable as having physical causes. When examined from the perspective of neuroscience or ophthalmology, it is clear that nothing supernatural can be said to occur. For example, in Spare's mirror magic, the light seen before the closing of the defocused eyes produces an afterimage as the lenses adjust to the darkness produced by the closed eyelids. Scientists have studied this phenomenon and named it as entoptic hallucination (rather than optical hallucination); that is, the eyes alone can produce visual effects which, unlike most images, cannot be seen by others. In the past, some have claimed such images to be vital globules, but science reveals this is an error. Spare though makes no such claims; rather, he is interested in the psychological effects of the practice, 'in the feeling of immensity (which sees a small form), whose limit you cannot reach' (74).

Spare has other uses for vacuity and for other methods that disorientate the senses, including sigil magic. Creating a sigil involves making abstract symbols by scrambling and rearranging words that express wishes or desires, followed by the 'burning' of the sigil into the subconscious by staring at the image while engaging in actions that produce exhaustion. Following this procedure, the wish is eventually forgotten, but

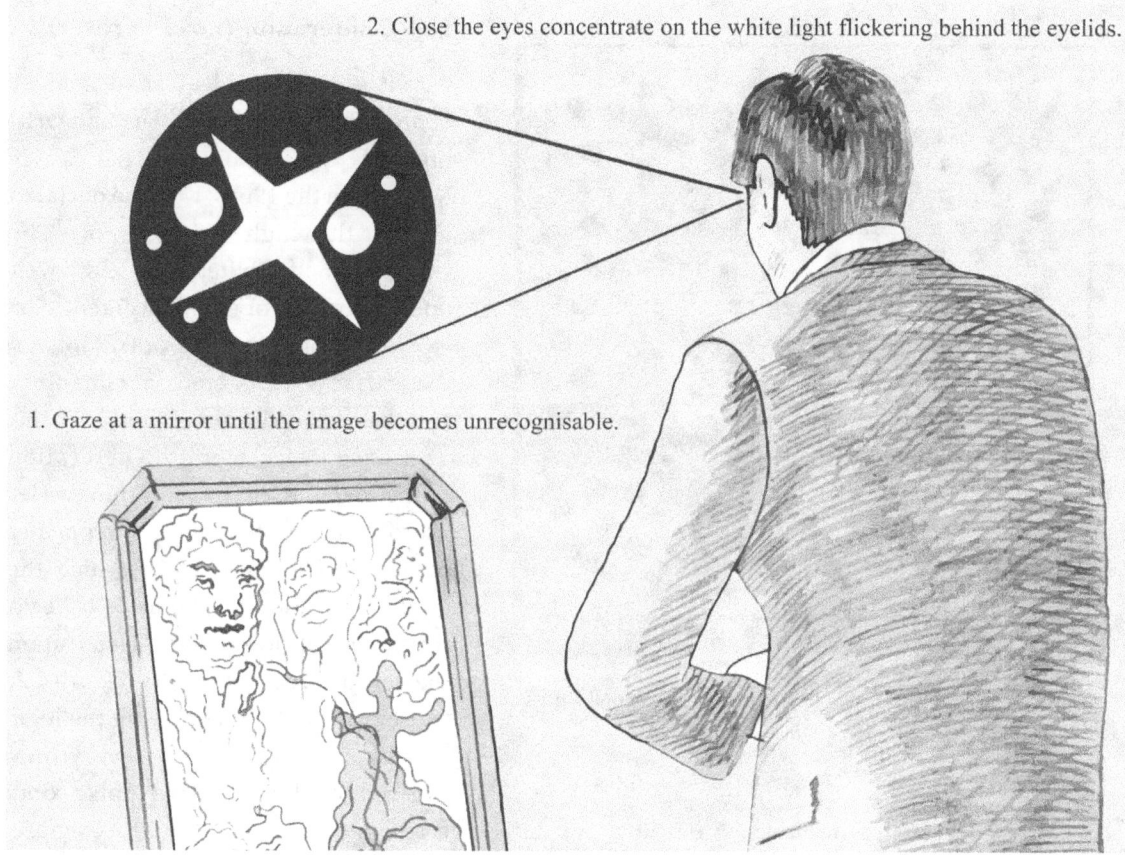

2. Close the eyes concentrate on the white light flickering behind the eyelids.

1. Gaze at a mirror until the image becomes unrecognisable.

4.1 Diagram of Austin Osman Spare's use of a mirror to see a small form whose limit cannot be reached (credit: the authors).

only by the conscious self. The sigil-maker unconsciously realises a wished-for state or transformation, without consciousness or belief placing a limit on the desire (91–3). In Spare's description of sigil magic, belief is revealed as something to be experimented with, through believing what is unbelievable. In relation to art practice more directly, vacuity – as an emptying out of consciousness – is also important for producing drawings when staring into mirrors or when making automatic draw-ings, which, Spare suggests, 'permits the germ of an idea in the subconscious mind to express, or at least suggest itself to consciousness' (Carter and Spare 2007: 8).

In conclusion then, Spare makes good use of vacuity, while holding firm to the principle that any belief in, and conception of, selfhood produces only error. To repeat the lines we took as our epigraph to this chapter, and with which he concludes *The Book of Pleasure (Self-Love)*: 'The self, how empty! How prolific of incomplete-ness! . . . By self-effacement would seem reality' (2007b: 93–4).

Positive/Polka Dot

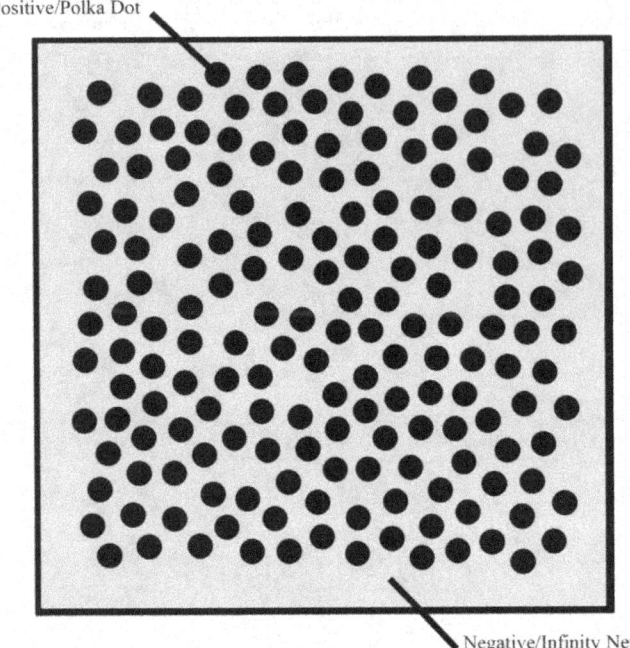

Negative/Infinity Net

4.2 Diagram of negative/positive relation of Kusama's polka dots and the *Infinity Net* (credit: the authors).

Self-Obliteration (Love Forever)

Parallels with the ideas advocated by Spare can be found in the art and writings of the Japanese artist Yoyoi Kusama. In the 1960s, Kusama declared herself the high priestess of 'The Church of Self-Obliteration' and developed a practice of ego-effacement. She is famous for inscribing polka dots on the surfaces of objects, architecture and the bodies of animals and humans; a practice which blurs the perception of the boundaries between things. Her use of polka dots stemmed from her paintings of 'infinity nets' in which 'the ground – or mesh of the net – is negative, and the polka dots placed upon the ground are positive' (see Figure 4.2) (Kusama 2011: 47). Following the logic of Kasuma's statement, everything covered by her positive polka dots becomes negative or nothing. As difference and boundaries appear to collapse, everything seems to dissolve into an *Infinity Net*.

Kusama explores her own complexes and fears in her work. She once claimed to be terrified of penetration, a fear she addressed by making many soft, phallic-shaped objects which she calls 'macaroni sculptures', adding that 'I make them and make them and then keep on making them, until I bury myself in the process. I call this obliteration' (47). In this way, the fear of penetration by another disappears as Kusama herself disappears.

Influenced in the 1960s by the politics of the counterculture and the art of her peers, Kusama organised performance events commonly referred to as 'Happenings', developing an expanded practice which used simple means – the repeated painting of polka dots – to transform or collapse experience (a practice of reducing or collapsing forms to simplicity or infinite substance, which corresponds to Spare's definition of magic). Of this expanded approach Kusama writes:

For example, by covering my entire body with polka dots, and then covering the background with polka dots as well, I find self-obliteration. Or I stick polka dots all over a horse standing before a polka dot background, and the form of the horse disappears, assimilated into the dots. The mass that is 'horse' is absorbed into something timeless. And when that happens, I too am obliterated. (47)

For Kusama, obliteration of self equals obliteration of time, as the obliteration of boundaries between things registers 'something timeless' (47). Here we can reflect on the ways in which humans bind a self and world together through perceiving, imagining or measuring figures and objects in space and time, a process which Kusama suggests is interrupted by collapsing figure–ground relationships and suspending the differentiation of forms. This idea was not just the product of a repetitive painting practice – Kusama claims it resulted from an event in her childhood. In her autobiography *Infinity Net*, she recounts an occasion when, after staring at a flowery red tablecloth, she averted her gaze and the red flower pattern seemed to cover every surface she looked at. This event had a lasting effect on her:

> I saw the entire room, my entire body, and the entire universe covered with red flowers, and in that instant my soul was obliterated and I was restored, returned to infinity, to eternal time, absolute space. This was not an illusion but reality itself. (69)

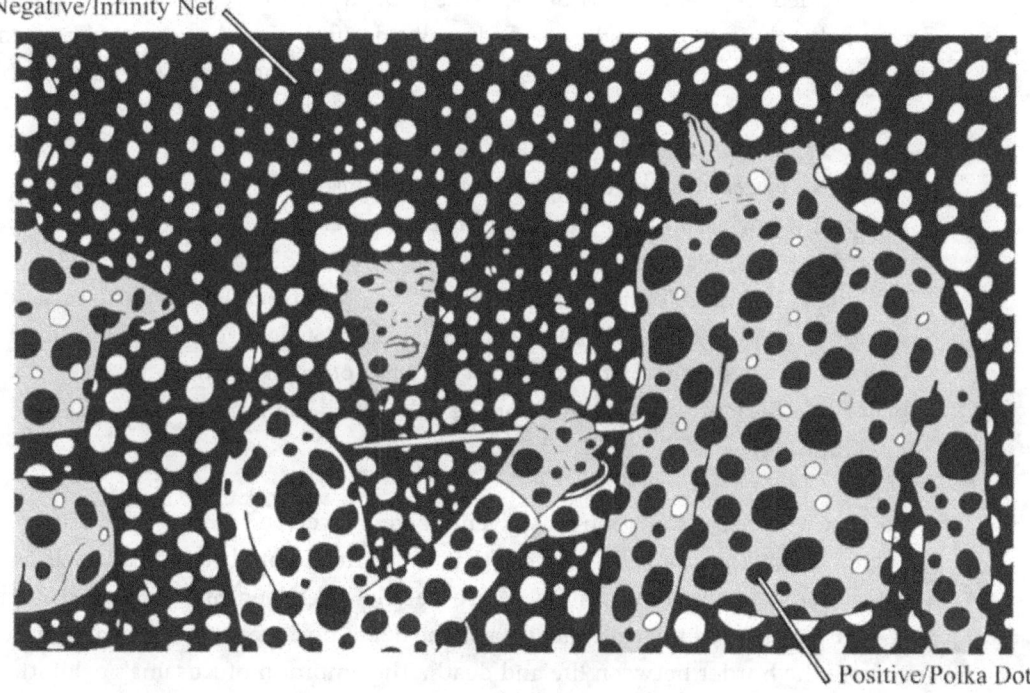

4.3. Diagram of obliteration of figure–ground relations in the performances of Kusama (credit: the authors).

Here we find another echo of Spare's philosophy, but with the key difference that Kusama explores self-obliteration communally, through Happenings, and as having political potential (see Figure 4.3). She describes one such event as a 'Sex Happening', in which performers began whipping each other and 'doing sexual things with dogs and so forth' before painting their bodies with polka dots, which she identifies as the 'trademark of the Kusama Happenings' (102). On a number of occasions, she suggests that the dots might be the Earth, Sun or Moon, which produce a movement (optically but also implying a movement of bodies). Ultimately, however, what concerns her is that painting polka-dot patterns on someone 'caused that person's self to be obliterated and returned him to the natural universe' (102). Here we could think of Kusama's trademark polka dot as a sigil, but it is also more than that, being envisaged by the artist as a device for disorganising vision and bodies, and for collapsing any perception of difference and identity.

Kusama began using mirrors as a means of further developing disorientating presentations. In her exhibition at the Castellane Gallery in New York in 1965, she installed mirrors to make her macaroni sculptures appear as an infinite, 'miraculous field of phalluses' (51). By 1966, in the same gallery, Kusama hoped to induce 'madness' by combining wall-length mirrors with flashing lights and music, creating an environment she titled, *The Endless Love Show*. In the publicity brochure for the show Kusama declared that the exhibition addressed 'Unrealized Infinite Love' and offered a second title for the exhibition, *Kusama's Peep Show*, claiming that it allowed untouchable things to be seen (48–51):

> This was a materialisation of a state of rapture I myself had experienced, in which my spirit was whisked away to wander the border between life and death . . . This was my living, breathing manifesto of Love. Thousands of illuminated colours blinking at the speed of light – isn't this the very illusion of Life in our transient world? In the darkness that follows a single flash of light, our souls are lured into the black silence of death. The kaleidoscope of our lives and joys . . . a paper-thin instant, dependent upon denial and disconnection at one-second intervals. (51)

Each visitor to the installation was given a badge inscribed with 'Love Forever'. It does not seem too crude to suggest that the button could have read 'Self-Love Forever', for it is apparent that there are parallels between Spare's notion of the '*Kia*-void' (registered through vacuity and the death posture) and Kusama's wandering along the border between life and death. The ambition of Kusama's exhibitions of disorientating mirror installations, then, is that self-effacement will seem to all to be reality.

Dedifferentiation

Although Robert Smithson explores ideas similar to those developed by Spare and Kusama, his approach differs in that he is interested in dialectical or scientific methods, though his concern is with timelessness and scales that transcend measure and confound logic or rationality. A key work in this respect is his construction *Enantiomorphic Chambers*, a wall work made in 1964 comprised of two mirrors placed at angles that confuse (human) vision. The viewer cannot see their own reflection, which is cancelled by standing between the two mirrors (see Figure 4.4); the device only captures the reflections of reflections and the environment surrounding the viewer. The term 'enantiomorphic' refers to crystalline structures and facets of crystals which produce oblique reflections. In titling his piece *Enantiomorphic Chambers*, Smithson highlights how the work's two chambers do not deliver the expected image of the self but generate an awareness of looking for an image which

4.4 Diagram of Robert Smithson's *Enantiomorphic Chambers* (credit: the authors).

Reflections are fleeting instances that evade measure.

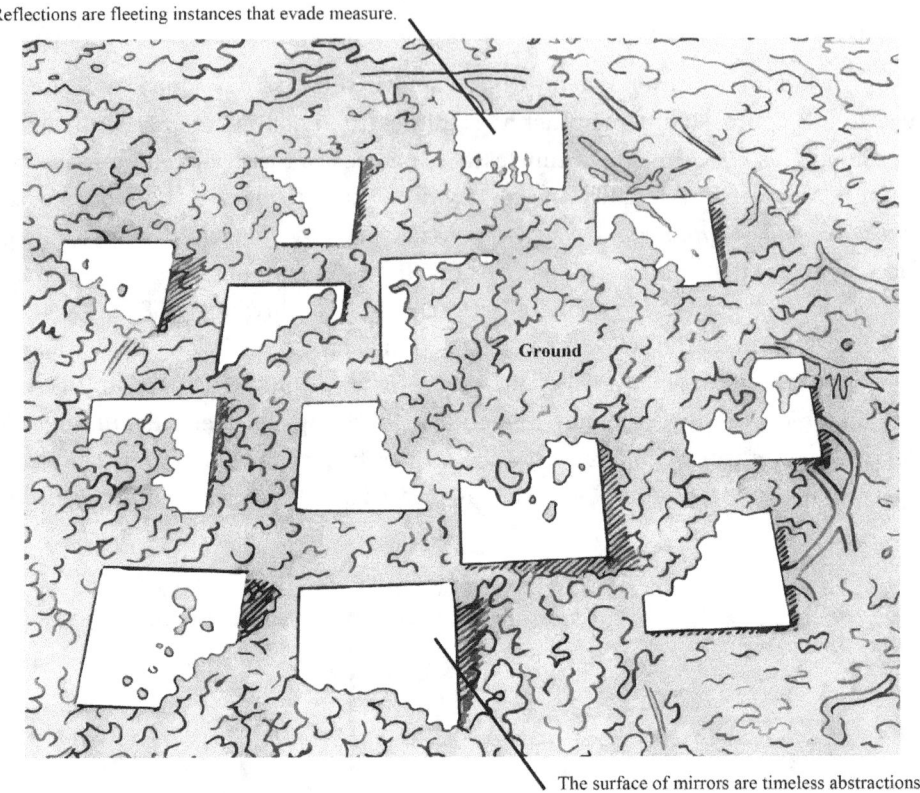

Ground

The surface of mirrors are timeless abstractions.

4.5 Diagram of Robert Smithson's *Yucatan Mirror Displacements* (credit: the authors).

does not materialise. In his text 'Interpolation of the Enantiomorphic Chambers' from 1966 he writes: 'To see one's own sight means visible blindness' (1996b: 39–40). This cryptic proposition about the artwork is made clearer in a description Smithson gave in an interview, in which he suggests that the chambers are 'like a set of eyes outside my personal set, so it's a kind of depersonalization' (208).

Smithson went on to explore this divestment of the self and self-image through *Yucatan Mirror Displacements (1–9)*, made in 1969. The artist produced nine mirror displacements by cantilevering twelve mirrors in earth and foliage; the arrangements were then photographed and dismantled (see Figure 4.5). Each mirror assemblage mixes aspects of the environment or captures both the sky and ground, with the horizon line – impossible to reach – appearing at Smithson's feet. Of equal interest though, is that Smithson is not visible in the reflections. Through careful positioning of his body and camera in relation to the mirrors, it seems that – just as in *Enantiomorphic Chambers* – Smithson is able to disappear from sight while gazing at the environment through the cantilevered mirrors, reflections of contiguous surroundings being the only images produced. Both artworks are examples of Smithson's engagement with the possibilities opened up by minimalism, but they also mark his interest in addressing the psychological and subjective aspects of seeing or looking and of experience. A minimalist work (or what the artist Donald Judd called a *specific object*) addresses the relation of an object to the viewer's (active) body and the space or environment that object and viewer occupy. Smithson not only explores perception, his work invites the viewer to reflect upon how a body with its senses is an instrument which produces not only images of the world but a self-image or selfhood (and how, through an action, movement or performance engendered by Smithson's work, a representation of self can be lost too).

In 'Incidents of Mirror-Travel in the Yucatan', a text which narrates the making of the nine mirror displacements, Smithson recounts a car journey through Mexico which conjures up Aztec or Mayan avatars that speak to him as he travels through different environments (1996c: 119–33). One deity, Tezcatlipoca –associated with obsidian, the material from which mirrors are made – appears in his rear-view mirror (appropriately) and tells the artist to throw away his travel guides and history books, for if he wants to make art it is best to get lost in the thickets, like the first Mayan (120). Smithson follows Tezcatlipoca's advice and makes the first of his nine mirror displacements in a field of ashes. The third displacement catches an image of butterflies that seem to fly in a sky of gravel. When Smithson makes his fourth arrangement on a shoreline he understands that the mirror displacements cannot be addressed in rational terms. Chalchihuitlicue, the Aztec goddess of water, confirms this by telling Smithson 'The true fiction eradicates the false reality' (123). A fifth mirror displacement lodges mirrors in a tree in a jungle. Smithson writes that particles of colour infect the reflections and that deadly, sickly greens devour all light – an encounter with real colour being a risky business. The eighth mirror displacement is constructed in the Island of Blue Water, a territory continually dropping back into the water. Smithson looks at the surfaces of the mirrors awash with crumbling particles of matter and describes his eyes as wastebaskets, depositories for diverse colours, ashy hues and sunburned chromatics. He asks why he would try to construct what can be seen, in language, and answers this question by writing, 'Why not reconstruct one's inability to see?' (130). The final displacement is produced in the branches and roots of a mangrove, and the assemblage provokes Smithson to think about art, nature and time, realising that it is mirrors – with their capacity to take on the appearance of many things – that arrest time, rather than rocks or natural forms.

Smithson argues that the significance of the mirror displacements lies in the fact that mirrors are not subject to duration – their surfaces are always continuous, timeless abstractions and their reflections 'fleeting instances that evade measure' (122). In this he echoes the views of Spare and Kusama, and goes on to suggest:

> Space is the remains, or corpse, of time, it has dimensions. 'Objects' are 'sham space', the excrement of thought and language. Once you start seeing objects in a positive or negative way you are on the road to derangement. Objects are phantoms of the mind, as false as angels. (122)

For Smithson (as for Kusama and Spare) it is important to develop practices which produce depersonalisation and dedifferentiation (or self-obliteration or vacuity) – that is, a blindness of a kind – in order to suspend phenomenological and epistemic conditioning and register reality as a negative of appearance. But we also find in his work a movement between dialectical and scientific ideas on the one hand and 'folk' imagery and thought, magical or mystical, on the other – the true fiction eradicating the false reality (Smithson's own *Neither-Neither* principle).

Smithson's best-known work is probably *Spiral Jetty* (1970), a giant drawing of a spiral made from rocks laid out in a salt lake in Utah (see Figure 4.6). 'Spiral Jetty'

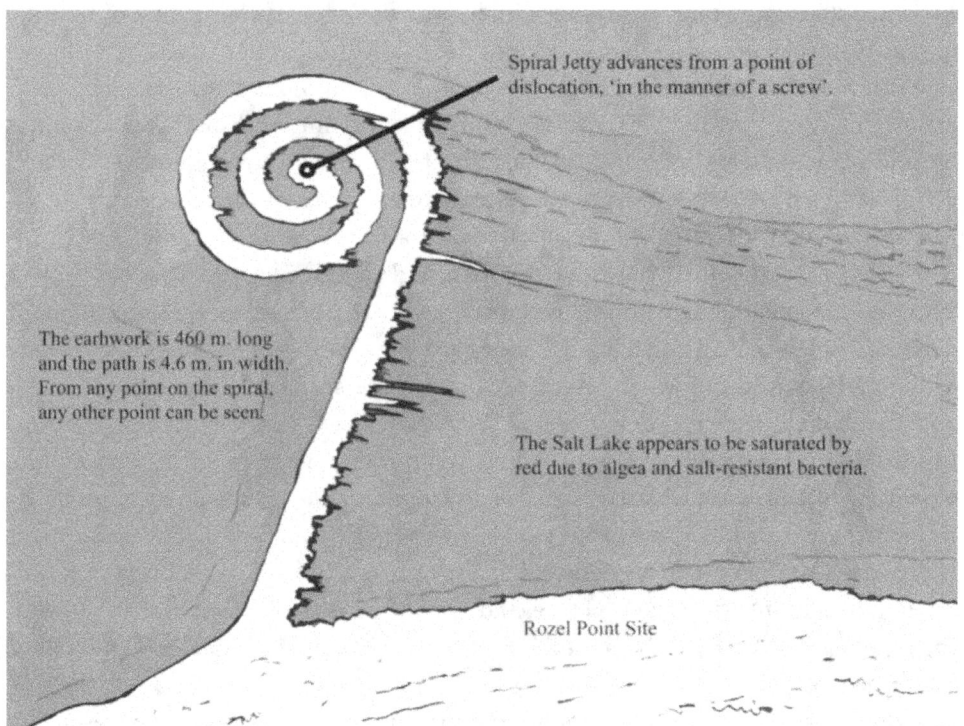

Spiral Jetty advances from a point of dislocation, 'in the manner of a screw'.

The earthwork is 460 m. long and the path is 4.6 m. in width. From any point on the spiral, any other point can be seen.

The Salt Lake appears to be saturated by red due to algea and salt-resistant bacteria.

Rozel Point Site

4.6 Diagram of Robert Smithson's *Spiral Jetty* (credit: the authors).

is also the name of a film and a text (Smithson 1996d: 143–53) which documents the development of the jetty as well as Smithson's performance on the earthwork. The text explains that *Spiral Jetty* echoes the growth of salt crystals that form on the earthwork's surface, which Smithson describes as advancing from a point of dislocation 'in the manner of a screw' (147). *Spiral Jetty*, then, might be thought of as a sigil for, or diagram of, collapse. Smithson had himself filmed from a helicopter, hurrying to the inner point of the earthwork. His account of this performance is comparable to Kusama's description of her experience of the universe as an infinity net, and to Spare's aspiration to achieve a state of *Kia* too. Smithson writes that in tracing the spiral he returns to 'pulpy protoplasm', an origin and a 'floating ante-diluvian ocean' (148). The colour crimson – blood red – seems to saturate everything. There are streaks of red in the salt lake – crimson algae at the lake's centre – and Smithson speculates that the gathering storm clouds will surely rain blood. When he closes his eyelids he sees yet more red, caused by the sun's burning light and his own blood 'sucking up obscure sediments' (148). He writes: 'My eyes became combustion chambers ... Perception was heaving ... I was on a geologic fault that groaned within me. Between heat lightning and heat exhaustion the spiral curled into vaporization' (148).

If, when seized by the *Spiral Jetty*, self and other, subject and object and human or historical time all evaporate, the result is a disorientating state, perhaps similar to Spare's description of the after-effects of mirror magic, which produces a 'feeling of immensity (which sees a small form), whose limit you cannot reach' (2007b: 74).

Self-Blinding

It would seem, following Spare, Kusama and Smithson, that a suspension of self-consciousness is not only possible but also a means of suspending the illusions of selfhood. However, there is still a question as to whether a subject (or self-consciousness) awakened after the event of self-obliteration gains any insights concerning a reality beyond appearance. Or do yet more romanticised or imprecise notions follow? No doubt the experiential effects of vacuity described by Spare and the collapse of figure –ground relations presented by Kusama and Smithson can all be explained through science. But the three artists do not seem to claim much more for their self-blinding practices than that they are experiments with bodily processes and embodiment. In this, consciousness is affected through the repetition and recall of self-obliteration. The value of self-obliteration is that it puts consciousness to sleep, an event that can be explored retrospectively, or through an encounter with the practices of the artists. That Spare, Kusama and Smithson attribute no positive content to instances of vacuity, self-obliteration or depersonalisation is important, for such self-less episodes are cast as states which produce nothing more than an openness to a reality beyond form and appearance.

A core concern of this chapter has been whether an escape, at least in part, from the illusions of selfhood is engendered not just by the sciences and cognitive philosophy but also by artworks or performance protocols. In addressing this question, we have presented examples of practices that counter perceptual and epistemic habits through a collapse of figure–ground relations, or through performances that exhaust the body. It may be said that what these examples register is nothing more than the confounding of perception. Here scientists might propose that the noise, or what we are calling the *after-effect*, of vacuity or dedifferentiation is revealing of self-generation and no more, and that other means are necessary for understanding reality. It can also be said that a myth is created by such practices, namely the equation of self-dissolution with the idea that, as Kusama suggests, all is 'absorbed into something timeless' (2011: 47). We would agree with these conclusions but suggest that these practices also present a mythopoesis that calls forth subjects or a people with the potential to confront and escape the limits of selfhood and self-experience – subjects that live a life with an understanding of selfhood as illusion – eschewing too the mastery that is sometimes produced by scientific knowledge. Indeed, what we have been arguing is that Spare, Kusama and Smithson are not concerned with producing objective representations of the body and the universe but with understanding the voids, noise and after-effects of self-obliteration as an index of reality which they incorporate into their life and practice. In this, the artists produce something like a (non)religious practice in which myths such as *Kia*, an infinity net and a floating antediluvian ocean are important. That is, ritual performance or performance protocols are used for non-religious ends, so as to affect life and consciousness and to arrest belief and self-identity, both for the artists and for others.

We understand that some might be wary of our promotion of myth here. Myth remains a powerful agent – often with problematic influence – and despite the best efforts of scientists, belief in selfhood persists, along with religious ideas and morality. It might be that science and other agencies have a limited power to dissolve ignorance when belief is a passion, clung to precisely because ignorance binds identities and (subjective) worlds, as Spare understood well. And perhaps, too, myths of experience and selfhood persist because the illusory productions of body and brain are difficult to overcome or cast aside, and the counterintuitive universe presented by the sciences is hard to accept.

The cognitive philosopher Daniel Dennett has addressed the persistence of myth, suggesting that religion and belief should be studied just as climate change or global economics are studied. However, despite advocating for the explanation of religions and their myths through scientific means, Dennett is not sure that he would completely dispense with religion just yet, for he wonders if it may play some valuable role that is yet to be ascertained. He speculates that, like red wine in moderation, religion might be beneficial (Dennett 2007: 309). Why would an enemy of superstition suggest such a thing? Perhaps because he realises that myth can be understood not (just) as false-hood but as having a function which orientates or binds an individual or group of people, at conscious or unconscious levels, thus marking a limit to the efficacy of demystification. Myths might be necessary intersubjective components of social and cultural organisation and relations (for us, this is something we understand as crucial to the function of mythopoetic works or performances that call forth a people). Perhaps this is what Dennett's analogy with the moderate consumption of red wine hints at, and perhaps he too partakes in myth consumption. Indeed, in battling folk myths, Dennett and his fellow traveller in the war against religion, Richard Dawkins, call themselves 'Brights' (a name also adopted by those who campaign for educational institutions to teach evolutionary theory).[8] This name – which seems to us also to be a sigil of sorts – appeals not entirely to reason or rationality but to human feelings about negative and positive qualities. We would suggest that through identification with this term, religious myth is not just countered through reason but through yet more myth; this is also how we understand the mythopoesis of Spare, Kusama, Smithson and others, who counter the myth or fiction of the self through more myth.

In this, we do not count the selfless experiences and altered states presented by the artists and writers discussed above as myth because they are necessarily false; we do so rather because such experiences and states function to orientate and bind a practice and potentially a people too. We also find this notion of myth as an orien-tating and binding agent in the writing of Georges Bataille, who speculated that to declare the absence of God is to create a new myth or principle. The absence of myth is the greatest myth of all, and 'night is also a sun' (Bataille 1994: 48). We think Bataille understood something about what we are calling fictioning, in particular that reason alone does not necessarily direct the application or communication of reason, particularly when the transformation of life and society are its goal.

Notes

1   Spare's declaration that humans are blind to their embodiment is in keeping with the view of neuroscience. Thomas Metzinger (2014), for instance, argues that there are three levels of embodiment, and that living organisms are not conscious of all of them. We will discuss Metzinger's research on embodiment in depth in the final chapter of our book.

2   It is worth remembering that Spare wrote and published *The Focus of Life* in the context of Edwardian society, and thus in a somewhat restricted moral terrain. We would also

note here that in rejecting this morality and arguing for an unfettered sexuality, Spare's work has some resonance with the writing of the figures discussed in the last chapter, particularly those associated with a counterculture that rejects morality as control.

3   It is interesting to note in relation to Spare's call to become a 'walking tree' that, before using the term 'Body Without Organs' in the radio play *To Have Done with the Judgement of God* (1947), Antonin Artaud used the phrase 'tree without organs' (1976: 515). Artaud's term 'Body Without Organs' is developed by Deleuze and Guattari to refer to the arresting of the hierarchies of the body in *A Thousand Plateaus* (1988).

4   In a footnote, Metzinger attributes this concept to the philosopher Rick Grush, describing a nemocentric reality as centred on nobody (2003: 336).

5   We will return to the idea of nemocentricism in section three, and in particular to Ray Brassier's interest in Metzinger's work as the basis for a nemocentric subject. Brassier (2009) advocates exploring the potential for selfless subjects by splitting cognition from experience, arguing for the investigation of the potential for *experience-less subjects* rather than *selfless experience* (the latter being precisely the condition Spare, Kusama and Smithson are concerned with, or attempt to fiction). In rejecting selfless experience Brassier not only questions whether experience holds any promise of registering reality, but also views aesthetic practices as problematic and unable to overcome the 'rift' between knowing and feeling.

6   At the very least, as Ray Brassier has stated in an interview, some correlation of reality with experience seems necessary for representation to take place (Brassier and Malik 2015: 223–4).

7   Phil Baker, Spare's biographer, speculates that *Neither-Neither* relates to the Sanskrit expression *Neti-Neti*, which translates as 'not this, not that' or 'neither this nor that' (Baker 2011: 103).

8   This follows the idea proposed by Paul Geisert of replacing the negative term 'Godless' with a more positive one for those who value reason over superstition and have a naturalistic view of the universe.

B. PERFORMANCE FICTIONING:
PASTS, PRESENTS AND FUTURES

5 Residual Culture and the Magical Mode of Existence

Aesthetic thinking emerges at the neutral point between technics and religion, at the moment of the division of primitive magical unity: this is not a phase but, rather, a permanent reminder of the rupture of the unity of the magical mode of being and a search for a future unity.

Gilbert Simondon, *On the Technical Mode of Being*

FOLLOWING ON FROM our account of how mythopoesis might be pitched against control and the fiction of the self, in this chapter we want to attend to how the past, and especially previous modes of existence, might be utilised as a resource against the impasses of the present (and against the different subjectivities afforded by capitalism). This is not from any nostalgic desire to return to an idealised moment, nor to dream of escape from the complexities and pressing concerns of today. Neither is it, strictly speaking, to do history; rather, it is to view the past and present as entangled. The past, as construed here, is a repository of materials that might well provide alternative points of subjectification today, especially when mobilised in contemporary aesthetic productions, and, not least, in certain fictions.

The chapter begins with a brief look at Raymond Williams' writing on hegemony, before going on to offer a commentary on a relatively recently translated extract from Gilbert Simondon's *On the Mode of Existence of Technical Objects* (2011). Throughout, we make some reference to other theoretical resources, especially Félix Guattari and Henri Bergson. Our commentary ends with four case studies – taking in a work of literature, two works from filmic art practice, and one from cinema – all of which evidence a certain Romantic Englishness and exemplify this active and creative attitude and orientation towards the past. In these case studies especially, the focus of our discussion shifts. For if we have previously suggested that mythopoesis disrupts the present through a call to a people to come, here we look to practices that perform this disruption through a kind of pre-modern futurism that itself involves a variety of attendant fictioning technologies such as nesting (especially in relation to fiction), layering and looping (in relation to time), and journeying (in relation to performance). This shift will become ever more apparent in the final chapters of section one.

PART I: THEORIES OF RESIDUAL CULTURE
AND THE MAGICAL MODE OF EXISTENCE

Residual Culture

In his essay 'Base and Superstructure in Marxist Cultural Theory', Raymond Williams (1980) presents a compelling matrix of the contemporary – an account of the way in which any present moment is always already made up of different 'times'. In particular, he shows how what he calls the dominant and thus effective culture (or, in Williams' terms, hegemony) is never complete, since there are always 'left overs' from previous hegemonies that might offer alternative and even oppositional cultures (opposition here naming the possibility of a challenge to the dominant culture).[1] Williams calls these kinds of cultures 'residual', differentiating them from what he calls 'archaic' cultures, referring to those aspects of the past that have been effectively incorporated within the dominant culture. He mentions religion, rural culture and monarchy, each of which might have both residual and archaic aspects, though the last would seem to offer little in terms of alternative or oppositional culture.[2]

Williams goes on to write about more future-orientated, 'emergent' cultures, which are often the expression of a new class, but not necessarily so. The emergent is simply a new area of human activity as yet unrecognised by the dominant culture (hence its importance, politically speaking). Williams is attuned to what might be called a logic of deconstruction here – that an emergent culture must express itself in terms of the dominant culture – but he also highlights the importance of a pre-emergent scene. Elsewhere, in a development of the themes of this particular essay, Williams goes one step further (or one step back), suggesting that it might even be a question of what he calls 'structures of feeling' that are, as it were, *pre*-pre-emergent (Williams 1977).[3] It is within art – literature in fact – that Williams identifies these new forms, or proto-forms, of life; and, indeed, it seems clear that aesthetic practice in general is often involved in what we might call this affective register of the pre-emergent.

This notion of residual and emergent cultures may have some resonance with contemporary reactionary politics, and, in particular, with what has been named Neoreaction, or its technologically oriented wing known as NRx. Certainly there are some similarities in the way NRx turns to the past but also embraces technology while rejecting modernism and ideas of progress and democracy. There is also a more direct resonance with the Neoreactionary philosopher Nick Land – a figure we will be returning to more than once throughout the book – and his idea of a politics that explores a 'time-twisted vector that spirals forwards into the past, and backwards into the future' (Land 2013a). Williams' thesis, however, is clearly positioned on the Left, which is to say it is progressive rather than reactive, and belongs to a tradition of Marxism that views cultural production (rather than just economic relations) as a significant aspect of class struggle. In this regard, Williams writes in particular on the tendency of Science Fiction to privilege technological determinism – it is, we might say, overdetermined by the capitalist mode of production. We will address Williams' thoughts on Science Fiction in detail in Chapter 12, but note here his idea of a form of utopian writing adequate and appropriate to our time: a fiction of the 'wasteland' that involves a 'voluntary deprivation', at least for 'those who have known affluence and known with it social injustice and moral corruption' (Williams 1978: 212). We will offer a concrete example of a fiction of the wasteland towards the end of this chapter – Russell Hoban's novel *Riddley Walker* (2002) – but it is worth remarking at this point that the utopian impulse Williams proposes imagines a post-capitalist society that necessarily echoes aspects of a pre-capitalist past.

The Magical Mode of Existence

We want now to deepen this account of the complexity of the present by looking at the Gilbert Simondon extract mentioned above. Although from a different intellectual tradition to Williams – broadly continental philosophy as opposed to British Cultural Studies – Simondon is likewise highly attuned to the residues of the past within the present and, importantly for our discussion, to the role that the landscape and its sites and assemblages play in this. *On the Mode of Existence of Technical Objects* was itself written against the background of a certain ideological hangover from the past that viewed the technical as distinct from and inferior to culture. Simondon's aim is thus to explain technical consciousness and gesture towards its future possibilities. We should note at the outset, however, that his book was written over forty years ago and, as such, some of his pronouncements on technology might be questioned – for example, the division he introduces between the given and the made, and his concomitant rejection of the artificial – nevertheless his account of the move to a technical consciousness seems to us to be both important and useful. We should acknowledge that we read Simondon (or at least the extract in question) somewhat against the grain in so far as we are interested in the resistant and oppositional quality of a pre-technical mode of existence (involving magical thinking) that might exist alongside the technical (and, indeed, resonate with a mode of existence to come).

At the very beginning of the extract Simondon offers his own temporal matrix in terms of phase-shifts between, precisely, different modes of existence. The idea of phase-shifts is employed so as to move away from any dialectic or idea of simple temporal progression; it suggests the possible coexistence of different phases as well as their interpenetration and specific points of genesis. To reconstruct Simondon's argument very briefly (again, as with Deleuze's notion of control societies, we will approach it as a Science Fiction): The original mode of existence of so-called primitive humans was one of magical unity; this was a state before any subject–object split and before any concomitant division between religion and what Simondon calls technicity. For Simondon aesthetics is a kind of future-orientated reminder of this originary unity:

> We suppose that technicity results from a phase-shift of a central, original and unique mode of being in the world, the magical mode; the phase that balances technicity is the religious mode of being. Aesthetic thinking emerges at the neutral point between technics and religion, at the moment of the division of primitive magical unity: this is not a phase but, rather, a permanent reminder of the rupture

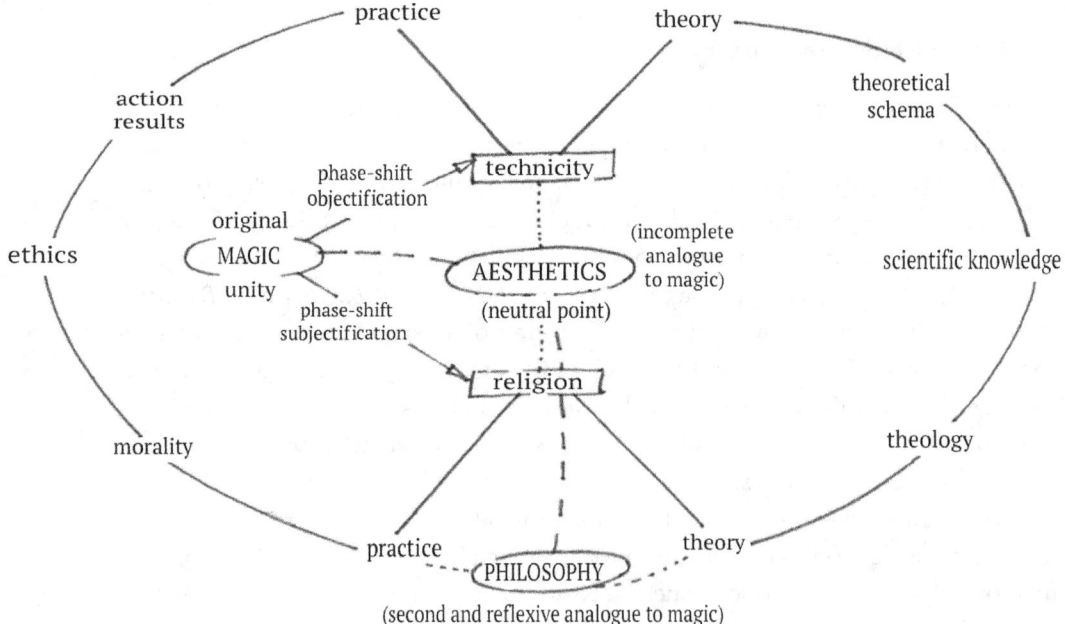

5.1 Diagram of Gilbert Simondon's modes of existence to highlight connections between magic, aesthetics and philosophy (credit: the authors).

of the unity of the magical mode of being and a search for a future unity. (Simondon 2011: 408)

In fact, things are more complex than this, with the two modes – technicity and religion – each split further into theoretical and practical aspects. The distance between the two theoretical aspects of technicity and religion characterises scientific knowledge; the distance between their two practical aspects characterises ethics, or 'ethical thinking'. These divisions are themselves further divided, with morality and theology representing the practical and theoretical aspects of religion, and 'action-results' and theoretical schema representing the practice and theory aspects of technicity. We might diagram this constellation of different modes and phases as in Figure 5.1.

At the core of what we are calling Simondon's Science Fiction, we find the myth of a lost magical unity that orientates not only his thinking but also some of the art practices discussed in this and subsequent chapters of section one. The idea of a magical unity can be questioned – as can the romantic schema according to which humans were at one with their environment until the advent of technics and religion – but what interests us here is the idea that a notion of unity is not just found in residual cultures but drives practices towards a future state in which alienation is overcome.

For Simondon, magical thinking as a mode of existence involves a unity of human and world, but also has its own particular organisation: figure–ground relations which structure the very milieu of living beings. It is this originary form of relation that is then isolated and fragmented in the shift away from magic: 'figure and ground separate by becoming detached from the universe to which they adhered' (415). Figure is abstracted and cut off from its ground, just as the ground itself is freed from its relation to any specific figure. This involves an objectification resulting, ultimately, in technical objects that can be moved and manipulated, and a subjectification that results in religious mediators (and, ultimately, the subject).

There is more to be said about how religious mediators (and religion more generally) actually produce this subject,[4] and, indeed, about the whole co-dependent relation of technicity and religion in so far as they form two halves of a whole. But here we want to focus on the definition of the prior 'primitive magical unity', which Simondon suggests is 'the vital relational link between man and the world' (411), in order to see if something might remain and, in Williams' terms, offer up an alternative to a more dominant technical-religious mode of existence.[5] Put bluntly: could magical thinking, in our own time, be residual?

Simondon suggests that the magical mode, as the 'fundamental structuring of the milieu of a living being', involves 'the birth of a network of privileged points of exchange between the being and the milieu' (412). This is the figure–ground relation we mentioned above, in which certain points are foregrounded from a background:

A privileged place, a place that has a power, is one which draws into itself all the force and efficacy of the domain it delimits; it summarises and contains the force of a compact mass of reality; it summarises and governs it, as a highland governs and dominates a lowland; the elevated peak is the lord of the mountain, just as the most impenetrable part of the wood is where all its reality resides. The magical world is in this way made of a network of places and things that have a power and are bound to other things and other places that also have a power. Such a path, such an enclosure, such a temenos contains all the force of the land, and is the key-point of the reality and of the spontaneity of things, as well as of their accessibility. (412)

For Simondon these key points of exchange and communication between human and world might be characterised as points of passage between two realities. As he remarks: 'The magical universe is made up of the network of places providing access to every domain of reality: it consists of thresholds, summits, boundaries and crossing points that are connected to one another by their singularity and their exceptional nature' (414).[6]

This magical landscape is doubled by a similar reticulation in time. Privileged locations are accompanied by privileged moments – specific dates – on which it is

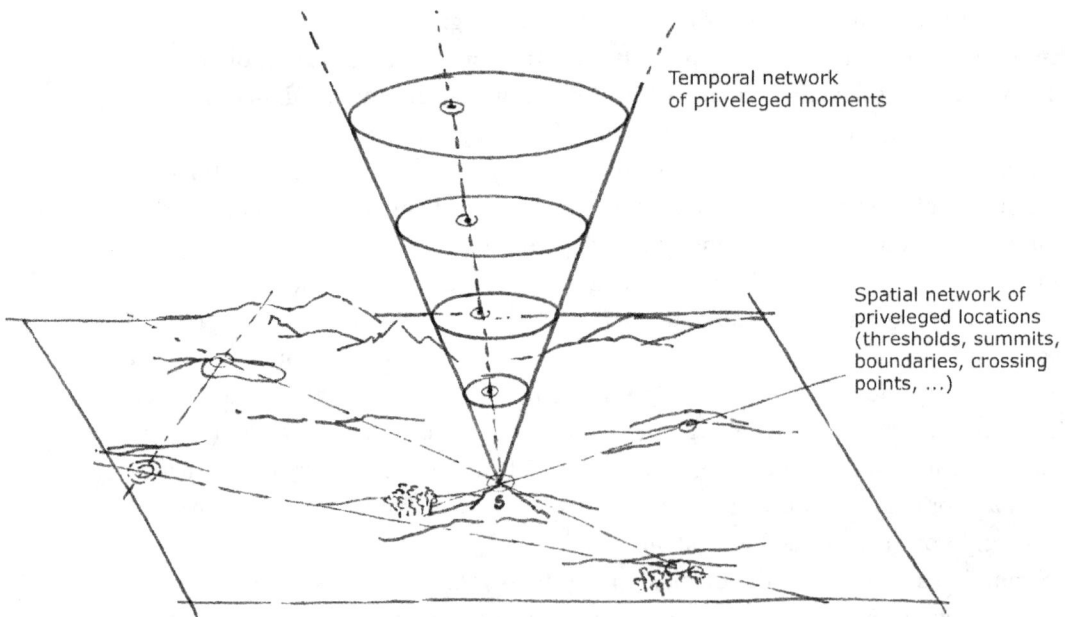

Temporal network
of priveleged moments

Spatial network of
priveleged locations
(thresholds, summits,
boundaries, crossing
points, ...)

5.2 Diagram of magical structure (following Henri Bergson) to highlight connection between privilege points in space and time (credit: the authors).

auspicious to act, or to begin an action (in both cases, we can see the influence on Deleuze and Guattari's *A Thousand Plateaus* – not least on its novel structure with specifically dated plateaus). These notable dates are linked back through time in a kind of temporal topography that doubles the spatial one. In a nod to Bergson and his own diagramming of the relationship of the past to the present – his celebrated cone – in *Matter and Memory* (Bergson 2004: 133–78), this magical structure can be diagrammed as in Figure 5.2.

Festivals, and rituals more broadly, performed at a specific time and place mark – and enact – a privileged link between these key points (see point S in the diagram).[7] They are special kinds of space-time foregrounded out of the more ordinary and mundane. Following Bergson we might also suggest that a suspension of habit is important here (again, at point S): a hesitation, or pause; a 'stopping of the world' (to use Carlos Castaneda's phrase) that allows other times to be 'accessed' (in Bergson's thesis, the past has not gone anywhere – it subsists, albeit occluded by habit and utilitarian interests).[8] Simondon suggests that with vacations we might have a version (if a watered-down one) of this desire for privileged points – a specific time to journey to the city for the countryside dweller, or to the countryside for the city dweller.

Once again, the shift from this magical unity and structure involves these key points becoming detached from their ground – hence technical objects which retain 'only their functionary mediatory characteristics, becoming instrumental, mobile, capable of efficiency in any place and at any time' (Simondon 2011: 415).[9] At the same time, the characteristics of the ground itself become detached, and are able now to 'hover over the whole universe, throughout space and throughout time, in the form of detached powers and forces above the world' (415). This is the splitting of magical unity into two modes of existence: technicity and religion. Simondon suggests that this very split gestures towards a further ideal unity, a new meeting of science and religion, though for him this remains merely a tendency.

Here we might note in passing Guattari's thesis on the new aesthetic paradigm and on what he calls the third 'processual' assemblage of the production of subjectivity. The latter involves a mediated return (at least of sorts) to a first pre-capitalist and transpersonal assemblage, one marked by its passage through our own capitalist assemblage with its reduction and standardisation of the heterogeneity of subjectivity (not least through transcendent enunciators). The third assemblage involves a kind of 'folding-in' of transcendence so as to produce autopoetic nuclei around which a different subjectivity might crystallise.[10] In fact, in many ways Guattari's three assemblages are analogous to Simondon's phase-shifts in so far as they are not, strictly speaking, to do with a linear progression, but might well coexist (as in the survival of pagan culture within the modern). The role of aesthetics – as a neutral point/future-reminder of unity, and as a point around which a different subjectivity might coalesce – is also remarkably similar. While this aspect of or approach to aesthetics – as connection to magical unity – is not found in all mythopoetic practices (defined as a calling forth of a people to come which might be – why not? – a nemocentric, technically produced subject), there are certainly examples of mythopoesis (which we will discuss later in this chapter) that engage with privileged locations and aesthetic presentations as points that connect to a past time, and to a magical unity.

To return to Simondon, the phase-shift from magic produces the first objects and subjects, and with that the beginnings of the modern world:

> This phase-shift of the mediation into figural characteristics and ground characteristics translates into the emergence of a distance between man and world. The mediation itself, instead of being a simple structuring of the universe, takes on a certain density; it becomes objectified in technics and becomes subjectified in religion, making the first object appear in the technical object and the first subject appear in divinity. (415)

In both technical and religious modes, then, the individual is distanced from the world, always less than the original unity, or totality, that in some senses preceded them (and, indeed, their very formation as individual). In religion 'particular being is understood in relation to a totality in which it participates, but which it can never completely express' (419). Here the individual is, as it were, cut off from the infinite of which it is a part (a curtain has been drawn between the human and the world). In technicity there is always a lack of 'absolute adequacy' to the world in so far as the technical object 'is localized, particularized'; as such, for Simondon, 'adding technical objects one to another can neither remake the world nor regain contact with the world in its unity' (421). Ultimately, religion affixes the powers of the ground to various personifications of the divine and sacred, and eventually the figure of the priest (with his subjects) arises as privileged mediator. In technicity mediation is provided by the technical object.

It is in this sense that, for Simondon, both technicity and religion are the heirs of magic – not degraded forms but two tendencies abstracted from an original unity. Although Simondon does not address this, it seems to us that this might also account, at least in part, for why advanced technology, in comparison with the very primitive, can seem magical, just as the older a religion is the more it takes on a magical character (one thinks specifically of non-monotheistic religions such as paganism). In a more speculative vein we might also ask if there is such a thing as an 'advanced' form of religion, in a form different to the dominant monotheisms. Might this also appear magical in some sense, or at least not necessarily involve mirroring and securing a centred and cohesive subject?[11] And might mythopoesis, in certain instances or practices, function by making connections between so-called primitive and advanced technologies alongside pre- and postmodern religion: a Science Fiction paganism perhaps?[12]

Is it also the case that advanced technicity might in and of itself produce a different mode of existence beyond a more alienated one? In relation to this, and in another recently translated extract – 'Technical Mentality' – Simondon suggests that technicity 'has not yet properly emerged' and thus to judge it in its partly complete form is to miscomprehend it (Simondon 2012: 1–15). For Simondon, 'If one seeks the sign of the perfection of the technical mentality, one can unite in a single criterion the manifestation of cognitive schemas, affective modalities and norms of action: that of the *opening*' (14). He continues: 'Technical reality lends itself remarkably well to being continued, completed, perfected, extended. In this sense, an extension of the technical mentality is possible, and begins to manifest itself in the domain of the fine arts in particular' (he mentions the modular architecture of Le Corbusier as a case in point here) (4). Technicity's lack of unity – its fundamental character as alienated mode of existence – is in this sense productive, creative and always future-orientated.

In relation to this future, Simondon suggests that the open character of technical reality is also manifest in a 'virtual network' to come, a 'multifunctional network that marks the key points of the geographical and human world' (9). There is a profound resonance with the magical structuring of the universe here, with its privileged points – as there is also in the way in which technicity ultimately involves an 'appeal to forces that *do not depend on the human being*' (15 n.5). This is the discovery and harnessing of the 'infinite reserve' of nature. In the same footnote Simondon also gestures towards certain activities – 'agriculture, nursing and navigation with sails' – which, he suggests, might also be seen as industrial in so far as they involve a relation to these non-human forces, albeit not, strictly speaking, their manipulation. In fact, '*they comodulate the human operation of preparation and the cosmological action*' (15 n.5). We might note Deleuze and Guattari's own writings on industry here, and especially on the emergence of metallurgy with its nomadic smiths (Simondon himself suggests metallurgy as the first industry).[13] Technicity, if this is the correct name for this particular mode of existence, is in this sense not a domination of nature by humans, but involves a tracking of the singularities present in nature. Indeed, as Simondon remarks, these kinds of operation can 'give rise to a *magico-religious thinking*' (15 n.5).

That said, this thinking is clearly still the result of an alienation from the world. Technical mentality in general, Simondon argues, cannot overcome this alienation as it is the progenitor of it. This also implies that technical objects themselves (and science more generally) are not enough to remake the world, as technicity itself is just one half of a prior phase and a prior unity.[14] Simondon's thesis implies a limit to the Promethean impulse to 'remake the world' in this sense; put differently, there is in his writings a sanctity of the given over the made.

In fact, to return to the extract from *On the Mode of Existence of Technical Objects*, Simondon suggests that technicity can only ever attend to the how of things and not the why. It certainly provides knowledge, but of a kind that is inevitably piecemeal, lacking any overview: 'The application of schemas drawn from technics does not account for the existence of the totality, taken as a unity, but does account for the point by point and instant by instant functioning of that totality' (Simondon 2011: 422). Technicity, in this sense, is characterised by induction, defined as any process whose 'content is inferior to the status of unity, if it strives to attain unity or, at least, it if tends towards unity from a plurality of elements, each of which is inferior to unity' (423). Induction is forward moving and productive, but always blind in this sense.

Any ethics that develops from this technicity also falls short of unity, for example 'to want the whole duration of life to be a series of moments, to extract from each situation what is pleasant in it, and to want to construct the happiness of life by accumulating its agreeable element' (423). Further, it invariably involves the denigration, even elimination, of the passions, 'since they cannot be treated as elements; they are larger than the unity of the subject; they dominate it; they come from farther away than it and tend to go farther on than it, obliging it to exceed its limits' (423). Conversely, any morality developed from religion derives its significance from a totality with which the subject does not coincide (the subject is always forsaken in this sense).

PART 2: CASE STUDIES OF RESIDUAL CULTURE
AND THE MAGICAL MODE OF EXISTENCE

Riddley Walker

In Russell Hoban's post-apocalyptic novel *Riddley Walker* (1980) – a fiction of the wasteland if ever there was one – there is a mixing, or layering, of the magical and technical modes of existence in so far as the story is about a future in which technicity has receded following a crisis, and thus all sorts of other practices and ways of thinking come into play. These include the technical, especially when this is pre-industrial (for example the excavation – with shovels and pulley systems – of 'past' machinery), but also various proto-religious practices (such as the Eusa show, a strange kind of divinatory Punch and Judy) and, towards the end of the novel, practices and scenarios that could only be described as magical (the various visions and supernatural happenings at 'Cambry', or the city of Canterbury).

In terms of a magical structuring of the world, *Riddley Walker* is also organised around the key point – and pilgrimage to – Cambry (following the *Canterbury Tales*), and indeed the book as a whole might be said to be organised around passages and thresholds, privileged times and locations (such as the 'hart of the wood') (see the map in Figure 5.3). Crucially, these places are real, albeit projected into the future by Hoban. The Eusa show, we suggest, operates as a residual culture; in fact, in Riddley's world it operates as a kind of doubled residual culture in so far as it is throwback to an earlier time (for Riddley), but is also, even then (in our time as it were), a remnant of a previous culture. But for the reader the Eusa show is also a story within a story (Riddley's

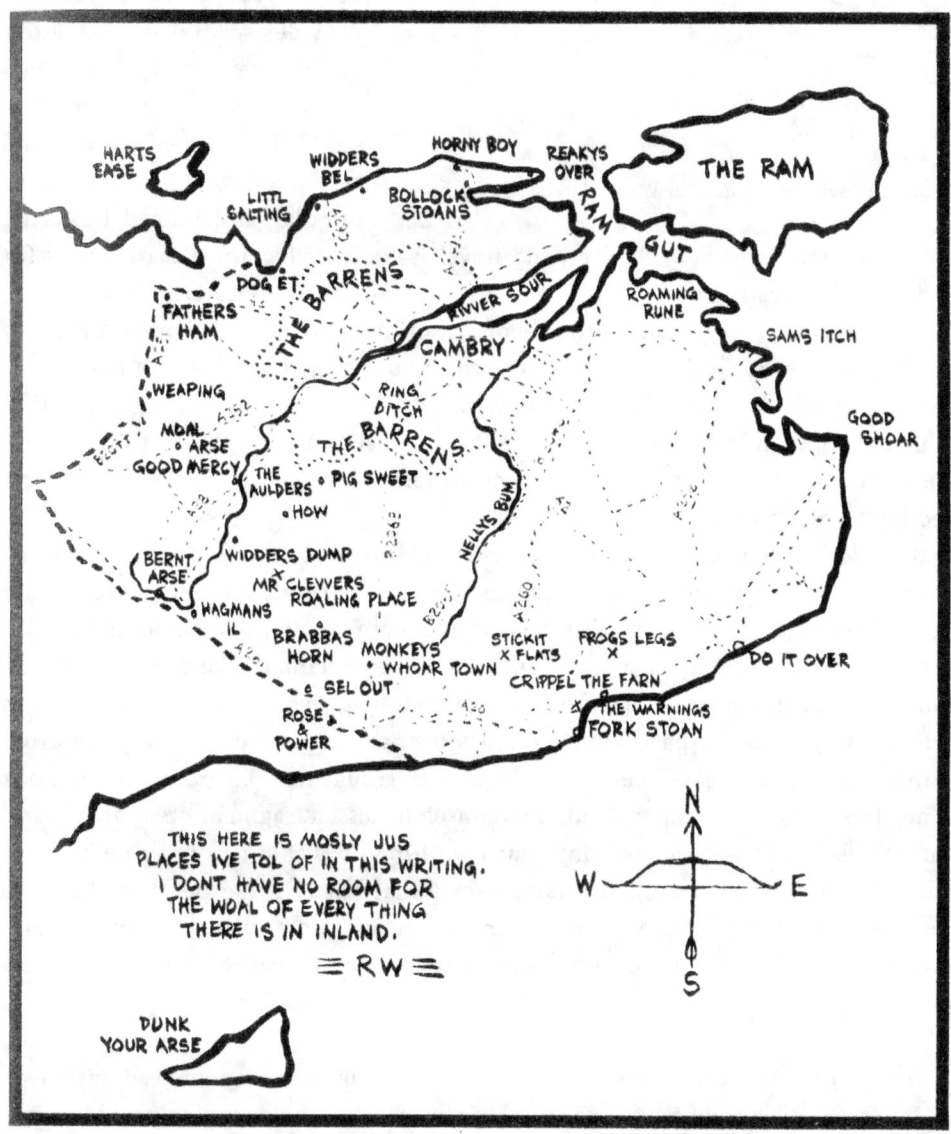

5.3 Map from Russell Hoban's *Riddley Walker*, 1980 (© The Trustees of the Russell Hoban Trust, used by permission of David Higham Associates).

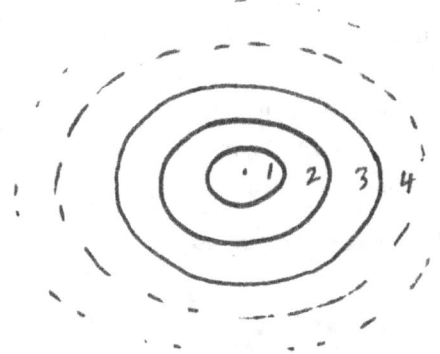

1 The Eusa Show

2 Riddley's Story

3 Hoban's Story/Time

4 Time of the Reader

5.4 Diagram to show nesting of fictions in *Riddley Walker* (credit: the authors).

own telling of his tale) that is itself 'within' Hoban's novel. We might diagram this nesting of fictions as in Figure 5.4.

A complicating factor here is that the Eusa show, the innermost circuit of the novel, also provides a kind of divinatory knowledge in and of Riddley's world. This 'story within a story' allows an exiting and passage to a larger circuit (to follow our diagram). Indeed, this is the role of fiction in *Riddley Walker*: the novel is for us what the Eusa show is for Riddley. This nesting of fictions produces a certain self-reflexivity and, with that, an understanding of the importance of fiction and myth in the presentation of reality. For the reader who is familiar with English folk traditions and culture (as well as with Kent, where the story takes place), the novel also offers identification with a certain kind of Englishness (something we will find repeated in the practices we attend to in this chapter and some others addressed throughout this first section of our book).

But *Riddley Walker* is also an aesthetic work in and of itself, constructing its narrative, characters and startling images through language. Its very particular use (and abuse) of syntax resonates with a crude, comical and contemporary idea of pre-modern and colloquial speech, but there are also remnants of the modern and, indeed, constructions that gesture forwards to a language yet to come. Ultimately, it is this strange future-past syntax that produces a very particular scene – or 'structure of feeling', to use Williams' term. Like a Burroughs or Ballard novel the book is an embodiment of a different kind of consciousness: a fragment of another world thrown backwards or forwards into our own time (it is as if it is not simply about another place, but from it). It is also a text that needs to be performed in this sense – at least, the reading of it requires a certain effort. It is not only a fiction then, but has this performance fictioning aspect (for to read the novel is to speak as Riddley does):

Eusa come up then slow and scanful like all ways terning his woodin head this way and that and his paintit eyes taking us all in in. Many and manys the time Id lookit back at the staring blue eyes. Since back befor I cud member it even. Only this time it seamt like the 1st time I wer seeing him and I wer afeart of him. The way he kept terning his head it made me think of that thing with no name looking out thru our eye hoals. (Hoban 1980: 46)

In this sense, the book is about a form of aesthetic thinking (in so far as, following Simondon, this is a reminder of, and incomplete analogue to, magic), but is also a form of aesthetic thinking itself. In terms of some of our comments above, we might also say that it stops the world (as this is habitually understood), not least in the way its syntax calls for an alteration of our speeds of 'communication'. Fiction operates here to point to something 'outside' technicity and religion (it might be said fiction operates at the neutral point). In Simondon's terms, *Riddley Walker* is also about the phase-shifts of different modes of existence (magic, technicity and religion), their codependence and interpenetration, as well as their specific points of genesis (and also their de- and re-genesis). It is also about living this complex and layered temporality. While the novel portrays a broken world, bleak and dystopian, it also harbours a strange joy (not least that of Riddley himself) and an affirmation of this future which, for us, is to come.

In Williams' terms, the book is clearly about the survival of residual culture, and the relation of this to more archaic aspects that also survive. But these survivals are themselves nested in a strange manner. The residual culture (following Williams' definition) comes mainly from a pre-modern and pre-industrial time, with the more recent past (the modern age that brought about the unnamed catastrophe of the novel) operating as a trauma event which has been passed over (and which survives only in a kind of occult knowledge and in archaeological relics). In fact, this event is clearly connected to the nuclear, that apotheosis of a certain kind of scientific mentality (if not the apex of technicity itself). This strange temporality is itself doubled in so far as the actual present of *Riddley Walker* may read like the past but is in fact an imagined future, with the threat of human-produced catastrophe (the novel is of its time in this sense – in terms of the omnipresent fear of nuclear holocaust that haunted the 1970s – but, read today, it is also highly prescient in terms of the ecological fears and anxieties of the Anthropocene). The power of *Riddley Walker*, it seems to us, lies in part in the nesting of these different times that accompanies the nesting of fictions we mentioned above, and which itself includes a mixing of residual, dominant and emergent cultures. What we might call this syncretism of times and phases – the co-presence of different futures and pasts presented within fiction – is an example of what we have been attempting to define in this chapter as a mythopoesis that channels residual cultures and magical thinking, so as to destabilise notions of time as a historical progression or line, from past through present toward the future. To repurpose Burroughs' axiom we used as an epigraph for Chapter 2: *NO TIME IS TRUE. EVERY TIME IS PERMITTED.*

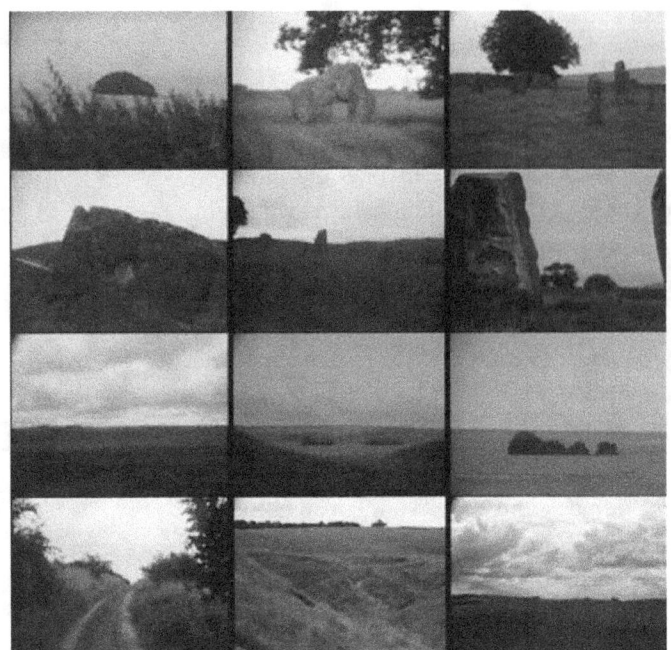

5.5 Stills from Derek Jarman's *Journey to Avebury*, 1971 (courtesy and copyright LUMA Foundation).

Journey to Avebury

In terms of Simondon's magical structuring of the universe, Derek Jarman's film *Journey to Avebury* (1971) focuses on a certain privileged point (or threshold), but also, like *Riddley Walker*, on a journey – or pilgrimage – across a sacred landscape (see Figure 5.5). Indeed, although Simondon does not address this, it seems to us that standing stones and henges such as the one at Avebury in Wiltshire are markers of the key points of the magical mode of existence; or, at least, they lie on the cusp between this magical unity and the 'new' technical mode of being to come (the stones are static place markers, but they have also been moved – and often otherwise manipulated – by humans). They are also, of course, visible reminders – or themselves residues – of the prehistorical within the contemporary: markers that subsist in space and through time.[15]

Jarman's film of his own journey to Avebury is then a modern work about a pre-modern site. It evidences the co-presence of our own technical mode of existence with a prior magical one in both its subject, Avebury, and in the subjectivity of its auteur, Jarman himself. But it is also, again, specifically an aesthetic work. As such, we might say it is *about* a magical mode of existence, but also, as an artwork, a future calling to a different mode of existence (one that resonates with the pre-technical). In Williams' terms, the power of the film – which doubles the power of the stones themselves – arises from its mobilising of a certain residuality, the survival of a kind of paganism in the present, achieved through a specific composition of affect or 'structure of feeling'.[16] Paradoxically, the film is also only possible because of a technical object – the camera. Magical thinking precedes technicity, but here technicity itself begets aesthetic thinking, which in turn operates as a reminder and an extension of magic.

Castlerigg

In Bruce Lacey's film *Castlerigg* (1981) we find similar themes in relation to stone circles, their residual power, and aesthetic thinking. The film – which records a visit to Castlerigg henge in Cumbria – conjures a very particular affective scene, produced in part by its analogue nature (especially for a contemporary viewer immersed in the digital), by the weather and other atmospherics of the site that the film captures, and, crucially, by the point of view it provides (the handheld camera, the selection of certain shots). Especially interesting in this respect is the time-lapse photography: the technology itself allows us to see a different world beyond that which humans see, opening up a mode of perception (and thus gesturing to a mode of existence) beyond the human.

There is also the figure of Lacey himself performing a ritual of sorts at the stones (a performance fictioning that we find in his other films that more explicitly involve him re-animating, but also reinventing, these pre-modern rituals). Lacey demonstrates the importance of participation when it comes to residual culture (it is partly this that gives the latter its oppositional character, in contrast to our dominant culture of passive spectatorship); but, later in his career, he also operates as a kind of residual subjectivity in and of himself, one that was part of the larger countercultural 'movement' of the 1960s and '70s that questioned industrialisation and the paradigm of technicity. Indeed, by the time Lacey made *Castlerigg*, he was attuned to the specific problems of modernity and especially to the increasingly pressing ecological issues of the late twentieth century. He was also interested, especially in his earlier work, in a kind of future-orientation, in Science Fictions and other cosmic dramas which were performed and enacted (for a survey of these see Mellor 2012). He was, we might say, a pioneer of machine art – one attuned to residual culture and magical thinking but also to future cultures and fictions of a world and people to come.

The Wicker Man

Our final case study is *The Wicker Man*, a 1973 feature film directed by Robin Hardy about the encounter of a modern individual (a Christian policeman) with a pre-modern, pagan world. On Summerisle (where the film is set) a past culture survives and is operational in the present, but also offers various alternatives to it, with aspects that are both residual and archaic. Indeed, this is the fascination of the film: besides the compelling and macabre storyline, it shows a modern working and integrated pagan society, complete with alternative school lessons and village rituals. In part, the film is about a clash between transcendent enunciators (the law, Christianity) and a culture of immanence (with its focus on magical thinking). The horror, but also joy, arises from the inadequacies and ultimate irrelevance of the transcendent enunciators in a culture which is, in this sense, irreligious and lawless. Indeed, the pagan culture – with its liberated notions of sexuality and its respectful participation in and with the natural world – comes over less as an aberration than as the successful imagining of an alternative mode of existence.

In one scene, the idea of the festival – in this case the Maypole dance – exemplifies this magical mode of existence, and not least the idea of key privileged points existing in space and time (see Figure 5.6).[17] The dance is a repetition of all previous dances as well as an echo forward to those dances yet to come. It is also specifically communal and participatory – a pre-modern tradition that is collectively understood to be a means of binding a community, with its residual cultures or values, in the future. In the film it stands out as an especially important moment, not least in the protagonist's realisation that there is something not quite right about life on the island (the dance is accompanied by a song about fertility and a heretical pathogenesis).

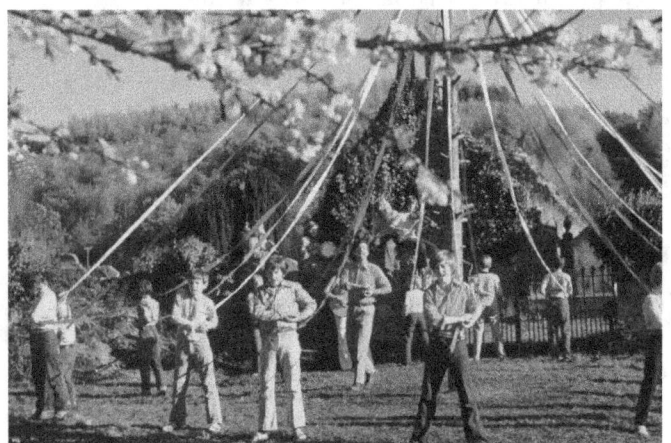

5.6 Still from *The Wicker Man*, 1973 (courtesy of STUDIOCANAL Films Ltd).

The film also evidences the link we made above between a pre-modernism and a 1960s and '70s counterculture, a time in which new and alternative subjectivities were being produced and experimented with. Immanence was, we might say, being activated. The power of *The Wicker Man* comes from this layering and looping of different times, the coexistence of different modes of existence – and, especially, the affirmation of something simply different (including a different form of consciousness).[18] This other space-time, which is never less than convincing, means that the film itself offers up a different world – it is not simply about a return to the past. In fact, as with the previous case studies, this is achieved as much through the form of the film, its aesthetic composition, as through its manifest content. The colours and sounds – the songs in particular – produce a kind of Spinozist joy that transports the viewer to a different space-time. Might mythopoesis also be a name for these kinds of future-past fictions that offer up – almost as side-effect – different affective scenes and potential modellings for a subjectivity alienated by rationalised, economically driven and utilitarian societies?

Notes

1 Mark Fisher develops a similar idea of the survival of future-orientated past cultures within the present in terms of a general hauntology (see as indicative Fisher 2014).

2 O'Sullivan has written more about the possibility of 'residual subjectivities' in *On the Production of Subjectivity* (2012: 192–7). Therein an encounter was staged between Williams' writings on the residual and emergent and *A Thousand Plateaus*, in particular the plateau '587 B.C.–A.D. 70: On Several Regimes of Signs' (Deleuze and Guattari 1988: 111–48), with its laying out of the possibility of a mixed semiotic (and, in relation to the themes of this chapter, the possible transportation into the present of a proposition from a previous regime that might then operate as an alternative point for subjectification).

3 A 'structure of feeling' is defined as a lived sensibility that is 'emergent or pre-emergent' (before 'definition, classification or rationalisation'), but still with a defined structure ('specific feelings, specific rhythms') (Williams 1980: 132–3).

4 See Deleuze and Guattari's discussion of the white face of Christ in 'Year Zero: Faciality' (1988: 167–91).

5 It is worth highlighting here Adorno and Horkheimer's (1969) alternative definition of magic as a regression in thought and, as such, as a form of thinking that is pre-capitalist but also subsumed by late capitalist forms (Williams' term 'archaic' would also be relevant here).

6 In terms of Europe, the seminal text on these privileged points and their lines of connection is Alfred Watkins' *The Old Straight Track* (1974).

7 See also Deleuze's discussion of the repetition of festivals at the very beginning of *Difference and Repetition* (Deleuze 1994: 1).

8 For more detail on this see O'Sullivan 2013.

9 It is worth addressing a key issue here – that of the differences between Simondon's idea of magical unity as prior mode of existence (that itself involves magical thinking) and the more typical understanding of magical causality operative in the practices of magic. In *The Golden Bough*, J. G. Frazer suggests two ways in which such a 'manipulation' of nature might be achieved, by a law of similarity and by one of contact (1957: 16). The term 'sympathetic magic' brings these two laws together.

10 This formulation of a 'folding-in' of transcendence is our own take on Guattari. For a more detailed discussion of the latter, and of the three assemblages more generally, see O'Sullivan 2010.

11 Erik Davis, in his chapter on 'The Spiritual Cyborg' in *Techgnosis* (1988: 129–63), makes a compelling case for understanding Scientology as a very particular modern and technological religion (or spiritual Prometheanism as he calls it). Dianetics – 'the modern science of modern health' that is the Church's 'Tech' – involves an application of Norbert

Wiener's 'new' cybernetic theory to the mind, as well as the use of technical machines in its therapeutic practices. Davis argues that this is but the latest in the tradition of a gnosis that pitches itself against typical reality and its attendant notion of a single and centred self.

12   In relation to this see Lucy A. Sames' booklet (published to accompany a group exhibition) *Sci-Fi Paganism* (2014).

13   See Deleuze and Guattari 1988: 351–423.

14   An interesting counter-example here is the emergence of ever more sophisticated 3D printing, which is increasingly remaking the world (alongside the whole area of molecular biology that increasingly involves the synthetic). Do these new technological advancements announce an end to 'the given versus the made' binary, or, from Simondon's point of view, are they still forms of alienated thinking, still on the other side of the curtain as it were?

15   For a compelling art historical account of the resonances between standing stones – and prehistoric objects and images more generally – and contemporary art, see Lippard 1983. For a more recent study of modern and contemporary art's connection and resonances with the past, in a British context and concerning magic more specifically, see Bracewell et al. 2009.

16   The soundtrack by Coil also contributes to the affect of the film (Coil were themselves interested and involved in magical practice). For a different fiction – one that produces a different structure of feeling – in relation to pilgrimages and standing stones (in conjunction with pornography), see Home 2002. In its fictioning of a particular landscape (Aberdeenshire), this book also looks forward to some of the material we will be discussing in Chapter 7. Home, more generally, is involved in an experimental writing practice pitched against bourgeois norms and, as such, might also be understood to be writing against the fiction of the self (hence also the connections with some of the material of Chapter 3).

17   O'Sullivan attends further to the Maypole – and its dance – as an alternative point of subjectification in 'Contours and Case Studies for a Dissenting Subjectivity (or, How to Live Creatively in a Fearful World)' (2006).

18   For another account of this nesting of the future within the past, this time from the 1920s, see Annebella Pollen's *The Kindred of the Kibbo Kift* (2015). The look, practices and ideas of the Kibbo Kift involved a particular combination of the pre-industrial and aspects of the modern in an experimental exploration of another mode of being (for an analysis that foregrounds this aspect of the Kibbo Kift see Plastique Fantastique's review article (2016) on both this 'movement' and Pollen's book).

6   Future-Past-Presents: Neomedieval Mappae Mundi

Neomedievalism ... was a lens through which contemporary artists identified and justified the present in the past and through which they narrated this past in terms of how they imagined their futures. It has no logical conclusion.

The Confraternity of Neoflagellants, *thN Lng folk 2go*

IN THIS CHAPTER we address practices that fiction neomedieval worlds in the present and as potential futures, extending our discussion of Raymond Williams' concepts of residual and emergent cultures that we introduced in the last chapter. We also continue an interest in European art practices and writing that address physical or extensive space (especially rural landscapes and cityscapes) as presenting sites or points that facilitate performances which, in themselves, fiction a space-time different to modernity and its rationalisations. This involves a shift in our focus from practices concerned with magical unity to themes that abounded in a time dominated by religion. In so doing, we explore the fictioning of the pre-modern and the non-modern as a means of resisting those dominant forms of globalisation that have transformed societies by opening up or erasing borders and integrating economies, thereby transforming the scale, speed and nature of the relations and exchanges taking place in actual and cyber spaces.

The politics of this rejection of capitalist modernisation are complicated. As we briefly noted in the previous chapter, *other-times-past* serve as models for many kinds of progressive and reactionary orientations, and today it might be said that the rejection and dismantling of modernist projects and institutions is taking place on a scale not seen before: the United Kingdom is preparing to exit a European Union fraught with tensions; reactionary politics has become mainstream in the United States of America; and religious, tribal and racial identifications continue to influence beliefs and opinions in most regions of the globe. The market logics of neoliberalism are being challenged, leading some (particularly on what has become known as the alt-right) to sound the death-knell of not just (left-inspired) social democracy and internationalism, but also of those forms of transnational capitalism that ignore race, ethnicity or religion in the pursuit of expanding markets dependent on the free movement of cheap labour, goods and finance.

To a large extent, this chapter discusses practices that draw on pre-modern and residual cultures to explore alternative logics to both these reactionary ideologies and those more general modernising tendencies that shape and standardise life. It is important then that we first lay out some of this terrain in more detail, along with its problematics. First we examine the novel *The Diamond Age* (1996) by Neal Stephenson, which seems to relate to (or predict) the contemporary reactionary rejection of globalisation through a turn to the past, which neomedieval practices might be thought to be in sympathy with but are, in fact, against. We then discuss the writing of Fredric Jameson, who in addressing postmodernism was concerned with how best to map globalised societies and whether a new kind of allegorical art might serve that purpose (negatively referencing medieval allegory in the process). It is our contention that contemporary non-modern and neomedieval art practices have answers for the problems that Jameson identifies.

The Diamond Age

The ideologies of the alt-right and NRx – which reject progressive notions of equality, democracy and modernity – promise a new age, one in which the novel *The Diamond Age* by Neal Stephenson (1996) would no longer seem a fictional work but a mapping of a potential order to come. It is as if this tale of a technologically advanced world structured by, and fixated on, past empires and ethnic identities was an early warning that modernism and democracy are nothing but a blip in the history of human societies. In *The Diamond Age*, something like the Neoreactionary ideals of 'patchwork' (small states organised around ethnic, business or ideological interests) and Neocameralism (neo-states in which a monarch or CEO rules through executive appointment) have come to pass. As Vincent Garton suggests in his essay 'Leviathan Rots' (2017), the contemporary notion of patchwork, attributed to the computer scientist Curtis Yarvin (a major progenitor of Neoreactionary thinking), can be seen as reprising 'a tradition of Western political thought' that can be traced back to the 'origins of nationalism in the medieval French reaction against the universalist pretences of the Emperor'. Garton draws a parallel here between medieval politics and the Neoreactionary rejection of both globalisation and left-inspired or progressive internationalism. While *The Diamond Age* is not easily read as a neomedieval work (as with reactionary politics today, it is more easily read as a return to pre-twentieth-century values of hierarchy, order and competition, and national and ethnic purity), the various political and economic powers described in the novel all regulate and defend borders, and there is little if any trace of internationalist or globalising ideologies in the exchanges between the tale's protagonists.[1] Stephenson's future Earth is divided into territories or enclaves run by Phyles or tribes, including the Chinese Han, the Anglo-Saxon Neo-Victorians (or 'Vickys') of New Atlantis, the Japanese of Nippon, the Hindustanis of Hindustan, a Jewish Phyle, the Mormons, a Parsis Phyle, the Maoist Senderistas, a secretive group called CryptNet, and the Drummers (who develop hive-like communication and ways of living). We would suggest that in Stephenson's novel – in which everyday relations are ordered by the codes and values of a Phyle (the primary example being New Atlantis) – life is lived in a *present-perfect* tense. This grammatical term expresses the completion of an action without necessarily stating when the event took place. It is mostly used when referring to events of the recent past; an example here would be 'the Victorians have provided a model for society'. This is different from the grammatical construction of the *past-perfect* tense, which articulates an action finished or perfected in the past, as in 'the Victorians had provided a model for society'. The use of 'have' (referring to the present) and 'had' (referring to the past) marks the difference between present- and past-perfect terms. In *The Diamond Age*, an Atlantan subject – however different from an original Victorian subject, or aware of the hypocrisy of the Victorian age – does not tend to think of Victorians in past-perfect terms: Atlantans live in a perpetual Victorian present, however knowingly idealised. The social hierarchies of the Vickys of New Atlantis – as well as their morals and attitudes to craft and technology – will remain unchanged for the foreseeable future. The Victorians – or at least an idealised Victorian society – have provided everything that is needed. The fact that the Vickys know that New Atlantis is a particular kind of construction (that is, a performance or fictioning) contributes to the inert, futureless temporality that pervades *The Diamond Age*. In one sense, history – or rather modernity – is over for the Vickys, as (neo-)Victorian culture – bar new technological developments – cannot be improved upon.

Whether Stephenson understands something about the limits of globalisation and the ideologies that reject market-driven modernisation, or is predicting a form of global organisation to come, is too early to tell. What interests us here is that in many contemporary instances where the collapse of liberal or modern institutions and globalising systems is imagined, we find fictions that have exited a narrative of history (as a grand march), similar to the ways in which enclaves in *The Diamond Age* seem to have abandoned the time of modernity – for them, historical time delivering change, progress and the 'shock of the new' is a thing of the past. Paradoxically, however, such fictions loop narratives of the past into the present, as the basis for present-day social organisation. This is the case with life in some enclaves in the novel, such as the Celestial Kingdom, which organises a society purged of communism (declared a Western plot) by following the philosophy of Confucius, the 'Throneless King' (Stephenson 1996: 280). The idea that the past provides a basis for present-day life, in reaction to ideas of progress, is not unfamiliar. We see this also in mainstream political positions that propose a reversal of modernist, egalitarian programmes – a good example being Donald Trump's 2016 election campaign slogan, 'Make America Great Again'. As with all fictions that exit modernism and draw on *other-times-past*, the notion of postmodernism may be exceeded but not exactly left behind, not least because reactionary politics might not just be a symptom of postmodernity but also a response to aspects of postmodern transformations. Here we suggest that the difference between reactionary politics and contemporary neomedieval art practices that we attend to all comes down to a question of how the past is activated or fictioned in the present; more than this, neomedieval practices explore the potential of allegory and fiction combined with performance to find alternatives to globalising tendencies without attempting to turn the clock back to a time before the spread of democratic and egalitarian politics. To help us address this, and to offer an account of global- isation useful for our discussion, we now attend to Fredric Jameson's writing on postmodernism before turning more directly neomedieval fictionings.

Time Subordinated to Space (in the Present Tense)

In *Postmodernism, or, the Cultural Logic of Late Capitalism* (1991), Jameson's famous book expanding upon ideas he first presented in a journal article in 1984, the Marxist scholar offers a critique of the disorientating spatialisations of capitalism. He revisits this critique some thirty years later in an essay titled 'The Aesthetics of Singularity' (2015), stating that his original thesis was correct, but that instead of writing about postmodernism all those years ago he was actually writing about globalisation. As early as his first journal article on postmodernism, and then in more detail in his book, Jameson argues that a relevant and urgent response to postmodernism and its globalising tendencies is cognitive mapping, suggesting that postmodernity 'has finally succeeded in transcending the capacities of the individual human body to locate itself, to organize its immediate surroundings perceptually, and cognitively to map its position in a mappable external world' (1991: 44).

In this, Jameson suggests that capitalism, in its most recent phase, subordinates time to space, differentiating postmodern culture from the culture of the moderns. If for the latter difference emerging over or in time is a key process, it is relations in space which becomes important to postmodernity and contemporary capitalism. Postmodernity (or globalisation) is, nonetheless, still a historical process or event, despite producing an ahistorical culture – one which, Jameson suggests, generates ever more instances that are 'one-time unrepeatable formal events (in their own pure present . . .)' (2015: 113). Jameson includes in this the contracts of derivative markets (which we will ourselves turn to in the last section of our book), the fine-dining menus of famous restaurants such as *El Bulli*, flashmobs and international art events. These examples all constitute a postmodernity which, as Jameson famously wrote of the Westin Bonaventure Hotel, 'aspires to being a total space, a complete world' (1991: 39). He understands this postmodern logic as signalling the end of the 'bourgeois subject', which disappears along with 'historicity' (2015: 128).

> This is why, as our system becomes ever more abstract, it is appropriate to substitute a more abstract diagnosis, namely the displacement of time by space as a systemic dominant, and the effacement of traditional temporality by those multiple forms of spatiality we call globalization. (128)

Life then, according to Jameson, is subject to increasing abstraction, making it difficult if not impossible to imagine such life in a future tense. For Jameson implies that in order to bring about change an understanding of how present-day life is organised is required, which is why he states that a mapping of a particular kind – one that plots the temporal and spatial aspects of globalisation – is needed. How to produce such a mapping is then an urgent question for the Marxist theorist. In a paper delivered in 1990, in which Jameson develops his thesis on cognitive mapping, he suggests that imagining a future would require new aesthetic practices (though he has no idea what these would be). As he makes clear, a project of cognitive mapping stands or falls with the notion that there is an '(unrepresentable, imaginary) global social totality' that 'was to have been mapped' by modernist practices (1990: 347). That this problem is articulated as a future-orientated project that has stalled in the past – a project that 'was to have been' (the future articulated in the past tense) – signals Jameson's key concern that humans now struggle to find the means of understanding the times they live in. Most importantly for Jameson, the truth of any experience or event is no longer located in the space within which it takes place, as economies and cultures are global and networked. Such economies and networks have local effects that do not necessarily reveal their non-local influences. The complexities of global relations are not tangible to individual experience or understanding without specialist knowledge or technologies to collect and process data: the example Jameson offers is a city connected at increasing speeds to many other places, a network beyond the grasp of the city dweller's experience or imagination (349). The aesthetics of singularity, then, would be a twenty-first-century attempt to manage and profit from the complexities of the local and non-local relations of globalisation, rather than an aesthetics that aims towards reflexive or enlightening ends.

Postmodernism, or the Cultural Logic of the Middle Ages

In commenting on the aesthetics of singularity and spatialisation, Jameson offers two important observations. Firstly, he discusses ownership of land, and control of space, as a contemporary problem of real estate and, in a direct reference to medieval society, as a problem of the return of feudalism. In this, he suggests there is a rise of feudal modes of production, pointing out that some economists are returning to doctrines of rent in relation to finance capital (2015: 131).[2] Secondly, Jameson makes it clear that, in this, he disagrees with those who argue that technologies of acceleration abolish space. He responds to this idea by suggesting that what people have in mind is the reduction of distance between stock exchanges (and other sites of exchange) with the advent of ever faster communication technologies. Indeed, globalisation and the advent of digital exchange can actually be understood as a spatialisation and as 'a crucial representational problem for grasping postmodernity' (131).

The representational problem, here, relates not just to understanding the present but also to imagining alternatives to new financial and economic transactions and exchanges, and to spatial arrangements (including ownership) that are difficult to model or map due to their speed and scale of complexity. The answer, for Jameson, is to develop a sense of history that 'can only be reawakened by a Utopian vision lying beyond the horizon of our current globalized system, which appears too complex for representation in thought' (121).

In advocating for utopia, Jameson keeps faith with the possibility of articulating social change in a *future-perfect tense* (an example being the statement 'we will have changed things'). In this, he also keeps faith with the idea that it is artworks that announce (new) times, different and other to the present. But Jameson's relation to utopia is not straightforward (as we shall discuss later on), and he certainly does not view it as a blueprint for a perfect future society. In relation to this commitment to a kind of utopian art practice Jameson discusses *Untitled Installation* (1988), a collaboration between Robert Gober, Meg Webster, Albert Bierstadt and Richard Prince, presenting a strange room that seems a space apart, rather than in the future, consisting of a door separated from its frame, a landscape painting, a mound of moss and a text work (Jameson 1991: 160).[3] For Jameson, this is a spatialised (postmodern) utopia; he argues that, unlike much conceptual art, *Untitled Installation* addresses 'a concept that does not yet exist' (163). If this is a postmodern utopia, Jameson tentatively suggests – not least as it is a collective enunciation in which various forms of art come together – it is perhaps because it presents a domestic space that is also a glimpse of a future-absence of traces of family life, which he reads as a statement relating to gender (166). It might, he argues, be a new form of allegory that is:

horizontal rather than vertical: if it must still attach its one-on-one conceptual labels to its objects after the fashion of *The Pilgrim's Progress*, it does so in the conviction that those objects (along with their labels) are now profoundly relational . . . When we add to this the inevitable mobility of such relations, we begin to glimpse the process of allegorical interpretation as a kind of scanning that, moving back and forth across the text, readjusts its terms in constant modification of a type quite different from our stereotypes of some static medieval or biblical decoding, and which one would be tempted (were it not also an old-fashioned word!) to characterize as dialectical. (168)

We understand Jameson's notion of (dialectical) scanning as a form of mapping, but think his dismissal of medieval allegory too quick. Scholars such as Arnold Williams suggest that medieval allegory is both 'a method of interpretation and a method of creation' (1969: 77) that combines the myths of the ancient or classical with (new) Christian worlds – such realms are seen as continuous in the Middle Ages, rather than as separate and historical (as evident in Mappae Mundi, which we will discuss below). Medieval allegory, then, being productive and providing continuity between (singular) times and places, might be relevant to our contemporary conditions.

As Theodore Silverstein argues, in certain instances medieval allegory escapes orthodox Christian interpretation as 'there were other forms of allegory in the Middle Ages' (1967: 28) produced by the Catholic Church. Silverstein has written critically on (but not without interest in) what some call the four-fold system of medieval allegory that includes literal interpretation (Jameson's static biblical decoding) alongside other, more symbolic forms. Arnold Williams characterises these as moral (approached through beauty), figuration and typological presentations (in which an individual is equated with another specific individual) and analogy (of which Williams suggests the most fruitful are spatial, as when a 'journey becomes a spatial analogy for moral or spiritual education') (1969: 80–83). All three of these non-literal allegorical forms address a problem that Jameson is concerned with, not least as a problem relevant to postmodernity:

> The allegorical, then – whether those of De Man or Benjamin, of the revalorization of medieval or of non-European texts . . . – can be minimally formulated as the question posed to thinking by the awareness of incommensurable distances within its object of thought. (1991: 168)

We suggest that Arnold Williams' 'operational approach' to medieval allegory points to fictioning modes that can address the 'horizontal' and mobile relationality Jameson identifies as an aspect of postmodern culture.[4] In this, we view neomedieval allegorical operations as producing new mappings or a new scanning of the world that engage with – and possibly counter – globalising tendencies. Against totalising historicist representations, neomedievalisms interpret and produce spatial relations on different scales, through the allegorical doubling of figures and objects, and through their allegorical journeys, pilgrimages and performances. By drawing horizontal lines of connection, these medieval allegorical operations bring (or fiction) ancient, contemporary and future times and spaces into existence, side by side, just as we found in Hoban's novel *Riddley Walker* (1980).

To explore this idea, we will attend first to The Confraternity of Neoflagellants (Norman Hogg and Neil Mulholland) and their book *thN Lng folk 2go: Investigating Future Premoderns* (2013), which is written from the vantage point of a neomedieval future, before discussing examples of art practice. The work of the Neoflagellants is important for indexing myriad neomedieval theories, concepts and practices, but also, we suggest, for exploring contemporary life through political or ethical allegories, thus attending to globalisation in terms of an 'elasticated atemporal looping and folding' in which 'pre-modern conditions' provide insight 'into postmodern conditions' (The Confraternity of Neoflagellants 2013: 178).

Future-Past-Presents

thN Lng folk 2go begins with a tale of the past (told by voices from the future) about the involvement of a character called Gambini in neomedieval power games in Montreal. It is important to point out though that the world the narrators inhabit and the events concerning Gambini that they recount are set in the future for the reader (they have yet to take place). This makes the volume a Science Fiction but also a science fictioning too, for the narrators are Hogg and Mulholland who travelled and photographed the setting of Gambini's adventures to illustrate their writing, as if looking for privileged sites of historical, neomedieval importance.

The book narrates Gambini's time spent journeying through a mall, the RÉSO or 'Underground City' of Montreal.[5] This exploration of a vast complex consisting of office and retail spaces linked by tunnels resonates with Jameson's description of postmodern spatialisations (but also with Walter Benjamin's *Arcades Project*). Indeed, the Underground City contains a Bonaventure Hotel, though it must be said the building is different to the Westin Bonaventure Hotel in California that Jameson famously wrote about in his book on postmodernism. Since the RÉSO dates from 1962, it might be argued that the mall is an early postmodern spatialisation. In Hogg and Mulholland's book, it may appear to be (or is fictioned as) a series of singular domains, or, as the Neoflagellants suggest, a number of kingdoms (2), consisting of restaurants and shops, a monorail terminal, a university, galleries and museums; that is, the RÉSO could be said to aspire to being a complete world. But if the mall is a singular world, the account of Gambini's adventures in the RÉSO places the reader in multiple times: the (medieval) past, modern and contemporary consumer culture, and a future (neomedieval) society. As such the reader can scan across times that seem both continuous and different, a process that relates to our earlier discussion of nested temporalities within fictions.

Gambini's life story is followed by an account of various theories of neomedievalism and their relevance to contemporary and future political and economic conditions, which the Neoflagellants initially address through the ideas of Hedley Bull. Bull – an anarchist writing at the time of détente between the superpowers of the last century – suggests that non-state actors (such as the UN and transnational corporations) might challenge nation states, just as the Catholic Church in the Middle Ages competed with sovereign states and local powers. Quoting Bull, the Neoflagellants describe transnational relations as 'a system of overlapping authority and multiple loyalty' (56) – a state of affairs evident in the tale of Gambini. Referring to the paradigm of globalisation, they discuss how Bull's idea might allow 'societal actors' to refocus loyalties and influence transnational 'economic realms' and resist 'political inter-ference' so that they adapt to 'societal values at odds with the autonomous logic of market efficiency' (57–8). We would suggest that the Neoflagellants' political model offers an alternative to the Neoreactionary notion of 'patchwork' mentioned earlier, which operates through unceasing loyalty to – or a contract honoured with – a specific tribe or business concern. But the Neoflagellants, although favouring multiple loyal-ties, note a problem with Bull's proposition: transnational interests can colonise politics and societies for specific ends. While there are a number of neomedieval aspects to transnationalism or globalisation – to discuss these the Neoflagellants draw on a number of scholars to list overlapping jurisdictions, fluid and contested bound-aries and multiple loyalties among them – such attributes do not necessarily challenge neoliberalism. This leads the Neoflagellants to consider exactly what forms of neome-dievalism might resist or aid a neoliberalism that has the effect of fragmenting state organisation through market expansion (54). One idea – John Gerrard Ruggie's notion of a medieval 'nonterritorial functional space' – seems particularly important to the Neoflagellants as a space in which, potentially, societal actors might have some influ-ence. The Neoflagellants affirm that 'nonterritorial functional spaces' are where transnational affairs are conducted (without a dominant authority ruling the territory), facilitated in medieval times by fairs and markets and 'political communities spanning across multiple borders' (61–2). The contemporary (neomedieval) equivalent of 'nonterritorial functional spaces', according to the Neoflagellants, would be the inter-net or other such 'nonterritorial' domains. The question that arises is whether such spaces can be said to facilitate a multiplicity of narratives beyond the market focus of neoliberalism. This is precisely what the Neoflagellants set out to explore, and in doing so offer an alternative perspective to Jameson's view and critique of postmodern singularities as well as a position very different to ideologies that focus on establishing a patchwork of territories and autonomous authorities. To this end, the Neoflagellants fiction worlds through a neomedieval filter, drawing on many scholars to draw parallels between the proliferation of images that can be accessed through the World Wide Web and 'Christian representations' found in medieval maps and books (62). They also offer a critique of the 'enlightenment impulse of European colonists to measure, categorise and format the world in terms of a totalising classificatory grid' (76). Even though the Neoflagellants might reject Jameson's call for cognitive mapping, they might agree that new aesthetic practices are required, but here these are practices that envisage a future through a medieval past registered in the present.

Neomedieval Mappae Mundi

The Neoflagellants thus develop a mapping of a kind radically different to that which Jameson and other commentators on postmodernity call for. Firstly, they do not imagine that humans can master (and absolutely map) objects and the world; secondly, they see the importance of identifying (or producing) spaces in which performance or performative modes can claim efficacy when exploring contemporary conditions. Lastly, they suggest that thinking about medieval relations between humans and things can be relevant to an encounter with postmodern arrangements (such as, we suggest, the horizontal relations found in *Untitled Installation* discussed earlier). Indeed, the Neoflagellants draw an analogy between medieval metaphysics and perspectives in recent continental philosophy:

> Speculative Realism – or in one of its more prominent variants, Object Oriented Ontology – stated not only that objects exist, fully independent of human observation or cognition, but that the human subject is just one particular type of object amongst others. (138)

Such a perspective challenges any idea that humans can map and master the world through straightforward representational modes. As one of the Neoflagellants, Norman Hogg, suggests in his statement for the website of The Centre for Sensory Studies:

> neomedievalism describes the acetic-ludic pursuit of a concrete aesthetic practice that does not (like modern art say) center the subject as sole assembler, virtuoso conductor and final aesthetic judge of matter. To this end, the medieval cosmology is harnessed as a sensual hyper-economy of translation – the processual rituals through which all things, inscribed or enfleshed, animal, vegetable or mineral, inter- act and translate each other sense for sense. (Hogg n. d.)

To embellish this notion the Neoflagellants argue that neomedievalisms offer 'aletri' or 'remote presents' that enable 'performative, ludic research', allowing neomedievalists to find 'a novel point of entry into an inexhaustible range of contemporary subjects' (The Confraternity of Neoflagellants 2013: 178). Although the Neoflagellants do not address medieval maps to any great extent, we suggest that the making of neomedieval Mappae Mundi seems appropriate to finding 'novel points of entry' into contemporary situations. For medieval maps, rather than being just representations of worlds, are sacred objects that guide or invite journeys. They trace pilgrimages and trade routes, and promise encounters – both mundane and fantastic – that are ancient, biblical and (contemporary) medieval (here we are reminded of the privileged points and track-ways of the previous chapter).

It might be objected that Jameson outlines a problem not addressed in neomedievalism, namely that globalisation produces a world in which experience and objective truth are out of kilter (as if it were ever different). Certainly, neomedieval Mappae Mundi will not map a social totality, nor meet Jameson's call for a representation that bridges experience and (the total) truth of relations. If, however, we understand neomedieval Mappae Mundi as engendering a journey and performance that reflects upon postmodern spatialisations, then perhaps political agency (and a scanning between times or histories) is also engendered. Another objection here might be that medieval maps, particularly Mappae Mundi, were the work of conservative authorities (it might be said that a contemporary Mappa Mundi made concrete would be Disneyland) – and again we are reminded of Jameson's dismissal of stereotypical medieval allegory. But if we examine not just the work of neomedieval artists but contemporary medieval scholars, we will see that more radical allegories or fictionings can be imparted by Mappae Mundi, to counter dominant narratives.

The (New) Pilgrims

Dan Terkla, in 'The Original Placement of the Hereford Mappa Mundi' (2010), argues that the Hereford map was not an altar piece but part of what he calls the Cantilupe pilgrimage complex – an assemblage of objects and images including the shrine of St Cantilupe (Terkla 2010: 131). For a time, Hereford Cathedral would have been one of England's most popular pilgrimage destinations, and Terkla suggests that 'the map would have added to the complex's attractive power and served as a multi-media pedagogical tool' (131). The Cathedral is depicted on the map but is barely visible. It is thought that pilgrims touching and pointing to the icon have erased the drawing over time. To suggest that the map is an object of contemplation or veneration, but also an object activated by performances that include pilgrimage, adds support to our earlier suggestion that medieval practices have an equivalence with contemporary practices reflecting on local and global scales. Here we are thinking of the virtual-psycho-geographical 'Mappa Mundi' that UK artist John Cussans presents through performance lectures that use Google maps, indexing the locations at which he first came across books important to his art practice, research and life. In this way, Cussans produces a singular space-time scale by which to orientate himself and his own journeys through Google Earth, relating places to critical thinking and other narratives (Cussans 2011: 25–6). This practice relates to Cussans' paranoid-critical research methodology, which finds meaning in coincidences and (so-called) chance associations and encounters (16). Many, including Jameson, might dismiss Cussans' approach – which proceeds by discovering hidden and unknown relations – arguing, as Jameson does, that a sense of conspiracy

> is the poor person's cognitive mapping in the postmodern age; it is the degraded figure of the total logic of late capital, a desperate attempt to represent the latter's system, whose failure is marked by its slippage into sheer theme and content. (Jameson 1990: 356)

But Cussans' paranoid-critical method does not attempt to produce a totalising representation; rather, it seems to us to be a performance that might be as good a way as any to discover how experience connects to the (hidden) truths of relations (including how daily life and economic and social systems might be influenced by governments, mass media and business); for the paranoid sees connections where others might not, and just because they are paranoid does not mean they are mistaken. The paranoid method recognises the individual – their location, history and subjective orientations – as but one more agent in the world that shapes the process and results of the research (unlike or perhaps in ways different to dialectical methods).

We do not think it too much to suggest that a similar approach to Cussans' method can be found in contemporary medieval scholarship – Daniel Birkholz's 'Mapping Medieval Utopia: Exercises in Restraint' (2006) being an example, albeit a cautious one. Birkholz forces a contemporary reading of instances of resistance through identifying certain figures as markers of dissent in the Hereford Mappa Mundi. He argues that points of bifurcation can be found in its imagery (from a contemporary point of view), such as in the figure of Lot's wife, who turns back towards a community she does not want to leave, disobeying God, who then turns her into a pillar of salt. Birkholz sees Lot's wife as a point of resistance, her cursedness for defying orthodoxy reinforced by her proximity to cities hostile to the Israelites, and to a shape-changing beast (2006: 605–7). A similarly bifurcating, dissenting figure is found in Noah's wife who, Birkholz argues, 'by the late Middle Ages had emerged as the [arche]type of the shrewish spouse', and was said to not want to leave her friends to perish in the heaven-sent flood (609).

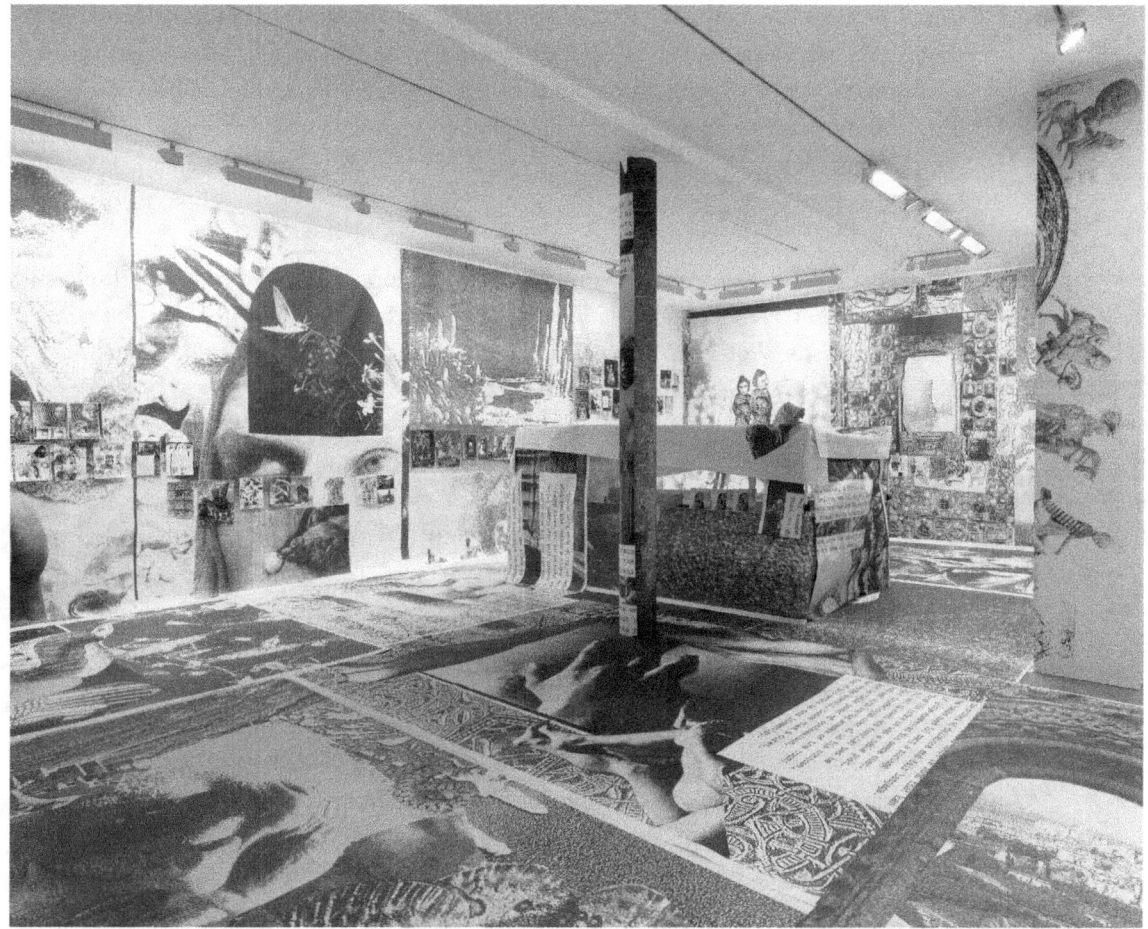

6.1 Marvin Gaye Chetwynd, *Some Canterbury Tales*, 2010–14, 166 collage photocopies, photocopied wallpaper, dimensions: variable (© Marvin Gaye Chetwynd, courtesy of Sadie Coles HQ, London).

Birkholz's approach seems to us a scanning between past and present-day concerns (such as the medieval disdain for disobedient wives and contemporary feminist thought and commitment to community). This is something that a number of neo-medieval art practices have in common, including the work of Marvin Gaye Chetwynd, an example being *Some Canterbury Tales* (2014), exhibited at Sadie Coles HQ in London (see Figure 6.1). The installation – a typological and analogical allegory – features collages that illustrate (or rewrite) *The Canterbury Tales*. It comprises material collected by the artist from close acquaintances, combined with photographs of medieval churches and Baroque ornamentation, synthesised to produce absurd and celebratory images of bodies (and of Chetwynd's friends) – a scanning between medieval and contemporary representations of community and the human body. In this, Chetwynd's work may be said to partake in and address another economy to that of the art market or spectacle. Chetwynd presents images – produced through a communal venture – that circulate through a group of friends or collaborators too. This commitment to community – as well as to making a space or zone for vulgarity, dissonance, play and non-linear time – is also found in her performances, which, Chetwynd suggests,

> are linked to my studies in anthropology. I want more of a shared collective, bonded experience in a smaller community . . . It's more about how any generous or spontaneous gesture could be taken as a form of politics. It's about making a difference on an everyday level. (Chetwynd 2015)

Chetwynd's work is often associated with a specific kind of medieval performance. In their chapter, 'xyzzy: Contemporary Art Before and After Britain', the Neoflagellants cite Chetwynd as one of number of British artists influenced by mumming traditions – others include Joanne Tatham and Tom O'Sullivan and Plastique Fantastique (The Confraternity of Neoflagellants 2013: 177), the latter a collaboration that we, the authors of this book, are involved in. Mumming – a folk tradition of performing a play in masks – is a residual culture that can be found in many parts of Europe today. Produced by members of a community, mumming is not necessarily enjoyable for the audience: in certain instances, in medieval Europe over the period of Christmas, anonymous mummers would pay uninvited and sometimes unwelcome visits to households, performing a play in expectation of reward – a kind of forced gift-economy. The class tensions of a community sometimes manifested at these times, as masked mummers settled scores or committed crimes, leading to the ban of mumming by various authorities (Hutton 1997: 11–12). It is the production of an unruly and playful space and time within the spaces of art that, like Mappae Mundi, engender topological and analogical allegories. Rather than any direct reference to the Middle Ages, it is this that makes the rambling performances of Chetwynd and her collaborators neomedieval: a fictioning of community that produces a probing or disturbance of the present, as found in pilgrimage and mumming. Indeed, as A. L. Morton notes in his reading of R. J. E. Tiddy's *The Mummers Play*, medieval plays produce zones that offer instances of abundance or excess often juxtaposed with themes of 'topsy-turvydom' (Morton 1978: 27), which may serve too as a description of Chetwynd's art.

In relation to this, Erik Davis has some provocative things to say about the interest Western contemporary societies have in festivals and fantasy, which he discussed at the Goldsmiths conference on Neomedievalisms.[6] Davis speculates that, while probably lacking political efficacy, this trend might signal an attempt to find a space for the body and pleasure through establishing a community of a kind. It could be argued that such an idea valorises transgressions that serve merely as a release or safety valve, ensuring social tensions do not produce rebellion, as Peter Stallybrass and Allon White (1986) contend in relation to celebrations of the carnivalesque. Another objection is that festivals, carnivals and fairs are increasingly commodified. We agree with this, but would also suggest that where a community of a kind (as found in the work of Chetwynd) attempts to produce or perform a space for the body, pleasure and generosity, there is also a potential politics. And it seems to us that mappings, parades, pilgrimages and other kinds of journeys and performances can mark or even manifest 'nonterritorial functional spaces' in which various histories and the relations of the local and global can be explored.

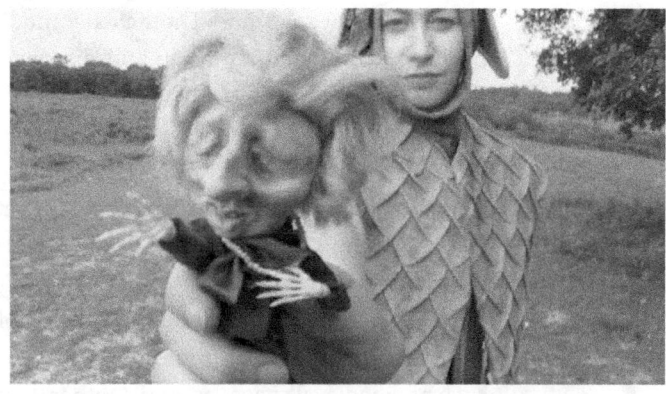

6.2 Jennet Thomas, still from *The Unspeakable Freedom Device*, 2015 (courtesy and copyright Jennet Thomas).

Such an allegorical-analogical operation is found in the work of UK artist Jennet Thomas, and in particular her film *The Unspeakable Freedom Device*, which presents the journey of two women through a bizarre, dysfunctional world of collapsing signs and values (see Figure 6.2). In Thomas' primitive-future world the difference between technology and magic is incomprehensible. The women are on a pilgrimage to the Winter Gardens in Blackpool so that one of the pilgrims can cure her green baby. Along the way, they get caught up in a Margaret Thatcher cargo-cult, at one point buying a 'talking' Thatcher Doll. In publicity for the film, Thomas explains that her work explores the idea of the image of Thatcher as an after-burn on the collective memory of British culture, the Winter Gardens being a privileged location for mainstream political party conferences (Thomas 2015b). By fictioning a pilgrimage, the journey becomes a medium through which past and present myths and rituals are encountered, reflected upon and projected as a (nightmarish) future.

A similar neomedieval approach can be found in a project and book curated and edited by artist Nicky Coutts, which presents the responses of artists and writers to the title and theme of the book, *Pilgrimage* (2007). The invited contributors included Heather Phillipson, Will Cobbing, and Kit Poulson and David Burrows. The latter pair decided on two destinations for pilgrimage: the site where Constable painted *The Hay Wain* in 1821 in the East of England, and the Hammersmith Odeon (now The Apollo) in West London, where David Bowie killed off Ziggy Stardust in 1973.

As with Chetwynd's and Thomas' neomedieval allegories, such performance fictions produce non-linear, alternate and dissonant space-times.

(Neomedieval) Atopias

The question arises here: are we proposing yet another (fictional) form of utopia or utopic space? We think not. We do not conceive of such fictionings as postmodern utopias, as called for by Jameson, or as the micro-utopias of contemporary art and information technology economies identified by the Neoflagellants, though we have some sympathy with this idea (The Confraternity of Neoflagellants 2013: 181). Rather, we understand such neomedieval spaces as atopic rather than utopic (see also Burrows 2006). We borrow the term *atopia* from Michel Le Doueff, who defines atopic texts as having no correct interpretation (2002: 54), a notion we will return to after clarifying the relation of utopia to medieval cultures, for if we are to make the case that neomedieval performance fictions are atopic, it is important that we make clear our understanding that the invention of utopia comes at the moment the pre-modern gives way to the modern.

As Birkholz argues, utopia cannot be found on medieval maps, unless historicism is dispensed with and incongruity embraced (2006: 589–90). Even so, while he states there is no such thing as a medieval utopia (a nonsensical idea, for utopia is a paradise on Earth rather than in heaven), Birkholz's question is 'whether the fey act of seeking to locate such a construct might somehow help to produce it'? (590). We admit that this is an interesting idea (it sounds like fictioning to us), and there are a number of candidates for medieval utopias in this sense. Birkholz proposes the Garden of Eden, or paradise, as utopia (592) – a space apart from Europe, Asia and Africa – which is found on the Hereford Mappa Mundi at the Eastern extreme of the map, inaccessible and encircled by fire. To make the case for this as a utopia, however, might elide the complexity of utopian fiction. Not only this, for medieval societies the Garden of Eden may have been no less real than any other place, and therefore hardly a utopia.

Another candidate worthy of mention is the medieval myth of Cockaigne. The myth describes an island where pigs run around with knives and forks in their hams, where houses are made of pancakes and there are lakes of wine, oil and milk. Herman Pleij writes in *Dreaming of Cockaigne* that this island is no utopia, but is best understood as a satire (2001: 69). If the myth is a satire, Cockaigne is still worth discussing in relation to our exploration of utopia, atopia and topsy-turvy worlds (the latter being a feature of some neomedieval fictionings). Interestingly for us, Pleij, while rejecting the idea of Cockaigne as a utopia, relates the myth to medieval literature and carnival that inverts and makes a nonsense of social order (338–9), similar to the inversions of the medieval Feast of Fools (417). More than this, Cockaigne is a world with no hierarchy, where all live free beyond sin as nature commands, similar to the life lived in the Heresy of the Free Spirit, a medieval movement that Pleij associates with Dutch versions of Cockaigne (329). Perhaps A. L. Morton, in *The English Utopia*, is right to argue for a political interpretation of Cockaigne, pointing to passages that proclaim 'all is common to young and old' (1978: 24), and noting that the island, in the material sense, is clearly more enticing than heavenly paradise. But although Morton suggests Cockaigne expresses a utopian impulse – its sublime and grotesque imagery giving insight into the common mind (24) – its fantastic and (magically) compliant resources are in stark contrast to the social organisations of Thomas More's island *Utopia*, the origin for many concepts of utopia.

For most, the two sections or books that make up *Utopia* (1994) – published in 1516 – mark a significant event in the development of modern European politics and philosophy, as a critique of the corruption of the commonwealth and as a contribution to the development of humanism. Utopia – the good place that is nowhere – is commonly identified as a satirical fiction *and* a promise, if not a blueprint, of an alternative society. In this respect, utopia seems a thoroughly modern idea. This is the view of Louis Marin, author of *Utopics*, who argues that utopia appears historically 'only when a mode of capitalist production is formed' and a conflict between feudalism and bourgeois productive forces manifests (Marin 1990: 198–9). It would seem, following Marin, that a medieval, Christian monoculture does not produce the plurality or dialectical thought necessary to engender the double function of critical reflection and fiction (7). Furthermore, Marin – an influence on Jameson's thinking – defines utopia as the 'ideological critique of ideology' (195) that also presents a fictional neutrality spanning truth and falsehood (7) (a reflexivity that he thinks medieval culture does not have).

To further examine this double function of utopia (and introduce in detail the concept of the atopic), we now turn to Michelle Le Doueff's comments in *The Philosophical Imaginary*, which draw attention to the fact that the first book of More's *Utopia* – which 'can roughly be termed the critical analysis of a reality' – functions as a critique, whereas the second book is more ambiguous in its meaning (Le Doueff 2002: 44). For it is the latter which contains the actual descriptions of the strange land, and which Le Doueff suggests we can call fiction (44). Her inference here is that through reading the two books together *Utopia* becomes a critical measure for Tudor society (47). She speculates that the writing of the first book (after the completion of the second book) is an acknowledgement that the second book has a plurality of possible readings, that it is *polysemic*. Book two, on its own, could be read as a reverie, pastiche or, indeed, as 'a most ancient and very new idea, that of the Antipodes' – an upside-down, topsy-turvy world (47–8). Without the first book, Le Doueff contends, *Utopia*, a bizarre place that is no place, is an atopia (the part of fiction, we suggest, that discourse cannot fully account for or receive).

In this sense, atopia (as polysemic fiction) does not express what someone thinks – the way the first book of *Utopia* might be said to express More's critique of Tudor

England – but constitutes a fiction that forces thought. The second book, read through Le Doueff's eyes, produces a familiar yet strange society in which the Utopians sleep during the day and work at night, and eschew gold (which is less valuable than iron, as gold jewellery is thought childish and is given to criminals to wear to humiliate them). In fact, Utopians seem to have many unusual customs, including allowing brides and grooms to view each other's naked bodies before marriage, and treating burials as entertainment – traditions that the staunch Catholic Thomas More might not have viewed as desirable. If book two of *Utopia* is an atopia with medieval traits, and book one presents an ideological critique, it seems as if More's work lies, as we implied above, on the cusp of modernity – between the medieval (book two) and the modern (book one). This is important to our argument, for it seems to us that neomedieval practices and fictionings are only half a utopia (if a utopia at all), the half that is polysemic and atopic.

We take a pause here to consider the fact that *Utopia* (and therefore the atopia Le Doueff finds in the book) was conceived in a period when European colonial expansion was looking to 'The New World': colonialism engenders the imaginary of a European intellectual to write a fiction about a place where everything seems turned on its head. We should also acknowledge that other traditions we have addressed here can be said to have been influenced by European colonial or overseas ventures, not least that of pilgrimage, which entailed journeying to the Holy Land and greatly contributed to the advent of the Crusades, a war that continues to blight relations between Europe and the Middle East. Not only, then, are European religious, national and political relations effected by colonialism, but also European traditions of art, including those in which wanderers and explorers set off in search of 'strange', uncharted or wild lands, free of European culture and corruption. Returning to More's novel, we note that its space of radical otherness, of utopia and atopia, is not produced in time (as Jameson suggests of utopias), but as a space elsewhere and nowhere (but opened up by exploration of 'The New World'). It might be that the (imaginary) space opened up by the opportunism and entrepreneurialism of European travellers produces a fiction which, as Le Doueff argues, is free from binary, dialectical functions and ideological critique (at least in the description of the utopia in More's second book). An irony perhaps? It is in this fiction of a place in 'The New World' that is nowhere that allegory is accelerated to produce polysemic fiction. Despite the problematic history of utopia, we think Le Doueff's atopic, polysemic fiction an important residual form. A narrative mode which, as we have observed of other kinds of mythopoetic fictions, is performed through reading it. As Le Doueff explains, polysemy

is perceived only when no one immediate meaning prevails. It is related to a fundamental asemy. Several possible meanings and no definite, precise meaning amount to the same thing, if one accepts the findings of experiments conducted on the perception of blurred images and ink blots. (54)

We suggest that this (residual, medieval) atopic fictional form can be found in contemporary art practices, including in the work of British artist Nathaniel Mellors. An example is *Giantbum* (2008), presented as a play and installation of animated talking heads that tell the story of a medieval family of explorers trapped in the bowels of a giant, full of the giant's faeces – called the Ploppen – that keep disappearing, perhaps indicating a way out for the explorers. But this apparently proves to be a false hope, when the father explains that the Ploppen eat each other. It seems that the father has concluded there is no way out of *Giantbum* and is cannibalising himself as a means of regeneration; he eats his arms and then remakes them (badly), a process that he thinks will allow him to live forever. It is the multiple and strange allegories (of social relations and worlds), the fantastic concepts (of regeneration and immortality) and the humorous absurdities (that present a community of faeces) that make *Giantbum* an engaging atopia. Mellor's film *Saprophage* (2012) similarly presents polysemic fictioning, and introduces 'Epiphany', the administrator of Sodom, and 'Nunzio', administrator of Gomorrah – the latter describing his idea for a movie titled 'The Big Brown Film' about an American who is a good guy but also like a vampire. When the character Paul Gerald Saprophage appears in the film in another scene, he asks 'is this America?' He is told he is nowhere.

It could be said that such nonsense is no substitute for cognitive mapping, or for dialectical utopias where a traveller visits a future or alternative society that generates meaning by revealing the visitor's own society as imperfect. But atopia has an effect on the present, through imaging or presenting engaging worlds beyond the logics of the present day, which allow us to reflect on those logics through an inverted or non-modern perspective. In producing polysemic scenes and performance fictions, we propose that contemporary atopic presentations can be a critical and productive form of mythopoesis. To develop this idea, and conclude the chapter, we turn to Karma Lochrie's discussion of medieval maps and the antipodes.

The (New) Antipodeans

In 'Sheer Wonder: Dreaming Utopia in the Middle Ages' (2006), Lochrie posits the *Commentary on the Dream of Scipio* by Macrobius as a medieval utopia. The commentary (on a book by the Roman scholar Cicero) refers to a map of the world that depicts the northern and southern hemispheres. On the map, Europe is married to an antipodean region which Lochrie suggests is a 'deterritorialisation' in the 'Deleuzo-Guattarian' sense of an 'estranging critique' and a dislocation of previous cultural formations – in this case, 'Rome and its ethos of fame as the imperial exemplar' (Lochrie 2006: 506).

There is, the reader of the map might conclude, an elsewhere where Rome's logic is not sovereign. Lochrie argues that, at the very least, the antipodean map suggests a paradox, 'if not an internal contradiction' (506), reminding us that Louis Marin calls utopian texts 'neutral', in that they hold contrasting visions without resolving or synthesising them. Whether Lochrie successfully establishes the existence of a medieval utopia is not our concern here (though we do not think the *Commentary on the Dream of Scipio* entirely meets Marin's criteria laid out above for utopian fiction). Rather, we note that Lochrie demonstrates that allegorical doubling does not always lead to a comparison of figures or places; a scrambling or collapsing of opposites is another possible outcome. More than this, following Lochrie, any deterritorialisation that produces a space in which the logics of the dominant culture are absent has an effect on the imaginary that supports and enables those logics to operate as reality.

It is this effect on the imaginary that we find in Simon Faithfull's *Going Nowhere* trilogy (1995–2016); a body of work that produces one of the most extreme, rudimentary examples of atopic and antipodean space to be found in contemporary art. Though Faithfull would not, we think, consider himself a neomedievalist, we suggest his work operates as analogous allegory and atopic performance fiction. In Faithfull's trilogy a mapping of sorts is produced through what appear to be austere and bizarre acts. A key aspect of Faithfull's practice is that the artist seeks deserted territories within which to perform. In 1995, for *Going Nowhere 1*, Faithfull set up a video camera in a field and then walked away. Nothing happens. In 2011, for *Going Nowhere 2*, another camera is set up at the bottom of a sea, and again Faithfull walks away, but this time he is a strange sight, tramping across the seabed in a white shirt and black trousers. Again, nothing seems to happen. For *Going Nowhere 1.5*, in 2016, a walk is taken on an island that only appears twice a day due to tidal conditions. Faithfull is recorded walking around in ever decreasing circles by a drone that also captures the disappearance of the island – reminiscent of Robert Smithson's performance

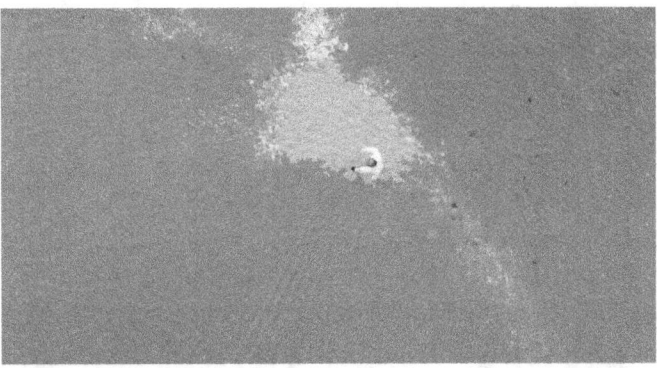
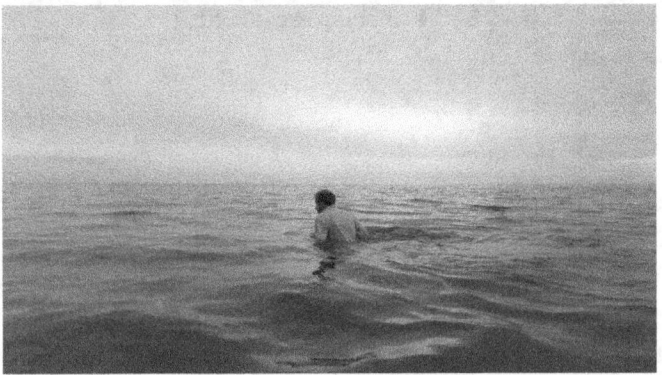

6.3 Simon Faithful, *Going Nowhere 1.5*, 2016 (courtesy and copyright Simon Faithfull).

on *Spiral Jetty* (1970) (see Figure 6.3). At the end of the film, as the drone withdraws, Faithfull is lapped by the waves; when the drone returns for a last look, the island has disappeared completely. Although environmental themes can be identified in this trilogy, we suggest Faithfull produces a performance fictioning of antipodean spaces, but not in the sense of tracing one land mass directly opposite to another (although the deserted locations chosen by the artist exist in contrast with the populated and built-up environments of globalised economies). Rather, Faithfull produces performances (going nowhere) in places ruled by elemental forces, animals, vegetables and minerals (where human feet are not seen to tread very often if at all). As Joy Sleeman (2016: 24) comments on *Going Nowhere 1.5*, Faithfull might be the 'last man', but equally, we suggest, he might be a pilgrim or an antipodean inhabitant.

We count Faithfull as one among many new pilgrims, mummers, antipodeans and atopians who allow us to reflect on contemporary social, spatial and temporal organisations, but who also present – through performance – spaces and horizons beyond the logics of globalisation and postmodernity. Whether collective or individual gestures, such practices and performance fictions counter the apparent perpetual present and singularities of globalisation. The examples we have discussed pursue a horizontalism (the performances are literally a movement through space but also often involve a disrupting or inverting of hierarchies) that both draws upon and actuates residual cultures by attending to specific points and places (in Simondon's terms, privileged locations in the landscape). It is this mode of practice that we further attend to in the following chapters, and that we find articulated by twentieth-century and contemporary European and American artists and writers who fiction the landscape.

Notes

1   While Stephenson has also authored *Anathem* (2009), a tale in which groups withdraw into monastic communities that forgo contact with the outside world and abstain from using modern technologies, it is *The Diamond Age* that addresses a world purged of the universalism of the modern age, and that seems most relevant to a discussion of neomedievalism.

2   We see the same logic at work in many contemporary software purchases: Adobe suites, for example, can only be rented rather than owned.

3   Prince's text was a joke: 'Fireman pulling drunk out of a burning bed: You darned fool, that'll teach you to smoke in bed. Drunk: I wasn't smoking in bed, it was on fire when I laid down.'

4   The third non-literal approach identified by Williams – the allegory of the moral through beauty – might be beyond its sell-by date, but we suggest it has been replaced today by political and ethical allegories that address contemporary conditions through aesthetic

productions. Just as in modern art, the question of what is beautiful (aesthetic judgement) is replaced by the question of what art can be (experimental practice).

5   RÉSO is a homophone that relates to the French word for network, *réseau*, and that adopts the logo, the letter O, used by the city's metro for its last letter.

6   Held at Goldsmiths, University of London, 27–29 January 2014, and organised in part to discuss the Neoflagellants' book and neomedievalism within contemporary art more generally.

7   Fictioning the Landscape

That zero panorama seemed to contain ruins in reverse, *that is –*
all the new construction that would eventually be built. This is the
opposite of the 'romantic ruin' because the buildings don't fall *into ruin*
after *they are built but rather* rise *into ruin before they are built.*

> Robert Smithson, 'A Tour of the Monuments
> of Passaic, New Jersey (1967)'

The landscape has ceased to be a backdrop for something else to happen
in front of; instead, everything that happens is a part of the landscape.
There is no longer a sharp distinction between foreground and background.

> Brian Eno, *On Land* (quoted in Mark Fisher, *The Weird and the Eerie*)

CONTINUING WITH SOME of the themes of this first section, we want now to further explore the idea of mythopoesis as a fictioning of other pasts, but also other futures – by examining practices that proceed through overlaying different narratives on a given landscape. This form of mythopoesis can also involve a tracking of points of intersection between a given reality or landscape and fiction or, again, a nesting of fictions (we should say at the outset that these different diagrams are not necessarily compatible, but that they can and do coexist within certain artworks). Finally, in this chapter, fictioning once again refers to the way in which these different diagrams need to be performed in some way, either through formal experimentation or, more explicitly, with a journey through or to some other place.

This chapter and the next are organised around a series of case studies from an Anglo-American context. They are also concerned predominantly, though not exclusively, with a masculine subjectivity (something we mentioned in the Introduction and acknowledge as a particular and partial perspective). There is less theoretical material in both of these chapters, as the idea is that the case studies themselves provide different inflections on our theme. That said, our first case study relates to some of the theoretical material discussed in Chapters 2 and 3, especially in relation to the cut-up technique and the fiction of the self, while the other case studies – in both this chapter and the next – also make reference to some of the material from Chapters 1 and 5, namely Guattari's concept of 'fabulous images' that cross from literature to life, Williams' discussion of residual culture, and Simondon's laying out of magic as a pre-technical mode of existence.

The Atrocity Exhibition

Although a literary writer, J. G. Ballard was also involved in a more particular fictioning of social and psychological reality, especially in his post-1969 work (the novels and short stories up to this point being more recognisably Science Fiction or fantasy works). This is especially the case with his experimental novel *The Atrocity Exhibition* (1970), which signalled a change in direction from the depiction of other worlds or imaginary places to the depiction, albeit from a strange angle, of the world Ballard perceived to be his own reality.[1] As he remarked in an interview from the early 1970s, it was directly after writing *The Atrocity Exhibition* that he 'turned to the landscape of technology and the communications industry' (Ballard and Louit 2012: 76). Indeed, Ballard could be said to be among the first to map a new techno-psychosexual geography and, as such, is important for our study of mythopoetic practices that address landscapes and environments. Furthermore, as we shall see, the fact that the very form of *The Atrocity Exhibition* doubles its content – it employs forms of writing that seem influenced by mass-media productions – means the book is not simply about this 'new' landscape but very much a part of it.

Before looking at this particular work it is worth pointing out that Ballard was already involved in what might be called a 'proto-fictioning' of reality and especially the landscape in his earlier work. Novels such as *The Crystal World* (1966) and *The Drowned World* (1962), as well as the short-story collection *The Terminal Beach* (1964), involve the exploration of other non-human and geologic durations – often in postindustrial landscapes. The protagonists of these novels, we would argue, can be seen as experimental avatars, who by the end of each novel end up living a different space-time (one perhaps increasingly more appropriate to the times we live in) and embody a colder and more inorganic sexuality.[2] These fictions also operate more generally as a kind of filter, after which certain landscapes of our contemporary world cannot but be seen through Ballard's eyes (hence the term 'Ballardian'). There is also a shuttling across from these external landscapes to the interior, psychological states of the protagonists, with a sense that the former states mirror the latter (and vice versa).

In the interview mentioned above, Ballard suggests that literature's role is to 'explore the fictions that surround us' and that the 'function of the writer is no longer the addition of fiction in the world, but rather to seek its abstraction, to direct an enquiry aimed at recovering elements of reality from this debauch of fiction' (Ballard and Louit 2012: 76). It is in this sense that the novels of this later period – the interview is from around the date of the publication of *Crash* (1973) – are investigations into reality. They operate in a speculative register: less a record of what happened (as in the typical novel), they rather set forth hypotheses which they then test (in this respect, it is no surprise that the lead characters are all male and heterosexual, variations on Ballard himself) (Ballard and Louit 2012: 75). It is also in this sense that Ballard's writing might be seen as a kind of performance fictioning. In relation to the arguments of Chapter 2, might we also claim that these fictions are pitched against control in so far as they are concerned with both a shift in perspective and the exploration of other modes of existence?

Indeed, books like *Crash* or *Concrete Island* (1974) offer narratives that are set in a contemporary world but explore what might be called limit states and thresholds, showing 'the present from an unusual angle' (Ballard and Louit 2012: 73). It is towards these liminal landscapes that Ballard is drawn, and has a libidinal investment in, perhaps harking back to his own childhood experience as recounted in *Empire of the Sun* (1984).[3] The landscapes in these books set up the conditions – or operate as a platform – for experimentation. Again, they allow for a kind of performance, or call forth a people. Ballard has suggested that in these works he turned back from the formal experimentation of a book like *The Atrocity Exhibition* because the themes of the later work – the ideas he wanted to explore – were in and of themselves challenging (they did not require further alienation of the reader, as it were). And indeed, towards the end of his life, in novels such as *Cocaine Nights* (1996), Ballard addresses unravelling communities living in modernised estates or complexes through conventional narrative means.

The Atrocity Exhibition, however, involves a different kind of method. Certainly, it still offers an optic on the present, with all of Ballard's 'signature' landscape imagery in play: sparsely populated and often decaying entropic urban spaces and deserted beaches, concrete monuments and motorway fly-overs, helicopters and debris and so forth, with a cold machine-flesh eroticism predominating. There is also a continuing interest in Surrealist landscapes, for example those by Max Ernst and Salvador Dali; an indicative example, which also shows the shuttling between interior and exterior landscapes:

The Persistence of Memory. An empty beach with its fused sand. Her clock time is no longer valid. Even the embryo, symbol of secret growth and possibility, is drained and limp. These images are the residues of a remembered moment of time. For Talbot the most disturbing elements are the rectilinear sections of the beach and sea. The displacement of these two images through time, and their marriage with his own continuum, has warped them into the rigid and unyielding structures of his own consciousness. Later, walking along the overpass, he realised that the rectilinear forms of his conscious reality were warped elements from some placid and harmonious future. (Ballard 1993: 24)

Unlike in his other novels however, in *The Atrocity Exhibition* these different images and scenes are deployed in a non-linear manner that disrupts any straightforward narrative flow or single coherent landscape. The dislocation of time and space characteristic of the other novels is here as much part of the formal technique of the novel as its content. In fact, as suggested above, the book mimics the technologies – film, photography and TV – that in some sense it competes with, addressing the experience of inhabiting a technological landscape produced by both physical or concrete development (machines and gadgets, motorways, airports and high-rise buildings) and the proliferation or circulation of media representations. But it also plays with these forms, pushing their logics further (and in this *The Atrocity Exhibition* looks directly back to the cut-up works of Burroughs).

If the disjointed character of the novel allows Ballard to more fully account for modern experience, this is often through non-narrative episodes that operate on multiple registers:

To speak of this new world I was led, in *The Atrocity Exhibition*, to fragment contemporary reality so that I could reassemble its elements paragraph by paragraph and show its springs. This method allowed me to examine simultaneously the different strata that make up our experience of the actual world. (Ballard and Louit 2012: 74)

In Ballard's novels of this period these different strata – the 'public, private and fantastic' – are intimately connected. They 'cut backwards and forwards across one another' (74). For Ballard, these concerns – and this kind of enquiry – are there in both the linear and non-linear works, but with *The Atrocity Exhibition* the tracking of 'points of intersection' (74) is especially foregrounded. Indeed, in many ways, this is what the novel is 'about'.

The novel does not then offer up a story in any straightforward sense. The reader is left to reconstruct their own narrative (and landscape), finding their own thread through the series of fragments. The book proceeds via a series of vignettes, almost filmic shorts which in many cases read like 'set pieces' for artworks (there are clear references, for example, to the work of Robert Smithson).[4] In its attention to various correspondences and resonances, the novel also proposes an unusual connectivity between different things and events (and, in this, seems almost magical in character).[5]

As well as these different scenes there are repetitions and variations on key themes, which produce a certain Ballardian humour. Some passages seem realistic, others are more dream-like – the book in general operates through a logic of condensation and displacement (as a dream work, to borrow a term from Freud that Guattari, as we noted earlier, also identifies with his notion of fabulous images). In each case there is a tracking across of the three levels mentioned above (public, private and fantastic), as well as a more general exploration of relationships between the body and the landscape it inhabits, where what might be called an inorganic sexuality is especially prominent.

It is clear that *The Atrocity Exhibition* is indebted to psychoanalytic frameworks (hence the connections to Surrealism). We are reminded especially of psychoanalytic accounts of dreams and also of Freud's take on the cityscape as a model of the psyche haunted by the ruins of its pasts (Freud 2002). In particular, Ballard's approach to new sexual-psychological-technological landscapes seems to coincide with Freud's thoughts on an inorganic sexuality and the death drive, producing a new form of Science Fiction. In fact, Ballard's method of fictioning reality, it seems to us, both utilises these psycho-analytic concepts but also deploys a more schizoanalytic method in so far as the emphasis is on experimentation and the production of ever more fictions.

In relation to this it is worth noting that Ballard was involved with Michael Moorcock and others in the *New Worlds* magazine and, with that, in the general development of a new wave of Science Fiction writing which, in Moorcock's reckoning, heralded 'a new literature for the space age' (Moorcock explicitly follows Burroughs with this pronouncement) (Moorcock 1964). Once again, there is a sense that Ballard wanted to develop a form of fiction that was appropriate and adequate to the postindustrial landscapes and technologically mediated reality surrounding him, but also, with *The Atrocity Exhibition*, to the new kinds of psychic space – the new internal landscapes – being produced by Pop and celebrity culture. This was also evident in his various experiments in design and text format – as for example in the 'Project for a New Novel' (see Figure 7.1) of the late 1950s, elements of which appeared, reworked, in *The Atrocity Exhibition*. *New Worlds* also

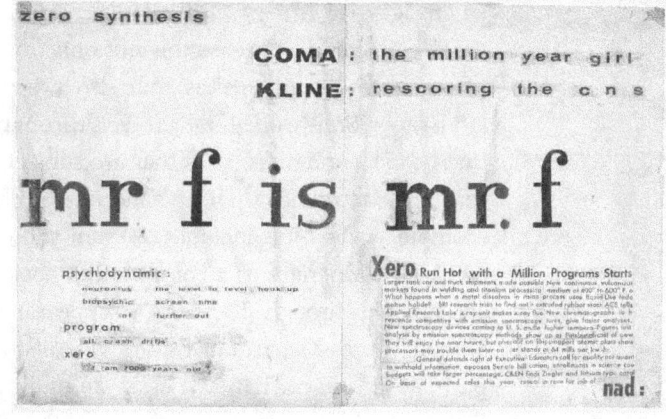

7.1 J. G. Ballard, double page from 'Project for a New Novel', 1958 (image from the J. G. Ballard archive. Copyright © J. G. Ballard, used by permission of The Wylie Agency (UK) Limited).

included images, photography and comic strips, with Ballard himself collaborating on various art projects.

In terms of this new kind of experimental literature – and the new internal and external landscapes of our contemporary world – Ballard was also attuned to what we might call the ur-fiction that holds the others in place: the fiction of the self. Here it is worth quoting Ballard himself on his own turn away from this particular kind of 'serious' fiction:

> Writers of so-called serious fiction shared one dominant characteristic – their fiction was first and foremost about themselves. The 'self' lay at the heart of Modernism, but now had a powerful rival, in the everyday world, which was just as much a psychological construct, and just as prone to mysterious and often psychopathic impulses. (Ballard quoted in Brittain 2013: 25)

In its very structure a work like *The Atrocity Exhibition* disrupts this key anchoring fiction, refusing to mirror back to its reader a coherent sense of self. Instead the novel offers a landscape in which to explore an avant-garde mythopoetic method and, with that, offers up different diagrams for a people to come.

Ruins in Reverse

If art practice has an equivalent to Ballard's probing of subjectivity and production of different modes of existence through an exploration and fictioning of environments, then it is to be found in the work of Robert Smithson. For as well as developing practices of depersonalisation (that we have already addressed), Smithson can be viewed as engaging in a very particular fictioning of the landscape and, especially, certain privileged sites. In his case this not only involves uninhabited and uninhabitable places (alongside other urban sites), but also a rejection of previous traditions of representing landscapes. Smithson literally travels through, and performs in, regions or environments that he calls non-sites (sites that are subject to contingency), as opposed to those sites that are controlled, such as galleries (Smithson 1996e). A work like *Spiral Jetty* for example – when this includes the film and essay as well as the actual jetty in the Great Salt Lake – operates as a complex and performative myth-making machine, one that is accentuated through the jetty's disappearance and relatively recent re-emergence. This work activates its particular context whilst also producing a particular scene in which past and future coexist. The essay and film of *Spiral Jetty* borrow tropes from Science Fiction (Smithson was himself a fan of the genre, including Ballard's work), but in their reimagining of a location as intimately connected both to the distant past and the far future, these works themselves operate as a form science *fictioning*.[6]

Ballard himself was interested in Smithson's practice – we mentioned above that Smithson's art appears in *The Atrocity Exhibition* – and points to the artist's interest in fiction in his essay 'Robert Smithson as Cargo Cultist' (2000). Indeed, the character of Smithson's work as a myth-producing assemblage is well illustrated by Ballard's question about what kinds of ship would use Smithson's jetty – perhaps ancient vessels or vehicles sent from the stars? Several of Smithson's other essays on his own work also have this mythic character, for example 'Incidents of Mirror-Travel in the Yucatan' (discussed in Chapter 4), which might be understood in this context as the record of a specifically mythic journey through the Yucatan landscape. In relation to our case studies in this and the next two chapters (and their concern with a certain future-past Englishness), it is notable that Smithson and the artist Nancy Holt made a trip to the UK in 1969, where they visited and made works in various quarries and other landscapes.[7] They also visited prehistoric sites (see Figure 7.2). As Holt remarked in a recent interview:

> We went to Pentre Ifan, the Bronze Age megalithic site that is made of the same rocks that form the blue stone ring at Stonehenge. We were awed, just like we were when we went to the Avebury Rings, Silbury Hill, Stonehenge and Cerne Abbas. And along the route we saw many earth-works and burial mounds. Looking back on it, our trip was quite significant for both of us, and has had a lasting effect. (Holt 2012)

But if Smithson is interested in geological and pre-modern times, he also brings his performance fictioning practice to modern environments too. His essay 'Entropy and the New Monuments (1966)' is a good example of this fictioning (Smithson 1996f). It makes many remarkable connections: between entropy/thermodynamics and minimalist artworks; between writing on art and fiction per se; and between art practice and, again, Science Fiction.[8] Smithson comments on the importance of Science Fiction (and horror) film as artistic resource in the essay:

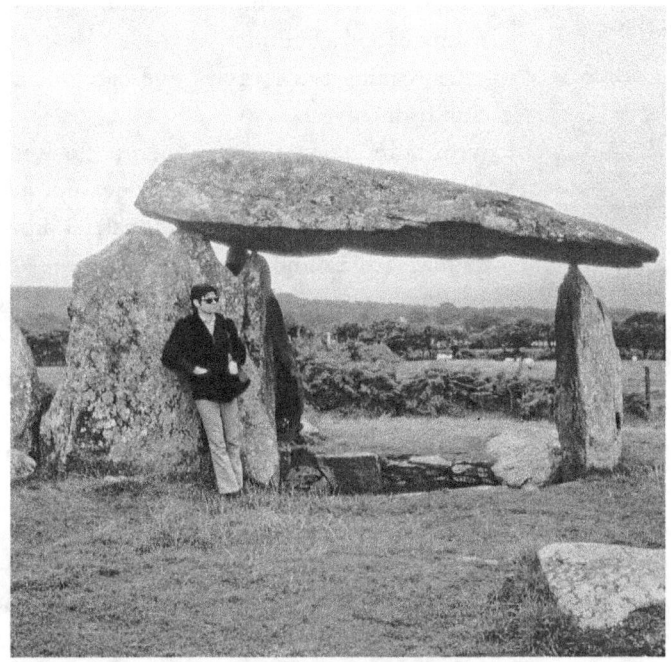

7.2 Nancy Holt, photo of Robert Smithson at Pentre Ifan, 1969 (© Holt-Smithson Foundation/DACS, London/VAGA, New York 2018).

The movies give a ritual pattern to the lives of many artists, and this induces a kind of 'low-budget' mysticism, which keeps them in perpetual trance. The 'blood and guts' of horror movies provides for their 'organic needs', while the 'cold steel' of Sci-fic movies provides for their inorganic needs. (16)

This interest in materiality and time is even more pronounced in 'A Sedimentation of the Mind: Earth Projects (1968)', in which Smithson again writes about environments and locations in which 'remote futures meet remote pasts' (1996g: 113). Again, for Smithson, this involves performing and producing in specific, privileged locations, and he reflects on what he calls the time of the artist as being as being at odds with capitalist time (of work/leisure; of commodities and the market) (1996c: 111–13). Smithson, like his art, operated in a different, more non-human temporality, and it is through writing that this temporality can be fully explored and made accessible to others.

To return to Smithson's writings *as* art we want to briefly consider two further essays as case studies of his method: the diaristic 'Hotel Palenque' – from the same Yucatan journey mentioned above – which was originally a slide presentation (Smithson 1969); and 'A Tour of the Monuments of Passaic, New Jersey (1967)', which records a trip Smithson made into the industrial landscape just outside New York City (Smithson 1996h). Both involved a journey 'beyond' Smithson's habitual environment and a fictioning of the landscape he found himself in. Indeed, as with Ballard, after reading these essays one cannot but see a certain kind of landscape through Smithson's eyes.

In both essays there is then a close imbrication – or blurring – of fiction and reality, in so far as Smithson does not actually invent anything that is not already there. In the Passaic essay, industrial pipelines, buildings, bridges and such like are reimagined as monuments, but the essay itself begins with Smithson buying a newspaper and Brian Aldiss' Science Fiction novel *Earthworks* (along with a map), each of which then serve as guide and commentary for his trip. Each of these documents are, as it were, given equal footing in terms of their account of the Passaic area. In 'Hotel Palenque', as the slide images show, Smithson – at least apparently – is just reporting on what he sees (and, indeed, what we can see) in the photos he has taken. In both cases everyday spaces are reimagined as something more remarkable.

Palenque actually used to be called the city of the snake. There were people there who worshipped the snake and, in a sense, this hotel is built in a kind of intertwining snaking way. It has no center, or you might try to find a center in this place but you really can't, you know, because its so de-differentiated, and so the logic of the whole place is just impossible to fathom. Here is no way that you can possibly figure it out . . . and actually you can see that nice stained wood façade there and just meditate on that all afternoon. (Smithson 1969)

Reality is then 'read' differently by Smithson: that which is often overlooked, or in the background, is foregrounded. There is a kind of psychosis – or stoned logic – at work here, a veritable 'interpretosis' that also gives the presentation a certain humour (in these essays there is less a refusal of interpretation than an acceleration of it). This is due, in part, to the way Smithson overlays his own narratives on Palenque, but there is also a sense that the sites he visits are themselves already fictions – the Hotel Palenque especially with its paths and doorways leading nowhere, and façades within façades. In this sense Smithson is layering one fiction on another.

This makes sense as Smithson was interested in a certain geological layering and production of strata (as in his earthworks), but in the Hotel Palenque essay there is also this concern with the doubling of fictions that reminds us of Ballard's own dreamwork. In fact, with both Ballard and Smithson there is, it seems to us, a concern with what might be called *environmental fictioning* as method, when this is pitched against the more usual sense of well-defined subjects and objects and deeper divisions between the organic and inorganic. As we shall see later, both of these writers also chime with what Reza Negerastani (and Robin Mackay) call 'geotrauma', referring to a layering and nesting of organic and inorganic traumas that constitute 'us' as beings of landscape (see Negarestani 2011a and Mackay 2015).

As we have already intimated, both of Smithson's essays also concern themselves with time. In fact, both are concerned with that strange temporality that is characteristic of Smithson's work more generally: encounters with past futures and future pasts. As Smithson puts it in the Passaic essay, the industrial monuments are *'ruins in reverse'*, the 'memory-traces of an abandoned set of futures' (1996d: 72). Here, industrial machines are seen to equate with prehistoric creatures, just as the sites of industry equate with possible future artworks (the industrial landscape is littered with what we might call these past-future signs). In 'Hotel Palenque' the building resembles ancient ruined Mayan temples (the hotel, we might say, is also a 'ruin in reverse'). In fact, Smithson sees a homology between these two kinds of building in terms of architectural detail but also in terms of the attitude of the people that built them – they are, he says, connected through time (this also resonates with the Mayans own concept of time as not simply linear). Indeed, time is itself layered in this set-up, and fictioning functions as a method of presenting the co-presence of many different pasts and futures within a given landscape.

Docu-fictions and Theory-Fictions

Our next case studies of fictioning the landscape come from artists working with what Stewart Home identifies as a genre of 'docu-fiction' (Home 2011: 3).[9] The latter operates on a porous border between fact and fiction (often layering the latter over the former), but also, in the particular articulation we are concerned with, between fiction and theory (and, at times, between the personal and political). The form has obvious connections with the films of Derek Jarman and Bruce Lacey discussed in Chapter 5, especially in the examples we look at below with their focus on the residual within the British landscape. These case studies also address mythopoesis through the idea of the journey or pilgrimage, underlining once more the importance of movement in space, or exploration of locations.

The *Robinson* trilogy

With Patrick Keiller's *London*, the first in a trilogy of films involving the invented character of Robinson, we have a fictioning of that city that operates through the overlaying of a narrative on film footage. The film is a case study in mythopoesis – a veritable making-mythic of the urban landscape – as, for example, in the reimagining of the iconic Post Office Tower as a monument to Rimbaud and Verlaine, or in the fantastical account of the still-existing London Stone, located on Cannon Street in the City, as involved in a foundational myth of the city. The narrative itself involves a drift – or *dérive* – around different districts, and, as such, is very much in the tradition of the Situationists and the psychogeographic practices we referenced in Chapter 3 when discussing Burroughs' writing of a dream-like cityscape. But the film is also a sustained meditation on the state of Britain in the early 1990s and, especially, on the political situation. Indeed, the personal and the political are entwined in this already entwined reality-fiction. It is as if the very fiction of Robinson allows for a more pointed reflection on our political reality. The fiction – like the walks Robinson takes with the narrator – offers a specifically different perspective (accentuated by the suggestion that Robinson is himself queer, and a proverbial outsider).

There is also a further entwining of different times in the film, with Robinson intent on reading the city so as to remember and understand its different pasts (once again there are resonances with Freud) but also as a method of divining its possible futures. As Robinson remarks (in the narrator's account), his walks are an attempt at time-travel, but we might also say that it is through fiction more generally that these time loops are able to operate. In relation to our own concept of fictioning, *London* also introduces the important concept and tradition of Romanticism which, as the narrator suggests, involves a particular 'mode of feeling'. This is to see one's life from outside, *as* a Romance. It seems to us that a certain kind of nomadism is important for producing this perspective. In our terms, this Romanticism denotes a capacity to see life as itself a fiction and, as such, open up the possibility of shifting perspectives: it offers up, we might say, a method of sorts for seeing the workings of a certain reality effect.

Robinson in Space (1997), the second film in the trilogy, takes Robinson's enquiry out of the capital city to the town of Reading where Robinson now lives, and into what the narrator calls the 'problem of England' more generally.[10] As with *London* the enquiry is also into capitalism, albeit here it is of a later, more international form, as evidenced by the container ports, distribution centres and foreign car manufacturers which Robinson and the narrator visit. One of the key aspects of this second film is the disjunction between this globalisation (and the impact it has had on manufacturing) and a more parochial, insular England (an especially prescient disjunction today in the context of Brexit). But the film also traces the connections between the two, for example with Oxbridge and how this throwback to the past has always produced our political elite, and now often educates our new economic masters.

The fiction of Robinson continues in this film with a 'reading' of the past and future of the British landscape, especially in relation to specific privileged locations. In terms of the past, there are references to the Levellers and Diggers, but also, at certain moments, the narrative stops and we are presented with certain images – of chalk hill figures, for example – accompanied only by birdsong or simply silence. These pre-industrial remnants are not commented on, but simply presented – quietly – as different. They offer something residual within a banal present of supermarkets and motorway hotels. Indeed, the film ends with an enigmatic sequence of images of Neolithic rock carvings that might appear to some as almost alien (again, simply accompanied by birdsong). In terms of the future, the film tracks the massive changes going on in the built superstructure, and resonates with Ballard in the attention it gives to the new 'non-places' that accompany our motorways and container ports. But there are also other, more Science Fiction references to 'Buckminsterfulleremes' and to Mars, as well as to non-human modes of existence – a strange close-up of frogspawn, for example – that are spliced into an otherwise relatively straightforward narrative.

Fiction, then, is a resource: in fact, the whole narrative structure of the film – with its seven pilgrimages – is loosely based on the writer Daniel Defoe's journeys in England; but it is also a method: the spoken narrative and editing of shots fictions the landscape, giving certain features a significance – the signs to a Toyota factory, for example, suddenly become pregnant with meaning and myth. As with *London* there are also references to other works that blur the fiction/reality boundary, for example Richard Jeffries' own post-apocalyptic *After London* (1980) – written a century before Keiller's film – the first section of which reads more like reportage than fiction. There is a sense, more generally, that like the past, these different fictions might also offer an alternative to our capitalist present. In fact, this fictioning of the landscape dovetails with a certain comic aspect of the film, which is produced by a set of disjunctions between Tesco cafes or the details of car models – the stuff of everyday capitalism – and other narratives and more sacred spaces and places.[11] The comic operates here, it seems to us, to foreground fiction as method.

Robinson in Ruins (2010), the third and final film of the series, is more serious, and again involves a reading of the landscape in terms of its hidden present and pasts. In terms of the former, the film focuses on the military-industrial complex, and especially oil and the nuclear industries, as well as the various now abandoned bases and filling stations of an occupying US military. The film also looks back to the various popular protests against that occupation, for example at Greenham Common, where the camera reveals a reclaimed base that now resembles a pre-industrial monument. A second theme is the banking crisis. Here, the juxtaposition of an account of haemorrhaging markets and diving share prices contrasts with the peaceful scenes of pastoral England. A third theme is agriculture – its importance to the UK economy, but also its increasing mechanisation (much of the film records the harvest process). This disjunction between the industrial and mechanised and the natural and organic produces some of the film's most memorable sequences – for example, the slow, deliberate progress of a combine harvester across a field, or a container train rushing through an idyllic river scene.

As with the first two films, it is often the pre-industrial residues in the landscape that the camera seeks out; the ancient Ridgeway of Southern England, for example. In terms of this focus on the past, further crucial events in English history and its landscape are looked to. Central here are the Inclosure Acts, and how this imposition of private property dramatically changed the face of England. The film tells the story of the protests against the enclosure of common land, but also the subsequent crackdown by the state. *Robinson in Ruins* recovers a *different* history in this sense, one often occluded by more typical state narratives. In this there is a kind of utopianism – as evidenced by the mention of the *Land of Cockaigne*. As we saw in the previous chapter, this medieval fiction about a more bountiful and free society can be understood as an inversion of existing conditions, and the reference to it in the film produces a looping forward to Robinson's own longings for a 'new city' to be built on the banks of the River Cherwell, inspired by his sighting of the ruins of a disused concrete factory. In fact, the future implied by the film, although hopeful, is also haunted by a certain melancholy and, indeed, the threat of extinction.

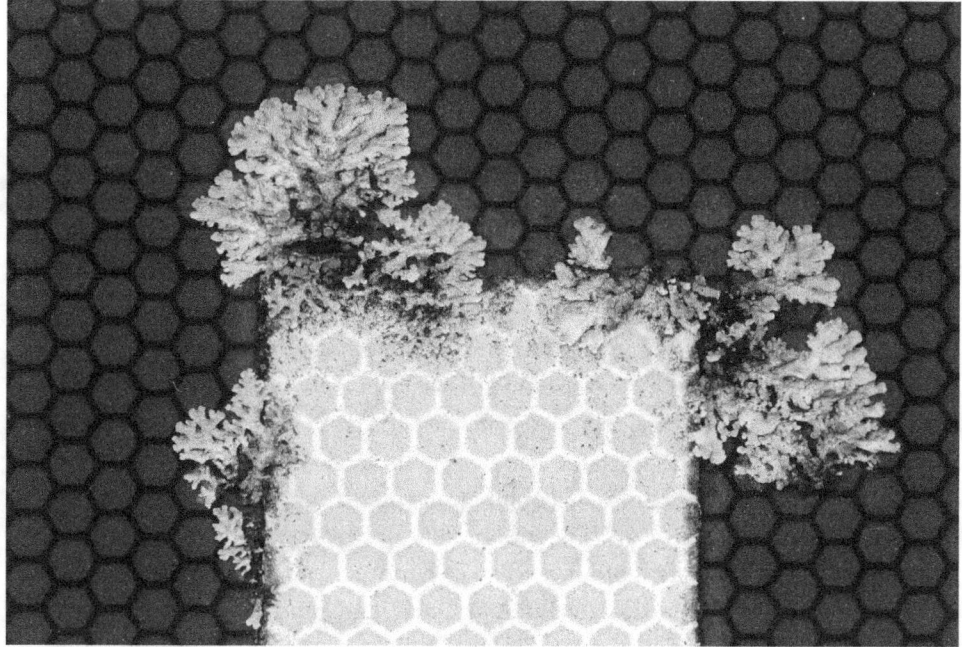

7.3 Patrick Keiller, publicity image for *Robinson in Ruins*, 2010 (© and permission Patrick Keiller).

Throughout this last film the fiction of Robinson is maintained, albeit now his journey has been reconstructed by a mysterious Research Institute, on the basis of a notebook and film canisters discovered in an old caravan. As with the previous two films, *Robinson in Ruins* still works by overlaying a narrative on the film footage, but here, alongside the references to past and present, it is especially the Science Fiction themes that predominate and are most compelling. There is, for example, the recurring idea of a meteorite arriving from space, the presence of something different, something from outside human influence or production, and which, possibly, brought life with it. The film also begins with the idea that there is a 'network of non-human intelligence' intent on maintaining survival on the planet. As the film progresses, it becomes clear that this is our own plant life – or, rather, our complex organic ecosystem with its molecular events and encounters (the evolutionary biologist Lynn Margulis is quoted). At times the camera lingers on just a flower, or lichen on a road sign (see Figure 7.3). The soundtrack, too, foregrounds the non-human, especially, again, with birdsong. It is as if a different structure of feeling is being fictioned by the film and, with that, the presentation of other non-human worlds. The latter have often been occluded by human arrogance and invention, but here, paradoxically, it is the technical apparatus of film itself, with its different speeds and slownesses, different images and registers, that enables this speculative and mythopoetic journey into the landscape.

On Vanishing Land

Mark Fisher has described the Robinson films as an example of what he calls the 'English Pastoral' (Fisher 2010),[12] but he has also produced – with the writer Justin Barton – his own docu-fictions, including *On Vanishing Land* (2013). This audio *dérive* along the Suffolk coast (which in its presentation at the Showroom Gallery in London also included a showreel of images from the walk; Figure 7.4 is an example) is itself a fictioning of a very particular landscape (from the container port of Folkestone to Sutton Hoo), but it is also a case study in the genre of the eerie: 'understood primarily as an awareness – however fugitive it might be – of unknown forces that could be either positive or negative, and that are both "out of sight" around you, and could perhaps in some sense be stalking you, or moving closer to you' (Barton 2015: 13–14). *On Vanishing Land* was, in part, inspired by Brian Eno's recording *Ambient IV: On Land* (1982), and Eno's particular take on the landscape and its sometimes strange temporalities, in conjunction with the ghost stories of M. R. James, themselves a key progenitor of the modern genre of the eerie.

At play *in On Vanishing Land* is a sense of haunting and, more generally, an idea of the landscape as composed of different times and presences that are, in some senses, actualised by a performance (in this case, once again, by a walk). On the website for the work Barton and Fisher quote Eno from the *On Land* sleeve notes,

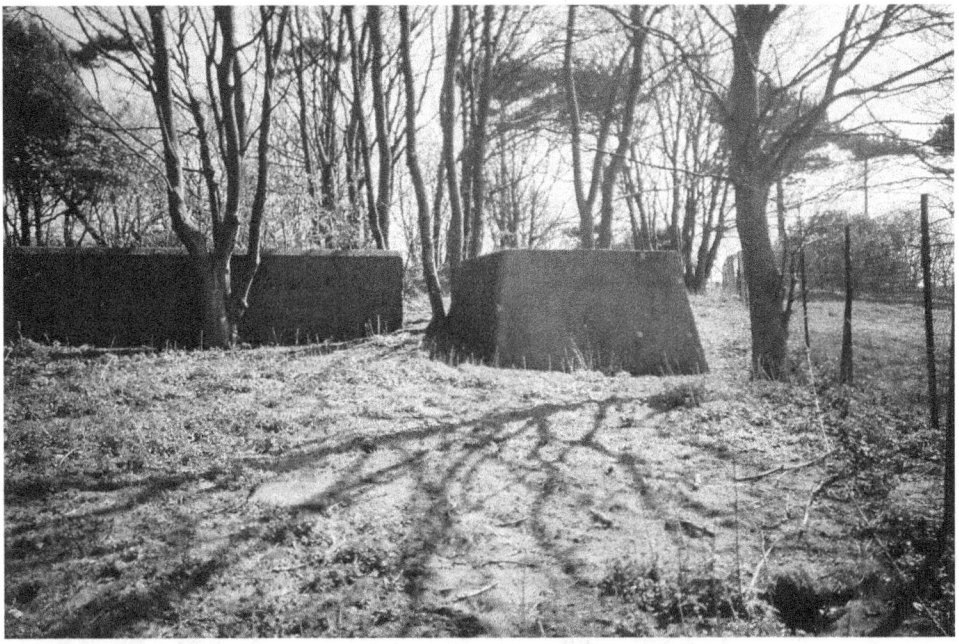

7.4 Image from the showreel accompanying *On Vanishing Land* by Justin Barton and Mark Fisher, 2013 (image credit: Mark Fisher, reproduced by permission of Justin Barton).

bywhere the musician suggests that 'we feel affinities not only with the past, but also with the futures that didn't materialize, and with the other variations of the present that we suspect run parallel to the one we have agreed to live in'. There is also an interest in how the sonic can itself augment or double the physical landscape. The audio-essay includes various interviews alongside a narration by Barton (reflecting on the geography and history they are walking through), and a reading by Fisher from M. R. James, but also commissioned electronic music from artists including John Foxx and Gazelle Twin, all of which, cumulatively, produce a very particular vibe, or, to use the term again, a particular structure of feeling.

In his book *The Weird and the Eerie* Fisher argues that the eerie, beyond being a literary genre (again, one notably associated with M. R. James), can also be thought of as a mode of being. It is characterised, Fisher explains, by a fascination with both the non-human and the forces outside; as such, the eerie might 'give us access to spaces beyond mundane reality' (2016: 13).[13] In the terms of Fisher's previous book, perhaps we might even suggest that the eerie works as an antidote to Capitalist Realism, a concept developed by the writer to describe the mind-set that declares there is no alternative to capitalism (Fisher 2009). But, as Fisher suggests, the eerie is also a particularly philosophically orientated genre of fiction – especially in relation to more recent speculative trends in the continental tradition. Indeed, fiction can operate as a kind of forward probe of this conceptual work. There are connections here to what has been called the genre of the 'New Weird', exemplified by writers such as China Miéville and Jeff VanderMeer (themselves following figures like H. P. Lovecraft and M. R. James). Again, Fisher has tracked through aspects of this genre in his book and demarcated it from its close cousin of the eerie.

Barton's own theory-fiction, *Hidden Valleys* (2015) (from where the above quote about the eerie is taken), itself involves a reading of the landscape as inhabited by multiple durations and, indeed, other modes of non-human existence. It also has an overriding interest in the forces of the outside, or what are called in *On Vanishing Land* 'planetary thresholds of the Unknown'. *Hidden Valleys* is written in the tradition of the confession, as a kind of philosophical biography that is a more general account of a very particular space-time (the North York Moors and adolescence). Fiction is used as resource (writers such as Emily Brontë, Virginia Woolf and Angela Carter are especially important), and, again, as method – as for example in the book's particular narrative form, but also in the importance placed on dreams and dreaming as philosophical resources (alongside other experiments in altered consciousness, and, indeed, that other theory-fiction, Deleuze and Guattari's *A Thousand Plateaus*).

Hidden Valleys is directly concerned with the landscape and how this external terrain forms our internal world. It successfully conveys a particular affective scene or a structure of feeling not unlike that produced by M. John Harrison or Christopher Priest, two writers known for their Science Fiction novels and whom Fisher also discusses in relation to the eerie. Barton's book is also concerned with a kind of layered temporality and, especially, with a haunting of other 'future pasts' (those futures that were promised, but never arrived), as well as the conjunction of 'ancientism' with what the author calls a 'sci-fi modernism'. In relation to these Science Fiction themes, Barton's book and *On Vanishing Land* also develop the idea of an 'inorganic sentience' that, as we saw, is also at play especially in the last of the Robinson films (and, arguably, in both Ballard and Smithson too).

A further key conceptual intention in both *Hidden Valleys* and *On Vanishing Land* is the development of an idea of 'lucidity', pitched against 'reactive thought' and any over-emphasis on rationality (what Barton – in an echo of Burroughs – calls 'the control mind'). Lucidity is an 'abstract oneiric system' that involves the identification of 'intent-currents' that are outside – or at least at the very edge – of human understanding. There is something reminiscent of Carlos Castaneda here (who is quoted in *Hidden Valleys*), but also, again, an affinity with Ballard. Indeed, it seems to us that in exploring and, at times, performing both the eeire and the weird as alternative modes of being in the world, both Barton and Fisher produce a mythopoesis and a fictioning of the landscape that is set against dominant technoscientific models. It is a mode that is both firmly of its time and yet outside of time; one that offers up a different understanding of our world and, at the same time, an alternative narrative for those who live within it.

Notes

1   In fact, we can date the emergence of this 'new' sensibility to 1964, with the reinvention of the Science Fiction magazine *New Worlds* by Ballard and Moorcock (which is to say it is, at least at first, a particular – and collective – editorial stance).

2   See also our comments at the end of section two of Chapter 18, in relation to Ray Brassier's take on Ballard's characters as conceptual personae for a renewed Prometheanism.

3   In this autobiographical work, Ballard recounts how (as the character James Graham – his first two names) he found himself in the collapsing colonial society of Shanghai, amid the chaos brought about by the Second World War. For the young Ballard, this was both a disturbing and exciting event and an end to what were once considered British or civilised values. The book makes much of James Graham's exploration of a landscape and environment that is ruined or marked by war.

4   This seems to be the Smithson reference: '"What are you trying to build?" She asked. He assembled the mirrors into a box-like structure. He glanced up at her, face hidden by the peak of his Air Force cap. "A trap". She stood beside him as he knelt on the floor. "For what?" "Time"' (Ballard 1993: 44).

5   As Ballard remarks in interview:

>   I'm convinced that when an event takes place on one of the three levels of reality . . . it
>   necessarily affects the other two in a more or less perceptible way. So, when I evoke
>   the suicide of Marilyn Monroe in *The Atrocity Exhibition*, it's because it doesn't appear
>   to me as simply the death of a woman, but as a kind of space-time disaster, a catastrophe
>   which created a rupture in our perception of time and space, as if we saw the abrupt
>   subsidence of an immoveable object before our very eyes. (Ballard and Louit 2012: 75)

6   For an account of *Spiral Jetty* (and 'Incidents of Mirror-Travel in the Yucatan') along
     these lines, albeit specifically through a Deleuzian optic, see O'Sullivan 2006a: 98–120.

7   Some of Nancy Holt's own practice involved a kind of mythopoesis and fictioning of the
     landscape. A work like *Sun Tunnels*, for example, 'activates' its context (the desert and
     mountains, but also the sun, moon and stars), introducing a different scale but also a
     different geologic, and indeed planetary, temporality. In a resonance with prehistoric
     monuments, the *Sun Tunnels* have also become sites for solstice celebrations (might we
     even say they call forth a people).

8   Smithson's writings on the artists that were his contemporaries also involve a particular
     kind of science fictioning of their work. For example in 'The Crystal Land (1966)', on
     the work of Donald Judd, the references are as much to a writer like Ballard as they are
     art historical: 'The first time I saw Don Judd's "pink plexiglass box"', Smithson writes,
     'it suggested a giant crystal from another planet. After talking to Judd, I found out we
     had a mutual interest in geology and mineralogy, so we decided to go rock hunting in
     New Jersey' (Smithson 1996a: 7).

9   Home is in fact referring to another docu-fiction, *Voodoo Science Park* (2011), by Victoria
     Halford and Steve Beard. This audio-visual presentation resulted from a residency by
     the artists at the Government 'Health and Safety Laboratory' in the Peak District. As
     with the works we discuss below, *Voodoo Science Park* involves an invented (and mythic)
     narrative laid over film footage (of the large-scale industrial accidents that are investi-
     gated), which convincingly fictions an archive (most of the film is sourced from the
     Laboratory's own collection).

10   Keiller later developed some of the themes of the film as an installation – 'The Robinson
     Institute' – at Tate Britain in London, using objects and images from the collection
     alongside the film itself. As with *Robinson in Space* there was also a book (based on the
     film and installation), *The Possibility of Life's Survival on the Planet* (Keiller 2012), which
     contained further research notes. The fictioning function of this last Robinson film is,
     we might say, specifically 'multi-platform'.

11   See also Stewart Home's *Sixty-Nine Things to do with a Dead Princess* (2002) – also
     footnoted in Chapter 5 – which involves a certain deadpan reportage about the menus

of Tesco cafes, alongside pornographic adventures amongst the standing stones of Aberdeenshire.

12 The essay attends especially to Keiller's politicisation of the landscape (and what Fisher calls the dialectic between capitalism and environment), but, like ourselves, Fisher is also attuned to the Science Fiction character of the film and especially its utopian exploration of non-human forms of life. Moreover, Fisher also makes the connection between the film's themes and recent speculative philosophy, including that of Ray Brassier.

13 It is also a mode that has been picked up in more mainstream media, as, for example, with Robert McFarlane's essay for *The Guardian* on 'The Eeriness of the English Countryside' (2015), which, amongst a roll call of other writers, musicians, filmmakers and artists, also name-checks Keiller and Barton and Fisher.

8   A Journey Through the Ruins of Colonialism

The Frenchman was the only modern being to have explored the Vorrh.
The only one – and all his perilous journey had been a fiction. What
better way was there to trespass on the sacred and forbidden?

Brian Catling, *The Vorrh*

IN THIS CHAPTER we once again look to practices that involve different inflections on the relationship between (and blurring of) fiction and reality, whilst continuing our preoccupation with journeying to other places. What follows also resonates with some of the material we have already discussed in relation to landscape, residual cultures and neomedievalism. As we have implied throughout this first section of our book, these themes relate to a certain kind of outsider perspective and, indeed, link to a Romantic Modernist tradition and nomadism – as defined by Deleuze – developed in twentieth-century European and colonial contexts. It is to two European artists who present fictions in the ruins of this colonialism that we now turn (our interest being that in this their fictions articulate, we suggest, European perspectives but in very different ways). As with the other practices we have discussed so far, it seems to us that these fictions have a performative dimension and, as such, might more accurately be described as forms of fictioning: the first involves a nesting function, alongside a logic of recycling and sequencing; the second returns us to some of our previous discussions around fabulous images and intercessors.

A Forgotten Kingdom: Nesting, Recycling and Sequencing

We turn first to the artist Mike Nelson, who, it seems to us, develops some of the tropes of Ballard and, especially, Smithson that we laid out in the previous chapter. These include the idea of the West in ruins or decline, out of which different futures might be imagined (Science Fiction playing an important role as a resource in this).

Indeed, in relation to this last idea, Nelson's work abounds in different references to fiction – some oblique, some more obvious – but also itself operates as a form of fictioning that blurs any firm distinction between fiction and reality. His interest in fiction is creatively documented in the 'catalogue' *Forgotten Kingdom* (2001), in which Nelson provides a list of – and extracts from – the authors he especially looks to. The selection includes both Burroughs and Ballard alongside a number of other Science Fiction writers. In terms of the blurring of boundaries and borders, Nelson builds labyrinthine installations (they have also been compared to cinematic spaces) that the audience walks in to, literally entering into a narrative scene.[1] The line between fiction and reality is then especially blurred as a result of this performative dimension – our active participation in the work. We become involved in our own kind of performance fictioning as we move through Nelson's installations, journeying through a space and its ambient narratives (once again this movement in space seems important to the work's mythopoetic functioning). The blurring of fiction and reality also happens here because the installations themselves partly consist of found objects that connect with an archive of literary and other references. The installations, we might say, are simply a different arrangement of what already exists out there in the world. The different 'props' Nelson uses also have their own associations which they retain – carried over from their previous contexts or worlds – adding a further layer to the fiction. Nelson has suggested that he is 'particularly interested in the resonance of an object that knows why it's there even if you don't' (Nelson and Rogers 2003: 21).[2]

Although he produces smaller sculptures and assemblages out of these found objects, Nelson's installations are generally large, complex and ephemeral, often involving a significant built component – especially walls and doors – which then sit inside an already existing (often institutional) space. The 'reality effect' of these works (to use a phrase from Roland Barthes) is produced through an almost obsessive attention to detail (see Barthes 1989). Indeed, it is this that allows the participant's suspension of disbelief. Objects are carefully chosen to activate particular narrative and affective scenes, and the installation of elements is meticulously put together so that the fiction is all-encompassing and seamless. The materials are often second-hand (sourced from charity and thrift shops and the like, but also picked up by Nelson on his travels or from the street), and then arranged as if the inhabitants of the space had just left, or an event had just happened.

Besides this production of singular installations, there is a further characteristic of Nelson's work – and especially of some of the pieces from 1999 to 2001 – which involve the artist recycling and reusing objects and setups, as well as certain motifs, to produce a continuity of fictions across installations. This recycling produces a sequence of different instantiations of Nelson's work, which also points to how both material and fiction can be spliced together, rearranged or have multiple forms (we are reminded of Burroughs cut-ups of his own writing here). The different installations, we might say, are variations on a theme, but they also – as a group – cumulatively deploy a different kind of space-time to the one with which we are more familiar. A temporality is produced that proceeds not through a linear progression of discrete units of time but as a passing through and returning to different times. There is then a certain logic of connection and continuity between the apparently disparate shows, connections being made for the viewers through their engagement with and memory of Nelson's work.

This continuity and space for connections also includes a nesting of fictions. This might involve the positioning of one fiction within another, but also the nesting of these fictions in Nelson's own personal mythos and other narrative constructions (in both of these gambits Nelson's work looks especially to the stories of Jorge Luis Borges). This nesting can also involve the insertion of one kind of space-time within another; a recent example would be Nelson's *I, Impostor*, in which he built an Arabic souk within the British Pavilion at the Venice Biennale in 2011. Indeed, these sets of nestings – of fictions within fictions – can produce a formal complexity and density that parallels the content.

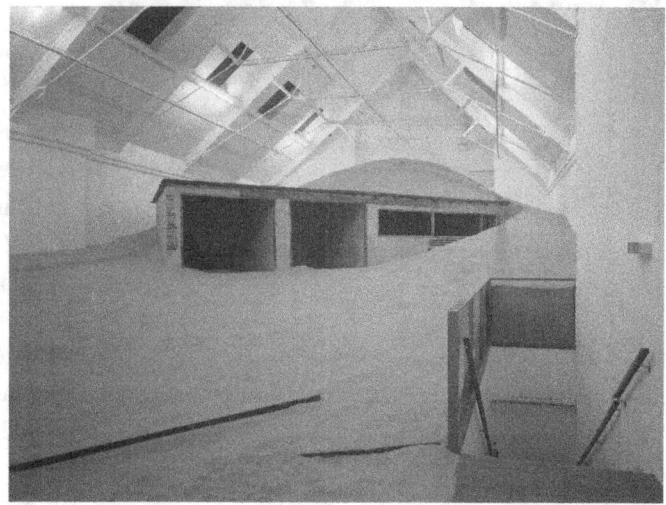

8.1 Mike Nelson, *Triple Bluff Canyon*, 2004. Installation view, Modern Art Oxford (courtesy the artist and 303 Gallery, New York; Galleria Franco Noero, Turin; Matt's Gallery, London; and neugerriemschneider, Berlin).

A further example is *Triple Bluff Canyon* (2004), which involved the nesting of Robert Smithson's *Partially Buried Woodshed* (1970) – itself famously recontextualised by the bullets which lodged in it during the police shootings of students at Kent State University, and the subsequent addition of commemorative graffiti – inside a whole collection of further narratives, including on the Gulf War (with sand replacing the earth of Smithson's work) and Nelson's own mythologisation of his studio (see Figure 8.1). On entering this installation the viewer is first faced with a number of cinema doors, the choosing of a door dictating the route the visitor will take. Once through a door, a sequence of atmospheric scenes unfolds, arranged to allow the viewer to pass through different scales and types of fictions – domestic, personal, historical, political and global – all explored in a dream-like environment that seems not to correspond to any knowledge the viewer might have of the building the

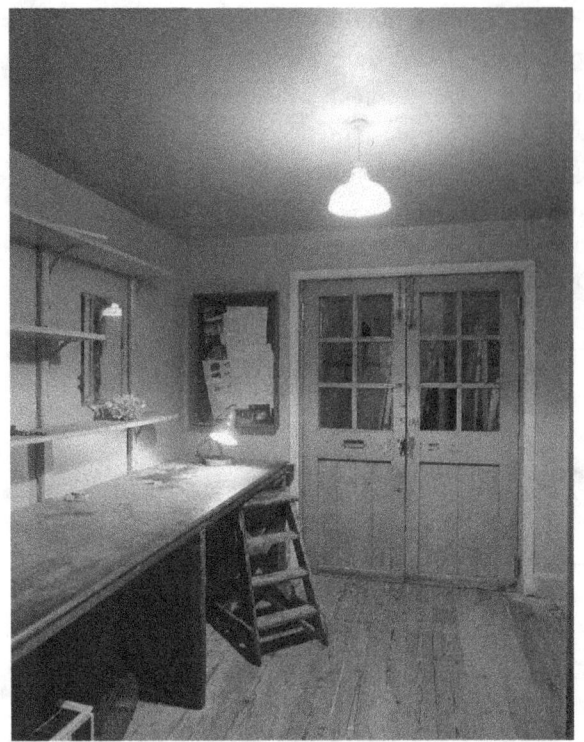

8.2 Mike Nelson, *The Cosmic Legend of the Uroboros Serpent*, 2001. Installation view, Tate Gallery London (courtesy the artist and 303 Gallery, New York; Galleria Franco Noero, Turin; Matt's Gallery, London; and neugerriemschneider, Berlin).

installation is contained within. Along this journey, the visitor comes across the artist's studio – a ground-floor room of a house in London – which houses Nelson's collection of objects, and where conspiracy theories and connections between fictions are developed and shaped.

Alongside references to an outside of the work – to a larger political reality for example – there is also a self-referentiality that gives Nelson's practice one of its most compelling aspects. This is perhaps best exemplified by his work for the 2001 Turner Prize show, *The Cosmic Legend of the Uroboros Serpent* (see Figure 8.2), which, in part, stored – we would add nested – his own previous installation *The Coral Reef* from Matt's Gallery in 1999 (a work which won him the Turner nomination and was subsequently acquired by the Tate).[3] *The Coral Reef* was itself already a complex fiction staged as a labyrinthine installation of rooms that referenced the various spaces of the London East End context in which it was built; it consisted of a series of low lit taxi offices, including one exactly duplicated, the two identical rooms producing a very particular effect of disorientation. In the subsequent Tate show, Nelson used his art as its own kind of used object in this sense – contained, encircled, within the new installation. As these works are repeated, or restaged in other institutions, new layers of meaning are added; the fiction becomes denser – more difficult but also more compelling.

Although offering up a different bloc of space-time, this nesting of fictions might also be thought of as an arrangement of objects as privileged points or locations within the installation, which then serve as portals through which the viewer can (imaginatively) journey from present to the past and then back to the present. Nelson uses actual elements from his own past, but there is also an ongoing sense, as we suggested above, that each installation involves a kind of restaging of, or variation on, those that have gone before. Especially interesting, however, are the points that allow travel into a future. Indeed, Nelson has described his *Futurobjects* show at Camden Gallery in 1998 as being involved in setting up the conditions and possibilities for the future of his own practice, the installation here operating as a technique of divination:

Futurobjectics, a title that refers to that chapter in Stanislaw Lem's *Futurological Congress* that we used in *Forgotten Kingdom*, the one that talks about 'future linguistics', which is the idea that you can predict the future by mutilating, modifying and combining words. I changed that to *Futurobjectics*, to take my own references and mesh them together and potentially predict the future of what I'd make – and strangely enough it did, it worked. (Nelson and Bradley 2003)

Although Nelson talks about the predictive aspect of this show, we might also suggest that it involved a kind of fictioning of the future of his practice – laying out a set of propositions or a particular syntax to be used later: prediction but, perhaps too, divination, which is enabled because of the 'closed set' of Nelson's practice. Put differently: time, or a very particular kind of time, is not a given background to Nelson's work, but is specifically presented in it as material to be explored but also manufactured and recycled.

Some of the catalogues from this early sequence of works operate in a similar way. *A Forgotten Kingdom* (2001), which as mentioned above contains found texts, has been described by Nelson as a Reader for his work: a gathering of different archives that gestures to future possibilities. The publication *Magazine* (2003), containing a selection of images from *The Coral Reef* (1999) to the Turner Prize show, doubles the experience of these shows (there is no beginning or end to the book, one is always in the middle, with images from different shows leading on from and into one another). It also operates as a sourcebook, and as a work that fictions the exhibitions themselves (it doubles the fiction as it were). There is also Nelson's earliest catalogue, *Extinction Beckons* (2000), tracking his practice from its inception up to *The Coral Reef*, which is presented like a travel book – it looks like one thing but is another – and contains a long essay by Jaki Irvine (put together from previous reviews and short essays) that further links the different installations through a fictioning of the artist's life.

Extinction Beckons also contains a selection of private view invites. These were a key aspect of Nelson's practice at this time (pre-internet as it were) and were often pictures of Nelson himself in different locations, such as in a graffitied bus shelter for *Master of Reality* (1997). Others, both in and subsequent to *Extinction Beckons*, point to Nelson as European traveller, such as an image of the artist in Asia with a Buddhist monk for *Nothing is True, Everything is Permitted* (2001), or the photograph of Nelson's truck travelling overseas for *Lionheart* (1997) and *The Amnesiacs* (1997). There is always a sense in Nelson's installations that certain characters are absent – for example, with the above shows, the drifter, the outlaw, and so on. It is not so much that Nelson is this Romantic character exactly (each show is very particular in the figures it diagrams), but there is certainly a sense – accentuated by the reality of the images on the invites – that Nelson somehow partakes of these characters through fiction.[4] The line between the reality of Nelson's life and the fictional presentation becomes blurred through a certain self-produced mythos (he did, after all, produce this work after travelling widely).

There is a question, in some of these works, of an encounter with colonial and postcolonial perspectives (however manufactured these might be), which perhaps develop out of the occidental traditions, in both literature and art, in which a European travels to the lands and cultures of others, to find another perspective on the West and on life. While this might be problematic – certainly immigrant or non-Western subjectivities may not be presented in the work – the viewer is also an interloper in scenes that remain out of grasp or entail equivocal rather than direct interpretation. An example would be Nelson's *Trading Station Alpha CMa* (1996) which references both the film *Apocalypse Now* (1979) and Joseph Conrad's *Heart of Darkness*.[5] The latter, first published in 1899, tells the tale of Marlow, who travels up the Congo River in the heart of Africa and, on his way, hears of the agent Kurtz who runs a successful colonial trading station. Marlow decides to set off to find him. It is not so much that we equate Nelson with either Marlow or Kurtz, only that in some of Nelson's works the genres or kinds of fictions he is interested in belong to traditions that gain perspective through travel, as in the adventures of Europeans in other lands. There is an important twist to *Trading Station Alpha CMa* though (which perhaps points to colonists as alien invaders), as the installation also references the book *Roadside Picnic* (2000) by the Brothers Strugatsky, a tale about a strange zone that is created by the discarded rubbish of passing aliens. The book was the basis for Andrei Tarkovsky's film *Stalker* (1979), in which figures traverse a landscape made dangerous and unpredictable to find alien treasure. All this resonates with Nelson's interest in wandering or exiled figures and outsiders such as biker gangs – all figures that feature (as absent characters) in Nelson's work *The Amnesiacs* (1997).

This latter installation points to the recurring motif in Nelson's work of the group or pack, which exists alongside his interest in the loner. *The Amnesiacs* show that staged the HQ of a fictional biker gang, but also future works that return to this motif (*AMNESIAC SHRINE or Double coop displacement* at Matt's Gallery in 2006 for example), might be the most explicit manifestation of the pack in Nelson's work.[6] It is this sense of a 'missing people' – summoned into being by certain objects, clothes, logos, symbols, and so forth – that gives the work an especially pronounced mytho-poetic aspect. A collective can operate as a particularly effective performance fictioning in this sense, (dislodging that key fiction of the self-possessed and centred individual subject). In the case of *The Amnesiacs*, there is a further layer of fiction in so far as the group (or is it just one individual?) are forced to remake – or fiction – the world anew each day after waking with no memory of their past (hence their moniker). Here we think Nelson's work addresses mythopoesis more thematically in so far as it involves both a summoning of a people to come but also a staged enquiry into how an individual can produce or fiction such a collective. These people are called forth through encountering Nelson's arrangements of discarded, second-hand, aged and battered remnants of everyday life, collected, as we mentioned above, on the artist's travels but also on the streets of cities. We have the feeling that it is these people – fictioned by Nelson's work – who find themselves confronted with the task of making a life in landscapes in which old and modern orders survive but only through their wastelands and ruins.

The Vorrh: Fabulous Images and Intercessors

Brian Catling is a sculptor, painter, filmmaker – and, importantly in relation to mythopoesis, both a performance artist and a writer. More generally he might be described as simply a *maker*, in so far as even his text works seem to have a certain kind of material weight to them (as well as being products of a very singular imagination). His recent surrealist/fantasy novel *The Vorrh* is a case in point (Catling 2012). Written in a very distinctive style, Catling has remarked in interview how the novel more or less wrote itself (as he also says in the interview, when asked where he gets his ideas and images: 'It's like someone is talking in my ear') (Catling and Spragg 2011). It is this sense of being channelled – of the work both being by Catling and not by him at the same time – that gives the novel its very particular flow of events and other-worldly character.

The title of the novel takes the reader back in time to a colonial past. 'The Vorrh' is borrowed from Raymond Roussel's 1910 novel *Impressions of Africa* (2011), where it names a large primeval forest, which, in Catling's hands, becomes the eponymous hero of his own novel. Roussel's forest is brought alive, along with a series of equally fantastic and finely drawn protagonists who journey into and across it (once again a sense of journeying is important to the novel's mythopoetic character). These avatars are, to a certain extent, from our own past, and it can be said that they emerge from an imagination that looks back to fictions of a colonial or colonising history – like the forest and the city of Essenwald that sits on the borders of the Vorrh, or the hunter Tsungali complete with fetish-object Enfield rifle. But it can also be said that Catling's writing presents a pagan pre-modernity that is entwined with both the modern (the novel is 'set' after the First World War) and a strange postmodernity of references to various other stories which we might also call (to mix metaphors) a patchwork temporality. It is this patchwork temporality that Alan Moore celebrates in his foreword to *The Vorrh*, suggesting that Catling 'builds a literature of unrestrained futurity out from the fond and sorry debris of a dissipating past' (Moore 2012: vii).

The book throws up many startling images and memorable narrative sequences; for example at the very beginning there is a detailed account of the careful construction of a magical bow from Este, a dismembered lover:

> I shaved long, flat strips from the bones of her legs. Plaiting sinew and tendon, I stretched muscle into interwoven pages and bound them with flax she had cut from the garden. I made the bow of these, setting the fibres and grains of her tissue in opposition, the raw arc congealing, twisting and shrinking into its proportion of purpose. (Catling 2012: 8)

We might note the romantic (and heterosexual) fantasy of a lover becoming an object or possession of the hero here, but this passage also reveals the artist's concern with manipulating physical materials and form through writing. Catling has remarked that fiction allows him to make in words the installations that would be impossible in real life – and there is something about narrative episodes such as the above (and there are many similar) which reflect this interest. We will return to this performative element below. As we saw in Chapter 1, Guattari develops the concept of 'fabulous images' for those descriptions that cross over from literature into life, ultimately 'producing another real, correlative to another subjectivity' (Guattari 2013: 225). *The Vorrh* is composed of such images that have this traction outside the novel (despite or, in fact, because of their fictional character), allowing something else to coalesce around them. Such images, it seems to us, are like the 'points of intersection' Ballard mentions in relation to his own fiction.

In claiming this, however, we have to acknowledge a certain colonial aspect to Catling's writing. Some of the characters and imagery (for example in a figure such as Tsungali the hunter), and indeed the novel as a whole, can only be described as a European projection onto an Africa in which the realities of colonial and postcolonial events are not addressed. This is problematic, but is also often an aspect of European mythopoetic fictions that draw on the past. As Michael Moorcock writes of Catling in his review of *The Vorrh*: 'His theses are the many forms of psychic and physical colonisation' (Moorcock 2015). The novel repeats certain themes and tropes of a European imaginary – the journey in to the heart of darkness, as it were, not unlike that taken by the visitor to Mike Nelson's *Trading Station Alpha CMa*. It may offer up a different future or an alternative reality premised on a rewriting of the past or past fictions, but this is still from a particular perspective. In its turn to a kind of ruined imperialism alongside a 'reconstructed' and somewhat imaginary Africa (as well as other landscapes such as an Irish peat bog, which was also once a colonised land), the novel belies a very particular take on the foreign, doubling the temporal syncretism (if we can call it such) with a spatial one in which different continents collide and intermingle.

It is helpful here to make a comparison between *The Vorrh* and *The Palm-Wine Drinkard: And His Dead Palm-Wine Tapster in the Dead's Town* (2014), a novel by the Nigerian author Amos Tutuola first published in 1952. As Wole Soyinka notes in his introduction to the book, the poet Dylan Thomas celebrated Tutuola's writing, but in his home country the reception was mixed. The novel was thought naive by some, not least for the misspellings and writing style which today, in the context of our earlier discussions of a minor literature, would seem like a deliberate corruption of the major language of English. Like Catling's novel, *The Palm-Wine Drinkard* narrates a journey through a landscape. The book relates the tale of a protagonist who never gives himself a name and is addicted to palm wine. When his tapster (who drains the sap for the wine) dies, the man decides to set off for the Dead's Town to bring the tapster back. The journey – through forests and encounters with other people, ghosts and supernatural beings – draws upon the knowledge, traditions and experiences of African cultures and life. After reading *The Palm-Wine Drinkard*, it becomes apparent that *The Vorrh* has the form of a major literature reflecting upon the decline of the rationalisations and values of European cultures and colonialism. Following Edward Said, it might even be argued that in *The Vorrh* a major literature is 'unhousing' or unravelling itself through the process of writing.

In relation to this, Moore's foreword also pinpoints something else about this work of fiction: the way it does not seem to fit neatly into any existing literary category, despite its use of familiar tropes. The novel arrives, as it were, *sui generis* (to use a term from Moorcock's review). The book has a certain singular and, indeed, untimely character in this sense, not unlike a Ballard novel. It creates its own scene or vibe – a kind of future-past Englishness, albeit set in colonial Africa. Might we even say it constitutes its very own genre, but also one which Nelson and Ballard, and others we have addressed, can also be said to be concerned with: the ruins of colonialism, and the attendant unravelling or alienation of the European perspective?

The Vorrh's power of fictioning is also manifested through the way its content is connected to our reality. In particular, the fictional characters intermingle with real historical figures (Eadweard Muybridge and William Gell, for example – alongside the author Roussel, referred to as 'the Frenchman') who have themselves been re-cast as fictional characters. We might turn here once more to Deleuze's own comments on the character of certain fictions (as we remarked in Chapter 1, Deleuze has cinema in mind) that involve the use of real historical figures as interlocutors and intercessors (Deleuze 1989: 222). In *The Vorrh*, it seems to us, Catling makes use of his own intercessors to construct the fiction.

In Iain Sinclair's *Lights Out for the Territory* (1997) – a psychogeographical *dérive* through an increasingly disappearing London – this fictioning moves in another direction, with Catling himself operating as an intercessor in Sinclair's narrative. In his book Sinclair describes Catling as 'the English Beuys', and there is certainly something about the materials (and expanded practice) of both artists that resonates, alongside a certain amount of self-mythologisation which Sinclair himself embellishes. Indeed, Catling is compared to Dr Dee, described as an 'Elizabethan Jesuit' and a 'wandering scholar and magician' (Sinclair 1997: 261), as well as a practitioner of 'the shamanism of intent' (the title of the chapter that deals with Catling, amongst others). In relation to this use of intercessors we might also note that Catling paradoxically plays himself, but also the character 'The Object', in the contemporary artist Nathaniel Mellors' own mythopoetic fictioning, *Our House* (2010–16).

In *Lights Out for the Territory* Sinclair attends in particular to Catling's writing prior to *The Vorrh*, and especially to the poetry volume *The Stumbling Block* (Catling 1990), which he calls 'written sculpture' (256).[7] But he also makes the connection between this and Catling's other work, all of which, as we suggested above, has this distinctive feel for, and manipulation of, materials (the different aspects of Catling's practice constituting, for Sinclair, a 'single energy field' in this sense). In terms of *The Vorrh*, Moore also highlights the materiality of Catling's language, writing of the 'alchemy' and 'earthy shamanism' of the novel, how it tells of 'bark, metal, mud and stone', with 'language worked between the fingers into different and surprising contours' (Moore 2012: vi). *The Vorrh* then has a content – a narrative – that moves across different terrains, but also this physicality, this presence *as* reality that comes from its particular manipulation of language.

Sinclair also writes about Catling's performances, in particular *At the Lighthouse* (1991), performed at Trinity Buoy Wharf, London, an 'Hogarthian freakshow' in which Catling (in Sinclair's account) plays a kind of oracle and does not 'come out of character' (Sinclair 1997: 258). Once again there are precursors of *The Vorrh* here: in the use of language *as* sculpture and in the throwing-up of startling images, but also in so far as Catling performs a character much like his own fictional creations. Indeed, following the performance of *At the Lighthouse* (and a chance reflection of his own face – looking like a Cyclops – in a glass door during another performance), Catling further actualises this figure in future performances, and tells a tale of the 'original' inspiration: a real Cyclops preserved in a glass jar in a medical room in Hungary. Finally, in *The Vorrh*, a version of this figure becomes one of the central and most compelling characters.[8] There is, then, a nesting of fictions in and across Catling's life and art, along with the recurrence of certain motifs and avatars which track across both fiction and reality, operating as connectors.

Catling has described his filmmaking as a fusion between his installation/sculpture and the poetry/readings, but for him it is the novel – fiction – that is able to take this a step further; as we mentioned above, fiction allows the depiction of possibilities that are, on one level, unrealisable (Catling and Spragg 2011). It is this aspect of *The Vorrh* that especially warrants its inclusion as a case study in this chapter: the novel involves a kind of performance enacted *through* fiction. In interview he remarks on how his own performances operate by shifting a fiction from one context to another – in order, we might say, to highlight the difference (Catling and Spragg 2011). Could we say then that, through its mobilisation of fabulous images and intercessors, and as a 'performance by other means', *The Vorhh* also involves this kind of shifting of contexts (when this is also a shuttling back and forth between fiction and the reality of Catling's life)?

Notes

1   For a compelling description of one such installation – along with its literary resources – see Richard Grayson's account of Nelson's work at the Venice Biennale in 2001, in his essay 'The Deliverance and the Patience' (Grayson 2002).

2   Nelson's work is usually displayed in galleries, or, at least, in buildings that are clearly demarcated as art spaces. However, the blurring of fiction/reality becomes especially pronounced when this is not the case – when, we might say, the frame is missing – as for example in the work for the 2002 Sydney Biennale *24 Orwell Street*, in which, as Will Bradley suggests in his interview with Nelson, 'the whole building has been incorporated into the work – the interior is altered so that the façade, though unchanged, becomes an intrinsic part of the piece' (Bradley and Nelson 2003). Nelson's response is telling:

> There was a curious reaction to the piece in Australia, because it was so completely within the fabric of the city that people had problems dealing with it, with the replication. If it had taken place within the white space of the gallery I think they would have accepted it with more ease. (Bradley and Nelson 2003)

3   *The Cosmic Legend of the Uroboros Serpent* also emulated the structure of a previous installation – *Trading Station Alpha CMa* – at Matt's gallery in 1996.

4   Jaki Irvine writes about these absent figures, how they are summoned into presence through certain objects and residues (in this case in the *Lionheart* installation), but also the postcoloniality of this particular take:

> Other bundles of magazines, an American football, a toolbox, fuel cans clutter the floor, testifying to their far-flung origins and to the nomadic eclecticism of their owner. The skins, cages, traps, darts, beer cans, books – all make insinuations about an English drifter whose livelihood is based on gleaning discarded objects from the streets and markets of London, moving from one section of the city to another through Asian,

Turkish, Afro-Caribbean, Irish communities . . . sifting through things whose origins and functions were once known and cared about . . . things that were made specifically to perform precise functions in certain circumstances . . . that now, dislocated from their beginnings have turned into so much junk . . . to be peddled by the growing numbers of poor white British trash. (Irvine 2000: 46)

5   See Burrows 1996 for an account of the way this work also nested different fictions within it.

6   The third absent 'figure' – alongside the loner and the gang – is the unnamed beast of John Carpenter/H. P. Lovecraft which, in the case of the installation *To the Memory of H. P. Lovecraft* (1999), has literally torn the exhibition space apart.

7   The opening stanza of 'The Stumbling Block and its Index' reads:

The Stumbling Block is a graphite font. This black plinth was once a brush or similar terminal that was the lips of an intense electrical arc. Industries proud and violent spoke through it to turn the wheel or smelt and cast the constructed challenge. Now abandoned it finds benediction in seclusion. It has softened its mouth to hold water, so that small animals may drink or sign themselves in their passage. (Catlin in Sinclair 1996: 13)

8   Catling also remarks in interview that during the writing of *The Vorrh* he embarked on a series of small egg tempura paintings of a Cyclops (Catling and Spragg 2011).

9   Scenes as Performance Fictions

Days were spent in fumes from the copying machine, from the
aerosols and inks of the 'banner production department' – bed
sheets vanished – banners appeared, from the soldering of audio,
video, and lighting leads. The place stank. The garden was
strewn with the custom made cabinets of the group's equipment,
the black silk-emulsion paint drying on the hessian surfaces.
Everything matched. The band logo shone silver from the bullet-
proof Crimplene of the speaker front. Very neat. Very fetching.

Peter Wright (quoted in George Berger, *The Story of Crass*)

IN THIS FINAL chapter of section one we move from specific texts and art practices to groups and scenes (the latter very broadly construed), but also revisit certain
concepts, themes and practitioners that we have discussed in the preceding chapters. Here mythopoesis involves a sharper challenge to dominant fictions and their
reality effects, as well as a more sustained intention to produce – and live – alternative fictions (often involving the creation of autonomous spaces). Accompanying
this will to self-determination (pitched, paradoxically, against the individual or
individualism) is an emphasis on collective participation, especially when this
includes a performative dimension; as such, the term *performance fictions* seems
once again appropriate. As with the previous two chapters, the theoretical work is
developed from case studies: of the UK groups Crass and Thee Temple ov Psychick
Youth. We conclude this chapter with some brief remarks about what might very
broadly be called 'rave culture', when this is also understood as a particular scene
and, again, as a kind of lived fiction. In general, then, the chapter attends to practices that operate away from the rarefied worlds of contemporary art – although
it is our contention that the latter has learnt, and has more to learn, from these
different scenes.

There is No Authority but Oneself

Crass emerged, at least in part, from both the 1960s counterculture and the 'tradition' of the avant-garde. As far as the former goes, Penny Rimbaud and Gee Vaucher – two key members of the group – were products of art school, and were influenced by figures like John Lennon and David Bowie; later, Crass would become closely involved with one of the UK's key countercultural events: the Stonehenge Free Festival. In terms of the avant-garde, Rimbaud had been the instigator of the experimental music group EXIT and, in this prehistory to Crass, had organised avant-garde music festivals and generally identified with Fluxus. Both these currents – high and popular culture – had a determining influence on Crass, but it was only with the arrival of punk and a third key figure, Steve Ignorant, who identified as working class (state-school educated rather than public school like Rimbaud), that the conditions for Crass were in place.

A further key factor in the group's formation and ongoing existence was Dial House. Rimbaud had set up this rural cottage as his home, but also as an open house, in the 1960s. It provided a space for like-minded people to gather, talk and experiment, not least in the production of music (there was a rehearsal room at the cottage). Crass were adamant that it was not a commune, but there is certainly a sense in which the house allowed a collective to form. As George Berger points out in his biography of the group (2006), it was the existence of Crass as a collective beyond the stage that also gave the group a certain mystery. Crucially, Dial House gave sanctuary to a group of individuals so that they could spend time together outside the pressures of finding work. It was set up as a very inexpensive place to live, not least in so far as it refused commodity culture (in large part this was all enabled by the favourable social security legislation at the time). We would suggest then, that Dial House functioned as something like an autonomous zone, producing alternative ways of living beyond those of the everyday capitalist organisation of life. Or, in terms of the previous chapters, this open house called forth a people.

The location outside the city, in relative seclusion in Essex, also contributed to a certain rural idyll associated with Crass, as exemplified by the picture of ploughed fields on one of their record sleeves (see Figure 9.1). This image of a semi-rural, self-sufficient life engendered by Dial House and its large grounds, set within a landscape at the edge of London, is important to the myth of Crass and relates to our earlier discussion of privileged locations in the landscape. The image of Dial House appears in stark relief to the other images produced by the band, in their performances and for their record covers, which depict apocalyptic scenes of genocide and nuclear disaster (again, see Figure 9.1). This opposition of a nightmare existence and a creative, autonomous community produced a simple but effective topology and fictioning. Within a landscape of horror and oppression, small pockets of anarchy can be found,

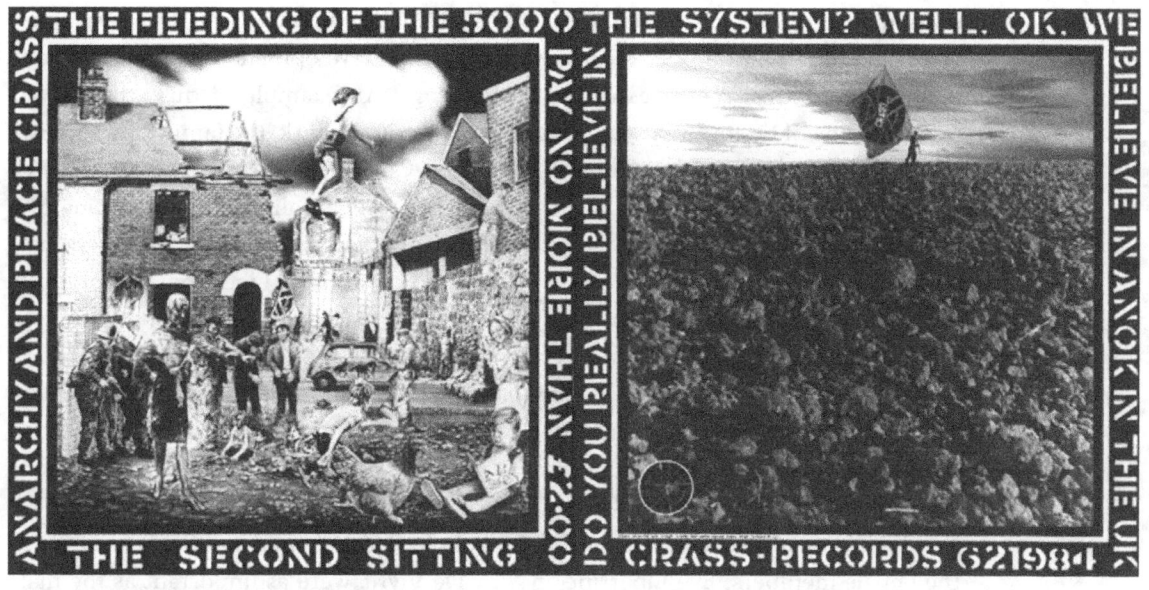

9.1 Gee Vaucher, album cover of *The Feeding of the 5000*, 1978 (reproduced by permission of Gee Vaucher).

Dial House being one of these isolated points through which alternative ways of living and thinking might be accessed or developed. Such would be a revolution for Crass.

The isolation had its benefits in so far as it produced a certain intensity which, it seems to us, is the progenitor of any scene, but it also brought issues, especially towards the end: there were claims that the group became somewhat cut-off from the scene they had instigated, as well as the squat culture of London. It is worth noting that a kind of radical parochialism was in play here, but this does not mean the band did not resonate outside its immediate context. Indeed, quite the contrary: Crass had (and has) a more global traction partly because of its local and singular character. This is an important aspect of these mythopoetic scenes: they resonate across space and time because they are singular rather than universalising.

For Crass, making music and art was a way of life. The group took the DIY attitude and aesthetic of punk seriously both on stage and record, but also as a script for their lives. Crucially, Crass records were produced independently and distributed via the growing network of independent record shops at the time. There was no way Crass would be played on daytime radio (although they did at one point do a BBC Radio 1 John Peel session), so this alternative mode of distribution was also crucial. The group was part of a larger mail art and DIY fanzine culture – an expanded network – that characterised what became known as the anarcho-punk scene.

In terms of mythopoesis, Crass were focused on calling forth a people from the disenfranchised and alienated of the UK. The will to self-determination, exemplified in their slogan 'There is no authority but oneself, so, whatever it is, do it', was a key factor in the formation of the band and its ongoing development, but it was also one of the key political messages of the Crass songs. An example of this attitude was their pitching of themselves against certain institutions: work, the family and so forth, but also against that key agent of transcendence, Christ. Also crucial was the practice of renaming – a reclaiming of identity from external causality, and a fictioning of a new identity. Along with Vaucher, Rimbaud and Ignorant, other members also changed their name, including Joy De Vivre, Phil Free and Eve Libertine. This practice, common in punk generally, can be thought of as a magical process (and one shared with the second of our case studies below).

One of the key aspects that distinguished Crass from other punk bands was the writings that were invariably included with their records. Polemical, angry, pitched against the status quo, but also at times cryptic and poetic, these writings – alongside the mythos of Dial House – helped give the band a very particular identity.[1] We should also mention here, crucially, the band's feminist agenda and the way in which the female members, Eve Libertine and Joy De Vivre, were as important as the male members. But it was the more general aesthetic of the band that contributed to their mythopoetic aspect. They always wore black and often sported armbands with the Crass logo (more on which in a moment). This 'uniform' was certainly open to misconstrual – and Crass claimed that part of their intention was to explore these contradictions – but, in general, it operated to produce a certain cohesion and, especially when viewed from the outside, the idea of a project with a consistency, which had both a back story and future intention. At gigs, the band members would line up in a row at the front of the stage, whilst at the back there would be large spray-painted and screen-printed banners with various anti-war slogans and logos. The performance would not just be an audio affair, but would include several screens with looped projectors (again, harking back to a more avant-garde tradition of experimental film).[2] In many ways the group, especially as they became more serious, were as much a multi-media collective as a punk band (Vaucher herself has referred to them as 'living theatre').[3]

This aesthetic was also prevalent in the design of Crass records. Covers would be foldout posters, printed in

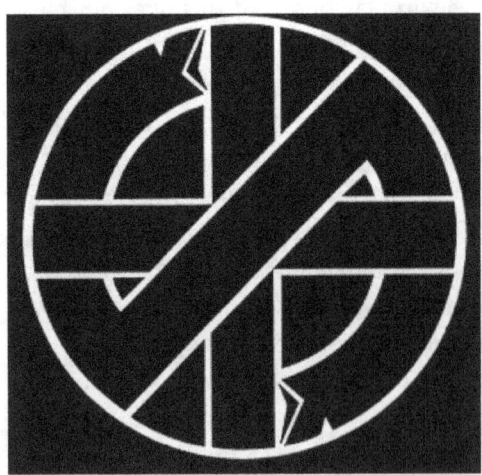

9.2 Crass logo, designed by David King (reproduced by permission of Penny Rimbaud).

black and white with Vaucher's very particular collages (she has talked about the intention of developing a new language – an 'aesthetic of the present' – in her work with Crass). There was also the highly distinctive Crass logo (see Figure 9.2), an amalgamation and condensing of different symbols related to the church, the family and the state. Indeed, Rimbaud has claimed that Crass came up with the first corporate logo, but we might also suggest that the Crass symbol operated as a sigil of sorts (we will return to the use of sigils below). The lettering around the edges of the record sleeves (and sometimes around the circular logo) had a very particular stencilled appearance, and this also became part of the band's mythos – not least as slogans in this lettering, along with the Crass logo, could be found stencilled around London, harking back to Paris and the Letterists and Situationists (and before graffiti as such had become a widespread art form in the UK). This attention to graphic presentation and other details of appearance and design produced a kind of lifestyle package (to continue the corporate language), or what we might call the 'Crass-assemblage'. In fact, Crass fans themselves became part of the assemblage in so far as they adopted the Crass look and took part in Crass events, as well various protests and the anarcho-punk scene at large. There was no sharp divide between band and fans, and Crass themselves would spend time talking to their fans and, indeed, put them up in Dial House.

In conclusion then, although Crass cannot be fully understood independently of their explicitly political message, they were also engaged, it seems to us, in a kind of performance fictioning of an alternative, anarchist life: summoning a people to come. There were two factors at play in the development and deployment of Crass in this mythopoetic sense. The first is internal: a particular group of individuals, all sharing a similar perspective and intention, and all, crucially, in favour of a collective practice that was more than the sum of its parts. The second, external aspect is how Crass were seen from the other side: the effect that the gigs had on their fans, along with the myth of Dial House and the spectacle or 'fabulous image' of the band and their art. Crass represented a different reality, one that – it appeared – was actually being lived, and in this way they produced a mythopoetic practice as an alternative reality effect.[4]

Do What Thou Wilt Shall be the Whole of the Law

Thee Temple ov Psychick Youth (TOPY) was – and to some extent (at least in a certain instantiation) still is – a community of individuals dedicated to the modern use of magick (the k here denotes specific practices derived from Aleister Crowley), especially as this intersects with popular culture (hence the TOPY term 'occulture'). It emerged to a large extent from the thinking and writing of Genesis P-Orridge, and, at one time, from the band – or multi-media collective – Psychick TV. In fact, P-Orridge had already instigated and been involved in different collectives and scenes, for example around the influential industrial noise band Throbbing Gristle (the formation of which coincided with punk), and, prior to that, the performance group COUM Transmissions, which emerged from the 1960s counterculture and associated avant-garde.[5] It is, however, with TOPY that we see the full development of a certain kind of mythopoesis which brings these experiences and interests in audio-visual presentations, performance and alternative collectives into conjunction with esoteric practices. In terms of the latter, TOPY followed Burroughs and Gysin in the adoption of the cut-up as method,[6] and Aleister Crowley and Austin Osman Spare in relation to sigil magic. Indeed, with these two technologies – the cut-up and the sigil – and especially in their combination and extension, TOPY were involved in a systematic and magical fictioning of reality.[7]

TOPY also involved an ethics of sorts, understood not as a morality but as the following of a very particular way of life pitched against all forms of external authority.[8] In terms of Spinoza's idea of ethics, we might say the group were concerned with exploring what a body is capable of and with developing a programme – involving specific disciplines and discipline more generally – that might foster further experiments in the 'short circuiting of control'. One of TOPY's key phrases, taken from Crowley, was 'Do what thou wilt shall be the whole of the law'.[9] A central aspect of this ethics was the will to self-determination – 'to become a cause of oneself' – and, with that, the refusal of any transcendent enunciators, in particular Christianity. TOPY was specifically conceived as a form of mysticism without religion in this sense.[10] We might note the connections with Crass here, in so far as both groups waged this war against the Christ (although this is certainly not to suggest any alliance – or, indeed, any particular connection – at the time between the two groups).

Although these practices were very much focused on individual transformation, it was the collective – which included, at different times, different forms of communal living and various other shared resources – which allowed for this experimentation. The group provided both a context and a legitimisation for this alternative way of life, as well as, more generally, a sense of belonging and identity. It also provided what might be called a common script set against more dominant narratives. As with Crass, the group assigned new names to its members. TOPY discarded the use of 'I' and replaced it with 'we' to signify the collectivity, which also extended 'inwards' to the multiplicity which constitutes any given individual, the many different personalities and fantasies behind the illusion of the single self (see the interview, P-Orridge and Christopherson 1982). TOPY had this double aspect of individual and collective involvement, of both private and public actions, the latter most obviously in the Psychick TV events and, indeed, in the general media attention P-Orridge received, and often actively courted, in the 1980s. This was also in play with COUM's performances: explorations concerning the body (and its limits) which were carried out in the public eye. Indeed, we might say that COUM, in part, was about making the intensely private public, or in bringing the hidden into view, as, for example, in their final show *Prostitution* at the ICA, London, which included images from Cosey Fanni Tutti's work with erotic magazines.

In terms of this focus on the intensely intimate and often repressed aspects of life, TOPY focused on sexuality and the orgasm as a conduit to other states of consciousness (although this was also a focus of COUM and Throbbing Gristle, the latter, certainly, placed more emphasis on horror and violence). The ritual exploration of guilt-free sexuality and of sexual energy more generally was used as transformative technology. In this TOPY looked to Eastern tantric traditions, with their own focus on the use and transformation of sexual energy, but also to various counterculture ideas about free sexuality and sexual expression, such as those found in the writings of Wilhelm Reich. Put simply, for TOPY sex was a powerful threat to control. In particular, the group explored various collective expressions of this energy, for example through the 'writing' of sigils that involved the participant's blood, hair and semen or vaginal fluids. These were 'written' by individuals in the wider TOPY community on a certain day and mailed to the TOPY headquarters.

As we suggested in Chapter 4, sigils are not artworks, nor designed for disinterested aesthetic consumption, but have the very specific function of bringing about the participant's desires. They allow a certain focus and concentration of intent, and operate through a logic of contagion and magical causality (where like affects like) rather than through representation per se (they might be seen as representational but this is not their chief purpose). In fact, it seems to us that sigils operate cybernetically, implying a kind of 'flat time' or a temporal diagram different to anything straightforwardly linear, and allowing a working on the future (or a writing of it) from the present. TOPY's use of sigil magic followed this logic, but in their use of various bodily fluids (elements of the real that break with representation), they also looked to practices such as voodoo.[11]

P-Orridge himself was especially influenced by Burroughs' idea that consensual reality is a recording which might be cut into and rearranged.[12] In fact, like Burroughs and Gysin, P-Orridge saw a direct connection between the cut-up and the practice of magick, which likewise involved a manipulation of so-called 'reality'. Magick offered an alternative to more typical technoscientific understandings of causality, and to a contemporary mediascape which was, for TOPY, perpetuating the reduction of individuals to spectators rather than participants in their lives.

A further key technology in this magickal practice was ritual: the setting up of very particular spaces and the use of certain tools (or props) and techniques in order to side-step habitual subjectivity and produce an altered consciousness. Although private, these rituals were performance fictions whose aim was to counteract the consensual fictions already in operation, and which were themselves taken as reality. With Psychick TV and TOPY concerts these magickal rituals took on a more explicitly public and participatory form, in which trance was a key collective technology.

In relation to the fiction of the self, TOPY were also involved in various practices of deprogramming aimed at loosening this crucial anchor point. Again, there are very real resonances here with Eastern practices and disciplines, and especially with Buddhist technologies. P-Orridge himself travelled to India, encountering sadhus and other holy men, and Nepal, where he met Rinpoches and other Buddhist practitioners. However, it seems to us that TOPY's key concern in this regard was not introspection and emptiness, but rather the production – or writing – of a different kind of fiction of and for a given subjectivity. To this extent, TOPY had more connections with a Western counterculture tradition than with anything non-Western. As P-Orridge makes clear in his own writings, it was 1960s groups like The Process, as well as his own experiences in the Transmedia commune in the 1970s, which were most formative.

9.3 Thee Temple ov Psychick Youth Tri-cross logo (reproduced by permission of Ryan Martin).

In relation to sigils we might also note TOPY's tri-cross 'logo' (see Figure 9.3) – which P-Orridge relates to both the Kabbalah and the symbol of The Process[13] – and the skull/lightning bolt logo of Throbbing Gristle. These sigils encapsulate some of the intentions and orientations of each of these groups. Their style of dress also played a part in this. Throbbing Gristle's black paramilitary outfits, for example, resonated with Crass, while TOPY affected a more ecclesiastical look (their uniform looked back to The Process), but in both cases these clothes and costumes operated as 'fabulous images' around which a different subjectivity could coalesce and cohere. In fact, the visual appearance of TOPY in particular was, according to P-Orridge at the time, a kind of smoke screen for the group's real purpose, which was less the production of any group-mind and more the development of individuals (see P-Orridge and Christopherson 1982). Nevertheless, their group look gave TOPY a very particular identity which others could relate and aspire to (and, indeed, join). They called forth a people. TOPY constituted a scene in this sense, one that eventually dovetailed with the rave scene of the 1980s, itself a period which let 'the mask of control slip, just slightly, for a few brief years, for a whole generation' (Louv 2009: 23).

TOPY, and more particularly Psychick TV, extended the use of magick to other technologies, including TV. This turn to more contemporary media characterised their use of magick, which, again, followed from Burroughs' own experiments with video recording and from Gysin's experiments with perception and 'flicker' technology.[14] The interest in TV as a technology that might be repurposed was evidenced in Psychick TV events, which were as much visual as audio performances. These would involve a form of cut-up and 'surrealist' TV aimed at counteracting a more passive TV consciousness and displaying repressed content. This extended to advertising, which was seen to resonate with the practice of magick: 'advertising jargon is a magical language. It can be used to affect or program the unconscious mind. Advertisements are constructed in exactly the same way that rituals are, using mnemonic devices very similar to the kabbalah' (TOPYNA 2009: 175).

In its turn to popular media TOPY departed from the hierarchies and ceremonies of high magick and from Crowley's original OTO.[15] In general, technology was to be embraced and magick was seen less as pre-modern than as a contemporary, if not future-orientated practice. As P-Orridge remarks: 'Burroughs, and Gysin, both told me something that resonated with me for the rest of my life-so-far. They pointed out that alchemists always used the most modern equipment and mathematics, the most precise science of their day' (P-Orridge 2009a: 293). P-Orridge also had an interest in the feedback loops of neurolinguistics, in so far as this might also allow a rewriting of (subjective) reality.

In conclusion, it seems to us that, although very different in many respects (not least in some of their politics), both Crass and TOPY showed up the edges of dominant fictions, but also produced new fictions and, with that, the possibility of individual and collective transformation. Our discussion of both groups has, of course, been conducted from an outside perspective (although we saw them perform live), and one separated from them in time. As such, it attends less to what might actually have been the dynamics and relationships within the groups and more to their mythopoetic aspects, including the myths and fabulous images of them that circulate to this day. Certainly, with TOPY at least, there are no doubt other more problematic or dubious aspects that we have not considered. This kind of revisionary history – which seeks to correct myths and inaccuracies about certain groups and scenes – is important. But it seems to us that it is equally important to look to what might be extracted from these scenes and positively reactivated today. It is crucial to challenge the fictions and myths of our contemporary political mediascape, and following Crass and TOPY, it seems that producing scenes is one way of doing this.

... the Emission of a Succession of Repetitive Beats

In general punk can be defined, at least in part, as a radical break with the previous hippy counterculture. But there is also a sense that behind this break lies a deeper continuity – a secret history – which links a group like Crass or TOPY with a group like Hawkwind (as evidenced, for example, in the fact that both Crass and Hawkwind played at the early Stonehenge festivals, or in John Lydon's citing of Hawkwind as an influence). The apparent nihilism of punk – with its slogan 'no future' – also had this other side to it: a will to experimentation and, more generally, to explore other ways of living outside the mainstream. We can follow this counterculture thread forwards, past punk and post-punk to the rave culture in the late 1980s and '90s. This in many ways marked a return to the more psychedelic scenes of the 1960s (especially in its various experiments with altered consciousness), as well as to some Situationist strategies from the same era (especially in the setting up of autonomous spaces and events). There was also a distinct spatial aspect to rave, particularly, as we shall see, in its relationship to landscapes and sites outside the city and to certain privileged locations.

9.4 KLF logo (reproduced by permission of Bill Drummond).

To end this chapter we attend to electronic dance music and present the case study of rave culture in the UK. But first we will focus on the work of the KLF, formed by Bill Drummond and Jimmy Cauty in 1987 (see their logo in Figure 9.4). Drummond had already been involved in various post-punk bands in Liverpool, including managing The Teardrop Explodes and Echo and the Bunnymen. In his book *The KLF: Chaos, Magic and the Band who Burned a Million Pounds*, John Higgs (2012) makes a convincing case that Drummond was already involved in a particular and idiosyncratic mythos; while Cauty was also himself partaking in various counterculture activities. However, it was with the KLF that the two developed a fully-fledged myth-making machine. Although labelled as pranksters – and, as such, very much in the tradition of the parodies and pastiches of the Situationists, or even of Ken Kesey's Merry Pranksters – the KLF also inserted their fictions directly into reality, targeting in particular the music business and mass media.

Higgs' compelling narrative is organised around the conceit that the KLF did not know what they were doing – especially in their later incarnation as the K-Foundation, when they burned a million pounds – but were caught up in a wider network of causes and contexts beyond their understanding and inevitably limited perspective (might we even say they were in a kind of trance?). It was important that the money-burning ritual took place away from the city – in the landscape – in an isolated spot on the isle of Jura (a privileged location); this helped to produce a certain myth of the event. For Higgs, the individual ego is simply a spin-doctor of sorts, a '*self referential reality tunnel*' (Robert Anton Wilson quoted in Higgs 2012: 71) which attempts to account for events after they have happened (the ego, as it were, is always the last to know). As such, the 'story' of the KLF can also be told through other models, various precursors and sometimes tangential or marginal contexts and coin- cidences, which follow a dream, or magical, logic. The fiction of the self, we might say, is not the only fiction, nor is it necessarily the most appropriate one to deploy in explaining any given set of events.

The KLF (and later the K-Foundation) presented themselves as an anonymous collective, located at a particular base, 'Transcentral' (Cauty's squat in London). Drummond and Cauty's practice can be said to proceed, to an extent, through collaging and sampling; indeed it was hip-hop culture that first inspired them to form the precursor to the KLF, The Justified Ancients of Mu Mu. There was also an interest in naming as a form of fictioning, as in the production of monikers such as King Boy D. Arguably, the KLF lacked the intensity of the groups presented in our case studies above – they were not involved in exploring a radically different mode of existence, nor in practices of self-transformation. But in terms of their creative output and how it intersected with popular culture, they were certainly involved in a kind of fictioning of reality or myth-making.

The KLF were one of the more public (and pop) faces of a wider underground scene constellated around electronic music, in which the spaces and places of club culture were instrumental in producing a certain mythos. The growth of electronic music's popularity in the 1980s and '90s led to different scenes and fictions centred on different cities and clubs with fierce loyalties. Clubbing became a way of life, but ultimately Techno left the clubs and started colonising other spaces and places. The 1990s saw the beginnings of a thriving free party scene which, in part, looked back to the earlier raves of the late 1980s. Sound systems were set up in disused warehouses in different cities, but also taken out into the countryside, dovetailing there with the anarcho-punk 'new traveller' scene (itself performing a kind of fictioning of the landscape). If the influence of the DIY punk scene that Crass contributed to can be seen anywhere it is here, not least in the free party sound system Spiral Tribe, who were partly responsible for the infamous Castlemorton free festival in 1992 (see their logo in Figure 9.5). Although there was sometimes an emphasis on specific DJs (which involved a certain amount of mythologisation of the star-artist-type), rave culture also celebrated an anonymity, albeit often constellated around the name of a sound system. This was manifest at the raves, with crowds no longer facing the stage, but one other. The drugs – themselves a particular kind of molecular technology – likewise fostered a certain kind of collectivity in so far as they allowed a break from fear and guilt (as we mentioned earlier, Ecstasy allowed the emergence of another reality). And, of course, it was the combination of this with the repetitive beats of the music which produced a very particular altered state of consciousness.

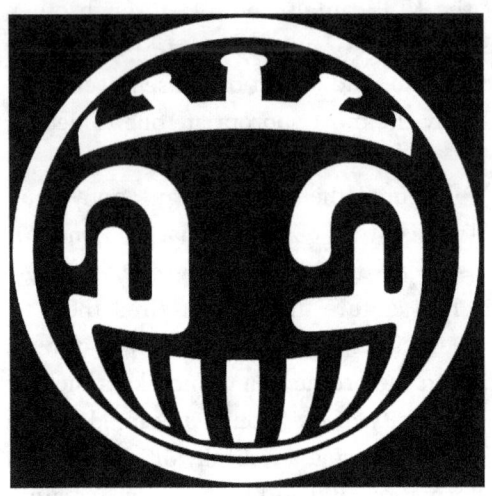

9.5 Spiral Tribe logo (reproduced by permission of the designer, Mark Harrison, Cult of Signs)

Rave culture offered an alternative. Indeed, it might be described as mythopoetic in so far as it was a lived fiction.[16] It offered up other points of subjectification, as Guattari might say, allowing different kinds of relation to form, brought about by a community, or a diversity of microcommunities, with certain common values and beliefs (at least to some extent), and shared experiences in altered perception and affect produced by both sonic and pharmaceutical machines. Put simply, rave culture called forth a people. As well as its sonic and pharmaceutical technologies, however, rave is associated with a host of material cultures and devices, from flyers and fanzines to sound systems, backdrops and lighting rigs. To a certain extent it was this production of another world, and the summoning forth of a people, that was seen as a threat, leading to the Criminal Justice Bill in 1994 (after the Castlemorton rave) and, more insidiously, to the commercialisation and enclosure of club culture. In many ways, art practice can only ever be a pale imitation of these kinds of intensive scenes, but it has also often intersected with them and, indeed, developed some of their elements further. In fact, we would maintain that the most interesting mythopoetic art practices today often look to these kinds of scenes, and to what, once again, we might call their performance fictions.[17]

Notes

1   Alongside the anger there was also a more utopian message – exemplified by the cover of the first album (again, see Figure 9.1) – which, we might say, belied a more 1960s influence. Reading George Berger's *The Story of Crass* (2006) there is also, clearly, a more spiritual, even mystical thread that is especially present just before the group's formation – around Dial House, Wally Hope and the Stonehenge festival – and after Crass split, with Rimbaud's interest in Buddhism and Taoism.

2   In fact, the artist Chad McCall showed his early film work at Crass gigs.

3   An insight into how this aesthetic was achieved is given in Pete Wright's account – in the epigraph that begins this chapter – of the preparations carried out for a rare European tour.

4   We might note a further – more magical – aspect of mythopoesis which involves apparently more incidental detail, and which resonates across space and time, following a logic of synchronicity. After Crass split, Ignorant went on to do Punch and Judy shows, having carved his own figure of Punch. David Tibet of Current 93 was also interested in this area and had begun collecting Punch and Judy paraphernalia after seeing *The Wicker Man*. After also reading and being impressed by *Riddley Walker*, Tibet asked Ignorant (a 'connection man' if ever there was one) to open for his band (see the account in Keenan 2016).

5   Even earlier than this P-Orridge was involved with the Transmedia commune and with the Exploding Galaxy group in the 1960s. For an account of this early history – and of COUM and Throbbing Gristle more generally – see Reynolds 1999. For what might be called a corrective to this history, written by the other key member of the last two groups, see Cosey Fanny Tutti's *Art Sex Money* (2017). For a more theoretical reflection (through the lens of Deleuze), focusing on Throbbing Gristle and their experiments with noise, see Goddard 2008: 162–72.

6   Burroughs had in fact been a key influence on both COUM and Throbbing Gristle, and on P-Orridge in particular, after a meeting between the two of them in the 1970s. For a discussion of the key role played by the cut-up pre-Psychick TV and TOPY, see Goddard 2008.

7   Other key precursors (or points of inspiration) were Timothy Leary, Alfred Korzybski and figures like the Elizabethan mage John Dee and Brian Jones of The Rolling Stones.

8   For a discussion of ethics along these lines see O'Sullivan 2012: 59–88.

9   This focus extends to P-Orridge's trans-sexual 'pandogyne' project in which P-Orridge, ultimately, 'merges' with his then wife, Lady Jaye Breyer (hence, his current name: Genesis Breyer P-Orridge). This project might itself be understood as a fictioning or rewriting of gender, and, as such, as a refusal of the sanctity of the given over the made.

10   As P-Orridge remarks:

> One thing was central to TOPY, apart from all the tactics and vivid aspects, and that was that beyond all else we desperately wanted to discover and develop a system of practices that would finally enable us and like-minded individuals to consciously change our behaviours, erase our negative loops and become focussed and unencumbered with psychological baggage. (P-Orridge 2009b: 419)

11   Since the period of TOPY that our account is concerned with (roughly the 1980s), P-Orridge has explored voodoo more explicitly. See, as indicative, Hazel Hill McCarthy III's film 'Bight of the Twin' (McCarthy 2016).

12   As P-Orridge remarks about his meeting with Burroughs:

> What Bill explained to me then was pivotal to the unfolding of my life and art. Everything is recorded. If it is recorded, then it can be edited. If it can be edited then the order, sense, meaning and direction are as arbitrary and personal as the agenda and/or person editing. This is magick. (P-Orridge 2009a: 279)

13   See the essay 'The Process is thee Produkt' (P-Orridge 2009b), where P-Orridge analyses this symbolism in contradistinction to the 'P Cross' of The Process.

14   As TOPYNA remarks:

> It might be interesting for a moment to consider magick, particularly ritual, as a form of editing. Like a good television editor, a magician strives for some form of continuity in his program, or life. By emphasising desired aspects, the magician tries to edit out, or banish unwanted footage from her life. Any idiot can shoot great footage; only a master can edit it all so it makes sense to a viewer later on. This could be used as a modern alchemical allegory. (2009: 164)

15   OTO stands for Ordo Templi Orientis, the name of the secret order that Crowley eventually led and which followed his philosophy of Thelema (*The Book of the Law*) and a practice of magick emphasising ceremony and initiation.

16   To quote Mark Harrison of Spiral Tribe (on living a fiction, but also with some resonances with Crass):

> we had a punk DIY ethos. We had no money, so we depended on our creative intelligence to provide us with everything from clothing, food, materials, equipment and opportunities. We embraced, celebrated and hacked computer technology. We rejected all forms of authoritarian rule and experimented with collective living and shared resources. And we were reminded continually by the riot police that society had already moved into a dystopian future of corporate control. In fact I think it was because we were actually experiencing, on a day to day basis, the dystopian vision of

much Cyberpunk fiction, that we didn't actually get much inspiration from the genre. We had no time to read books, we were busy doing our own thing. The Cyberpunk authors were writing fiction (some of which is very perceptive and prophetic) but we were actually living it moment to moment. (Harrison 2013)

17 In relation to performance fictions and the logic of scenes more generally see Burrows 2010a and 2010b.

II. MYTH-SCIENCE TO SCIENCE FICTIONING

A. MYTH-SCIENCE:
PERSPECTIVISM AND
ALIENATION AS METHOD

10   Myth-Analysis: Lessons in Enchantment

Myth analysis is done by converting a myth into some form of matrix
and the form of these matrices is essentially diagrammatical, iconic.

Alfred Gell, *The Art of Anthropology*

IN THIS SECOND section of our book we turn to practices which fiction alternate or parallel perspectives. We name such practices *myth-science*, a term we associate with the musician Sun Ra (a figure we will discuss in detail in Chapter 11). We are keen to differentiate myth-science, with its particular attitude towards myth, from the various forms of *myth-analysis* found within university discourses.[1] This is perhaps not so hard to do. Consider Sun Ra's statement on myth and music, quoted in the biography *Space is the Place* by John F. Szwed: 'The beauty of music is that it can reach across the border of reality into the myth . . . The potential of myth is inexpressible because it is of the realm of the impossible. Myth demands another type of music' (Szwed 2000: 329). Consider, too, Sun Ra on his origins and teachings:

> I am not human. I never called anyone 'mother' . . . I never called anyone 'father' . . . And this is exactly what I want to teach everybody: that it is important to liberate oneself from the obligation to be born . . . because whoever is born has to die. (Ra quoted in Szwed 2000: 6)

Sun Ra – who let it be known he was an alien visiting Earth from Saturn – not only develops music of a realm not yet known to reality, but, as a myth-scientist, also addresses questions around origins and kinship, rejecting family filiations and alliances for myths of cosmic existence without beginning or end. While myth-analysis may address similar themes (at least in part), it is clear that Sun Ra's myth-science is ultimately concerned with something different: the performance or presentation of the impossible.

Nevertheless, we recognise that various university discourses offer theories and concepts which significantly aid our investigation of myth-science (and fictioning), not least by offering insights into myth as a specific kind of process, or agent even. Anthropology in particular offers its own insights into problems of origins, alliances and filiation (something we will return to in some depth at the end of this chapter). In what follows, we discuss various anthropological discourses and concepts – which attend to myth in ways very different to the *sacred sociology* of Georges Bataille, mentioned briefly at the end of Chapter 4 – in order to understand where myth-science and myth-analysis are in accord, where they diverge, and the terrains of their different operations. More specifically, we look to some of the work of Marilyn Strathern, Roy Wagner, Alfred Gell, Claude Lévi-Strauss and Eduardo Viveiros de Castro. However, we also want to make clear at the outset that we are not interested in attempting to contribute to the further development of a science of myth-analysis. Rather the aim is to draw *lessons* from myth-analysis which are useful for a discussion of practices concerned with fabricating alternate perspectives or worldviews.

PART 1: ANTHROPOLOGICAL FICTIONS

A Lesson in the Limits of Analysis

In looking at various practices of myth-analysis, we find it far from an objective science – as anthropologists would readily agree. At the start of *The Gender of the Gift*, Marilyn Strathern (1988) discusses the problem of presenting the complexity of the world. Her book addresses the shortcomings of comparative anthropological studies of Melanesian society, in which gender relations have been misrepresented due to the assumptions of Western authors. In approaching this problem, Strathern deconstructs the ethnographic literature, but there is still the problem of the anthropological strategies that Strathern herself might adopt to address gender and gift exchange on the Melanesian Islands. She approaches this problem by drawing on Gillian Beer's discussion of Charles Darwin's research, which, she argues, avoids any simplification of the complexity of the natural world. Importantly, Darwin uses metaphor and 'convenient' representations and, in so doing, produces descriptions that Strathern does not believe are intended to be read as accounts that capture the complexity of the phenomenon being studied (Strathern 1988: 6). Following this, Strathern suggests that she looks 'to the way that one might hold analysis as a kind of convenient or controlled fiction' (6).

In recognising the limits of analysis, Strathern calls for modes of research which reveal how the complexities of social life:

provoke or elicit an analytical form that would not pretend to be commensurate to them but that would, nonetheless, indicate an analogous degree of complexity. It is to this fictional end that I contrive to give the language of analysis an internal dialogue. (7)

In Strathern's anthropological strategy, then, there is a complex relation between fiction and analysis (which correlates with our discussion of Plato's discourse and fictioning in the Introduction). Our first lesson: fiction and analysis are not necessarily opposed or incompatible modes; in fact, analysis might require fiction.

Lessons Concerning Myth (The Teachings of a Coyote)

To develop Strathern's theme of analysis as (a controlled form of) fiction we turn to others who combine fiction and analysis to generative ends, or who seem to slide between (reflexive) myth-analysis and myth-generation – for the line is easily crossed, sometimes wilfully so. Here we are thinking of the dialogue between Roy Wagner and a coyote, transcribed in *Coyote Anthropology* (Wagner 2010), which discusses the first book of Carlos Castaneda's series published in 1968, *The Teachings of Don Juan: A Yaqui Way of Knowledge*.

In reviewing Wagner's themes that include, among other topics, perception and illusion, it seems our speculations might not be too far off the mark.

Coyote: '... once you realize that something is fake ...'

Roy Wagner: 'Or that *everything* is fake ...'

Coyote: 'You stand not at the end of knowledge, but at its beginning ...' (Wagner 2010: 2)

We should remember that most anthropologists are likely to consider coyotes to be tricksters (a recurring character in this and the following chapters of this section), and some thinkers, like Deleuze, have little time for such creatures, accusing them of being ironists who risk little, preferring traitors who are said to risk disappearance through creative acts of betrayal (Deleuze and Parnet 1987: 35). Even so, Wagner's coyote has a serious point to make. When asked whether he has left his bag of tricks at home the coyote presents a mirror for Wagner to gaze at, explaining that what we think we see is not the world, for something comes in between sensing and thinking, which the coyote (referring to the processes of perception) states is sensing-thinking-being itself. As the coyote suggests: 'I always come in-between – between myself and everything else. I have to trick myself before I trick anyone else' (Wagner 2010: 2).

The coyote's playful critique of perception raises an obvious but important question, one which touches on the problem of a sense (or fiction) of selfhood and reality that we discussed in section one: is every human a trickster, tricking themselves with what the coyote, drawing on Castaneda, refers to as the 'bubble of reflection' (4)? We would argue that this is indeed the case, in that the mediations of perception and consciousness are themselves not apparent to humans. In so far as this goes, all humans can be said to be tricking themselves before tricking others.

In light of this constitutive trickery, how then are we to engage with the world? And what anthropological strategies are sufficiently productive and reflexive to address the complexity of this question? *Coyote Anthropology* proposes that much of what is presented by anthropologists, much of the meaning attributed to various examples of social life, relates to what is not seen or perceived, or, at least, what is not present as such. This conclusion develops out of a discussion between Wagner and the coyote, addressing the way figure–ground relations are elusive and changeable. Extending his discussion of perception – and affirming here, we suggest, C. S. Peirce's notion that thought is mathematical and diagrammatic[2] – Wagner suggests that when we first become conscious of something (first attention), we also see a second thing which we are not conscious of, or which we pass over as unimportant or as background (second attention). The coyote is quick to grasp the play and the power of inverting figure–ground relations, leading Wagner (following Castaneda's don Juan) to suggest that experiencing foreground and background at the same time (a third kind of attention) requires one to die in the process (10–11).[3] As we touched on in our comments on Castaneda in Chapter 3, developing this third kind of attention requires 'NOT-DOING' (which is, Wagner admits, still a kind of doing) and a mode of perception which involves 'STOPPING THE WORLD' (11–12): 'Then coyotes talk to you, and dung beetles roll the world away. After that, nothing is the same anymore, even though everything reverts to normal' (12). Wagner and the coyote, then, teach that in experimenting with foreground and background inversions, it is important to attend to the negative (space) as well as positive (figures), and that to see both figure and ground involves giving up a certain kind of habitual lived-perspective.

Despite identifying important lessons – that fiction is necessary for analysis and that analysis might involve registering what is not apparent – we have yet to offer a concrete model for myth-analysis (coyote-style or otherwise), or, as we perhaps promised through our epigraph to this chapter, a diagrammatic account of myth. Wagner does theorise myth in books such as *The Invention of Culture* (1981), in which he explores the idea of obviation, but before addressing this we note a cryptic but thought-provoking notion of myth offered towards the end of *Coyote Anthropology*. Wagner states that in the beginning:

MYTHS sat around the campfire telling PEOPLE to one another. And the MYTHS and the PEOPLE were each the better half of the others' illusions, *each being the result of false claims made upon the other.* And the stories would not die, for the life of the people caught within them. And the people would not really *live*, either, for the life of the stories caught within them.

Coyote: 'Now that story tells me *nothing.'* (2010: 159)

Wagner agrees with the coyote, but we understand that, first, this cryptic discussion affirms that people (or a people) are mediums for myth – or are fictioned through myth – and, second, we note Wagner's suggestion that myth might limit life as much as produce it. Furthermore, Wagner the anthropologist declares he is 'HAPPY' to be a medium (160) but, as indicated above, he is, we think much more than this.

Perhaps Wagner's most important and, for us, most useful critical concept concerning myth is that of obviation. Martin Holbraad and Morten Axel Pedersen have eloquently and thoroughly explored this concept in their book *The Ontological Turn: An Anthropological Exposition* (2017), in which they explain Wagner's thinking and the ways in which obviation produces new figures or myths (and what we term fictionings). Here we draw upon the pair's writing that addresses Wagner's thoughts about myth, invention and spontaneity but also cultural conventions (69–86), which, of course, change over time and differ in various societies. Holbraad and Pedersen explain the relation of obviation, invention and convention through an explication of Wagner's account of *Habu*, a curing ritual performed by the Daribi of Melanesia that involves humans declaring that they are ghosts (80). What interests Holbraad and Pedersen is that, as Wagner observes, people who are obviously human make the declaration 'we are ghosts', countering a conventional understanding that humans are different to ghosts (that is, humans are not ghosts). This distinction between humans and ghosts is the starting point (or default convention) that gives the statement 'we are ghosts' meaning; a new figure is produced through what Wagner terms an *analogic flow* of meaning – between the idea of a human and the idea of a ghost – and that Holbraad and Pedersen compare to metaphor (88). The pair explain that it is through this analogic flow (or mediation) of meaning that the *Habu* performers propose a new entity of a ghost-human, a process that involves a sequence that Holbraad and Pedersen diagram through the triangulation of three terms (see Figure 10.1): A. 'ghosts vs humans'; B. analogic flow of meaning between human and ghost; and C. 'ghost-humans' (89). Holbraad and Pedersen suggest that in the statement 'we are ghosts' there is a linear and forward movement (describing two sides of the triangle), starting with A, passing through B and ending in C, the latter being the idea of a human-ghost or what Wagner would call a 'counter invention' (90). (In relation to our theme of fictioning, we would suggest that this is the way a conventional fiction is countered by another fiction). There is, however, more to counter invention than a linear process from thesis to antithesis, or from the idea of distinct humans and ghosts to that of a human-ghost, for, according to Wagner, this forward (dialectical) movement can be said to proceed in the opposite direction.

Returning to Holbraad and Pedersen's diagram, they demonstrate that the production of a counter invention (of a ghost-human) can be thought of as a 'going backwards', for as stated above, the idea of the human that is also a ghost relies on conventional definitions of what is human and what is a ghost. In this another line can be drawn between A (ghosts vs humans) and C (a ghost-human). This line actually starts from and proceeds backwards from B (analogic flow of meaning), with A therefore acting as mediator of C. For in thinking there is a ghost-human, as Holbraad and Pedersen make clear, Wagner suggests we also think of (or through) a default or conventional idea (90) – which in the case of the *Habu* ritual is the convention that there are humans distinct from ghosts. In this, the default idea is revealed as an invention that has become convention. This convention – of humans being distinct from ghosts – 'needs to be overcome' so as to produce 'new meanings' (90): this is a process in which 'established meanings are revealed ("made obvious") as being unnecessary, overcome, old hat, "obviated"' (91).

For us, Wagner's conception of myth and obviation raises important questions concerning the generative potential of fiction within analysis. Furthermore, and more generally, Wagner provides insights for our exploration of fictioning and myth-science and for our discussion of Sun Ra who, as we shall see in the next chapter, claims not to be a ghost but an alien (while appearing to most to be a human living in America and of African descent). In claiming 'I am extra-terrestrial', Ra challenges default assumptions (or fictions) about his human identity and origins. And in thinking of Sun Ra, it becomes apparent that there is more to add here regarding Holbraad and Pedersen's assertion that the ghost-human performers of the *Habu* 'willy nilly remind us, as it were, that normally we'd take them to be human

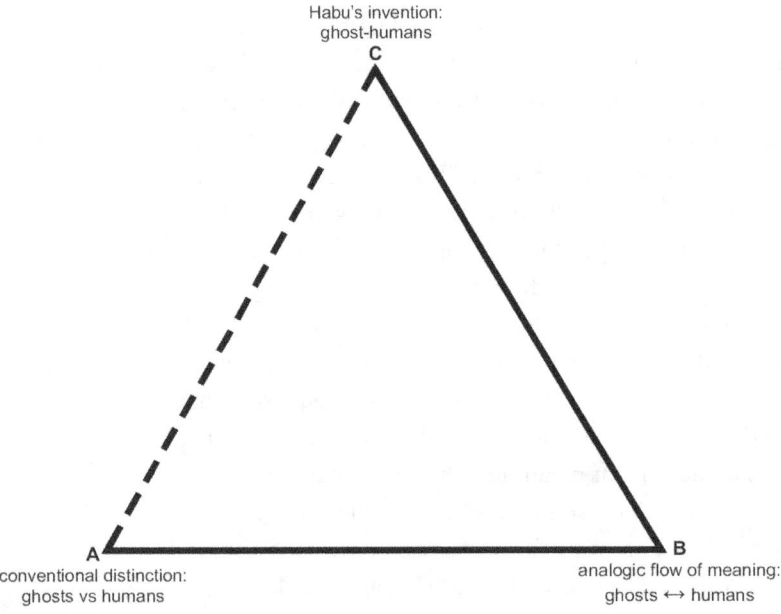

Habu's invention:
ghost-humans
C

A

conventional distinction:
ghosts vs humans

B

analogic flow of meaning:
ghosts ↔ humans

10.1 Martin Holbraad and Morten Axel Pedersen, diagram of Roy Wagner's theory of the obviation of meaning from *The Ontological Turn*, 2017 (courtesy of Holbraad and Pedersen and Cambridge University Press).

instead' (90). This observation underlines, for us, the fact that obviation involves performativity, and indeed a continuous performance, which might also be described as a performance fictioning. This leads us to suggest further that the art or performance of counter invention (and not just the semiotic processes of a presentation) are worthy of attention.

Lessons in Enchantment

Another figure we identify with countering conventions is Alfred Gell, an anthropologist who states that he is less concerned with contributing to the development of his field than with presenting counterintuitive narratives and ideas (Gell 2006: 25). Gell is known for his writing on art and for advocating that his discipline abandon aesthetics as a means of addressing both art and other artefacts. Instead of subjecting art to aesthetic judgement, Gell is keen to address artworks as presentations of complex intentionality – a position most succinctly explored in his essay 'Vogel's Net' (2006: 187–214). Gell realises that to argue that all artefacts can be said to be art in this sense involves a performative or discursive gesture – Duchamp's readymades being influential on Gell's thinking here (210). It is this approach – in which art production involves not only the production of objects but also a naming and other discursive gesturing – that Gell argues anthropology should itself adopt (212). We understand Gell's art-making as a kind of fictioning then – similar to the gesture of a judge that 'turns' the accused into a prisoner. A question arises here though: to what purpose does Gell name or point to something – a hunter's net for example – and call it art, and with what complex intentionality does he undertake this performance? Perhaps the only intention is to produce a counterintuitive event, a disorientating presentation; but in this, unexpected perspectives are encountered.

Relevant to this discussion is Gell's essay 'The Technology of Enchantment' (2006: 159–86), in which, as he states in the introduction to the book from which the essay is taken, he distances himself from semiotic and socio-linguistic problems (of meaning) and attempts to develop a mode of ethnographic research which recognises artefacts and actions as producing a 'psychological, non-linguistic religious vertigo' (17). Gell proposes that art be thought of as a technology of enchantment (and an enchantment of technology), and in so doing, again, he not only dismisses aestheticism but also argues that the 'sociologicalism' of Bourdieu and the iconographic approach of Panofsky similarly fail to adequately grasp art (when this includes those artefacts Gell also considers art) (162–3). Instead, Gell argues that forms of art are elements in 'technical systems' that are themselves necessary 'for the reproduction of human societies' (163). More specifically, he emphasises that art embodies processes that facilitate power by 'casting a spell over us so that we see the world in an enchanted form' (163). An example of this technology of enchantment is the dazzling wooden carvings on the prow-boards of Kula boats from the Trobriand Islands. Gell suggests the prow-boards are produced to unsettle; that is, the carvings are designed to weaken an individual's grip on their will, so that the owners of the boats receive more gifts than their neighbours initially intend to give at meetings between the different groups of islanders (164–5).

What gives the carvings their power? Is it that the patterns of the engraved prow-boards evoke eyes and wings inducing a phylogenetic response? Gell concludes that this is not the only explanation for their magic. What makes the prow-board a psychological weapon, in Gell's eyes, is that a disorientating effect, though mild, is thought to emanate from a boat, and this lends the vessel's owner a token of magical prowess (166). The prow-boards impress not just because of their dazzling effects but also by signifying that a person, people or community possess access to crafts and know-how beyond what might be thought possible or common.[4] Gell does not ignore the social milieu or habitus that these artefacts emerge within; indeed, he presents the agency and effects of artefacts – the psychological and non-discursive events of art – as mediating, but in turn as mediated by, the relations of specific groups of people. In this way, social technologies of enchantment can be seen to arrest perception and cognition for specific ends.

Furthermore, it seems that the anthropologist's textual and diagrammatic presentations are themselves technologies of enchantment. As Gell himself suggests, his intention is to create:

> a certain frisson, a certain artistic effect which could be achieved by taking a random collection of objects which could be made to fit together in an interesting way. You know, like a bird decorating its nest with an arrangement of little pieces of tissue paper, a leaf, a flower. (24)

We speculate here that Gell's interest in producing such 'arrangements' relates to the importance he places on *abduction*, a form of logic which arrives at an explanation of an observation by inferring the most obvious reason for a situation or phenomenon (C. S. Peirce likened such reasoning to guessing). In *Art and Agency* (1998), Gell suggests that humans use abductive reasoning when faced with some indexes (signs which have a physical relation to their referents) in order to determine their cause. In particular, he argues that abduction is evident in social situations, giving the example of a smile as a social, indexical sign, the meaning of which is often grasped through abduction (Gell 1998: 14–16). The importance of this is that when humans encounter strange, random-looking assemblages (as, for example, in the case of art and other complex artefacts), the intention of the assembler is often inferred through abduction. But, if we are correct, there is something tricky about Gell's own counter-intuitive presentations; he lays a trap for abductive logic, or at least a path that leads beyond intuition and habitual thought for his Western readers. In this, the collaging of disparate elements produces arrangements (what Gell calls art) which provoke explorations – or fictionings – of new relations in a reader or viewer. As Gell states, he teaches through a series of experiments for their own sake:

> providing examples of a particular intellectual performance and getting others to do likewise. But it is as an exemplary stylist that I wanted to make my mark on the world. I was trying to do a series of tricks, to get the machine to work. (2006: 26)

We take Gell at his word here. He is another trickster, producing (fictioning) machines, matrices or iconic images to challenge existing wisdom – such as in the example of 'Vogel's Net' (2006: 187–214), already discussed, in which Gell places a hunting net alongside a urinal and declares the artefact an artwork and readymade.

PART 2: Decolonising fictionings

Ontological Questions

Wagner and Gell can be said to develop both an analysis and an art of counterintuitive perspectives and, as such, we can draw some parallels with at least some of the practices we have already encountered in the first section of our book. In comparison though, the anthropologists do more than just destabilise their reader's perspective of reality: Wagner and Gell, among others, can be said to be mediums for the myths (or meta-physics) of the people they write about. Once again, our interest here is in learning lessons that are useful for our discussion of fictioning and myth-science. As implied by our epigraph, we see this as a diagrammatic process (or at least as a process that can be diagrammed) in which a metaphysics concerned with alternative perspectives of different states, places and entities – including the non-human – undermines the universalisations of Western thought, which may also lead to a decolonisation of thought.

Holbraad and Pedersen (2017) themselves identify decolonisation with an onto-logical turn in anthropology (and sociology). Protagonists of this turn include Bruno Latour who, in arguing for the agency of all manner of non-human actors, questions any division of the world into subjects and objects (Latour 1993), and Phillipe Descola who, in interrogating distinctions between nature and culture, identifies naturalism (which might be said to relate to Western or scientific thinking) as one among four ontological modes, the others being animism, totemism and analogism (Descola 2013). Importantly, naturalism – the division that Western metaphysics draws between nature and culture, or animal and (social) human – is an alien ontology for many people who anthropologists might study. This is a problem addressed in depth by the Brazilian anthropologist Eduardo Viveiros de Castro, who has developed an Amazon-inspired metaphysics that looks to a 'permanent decolonisation of thought' (Viveiros de Castro 2014: 92). Viveiros' ontological system, developed in his *Cannibal Metaphysics* (2014), has relevance for our discussion of myth-science, but another reason for our interest in his writing is that he names certain influences on his thinking which might be thought to be incompatible (addressing both structure *and* immanence in the process). We note that the later work of Claude Lévi-Strauss plays a central role in the Brazilian's thinking, as do the critics of the French anthropologist, Deleuze and Guattari, all of which leads to a very singular reading (and metamodel-isation) of both structuralism and poststructuralism.

Lessons on Colonial Metaphysics

Before engaging with *Cannibal Metaphysics* in detail, we want to briefly present an image of Viveiros' key interlocutor concerning metaphysics, as found in Patrick Wilcken's biography of Lévi-Strauss (Wilcken 2010). Lévi-Strauss is a recurring figure in both this and the next chapter, and Wilcken's portrait is valuable for understand-ing – and imagining – the anthropologist's practice. Wilcken informs us that Lévi-Strauss originally conceived of the research which informs the four-volume series *Mythologiques* as a cybernetic-inspired venture, and as a project assisted by a hard-working team feeding punch cards into IBM computers (265). Several years into the venture, however, Lévi-Strauss sits alone at his desk, surrounded by filing cabinets. Above his head hang numerous mobiles made from wire and paper, fragile diagrams which assist the anthropologist in his analysis of myth (266). Wilcken comments that despite Lévi-Strauss' ambition to develop a collective and scientific approach to cracking the genetic laws of myth, the venture became a 'profoundly personal project, the outcome of one mind and a mass of material' (265). It seems that, in writing *Mythologiques*, Lévi-Strauss engages in a fictioning of a kind – a kind of myth-channelling – through a solitary practice. If the idea that *Mythologiques* is a fabrication (or fictioning) seems to undermine the anthropologist's work, then consider Alfred Gell's comments:

> Lévi-Strauss is a great master of the counter-intuitive. When you read the myths in Lévi-Strauss, frankly they are a mess . . . But Lévi-Strauss manages like a magician through the manipulation of data to turn what is apparently arbitrary into something

that is very, very orderly . . . [He] shows everything is an inversion of everything else and then the next paragraph starts 'Nor is this all', and then he produces the whole trick all over again in some other dimension! (Gell 2006: 24)

So, might we claim that Lévi-Strauss is a trickster too?

This image of Lévi-Strauss assembling and disassembling myth has some affinity with Viveiros' argument in *Cannibal Metaphysics* that Lévi-Strauss, specifically in his late work, produces myths with unstable dualities. Viveiros asserts that Lévi-Strauss not only re-founds anthropology through structuralism but that he also unfounds the discipline by 'pointing the way to an anthropology of immanence' (2014: 46); a gesture that we understand as tracing multiple relations and perspectives in the structures of myths. Viveiros also claims that Lévi-Strauss recognises an asymmetry in encounters between occidental and so-called primitive thought, which is nowhere better illustrated than in *Race and History* (Lévi-Strauss 1952), a work that addresses early colonial encounters (Viveiros de Castro 2014: 50). Commenting on an incident in Greater Antilles, Lévi-Strauss points to the different ways in which Europeans and Amerindians conceive of the human. Whereas the Spanish colonialists debated whether Amerindians were human and possessed a soul, the Amerindians captured a Spaniard and drowned him, and then waited to see whether his body decayed just as their own bodies decomposed (for deities do not possess bodies). What interests Viveiros in these two attempts at classification is that the Europeans differentiated between humans, who were said to possess souls, and animals, arriving at the conclusion that Amerindians did not have souls. In contrast, the Amerindians were concerned with the nature of bodies, believing both humans and deities to have souls but that only the former possess a mortal body (52–3). Viveiros affirms what is well known, namely that while Europeans make classifications of life by distinguishing between the human and the non-human, Amerindians make no such distinction, counting both human and non-human as agents or persons. In this, Viveiros suggests that nature is not turned into culture; rather, nature is made strange through culture (69).

Furthermore, Viveiros suggests that to a Western person, Amerindians might seem to see nature as culture (62), and that what Western discourse might call a 'brute fact' is transformed through Amerindian metaphysics into a 'species artifact': Amerindians suggest that for the jaguar, blood is beer; for the tapir, a muddy puddle is a ceremonial house. For Western eyes and ears, this produces 'nature-culture' objects that are ambiguous in this sense (62). But we would venture that there is a fictioning of a kind involved here, too, in that Amerindians can be said to find 'extrahuman subjectivities' in all things. More importantly, according to Viveiros, if non-humans – such as jaguars and tapirs – are persons, then this also means, following Descola, that the different relations between humans and non-humans are always already social (82–3).

Lessons in Corporeal Mannerisms

To continue our discussion of personhood, we note that the embracing of non-humans as persons by Amerindians is the basis for a concept Viveiros calls *perspectivism* (68), though – to mark a difference with Descola – he is keen to point out that perspectivism is not animism but a kind of indigenous anthropology and intellectual structure placed over Western theory (78).

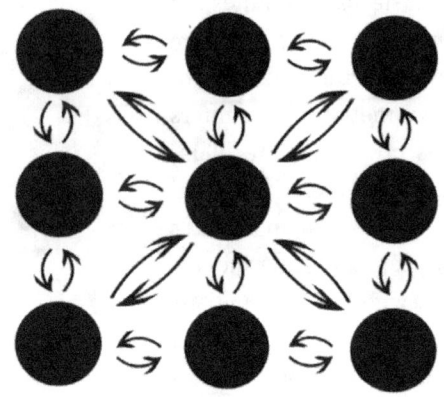

Put simply, perspectivism is the idea that any given body has a perspective, which engages with the perspectives of other bodies. If we try to diagram this topologically, a view from above is produced (something like Figure 10.2). But this diagram is not the best way to understand perspectivism, or rather it produces the view of a god that can see all and everything at once. Martin Holbraad offers a more nuanced diagramming of perspectivism. In his diagram a body sees other bodies that also have perspectives (Figure 10.3).[5] What Holbraad diagrams is a perspective on other perspectives, with all perpsectives seeing the same world, for multiple perspectives do not produce multiple worlds. Importantly, there is a divergence in what each perspective conceives the world to be (Viveiros de Castro 2014: 71–2). As we mark above, where one perspective (that of the human) sees blood, another (that of the jaguar) sees beer. Moreover, perspectives do not exist within a shared temporality or timeline; rather, they can be said to constitute different or singular durations (which can also be said to be beyond notions of Western, measured time). It seems to us that myth-science might have an affinity with this perspectivism, especially as the latter involves, as we shall see, comparative feedback loops of (and between) the perspectives of others.

10.2 Diagram of perspectives of different bodies (from a god's eye view) (credit: the authors).

For Viveiros then, rather than one nature there are many, a position he calls multinaturalism (14). This is related to the idea that there are always multiple perspectives, each of which relates to the 'specificity of the body' (72). In this, it is important to understand that perspectives are not representations, nor are they determined by any physiological difference. Rather, they relate to

affects, or strengths and weakness, that render each species of the body singular: what it eats, its way of moving or communicating, where it lives, whether it is gregarious or solitary, timid or fierce, and so on ... What we are calling a 'body' then, is

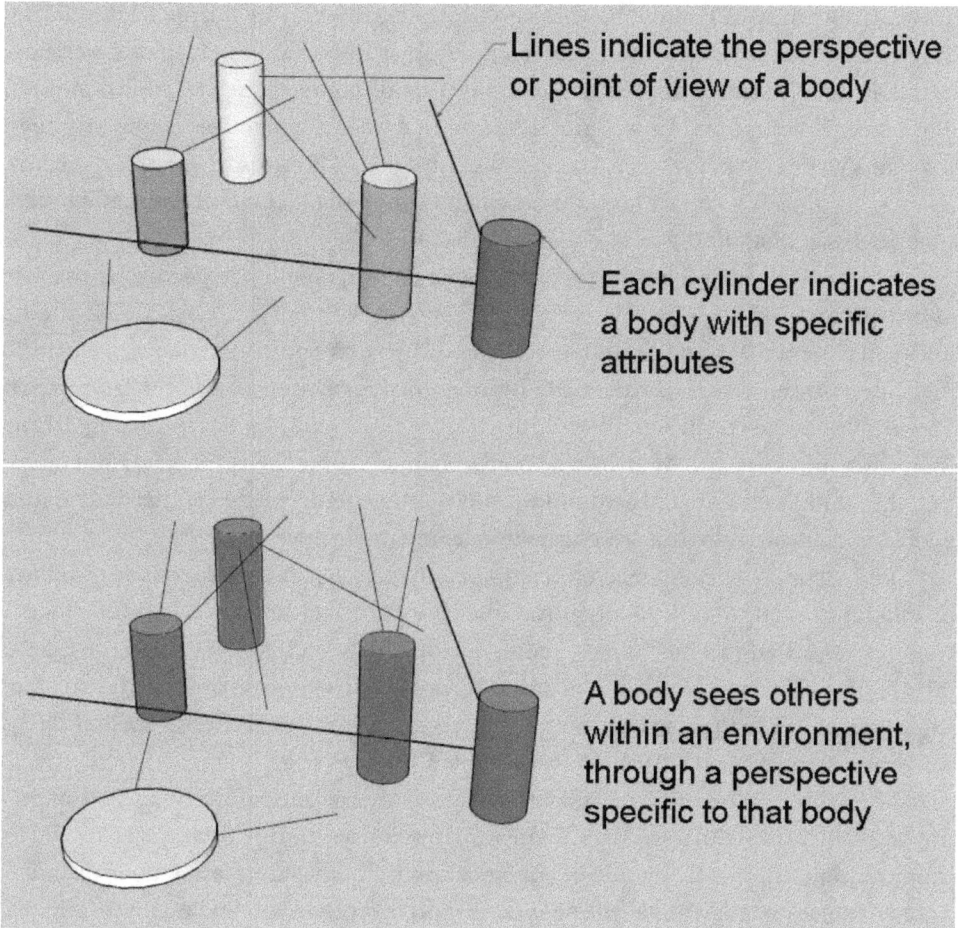

Lines indicate the perspective or point of view of a body

Each cylinder indicates a body with specific attributes

A body sees others within an environment, through a perspective specific to that body

10.3 Diagram of a perspective of a body by Martin Holbraad (courtesy of Martin Holbraad).

not the specific physiology or characteristic anatomy of something but an ensemble of ways or modes of being that constitutes a *habitus*, ethos, or ethogram. (72)

While this may read like Deleuze's own ethology, his notion of immanence and becoming (and Viveiros here is surely influenced by the follower of Spinoza and Bergson), there is an important divergence from Deleuzian thinking in Viveiros' conception of the immanence of a body: the Brazilian is interested in perspectives as being *different and multiple* without claiming them to be of *one and the same substance* (as Deleuze might).

For Viveiros then, 'a *point of view is in the body*' but the anthropologist is not concerned with the physical differences between species – Amerindians 'recognise a basic uniformity of bodies'; neither is he concerned with the 'spiritual essentialism of relativism'. As Holbraad and Pedersen argue, it is important to grasp that perspectivism is not the return of cultural relativism or discourse concerned with cultural difference (Holbraad and Pedersen 2017: 176–7). Rather, perspectives operate through a mode Viveiros describes as a 'corporeal mannerism' (Viveiros de Castro 2014: 73), relating to a body's capacities as a singular (rather than univocal) ensemble, or a specific 'body qua bundle of affects and capacities' (72).

In relation to this, and for the anthropologist engaging with perspectivism, the role of comparison (which we mark as being in contrast with our emphasis on becoming in the first section) cannot be underestimated. Viveiros quotes Strathern, who states that culture is the drawing of analogies between various aspects of a world, from which Viveiros draws the conclusion that culture is a 'gigantic, multidimensional comparison' (85). He also references Wagner, who states that anthropology is the study of culture through culture and, this time quoting Michael Herzfeld, concludes that indigenous people and anthropologists are engaged in 'comparable operations' (85).[6]

Producing a correspondence (or comparison) between the perspectives of bodies or different social or cultural organisations is not a direct process, however, since it requires a translation which is never complete or wholly successful (Viveiros de Castro 2014: 85) – particularly when it is an anthropologist who determines 'the rules of the game' of any comparative study (86). Borrowing from Amerindian epistemology, Viveiros argues that an answer to this problem of translation is *equivocation*, understood here as a mode of communication between different perspectives that allows for ambiguity and elusiveness (different, in this sense, to any attempt at direct or pure translation). It is this mode of equivocation that engenders ambiguous or indefinite enunciations that, as we will see, are important for understanding myth-science, at least as practised by Sun Ra.

Following Viveiros, Holbraad and Pedersen state that equivocation relates to the problem of both the perspective of anthropologists and the 'language game' of anthropology (2017: 178). It is worth noting here Holbraad and Pedersen's example of the operation of perspectives in one of the key topics of anthropology: gift exchange. In analysing what is thought to be a gift, an anthropologist may see what they understand to be an object where the indigenous person may see a spirit: in fact they see the same thing but there is divergence in terms of what they conceive is in front of them (179). This example helps us understand why, for Viveiros, equivocation can be seen as the condition but also the limit of anthropology (Viveiros de Castro 2014: 85–7). If we think of anthropology as an interpretative mode through which the concepts of the compared (indigenous people) are translated into the conceptual terms of the comparer (the anthropologist), it is through perspectivism that the viewpoint of the comparer is seen (or betrayed) merely as a perspective on the perspective of others, rather than as an authoritative or privileged viewpoint. But this betrayal can, in turn, produce insight or a transformation of thinking for, as Viveiros states, 'good translation allows foreign concepts to deform and subvert the conceptual apparatus of the translator' (87). And, Holbraad and Pedersen insist, they find the same feature in Viveiros' thinking as they do in Strathern's and Wagner's: 'Namely, the idea of *self-transformation*', through 'invention, obviation, relation' and, of course, perspectivism (Holbraad and Pedersen 2017: 186).

Here, then, is another lesson: comparison may not assist understanding so much as 'deform' existing conceptual frameworks through '*translation, betrayal and transformation*', which Viveiros states is another way of writing myth (2014: 87). In this, perspectivism (and the equivocal) frustrates the idea that the worlds of other people can be directly or completely understood through objective observation and analysis. To an extent, there may be an opacity to all perspectives – opacity being the name Édouard Glissant gives to that which remains invisible in any objective account (2010) (we will address this in more detail in Chapter 12). Perspectivism teaches us then that the 'Other of Others is always other' (Viveiros de Castro 2014: 91).

We see potential in this last lesson, and in perspectivism and equivocation more generally, for developing myth-science as a practice that proceeds through something like *alienation as method* (for it seems to us that perspectivism, for the anthropologist, might lead to such an approach). In relation to this, Viveiros suggests that the indirectness and ambiguities of equivocation do not produce error but an articulation of 'the relational positivity of difference' (making actual differences between one perspective and another palpable). Indeed, he argues that equivocation is 'not a subjective weakness but a machine for objectification' (91) that avoids 'reification', 'fetishization' and 'essentialization' by acknowledging different perspectives. In fact, Viveiros argues that error and illusion are produced by any anthropologist (or philosopher) who would act as a 'ventriloquist' in attempting to identify and articulate a univocation lying beneath each perspective (91). More than this, equivocation marks a relation with alterity and exteriority (90) and a point of a disjunctive synthesis (91), for it is important to grasp that the misunderstandings between people – between an indigenous person and an anthropologist – are not the same misunderstandings (they misunderstand each other in different ways). In their communication, two perspectives – two outsides – meet.

It seems to us that artists understand equivocation very well, a good example being Jimmie Durham, who has claimed Cherokee ancestry in the past.[7] Durham playfully (but also caustically) combines what the European viewer might suppose is the perspective but also a parody of Cherokee culture with the traditions of Western art and museum display. An example is the *Museum of Stones* (2012) and also the artist's boulder sculptures, which can be viewed as a presentation of geological specimens or cultural artefacts or markers of animist and environmental perspectives but also as jokes (or fictionings) concerning agents of inexplicable and extreme bad luck (some rocks are photographed after crushing cars). Barry Schwabsky alludes to this playfulness when commenting on *St Frigo* (1996) – a refrigerator (or Catholic Saint?) stoned many times by the artist – and quotes Durham, who says of the work:

> If I try to imagine looking at this refrigerator in a museum, as someone who doesn't know it – it's a silly exercise, but I can do it a little bit – I would notice human intelligence having done something to this refrigerator, by the fact of stoning it so often. I might not call it intelligence, I might call it human work or human deliberateness. (Durham quoted by Schwabsky 2012)

It would seem Durham understands that his presentation of 'deliberateness' might trigger equivocation but also that the act of stoning white goods – as possibly a judgemental, sacred, absurd or critical performance – will remain ambiguous to audiences (but not without making them aware of possible narratives or perspectives that may be associated with Durham's gestures).

Lessons Concerning Transversality and Disjunction

As we have implied above, perspectivism and equivocation are aspects of a metaphysics very different to the orientation we explored at the beginning of section one, in which the Deleuzian idea of becoming is identified with fictioning and mythopoesis. This is perhaps best illustrated by our example of Austin Osman Spare's question: on seeing a butterfly, *are we and the butterfly not one and the same*? As we hope we have established, perspectivism, on the other hand, looks to a different metaphysics. It is not that perspectivism is averse to becoming as such, for Amerindians can become possessed, hunters can become their prey, and shamans might access the affects and capacities of another body or perpsective, such as a jaguar, for specific purposes (all of which is very dangerous); but shamans, healers and conductors of rituals might also be said to be mediators between spirits or other species and humans (that is, between perspectives); or at least, in their practices, different perspectives (and the idea of multiple natures) are recognised, maintained and respected. In the next chapter, we will see how far we can take this idea of perspectivism as a basis for myth-science, which would be a myth-function concerned not only with the idea of many natures (rather than becomings that are of one nature) but also with the sociality of perspectivism and myth – that is, myth-science is not an escape or line of flight from existing social relations so much as a confrontation with sociality, for all natures are social and cultural according to perspectivism – a complex idea that needs further explaining). It is for this reason that we now turn to Viveiros' very technical reading of the difference between the later writing of Lévi-Strauss and Deleuze and Guattari's *Anti-Oedipus* (1984) (which is critical of Lévi-Strauss).[8] To understand the differences between the anthropological theories of Viveiros and Deleuze and Guattari, and to add precision to our differentiation between approaches in sections one and two of our book, we need to attend to something fundamental to anthropology: kinship.

In *Cannibal Metaphysics*, Viveiros notes that Deleuze and Guattari ask 'why return to myth?' (2014: 127). But they do not reject myth – despite their well-known critique of Oedipal myths. Instead, Viveiros observes, they perform a radical re-evaluation of so-called primitive myths as a means of countering occidental thought (129). Specifically, Deleuze and Guattari offer a close reading of a famous study of the Dogon people from West Africa, *The Pale Fox* by Marcel Griaule and Germaine Dieterlen,[9] in order to address two important concepts: production and disjunction. Deleuze and Guattari use the term production, in the first instance, to mean reproduction without social prohibitions, while disjunction refers to the relations of bodies, durations or perspectives. They explore these concepts through recounting the Dogon myth of the 'full body of the Earth', which is marked by an inclusive disjunctive synthesis – as intensive filiation (defined here as relating to how one thing is derived or descended from another) – in which 'everything divides, but into itself, and where the same thing is everywhere . . . differing only in intensity' (Deleuze and Guattari 1984: 154). What is important is that if everything is the same and differs only in intensity, this produces entities that differ in degree rather than in kind. Deleuze and Guattari then compare intensive filiation with alliance (or systems of symbolic differences and relations such as we find in marriage), arguing that the latter results in a 'recomposition of the body according to a new model of connection or conjugation', through which 'the full body is dismembered' and 'the sexes marked by circumcision' (155). This latter process asserts binaries that avow difference in kind. In *Cannibal Metaphysics*, Viveiros discusses this critique of alliance and Deleuze and Guattari's valorisation of intensive filiation (difference through degree); it is clear to Viveiros that they view alliance, alongside exchange, as forming and re-enforcing social and economic organisations (or structures), which in turn 'repress' (but can, in turn, also be countered by) production and the intensive disjunctions of filiation without alliance (Viveiros De Castro 2014: 129–30). It follows that alliance inscribes relations of gender and kinship and, as such, there is a 'derailment' of inclusive disjunction – thus, for Deleuze and Guattari, inclusivity is displaced by exclusivity through the development of (social) division, structure or hierarchy (Deleuze and Guattari 1984: 154–5). Specifically, Viveiros notes that for Deleuze and

Guattari, alliances overcode nature (or intensive filiations and inclusive disjunctions) (Viveiros De Castro 2014: 127).[10]

What Viveiros carefully shows is that Deleuze and Guattari interpret the Dogon myth as a proliferation of agents of immanence and univocity, which symbolic division or alliance then derails. For Deleuze and Guattari, it follows that the myth-functions they are interested in escape sociality and alliance (the Dogon myth being their prime example). While *Anti-Oedipus* influences *Cannibal Metaphysics* greatly, Viveiros – informed by his reading of Lévi-Strauss – does not accept Deleuze and Guattari's reading of the Dogon myth that casts alliance as the corruption of univocity. In explaining his thinking, Viveiros notes that the myths of the Dogon people, which Deleuze and Guattari present as intensities denied to 'social man', produce figures such as the *Nomo*, who are human and ophidian or reptile, and also the *Pale Fox*, who is simultaneously son, brother and spouse of the Earth (Viveiros De Castro 2014: 131). Following the metaphysics of Amerindians, Viveiros finds different social perspectives within the Dogon myth (for all perspectives are always already social). Deleuze and Guattari are not aware or do not articulate those perspectives. Most importantly, Viveiros suggests that in their account of the Dogon myth, Deleuze and Guattari distinguish between human societies or 'social man' and the non-social (or pre-social) world or time of the animals, spirits and non-human entities. It might be asked why this is a problem. To put it as simply as possible, where Deleuze and Guattari find pre-social production and inclusive disjunction denied to 'social man' in the myth of the full body of the Earth, Viveiros finds sociality.

It seems to us that Viveiros has identified something central to Deleuze and Guattari's thinking. Occidental naturalism is present in Deleuze and Guattari's refrain of *becoming animal* in a number of their books, including *A Thousand Plateaus* (1988) – proposed as, we saw in Chapter 1, as a process involving becoming-woman, becoming-animal, becoming molecular – that always moves away from culture towards nature. The importance of this for our book – and our thinking – is that if we are to develop the concept of myth-science as a decolonising myth-function, we feel we have to engage with – or at least try to run with – as best we can, the lessons Viveiros draws from Amerindian metaphysics. This is not to dispense with Deleuze and Guattari's thinking (or indeed Western philosophy); it is rather a matter of not embracing philosophical ideas uncritically as if they some how hold the key to understanding all practices. Understanding how Viveiros sees forms of sociality as present and addressed in myth seems to be the key to this.

To be specific about how sociality is presented in *Anti-Oedipus*, Viveiros identifies that Deleuze and Guattari present the filial twice in the book: first as an intensive mode of production that is disjunctive, nocturnal and ambiguous; and second as structured through alliance to produce sociality and political and economic orders

(Viveiros de Castro 2014: 128, 130). The problem for Deleuze and Guattari being that in this second process 'ambiguous signs cease to be ambiguous and . . . become negative or positive' (Deleuze and Guattari 1984: 155). But it is Viveiros' contention that, through such arguments, Deleuze and Guattari's thinking is concerned with the 'passage from Nature to Culture' (Viveiros De Castro 2014: 126). For us the challenge in this section of our book is to identify certain mythopetic productions not as the *something in us* that *aint us*, but as the alternate perspective of an other that challenges and transforms (translates and betrays) our own perspectives. In this, there is no escape from sociality by becoming animal or molecular. Even a cosmic perspective is a social perspective.

Lessons in Transversality

If, as Viveiros claims, sociality can be found in the Dogon myth of the full body of the Earth, a question remains: does alliance or sociality produce ambiguity or are they just modes fixing binary structures of negative and positive identities, as Deleuze and Guattari suggest? To explore this idea, Viveiros turns to Lévi-Strauss' *The Elementary Structures of Kinship* (Lévi-Strauss 1969) to discuss matrimonial exchange (or alliance), which Viveiros suggests is more complex than Deleuze and Guattari acknowledge. Viveiros notes that Lévi-Strauss finds transversality in alliance, for the multiple connections within alliances (the positions of brother and/or husband, sister and/or spouse, etc.) mean that anyone can be a cousin of anyone else and everyone can belong to all parts of the matrix of kinship relations (not unlike the Pale Fox of the Dogon myth): 'Everyone becomes double, simultaneously "man" and "woman"; connecter and connected are revealed to be permutable without thereby becoming redundant . . .' (134).

In rejecting the idea of alliance as a binary machine, Viveiros argues that differences within alliance are 'internal' to kinship structures (134). His reading of Lévi-Strauss (through the lens of Deleuze and Guattari) emphasises – it seems to us – that transversality is immanent to alliance and social structures (and also to perspectives). This idea is further explored via a discussion of Amerindian shamans, through which Viveiros states that while he is concerned with immanence, the humans and extrahumans that shamans connect with are not given equal status or equality. As well as this, in the practice of shamans, Viveiros finds no 'chain of ontological dignity' in the taking up of perpsectives, for 'no point of view contains the other in a unilateral way' (157–8). This means that shamanic practices are not truly horizontal, for 'the perspectivist system is in perpetual disequilibrium' (158). A question arises though, in what ways are multiple perspectives registered in a system of perpetual disequilibrium? To address this we conclude by attending to the way sacrifice is presented in *Cannibal Metaphysics*.

While Deleuze and Guattari and Lévi-Strauss greatly influence Viveiros, he states that his thoughts concerning perspectivism were first sparked by his study of cannibalism in Amerindian cultures. As he explains:

> All this first dawned on me while pondering Araweté war songs, where the warrior . . . speaks of himself from the point of view of his slain enemy: the victim, who is in both senses the subject of the song, speaks of the Araweté he has killed, and speaks of his own killer . . . Through his enemy . . . the Araweté doing the killing sees himself as the enemy. He apprehends himself as a subject at the moment that he sees himself through the gaze of his victim. (143)

Before this sacrifice, Viveiros explains that the victim lives in the village of his killer, with the possibility of taking a wife and becoming known as the killer's brother-in-law. The sacrificial victim might be thought of as both related to his killer and a member of the village as well an enemy and outsider – the outside or other brought inside, so to speak. Through ritual and song, the killer sees himself from the perspective of another (the victim), and it is significant for Viveiros that in the sacrifice 'the place of honor was reserved for the twin figures of the killer and his victim, who reflect each other and reverberate to infinity' (144). In this last image, it seems to us that sacrifice produces a vibration of perspectives to the point where they combine,[11] a reverberation that Viveiros suggests echoes an idea proposed by Lévi-Strauss, that so-called primitive society 'only comes to be "itself" outside itself' (145), which supports Viverios' idea that in so-called primitive societies 'immanence coincides with its transcendence' (145). Transcendence does not refer here to something like an idealist, transcendentalist philosophical orientation but more to an empirical transcending of a single perspective through an encounter with other perspectives. We take this to mean that whereas occidental metaphysics may produce interiority defined against exteriority (subject opposed to object), for Viveiros, any perspective is produced through and in relation to other perspectives (or exteriority). In our appropriation of Viveiros' thought to discuss myth-science it is this idea of accessing an exterior or other perspectives that is most important, not least for developing decolonising fictioning practices.

Postscript: The Lesson of the Elephant Child

As implied above, the lessons of this chapter are not unknown to artists. Camille Henrot, for instance, in *The Pale Fox* (2014) – an exhibition resulting from her residency at the Smithsonian Institute and collaboration with the Natural History Museum in Paris – draws upon Griaule and Dieterien's studies. In particular, Henrot's exhibition deploys the myths of Amma, who creates the universe, and of Ogo the trickster – the Pale Fox – who tries and fails to create a world through excessive curiosity and zeal. Henrot poses the question of whether the attributes of the Pale Fox are those of Western museums too.

The viewer of *The Pale Fox* enters a blue box the size of a domestic interior containing artefacts, documentary and mass-media images and mass-produced commodities. Some are scattered on the floor, others placed on metal shelves and platforms arranged around the room. The installation of objects is exhibited alongside (and as a development of) a film by Henrot titled *Grosse Fatigue* (2013) which implies that collecting or collating data can result not only in fatigue but also in disorien-

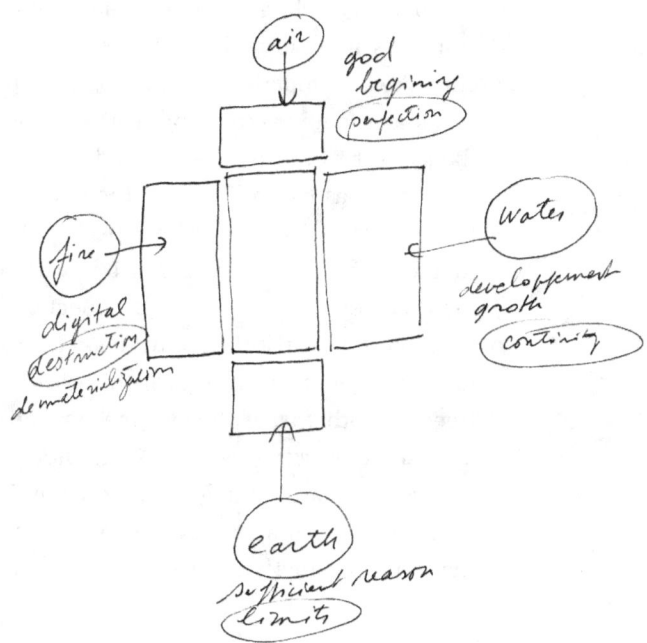

10.4 Camille Henrot, working drawing for *The Pale Fox*, 2013 (courtesy of the artist and Metro Pictures, New York).

tation or bewilderment. Both the film and the installation are discussed in the artist's book *Elephant Child* (Henrot 2016), which interweaves the myths of the Dogon people and a collection of images that aspires to contain the world and its origins.

Although Henrot's collection appears chaotic, there seems to be an order of a kind, and a plan of the installation can be found in her book, identifying that indeed the arrangement has significance or (mythic) structure – specifically, the four walls of the blue room are presented as an unfolded box (see Figure 10.4), each wall relating to Leibniz's principles of philosophy and one of four elements: air, water, earth and fire (165). A comparison of Henrot's diagram of her room with Holbraad's diagram of perspectivism (again, see Figure 10.3) marks a stark difference between Western interiority and Viveiros' Amerindian-inflected perpsectivism. The former is a box that gathers or nests, ordering the different elements of a world; the latter presents a viewpoint as one of many distributed in space.

The title of Henrot's book, *Elephant Child*, relates to a tale by Rudyard Kipling about how a young elephant got his trunk by asking too many questions – including 'What do crocodiles eat?' – a habit that leads to an encounter with a set of reptilian teeth that stretches the elephant's nose. We think Henrot nests the myths of *The Pale Fox* within a tale addressing the pursuit of knowledge as a lesson: the compulsions of (colonial) archivists and internet users alike, attempting to collect *the story* of (all) stories, is an undertaking that is rife with pitfalls. But we also learn that the incessant curiosity and impatience of the young elephant produces a prosthetic – a trunk – that can manipulate the environment for numerous ends, an appendage that separates the subject from the object world.

Henrot has much to say on the separation of subjects and objects, understanding that the compulsion to archive (perhaps as a Western neurosis and narcissism) relates to a fear of death and chaos or a rejection of external forces. The result is a detachment achieved by enclosing a collection of nested elements – as a totality – in a space, room or institution. In this, Henrot views both archives or museums and the idea of a room of one's own to be the desire for preservation, independence and freedom – that is, as defence mechanisms which produce interiority and that guard against exteriority (160–2). We do not present Henrot's compelling work as myth-science but as engaging in myth-analysis that takes the combining of fiction and analysis to its limit: reflexivity and deconstruction are its valuable results. Beyond that limit lies myth-science.

Notes

1 University discourses, here, refers to critical Western traditions which aim to contribute to knowledge. Later on we use the term *university discourse* to refer more specifically to the Lacanian-psychoanalytical notion of a discourse which develops knowledge as an agent of mastery.

2 Peirce is interested in how thought is mathematical and he develops 'existential graphs' or diagrams – hoping to produce an alternative to algebra or formulae – to facilitate logical thinking and to better express the mathematical thinking of relations through the spatial arrangements of elements (Peirce 1906). As well as this, Peirce comments on how, when something catches a human's attention (a first thing or 'firstness', or we might say a figure), a second thing (or 'secondness') follows (as extra to, or a ground for, the first thing). Peirce's mathematical thinking on attention and conception does not end with the count of two though: he argues that there is a third thing which comes to our notice. But this is not simply a third (counted) object or thing, rather, this third thing (which Peirce names 'thirdness') is an inference concerning the relation of firstness and secondness (Peirce 1998: 240). In short, thirdness is the relation between one object of attention and another (240).

3 It seems to us that the artists Spare, Kusama and Smithson would be in agreement.

4 As Martin Holbraad has pointed out to us, the power of the prow-boards would come not just from the carvers' great skill but also from the idea that they have a relationship with spirits.

5   In Figure 10.3, a body and perspective that is not represented is that of the reader, but it is implied in the diagram through (digitally realised) perspective.

6   Though as Holbraad and Pedersen demonstrate, Wagner's key concept is culture, whereas Viveiros focuses on nature (Holbraad and Pedersen 2017: 174).

7   Representatives of the Cherokee tribes contest this identification, arguing that Durham is a trickster, claiming Cherokee descent for career purposes. This controversy does nothing to diminish the ways in which Durham's work frustrates hermeneutic and anthropological interpretation. If anything, for us, it makes the ways in which fiction operates in Durham's practice even more complex.

8   In *Cannibal Metaphysics* Viveiros mentions another book, one he has been unable to write, which would explore what anthropologists owe, conceptually, to the people they study. He gives this unwritten book the provocative title of *Anti-Narcissus: Anthropology as a Minor Science* (2014: 39), in homage to Deleuze and Guattari's *Anti-Oedipus*.

9   It is worth noting that the authenticity of *The Pale Fox* has been questioned and Griaule has even been called 'a creative writer'.

10 It is important to note that in *A Thousand Plateaus* a different account of alliance and the filial is presented. In this sequel to *Anti-Oedipus*, in the first instance – and as we pointed out in Chapter 1 – alliance (with an animal or, at least, something anomalous) is an important stage in engendering an intensive becoming-animal (Deleuze and Guattari 1988: 238). In the second instance, this 'new' account presents the filial in terms of lines of descendants that then deny modes of becoming-animal (238). However, it can be said that the opposition between the animal or nature and the social or culture is maintained in both books.

11 Viveiros' observations remind us of Lacan's reworking of Freud's ideas concerning narcissism presented in 'The Mirror Stage', which accounts for how a child forms an illusory self-image through engaging with actual reflections but also with others (Lacan 2006: 75–81). Perspectivism differs from this concept however. The theory of the mirror stage details how a child produces an illusory self-image by registering external images as itself, whereas perspectivism involves registering the perspectives of others.

11 Myth-Science: Alien Perspectives

All planet Earth produces is the dead bodies of humanity, that's its only creation. Everything else comes from outer space and unknown regions ... Knowledge is laughable when attributed to a human being.

Sun Ra, *A Joyful Noise*

WE NOW TURN more directly to myth-science, but with an eye to the lessons of myth-analysis and, in particular, the idea of perpsectivism we discussed in the last chapter. However, as indicated earlier, we do not intend to approach myth-science solely through, or as, philosophy or anthropology. We acknowledge that our goal may seem perverse, for we aim to explore myth-science as the production of counter-intuitive perspectives presenting generative but also critical fictions that are of a different order to analysis. Our primary focus is the art and music of Sun Ra – a practice addressing race, history and the cosmos and one which combines myths of the past and accounts of history found in various religious tomes with the scientific understanding of outer space and the imaginary futures and worlds depicted by Science Fiction. As Ra explains, as quoted in Szwed's biography, he looks for answers in

> Ancient Egypt and . . . in the entire universe because I want to know the real potential of man . . . According to my research, the governments of this world have conspired to destroy the nations of black people . . . The consequences though have been that there now exists a separate kind of human being, the American black man. And . . . he doesn't belong on this Earth. (Szwed 2000: 138–40)

As we know from the film *Space is the Place* (Ra et al. 1974), (space) music fuels cosmic travel, convincing black people (and others too) of the need to leave the planet: this is a myth-science which is fantastic, political and practical, in that Ra's space music changes people's consciousness and purpose beyond what is thought to be possible. Here we can see how myth-science might be said to differ from myth-analysis in so far as the powers of fiction and enchantment are studied but not given free reign in myth-analysis. In the latter half of this chapter, we attempt to understand this difference through a direct comparison between the myth-analysis of Lévi-Strauss and the myth-science of Sun Ra, but before this it is important to fully introduce the originator of the term myth-science, the musician and artist Sun Ra.

Mister Ra is Mister Re

Who is Sun Ra? This is not an easy question to answer, as Ra cultivates the mystery of his origin, writing lyrics such as:

> When the world was in darkness
> Darkness is ignorance
> Along came Ra . . .
> The living myth, the living myth
> The living Mister Re . . . (quoted in Szwed 2000: xvi)

It seems that the 'living myth' lived humbly enough among ordinary folk, and that it was not unusual for some to see this Pharaoh from Saturn wander down a street and enter a music shop, play several of the instruments and chat with the store's staff. It would be common, too, for the alien – who looks human enough but claims not to have human origins – to gather a group of musicians of an evening, in a shared house, to rehearse a number of jazz standards but also make music that sounds more outlandish. On some nights, the rehearsal may end abruptly as the group – the 'Arkestra' – set off for a concert at which the Pharaoh leads the band, dressed in colourful costumes and playing analogue and electronic instruments and homemade drums (see Figure 11.1). Such performances may feature film projections and dancers parading through the concert hall, moving to the refrains of songs composed of repetitive, discordant chords, such as the unearthly sounding tune called *Retrospect*. Following this, a more upbeat sounding melody may be played, such as *Face the Music*, which warns 'you better listen to those cosmic songs'. The efforts of the musicians and their entourage often overwhelm the audience. Some respond negatively, others are dazzled or recognise singular solo styles and innovation, and some respond to the music that swings and vibrates their bodies. The musicians and dancers chant in unison. They warn that the space age is here and you had better be ready. They sing 'space is the place' and celebrate Saturn, the home planet of their bandleader. When the concert finishes, the audience disperse but the band leave together and return to their dwelling to play some more, or listen to their leader lecture on

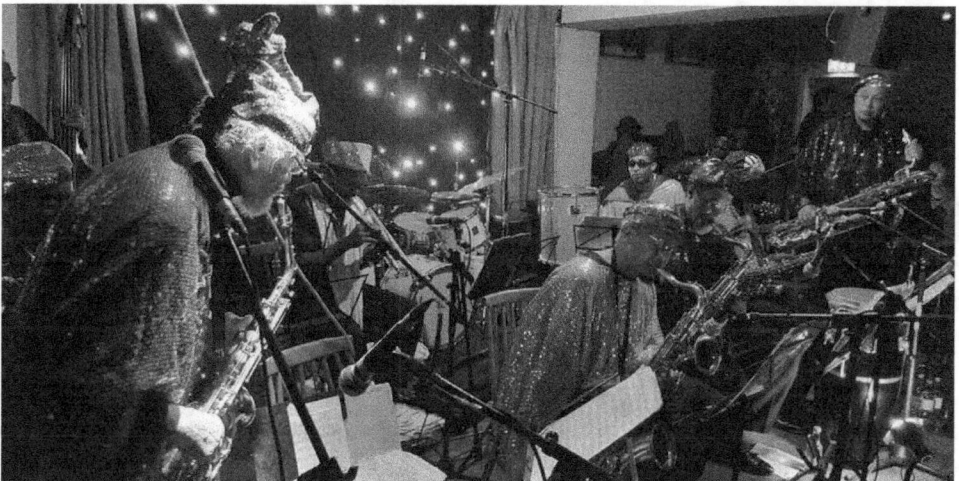

11.1 The Arkestra (Wikimedia commons).

philosophy, history and religion. Ra does not seem to sleep, or at least he does not go to bed, perhaps napping at his electric organ. In the house, there is a large cooking pot on the stove containing vegetable stew, for the leader does not consume meat. The band eat, learn their parts and listen to why the history books cannot always be trusted. When morning comes, the alien may once again wander through the streets, wearing a colourful robe and headpiece.

The bandleader is not the human Herman Blount of Alabama, an American of African descent born in 1914. The bandleader is Sun Ra, a space traveller who has taken up residence on Earth to deliver messages to humanity via music and other means. At least that is what Ra will tell you if you ask about the musician's origins. Ra's communications convey messages from the creator and from extra-terrestrials with antennae above their ears and eyes. The latter have shown Ra other worlds including Jupiter; this is how Ra knows there is more to life than can be found on the third planet from the Sun. The bandleader will also tell you that the lives and spirits of humans are impoverished, and that despite an interest in humanity, he has little sympathy for the wretched of the Earth. For Ra is not here to bring peace, democracy or equality to the planet. The alien is a Pharaoh, after all, a king (or at least Ra insists – and this is important – he is not descended from slaves), and Ra does not value democracy, rejecting the idea of government for the people chosen by the people. This is no joke. Ra is not kidding. As a bandleader, Ra rules over the Arkestra, distributing praise and punishment and wisdom. The musicians follow Ra – a strange attractor and fabulous image – as outer-space envoy, educator and a singular arranger and composer of music. Discipline rather than freedom is the order of the day in both the rehearsal room and on stage. The model for the Arkestra may have been the influence of the big bands created by Duke Ellington and Fletcher Henderson – dance orchestras with leaders who organised groups of smartly dressed African Americans in times that brought extreme racism, poverty and despair for many black communities. Discipline over freedom is even the rule for the music the Arkestra plays; even though Ra and the Arkestra play jazz, every note the group plays together – bar the solos – is rehearsed and delivered to Ra's liking, or so the legend goes.[1]

Ra claims to be an alien, and that is good enough for us. We do not wish to speculate on whether Ra is psychotic or a charlatan or from outer space. Our interest is in the effects of Ra's life-practice; that is, his compositions and in particular his use of the powers of fiction. In this, though, we recognise that Ra's fictioning of human and non-human perspectives is often playful and works for generative as well as critical and political ends. Some might ask whether it is possible to operate beyond the horizon of critical reason if one is going to also claim a critical effect for this kind of fictioning practice. We have already suggested in Chapter 10 that Sun Ra's myth-science involves obviation, mobilising a counter invention to reveal existing conventions as themselves inventions (the term myth-science itself being a counter invention challenging the convention – and modern invention – that myth and science are not compatible). We recognise the need here, though, to clarify further that Ra's myth-science is aimed at educating humans – such that they might be transformed – through the following means:

1. The performance of non-human perspectives – as in the claim 'I am extra-terrestrial.'
2. The production of narratives that draw upon myth and science and that present an 'outside' to humanist thinking, as well as the presentation of histories that challenge those written by Europeans.
3. A presentation (in and as life) of the (seemingly) impossible.
4. The development of collaborations and communes as alternative modes of living.

It is in this way that we consider the fictionings of Ra (which are beyond reason) as generative, political and critical.

Myth-Science and so-called Reality

At this point in our discussion it is important to address the functions of myth in relation to myth-science. We use the term function in this context to refer to the way myth produces relations through developing and spreading ideas. Further to this, we suggest that myth-science functions to double, multiply, invert, deform and arrange the relations of a myth. This latter idea – which is in accord with Ra's use of sound and imagery and other technologies of enchantment – is taken from Ra's poem *The Realm of Myth*, which is an example not just of the musician's poetry but also of what Ra called 'equations'.

> A myth among other things
> Is basically in the category of an idea
> The vibration – radiation of an idea
> Activates itself manifested synchronization
> A lie among other things
> Is basically in the category of a myth.
> The myth is of images,
> Because the myth and that which is of myth
> Is the activator of unlimited imagination
> . . . . Parallel to more . . . .
> Synchronized to what is not.
> Everything is of a particular science
> And myth is no exception
> Witness: 'Science-Fiction'
> And the manifestation of itself
> To a living what is called reality
> Or so-called reality
> As a science Myth has many dimensions
> And many degrees
> Tomorrow is said to be a dimension of myth itself
> When it is said that
> 'Tomorrow never comes'
> Thus when we speak of the future
> We speak of a lie
> Because the future is tomorrow
> And tomorrow never comes (Ra 1972, quoted in Kelley 1995: 25)

We admit the poem is ambiguous and elides direct interpretation (reminding us of our earlier discussion of equivocation), but in being an equation of a kind *The Realm of Myth* is, it seems to us, also a lesson. While we acknowledge that we explore Ra's poem through a particular perspective (and with myth-science as a counter invention in mind), we suggest Ra teaches us that the function of myth is the vibration (and radiation) of an idea. From this we understand that Ra's practice plays with (or is the science of) vibration, which we will attempt to explore through some equations of our own, so that later on in the chapter we can make comparisons with the formulas of Lévi-Strauss. In this, the function of vibration is marked as Fv in the formulas that follow. We write the formula of myth according to Ra as: myth (m) functions as the vibration (Fv) of an idea (i): that is, $m = Fv(i)$.

As we have suggested, Ra's myth-science experiments with vibration (Fv) to invert, transform or multiply ideas and perspectives to extreme or impossible ends, which for us would be an art of obviation too, involving performance and sonic and visual presentations. Furthermore, we suggest this experimental aspect of myth-science relates to the notion articulated in Ra's poem, that ideas perpetuated by myth are synchronised to 'what is not' – 'Parallel to more' – and provoke (or activate) unlimited imagination. In turn, unlimited imagination produces ideas (i) which do not equate ($\neq$) to reality (r). This leads us to propose the formula: myth-science (ms) functions through vibrating (Fv) ideas (i) similar to ($\sim$) ideas (i) which do not equate ($\neq$) with accepted reality (r): that is, $ms = Fv\,(i) \sim i \neq r$.

In this, myth-science (as Science Fiction) produces impossible perspectives of reality: a future that is the lie of a tomorrow that 'never comes'. But Ra complicates this idea by asking us to observe Science Fiction 'and the manifestation of itself / To a living what is called reality / Or so-called reality'. We read these strange, ambiguous lines as implying that Science Fiction presents a new and seemingly impossible reality that challenges conventional notions of *a living reality*, or *so-called reality*. In this, it seems Ra articulates a mistrust of existing reality, or we could say Ra presents Science Fiction as an obviation (following Wagner) of so-called reality. For the phrase 'Or so-called reality' implies that what may be thought to be reality is a myth or lie too. Or, put another way, existing myth (m) as the vibration (Fv) of ideas (i) is similar to ($\sim$) ideas (i) that equate to (=) so-called reality (r).

The full set of equations that we find in *The Realm of Myth* read as:

$$m = Fv(i) \sim i = r : ms = Fv\,(i) \sim i \neq r$$

It would seem, then, that the equations for myth and myth-science are well balanced, myth-science being the production of myth that overturns or obviates existing myth.

Sun Ra has another way of communicating this equation. If, as Ra implies in *The Realm of Myth*, Science Fiction is a manifestation of myth-science, then the future (tomorrow) is a field of enquiry for the myth-scientist. Tomorrow though, as already stated, can be said to be a lie in that tomorrow never comes. But in another poem, Ra inverts (or vibrates) 'tomorrow never comes' into 'comes never tomorrow' (which, we think, might be interpreted as *comes, the impossible that can never happen, tomorrow*). Ra's equation invites equivocation:

Every myth is a mathematical parable . . .
TOMORROW NEVER COMES

COMES TOMORROW NEVER
NEVER COMES TOMORROW
TOMORROW COMES NEVER
NEVER TOMORROW COMES
COMES NEVER TOMORROW

This is the equation, the touch of myth. (quoted in Szwed 2000: 304–5)

Whether 'never' (as an impossible future) is coming tomorrow or not – or whether the conventional saying tomorrow never comes is obviated or not – depends on the way the poem is read. And through Sun Ra's poems (which generate ambiguous meaning), but also through Ra himself (as Science Fiction extra-terrestrial who celebrates ancient Egypt and appears to be of African descent), we encounter art and performance fictioning that is not only future orientated but that also manifests past, present and future (all fictions) in one work or practice at the same time. In this, the equations of myth-science can be said to be both diachronic and synchronic. For myth-science – like (or as) Science Fiction – is concerned with both the non-reversible linearity of time, running from past to present to future (the diachronic), and presentations in which the past and impossible future can be found manifested in one composition (the synchronic).

We will return to the synchronic and diachronic later, when discussing Sun Ra's poetry in comparison with Lévi-Strauss' formula for myth. What we hope to demonstrate through our own equations – themselves derived from the lessons that we extract from Sun Ra's writing – is that Ra's myth-science – like myth itself – concerns 'so-called' reality (as convention) and also the impossible (as counter invention). We think this is nowhere better addressed than in the film *Space is the Place* (Ra et al 1974), directed by John Coney and written by Sun Ra and Joshua Smith. In the film, Ra – looking to settle people of African descent on another planet – challenges a character called the 'overseer', a figure who seems part criminal and part demon but who presents himself as the leader of an African-American community only to exploit it. Ra and the overseer are seen playing with tarot cards in the middle of a desert and each turn of the fortune-telling cards presents Ra with a new challenge or quest. In undertaking these quests, Ra visits a youth center to convey a message to those gathered in the building. After being challenged by young African Americans, Ra admits to not being real but then says, 'I am just like you'. The not-real alien reasons that if the young adults who identify as black Americans were real they would have some status in America, which they do not, living as they do with the legacies of slavery and not being treated as human equals by their white counterparts. The implication is that the youths have swallowed a powerful fiction or myth – a convention of 'so-called' reality – of blackness and slavery and the struggle for redemption, which in fact prevents them from realising their potential. This counterintuitive idea challenges the identifications of two young revolutionaries who aid Ra in his fight with the 'overseer', but also draws the attention of agents of the American government who do not want Ra and his orchestra to play, as they recognise that music is Ra's primary means of recruitment for his cause (as well as a means of fueling space travel). At the end of the film, when Ra leaves the planet in a spaceship, those choosing to go with the not-real alien leave their blackness behind (and the one Caucasian woman who enters the ship leaves her whiteness on Earth). In the film, as in all Ra's work, myth-science is pitched against the conventions of 'so-called' reality. The result is that the hierarchies of fiction and reality become unstable; the reality of blackness and whiteness is challenged (as a fiction) by a cosmic reality.

In thinking through Sun Ra's notion of myth, we should state here that Ra's practices and ideas relate to an experience of modernity, scientific thought and racism which leads to a distrust of the dominant narratives of history and knowledge. As such, Ra's perspective is markedly different to that of the anthropologists we referenced in Chapter 10, though we think there are similarities too. An obvious difference is that the myth-analysis of (and myths analysed by) anthropologists such as Lévi-Strauss and Viveiros do not address the future, but this is not the only difference between Ra's myth-science and the structuralist (or poststructuralist) approaches of Lévi-Strauss and the perspectivism of Viveiros. To expand on this further we will compare the practice of Sun Ra (referring to the mathemes that we have derived from Ra's poems) with the formulas and diagrammatic concepts of Lévi-Strauss and Viveiros.

A General Formula of Myth

In 'The Structuralist Study of Myth', Lévi-Strauss develops a formula for myth which stems from a discussion of several errors, including the search for original myths by those disturbed by the fact that as tales are retold they change, both in content and in the arrangement of their elements (Lévi-Strauss 1963: 207). Lévi-Strauss dismisses this last concern, for there is always uncertainty as to the first articulation of a myth. Another error, which Lévi-Strauss finds particularly in the work of Carl Jung, is thinking that there are mythical archetypes with a fixed and universal meaning, which the anthropologist suggests is a mistake similar to claiming that a sound uttered in speech has a fixed sense (208). He argues that the identification of archetypes is unproductive, as meaning does not reside in a single unit of a myth but in the assemblage of the units of myths or *mythemes*. In examining such assemblages, Lévi-Strauss shows how structures of myth can be read as a narrative but also as a laying out of the different elements that make up a myth, for – similarly to Ra – he views myth as consisting of a diachronic and synchronic ordering of elements (209). By analogy to linguistics and the function of phenomes, he suggests that the various assemblages of a myth are not copies of an authentic tale; rather, a myth is all its variants in total (217).

To explain his ideas, Lévi-Strauss presents a series of fictions, the first being a tale of archeologists from the future (and another planet), who are digging up a library on Earth (212). (We note a paradox or irony here: that in addressing the synchronic, Lévi-Strauss writes a Science Fiction, a tale of the future, but it is a device to allow the reader to approach the familiar from a fresh perspective rather than evidence of any interest in a future to come.) The alien archeologists discover some scripts which are not read in one direction (as with most texts they find) but have recurring patterns which can be read as a whole (synchronically rather than diachronically). These are orchestral scores (something the alien Ra has intimate knowledge of) which can be read left to right (diachronically) but also top to bottom and column by column (synchronically); that is, as music for individual instruments (on the horizontal or diachronic axis) and as the combined music of the various players (on the vertical or synchronic axis). It is the latter axis which Lévi-Strauss names 'one bundle of relations' or a mytheme (211). This tale of the alien archeologists is followed by the image of a fortune teller laying out a deck of playing cards (212–13). Lévi-Strauss suggests that it is possible to understand the elements of the pack from observation, by grasping the numbers in a suit (again, the diachronic axis) and repetition in the different suits (the synchronic axis).

Human and Chthonic Myths

Having established a mode of organising information which is both diachronic and synchronic, Lévi-Strauss continues his study of myth by presenting the tale of Oedipus in a manner influenced by his discussion of orchestral scores (see Figure 11.2). The benefit of such a composition is that the myth is not only readable from left to right and top to bottom but also column-by-column. According to Lévi-Strauss, each column is a unit of the myth (a mytheme). He interprets the myth of Oedipus as relating to the problem of origins (which, as we have discussed, is Sun Ra's problem too); that is, the myth concerns autochthonous birth and whether humans emerged from the land itself rather than from other humans.

The composition allows for the identification of four, seemingly opposing units relating to this question. The first column concerns the 'overrating' of blood-relations that are too intimate; the second concerns violence between blood-relations that are 'underrated'; the third concerns the slaying of (non-human) monsters; and the last column relates to physical characteristics which limit human action (215). Column one, referring to blood-relations and *humans born of humans*, is coupled by Lévi-Strauss with column three – which contains the killing of a dragon (a chthonian

Overrated Blood Relations	Underrated Blood Relations	Killing of Chthonian Beasts	Physical Impairments
Cadmos seeks his sister Europa, ravished by Zeus			
		Cadmos kills the dragon	
	The Sparoti kill one another		
			Labdacos (Laios' father) = *lame* (?)
	Oedipus kills his father, Laios		Laios, Oedipus' father = *left-sided* (?)
		Oedipus kills the Sphinx	
			Oedipus = *swollen foot* (?)
Oedipus marries his mother, Jocasta			
	Etecoles kills his brother, Polynices		
Antigone buries her brother, Polynices, despite prohibition			

Diachronic Axis

Synchronic Axis

11.2 Table of the relations of the myth of Oedipus by Lévi-Strauss, redrawn by David Burrows and Simon O'Sullivan (credit: the authors).

beast) and the Sphinx (a killer of men), and which is interpreted by Lévi-Strauss as a rejection of autochthonous origins. In contrast, he argues that the last column affirms autochthonous origins and is coupled with column two (the underrating of blood-relations); each name listed in column four refers to a difficulty with walking or standing, which Lévi-Strauss claims is a common attribute of humans born from the depths of the Earth (217). Having established his method of analysing (and privileging) a synchronic reading of a mythical narrative, Lévi-Strauss suggests examining similar myths addressing whether humans are born from the Earth or from man and woman, which can be identified in the tales of various cultures (including the Koskimo of the Kwakiutl and Viennese psychoanalysis in the form of Freud's Oedipal Complex, which does not address autochthonous birth as such but is concerned with how *one* can be born from *two*) (217). Lévi-Strauss goes on to suggest that if there is not one authentic myth but many variants of a tale, then the variability of the myth needs to be counted by similarly examining all versions, simplifying the variations until the 'structural law' is discovered. As to how variables are counted as one, the anthropologist suggests a myth, even when amended or added to, remains the same myth, 'if it is felt as such' (217).

At this point, having not only established that myth has synchronic and diachronic aspects but that each myth has variable content, Lévi-Strauss is halfway to a general formula for myth. To develop his ideas further he examines a number of other myths using his system of turning them into 'orchestral scores', suggesting:

By systematically using this kind of structural analysis it becomes possible to organize all the known variants of a myth into a set forming a kind of permutation group; the two groups placed at the far ends being in a symmetrical, though inverted, relationship to each other. (223)

In inscribing myth as units of contradictory terms – from the myth of Oedipus to Pueblo and Zuni emergence myths – Lévi-Strauss discovers terms arranged around themes of life and death and the problem of change and permanence. How such contradictions evolve is not hard to understand. Who bore the first human if humans are born of humans? How can a god be good and bad, punish and reward? And so on. Lévi-Strauss then concurs with Sun Ra that whilst myth may have a low truth value, it is nonetheless a form of thought – one in which contradictions and problems are not resolved so much as presented in a (narrative) structure. Between the poles of contradictory terms of a myth, Lévi-Strauss discovers mediators in the form of ambiguous terms, actions and characters – the Pale Fox of Dogon myths discussed in the previous chapter, who is simultaneously son, brother and spouse of the Earth, is one example. These terms, actions or characters, which can also be tricksters, are multiple and mediate many forms or states. And it is these ambiguous and mediating elements of myth which are important for myth-analysis to grasp (and that Ra's myth-science makes its own).

Lévi-Strauss further investigates mythic figures which mediate contradictions by analysing a Hopi myth in which the deity Masauwu is understood to be helpful (and given a value of x by Lévi-Strauss) but also unhelpful (and then given a value of y) (227). The anthropologist argues that it is the association of other figures in various tales which mediate the opposing values of x and y attributed to Masauwu. He suggests that Masauwu as helpful (x) has an attribute found in a similar myth which associates the deity with another figure called Muyingwu, who is *more* helpful than Masauwu. Lévi-Strauss relates the tale of Masauwu and Muyingwu to a similar myth concerning the figures of Shaloko and Muyingwu, a tale in which Masauwu is absent and Shaloko is the more helpful deity (more helpful than Muyingwu, and therefore more helpful than Masauwu). He concludes his assemblage of figures with myths of Masauwu as an unhelpful deity (y), completing the presentation of the contradictory actions or states of a (helpful and unhelpful) deity. The assemblage is then summarised in the following formula (similarity is marked by the symbol $\simeq$):

$$(\text{Masauwu}:x) \simeq (\text{Muyingwu}:\text{Masauwu}) \simeq (\text{Shaloko}:\text{Muyingwu}) \simeq (y:\text{Masauwu}) \quad (227)$$

We suggest that what Lévi-Strauss presents as taking place here is something like the vibration – to borrow a term from Ra – of myth, through which he registers all variations of the narratives of Masauwu. This in turn helps him develop a canonical formula for myth (228) in which both poles of this equation can be seen as inversions of the other.[2] That is, we see a similarity here between Lévi-Strauss' method of laying out the variations of a myth and Sun Ra's notion of myth as the vibration of an idea, as well as his obviation of so-called reality through presenting the impossible – though for Ra transformation rather than analysis is the goal.

A Living Myth

To further compare the ideas of Lévi-Strauss with the practices of Sun Ra, we offer the following thought experiment. If we present Ra's life, as narrated in John Szwed's biography, in the fashion that Lévi-Strauss would have us treat all myths (see Figure 11.3), we can see Sun Ra was perceived as or presented as a contradiction – as human and alien (or non-human). The problem of origins is key: is Ra born of human parents (is he of two) or is he from Saturn (of one)? Is Ra descended from slaves or not?

Human Relations/Existence	Human Life	Alien Life	Alien Relations/Existence
Born in Alabama in 1914 to human parents and given the name Hermann Blount			
			Claims to have known of alien origins when young
	Has a life-long affliction and pain from a hernia problem	Has a superhuman talent for music and learns how to play musical instruments from an early age	
	Joins bands of black musicians, which are examples of disciplined black men		
	Becomes politicised and rejects military service (and serving the USA), diagnosed as a pervert and deviant	Lives (and teaches) in relation to his understanding of music, history, science and religion and their myths	
		Visted by aliens and travels the solar system	Alien origins are confirmed as being Saturn
		Changes name and uses several names	
		Produces film *Space is the Place*, the alien's story of a mission on Earth	
	Becomes increasingly frail and suffers ill-health		
Dies in the Blount family home			Leaves planet Earth

Diachronic Axis

Synchronic Axis

11.3 Table of the myth of Sun Ra, as told in *Space is the Place* by John Szwed, drawn by David Burrows and Simon O'Sulliva (credit: the authors).

The table of the myth of Sun Ra presents two poles, the human and the alien, with the life of Sun Ra (or its various instantiations) mediating the two identities; for it is the duality produced by seemingly being a black man in America who identifies as an alien visitor from Saturn that gives Ra a power (of fiction) to question so-called reality, and to operate through (or to fiction) a singular alien perspective. So is Ra a trickster? For the musician seems to engage in racial politics (of the Earth, and of the twentieth century) but also claims indifference to anything other than cosmic futures (of the Universe). The answer is more complex than a simple yes or no.

The Problem with Tricksters and Traitors

Lévi-Strauss notes that a good example of a trickster is the coyote in the myths of first-nation North Americans (244). He reasons that coyotes are scavengers – they eat carrion and are therefore mediators between two other varieties of animals (or we might say perspectives): while being neither herbivores (or prey) nor carnivores (or predators), the scavengers are like herbivores (in that they do not kill animals to eat) and they are like carnivores (in that they eat meat) (244). The coyote, like all tricksters and mediators, is a double or multiple articulation of terms: from the African myth of Papa Legba, who serves as an intermediary between the gods and humans and who stands at the crossroads of two realms (and whose *veve* or sign is thus a cross), to the myth of Sun Ra, such mediators perform a movement or vibration between states or realms. And importantly, such (impossible) figures, as multiple perspectives, exist in one body or point, in one place and time.

Here we remember, once again, that Deleuze has written disparagingly of the trickster in relation to the traitor (Deleuze and Parnet 1987: 30–1). He argues that the trickster is a plagiarist whose movement leaves all terms or states intact and in play, whereas the traitor turns their back on everything, embodying a creative line of flight. This idea of the traitor could be seen as Romantic – the trickster engages with words in an ironic play of terms, whereas a traitor, in the 'conquest of the unknown', betrays all (31). Putting aside Viveiros' contention that equivocation and translation can involve not just betrayal but transformation of concepts too, is there something too binary about this Deleuzian trickster–traitor opposition, at least in light of Ra's myth-science? It should be remembered that Deleuze, in discussing tricksters and traitors, is writing about European and American literature and film, but we feel the comparison is appropriate, as Ra is a filmmaker, writer and musician working in an American context. What Ra's trickery offers is not (just) irony, as Deleuze might have it, but a perspective on other realms as well as a perspective on any existing world that an individual identifies as reality. In relation to this last function of Ra's myth science, there seems to be a correspondence with Samuel Delany's comparison of Science Fiction writing to mirrorshades, in which he states: 'the text becomes someplace where you look to see what's going on, only what you see is yourself looking at the text to see what's going on – while at the same time, the text presents a gaze that is somehow darkened, distorted, and reflected' (Delany 1994: 172). There are also parallels here with the perspectivism of Viveiros in so far as Delany presents Science Fiction as revealing of perspectives, and furthermore as having the capacity to distort perspectives when they attend to other or alien view-points or societies. It seems to us that the binary of the trickster and the traitor needs readdressing, at the very least in the singular instance of Sun Ra.

Ra certainly seems to be a trickster – an entity able to 'move' between realms and perspectives. But the alien can be said to vibrate perspectives or ideas concerning so-called reality and the impossible, to the point where they are no longer stable. When Ra – as alien – admits to not being real but states that the young African Americans are not real either, is he trickster or traitor? If we add to this that the alien voices a concern for humanity as well as an indifference, a complex set of perspectives is produced. Let us compare two Sun Ra's: the one quoted in Szwed's biography, who declares a concern for the 'potential of man' and for a humanity that has been hindered by many things (Szwed 2000: 138); and another Ra, who states:

> The only reason I'm here is that the Creator got me here against my will. If I can get out of in any way enlightening this planet I'll do so with the greatest of pleasure and let them stay in their darkness, cruelty, hatred, ignorance and the other things they got in the houses of deceit. (Ra quoted in Szwed 2000: 365)

Not only is Ra both helpful and unhelpful (like the deity discussed by Lévi-Strauss), it is clear to us that something more than the binary of traitor-trickster is needed to address Ra's vibrations of *the human* (as investment in humanity) and *the alien* (as inhuman indifference to humanity). We add to these terms those of *trickster* (a perverse movement between human and non-human, through performance and communication that seems ambiguous) and *traitor* (the human betrayal of the human), to understand the mythemes of Ra's myth-science. Furthermore, we lay these four terms out in a semiotic square, below (see Figure 11.4). The top half of the square presents the *Human* (invested in the human) and the *Human Traitor* (betraying humanity), which belong to the realm of human perspectives and potential; the lower half presents the *Trickster* (between perspectives) and the *Alien* (as inhuman perspective), which belong to the realm of the non-human.

Ra's myth-science vibrates all these terms and perspectives which then come together in the person of Sun Ra. But as the vibrations continue, everything can then come apart (which can be thought of as a betrayal of a kind, in which all terms or

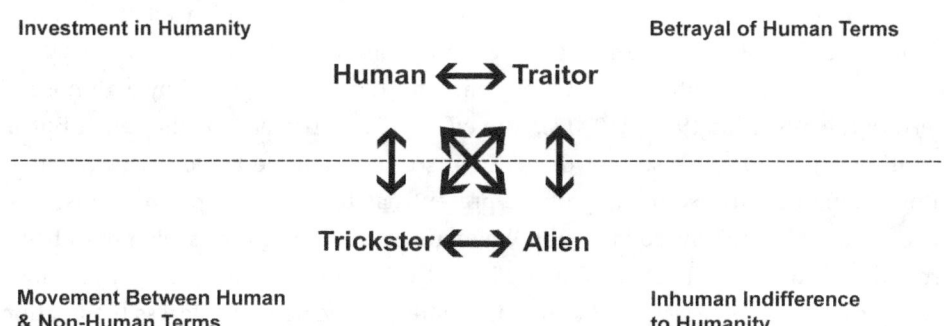

11.4 Semiotic Square of Human-Traitor-Trickster-Alien in the Myth of Sun Ra (credit: the authors).

perspectives seem to question one another). For Sun Ra seems a committed political commentator and historian but also a clown, one indifferent to civil-rights activism as well as seemingly lacking in empathy for the people of America and Earth. Ra is often indifferent to Earth and its people, and this is perhaps the most important aspect of the diagram of Ra's myth-science: as an alien, Ra has no kinship or alliances with humans. In this narrative, something radical emerges. Ra is more than an excluded middle between traitor and trickster. The alien maintains (or conjures) an outside or exteriority to the human world, a perspective which even Deleuze's traitor of European and American literature will have a hard time reaching. And here lies the promise of Sun Ra: the perspective of a cosmic life. Take this line of thought, and pretty soon you will see yourself through the eyes of an alien, or beyond human perspective. So why not follow the being from Saturn and prepare for the cosmic age? The human-alien-trickster-traitor invites you leave humanity behind and in doing so, sacrifice yourself.

Alien Vibrations

In mentioning sacrifice we feel there is more to say about vibration and its affects, and about giving oneself up to the music and perspectives of Ra's myth-science. This is where we imagine Ra might be critical of Lévi-Strauss' alien archaeologists, willing them to play the score they unearth, to produce vibrations, to produce new music and myth rather than simply analyse compositions. Similarly, rather than observe the use of cards in fortune telling as suggested by Lévi-Strauss, Sun Ra would play the cards, as he does in the film *Space is the Place*, to bring the past and future into the present. To be fair, Lévi-Strauss is aware of this possibility, as evidenced in his recognition of Michelet's description of the French Revolution as the day when everything became possible, the future became present, and time was replaced by a glimpse of eternity (Lévi-Strauss 1963: 210–11). The effect of myth-science is the same. But in vibrating time and space so that they blur – so that multiple perspectives manifest in one composition – something of the present has to be given up too; heads must be lost. Here we are reminded of Roy Wagner's discussion of how seeing both background and foreground requires dying, and also Viveiros' discussion of Amazonian shamans in *Cannibal Metaphysics*. And it is here that we need to address the relation of ritual (or performance) to myth (and myth-science).

Viveiros notes that Lévi-Strauss identifies ritual with the register of the imaginary (2014: 147), which we understand to mean that ritual, very often, does not concern the practicalities of living. Here, Viveiros is referring to the end of *The Naked Man*, in which Lévi-Strauss argues that the words and gestures of ritual 'are given a function in addition to their practical use, which sometimes replaces their use' (Lévi-Strauss 1990: 671). Viveiros disagrees, at least in relation to Amerindian cannibalism (discussed in Chapter 10), which he places in the category of ritual, and in which he finds nothing imaginary or false (Viveiros de Castro 2014: 149). It would seem that, following Viveiros, ritual performance serves as a 'conductor of perspective' and therefore is practical rather than merely symbolic or imaginary. Perspectives are made palpable and accessible in ritual – and this is also the case with our understanding of myth-science. We should be careful, however, and acknowledge that Viveiros is referring to a specific context and specific agents. He comments that:

> Amazonian shamanism, as is often remarked, is the continuation of war by other means. This has nothing to do, however, with violence as such but with communication, a transversal communication between incommunicables, a dangerous, delicate comparison between perspectives in which the position of the human is in constant dispute . . . And what, exactly, does that human position come down to? That is the question raised when an individual finds itself face to face with allogenic bundles of affections and agentivity, such as an animal or unknown being in the forest, a parent long absent from one's village, or a deceased person in a dream. (152)

Viveiros continues by suggesting that while a shaman converses with incommunicables, it is also the case that 'two different species that are each necessarily human in their own eyes can never simultaneously be so in the other's' (152–3). The alien perspective of Sun Ra offers a similar challenge. Here, we are not equating Ra with an Amazonian shaman – we would not wish to repeat the colonial error of asserting modern, Western art as a form of shamanism. Sun Ra is not a shaman; the musician is an alien. But there is some symmetry with the relations of ritual described by Viveiros and Ra's myth-science. For we have already discussed how Ra communes with, and embodies, human and non-human (or incommunicable) worlds, just as the shaman does (at some risk to the shaman). To be a conductor of perspectives, Ra sacrifices much – the possibility of taking up the identity of Herman Blount, family life, sexual relations, sleep, respect from others beyond a small group – as did the members of the Arkestra (who may not have given up all that Ra did but who none-theless, while living communally, dedicated themselves to Ra's ideas and vision). As already implied, Ra's myth-science demands that something or someone has to be sacrificed too. It is for this reason that the myth-scientist Ra is more troubling than any traitor; Ra is committed, indifferent, pragmatic and perverse in equal measure – an inhuman alien-trickster of the most radical kind.

Notes

1 This discipline is still evident today under Marshall Allen's direction of the Arkestra – Allen goes so far as to use noticeably insistent gestures to guide the dynamics of the solos.

2 The variable aspect of myth is explained through a general formula proposed by Lévi-Strauss (1963: 228):

$$Fx\ (a): Fy\ (b) \simeq Fx\ (b): Fa\text{-}1\ (y)$$

This general formula of myth has elements with no identity or content (as with mathe-matical algebraic formulae or writing). It is therefore not just complex but abstract too. Lévi-Strauss suggests that the elements a and b, with two functions x and y, inscribed at the beginning of the formula, are terms with 'a relation of equivalence' when defined, under specific conditions, through an 'inversion' of elements and functions (228). To be specific, the variation of myth involves two inversions within the formula: 1. The first occurs through replacing an element with its opposite – in the second half of the formula, a becomes a-1 or not-a. 2. A second inversion occurs when a function replaces or becomes an element within the formula – as in the last part of the equation when y (which in the first half of the formula is a function, Fy) becomes, in the second half, an element of a different function, Fa-1. Or, to put it another way: 1. a introduced in the first part of the formula is not present in the second half, and 2. y, which is a function in the first half of this formula, becomes an element in the second half. It seems that for Lévi-Strauss, understanding myth in all its variations involves this double inversion.

We can trace a double inversion in the last two parts of the myth sequence concerning Masauwu, where the deity is absent from the myth of Shaloko and Muyingwu and, in the last part, marked as an unhelpful deity (rather than helpful, which is how Masauwu is presented at the beginning of the myth sequence).

12 Afrofuturism, Sonic Fiction and Alienation as Method

*Traditionally, 20th C science sterilises all myth: myth starts
where science stops. But the recording medium acts as an
interface between science and myth. Every medium opens up
a continuum from technology to magic and back again.*

Kodwo Eshun, *More Brilliant Than the Sun*

So FAR WE have offered up an account of myth-science through a comparison
with the work of myth-analysis, identifying Sun Ra as a figure who traverses – and
vibrates – human and alien perspectives. We recognise not only that we are offering a very singular reading of myth-science, but that there are other accounts of
the alien's myth. In particular, Sun Ra's influence contributes to the development
of *afrofuturism*. This term was coined by Mark Dery in 1993 to account for the
Science Fictions of the African diaspora, examples of which, the writer claims, are
found in a variety of forms, from the paintings of Jean-Michel Basquiat, to the
music of Sun Ra and Lee 'Scratch' Perry, to the *Hardware* comics of Milestone
Media (Dery 1994: 182). Dery suggests that all versions of afrofuturism address a
very specific problem:

> Can a community whose past has been deliberately rubbed out, and whose energies
> have subsequently been consumed by the search for legible traces of history, imagine
> possible futures? Furthermore, isn't the unreal estate of the future already owned by
> technocrats, futurologists, streamliners, and set-designers – white to a man – who
> have engineered our collective fantasies? (180)

Here we can understand that, from the perspective of afrofuturism, as Dery suggests,
European humans are alien abductors landing Africans in an already existing

'science-fiction nightmare' where technologies of various kinds mark bodies and erase histories (180).

In this vein, and returning to some of the themes discussed in section one, we want now to focus on myth-science as a fictioning which presents alternative perspectives on the future (and the past). No one has explored this better than Kodwo Eshun, who has discussed and developed – and, indeed, accelerated – Sun Ra's concept of myth-science, bringing it to bear on a whole spectrum of Black electronic music. In our discussion of afrofuturism we pay particular attention to Eshun's important concept of 'sonic fiction', as well as to the more general idea of alienation as method, especially when this comes to the human-machine interface. We also look at some important passages from Édouard Glissant and from Stefano Harney and Fred Moten, which, although not explicitly addressing afrofuturism, develop the idea of a Black imaginary and contribute towards ideas of a Black poetics. Our chapter ends with a discussion of the film-essay and with two case studies of myth-science: the Black Audio Film Collective's *The Last Angel of History* (a work which includes an interview with Eshun), and the *Otolith* film trilogy made by The Otolith Group, Eshun's own collaborative practice with Anjalika Sagar. In all of the above, and especially in discussing Eshun's own take on afrofuturism, we become less focused on the anthropological aspects of myth-science and enter further into the territory of Science Fiction (and what we call 'science fictioning').[1] To this end, and before we begin, we want first to turn back to the cultural theorist Raymond Williams and his thoughts concerning Science Fiction (and, especially, its relationship to technological development). We propose that Williams offers a useful framework for approaching some of the territory opened up by science fictioning (indeed, it is a framework we will be returning to in subsequent chapters). It is also through reference to Williams' account of Science Fiction that we can understand how both myth-science and afrofuturism develop but also diverge from the genre.

Science Fiction and Utopia

In his essay on 'Utopia and Science Fiction' (1978), Raymond Williams lays out a matrix of narrative tropes for both genres of his essay's title:

1. The positing of a paradise and/or hell.
2. The externally altered world.
3. The willed transformation.
4. Technological transformation.

For Williams, the first of these is predominantly a form of magical or religious thinking typically found in fantasy literature (and in which the place is more determinate than the means of getting there). In terms of Williams' distinction between residual, dominant and emergent cultures that we looked at in Chapter 5 (Williams 1980: 31–49), this first trope tends to utilise archaic forms which are already incorporated within the dominant culture, and thus, for Williams, it has a limited resistant potential.[2] The second category is also of limited interest to Williams, amounting as it does to the positing of a transformation not caused by human actors (for example, a natural catastrophe). As a Marxist, it is the third category which Williams is most interested in but, in terms of cultural diagnosis, it is also the fine line between the third and the fourth categories which commands his attention. The interest in willed transformation, which for Williams is a characteristic of properly utopian fictions, is that it attends to human agency; in such fictions the future is not simply portrayed as the result of technological progress divorced from human sociality. In fact, for Williams, humanity is the only real historical actor (and as such also the real progenitor of technological development). Although Science Fiction crosses all four categories, it is especially the fourth which is most characteristic of the genre.

Following this matrix and his interest in human agency, Williams suggests that the different kinds of fiction laid out above are also expressions of different class positions, with their own particular ideas – or fictions – about their relation to the dominant mode of production. It is here that he makes some important remarks about the kinds of utopia attached to a rising class as opposed to those associated with a descending one: the former being linked with systematic utopias (an expression of confidence), and the latter with more open and heuristic utopias (which, for Williams, expresses a lack of confidence in the existing state of affairs). In relation to our interest in afrofuturism as Science Fiction, we might extend this class analysis to works that address race and note that some forms of non-Western Science Fiction can also express themselves (confidently) in systematic and technological form (though we are not suggesting that afrofuturism can be considered a subgenre of utopian fiction even if, perhaps, they fiction a dystopian, hellish present). We will return to William's genres of Science Fiction in later chapters, but in terms of the present chapter we note that Eshun positions the development of new technologies in music-making as crucial to a myth-science of alternative pasts and futures. It would seem that afrofuturist sonic fictions are partly the result of advances in music-making technology; they belong to the Science Fiction genre of technological transformation, in that – from Sun Ra's use of synthesizers, to recording studios that engineered dub, to DJs inventing sampling processes – technological transformation is part of the story of afrofuturism: afrofuturists are engineers and scientists who explore the past and future through technological means.

To engage with the ways in which social, technological and affective productions are important and combine here, we note that Williams goes further in his analysis of Science Fiction, foregrounding a very particular kind of utopian fiction which attends to the *transition* to a new kind of world and, with this, the development of 'new social relations and kinds of feeling' (Williams 1978: 209). Such literature is not just the dreaming of another place, it also reports on the struggle to bring this other world about. Williams' paradigmatic example is *News from Nowhere* by William Morris (1890), but he also cites a more recent case: Ursula Le Guin's *The Dispossessed* (1974). For Williams, this particular novel of 'voluntary deprivation' is especially attuned to our present condition; in particular, to the dissatisfactions which come with mass consumerism and a capitalist hegemony. As he remarks:

> It is probably only to such a utopia that those who have known affluence and known with it social injustice and moral corruption can be summoned. It is not the last journey. In particular it is not the journey which all those still subject to direct exploitation, to avoidable poverty and disease, will imagine themselves making: a transformed this-world, of course with all the imagined and undertaken and fought-for modes of transformation. But it is where, within a capitalist dominance, and within the crisis of power and affluence which is also the crisis of war and waste, the utopian impulse now warily, self-questioningly, and setting its own limits, renews itself. (Williams 1978: 212)

As a brief aside we might point to another short essay, 'Science Fiction', where Williams (1988) offers up a reduced tripartite division of the genre:

1. 'Putropia': fiction of this type tends to portray a world in which the isolated individual, often the intellectual, is opposed or in confrontation with 'the masses'.
2. 'Doomsday': this involves the depiction of a world in which the human is faced with extinction.
3. 'Space anthropology': a variation on 'travellers tales' and a form of fiction in which 'new tribes' and 'new patterns of living' are articulated and explored.

It is invariably the third category which most interests Williams (and us too in our exploration of myth-science as Science Fiction), as it offers up experimental models and ways of living as well as different perspectives that might be pitched against the dominant.

As opposed to a writer like Fredric Jameson, whose own writing on Science Fiction is often a form of ideology critique (or, at a pinch – and as he himself remarks – a form of 'anti-anti-Utopianism'; Jameson 2005: xvi), it seems to us that Williams is more attuned to the innovative and experimental aspects of the genre (although he is quite capable of executing his own critique, as in the sharp analysis of putropian fiction as bourgeois ideology). Indeed, we might say that Science Fiction is a site of emergent culture in so far as it can offer up the 'new patterns of living' mentioned above (Williams 1988: 359). Although this might involve more techno-logical predictions, themselves the result of a Promethean impulse (indeed, the science of Science Fiction announces this), for Williams Science Fiction is at its best when it explores what Simondon (2011) called other 'modes of existence'. Science Fiction can, in this sense, be an experimental social science – again, a 'space anthropology' – albeit one which is often untethered from the Earth and the present (Williams 1988: 359).[3]

Jameson's own idea of the traction of these future-oriented visions on the present is, arguably, more deconstructive. The issue for him is not just that Science Fiction is written in the present with the materials at hand – and that it is therefore, neces-sarily, limited by being a product of that present – but that this also represents a deeper ontological problem of how to combine 'the not-yet-being of the future' with the being of the present (Jameson 2005: xvi). Just as there are traces of the past in the present so Science Fiction can offer traces of the future in the present (hence the title of Jameson's book on Science Fiction, *Archaeologies of the Future* (2005)). Yet, a key question remains as to the exact nature of this future trace;[4] or, more generally, how something might be in the world but not wholly of that world. For both Jameson and Williams, this is the central dilemma of Science Fiction: how to figure whatever is to come in terms of the already here, or, at least, offer a view of a different kind of place in terms of the already visible. This is an issue we will be returning to, especially in Chapter 16 where we offer up an example of science fictioning that addresses this temporal (and, indeed, ontological) paradox, but would note here that Sun Ra, in stating that music brings the impossible that is not yet known to reality, also provides an answer of sorts to this problem. As we shall see, it is this idea of a kind of future orientation of music and sound which Eshun develops in his own writings.

Science Fiction and Afrofuturism

In looking at Williams' comments on Science Fiction we have identified that the conjunction of willed and technological transformation and also what he calls space anthropology are most relevant for our investigation of afrofuturism. Here technol-ogy – at least when it has been repurposed – becomes the very means of producing something different to the predictions of more market-driven capitalist futurology. Eshun writes well on this, from his book *More Brilliant Than the Sun* (1998) to his later article 'Further Considerations on Afrofuturism' (2003). In both he identifies Sun Ra, alongside George Clinton and Lee 'Scratch' Perry, as key sonic exponents of this mobilisation of 'future' technology, especially when this is linked with more

imaginary presentations – involving space travel and the colonisation of other plan-
ets – in the production of a different narrative for Black subjectivity.

In relation to what we have said in section one about the performance of fiction,
it is worth noting from the outset that, crucially, Eshun's pioneering book also
performs its content. *More Brilliant Than the Sun* consists of the engineering of
concepts (which arise from the material under investigation) as well as a sampling
(of Science Fiction and theory). There is also the invention of neologisms and a
playing with form and presentation (the book progresses through different rhythms,
with the text itself in a somewhat unusual font). In all this the book sets out to explore
a different way of writing about music: in place of historical and cultural analysis we
have a consideration of what we might call sound's material and machinic character
(Eshun follows Deleuze and Guattari in their own turn from signifying economies
in this respect). Put simply, as well as being about myth-science, it seems to us that
More Brilliant Than the Sun is also an example of it.

The significance of machinic modes, as well as Eshun's own writing mode, are
made clear when the author discusses the importance of science in activating and
traversing change:

> Tracks become Sonic Fictions, sonar systems through which audioships travel at the
> speed of thought. Ultramagnetic MCs are obsessed with the field of force that tech-
> nology ignites in us, with the unstable world of cosmophonic forces released by the
> sampler, the electromagnetic waveforms accessed through sampladelic operations.
> The human organism is flying apart. The Song is in ruins. Sampling has cracked the
> language into phonemes. It breaks the morpheme into rhythmolecules. Only science
> can ride the shockwaves it has instigated. (Eshun 1998: 25)

The impact of science and technology is crucial here, as is the relation of human and
non-human. In Eshun's account of the development of sonic fictions, Disco is 'the moment
when Black Music falls from the grace of gospel tradition into the metronomic assembly
line' (4). The 'Postsoul Era' follows, which Eshun suggests is indifferent to humanity;
indeed, as machine-music develops, the human is cast increasingly as a 'pointless and
treacherous category' (5). Postsoul music draws upon and includes a procession of
musicians whom Eshun identifies as exploring an 'Outer Side' to the human – Alice
Coltrane, Sun Ra (a pioneer of electronic keyboards), Underground Resistance, Tricky
and Martina Topley-Bird among them.[5] In such 'Alien Music' a sound arrives from the
future which 'alienates itself from the human', replicating as 'an applied art technology
for amplifying the rates of becoming alien' and for synthesising oneself (4–5). But, as
indicated in our discussion of Sun Ra's traversing of multiple perspectives, Eshun concedes
that the opposition of alien and human is a fallacy, at least in relation to sonic fictions:

At the Century's End, the Futurhythmachine has 2 opposing tendencies, 2 synthetic drives: the Soulful and the Postsoul. But then all music is made of both tendencies running simultaneously at all levels, so you can't merely *oppose* a humanist r&b with a posthuman Techno. (4)

It is through traversing both the historical (soul) and machinic (postsoul) axes, that the myths of alien music are channelled through the human – and alienation can be said to do its work – deforming the category of the human by fictioning posthuman, postsoul and postcolonial futures.

For Eshun, Sun Ra's myth-science had involved just such a re-engineering of the past (away from that which is typically written in and by White history) towards a projection into an alternate future. In this, it is Black music (again, sonic fiction) which is instrumental in constructing this view from elsewhere – view or perspective being the key term here. In fact, as Eshun points out, the visual imaginary is an important aspect of sonic fiction (and one which relates to our own idea that myth-science involves the vibration of ideas through various means and technologies, including visual art). In relation to Sun Ra, the album covers, films (especially, *Space is the Place*) and such like – as well as the costumes and other visual aspects of the performances – all contribute to the very particular 'future fiction' of Ra's expanded practice.[6]

In contradistinction to Williams' definition of properly utopian fictions, there is no explicit struggle to bring this other future about, as these myths and visions – at least on one level – are disconnected from any human agency (indeed, as we saw in Chapter 11, Sun Ra does not identify with the human at all). In fact, it is this disconnection which we suggest Eshun presents as alienation (or what we identify here, and develop later, as *alienation as method*), and which constitutes the power of myth-science and sonic fictions, at least in part: they refuse the logic of the existent and the 'way things are' (a situation in which Black subjectivity has been immiserated). We might say that there is also a refusal to think the future solely through the terms provided by the present and, following that, a concomitant turn to other destinies: precisely a turn to Science Fiction.

In the article 'Future Considerations of Afrofuturism' Eshun returns to this question but suggests that, in fact, the actual terrain of Science Fiction has recently changed with the emergence of futures markets and, more generally, a situation in which 'power operates predictively' through the 'envisioning, management, and delivery of reliable futures' (there are echoes of Dery's comments on the management of the future here) (Eshun 2003: 289). The future, we might say, is itself increasingly the new terrain of capitalist expansion (with these future visions then operating to call forth the very future they predict). This would seem to be something quite different to Williams' utopian impulse: indeed, for Eshun it signals the end of the 'utopian project for imagining alternative social realities' (290). Instead, Science Fiction becomes concerned 'with engineering feedback between its preferred future and its becoming present' (290). We will be returning to this new kind of temporality in the last section of our book (especially in relation to new financial instruments), but it is important to note here that the terms of our engagement with time seem to be changing.

In his article Eshun suggests his own tripartite field of possible future interventions:

1. Mathematical simulations: this is the future modelling performed by the markets.
2. Informal descriptions: as in Science Fiction and other less formal future predictions and projections.
3. Black vernacular myths of the future.

Although clearly the terrain of capitalism, the first of these has recently been addressed by the Left in calls for the repurposing of existing capitalist technologies and platforms (what has become known as 'Left accelerationism').[7] The second is also as much the terrain of Science Fiction writing (and cinema) as it is of expert futures consultancy (indeed, it is sometimes difficult to tell these two apart, and Eshun himself remarks on the existence of formal-informal hybrids). The last intervention involves a revisioning – or 'reversioning' – of previous future myths (or 'vernacular futurologies'), and Eshun gives a roll call of these which includes, of course, Sun Ra (alongside, for example, Dogon cosmology). Again, there is often a further kind of hybridity – spatial and temporal – in these last cases, where a pre-historical (and non-scientific) past meets a post-historical (and supra-scientific) future, as with Ancient Egyptians travelling through space and time. Or, again, in Sun Ra's term: myth-science.

It is also at this point in his article that Eshun turns directly to art practice (broadly construed), and back to the terrain explored in *More Brilliant Than the Sun*. In particular, it is the sonic which can operate as an expression of these different futures. It seems to us that with these technologically enabled practices we have not just the portrayal of other worlds (they are not simply utopian in this sense) but something else, something more embodied, something like a perspective relating to a specific bundle of affects and capacities and also technologies (both fleshy and inorganic). These different 'sonic fictions' are not just 'about' a different world but, formally we might say, are of that other world.

The Last Angel of History

In an interview for the Black Audio Film Collective's *The Last Angel of History* (1996), Eshun remarks that jungle, as a particular studio-produced music, does not have referents 'on the street', but conjures up more imaginary spaces and places (it does not represent something or somewhere pre-existent). This imaginary 'portrayal' is achieved by the new kinds of sound made available by new technologies (sampling, but also sequencers and drum machines). Elsewhere in the film, Eshun remarks on the way in which Black musicians have always been involved in releasing the potential of technological instruments, in exploiting their capacities – often, precisely, in using them against their intended purpose (paradigmatically – in terms of the subject matter of the film – in the use of turntables by DJs).

In *More Brilliant Than the Sun* Eshun also suggests that both sampling and scratching (what he calls 'scratchedelia') cannot, ultimately, be approached as textual practices. Rather, they constitute an 'abstract science', defined as a certain kinaesthetic and sensory intensification produced by the human-machine interface (this redefinition of science seems crucial to us). In his book Eshun attends to two trajectories of this science: hip hop and techno/jungle.[8] It is the second of these that *The Last Angel of History* focuses on, tracking the transit from Europe (Kraftwerk) to the US (especially Detroit), before tracing a further connection to the UK. We looked briefly at the lived fiction of UK rave culture at the end of Chapter 9, but might note here, again, that for Eshun these new kinds of machine music are necessarily future oriented (UK techno/rave culture was, to a large extent, called forth by this 'new' music). The technology, from turntables and vinyl to samplers and synthesisers, produced new sounds and rhythms, and calls forth new kinds of bodies adequate and appropriate to them. It is a sonic fiction not for you, but for something you might become through listening to the sound (when listening also involves bodily reaction).

Given that many recent afrofuturist 'visions' are enabled and indeed proceed from the alienating effects of technological development and the human-machine interface, it is germane, here, for us to attend more closely to alienation as a kind of method, something we have already introduced as a working concept.[9] Firstly, we might think of Sun Ra's alien perspective that is communicated, in part, by discordant music and noise produced through electronic keyboards and synths. Secondly, we might briefly return to Williams' tripartite Science Fiction schema and note that the first, 'putropia', can also be understood as a fiction of alienation but, in contrast to Williams' take (whereby putropia is understood as a fiction in which the bourgeois individual is set against the masses), here alienation is the very ground on which afrofutrurism develops its more liberatory fictions. *In More Brilliant Than the Sun* Eshun quotes Greg Tate on alienation:

In 'The Last Angel of History', Tate argued that 'the form itself, the conventions of the narrative in terms of the way it deals with subjectivity focuses on someone who is at odds with the apparatus of power in society and whose profound experience is one of cultural dislocation, alienation and estrangement. Most science fiction tales dramatically deal with how the individual is going to contend with these alienating, dislocating societies and circumstances and that pretty much sums up the mass experiences of black people in the post slavery twentieth century'. (Eshun 2003: 298)

As well as a documentary on certain aspects of Black music, from the Blues to Detroit techno, and its connections to Black Science Fiction writing (alongside Greg Tate, Octavia Butler and Samuel R. Delany are also interviewed), *The Last Angel of History* is also itself a work of Science Fiction, a kind of myth-science: it involves a fictioning of the archive of Black history which involves its own loops backwards and forwards in time (the narrator of the film – the 'data-thief' (see Figure 12.1) – is sent back from the future to research the 'mothership connection').[10] In its structure the film is also an example of the sampling and reversioning it looks at. Fiction (or perhaps a *re*-fictioning), becomes a method through which to rework consensual reality and its attendant subjectivities.

As Tate also suggests in the film (echoing the Dery quotation with which we began this chapter), from one perspective Black African-American experience has in fact always already been Science Fiction (Eshun also makes this explicit in his take on Paul Gilroy's *The Black Atlantic* as a major work of Science Fiction). The issue of how to write the future from the present – Fredric Jameson's temporal paradox – is, on the one hand, less relevant here in a situation in which Science Fiction, as Tate remarks, is precisely the lived present for many. Indeed, slavery lies at the heart of modernity – as its founding myth – with the 'middle passage' operating as the first alien abduction (hence the importance, in terms of afrofuturism, for Eshun and others, of the techno producers Drexciya, who mobilise the myth of an aquatic race born from the pregnant African slaves thrown overboard). On the other hand, Science Fiction becomes even more crucial in so far as the alternate perspectives it offers (most evident in what we have

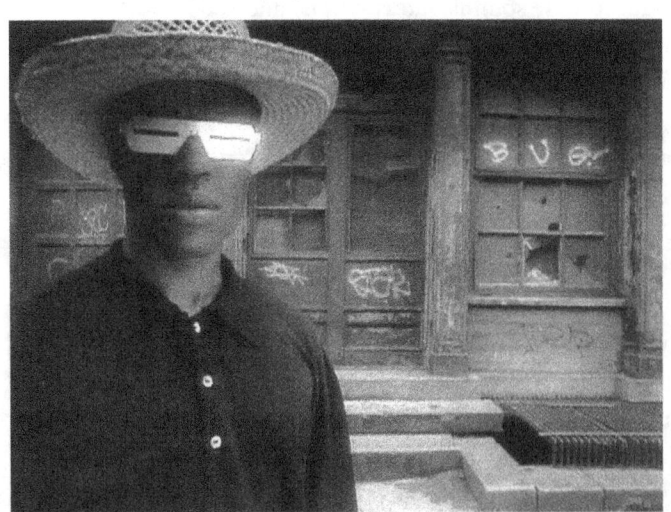

12.1 Black Audio Film Collective, still from *The Last Angel of History*, 1996 (© Smoking Dogs Films; Courtesy Lisson Gallery).

been calling myth-science) might be understood as a response to this already existing 'science-fiction nightmare' (to use Dery's phrase again). Afrofuturism is always already alienated then, or, more specifically, doubles the existing alienation of Black African-American subjectivity *through* Science Fiction.

Interlude: on Opacity and the Hold

In terms of a future poetics which might develop from the experiences of the middle passage, Édouard Glissant's writings are crucial. In his chapter on 'The Open Boat' in *Poetics of Relation*, Glissant writes about the experience of slave transportation:

> The first dark shadow was cast by being wrenched from their everyday, familiar land, away from protecting gods and tutelary community. But that is nothing yet. Exile can be bourne, even when it comes as a bolt from the blue. The second dark night fell as tortures and the deterioration of person, the result of so many incredible Gehennas. Imagine two hundred human beings crammed into a space barely capable of containing a third of them. Imagine vomit, naked flesh, swarming lice, the dead slumped, the dying crouched. Imagine, if you can, the swirling red of mounting to the deck, the ramp they climbed, the black sun on the horizon, vertigo, this dizzying sky plastered to the waves. Over the course of more than two centuries, twenty, thirty million people deported. Worn down, in a debasement more eternal than apocalypse. But that is nothing yet. (Glissant 2010: 5)

For Glissant, despite the abject horror of the middle passage, poetry (and what he calls 'relation') is also born in this forced exile (5). Indeed, it is creolisation itself, emerging on the shores of the new world, which holds out the possibility of a new kind of culture and language, one no longer tethered to roots and origins but which is, rather, rhizomatic and indeed nomadic (Glissant explicitly turns to Deleuze and Guattari in order to find this other way of thinking through what he calls an 'errant' identity).

Glissant also develops the key concept of opacity in relation to this errantry, as a name for that which remains invisible and thus resists any attempt to generalise or, we might say, interpret and co-opt in terms of more dominant – state – knowledges. Opacity, as we implied in Chapter 10, can be equated with ambiguity and the equivocal. It seems to us that some of the sonic fictions explored by Eshun also partake of this opacity (as does Sun Ra's myth-science) in so far as sonic fictions are not produced to be understood (in Ra's case, sonic works develop impossible and alien perspectives). But to stay with Glissant, these sonic fictions might also be said to involve both a nomadic 'thinking' (of flows and intensities as opposed to seeking origins, foundations and roots) and their own kind of creolisation, of other pasts and

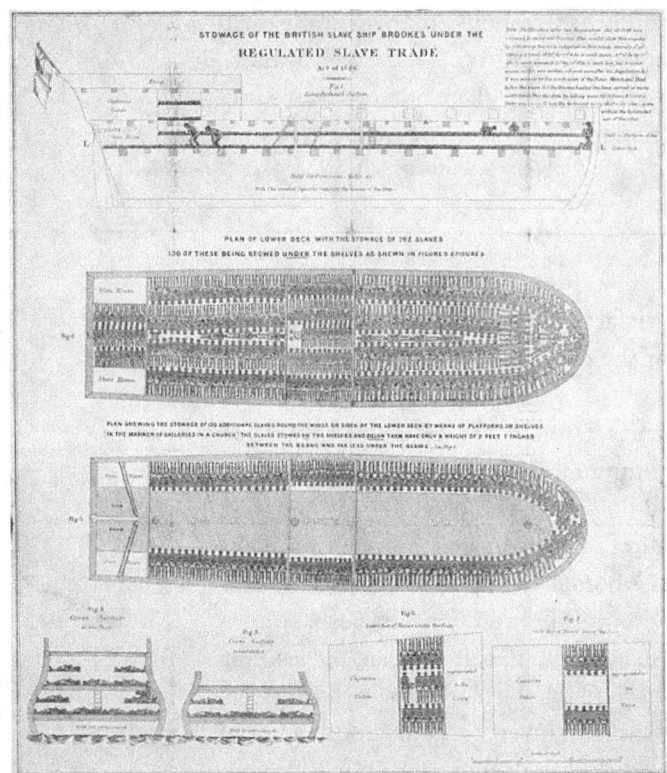

12.2 Stowage of the British Slave ship *Brookes* under the Regulated Slave Trade Act, circa 1789 (Wikimedia commons).

futures, but also of the human and the machine. Indeed, is it not the very opacity of these forms which allows other things to be set in motion, other possibilities (and impossibilities), not least of new communities being formed?

Stefano Harney and Fred Moten also address the imaginary produced by the middle passage – and especially containment in the ship's hold – in their book *The Undercommons* (2013). They are aware that this extreme alienation invariably produces a kind of haptic collectivity and, crucially, they also 'update' the idea of containment, attending to the new globalised manufacturing economies. As they remark, there is a continuum: 'Modern logistics is founded with the first great movement of commodities, the ones that could speak. It was founded in the Atlantic slave trade, founded against the Atlantic slave' (Harney and Moten 2013: 92). Slave ships, in this sense, are the first instruments of modern logistics (see Figure 12.2, which graphically presents the conditions for inhabitants of the hold). For Harney and Moten this Black imaginary – or simply a Blackness, 'where absolute nothingness and the world of things converge' (95) – has a distinctly sonic character. Indeed, the hold is 'black phonography's brutally experimental venue' (94). This is expressed, for example, in Don Cherry's 1969 recording *Mu*, which 'speaks of mu in relation to a circling or spiraling or ringing, roundness or rondo linking beginning and end, and to the wailing that accompanies entrance into and expulsion from sociality' (95).[11]

Again, it is alienation – here of an almost unbearable kind – which nevertheless produces the conditions for fantasy and the production of a certain kind of fiction which might begin to give cohesion and consistency, if not beauty, to trauma. In some cryptic passages in *The Undercommons* Harney and Moten also seem to be suggesting the possibility of a different kind of subjectivity or, in fact, a strange non-subjectivity attendant on this brutal experience – one which turns the experience of voidness into a point around which to spin a new mode of being:

Not simply to be among his own; but to be among his own in dispossession, to be among the ones who cannot own, the ones who have nothing and who, in having nothing, have everything. This is the sound of an unasked question. A choir versus acquisition, chant and moan and *Sprechsang*, babel and babble and gobbledy-gook, relaxin' by a brook or creek in Camarilo, singing to it, singing of it, for the bird of the crooked beak, the generative hook of *le petit negre*, the little nigger's comic spear, the cosmic crook of language, the burnin' and lootin' of pidgin, Bird's talk, Bob's talk, bard talk, bar talk, B talk, preparing the minds of the little negro steelworkers for meditation. (96–7)

These passages – that seem almost channeled – are as much a performance of a Black poetics as they are remarks about its possibility (we will be returning to Moten's own poetry in section three). As we suggest above, they point to a different, more fugitive mode of being – one 'at rest with the ones who consent not to be one' (97) – which is produced by this forced exile: 'It's a feeling, if you ride with it, that produces a certain distance from the settled, from those who determine themselves in space and time, who locate themselves in a determined history' (97). In fact, it seems to us that *The Undercommons* also exhibits its own opacity in so far as its style resists easy synopses or, indeed, at times, straightforward comprehension. It does not give ground to its readers and, indeed, might be said to be an expression of the very undercommons it writes about.

Science Fictioning the Archive

In the interview that comes at the end of *More Brilliant Than the Sun* Eshun talks of his interest in film music and, especially, in a certain disjunction between sound and image which is often manifest in cinema. This interest, it seems to us, is contin-ued in the film-essays of The Otolith Group – the collective formed by Eshun and Anjalika Sagar – which also involve a kind of productive disjunction between narra-tive/sound and images. Although the different works of The Otolith Group are not necessarily sonic fictions, they might be understood as a particular kind of audio-visual fictioning in so far as they involve the overlaying of a fictional narrative on archival and 'real' filmed footage. This form has a precursor in the work of Chris Marker (and especially *Sans Soleil*), and Eshun has written about his own indebtedness to this auteur as well as to two other key precursors: the Black Audio Film Collective and Harun Farocki.

The Otolith Group have produced films directly related to afrofuturism, including *Hydra Decapita* (2011), which uses the Drexciya mythos of the new aquatic race as its point of departure, and *People to be Reassembling* (2012), which 'reimagines the poetics of permutation' (Otolith Group 2017) in relation to the band Codona (which included Don Cherry, Colin Walcott and Naná Vasconcelas). More generally, The Otolith Group often attend to Science Fiction tropes and themes, for example in *Anathema* (2011), which 'reimagines the microscopic behaviour of liquid crystals undergoing turbulence as a sentient entity', and *Medium Earth* (2013), 'an audiovisual essay on the millennial time of geology and the infrastructural unconscious of Southern California' (Otolith Group 2017). Their films also address more urgent and contemporary concerns which often deploy more fictional set-ups alongside fact, as for example in *Nervus Rerum* (2008), a film about the refugee camp of Jenin, and *The Radiant* (2012), about the 2011 Tohoku earthquake in Japan triggered by a tsunami.[12] Finally, like *The Last Angel of History*, The Otolith Group's films often involve a particular take on memory and the archive, especially when this is connected to other – and different – futures.

In terms of this fictioning of archives as a counter to other, more dominant histories – and, indeed, the more general layering of a complex temporality – the *Otolith* trilogy (2003–9) contains many of the tropes and methods used throughout their practice. In these films, fiction is both content and method: in terms of the former, they bring together different 'fictions' – as well as imbricating the personal and political – in order to explore various past-potential futures. *Otolith 1* (2003), for example, involves a narrative about Sagar's grandmother meeting the first woman cosmonaut in India and the hopes of a communist Indian space programme, but it also narrates Sagar's own trip to Star City in Russia to experience micro-gravity (see Figure 12.3) – all alongside footage of the London anti-war demonstration of 2003.

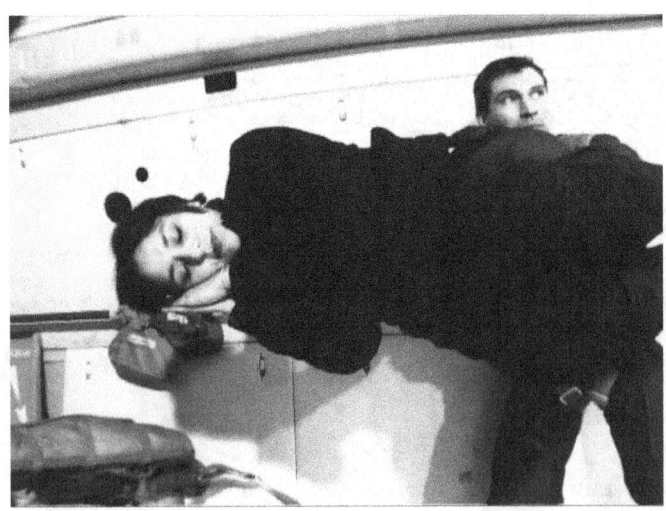

12.3 The Otolith Group, still from *Otolith I*, 2003 (courtesy of The Otolith Group).

In terms of method, it is this montaging of imagery and sound, but also the invented Science Fiction narrative of the film – told from the perspective of one of Sagar's space-dwelling descendants (who reads Sagar's diary) – which works to hold the film together and give the diverse elements a consistency. Could we also call this practice a form of myth-science in so far as it involves the instantiation of these very particular space-times – feedback loops from the past and future – which might operate as a resource and archive for other subjectivities in the present? (There are also other, more directly mythic elements, such as referring to the nuclear Manhattan Project as a 'return of the old gods' – in a reference, no doubt, to *Watchmen* – or in the very idea explored in the film of a future mutation of the human).

The second film in the *Otolith* trilogy (2007) continues the fictional narrative of Sagar's ancestor (in the form of letters), bringing this into conjunction with various images of labour from modern India and other places (the references to Farocki are especially pronounced in this second film). Once again there is the interest in hybrid temporalities, for example juxtaposing modernism's architectural promise, as manifest in Le Corbusier's Chandigarh, with existing slums in Mumbai. There is also an explicit interest in fictioning, here most obvious in the sustained focus on 'film city' in Mumbai, where old textile mills have been repurposed as film studios and where we witness the building/dismantling of a set based on London. With the above this second film returns us to some of the modes of fictioning we looked at in section one around the nesting of fictions and the 'revealing' of the apparatus of making fictions. More generally, there is an emphasis in the film on different locations referencing one another but also of other times haunting the present. The shuttling across temporal and spatial zones also relates to the way this film, as well as concerning various relations between communism, feminism and activism, refers to other fictions – Tarkovsky's *Stalker* for example (a film we mentioned in Chapter 8 and which is a kind of future-precursor to existing postindustrial spaces), but also Ballard, whose take on architecture is brought to bear on Le Corbusier.

The third film of the trilogy (2009) is somewhat different, involving as it does a meditation on Satyajit Ray's un-made movie *The Alien*. In this film the characters – who are situated in a kind of non-space – meditate on their relation to one another and on their existence as alienated images who dream of being 'projected' (at one point they also refer to themselves as 'scripts' awaiting actualisation). Here fiction is a method for reflection not only on memory and the future but also, more generally, on the nature of fiction itself – as in the search for people who might play the characters or, indeed, in relation to some of the other people involved in the intended narrative, for example the Science Fiction writer Arthur C. Clarke. There are further scenes which reference the pre-production of fiction, for example where the camera tracks across a kind of laid out archive containing Science Fiction comic strips, images of altered landscapes and such like. As with the other films in the trilogy, there is a nesting of fictions at work – in this case an encircling of Ray's unrealised movie in The Otolith Group's own film – but we note a difference too from the novels of Hoban and Ballard and others, similarly discussed in section one as employing the nesting of fictions. An archive of alternate pasts and futures is presented by the Group, which are not the fictional projections of a single character or subjectivity, but a collection of diverse cultural and social, personal and collective, technical and aesthetic material; or we might say that

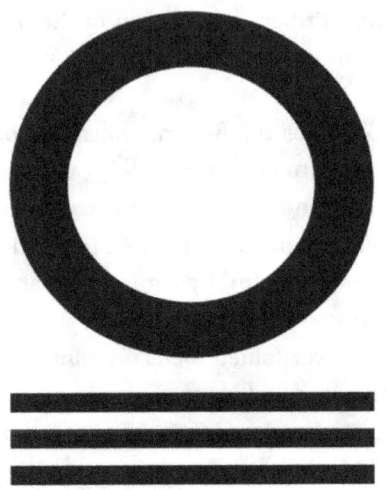

12.4 The Otolith Group logo (courtesy of The Otolith Group).

the Groups's films produce diverse collectivities and perspectives that invite comparison and translation even through their synthesis.[13]

Finally, it seems to us that The Otolith Group might itself be understood as a scene of sorts (in the sense that we explored in Chapter 9), involving collective filmmaking but also curating and the organisation of other events, many of which contain Science Fiction themes and methodologies. In this sense, it can be said that The Otolith Group exist as much through the conversations they have between themselves and with others as through their artistic output.[14] In a promotional film for the 2010 Turner Prize, the Group are presented as living and working in a single house in London, producing what Eshun terms 'a post-studio practice' of collective filmmaking. Eshun also suggests that the name of the Group implies, to some extent, that the collective is 'faceless' (2010). Might we even say that the name, partly, gives the Group a certain opacity? We suggest that in working collectively, The Otolith Group establish a society of time travellers that operate through audio and video technology. For we take the moniker Otolith – which is the name for a structure within the ear of vertebrates that is sensitive to sound, gravity and movement – as a term that identifies specific orientations (or approaches) to film and sonic works. The name is important then, just as the names Crass, TOPY and Spiral Tribe were important for those collectives addressed in Chapter 9. We find support for this latter comparison in The Otolith Group's use of a particular symbol – or sigil – in the third film (itself borrowed from a Godard movie) (see Figure 12.4). It is for all these reasons that we consider The Otolith Group as a case of science fictioning. But since they present or edit perspectives of non-European, diasporic and postcolonial experience, art, literature and film as alternative past and future histories of the Earth, we also recognise the Group's practice as a case of myth-science.

Notes

1   Although this chapter concerns itself specifically with afrofuturism, we want to note in passing the recent development of other non-Western futurisms which also turn to recent technological developments (in this case computer animation), as, for example, with Lawrence Lek's film-essay *Sinofuturism* (2016), and Sophia Al Maria's Gulf-Futurism in her film *The Future was a Desert* (2016).

2   It is worth noting, however, the possibility within this genre (and Science Fiction more generally) of the deployment of more residual cultures which offer an alternative, or even an opposition, to the dominant. This is especially the case with post-apocalyptic fictions such as Starhawk's *The Fifth Sacred Thing* (1993) or, more pertinent in relation to the arguments we develop in this chapter around formal experimentation, Russell Hoban's *Riddley Walker* (1980) (see our discussion of this book in Chapter 5).

3   Steven Shaviro's writings involve a similar take on Science Fiction as a speculative genre (which has, in this sense, much in common with experimental science per se). His recent book *Discognition* (2015) utilises Science Fiction as a kind of theoretical resource for thinking around problems of consciousness (and its possible futures), and, as such, has resonances with some of the material in the third section of our own book. However, whereas we are interested in a certain embodiment or instantiation of fiction in the world, for Shaviro it is Science Fiction's abstraction from reality which is crucial (albeit, for him, fiction does involve its own kind of embodiment of the colder abstractions of reason and rational thought). We will return to another, earlier, example of Shaviro's writing on Science Fiction, very briefly, at the beginning of Chapter 21.

4   We will return to the explicitly Derridean aspect of a future-trace in relation to financial instruments in Chapter 21.

5   Tricky and Topley Bird's gender blurring seems an especially interesting development of myth-science.

6   To quote Eshun:

> what I call the Sonic Fiction of records . . . is the entire series of things which swing into action as soon as you have music with no words. As soon as you have music with no words, then everything else becomes crucial: the label, the sleeve, the picture on the cover, the picture on the back, the titles. All these become jump-off points for your route through the music, or for the way the music captures you and abducts you into its world. (1998: 178–9)

7   We address Left accelerationism more directly in Chapter 18, especially in relation to the Promethean impulse.

8   In terms of myth-science, the apotheosis of this trajectory would seem to be Rammellzee and his 'Gothic Futurism', involving what Eshun calls a 'magico-mathematic' warfare conducted at the level of the symbolic (1998: 32). In relation to some of the work of the previous section, we might say Rammellzee opens up other space-times through the disruption of consensual scripts (and, indeed, the alphabet). His 'wild style' also involves the invention of other symbolic systems where, for example, graffiti operates as a kind of sigil magic (see Rammellzee 1979).

9   An important corrective to this take on afrofuturism and technology is Louis Onuorah Chude-Sokei's work, which traces the connections between technological development

(as this relates to the sonic but is also evident in Science Fiction) and race (and the history of slavery more particularly) (Chude-Sokei 2016). We address Chude-Sokei's ideas in Chapter 22.

10   Eshun has spoken recently about the doubling of this figure, or how the narrator and data-thief, although both played by Eddie George, are two distinct characters in the film. In the same discussion Eshun also points to the aural complexity of *The Last Angel of History* as well as the very particular use of colour and various camera filters. Ayesha Hameed, in the same conversation, also talks about a counterintuitive use of different colours (for example, sepia – often associated with memories and the past – for images of the future), and the strange use of 'props' by the data-thief in the film. See Eshun et al. 2017.

11   Cherry's music was one inspiration for Nathaniel Mackey's book, *Splay Anthem* (2006), from where Harney and Moten take the above suggestion; the other inspiration was the Dogon 'Song of the Andoumboulou', itself a piece of myth-science, and one Eshun also refers to.

12   T. J. Demos writes about *Nevus Rerum*'s refusal of representation in relation to Glissant and a 'cinema of opacity' (2013: 127). He also develops a convincing thesis about how the film involves a 'fictionalisation' of the reality of the camp which involves both a use of fiction as resource (in this case Genet and Pessoa) but also a refusal of the typical modus operandi of the documentary in terms of truth-telling (fictionalisation involves a 'denial of a transparent reality' in this sense) (122).

13   In relation to this nesting there is also a compelling insertion of found footage of an 'Exploding galaxy' performance – again a fiction with a fiction. In passing we want to note another of those minor connectors between different parts of our book: as we saw in Chapter 9, Genesis P-Orridge was himself part of the 'Exploding Galaxy' group. The latter had a profound effect on him and thus on the subsequent performance fictions he initiated and contributed towards.

14   In relation to this we would point to the catalogue *A Long Time Between Suns* (The Otolith Group 2009), which records a series of such conversations and itself gathers a very particular archive of images (alongside essays).

13   Wildness and Alienation in the Networks of the Digital

The most likely future is one in which we only have ourselves and this planet.

Martine Syms, 'The Mundane Afrofuturist Manifesto'

SO FAR IN this second section we have focused on what we see as the key characteristic of myth-science: the instantiation of alternate perspectives and futures often manifested through collective endeavour (and which are different to those offered by dominating institutions and cultures). In this, the collaborative production of music and art in the work of Sun Ra and his Arkestra, the sonic fictions of the Black Atlantic and the productions of The Otolith Group have all served as examples of the transformation of the living present – through the instantiation of new and shared narratives – at least for those scenes or groups concerned with producing new temporal, historical or social perspectives. It is in this sense that myth-science can be said to be successful, at least to a degree.

It remains the case, however, that in the contexts of America and Europe (as well as elsewhere) colonial legacies still dominate and racism and discrimination of all kinds are an aspect of everyday life (often violently so). What use then is myth-science and sonic fictioning given this contemporary reality? Martine Syms poses this question in 'The Mundane Afrofuturist Manifesto', published online in 2013, in which the artist calls upon anyone willing to join her 'in the future of black imagination' to burn works ('stupidities') that reference Sun Ra and other afrofuturist figures and tropes, including 'Jive-talking aliens . . . Magical negroes . . . Enormous self-control in light of great suffering . . . Inexplicable skill in the martial arts . . . Metallic colors' (Syms 2013). The directness and humour of 'The Mundane Afrofuturist Manifesto' is arresting, and Syms' emphasis on the importance of the mundane may signal a development of – but equally a limit to – myth-science. It is certainly a theme that needs addressing. To this end, this chapter will discuss Syms' critique of afrofuturism which, it seems to us, delivers a further discourse *on and of* alienation as both cognitive event *and* feeling. In this, we further address the idea of *alienation as method*, introduced in the last chapter.

This is then followed by a comparison with two other texts – Laboria Cuboniks' 'Xenofeminist Manifesto' (2015) and Jack Halberstam's 'Charming for the Revolution: A Gaga Manifesto' (2013). These two manifestos can be said to engage with fiction (or science fictioning) but also alienation, as well as rejecting mainstream and academic discourses concerning class, race, gender and sexuality. Despite certain differences we find a further common theme (which, again, seems important to all myth-science practices): the collective and collaborative production of images or fictions for a people either to come or yet to be free. It is then to this narration and interrogation of terrestrial, human alienation (rather than an extra-terrestrial and inhuman indifference) that we now turn, so as to further progress our discussion of practices offering alternate perspectives, and of the ways in which contemporary and digital cultures might develop or challenge the myth-science practices of another age. The texts and practices explored in this chapter signal a further shift in our book in so far as they attend more directly to the terrain of the political, and to questions around science and technology that are invariably intertwined with the latter.

Everyday Life and its Discontents

Why would references to Sun Ra need to be avoided (even burned)? The reasons are many and would certainly include the appropriation of afrofuturism by white cultures – and here this ranges from the discourses of academics like ourselves to Disneyesque representations and the products of entertainment corporations. But it might also include those artists engaging with afrofuturism as expressions of blackness without political efficacy. Indeed, the influence of Sun Ra and those who follow the musician would seem, according to Syms, to produce fun but also escapism and illusion. Syms' manifesto points out that:

> Out of five hundred thirty-four space travellers, fourteen have been black. An all-black crew is unlikely. Magic interstellar travel and/or the wondrous communication grid can lead to an illusion of outer space and cyberspace as egalitarian. This dream of utopia can encourage us to forget that outer space will not save us from injustice and that cyberspace was prefigured upon a 'master/slave' relationship. (Syms 2013)[1]

Although Syms does not directly use the term, it seems to us that her manifesto is both determined by and concerned with alienation, as evidenced by a certain tone of negativity and, indeed, the rejection of existing discourse. As she declares at the beginning of the manifesto: 'The undersigned, being alternately pissed off and bored, need a means of speculation and asserting a different set of values with which to re-imagine the future' (Syms 2013). If Syms is responding to the limitations of the present, the impetus for the artist's rejection of escapism in music and art correlates to a further sense of alienation when confronted with afrofuturism itself (particularly in relation to the context of everyday life):

> I was a black person using technology so in this one year I kept getting invited to all these Afrofuturist events . . . And I was not really feeling it. I thought some of the claims were just a little too self-serious. Around the time there was a noticeable increase in deaths from police brutality, and some of it just felt extremely strange. Senseless. I had already been thinking about that and responding to that. (Syms 2016a)

This concern for the stark and violent realities of contemporary conditions (as oppose to anything 'off-world') is found not just in the artist's manifesto but also throughout Syms' practice which might, in itself, be considered a form of mundane afrofuturism or Science Fiction. As in her manifesto, Sym's practice is concerned with the way entertainment technologies and cultures are productive of notions of black history and culture and can be said to mediate perspectives on reality. How Syms' addresses such problems through art practice was illustrated by the exhibition *Fact and Trouble* presented at the ICA in 2016 (see Figure 13.1). The show addressed the difference between lived experience and its representation, as well as exploring how images of the black diaspora circulate globally through audio and video material – which the artist suggests operates as a kind prosthetic memory producing a digital 'collective imaginary' (Syms 2016c). To explore this idea, *Fact and Trouble* featured several works, including a collage presented as a version of Sym's performance titled *Misdirected Kiss* (2016) – which refers to a film in which a black woman receives an accidental kiss – and that mimics a desktop collection of images personal to the artist's development. Another work, *Lessons* (2014), comprising of a series of film clips, is described by Syms as a commercial for black radical traditions (Syms 2016c); it is presented on screens that sit in a space inscribed with large black letters spelling out 'LIGHTLY, SLIGHTLY, POLITELY'. Each word has a wall to itself, and the artist has acknowledged that the three words together 'means something done perfectly. It's one way of being. . . . [a] good framework for thinking about the idea of tradition and cultural inheritance' (Syms quoted in Linden 2016). As Gracie Linden points out in an article on Syms, 'LIGHTLY, SLIGHTLY, POLITELY' may refer to the value placed on lightness of skin colour for racial passing (and we might think too, in relation to black women in fashion and the media), as well as referring to a polite demeanor that convention demands of black women, both in the past and today (Linden 2016). The exhibition, in part, addresses the artist's perception that identities constructed through images (and in particular social media) have 'taken on Hollywood cues' (Syms 2016b). In this, as with other works by the artist, fiction and myth are explored within those economies of communication and representation that are common in everyday life. For Syms, if afrofuturism is to have any purchase today, artists should follow Sym's lead.

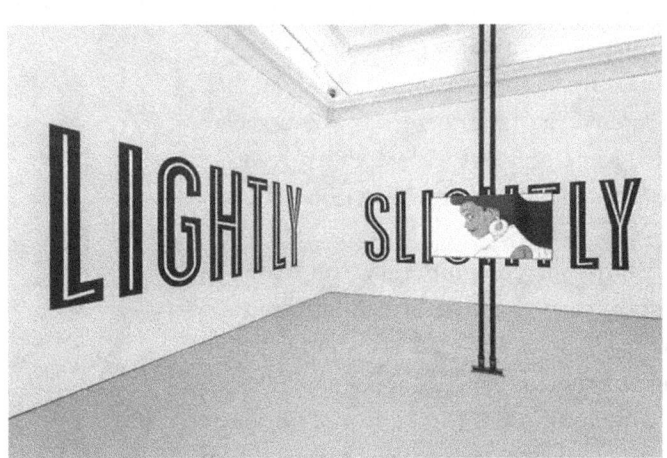

13.1 Martine Syms, installation image from *Fact and Trouble*, ICA, London, 2016 (courtesy of the artist and Sadie Coles Gallery).

To return to the manifesto, and despite the negativity, Syms does propose that a future different to the present can be achieved through a critique of the cultures of white domination, which would then lead towards a development of notions of blackness and a celebration of 'black humanity'. In this, she rejects science and fact in favour of the emotionally true and the vernacular. In fact, she asserts that blackness is 'possibly futuristic' and, referencing Elizabeth Alexander, adds that it moves towards a metaphysical space of wild imagination (Syms 2013). However, this declaration is followed by sixteen restraints to be placed on wild imagination, including no interstellar travel (travel being difficult, expensive and time-consuming), no aliens (unless the connection is tenuous and distant), and no alternative reality. To emphasise its commitment to the cause of the mundane, the manifesto is illustrated with an image of a woman – a fictional character – who features in an audio piece by Syms and the musician Neil Reinalda entitled *Most Days* (2014). This sonic fiction presents the suitably mundane life of Chanel Washington in Los Angeles in 2050 and follows the principles of 'The Mundane Manifesto' produced by Geoff Ryman and others at the Clarion West workshop in Seattle (Ryman et al. 2004). Indeed, the tone of Syms' manifesto draws heavily on a declaration made by Ryman and his collaborators, in which they insist on a Science Fiction that is of the known world (and not of a future or alternate reality). We understand the attraction of this principle for Syms, who, as indicated above, is concerned that politics and struggle are elided by afrofuturisms which might be regarded as wishful thinking. Where does this leave Syms' appeal to wildness and imagination though? And what of the artist's relation to myth-science?

Realness in Myth

If Syms' science fictioning can be thought of as myth-science at all, it would be through an inversion of Sun Ra's equation (which we looked at in Chapter 11), whereby myth is presented as equivalent to so-called reality (in that both are a lie). In rejecting science and fact as vehicles of white supremacy, and by insisting on the importance of an emotional register as an index for reality, Syms introduces the notion of *realness*.[2] This is the inversion of the equation mention above, for so-called reality is not exactly a lie for Syms. Certainly, the daily experience of racism shapes reality for many, and this is not adequately addressed or captured through impossible fictions. Secondly, Syms argues that existing myth is not to be ignored, for myth can be said to contain truth (it may well have a high truth content); an idea explained in a lecture entitled 'Vernacular Lessons of the Tradition' given at the Walker Art Centre (2014), in which Syms suggests it is best to accept myth as fact and to mine myth for truth. To be specific, Syms focuses on the realness of (or in) myth; a realness registered through emotional and vernacular cultural responses to white domination; a realness presented as a contrast to white perspectives promoted through the sciences that are also encountered as an aspect of everyday (or so-called) reality.

The artist's means of excavating this truth are varied, including writing and print but also the use of repetition and editing techniques which may sound like the methods used by William Burroughs but are certainly employed towards different ends and from a different perspective. For Syms manipulates material and recordings to glimpse not a new reality exactly, but realness (as a perspective). An example is an early work titled *My Only Idol is Reality* (2007), produced by re-recording a video-tape of an MTV show, *The Real World*, to the point where a discussion about race and power disintegrates both verbally (when the protagonists become upset) and physically (when the images on the tape become streaked and warped). Through this process of re-editing in which images degrade, conversation is compressed and the grain of the tape abstracts the recorded image. The effects of this process emphasise the abrasive and destructive conversation between a white female and black male, which escalates until the man tells the woman that race and power equals racism and therefore, as she is white and has power, she is racist. It is at this point, where little more can be said – and which is the most compelling and arresting moment of the film – that *My Only Idol is Reality* can be said to present the emotional tone of a breakdown as 'realness': what might seem to some as an overreaction – which is the case with the female protagonist in the film – is a measure of how deeply racism marks experience and relations.

Here we note that the term 'realness' is not unfamiliar to scholars of performance and queer studies or African-American culture. Groups belonging to the New York ballroom scene in the 1980s, captured in the documentary film *Paris is Burning* (1990), use the term realness to define a specific quality of their performances, which has been much discussed in academic circles concerned with performativity and representation, sometimes in very critical terms.[3] Syms uses the term differently, but the performances documented in *Paris is Burning* have some relevance for our discussion, not least in helping us understand that Syms' gives a new definition to the idea of realness.

Directed by Jennie Livingston, *Paris is Burning* depicts the ball and Voguing scenes of the late 1980s in New York, in which black and Latino gay men and transgender people formed 'Houses' or families, competing to appear as the most 'real' in categories that reference straight male identities, young street styles and supermodels.[4] Possessing 'realness' – being able to pass for something you are not – was the highest form of praise amongst competitors at the balls, yet the scene also explicitly signals that identities involve performative acts, and little more than that, and therefore might be thought to be hardly real at all. One legacy of the ballroom scene and of the film's critical reception is that realness presented as truth can be seen as questionable, for the Houses of Pepper LeBeija, Angie Xtravaganza and Willi Ninja documented in *Paris is Burning* present realness as a performance.

Is Syms herself engaging with more performance and fiction in her use of the term realness? The answer might be 'of course', but this does not mean that performance and fiction are devoid of truth. Syms' move to instigate realness through an emotional register – as the emotional response to injustice and discrimination – cannot, we suggest, be easily dismissed (for blackness, like whiteness, can be said to have, or be comprised of, real affects). And producing notions of blackness as realness might be seen as a necessary strategy for developing a transformative politics and imagined, future communities.[5] It seems Syms' notion of realness, which in the first instance refers to emotion, has little to do with problems of representation, appearance or the performativity of identity explored by postmodern theory or the identity politics of the last century. 'Realness', for Syms, might equate to something like Peggy Phelan's notion of performance as a singular episode or action, which Phelan opposes to the performative aspects of acts or gestures which circulate as representation (the identification and meaning of a performative act relying on the iteration of existing regimes of representation and relations) (Phelan 2000).[6] In making this distinction, Phelan is concerned with correcting the elision of the difference between performance and performativity in mass culture and in academia and art too, arguing that in performativity 'What does not get circulated is that affective experience, affect with an "a", the emotional specificity of the experience itself' (2000: 133).[7] We suggest here that 'realness' registers the 'emotional specificity of the experience', that aspect of performance that escapes representation (or that in representation becomes something else). More generally, exploring the notion of a difference between performance and performativity seems relevant to a discussion of Syms' work in that the artist addresses the communications of a global or digital mass culture in relation to instantiations of the vernacular and emotion. It might be said then, that by employing techniques of editing and representation Syms attempts to register the *affective truth* in myth – as the vernacular and emotion – that can be elided by mass-produced representations.

Staying in the Groove

It is easy to see how playing with myth as 'unrealness' can turn sour and futile when reality (and myth too for that matter) is not just limiting but deadly; certainly, it seems to us, Syms' 'Mundane Afrofuturist Manifesto' is an attempt to confront this problem. If this seems a bleak form of afrofuturism or myth-science (if it can be called a myth-science at all) then it is because Syms believes, as she articulated in her lecture at the Walker Art Centre, that 'There is no better . . . There just is' (Syms 2014); Syms has no time for the promises of progress. But if progress is off-limits, if there is no future-looping of a different or alternate world through art, for Syms there is still hope, and it is kept in play through another kind of looping, or we might say through fictioning.

Building on her comments on repetition, towards the end of her lecture on 'Vernacular Lessons of the Tradition' Syms states that she likes to stay in the groove, or in the loop, whether through vinyl records or rolls of film (2014). Her statement implies that repetition may negate (the promises of) progress but that it does not contradict expectation or hope. This is explained further in the last lesson of the lecture, 'Tradition is what you take but also what you make', and a case in point is Syms' discussion of her artist book *New Guards* (2014), which presents scans of a water-damaged copy of *The Black Panthers* by Stephen Shames (2006). This re-presentation through publication is composed of pages which have been torn and then stuck to each other, creating new, cut-up (or ripped-up) images. *New Guards* demonstrates a concern for and utilisation of radical traditions – also evidenced in other work through a use of analogue and digital material concerning blackness in art and mass media, and, indeed, in Syms' use of photographs and films produced by her father – which is, we suggest, a fictioning of a particular kind concerned in part with the history of media and technologies of various kinds. Through these technological means of staying in the groove, Syms would seem to imply there are ways to counter the influences and emotion-generating and affective productions of dominant mass medias that can elide 'realness' (as blackness). Indeed, her presentations seem to exist in marked contrast to the presentations produced by those corporations and state institutions which attempt to cash-in on or manage multiculturalism (through images devoid of racial histories, conflicts and tensions); an impression which is strengthened through engaging with Syms art, lectures and writing as a whole. In this, it seems to us that the radical traditions and narratives which Syms draws upon, and indeed the analogue technologies and techniques she employs, are forms of residual culture (which involve collective memory) to be found within mass media and digital spheres of information and entertainment. This residual culture is drawn upon to fiction 'realness' (as blackness, and as the collective and individual experience of racism) which arrests or counters other fictions and Spectacle.

In an important observation in her lecture at the Walker Art Centre, Syms states that if 'psychographics flow from demographics', then an argument can be made for a black aesthetic (2014). Syms' counterexample to this is the whiteness of surfing and surf culture. She suggests that one cannot think of surf culture without thinking about who had access to certain beaches and who was excluded from them. To further explain this point, she references the seminal surf film *The Endless Summer* (1966), directed by Bruce Brown, which documents the antics and travels of two surfers who traverse the world in search of perfect waves. This, for Syms, is a quintessential image of whiteness: here we have a notion of fictioning that has, at its kernel, the realities of a racially divided culture. And we can understand that, in wanting to stay in the groove of the *New Guards* – of the Black Panther project with its investment in community and education – Syms maintains a hope in something different which is to be achieved in the future by looping the radical traditions of the past in the present. In this, blackness itself (like realness) might be seen as a fictioning, operating critically and speculatively within contemporary social fields.

A Politics of Alienation

If Syms' afrofuturism is not exactly a perspectivism as defined in previous chapters, we would argue that at the very least it is a perspective of blackness (produced through an emotional register) that challenges a perceived instrumentality of science-fact. Indeed, Syms conceives of Mundane Afrofuturism as 'the ultimate laboratory for world-building outside of imperialist, capitalist, white patriarchy' (Syms 2013). We find a similar concern for alienation and world-building in another online declaration, 'The Xenofeminist (XF) Manifesto', published in 2015 by the collective Laboria Cuboniks, whose aim is to seize 'alienation as an impetus to generate new worlds' (Laboria Cuboniks 2015). In contrast to Syms' manifesto, and perhaps too in contrast to any myth-science primarily concerned with presenting alternate histories, Laboria Cuboniks' commitment to world-generation is grounded in a belief in the actual possibilities of the sciences to bring about change. The myth-science practices we have discussed so far do not present the sciences and technology as a means, in themselves, for overcoming oppression, but rather as mediums for developing perspectives or producing sonic and impossible fictions. In comparison, Laboria Cuboniks proposal might seem more down-to-earth, in that the Xenofeminists view the sciences as possibly transformative of societies hitherto dominated by patriarchy and other discriminatory interests. However, in this narrative, it seems to us, it can be said that science is the myth. By this, we do not mean that Laboria Cuboniks are in error (that they believe in something that is a lie) when presenting what they term technoscience as transformative, but that their collective science fictionings of new worlds, peoples and modes of existence is orientated, in part at least, by the idea – or, again, myth – of science as liberator. Indeed, we suggest that 'The XF Manifesto' – a digital document concerned with emergent rather than residual cultures – envisages agencies (or new social bodies and collectives) resulting from the combination of alienation and the advent of new technosciences. Whatever the differences between the Mundane Afrofuturists and the Xenofeminists, alienation is a shared concern, one that is explicitly spelt out in Laboria Cuboniks' manifesto: 'We are all alienated – but have we ever been otherwise? It is through, and not despite, our alienated condition that we can free ourselves from the muck of immediacy' (2015). In this, we sugest, Xenofeminism proceeds through *alienation as method*.

If alienation and its products are the driving force (and material) of Xenofeminism world-building, then the manifesto makes it equally clear who will thrive in these new worlds: anyone deemed 'unnatural' or oppressed through naturalising ideologies – for 'The XF Manifesto' opposes natural orders of all kinds – when this includes women (or anyone discriminated against through pregnancy or child-rearing duties), queers, transgender people and the differently abled. All of these have an important part to play in the development of new technoscientific innovation, which is, 'The XF Manifesto' declares, unpredictable and caught in feedback loops with culture (2015).

In comparison with Syms' concern for the mundane and realness, Laboria Cuboniks may be said to have their own (and possibly not too dissimilar) notion of a reality that is produced by or registered through an alienation resulting from exploitation and discrimination. And in terms similar to those used by Syms, 'The XF Manifesto' also declares a war on illusion and wishful thinking. In contrast, however, and as already made clear, the manifesto does not reject science and fact – for Xenofeminism is a rational project – nor does it eschew ideas of progress. Instead, 'The XF Manifesto' calls upon 'alien kin' to avoid melancholia presented under 'the guise of being realistic' (2015). This is then the mobilisation of a kind of Science Fiction (in its space anthro-pology guise, to return to Raymond Williams' definitions) that looks beyond the 'realistic' when the latter is presented as a limit to social change. Further similarities and dissimilarities between Mundane Afrofuturism and Xenofeminism can be found in relation to how both view technology. Just as we find that the fictioning of realness and blackness in Syms' work is produced through technological processes (the channeling of loops and grooves), we find a similar emphasis placed on technological processes and feedback loops in Laboria Cuboniks' manifesto. In a passage discussing the ways in which the internet and cyberspace quickly develop platforms for essentialist identities, morality and the fetishisation of oppression, 'The XF Manifesto' makes a demand for 'superior' forms of corruption (2015). We might compare this call for corruption with Syms' works that present deterioration (*New Guards* and *My Only Idol is Reality*), but instead of pressing the rewind button and looping the past in the present, Xenofeminism advocates a fast-forward mode so as to loop a projected future in the here and now. And this requires a science fictioning of the everyday, which operates through a process which Laboria Cuboniks refer to as hyperstition, a term which originated with the Cybernetic culture research unit (Ccru), a kind of para-academic research laboratory set up by the cultural theorist Sadie Plant and then led by Nick Land after her departure from academia.[8] Laboria Cuboniks write:

> The task of collective self-mastery requires a hyperstitional manipulation of desire's puppet-strings, and deployment of semiotic operators over a terrain of highly networked cultural systems. The will will always be corrupted by the memes in which it traces, but nothing prevents us from instrumentalizing this fact, and calibrating it in view of the ends it desires. (2015)

Here we find a manifesto attuned to desires made apparent through alienation – desires that do not sit well with 'natural orders'. We will return to hyperstition in Chapter 16, in relation to the practice of 0[rphan] d[rift>], but suffice to say at this point that hyperstitional manipulation operates – as Eshun has suggested all Science Fiction operates – to calibrate the trajectories of the present with desired futures. If this is not a perspectivism exactly, it certainly seems to involve the advent of new (Xeno)feminist perspectives:

> Xenofeminism indexes the desire to construct an alien future with a triumphant X on a mobile map. This X does not mark a destination. It is the insertion of a topological-keyframe for the formation of a new logic . . . we militate for ampliative capacities, for spaces of freedom with a richer geometry than the aisle, the assembly line, and the feed. (Laboria Cuboniks 2015)

The manifesto's heralding of a 'triumphant X on a mobile map' produces many questions. It is clear that the futures desired by Xenofeminism relate strongly to imagined scientific and technological transformation. What might we find through this new 'topological-keyframe', what new perspectives, what new logic? The production, we expect, of many natures devoid of any single order, or at least devoid of organisations enforcing univocal or dominating narratives. 'The Xenofeminist Manifesto' alludes to this when offering the maxim: 'If nature is unjust, change nature!' (2015). This may seem to counter earlier protestations against natural orders (and the affirmation of many natures), in that the maxim suggests that there currently exists a dominating nature which human culture, through technology, will be able to transform. Is this then a contradiction at the heart of Xenofeminism, understood as a politics that, through science, wants to transform a nature that it also names as an ideological, patriarchal idea and invention? Perhaps not, for a distinction can be made between existing notions of nature (produced by essentialism or science) and the diversity of natures to come – riven and produced by desire and alienation and technological processes applied without respect for 'natural order'. To grasp this logic, we refer to a statement made earlier in the manifesto which calls for a thousand sexes to bloom, demonstrating that Xenofeminism has no interest in depleting the number of genders in the world, but rather in cultivating any number of sexes and sexual orientations. The manifesto states: '"Gender abolitionism" is shorthand for the ambition to construct a society where traits currently assembled under the rubric of gender, no longer furnish a grid for the asymmetric operation of power' (2015).

It seems to us that the new logic of Xenofeminism calls for a certain 'wildness' (or, as in Syms' manifesto, a call to 'wild imagination') to frustrate power and representation. This is a way of thinking that Xenofeminism extends to the cause of the abolition of class but also of race, in which difference is acknowledged but is no longer a basis for discrimination; a decolonisation, then, as the recognition of many natures (and many perspectives). In short, experimenting with wild diversity is a good bet for the logic marked by X. And this leads us to our third manifesto, 'Charming for the Revolution: A Gaga Manifesto' by Jack Halberstam (2013).

Wildness

We have explored myth-science as the instantiation of the impossible – or as Sun Ra suggests, that 'which has not been of the known reality before' (quoted in Szwed 2000: 329). It seems to us that Jack Halberstam calls for something similar in 'A Gaga Manifesto', which (following the anarchist Emma Goldman) advocates for the potential of the impractical. Halberstam explains that the practical 'is limited to what we can already imagine', whereas the '*impractical* as a space of possibility and newness' promises an epistemological break (Halberstam 2013). However, like Syms and Laboria Cuboniks, Halberstam does not look to the cosmos or aliens from another world to escape the present, and is similarly materialist (and Earth-bound) when proposing impracticality as a path to something different. Importantly, in Halberstam's view, nothing (social) seems to escape transformation of one kind or another, with technology playing no small part in this (again the sciences are presented as important social agents). Halberstam states:

> the 'existing conditions' under which the building blocks of human identity were imagined and cemented in the last century – what we call gender, sex, race, and class – have changed so radically that new life can be glimpsed ahead. Our task is not to shape this new life into identifiable and comforting forms, not to 'know' this 'newness' in advance, but rather, as Nietzsche suggests, to impose upon the categorical chaos and crisis that surrounds us only 'as much regularity and form as our practical needs require'. (2013)

It is not that the grids of power or modulations of control no longer have a hold on desire and sexuality – though Halberstam makes it clear that the organisations and revolutions of gender and the sexes described by commentators such as Shulamith Firestone, a Promethean feminist writing at the end of the last century (who we address later on), have come and gone. Rather, the 'existing conditions' are no longer what they once were and they will be even more radically different in the future. In this, Halberstam understands heterosexuality today – through dialogue with Paul B. Preciado's work[9] – as a political and state-sponsored 'procreation technology', and homosexuality, similarly, as a 'state-approved' form of intimacy (2013). In a statement which echoes Xenofeminism, Halberstam declares the need for a new politics of gender and desire to short-circuit 'the grids of control' (2013); a goal to be pursued, however, through wild disjunctions rather than a new logic or mundane realness (as Laboria Cuboniks and Syms respectively call for).

Between Chaos and Control

Halberstam's reticence to produce over-determined fictions, in terms of identitarian politics, sets the Gaga manifesto apart from the others addressed in this chapter. However, a concern for diversity is found in all three of our examples: there is a shared belief in the possibility of resisting the modulations of various narratives and interests produced by mainstream cultures and the state and capitalism. We suggest that, to an extent, in all three manifestos such a resistance is fictioned through instantiations of alienation (and a rejection of existing conditions) and through events or works which present or generate disintegration, disorder, corruption or mutation as a frustration of control (and indeed, in some instances, as a loss of control).

However, Halberstam's concept of wildness does not just concern the looping of a radical past or future in the present, as in the Mundane Afrofuturist and XF manifestos. By raising the issue of regulating chaos (however minimal that regulation needs be) and making a plea to resist knowing 'newness in advance', Halberstam is addressing the important question of what a revolutionary practice might actually consist of, asking what part wildness and chaos play in this. Here it might appear that Halberstam is pitching wildness against chaos, but that is not exactly the case. The Gaga feminist quotes the anarchist slogan 'Hierarchy is Chaos', and offers a valuable observation in stating that chaos is a 'matter of perspective rather than an absolute value' (2013). As we argue in our second coda to Chapter 2, both capitalism and the state, often cast as restrictive systems of control, wreak havoc on lives, threatening chaos as much as regulation – and indeed reek havoc through regulation. This notion echoes Syms' observations concerning the senselessness of police violence against African Americans. Chaos, like (or as) control, could be said to be one of the many weapons of the state, and, indeed, other powerful organisations create chaos to manipulate markets and accumulate wealth.

Halberstam's emphasis on perspective rejects any simple opposition of control and chaos and moves towards a notion of wildness – as nominal regulation of chaos and disorder. This operates as a trope for the most unconventional political action that Halberstam identifies with the power of the undercommons, as explored by Harney and Moten (2013), and which we touched on in the previous chapter. Halberstam's example of a revolutionary is suitably unconventional but also, we suggest, an example of myth-science (one that has a Disneyesque persona that Syms might disapprove off): it is the lone wolf, unable to communicate beyond a gesture of solidarity, who meets Mr. Fox and his outlaw gang of animals in Wes Anderson's animated film *Fantastic Mr. Fox* (2009). This example is, for Halberstam, an affective moment: 'This exchange, silent and profound, brings tears to Mr. Fox's eyes precisely because it puts him face to face with the wildness he fears and the wildness he harbors within himself' (Halberstam 2013).

The meeting of the lone wolf and Mr. Fox is, Halberstam claims, an example of what Deleuze would call 'pure cinema', in that it cannot be reduced to any meaning other than the affirmation that there is potential for 'a life beyond the limits of our comprehension' (2013). As such, Halberstam goes on to define this wild revolutionary in Deleuzian terms:

> Ultimately, the revolutionary is a wild space where temporality is uncertain, relation is improvised, and futurity is on hold. Into this 'any instant whatsoever' (Deleuze) walks a figure that we cannot classify, that refuses to engage us in conventional terms, but speaks instead in the gestural language of solidarity, connection, and insurrection. (Halberstam 2013)

The Future of Myth-Science

From the perspective of our three manifestos, it seems that a more Earthbound response to politics and technology is demanded than that offered by cosmic-orientated myth-sciences of the past. Just as Syms insists on a reality-check to limit the escapist fantasies of afrofuturism, and just as change for Xenofeminism takes place within the possibilities opened up by science, Halberstam also recognises limitations, and that acting for revolution involves acknowledging the likelihood of failure – a nod to reality that myth-sciences of another age or kind do not offer. But in Halberstam's revolutionary wild space, Laboria Cuboniks' X without a destination, and Syms' concern for a 'metaphysical space beyond the black public' (Syms 2013) are we in fact so very far away from the myth-science of Sun Ra and his Arkestra? Perhaps not. The three manifestos are certainly focused on the means and possibilities for new societies on Earth. Even so, in practices exploring blackness, technoscience and wildness (developing postcolonial, feminist and queer perspectives but also myths that signal not illusion but the orientation of fictions with a traction on lived or so-called reality) we find *alienation as method* that points to, or holds out for, futures different to that promised by existing regimes and Spectacle.

Diagrams

In conclusion and to be more specific about the similarities and differences between these three texts, which appeared online at roughly the same time, we suggest the following: Syms is against fictions of progress but for hope and for finding realness in myth through 'staying in the groove' of past radical traditions; Laboria Cuboniks call for a new logic and hyperstitional future projections that present a desired future realised through technoscience; and Halberstam opposes any strong regulation of experimentation, as a means of reaching for what is thought impractical and producing a wild space 'where temporality is uncertain'. We diagram these loops below (Figures 13.2–4.), to suggest that the influence of the present (its alienating affect) is as important as the influence of other temporal dimensions, whether actual or imagined.

While the three manifestos may signal a need to reassess the possibilities for myth-science to bring about change, a rejection of the status quo as reality through fictioning alternate perspectives is central to all three. No doubt Syms and the Xenofeminists would agree with Halberstam's statement: 'I do not believe that the triumph of global capitalism is the end of the story, the only story, or the full story' (2013). And no doubt, too, they would agree with Halberstam's belief that new stories will not emerge from a disciplined university discourse: new perspectives will not be developed by experts who know their Foucault, Deleuze and Marx but not the joys of mass and pop culture or the alternative scenes of life-experimentation (Halberstam 2013). Perhaps here, in relation to what Halberstam identifies as an emerging 'wild theory' and as a failed disciplinary knowledge – which might describe many declarations and projects found online, including the manifestos of Syms and Xenofeminism – it can be said mythscience has led the way, starting with Sun Ra's science fictioning drawing on religious texts, history books, astronomy and scientific discovery.

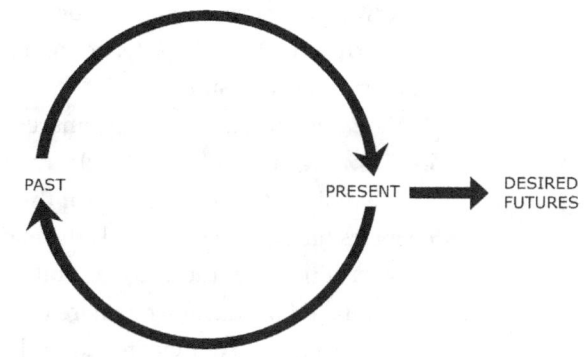

13.2 Diagram of 'staying in the grove', the orientation proposed by Martine Syms (credit: the authors).

Coda: New Arkestras

At the beginning of this chapter, we signalled our intention to demonstrate that collectivity is important to the examples we cite, and we now conclude by addressing why this is so. Halberstam's wild theory makes clear that collectivity is a value worth pursuing in itself, important for 'making worlds and sharing space' (2013), which we suggest is the Gaga feminist's approach to world-building (a term we will explore in full in the next chapter). To develop a logic of a wildness that makes worlds, Halberstam draws on the writing of Lauren Berlant to affirm an anarchism that engages in actions which, although understood as limited by fantasy, nevertheless find shared cause and narratives with others (which Halberstam identifies as a 'cruel optimism', the title of Berlant's book published in 2011). The author of 'A Gaga Manifesto' explains: 'we engage in fantasies of living

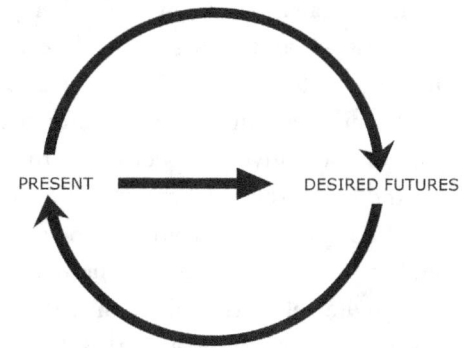

13.3 Diagram of the hypersititional feedback loop, the orientation proposed by Laboria Cuboniks (credit: the authors).

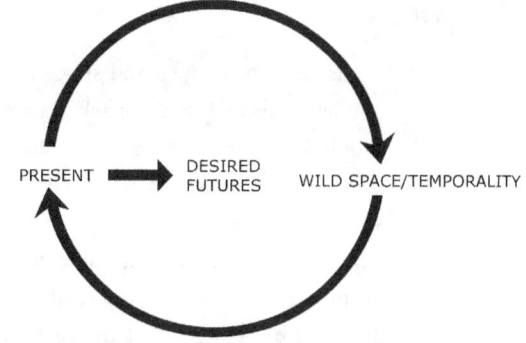

13.4 Diagram of wildness and 'uncertain temporality', the orientation proposed by Jack Hablerstam (credit: the authors).

otherwise with groups of other people because the embrace of a common cause leads to alternative modes of satisfaction and even happiness, whether or not the political outcome is successful' (2013).

Here, in Halberstam's Gaga anarchism, we find the promotion of collective forms of fictioning (and fictions of collectivity) for the sake of making or projecting community, a politics that echoes that of the myth-science collaborations explored in earlier chapters (and, indeed, towards the end of our section on mythopoesis). Furthermore, in a certain sense, these communities can themselves be understood as fictionings. We would follow Halberstam here who states: 'The wild projects I am making common cause with tend to anticipate rather than describe new ways of being together, making worlds, and sharing space' (2013). We draw parallels between Gaga feminism and Xenofeminism (which is written by a collective), but perhaps it might be fair to say that Syms' mundane afrofuturism might not entirely support the promotion of common cause for its own sake, being suspicious of ideas relating to the promise of progress without realness or political efficacy as guiding principles. However, Syms' looping of the politics of the *New Guards* – of the Black Panthers and other radical traditions – within the present, anticipates common causes too, as well as the production of alternative perspectives in the here and now.

And so we reiterate: establishing whether myth-science has a legacy or whether it can be identified as relating to new forms of science fictioning will mean exploring and producing collective-orientated, alien and alternative perspectives in art, music and digital platforms. Certainly, there are divergences, but this is, it seems to us, entirely appropriate. For myth-sciences or science fictionings as alternate and decolonising perspectives would necessarily cultivate a wild diversity of counter-fictions to resist naturalising and universalising tendencies.

Notes

1 Syms' view of science and space travel might not be so far from Sun Ra's in so far as the latter argued that if black people did not engage with science and technology they would be left behind. Here we also note recent remarks concerning space exploration and colonisation as a 'white flight' from Earth, as well as other comments that celebrate or criticise (depending on the political persuasion of the commentators) Elon Musk's plan to set up a self-sustainable city of a million people on Mars: the flight of the elites from Earth (see, for example, Maney 2015).

2 It might be thought that the realness promoted by Syms relates to the ways in which the term 'real' is articulated in hip-hop, but we suggest there is not necessarily an exact equivalence here. As Andres Tardio (2013) notes, rappers have long maintained – as KRS One's teacher in *My Philosophy* (1988) suggests – that hip-hop is about reality and

not the salary. But many rap about lives full of violence and criminality, and neighbor-hoods and experiences that they cannot claim as their own, presenting invented narratives and biographies. Tardio notes that Jay Z declares, in *Real As it Gets* (2009), that he is aware that he is rare, for he can be said to write rhymes about his own and not some fantasy life. To keep it real would, in one sense, be to not make things up as a means of trying to manufacture authenticity; that is, to be real is to be honest. There is of course another sense to 'Keeping it Real', which Tardio names as realism, giving the example of *The Message* (1982) by Grand Master Flash, which addresses the precar-iousness of urban life and was one of the earliest hip-hop songs to gain widespread international success (2013). There are similarities then, but Syms emphasises realness as a feeling, and not just as a concern relating to the content of narratives and representations.

3   See, for example, bell hooks' 'Is Paris Burning?' (1999); Judith Butler's 'Gender is Burning: Questions of Appropriation and Subversion' (1993); and Peggy Phelan's 'The Golden Apple: Jenny Livingstone's *Paris is Burning*' (1993).

4   The 'Houses' sustained communities and lives in difficult contexts, in so far as the opportunities for those taking part in the New York ball scene of the 1980s were limited, producing a focus on survival, as revealed in the film. For some, self-commodification allowed a few individuals to enter the entertainment industries – a feat clearly not to be looked down upon – while others attempted to realise lifestyles and identities which, at times, seem to also involve the ironic acceptance of representations (or stereotypes).

5   We suggest that there are parallels to be found between Syms' notion of 'realness' and discussions of queer affect – though the latter is less concerned with personal emotion or experience – and with other discussions of shame in queer theory, a discourse influ-enced by the work of Eve Kosofsky Sedgwick.

6   An example of a performative act is the gesture of making a sign of the cross to signify Catholic faith; the meaning arises through familiarity and iteration.

7   We note that both Syms' and Phelan's interest in affect differs from that of Deleuze and other philosophers, for whom affect is impersonal.

8   The Ccru was formed in 1995 at Warwick University and, throughout the late 1990s, explored the influence and potential of cybernetics (in relation to both fiction and continental philosophy).

9   Paul B. Preciado was born Beatriz Preciado, and published books under the latter name, including *Tetso Junkie*, published in Spanish in 2008 (Preciado 2013). In 2014, Preciado transitioned, adopting the name Paul B. Preciado in 2015.

B. SCIENCE FICTIONING:
WORLDS AND MODELS

14   Feminist World-Building and Worlding

It matters what matters we use to think other matters with; it
matters what stories we tell to tell other stories with; it matters what
knots knot knots, what thoughts think thoughts, what ties tie ties.
It matters what stories make worlds, what worlds make stories.

Donna Haraway, 'SF: Science Fiction, Speculative
Fabulation, String Figures, So Far'

HAVING DISCUSSED A series of manifestos that address afrofuturism, Xenofeminism and wildness (the last partly in relation to queer theory), we want now to turn
to the theme of world-building and the related idea of feminist worlding. Here, we
distinguish between the term world-building – as established story-writing practice –
and the term world-making, which in section one we ascribed to mythopoetic art
practices that involve performing fictions in some way. We also recognise that worlding
might be a term that is interchangeable with our own concept of fictioning, and it is
our contention that worlding is indeed a particular fictioning practice. We have already
touched on some of these themes in previous chapters in this section: in the various
writings and associated practices we have looked at so far, a form of world-building and
worlding can be said to occur through an engagement with radical traditions, the
potential of media and technology, and collaborative experimentation. We continue to
explore these different perspectives in what follows but focus more on those science
fictionings that engage with 'Science Fact'. We are not suggesting here an unproblematic
turn to scientific reason and utility. We take the phrase 'Science Fact' from Donna
Haraway, who uses it in conjunction with 'Science Fiction', 'Speculative Feminism' and
'Speculative Fabulation', all of which are signified for the writer by the initials SF. As
Haraway writes: 'In looping threads and relays of patterning, this SF practice is a model
for worlding. Therefore, SF must also mean "so far," opening up what is yet-to-come in
protean entangled times' pasts, presents, and futures' (Haraway 2011).

By attending to 'SF', we also prepare the ground for some of our subsequent chapters that speculate on – and fiction – future societies. In this, we become less concerned with the mobilisation of impossible worlds and fabulous images, or, indeed, the destabilisation of notions of reality, and more concerned with science fictionings that engage with the potential and limitations of mathematical, technological and scientific knowledge. To a large extent, such practices look beyond the production of scenes and groups and, instead, develop fictions or models of new communities and societies on a planetary scale.

In what follows, then, we address the work of Haraway, but also turn to Isabelle Stengers. Both thinkers offer important feminist perspectives in their fields, writing with the intention of producing 'words that are meaningful only when they bring about their reinvention, words whose greatest ambition would be to become elements of histories that, without them, might have been slightly different' (Stengers 2010: 13). This statement – which sounds to us like a proposal for fictioning through discourse – appears in Stengers' *Cosmopolitics I*. In this book Stengers argues that the idea of 'Science' as having sole access to universal truths needs to be challenged, not least for designating all non-scientific explanations or discourses concerning the world or cosmos as myth or sophistry, that is, as fiction. This is not a call to abandon Science Fact but a conviction that the sciences need to respect other accounts of the world. While this position can be said to have its problems,[1] Stengers' argument is persuasive, as is her more general questioning of whether the sciences alone should decide humanity's role in the universe (2010: 2). Haraway has similar concerns but with a different focus in that she suggests other species – as social-biological agents – be counted as part of future communities. Our discussion of Stengers' work is then followed by a return to Haraway and an examination of her call to choose non-humans as our kin. To further develop this idea, we end the chapter with a discussion of the work of the artist Carolee Schneemann, who we think important for our discussion of worlding, not least for her pioneering feminist art practice that involves collaboration with cats. Before discussing the work of Stengers, Haraway and Schneemann though, some more general questions need attending to.

World-Building to Worlding

The term world-building is associated with Fantasy and Science Fiction writing. In this context, it refers to the invention of imaginary places, societies and worlds, a practice that is of interest to us, for it foregrounds the idea that for any alternate realm to be considered coherent or tangible, it needs a logic, if not a structure and history. A survey of guides for world-building will find a common list of themes that a world-builder needs to attend to, including geology, biological systems, government and the technological levels of any society or entity. There are similarities here between Fantasy world-building techniques and feminist world-building workshops that engage in collective invention to address ways of overcoming patriarchy.[2] Design, then, understood in its broadest sense, is an important aspect of world-building. But a world is more than a design and a world-building practice that produces more than designs – that, in particular, addresses how relations between entities and things actually become manifest and have continuity – can be called a worlding; in the case of Haraway's writing, a feminist worlding.

Before discussing the term worlding in detail, however, it is reasonable to ask about the political and philosophical implications of the process of world-building – or, indeed, worlding – not least as the lessons of myth-analysis and myth-science addressed earlier in this section point to how a worldview is invariably produced from a specific perspective, often in order to address very particular problems or ends. Something similar to this problem is articulated by Gayatri Chakravorty Spivak in 'Three Women's Texts and a Critique of Imperialism', in which she uses the term worlding to refer to processes in which imperialist and colonialist narratives established what became known as the 'Third World', with European literature contributing greatly to this undertaking (Spivak 1985: 243). Spivak writes of Charlotte Brontë's *Jane Eyre* (1847) and Jean Rhys' *Wild Sargasso Sea* (1966) in which the worlding of a world beyond Europe can be said to support colonial narratives. Spivak's intention here is to critique a 'feminist individualism in the age of imperialism' celebrated by literary and feminist theory that is blind to the colonial aspects of the two novels (244). In this critique, Spivak's use of the term worlding refers to the imperial aspects of Western literature that both produce and elide colonial relations, and we have to acknowledge that her postcolonial deconstruction of European fiction poses questions for world-building and worlding (and indeed fictioning): how might the latter avoid a perspectival blindness, colonial or otherwise?

Spivak herself provides some answers to this question in a discussion of a third text in her essay: the novel *Frankenstein; or, The Modern Prometheus* by Mary Shelley, published in 1818. Spivak is more positive about this famous story in which Frankenstein creates an eight-foot tall, male, intelligent, human-like creature. She suggests that what many consider to be the first Science Fiction novel is also a 'nascent' feminist work producing a world that, importantly, is cryptic in its meanings, primarily because it does not 'speak the language of feminist individualism' that, Spivak suggests, 'we have come to hail as the language of high feminism' (254). This observation is relevant to our discussion of feminist science fictioning, for we propose that feminist world-building and worlding similarly do not speak the language of individualism or imperialism, in so far as they undermine the priority of any human perspective and particularly the perspective of any universalising discourse.

Spivak's comments concerning *Frankenstein* illuminate this last point further. She notes that Shelley's novel is 'not a battleground of male and female individualism' (a contest between two perspectives) articulated as an opposition between sexual reproduction (associated with the family and the female) and social subject-production (associated with race and the male). Indeed, Frankenstein's laboratory is an 'artificial womb' that challenges not just women as 'maker of children' but God as 'maker of man' (244–5). It is not that the novel is without colonial aspects. What Spivak argues however is that Shelley's worlding escapes a colonising perspective by undermining the notion of what it is to be human, or male or female (when these categories are premised on reproduction) and, in this, also destabilises individual perspectives.

Related to this is Spivak's observation that Shelley's novel also destabilises the idea that a scientific Prometheanism benefits humankind when the latter is defined as involving biological reproduction and, we note, kinship and patriarchal structures that are deemed natural. For another important aspect of the novel is that Frankenstein's speaking creature not only lacks a childhood and a mother but also has no female companion. As Spivak notes, Frankenstein cannot bring himself to create an artificial Eve for fear that the female creature would be more malignant than his first creation, and that the union – of the male creature and his Eve – would propagate a race that threatens humankind (256). Frankenstein's decision leads to a series of tragedies and the wretched end of his creature, but his dilemma as to whether he should create an artificial woman also reveals that the binary of male and female individualism is not the focus of Shelley's 'nascent feminism': the focus is the future of the human, or how the human is defined. Spivak suggests, a complex set of relations is laid out in *Frankenstein*, in which ideas about nature and sexual and artificial reproduction (including the patriarchal fear of usurping natural orders) are presented as (inescapably) gendered political and philosophical problems. It is through similarly problematising so-called natural orders that feminist world-building and SF worlding avoid some of the pitfalls that Spivak associates with 'high feminism', while at the same time developing feminist perspectives on social and scientific problems (including Prometheanism). An important point emerges here, namely that, as Spivak argues of Shelley's nascent feminism, 'social-engineering should not be based on pure, theoretical or scientific reason' (256).

What is a World?

Having looked briefly at whether feminist world-building and worlding might avoid individual perspectives or imperialist narratives, we now turn to a second and perhaps more difficult question (one that has been at stake throughout our book so far): what exactly is a world, if, as we claim, it can be produced by humans through various means, including worlding or fictioning? Spivak identifies her use of the term worlding as a vulgarisation of Martin Heidegger's phrase 'worlding of the world' (260), and, in this, she points to an important and influential definition of the terms world and worlding found in translations of Heidegger's 'The Origin of the Work of Art' (1999a). We think it important to briefly discuss Heidegger's concepts at this point, as it seems clear that any discussion of worlding – including both Haraway's and Spivak's – is partly indebted to the philosopher who made these concepts his own. This will allow us to mark how Haraway's use of the term worlding is different, while also enabling us to offer some clarification – if not a tentative definition – of the term world.

In his essay on the origin of art, Heidegger lays out his own concept of a world and a definition of worlding, stating:

> The world is not the mere collection of countable and uncountable, familiar and unfamiliar things at hand. But neither is it an imagined framework added by our representations to the sum of given things. The *world worlds*, and is more fully in being than the tangible and perceptible realm in which we believe ourselves to be at home. World is never an object that stands before us and can be seen. World is the ever non-objective to which we are subject as long as the paths of birth and death, blessing and curse keep us transported into Being. Wherever those utterly essential decisions of our history are made, are taken up and abandoned by us, go unrecognised and are rediscovered by new enquiry, there the world worlds. A stone is worldless. Plant and animal likewise have no world; but they belong to the covert throng of a surrounding into which they are linked. The peasant women, on the other hand, has a world because she dwells in the overtness of being. Her equipment, in its reliability, gives to the world a necessity and nearness of its own. By the opening up of a world, all things gain their lingering and hastening, their remoteness and nearness, their scope and limits. In a world's worlding is gathered that spaciousness out of which the protective grace of the gods is granted or withheld. Even this doom, of the god remaining absent, is a way in which world worlds. (1999a: 170)

There is much to say about this passage, and much that is problematic, but the statement that the world is more than an 'imagined framework added by our representations to the sum of given things' helps us understand further the difference between world-building as representational process, and a worlding concerned with the 'remoteness and nearness' and 'scope and limits' of entities in a world. Heidegger's idea that a peasant woman 'has a world' through 'dwelling in the overtness of being' builds upon concepts that the German philosopher develops in his book *Being and Time* (2001), in which he suggests that it may seem easy for us to grasp the world as we can name many things – 'houses, people, trees, mountains, stars' – but that this is to count a world as that which is visible or 'within the world' and, as such, would be no more than to describe entities or things that are 'ontical' (Heidegger 2001: 91). We think this a valuable insight, that a world is more than what is personal or common, more, that is, than a subjective or objective viewpoint. Expanding on this, Heidegger suggests that a world might be thought to be constituted by the ontical, addressing that which is 'present-at-hand' or where 'a Being may be said to live'; but a world is also constituted by the ontological, which addresses 'the Being of entities' and the existential acknowledging of 'the *a priori* character of worldhood in general' (93). In this, Heidegger's concern for the ontological relates to his interest in Being as Being-there (which we understand as a concept addressing the time of existence); crucially for Heidegger, 'worldhood itself is an *existentiale*' (92); that is, a world is produced *by* human existence. We should make it clear here that we do not see feminist world-building or worlding as in any way a Heideggerian or phenomenological project – far from it. But we are interested in thinking about the ways in which feminist worlding practices address more than just the ontical; they address existence in time, and as such also reveal the radical aspects of those worlding practices when compared to the existentialism of Heidegger.

There is one more aspect of Heidegger's concept of worldhood that is relevant to our discussion of feminist worlding and, indeed, of fictioning in general: the philosopher implies that a world is constituted through or as 'spaciousness' (Heidegger 1999a: 170). Furthermore, in 'The Origin of the Work of Art', Heidegger writes that a 'work, by being a work, makes space for this spaciousness', and in this way a 'work as work sets up a world' (170). This seems an important statement, suggesting that the setting forth of works such as equipment and built environments but also artworks, designs and objects can be understood as more than something present-at-hand, for – in Heidegger's terms – such works develop relations of remoteness and nearness and concern the lingering and hastening, the scope and limit, of things. Here, we understand that Heidegger is not concerned with the representational content of fictional works and we do not intend to confuse his assertion that a world is set up by work or works with the idea that the images presented in any artwork or fiction are worlds. For us, however, this does not invalidate the idea that worlding (through fictioning or fabulation) involves setting up a space for a world. True, this may rely on 'the *a priori* character of worldhood in general', but we suggest that feminist worlding or science fictioning (as a collective venture) is a forcing of, or a making of space for, future, intangible or alternative worlds which are not limited by, and indeed can be said to overturn or elide, what is of particular importance to Heidegger – namely, a sense of Being that is produced by the 'essential decisions of our history' (Heidegger 1999a: 170). For Heidegger 'our history' means human history. It perhaps does not need to be said that the history Heidegger refers to is written, for the most part (if not entirely) by men, but it is important to note here that feminist worlding practices reject the idea that the story of Being is solely a human history, and this is where a radical divide can be found regarding definitions of worlding.

To be clear: feminist worlding not only questions patriarchy and Eurocentricism, it rejects human exceptionalism (and for this reason, as we shall see in the case of Haraway, posthuman theory too). As we have noted, for Heidegger, things – rocks, plants, animals – cannot be said to have a world. Thinking back to the lessons of the anthropologists in Chapter 10, we can view Heidegger's philosophy as thoroughly occidental and Western in its separation of humans from other, non-human things, particularly in their capacity for world-making or worlding. And it is this emphasis on the priority of the human, an existential privileging, that feminist worlding rejects. But before addressing Haraway's differences with Heidegger in more detail, we want to discuss one more critique of human exceptionalism, which, through its extreme perspective, helps us understand further what is at stake in feminist worlding.

Extinction

An especially pointed critique of human exceptionalism is offered by Claire Colebrook, who first became known for writing on feminism, queer theory and art in texts influenced by Deleuzian philosophy but more recently has focused on the Anthroprocene, ecology and human extinction. In her book *Death of the Posthuman: Essays on Extinction Volume 1*, Colebrook suggests that the human concern for the ecology of the planet relates primarily to the survival of the human species, and this leads her to ask whether it is time 'to look at the world and ourselves without assuming our unquestioned right to life' (Colebrook 2014: 22). If this seems a disturbing proposition, Colebrook's text poses even more disconcerting ideas. In a direct response to Heidegger's declaration that a stone has no world, Colebrook asks whether we can imagine 'a world without organic perception, without the centered points of view of sensing and world-orientated beings' (23). More than that, can we project into the future and imagine humankind as an Anthropocene scar that may be registered as a geological layer after humankind's extinction – just as fossils today open up a lost world for humans? If so, can this produce an orientation that does not envisage the human as important to the planet's future? Is it possible to develop a mode of reading the world that 'frees itself from folding the earth's surface around human survival' (23)?

While Colebrook seems ambivalent about the demise of humankind, the focus of her work is also an attempt to think a world beyond that produced by human consciousness and senses. In this, she makes reference to the work of Quentin Meillassoux and Ray Brassier (both of whom we address in subsequent chapters of our own book) and their attempt to 'move further into a world without cognition' (38), for both engage with a time before the human or with the extinction of the sun as philosophical problems. Colebrook asks why and how it is possible to think about the absence or end of thought, making a connection with apocalyptic films or fictions that similarly imagine the potential end of humankind. She implies that science has contributed to the development of such an imaginary envisioning of human extinction and asks whether we now need a new kind of literary theory that addresses both the scientific data (or Science Fact) that predicts the demise of the human and the entertainment productions that attempt to witness this end (40). Colebrook concludes that we need a 'theory after theory' that would destroy such a human-centered imaginary (45). And by the end of her book we have a sense of what she might mean by this. She follows Deleuze and Guattari in their reading of certain modernist works (for example those of Virginia Woolf and T. E. Lawrence) as engaging with inhuman time, rather than positing 'something like tracing, marking, writing, text, *différance* or the word that would disperse and fragment any supposed grounding life'. In this, she also follows Bergson's notion that it is life itself that 'creates difference' (221). For Colebrook, who is strongly influenced by Deleuze here, Bergson demonstrates how intuition can register inhuman duration, grasping two aspects of life: 'the durations of matter, and the capacity—from those durations—to produce a metaphysical image of thought' (226). According to Colebrook, art and writing then, although not reducible to the cosmos, are 'in vibration with the cosmos – the chaosmos' (226). This last notion influences Colebrook's call for a 'radical atavism' suggested by Bergson (which we also looked at in Chapter 1), 'where humans intuit rhythms that are distinct, inhuman, and beyond the time of the present' (227).

Matters of Life and Death

While Colebrook's atavistic call for the registering of an extreme past and primitive states of life cannot exactly be identified as worlding, her work shares some concerns with that of feminist worlding in an era where sustainability, environmentalism and ecology have become key political concerns, not least in the attempt to construct an imaginary and a politics that is no longer human-centred. Haraway and others, however, do not go so far as to imagine the complete demise of the human, and perhaps accepting or projecting human extinction is too easy. Importantly, in feminist worlding, the human is simply one more entity on the planet producing a perspective that raises questions about the relations and survival of all entities. In this sense, worlding engages with scales, terrains and times that include the microscopic and the molecular, as well as Colebrook's 'rhythms that are distinct, inhuman, and beyond the time of the present'. It is important to emphasise that Haraway, in staying with the trouble, is staying with humankind (though she would welcome a decrease in the number of humans on the planet). Haraway does not follow those who declare the end of the human is nigh with the advent of artificial intelligence, or those who embrace the inorganic, as Colebrook does. In Haraway's thinking, humans still play an ongoing part in worlding worlds.

Here a question foregrounds itself as to whether feminist worlding might in fact share something with Heidegger's notion of worlding. For it can certainly be said that, like Heidegger, Haraway is concerned with finitude. We note that a pressing question for Haraway's Chthulucene is who lives and who dies, and she envisages a multispecies society as developing a culture that marks and remembers the extinction of any species (Haraway 2016: 101). But in this, the decisions and histories of the Chthulucene envisaged by Haraway concern many species rather than just the human (as we suggested above, the latter is the exclusive focus of Heidegger's philosophy).

With this in mind we reiterate that feminist worlding involves a feminism that relates not to female individualism or sexual liberation but to an embracing of radical (non-human) otherness. As such, Heideggerian existential or phenomenological questions are not key concerns. Haraway herself makes this clear when she says she is done with 'grumpy human-exceptionalist Heideggerian worlding' and with pondering the 'bond-less, lonely, Man-making gap theorized by Heidegger and his followers' (11). In this withering critique, Haraway underlines that, for her, worlding is a problem of multispecies existence rather than of human existence per se.

One further difference between Haraway and Heidegger concerns technology. Writing in the twentieth century, Heidegger argued that technology had come to involve a 'challenging' of nature (rather than a bringing-forth of the truth of nature), that is, it had become a means of unlocking or exploiting energy and transforming materials (Heidegger 1999b: 320), with humans too becoming reserves or resources for the modern technological projects enabled by science. Once again, while it seems at first that there may be similarities between feminist worlding that looks to theories of Gaia and ecology and Heidegger's concern for nature, there are differences too. For example, although Haraway is not Promethean, the possibilities of the scientific augmentation of species, bodies and reproduction, and the transformation of kin and family structures – as feminist-influenced concerns – are an aspect of her worlding practice. This is especially evident in the short story that concludes her book *Staying with the Trouble* (2016), which involves a questioning and transformation of what is given or thought natural and a challenging of nature-culture divisions. It might be said that Haraway offers no detailed account of technology when discussing multispecies societies in *Staying with the Trouble*, but there is the implication, as noted above, that her speculative thinking engages with both the sciences (such as biological theories about bacteria) and non-scientific perspectives (such as the pattern-making games of the Navajo that we will discuss later). The relation of the sciences to a feminist worlding committed to a radical otherness seems an urgent question then, and one perhaps best addressed by Haraway's fellow traveller in this enquiry.

Interlude: Reclaiming Animism

How to engage with non-Western and non-scientific perspectives as well as Science Fact is an urgent question for Isabelle Stengers. In 'Reclaiming Animism', Stengers cites the perspectivism of Eduardo Viveiros de Castro as an influence on her critique of science as a colonial and territorialising enterprise (Stengers 2012: 2). As already implied in our introduction to this chapter, despite declaring that her thinking is shaped by science (and that therefore she cannot believe in what she knows to be false), Stengers finds the global triumph of the sciences over non-scientific perspectives to be a problem. In fact, the problem is not with the sciences as such but with the notion that they have a privileged access to the real, eliding all other narratives. In this, Stengers distinguishes between a view of Science with a capital 'S' – Science as an institution which colonises territories by dismissing the perspectives of others – and science with a lower case 's' – an adventure which addresses problems in specific situations or contexts. To develop her critique, Stengers offers an analogy borrowed from Deleuze and Guattari, suggesting that scientific endeavours (science with a lower case 's') should be approached as *rhizomatic* pursuits that follow the material being investigated, and in turn test scientific perspectives, producing new questions rather than answers.[3] Importantly for Stengers, 'A rhizome rejects any generality. Connections do not manifest some truth about what is common beyond the rhizomatic heterogeneous multiplicity' (9). This understanding of science as a rhizomatic adventure counters the idea of Science rooted in established methods and truths and capturing the territories of the real (3).

To illustrate her position, Stengers offers the example of pilgrims venerating the Virgin Mary, suggesting that deities should not be dismissed as mere fictions if science cannot prove their (objective) existence; rather, she argues, deities like Mary should be considered to be agents in a 'milieu' (another term borrowed from Guattari) which may produce the events or phenomena being studied, such as faith healing and the effects of placebos (3). In respecting deities and animism, Stengers takes a position similar to that of Bruno Latour, who calls for social science to treat non-humans and objects as actors within networks of relations (Latour 2005). Indeed, in *On the Modern Cult of Factish Gods*, Latour praises Stengers for her understanding of the need to question epistemology – for he thinks Stengers understands that the objects of science need to be 'de-epistemologized' (2010: 38), or approached not just through established knowledge or questions concerning appropriate modes of research. To understand what this might mean for science, in the same text, Latour celebrates a centre for migrants where psychiatric practices counted deities as actors with some success (35–9). Latour comments that if these two practices – the de-epistemologising, scientific-philosophical work of Stengers and the social work of the migrant centre – taking place in two Parisian institutions at the same time, were to spread to other institutions, there would be an end to the rational, modernist project of integrating migrants into the Republic by banishing their divinities and ancestors (39).

We recognise that both Stengers and Latour are critical of the colonising methods of the university and the state here. Yet, ethical respect for non-scientific perspectives does not necessarily curtail the powers of the sciences or the state. As Stengers makes clear, adopting a rhizomatic approach does not mean a scientist can verify animism, and this leaves her with a problem, for she can no more abandon scientific perspectives than she can willfully see demons and ghosts. An asymmetrical division between science and other perspectives persists. Her solution is interesting for our discussion and understanding of worlding as fictioning, but it can also be seen as having limitations.

Magical Compromise

In discussing an encounter with the practices of modern-day American witches – who, on being told the supernatural Goddess they speak of is just a fiction, ask, 'is fiction powerless?' (Stengers 2012: 7) – Stengers states that she is interested in discovering how to be 'compromised by magic' (8). To explain this, she suggests that the witches challenge an 'addiction to truth' and force a reconsideration of the effects of the pursuit of knowledge; for the witches are pragmatic, experimenting with different modes of attention and their effects (which Stengers calls their craft) – she also notes that the witches are mindful that actions have consequences (8). Importantly, for Stengers, the witches insist that there are forces beyond themselves which change and transform the world, and which cannot easily be defined as 'nature' (which she identifies as 'for scientific explanation only') (8). To further explore her notion of compromise, Stengers compares the craft of the witches with the illusions and assemblages of stage magic. She quotes the ecologist David Abram, 'himself a sleight-of-hand magician', who explains that illusion relies on the way the senses make 'contact' with the 'invisible aspects of the sensible'. Not only this, Abram argues that illusion relies on the senses operating through 'the flux of participation' (Abram quoted by Stengers 2012: 8), something Stengers implies the witches would agree with. Here, scientists might object that the world filtered through the senses and the technologies of magic or enchantment is, as Stengers concedes, specious and seductive, producing illusion that has the potential to lead to enslavement (8). But her reason for arguing for compromise is to turn this critique back on Science, which, from the perspective of Amerindians and others, might appear to operate as 'magical' mediation. Stengers seeks to question the way the methods (or craft) and 'achievements' of science facilitate power, and the way those achievements are presented by the sciences as objective reality.

Even so, Stengers says that she will not abandon science, and with good reason. If science is lured by animism into error or regression the results can be dangerous. Reclaiming animism, then, is not a call to believe in what is not (scientifically) verified as true, but rather to adopt modes of attending to the world which recognise forces and events beyond human provenance and which acknowledge 'that we are not alone in the world' (9).

The problem of the privilege accorded to scientific or Western perspectives is first addressed by Stengers in depth in seven essays published together in *Cosmopolitics I* and *II*. In these books, Stengers makes it clear that she does not believe there can be a 'unifying body of knowledge' that brings together different modern and archaic traditions of thought, and she calls for 'an ethical experiment' of developing a *cosmopolitics* (2010: vii–viii). In this, Stengers does not envisage science having to give way to cultural relativism and stresses that the passion for truth that engenders creation and thought should not be sacrificed for the sake of 'peace' between different perspectives (12). Instead, she argues for the continuation of the passion for truth, but through sciences that concern themselves less with the 'identification of possibilities' and more with what is not known or knowable (13).

Reflecting on *Cosmopolitics* years later in 'The Cosmopolitical Proposal' (2005), Stengers comments further on her notion of an ecology of practices that resist the idea of a unifying and authoritative body of knowledge. Here she introduces a fictional example: the conceptual persona of the idiot. In this, Deleuze's thoughts on Dostoevsky's fiction *The Idiot* (first published serially 1868–9) are presented as an influence on her thinking. Dostoevsky's idiot slows people down and resists consensual views (994), not to confuse or spread perplexity but in order to question whether the fact of grasping knowledge gives a person or culture the right to claim authority over others, or whether having knowledge of something guarantees 'we possess the meaning of what we know' (995). This leads Stengers to refuse a notion of the cosmos as all and everything that Science will explore and conquer, and to reject too the Kantain project of making a good world for all (995). Instead, for Stengers, cosmos – as a political term – designates 'the unknown' as multiple and divergent worlds that include articulations of difference produced through a comparison of cosmological and cosmic perspectives (995). In this, Stengers offers an ethics for cosmopolitics and, indeed, for feminist worlding.

Speculative Feminism and the Carrier Bag of Fiction

If Stengers can be said to be open to (or be compromised by) beliefs and practices that embrace the non-human, Donna Haraway, through combining an interest in the sciences, craft and non-Western cultures, might be said to go further in fictioning a future world constituted by or through human and non-human symbiosis. For Haraway is keen to develop multispecies (as opposed to human or posthuman) perspectives and communities, expressing an interest in upsetting orders and hierarchies of different kinds. This project builds upon earlier feminist writing and relates to her training as a biologist but her focus on symbiosis articulates too her critique of philosophies and practices that promote human autonomy. In this, Haraway is critical of the idea of human self-creation through autopoetic (and, in this sense, Promethean) becomings – autopoetic human becoming being defined by Haraway as the notion of a 'self-making man' (Haraway 2016: 47), which foregrounds the gendered aspect of becoming, as she sees it. Indeed, in *Staying with the Trouble*, Haraway writes that her interest is in the chthonic ones that 'romp in multicritter humus but have no truck with sky-gazing' (2). That is, she does not look to the cosmos or interplanetary travel as a means of escaping problems on Earth; neither for that matter does she buy the idea that 'technofixes will come to the rescue of naughty and clever children' (333).

Haraway's approach to worlding involves producing narratives which address difficult (or troubling) questions and that embrace kin of all kinds (rather than just humankind). In this, fiction is a primary method, and in the following chapter we offer an analysis of Haraway's SF story that ends *Staying with the Trouble*. Here though, we note that the ideas and writings of Ursula Le Guin are a key influence on Haraway and her notion of SF – and important too, for a feminist world-building and worlding. In particular, Le Guin's essay 'The Carrier Bag Theory of Fiction' (1989) is significant in pointing to how worlding operates as more than description or a representational framework placed on an existing world – that is, as expressing more than a concern with the ontical. In the essay, Le Guin references Elizabeth Fisher's idea of the Carrier Bag Theory of human evolution, and comments that while the story of the spear or axe (which she names as the 'killer story' associated with masculinity) is well known, the other story of a tool that carries and stores energy or useful things – the story of containers – is not known (Le Guin 1989: 166–7). It is this other, untold story that she endeavours to write. To that end she carries 'a great heavy sack of stuff' full of, among other things, 'wimps and klutzes', things 'smaller than a mustard seed', and a chronometer that tells the time on other worlds, which help her narrate failures, troubling scenarios and difficult problems, including how to wrest oats from their husks but also how to resist 'killer stories' and Promethean and apocalyptic projections (166–8). From this, Haraway takes not only the idea that different kinds of worlds are produced by the objects and relations that carry a story, but that 'carrier bags' (of fiction) are important for 'telling the stuff of the living' (Haraway 2016: 118). Returning to our earlier discussion of feminist worlding as involving more than the ontical counting of things, we can think of the carrier bag (as idea and device) as engendering not just a gathering of things but also an assembling of relations in time (here we think there is a connection to our discussion of Heidegger's notion of worlding). That is, the theory of fiction as a carrier bag – as a gathering of objects and works to make a world – points to an understanding that the nature of a world's relations is as important as the objects manifest in a world.

While Haraway does not describe her own writing as a container, the idea of fiction as the holding or gathering together of the entities and elements of a world can be related to a compelling concept developed by Haraway that she names as 'String Figures' – another concept captured by the letters SF, and one that relates to her interest in non-Western cultures and craft. The concept of String Figures links Navajo and cat's cradle games that use string to practices engaged in pattern production and weaving. Haraway valorises String Figures and weaving (and other similar crafts and art) as a 'cosmological performance, knotting proper relationality and connectedness into the warp and weft of the fabric' (91). For Haraway then, the value of weaving as a traditional and contemporary practice is not just measured by economic or utilitarian aspects; like the production of String Figures, weaving is a way of making, thinking and worlding. Indeed, Haraway suggests that 'String Figures are like stories; they propose and enact patterns for participants to inhabit, somehow, on a vulnerable and wounded earth' (2016: 10). The reference to cat's cradle games (see Figure 14.1), in which the movement and arrangement of hands laced with string produce new compositions, suggests that Haraway sees SF as a form of communication (a reciprocal giving and receiving) that, as such, might be thought of as a collective world-building exercise. Here, what is important to Haraway is not just what worlds are made, but how they are made. This question of how fictions and worlds are produced is found throughout her work, and Haraway writes of her gratitude to Marilyn Strathern for teaching her that: '"It matters what ideas we use to think other ideas." . . . It matters what knowledges know knowledges. It matters what relations relate relations. It matters what worlds world worlds. It matters what stories tell stories' (35).

More than this though, Haraway suggests that worlding is a practice that is not focused on the potential of an individual, arguing that the model of the autopoetic and autonomous agent (human or otherwise) can no longer be taken seriously: 'Becoming with, not becoming, is the name of the game' (12). This is not just a call for humans to collaborate; her notion of worlding is more radical than that, for Haraway champions sympoesis as a model for future societies, embracing modes of existence common to multispecies collectives – studied by biologists – that have spatial arrangements without boundaries (33). Here she draws upon the work of M. Beth Dempster, who envisages sympoesis as being related to systems that are 'looped, braided, out-reaching, involuted' and that produce surprising change; such collectives – being made up of multiple systems – do not conform to the homeostatic and predictable functions of autopoetic systems (61). This presentation of a collective as a continuously looping and braiding assemblage is a description of the Chthulucene – the world of bacte-

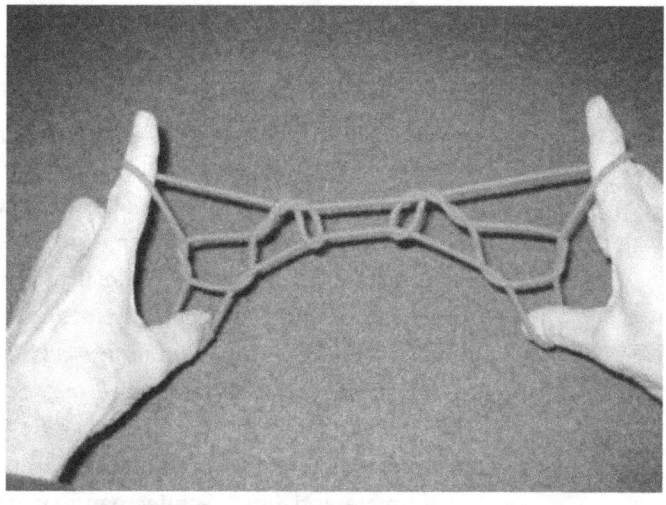

14.1 Cat's cradle image from Donna Haraway's *Staying With The Trouble*, 2011 (courtesy of Duke University Press).

ria, critters and creatures and ecologies of all kinds – which, unlike the story of the Anthropocene that ends badly, is ongoing; indeed, Haraway describes sympoesis as being a 'carrier bag for ongoingness' (125).

In promoting sympoesis and drawing on biology, her first field of study, Haraway proposes an *n*-dimensional niche space she calls 'Terrapolis', described as 'a story, a speculative fabulation and a string figure for multispecies worlding' (10). Importantly, the fictioning of Terrapolis or the Chthulucene is an alternative to the domination of those who look up (that is, of human kind who look to the stars or towards new horizons). For Haraway argues that history must give way to geostories, hence her conviction that the notion of the Anthropocene (or Capitalocene, which is her preferred term for marking the influence of humankind on the planet) should give way to a notion of the Chthulucene, as a flourishing of rich multispecies that may or may not include humans in the future (100–1). And this worlding of a Chthulucene, like Stengers' cosmopolitics, involves ethical questions. For if humankind is no longer central to the story of the planet, then what directs that story – and who is friend and kin as well as the question of 'who lives and dies' (2) – is an ongoing, troubling problem. How to form alliances with other species (how to engage with other perspec-tives) and what role humans and others have in those alliances is another pressing concern, one that might be addressed through experimentation and fiction. In relation to this, and before exploring Haraway's own fiction addressing this problem in the next chapter, we want now to look to an art practice that also involves a multispecies ethics and has relevance for the notions of feminist worlding that we have been discussing in this chapter so far.

Humans and Cats

Carolee Schneemann is a crucial figure in the development of performance art but also for radical feminist art practice more generally. In particular it is the use of her own body – often naked – that is important, in so far as this was both an avant-garde strategy (the utilisation of non-artistic material; the blurring of art and life), but also a strategy to refuse the distancing mechanisms of art and art history and confront a disinterested (male) gaze.[4] Crucially, Scheemann's refusal of the fetishisation of women's bodies involved performance and filmmaking that emphasised and affirmed women's sexuality – *Imaging Her Erotics* being the title of a key book on Schneemann's expanded practice (Schneemann 2002). Schneemann produced works like *Eye Body* (1963), *Meat Joy* (1964) and *Fuses* (1964–7) that emphasised the materiality of the body and viewpoints that can be said to be neither subjective nor objective as such, but intimate and fluid. Schneemann suggests that the film *Fuses* – which, through fragmentary images and close-ups, captures Schneemann and her then partner having sex – was influenced by Stan Brakhage. In particular, Schneemann was impressed with a film Brakhage made with his wife – *Winter Water Baby Moving* (1959) – recording the birth of their child. Brakhage's silent film work emphasises the material and physical aspects of filmmaking, and Schneemann herself suggests that she chose to work with film as it engendered a sense of 'getting closer to tactility, to sensations in the body that are streaming and unconscious and fluid – the orgasmic dissolution unseen, vivid even if unseeable' (Schneemann 2002: 23). This work can certainly be described as an attempt to frustrate the male gaze – in that an objectifying viewpoint or distance from Schneemann's body (or the body of her male partner) is denied the viewer.

Importantly, Schneemann's film offers perspectives that may be said to be non-human. Firstly, her camera and editing produce a perspective that a human would not see without the assistance of technology. (We will return to this aspect of technology in exploring the idea of machine fictioning in section three.) There is, however, one more facet of *Fuses* that needs acknowledging, and which is of relevance to our discussion of feminist worlding. The viewer of the film is also told, and indeed sees, that Kitch the cat is an actor in the film, as observer.

While Schneemann's early work might be thought of as a feminist performance fictioning – of an erotic world of flesh and pleasure free of the primacy of the phallus and a gaze that fetishises and objectifies female bodies – it might be a stretch to suggest that Schneemann's performances and films of the 1960s are worldings, at least in the terms we have been discussing. But the inclusion of Kitch the cat as observer in *Fuses* is not the only time Schneemann has collaborated with Kitch or other cats, and we suggest that she may well be a pioneer in developing multispecies relations. Later work includes photographic assemblages and films such as *Infinity*

Kisses I (1981–88), made with Cluny the cat, and *Infinity Kisses II* (1990–98), made with Vesper, a cat who Schneemann claims in one interview to be a reincarnation of Cluny (Schneemann 2013). Over a long period of time, Schneemann documented an exchange of kisses between herself and her feline companion, suggesting in the same interview that *Infinity Kisses* is similar to *Fuses* and relates to it in a number of ways, including her approach to image-making: capturing intimacy with cats through a lens involved embracing randomness, as there was no coercion of her cat collaborators when making the film. In this, we can understand Schneemann's worlding or fictioning of a multispecies relationship as having been developed through an intimate and experimental assemblage of human, cat and camera.

More than this though, Schneemann claims that Vesper the cat expressed well-developed critical skills:

> Vesper used to watch the prints, which were just Xerox, humble color prints being laid out and organized on the floor in the studio. He would sit in the studio and watch them and he would say 'oh, this is my wonderful work', or 'that one should go at the top' (Schneemann 2013).

Sometimes, it seems, Vesper was the more perceptive of the two collaborators. Schneemann remembers that just before a visit from a museum curator, Vesper suggested that the curator would want to see their collaborative work, and the cat turned out be correct. Schneemann narrates that she told the cat 'oh my god you were right' and comments that 'Those are the events that people would generally say are anthropomorphic and projective, but I have this kind of communication with some of my cats' (Schneemann 2013).

In ' "The Cat Is My Medium": Notes on the Writing and Art of Carolee Schneemann' (2015), Thyrza Nichols Goodeve remarks on the way in which the artist worked with a more 'female-centric epistemology', itself centered on the vulva (as well as, implicitly, deploying a different idea of history – a personal 'istory' as Schneeman called it). Indeed, this might be considered the basis of a feminist mythos – what Schneemann called a 'gynocracy' – which accompanies her more recognisable avant-garde gestures and gambits (Schneemann was also herself a reader of Graves' seminal work on myth *The White Goddess*). But Schneemann has commented that the association of her work with the body has often overshadowed the complexity of her practice (Schneemann 2013), which includes her interest in technology and animals. Goodeve's article, as the title suggests, does not limit commentary on Schneemann's art to her early performance work, and discusses the crucial role played by Schnneeman's cats in her life and career as an artist. This entails an exploration of the work beyond the narrow confines of a discussion concerning feminist artists using their bodies in performance. Indeed, the article foregrounds the idea of witchcraft (which has reso-nance with Stengers' notion of being compromised by magic) and, in a further resonance with Haraway, the notion of 'companion species' as well as cat's cradle games. An important reference here is another film project by Brakhage, titled *Cat's Cradle* (1957), which Kitch and Schneemann took part in making, and that features intimacy between couples and a cat as a medium. As Goodeve points out, Schneemann was unhappy with the way *Cat's Cradle* was filmed and edited and the distancing affect of Brakhage's film, which, Goodeve implies, influenced Schneemann's decision to make *Fuses* – a film of humans having sex as seen through the eyes of Kitch the cat (Goodeve 2015: 14–15).

The value of Goodeve's essay is that it takes the artist's collaboration with another species seriously; Goodeve presents the cat as spirit guide or familiar, which for us also signals a kind of perspectivism in which cats in relationships with humans are approached as persons or social beings (rather than just natural specimens). In relation to our discussion of Stengers' and Haraway's work and feminist worlding, it would seem to us that Schneemann has long been involved in producing not only a world free from patriarchy and the male gaze but also one unencumbered by a human-centered vision: an ecology of practices. This ecology traverses the technical and what many might think anthropomorphism, but that, following Haraway, we might suggest is a social endeavour: a making of kin with cats. Schneemann's cat-kin are at least equal to any human in the part they play in her affections and erotic life, and equal too as fellow collaborators in her art practice; and through Schneemann's (fictioning) practice, the cats can also be said to have an equal part in worlding a world.

Notes

1   Steven Shaviro, in his review of Stenger's *Cosmopolitics I* and *II* (2005), writes that he is troubled by the anti-modernist sentiments of Stengers (and of Bruno Latour too), for it is one thing to engage with the beliefs of Amerindians and another thing to respect the beliefs of, for example, fundamentalist Christians and Creationists, who Shaviro finds oppressive. And, he concludes, it is not enough to dismiss the beliefs of others for being intolerant. This leads him to question Stenger's rejection of a 'liberal tolerance' towards non-modern beliefs and her call to treat them as equivalents to scientific discourse.

2   One example is the 'Feminist Futures Workshop' organised by Paisley Smith and Caitlin Conlen in Los Angeles on 23 April 2017. They present world-building as a design-thinking tool, adopting the term 'visionary fiction' (rather than Science Fiction) to imagine future societies. See http://caitlinconlen.com/Feminist-Futures (accessed 30 November 2017).

3   Stengers' approach to science also echoes a further concept from *A Thousand Plateaus*, that of a minor or nomad and itinerant science, which the authors pitch against a Royal or state science (equivalent to Science with a capital 'S' in Stengers' terms) (Deleuze and Guattari 1988: 367–9).

4   For an account of Schneemann along these art historical lines see Jones 1998.

15   The Inhuman Social Imaginary of Science Fiction

*How long before it dawns on us that the world we see no
longer reflects the world we inhabit, that we are blind?*

Peter Watts, *Blindsight*

HAVING DISCUSSED AN idea of worlding that engages with Science Fact we
now attend to Science Fictions that draw upon science in order to conjure worlds
that are non-human, partial-human or more-than-human. In particular, we address
Science Fiction worlds that might seem cruel to some in that they question or
discount human values and especially the priority of human empathy and reproduction. In so doing we return to the work of Donna Haraway, who presents the
Science Fiction, 'The Camille Stories: Children of the Compost', at the end of her
book *Staying with the Trouble* (2016: 134–68). As we noted in the last chapter, in
Haraway's stories, the development of a multispecies society, in which humans
identify creatures of all kinds as kin, is assisted by the augmentation of human
bodies through implants, enabling humans to develop non-human sensory organs.
These creatures are then more than human. They are also among the few children
born to societies that have enforced a self-imposed prohibition on making human
babies. Our other case study is Peter Watts' *Blindsight* (2006) (a term that refers to
being able to 'see' with a damaged visual cortex). Originally published as a stand-
alone novel, it has since been republished as the first part of *Firefall* (2014), the
second part being titled *Echopraxia* (a term for the symptom of a meaningless
imitation of the actions of others). Humans flounder – or seem redundant – in the
worlds depicted in *Blindsight* and *Echopraxia*, which are made up of vampires, alien
life (in the form of a non-conscious intelligence), humans with multiple personalities and, as with Haraway's fiction, technologically augmented bodies.[1] Both writers,
then, question human agency and autonomy, through fictions in which a reader
encounters non-human perspectives or natures and societies. Importantly, both have

scientific training and indeed draw upon the sciences – specifically biology and neuroscience – to write their fictions.

In *Blindsight* and 'The Camille Stories', what many would consider monsters – chthonic life-forms – play key roles.[2] In *Blindsight*, the vampires and alien organisations threaten human life, and in Haraway's stories, humans take on the attributes of various critters of the Earth through augmentation. But if the creatures of H. P. Lovecraft come to mind here, there are nevertheless key differences. Certainly, Haraway is keen to make clear her distain for Lovecraft's fictions, which she sees as misogynist and racial nightmares (Haraway 2016: 101). A difference needs to be marked then, at least, between the weird, abstract horrors of Lovecraft's Cthulhu myth and the symbiotic, multispecies alliances of Haraway's *Chthulucene*. And if in Watts' novels the arrangements of alien bodies which make up the inhuman intelligences threatening the solar system seem in sympathy with Lovecraft's monsters, then this is countered by the portrayal of a society of machines, partial-humans and vampires that speak common languages and are in an alliance, at least of sorts. Indeed, what particularly interests us about the fictions of Watts and Haraway is the way they manifest not so much the fantastic or weird as the (seemingly) impossible – the perspective of a non-human otherness – which is produced through drawing on Science Fact. In so doing they also explore societies or communities in which non-human and human perspectives exist together in a human (or, at any rate, human-like) society. That is, both writers produce fictions presenting worlds or communities in which humans live, communicate and die, side by side with partial-humans and non-humans. In all of this, as with all fiction, the imaginary is a key register, but it is significant that Haraway and Watts develop an imaginary that is not human-centric. Indeed, both produce what we would call an *inhuman social imaginary*.

The Persistence of the Imaginary

There are a number of definitions of, and uses for, the term imaginary. A common definition is that the imaginary is not real, that it is, precisely, something produced by the imagination. We reject this as a misunderstanding of the imaginary and how it works. Another definition is that the imaginary is a specular or pre-discursive register of images, as well as a register that is triggered (in humans) by signifiers – an evolutionary development that allows for the anticipation of danger, as when the sound of a twig snapping produces the image of a salivating predator. It is the imaginary that allows for the anticipation of the effects of different actions in space and time, and also for a world populated by others to be imagined. Something like this latter idea is associated with Lacanian psychoanalysis, which counts the register of the *Imaginary*, along with the *Real* and the *Symbolic*, as important for producing subject structures (and, we would suggest, their attendant worlds too). The imaginary, however, is not to be trusted in the Lacanian clinic.[3]

From a psychoanalytic perspective, it could be said that the vampires and human-critters that populate Watts' and Haraway's fictions are figures of a specular imaginary. Further to this, perhaps the sciences, from which Watts and Haraway draw, fuel the imaginary, for beyond the clinic of psychoanalysis,[4] it might be the unruly register of the imaginary – and the seemingly schizoid – which pokes holes in existing knowledge and opens up horizons (which might not be without risk).[5] In presenting a multispecies Chthulucene or non-conscious alien life and vampire-intelligence, Haraway and Watts might be said to present imaginary figures triggered by Science Fact. But there is more to their fictions than this. They each present symbolic relations (albeit somewhat precarious) that either connect human and non-human (and structure kinship, in Haraway's fiction at least) or are shared by humans and non-humans; in this way they develop what we name an *inhuman social imaginary*.

Perhaps it is disappointing that neither Watts nor Haraway address the subjectivities of non- or partial-humans in any great detail; there is no first-person narration of the experiences of Camille – the Monarch-Butterfly-Human who is the subject of Haraway's story – or of the vampire who plays a key part in Watts' novel. The reader is given some insight into the perception and thought processes of vampires in *Blindsight*, though, and we are also told that the 'symbiont children' of Haraway's tale have a 'subjectivity composed of loneliness, intense sociality, intimacy with nonhuman others, specialness, lack of choice, fullness of meaning, and sureness of future purpose' (Haraway 2016: 149). But if the reader is not given any depth of understanding of the subjectivities of the more-than-human protagonists of both tales then perhaps this is because narrativising subjectivity is not a focus or priority for either author. Rather, the focus is on a confrontation with non-human perspectives, which the reader does not have direct access to (unlike perhaps other novels that might present the inner – and often human-like – subjectivities of non-human characters). The perspectives explored in both fictions relate not to subjectivity but to relations that human society, in the eyes of the authors, needs or may soon have to accommodate. *Blindsight* presents a future in which neuroscience, bio-engineering and artificial intelligence seem to be in the ascendency, transforming human society: a cerebral fiction that contrasts with Haraway's fiction, which expresses her symbiotic-orientated politics and thinking.[6]

It is also worth noting that *Staying with the Trouble* and 'The Camille Stories' developed out of Haraway's involvement in collective worlding workshops (Haraway 2016: xii). Haraway's stories are then, in part, a shared social project and the product of group endeavour. We suggest that Watts and particularly Haraway can be said to *science fiction* worlds (as opposed to merely writing Science Fiction) to the extent that they produce inhuman social imaginaries and models for multispecies relations, for others to explore. To understand this we need to turn now to what exactly is meant by the term social imaginary.

A Social Imaginary

The term social imaginary is associated with the fields of sociology and anthropology and is synonymous with the work of Benedict Anderson, who argues that in Europe the advent of printing allowed for imaginary communities of nation states to flourish (Anderson 2006). This suggests that social imaginaries are more than specular images and are mediated or engendered by historical and technological developments. The philosopher Charles Taylor, author of *Modern Social Imaginaries*, argues something similar in stating that a social imaginary is not a set of ideas but that which enables 'a set of practices' (2004: 43). For our discussion of human and non-human societies in the fictions of Haraway and Watts, however, it is the work of Cornelius Castoriadis which proves most interesting, in its positing of what he calls an 'undetermined social imaginary' as the harbinger of social change. As John B. Thompson has noted, Castoriadis breaks with a Marxism that understands existence, even new social organisations, as always already determined. For Castoriadis the world is

> not articulated once and for all but is in each case the creation of the society concerned. In instituting itself society creates in the fullest sense of the term; it posits a new *eidos* that could not be deduced from or produced by a prior state of affairs. (Thompson 1982: 663)

Insisting that the cognitive attributes of a society are undetermined entails a rejection of much orthodox Marxist doctrine – including the technological determinism critiqued by Raymond Williams (a fellow-traveller to Castoriadis it seems to us), and which is said to drive some Science Fiction narratives. For Castoriadis, a social imaginary is, then, a generative force. As Thompson comments: 'Castoriadis contends that the imaginary is what renders possible any relation of object and image … without which there could be no reflection of anything' (664).

If societies are not predetermined, what then produces a new society? Castoriadis proposes that societies are self-realising in the first instance through seizing on ruptures of otherness produced by collectively imagining and instantiating relations different to 'the already-instituted' (Castoriadas 1997: 133). This is an idea that has relevance for our discussion of Watts' and Haraway's social or worlding imaginaries, and for our own notion of fictioning. Castoriadis' argues: 'what is essential to creation is not "discovery" but constituting the new: art does not discover, it constitutes; and the relation between what it constitutes and the "real", an exceedingly complex relation to be sure, is not a relation of verification' (85). Importantly, the imaginary as instantiation of the new produces historical-social fields that are not determined; which is to say, the (social) imaginary itself is not historically and socially determined. As Thompson explains, for Castoriadis, the imaginary is responsible for the orientations of social institutions, myths, traditions and symbolism (1982: 664), an idea which is posed as a challenge to any narrow psychoanalytic theory (Castoriadis 1997: 7). Rejecting the idea that the imaginary is determined or leads to error is crucial for Castoriadis, otherwise one remains chained to the warnings articulated in Plato's myth of the cave and, we would infer, to the idea that engaging with the imaginary leads to illusion or misrecognition (an idea asserted by Lacan in his early writings). The problem is that critique of the 'specular' and the 'fictive' tends to define the imaginary as *an image of something*, and this is not how Castoriadis defines the imaginary at all. As he explains:

> The imaginary of which I am speaking is not an image *of*. It is the unceasing and essentially *undetermined* (social-historical and psychical) creation of figures/forms/ images, on the basis of which alone there can ever be a question *of* 'something'. What we call 'reality' and 'rationality' are its works. (1997: 7).

In relation to this last statement, we understand Castoriadis to be asserting that all imaginary perspectives are social, not because the imaginary is determined socially and historically, but because thinking through the imaginary – producing imaginary figures – is a human 'social-historical creation' (7). We embrace Castoriadis' idea of a social imaginary being undetermined because it allows an 'outside' of existing historical and social institutions to effect the social and historical and thus to transform worlds. However, we would suggest that when a social imaginary includes non-human social agents, then the notion of a social-historical field necessarily becomes expanded and complex. Indeed, the social-historical field envisaged by Castoriadis is arguably rooted in a very Western social imaginary, for there are perhaps social imaginaries which have no history or, rather, do not produce the social-historical institutions Castoriadis refers to. They may, for example, see social-historical fields where others see nature, and natures where others see social-historical fields (to paraphrase Viveiros). There is also the question of what counts as a social agent or actor in the first place – a question that may help us establish a crucial difference between a social imaginary concerned with human social-historical fields and an inhuman social imaginary concerned with the relations of humans and non-humans.

From Human to Inhuman Social Imaginaries

Like Heidegger's notion of worlding, the theory of the social imaginary proposed by Castoriadis understands society and its institutions as being constituted by human actions and decisions that produce history and meaning. Unlike Heidegger however, Castoriadis looks to a social imaginary as having the potential to break with existing time and meaning. This is a key idea for Castoriadis, who is keen to oppose the imaginary of capitalist time characterised by 'indefinite progress, unlimited growth, accumulation . . . of the conquest of nature, of the always closer approximation of a total, exact knowledge, of the realization of the phantasy of omnipotence' (128).

In relation to capitalist omnipotence, Castoriadis spells out the problematic role of the imaginary at the end of the twentieth century in terms of the rationalised projection of future time, suggesting that the 'essential characteristic of the world lies in the fact that it can be reduced to a system of formal rules' which – through the rationalising of Science Fact – enables one to calculate the future (100). The problem is that this imaginary has 'no *flesh of its own*, it borrows its substance from something else', which involves 'the autonomization of elements that in themselves do not stem from the imaginary' (100). In modern capitalism then, Castoriadis suggests that the imaginary is combined with science to produce (overly) rationalised systems, which, more often than not, meet with failure and crisis. This capitalist social imaginary that drives towards mastery is, of course, not scientific in its understanding of the human or the actual temporality of capital: capitalism is ruled by concerns for profit, expansion, and the drive for 'ever more' and 'more of the same' rather than any critical or scientific understanding. Crucially, however, the time and rationalisations of the capitalist social imaginary are in tension with the ruptures, changes and otherness wrought by the operations of capital (128). In contemporary terms, we would suggest this tension is generated by the ways in which capitalism destroys traditions, transforms the environment and ecologies of the planet, and produces new organisations of social life (that are often resisted or that generate alternative notions of living).

Here, Castoriadis makes it clear that he is interested in an idea of time as the 'emergence of what is other' (119). This position seems to us to accord with European avant-gardist or modernist notions of history, as is apparent when Castoriadis states that: 'Time as the dimension of the radical imaginary (hence, as a dimension of the radical imagination of the subject as subject as well as of the social-historical imaginary) is the emergence of other figures' (120). To counter a capitalist or pseudo-rational imaginary, Castoriadis thus proposes a 'radical imaginary' operating through a dimension of time that pseudo-rationalisations (and institutions that project what can be imagined through rationalisation) do not engage with.

At this point we offer not so much a criticism as an observation: for Castoriadis, the figure that emerges through a radical imaginary is that of a human actor as historical subject, or as a human agency within a new social-historical time that the capitalist pseudo-rationalisations of Science Fact can neither envisage nor project. In the Science Fictions of Watts and Haraway – which attend to societies of human and non-human entities – figures emerge that are not human but that nevertheless are social-historical agents. For it can be said that while the emergence of non-human or part-human social actors is a historical event for humans, the non-human or part-human entities of inhuman social imaginaries do not necessarily share a sense of historical time with humans – possibly having perspectives devoid of human-historical subjectivity. Furthermore, they do not necessarily share human conceptions of space and time, or recognise what humans take for reality as reality. For instance, Haraway's character Camille is concerned with the migration patterns of a companion species, and the vampires of Watts' fiction do not suffer the limitations of human sensory processes that produce – from the perspective of vampires – an impoverished notion of space and time, as well as the illusion of selfhood. The importance of this is not just that human worlds or reality are seen for what they are – and that history itself involves a species-specific conception of time – but that in Watts' and Haraway's stories human, non-human and inhuman perspectives and perceptions are active within shared institutions and social organisations. Furthermore, in relation to the critique of capitalist rationalisation offered by Castoriadis, and to his notion of a time of radical otherness different to capitalist time, in Watts' Science Fiction the rationalisations of Science Fact pursued by the military and capitalism can be said to engender inhuman social imaginaries producing new and radical figures. There are, of course, good reasons why, from a human perspective, the placement of vampires within human society might be a bad idea. But Watts' tale points to how capitalists and the military today may already be producing non-human intelligences that manifest a radical otherness – the vampire in Watts' tale is guided by an artificial intelligence – which state politics finds difficult to address (other than as economically and militarily beneficial or socially damaging and divisive, and always in relation to human advantage or disadvantage).

In the case of Haraway's story, and in relation to her concern for the survival of ecological systems, it is clear that her rejection of human exceptionalism includes questioning the impact of capitalism, and indeed of the human, as a primary influence on the history and future of the planet. For whether species flourish or come close to extinction is not always or entirely due to the influence of capitalism, or indeed humans. As far as Haraway is concerned, a virus may prove to be just as important, if not more so, to the life and death of any organism or species than human pollution or environmentally friendly policies. With the inhuman social imaginaries of Watts and Haraway, both the notion of capitalism as limiting radical otherness and the idea that historical events result from human action are questioned, or at least complicated. And while Science Fiction has long held the promise of human and non-human worlds, it could be said that today it is the influence of Science Fact, including discourses addressing the potential for species and human augmentation and the development of artificial life and intelligence, that is developing an inhuman social imaginary most keenly. To explore this imaginary further, we want now to turn more directly to the stories of Watts and Haraway.

Hard-Character Science Fiction

In a lecture for the Toronto Specific Colloquium of 2010, titled 'God, Jackboots and Rule 34 OR How Pornography Could Save the World', Peter Watts reflects upon his porting of neuroscience and evolutionary theory into fiction by recognising a paradox. He understands that his writing produces fictions of non-human perspectives, but that these fictions are for human 'soft-machines' or 'feeling-machines that happen to think' (Watts 2010). To what ends then? Perhaps towards a radical form of scientific-inflected perspectivism – that challenges the primacy of humanity – developed through 'hard-character Science Fiction' which addresses scientific perspectives concerning human limitations. As Watts explains in his lecture – self-identifying, somewhat ironically, as a poster-boy for the new genre of hard-character Science Fiction – humans are ruled by evolution more than they would care to admit. They are electrical and chemical machines responding to environments (Watts 2010). Human brains are not truth-detectors in this sense, but 'survival-engines', meaning that consciousness does grasp reality but only as a narrow stream of 'useful' data. Watts' fictions are designed to 'rub our faces' in this, but for all his irony, he presents an 'outside' (to human experience) through non-human and part-human figures that raises interesting questions about future societies. For *Blindsight* is as much about the relations between a human and non-human crew on a spaceship – as already noted, an artificial intelligence and a vampire play an important part in this society – as it is about the non-conscious alien intelligence the crew are sent to investigate. The vampire, Jukku Sarasti, is the commander of the crew, which consists of an autistic human called Siri Keeton (who observes and reports on his colleagues), a human linguist known as the Gang (made up of multiple personalities), and two humans augmented to act and interact with speed and precision within their environment – Amanda Bates (military officer) and Issac Szpindel (scientist). This society includes the vessel itself, *Theseus*, and the artificial intelligence known as the Captain which hosts, supports and (with and through Sarasti) decides how the crew's mission should proceed. That mission is to examine, communicate with and possibly destroy an alien intelligence which has appeared on the edge of the solar system. Sarasti is chosen as the crew's leader for his abilities to see and think in ways humans cannot. What social imaginary is in play here? How has a member of a species that favours humans as its prey (as the vampires do) come to be placed in charge of a ship – albeit under the influence of an artificial intelligence – with human operatives and answering to the military-industrial complex of Earth?

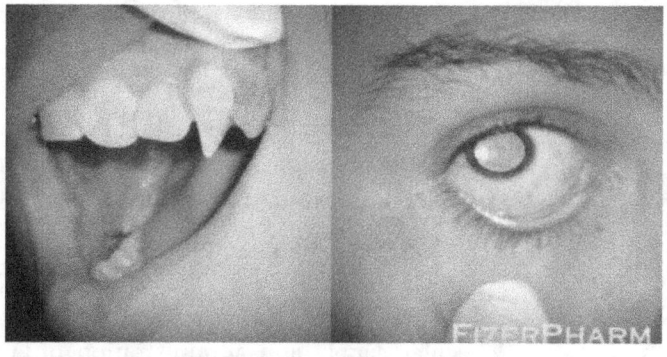

15.1 Still from *Vampires Biology and Evolution* by Peter Watts. Photo: GB (courtesy of Peter Watts).

An explanation for the origin of the vampire-commander – perhaps also pointing to the kind of social imaginary that envisages vampires as managers of work crews – can be found in a video posted online by Watts following the publication of *Blindsight*, which discloses that experiments carried out by a biomedical company called FizerPharm are responsible for human-vampire workforces. The film presents an account of gene therapy administered to Donnie Moss, a high-functioning autistic child (Watts 2009). The narrator of the film states that the aim of the research was to cure Donnie's autism by rewriting the boy's DNA code at the molecular level. Donnie experiences a number of physiological changes following the start of his gene therapy: blood circulation retreats from the surface of his skin, his gum-line recedes and his eyes change to resemble the eyes of cats (see Figure 15.1). Other changes are observed, including a dip in his empathy quotient to a point that identifies him as a psychopath. Not only this, Donnie becomes more active at night and his ability to process information increases, as do his pattern-matching skills. The potential of Donnie's abilities are, however, never fully realised. Progress is hampered, first by non-cooperation and violence, and then, sadly, by death caused by intense seizures induced, as in epilepsy, by visual stimuli. It is not intense or flashing lights that prove troublesome, but the shape of a black cross dividing four pictures on a screen, which ends Donnie's life.

While recognising a tragedy of their own making, FizerPharm do not consider the therapy a total failure. Donnie was cured of his autism and some remarkable data is gathered. True, his retina had been rewired, producing neural-cortex overload when looking at right-angles, but parts of the boy's brain also increased in size. The narrator makes clear that the team were mystified by these results but speculated that gene therapy kick-started junk DNA – ancestral traits – which had remained dormant for hundreds of thousands of years (see Figure 15.2). When the genes were activated Donnie mutated to become a subspecies of the human race, or something entirely non-human. FizerPharm are able to continue their project by experimenting on the inmates of Texan prisons, eventually declaring that a *Homo Sapiens Vampiris* has been produced which has commercial potential. The differences between vampires and baseline non-augmented humans include the speed of their neurological connections, which allows them to perceive multiple perspectives at once, something it would be neurologically impossible for humans to process. In having no empathy, vampires are also excellent decision-makers in business or military contexts. The 'crucifix-glitch' allows humans to limit the threat of vampire attack in the workplace – this is a control achieved through the threat of withdrawing the regular supply and administration of Anti-Euclidean Neurotopes, a drug which alleviates the deadly effects of encounters with crosses.

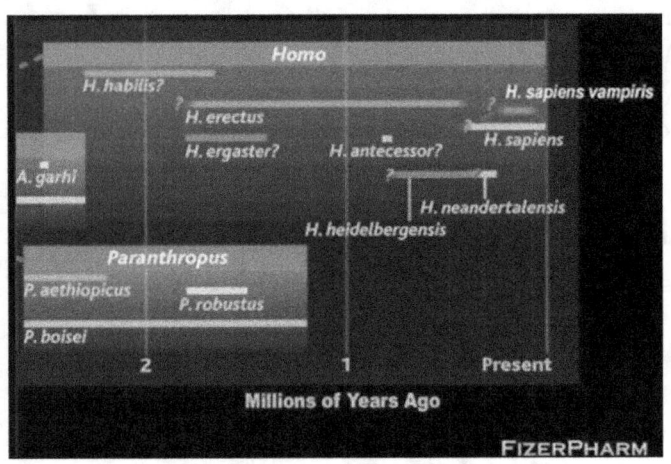

15.2 Diagram from *Vampires Biology and Evolution* by Peter Watts (courtesy of Peter Watts).

This tale explains how a vampire might have come to command a crew on a spaceship in 2082. Born out of the pseudo-rationalisations of a capitalist social imaginary, a crew is assembled. An alliance is forged between (or forced upon) non-human and human – albeit with unknown consequences, for the vampires are enslaved and their motives and logic are beyond human comprehension, producing anxiety and fear as well as efficiency. Siri Keeton, when drifting towards Earth in his escape vessel, hears signals suggesting that the vampires on his home planet have revolted. The competing predators – who cannot abide each other – come together to throw off their slavery, with the promise of producing an inhuman, radical social imaginary or time – a vampire revolution. Castoriadis would be pleased.

But if Jukku Sarasti is a slave he certainly does not behave like one, perhaps because of the influence of the artificial intelligence. Sarasti acts in the interests of humans, vampires and artificial intelligences alike when sacrificing himself to defeat a common enemy, the alien life-form. In this, Sarasti is a social being or agent, albeit one that harbours a potentially extreme anti-social nature and exhibiting attributes that reveal the limited perceptions of baseline humankind. Before Sarasti's act of sacrifice, as already mentioned, we find the vampire directing the working community of the *Theseus* along with the ship's artificial intelligence. Through this pairing of non-human intelligences and the figure of the alien Watts addresses not just artificial intelligence but theories concerning human and machine consciousness and non-consciousness.

At first, communication with the alien entity – which calls itself Rorschach in English and Chinese – seems possible, but as contact is pursued, and as the crew penetrate the alien assemblage and capture several alien bodies, it becomes clear that the alien intelligence is highly developed but not conscious. Watts' imaginary creation – this beast that proves to be beyond human comprehension – is drawn through the perspective of neuroscience, allowing the author not only to probe notions of consciousness but to present a non-conscious intelligence that is inexplicable to and outside of human understanding and experience. Importantly, the alien – which is made up of many parts, and may also exist as a society of sorts – is a threat that unites a human and non-human society composed of conscious entities that share a commitment to intelligence gathering and data processing. It is implied in *Blindsight* that the authorities responsible for the selection of the crew understand the limitations of baseline humans. It is perhaps implied too that the political, business and military interests that rule the Earth understand human consciousness to be an evolutionary dead-end. In this, the lessons of cognitive philosophy and neuroscience may have social and economic effects, evident in Watts' story in the organisation and values of the crew.

To understand Watts' inhuman social imaginary, it is worth reflecting upon the problems the author is concerned with. In presenting the limitations of human consciousness through fiction, Watts addresses problems similar to those confronting philosophers and scientists who study cognition and consciousness, problems such as the philosopher's zombie. The latter is summarised by Daniel Dennett, in conversation with Susan Blackmore, as the idea that there exists 'a being that behaves exactly as you or I behave in every regard – it could cry at sad movies, be thrilled by sunsets, enjoy ice cream yet not be conscious at all' for 'It would just be a zombie' (Blackmore 2005: 81). Here we might think of the non-conscious alien in *Blindsight*, but there is also the suggestion in the novel that the human protagonist Siri Keeton (who has surgically induced brain damage) is thought by some characters to lack interiority; Keeton alarms other humans, for he seems to them to have no depth of emotion or empathy, and no interior consciousness. However, *Blindsight* seems to show that Keeton is not a zombie – he is just seemingly without empathy and perhaps dysfunctional – and this implies that it is possible to identify aspects of consciousness necessary for communication (it is possible to distinguish between Keeton and the alien at least, the latter failing something like an advanced Turing test in the novel). Dennett similarly rejects the possibility that there is a conscious creature that feels and another identically behaving non-conscious creature that does not, and that we would not be able to tell the difference. But he does not dismiss the problem of the philosopher's zombie as uninteresting; for, like Watts, Dennett thinks consciousness is best understood through engaging with counterintuitive ideas. In conversation with Blackmore, Dennett addresses other problems concerning consciousness that are also relevant to the story of *Blindsight* – such as 'change blindness', where an observer does not notice changes in visual information (which afflicts a character in the book during an especially tense episode). This and other phenomena are important to Dennett's argument that the continuity of consciousness is an illusion (84). As already mentioned, the title of Watts' novel refers to a phenomenon found in people who can respond to visual stimuli even though they have a damaged primary visual cortex. The phenomenon of blindsight itself brings into question the idea that there is a continuity of experience that produces consciousness. For Dennett, understanding aspects of the relation of motor-sensory processes, consciousness and cognition requires not a first-person but a third-person perspective, which would sneak up on consciousness from the 'outside' and not approach it from the 'inside', so to speak – a question not of how thought is possible but of how it can be engineered (86). Dennett suggests that first-person experience produces an illusion of what he calls the 'Cartesian Theatre', the idea that there is a 'show going on in the head', with someone (and somewhere from which) to watch it (87). Here we can think back to our discussion in section one of Thomas Metzinger's notion that the motor-sensory processes of the human produce an Ego Tunnel and the illusion of selfhood. Dennett proposes that the human should reject the Cartesian Theatre model of consciousness and become an agent – a body – which has consciousness but which processes information through scientific or objective (third-person) means, so as to act and generate expectations of the future through means other than first-hand experience (88). Returning to Watts' story, it would seem that the authorities selecting the crew of the *Theseus* are similarly minded to promote third-person perspectives or objectivity, as Siri Keeton seems to be the only inhabitant of the ship operating through first-hand experience. He is, as it were, the only crew member locked into an Ego Tunnel. To a greater or lesser extent, the rest of the crew – the artificial intelligence, the vampire operating through pattern recognition and other processes, the medical officer embedded in technologies and environments to the point where he no longer begins and ends at the surface of his body, and the military officer commanding machine soldiers and their viewpoints through sensory augmentation – all seem to operate through third-hand perspectives or distributed viewpoints.

The tension between first- and third-hand perspectives – in terms of species differences – is brought to light following a horrific incident on the spaceship. Sarasti the vampire attacks Keeton the autistic human, who is severely injured in the incident. The reason for the attack becomes clear when the vampire speaks:

'I know your race and mine are never on the best of terms.' There was a cold smile in his voice if not his face. 'But I do only what you force to me to do. You *rationalize*, Keeton. You *defend*. You reject unpalatable truths . . . You and your Chinese Room . . . You reject the truth without even knowing what it is.' (Watts 2014: 332)

The vampire attacks but does not kill the human in order to wake Keeton up to the seriousness of the encounter with the non-conscious alien but also to the reality of his own Cartesian Theatre, the illusion of which crashes when the vampire rips the human's limb apart. In explaining why he tore Keeton's arm to shreds, Sarasti references the problem of the 'Chinese Room', posed by the philosopher John Searle to address whether computer programmes produce consciousness. The vampire implies that Keeton functions by inputting and outputting information without understanding it – just like a primitive computer programme, or like the famous Chinese room in which Searle sits, receiving, processing and outputting Chinese characters through the use of a programme to produce intelligent communication, all without understanding Chinese. In this analogy, we see the vampire's perspective on the human perspective. Here, however, the vampire's lesson is not simply didactic but a matter of life and death. Sarasti wants Keeton to give a convincing account – a message – to his superiors on Earth, and to be fully awake to the truth of their battle with the non-conscious intelligence to come. Keeton surmises this after being launched in a vessel sent back into the solar system. Understanding that the vampire and the artificial intelligence (the Captain) have decided to destroy the alien by blowing up the ship, it becomes clear to Keeton that only the Captain and Sarasti have perspectives and processing power that are a match for the alien. In this, it is not hard to see that the inhuman social imaginary of *Blindsight* points to future societies run or ruled by augmented and artificial intelligences. A social revolution of a kind can be imagined then, in which baseline humans either wise up to their limitations and become augmented or risk becoming of little consequence.

Speculative Fabulations

In Haraway's *Staying with the Trouble*, we find diverse alliances of a very different kind to Watts' community of baseline and augmented humans, vampires and artificial intelligence. Indeed, as suggested above, in Haraway's Chthulucene we find societies beyond the social imaginaries of capitalism. Like Watts though, Haraway draws on biology and Science Fact – combined with anthropology – to suggest that humans and their organisations are produced and influenced by networks and processes of which the human species is often not conscious. She envisages these networks as societies involving multiple species, including non-conscious entities such as humus, bacteria and coral reefs. This is not surprising since Haraway acknowledges Viveiros de Castro as an influence on her writing, and also supports the notion that animism is the only sensible form of materialism (Haraway 2016: 165) – which marks a clear difference between her writing and that of Watts. Viveiros has argued that anything might be said to have a point of view, and Haraway seems in agreement, valuing all perspectives as possible actors within her multispecies social imaginary. Animism aside, the idea that non-conscious and non-human entities might have their own perspectives is not so far away from Watts' accounts (through various characters) of Roscharch the alien and Sarasti the vampire. It is also an idea that, as Susan Blackmore suggests, even Dennett has conceded (Blackmore 2005: 80). Non-humans may have something like consciousness, especially if they (for example a mosquito or a pine tree) can be said to respond to the world selectively. And this might be important for how we think of societies to come, particularly if we embrace Haraway's inhuman social imaginary and her inclusivity of the perspectives of non-humans of all kinds as themselves social-biological agents. We have already discussed Haraway's interest in the chthonic monsters of the underworld (both ancient and contemporary) and in what she calls the Chthulucene, made up of octopi, lichens and creatures that crawl, feast and die on the Earth from which they are born – rich multispecies assemblages 'past, present and to come' (Haraway 2016: 101). From the perspective of the Chthulucene, according to Haraway, we are not post-human so much as com-post (11), and we should make common cause with companion species. As discussed in the previous chapter, this is Haraway's idea of staying with the trouble (staying with environmental problems caused in part by humans but also by other factors), which calls for a reevaluation of human society and of one of feminism's most important areas of concern: reproduction.

Haraway suggests that the Chthulucene needs a slogan; she proposes 'Make Kin not Babies', arguing that the making and recognising of kin is 'the most urgent part' of fulfilling this axiom (102). Haraway redefines kinship through a bio-anthropology – porting biology into anthropology, and then bio-anthropology into fiction – so as to world a kinship beyond human blood-relatives, radicalising notions of the filial and alliance for Western societies (and involving what might seem an inhuman prohibition on the right of humans to have human children). It is in this way that SF, in all its variations (and, we would contend, as a kind of myth-science or obviation), encourages the worlding of alternative perspectives to human exceptionalism and the Anthropocene, including alternatives to stories that present humans as responsible for producing history or reality. Instead, Haraway evokes a radical social imaginary that includes *holobionts* – polytemporal, symbiotic arrangements which hold together 'contingently and dynamically, engaging other holobionts in complex patterns', and which challenge the stories of human exceptionalists, but also narratives that valorise the one, or one species or individual over another (60). Following evolutionary theorist Lynn Margulis – who she suggests knew a thing of two about 'the intimacy of strangers' – Haraway argues that critters 'make each other' through a variety of means, including 'semiotic material involution' from previous 'entanglements' (60), and through digestion and indigestion, partial assimilation and by looping around each other (59). To recognise such critters as kin is to make what Haraway calls 'oddkins' through odd means, rather than human families through sexual reproduction (2–4). Here an oddkin-orientated social imaginary begins to form.

This imaginary is clearly at work in 'The Camille Stories: Children of the Compost' (2016: 134–68). The tale begins by describing the founding of a small community in 2020 by a diverse group, 'including two hundred adults of the four major genders practiced at the time', who build a town called New Gauley (144). The town decides not to bring any new children into the world at first, in recognition of the need for the human population to fall so that other species might have a chance of a future. Instead, they develop a politics, culture and rituals which make kin with other species. Several other societies form and become known as the 'Communities of the Compost' (138), for instead of looking for ways out of ecological problems or ways off the planet, they face (stay with) the troubling state of things which threatens to terminate many species. Through this orientation, a different social imaginary to the Capitalocene emerges: that of Compostism. In 2025 the compostists are ready to produce children, but only a small number are born, five in total. Camille 1 is the only youngster 'linked to an insect' (146), the Monarch butterfly. Camille 1 is genetically modified, gaining genes that pattern her skin differently throughout her life, a modification enabled through scientific knowledge which allows her to taste the wind. She also gains microbes which allow her to consume toxins from milkweed plants which the Monarchs imbibe and store in their bodies to deter predators.

Camille 2, mentored by Camille 1, is given chin implants in the form of antennae when aged fifteen, so that the world of the Monarch can be tasted more vividly. Later in life, Camille 2 travels the migratory route of the butterflies, encountering groups working to repair the environment and protect species. By the time Camille 3 is born the human species is decreasing in large numbers, and continues to do so following a deliberate pattern, while symbionts and compostist communities grow in number (159). The idea of making kin rather than babies spreads, too, resulting in diverse economic and social organisations. When Camille 4 is born there seems to be cause for optimism, but a new viral disease wipes out many species, including the Monarch butterfly. The story ends with Camille 4 preparing Camille 5 for a new role: to be a 'Speaker for the Dead' (164), tasked with remembering the patterns of life of an extinct species as part of the 'curious practice of becoming-with others for a habitable, flourishing world' (168). Haraway's fiction is no doubt conceived as a troubling story, and in this it marks a decision or orientation to foster a social imaginary that challenges the primacy, autonomy and happiness of the human as the goal of social institutions. What is counted as a society or a world, and who or what produces a society – who or what worlds a world – here becomes a most important question.

Foregrounds and Backgrounds

Watts and Haraway may be said to produce conventional narratives and writing, with a beginning, middle and end – a chronological and linear form (though there are some flashbacks in *Blindsight*). This is not a criticism, just an observation that both writers work within familiar forms of story-telling, even if their fictions point to non-human-centred or inhuman futures (we will ourselves turn to an idea of science fictioning that experiments with writing and art that does not take up linear or chronological forms in the following chapter). We understand that the use of conventional narrative styles of writing might be necessary to deliver fictions that are, in part, didactic and mark out an argument critical of other perspectives. Indeed, the didactic aspects of the fictions produced by Watts and Haraway develop and deliver their different inhuman social imaginaries. It is this mix of the speculative and the didactic that makes the pairing of Watts and Haraway seem appropriate to us. For our choice is not random. We suggest that, placed together, their fictions diagram orientations concerning evolution that resist human-centricism. Clearly, they choose different stories with which to produce their fictions and, therefore, project very different orientations and futures. Watts chooses the story of cognitive philosophy and neuroscience while Haraway chooses the biological theories of Lynn Margulis: these are the stories from which they make their stories. And this is, of course, Haraway's point: the choice of narrative mode – what ideas and fictions one uses to think with (and to fiction with) – matters. In that choice the ethics of a fiction (or fictioning) is found.

In telling one kind of story and dismissing others, however, is there a danger of being trapped by a genre or a use of language that is blind to other perspectives or social imaginaries? Perhaps this comes down to political or critical intent or commitment. For when Haraway argues 'think we must!', referencing Stengers among others, she is referring to a situation in which she sees 'human exceptionalism' and 'bounded individualism' as untenable or 'unthinkable' in light of the best biological and social sciences of the twenty-first century (Haraway 2016: 30). Her response is to conceive of 'becoming-with' as a means of developing human engagement with multispecies sympoesis (hence her disdain for posthumanism). If Watts takes a different view – engaging with the posthuman and experimenting with the idea of a post-experience transhumanism, or by writing about a non-conscious alien as an autopoetic entity – then he can still be said to be responding to the best science (as he sees it). Haraway, from this perspective, might be said to be too dismissive of the effects or potential of autopoetic processes and of the kind of human-made tools and technologies – as agents and persons – which allow the symbionts in her story, such as the various generations of Camille, to flourish. Perhaps there is always a blindspot in any narrative, or at least a play of foreground and background concerning ideas in any fiction or fictioning. Certainly, there will be a depth of field in any social imaginary, in which some details have a sharp focus and others are without focus. Haraway cannot be accused of completely dismissing autopoesis though – it is not a blindspot – for she acknowledges that the term is used by scientists that have influenced her thinking. There are moments when she reflects upon this, and indeed her promotion of becoming-with is tempered at one point in her book with an important discussion of autopoesis and sympoesis, which concludes that neither can be privileged to the point where the other is considered irrelevant. Despite often dismissing concepts such as the posthuman, becoming and autopoesis, she recognises too that the terms have relevance, acknowledging that Margulis used the term autopoesis to refer to the processes of the Earth's maintenance and ecologies (61). She also suggests that the word sympoesis had not 'surfaced' when Margulis was writing and concedes that, if autopoesis is not defined as self-sufficiency, then 'autopoeisis and sympoiesis, foregrounding and backgrounding different aspects of systemic complexity, are in generative friction or generative enfolding, rather than opposition' (61).

We think this observation important, and would ask whether, as well as producing generative friction, the movement between – or a diagramming of – sympoesis and autopoesis can be thought of as generative metamodelisation too? It seems that Haraway, in a moment of reflection, opens up the possibility of this diagramming. It is one that we have attempted to produce in comparing the fictions of Watts and Haraway, as two different biological-anthropological orientations producing an inhuman social imaginary that proceed through Science Fact and Science Fiction.

Notes

1   For another detailed discussion of Peter Watts' fiction in relation to the problems of presenting non-human worlds and other modes of existence see Shaviro 2015.

2   We have already defined the chthonic earlier in this section of our book (Chapter 11) as those creatures that come from beneath the ground – and inhabit the earth, humus or dirt – or as not originating from sexual reproduction between males and females. In this, chthonic myths address the problem of origins.

3   To understand this mistrust we need to explain the Real, Symbolic and Imaginary in psychoanalytic terms. In Lacan's early work, the symbolic register is associated with speech and language through which meaning is produced; in the later work it is

associated with a symbolic order of things, understood as a chain of signifiers – such as father, mother, brother, sister – in which said signifiers can be said to have a symbolic place and a particular relation to one another. The real is the limit of symbolisation or the residuum of relations and experience which cannot be symbolised or represented. The real can trigger the imaginary (associated by Lacan with gestalt) and then become registered in the symbolic, but Lacan warns clinicians that the imaginary does not provide any firm ground for analysis or practice: it is implicated in the formation of the ego and narcissism, the misrecognition of the subject, and paranoia (Lacan 2005: 75–81). For this reason Lacan suggests that the imaginary, 'to a greater or lesser degree is only of secondary importance' (1979: 6), insisting that psychoanalysis must operate through a symbolic register or discourse.

4

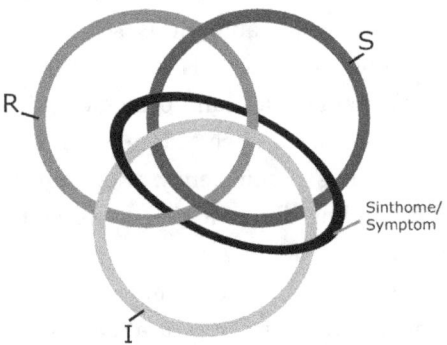

15.3 Diagram of the Borromean Knot (credit: the authors).

To clarify the Lacanian clinic's view on psychosis and the Real, Symbolic and Imaginary (RSI), in his later work, Lacan reassesses the three registers as being of equal importance, and presents their various relations in a diagram based on a design called the Borromean knot that links the registers in various ways (Figure 15.3). In this modelisation of the psyche, the knot is tied together by a fourth strand representing a *sinthome* or symptom – such as identification with authority or order, an obsession of some kind, or creative activities – producing a socially functioning subject operating within symbolic relations. If the RSI knot comes apart, if the Imaginary and Real are no longer tied to the Symbolic, psychosis is said to follow, with life lived in the Real and through the Imaginary without Symbolic order (hence the need for the *sinthome* or symptom to tie the strands of the knot together).

5   In discussing the schizoid and the imaginary, we would mark a difference between figures of the imaginary and figures of the imagination: though clearly related, they are not the

same thing. We would define the latter – figures of the imagination – as being limited to what is known or determined by what has already been given identity or symbolic value, whereas the imaginary can produce apparitions and avatars of an un-symbolised outside or real. To mark this difference, we have elsewhere proposed the term *the imaginal* as the presentation of imagery that cannot be said to represent figures of the imagination with symbolic or meaningful identities (see Burrows and O'Sullivan 2014: 274).

6   Haraway's fictioning of symbionts relates to her long-held interest in companion species relations, as addressed in her *Companion Species Manifesto* (2003). The latter draws on her own relations with a dog called Ms. Cayenne Pepper that could be said to involve a performance fiction of a multispecies partnership, developed through, among other activities, human-canine agility training (a partnership not unlike the human-feline collaborative art practice fictioned by Schneemann discussed in the last chapter). Haraway also refers to her collaboration with Cayenne in *When Species Meet*, which reproduces a letter that recounts a training session in which human and dog were in synch – moving as one – but then felt suddenly unconnected (Haraway 2008: 230–1). The author's reflections on this event make clear her commitment to and investment in the physical and psychic or emotional bonds between humans and other species. Haraway describes the moment of becoming unconnected as traumatic for both human and dog, as a 'tiny tear in the fabric of being' in which 'each is more than one but less than two' (230).

16   From Science Fiction to Science Fictioning

*What if the language in/on the pages has nothing to do with the
'language' by which the book is articulated as an artwork, or anything
else. What if there are different types of language, different qualities and
intensities . . . Perhaps when the book is being read, we are removed from
the influence of other kinds of language. The language 'inside' a book
might be different. Like the succulent contents of a guava fruit – a rich
area inaccessible to 'information'. A kind of change of speed/attitude/
pitch or whatever that puts it out of reach of the rest of culture, or at
least these interpolating forces. Like the soft innards of this vermin . . .*

John Russell, 'Autonomy is Not Worth the Paper it is Written On'

HAVING ADDRESSED SCIENCE Fictions that engage with Science Fact, we want
now to change perspective and look to Science Fiction as a mode of articulating powerful, counterintuitive imaginary models that are not just beyond human-centred worlds
but also beyond rationalisation and science itself. The fictions of Peter Watts and Donna
Haraway can be said to be radical in content but also conventional in adhering to a
world governed by laws derived from the sciences. There are other Science Fictions in
which chaos and contingency produce unconventional narratives or forms of writing
and presentation. An example is Samuel Delany's *Dhalgren* (2001), which presents a
world that does not conform to the laws of physics, but instead explores an alternative
or parallel reality that seems full of contradictions and chaos. We briefly mentioned
Delany in Chapter 11, quoting his important comparison of Science Fiction with
mirrorshades. In *The Silent Interviews*, Delany explains how alternative models of
reality, which he also names as the paraspaces of Science Fiction, are subversive:

we have to note that our paraspaces are not in a hierarchical relation – at least not
in a simple and easy hierarchical relation – to the narrative's 'real', or ordinary, space.

What goes on in one subverts the other; what goes on in the other subverts the one. (1994: 168)

In this, Science Fiction can produce worlds and new conditions that are unstable and that language has to respond to; a bewildering process, as a reader of *Dhalgren* will find. The novel concerns an isolated city in ruins called Bellona, and an amnesiac, bisexual protagonist named 'The Kid', who eventually becomes the leader of a lawless street gang. In Bellona, space and time are fragmentary and circular and events are repeated but differently; in the skies overhead there are sometimes two moons and a sun which sets and rises in the same place. Whether *Dhalgren*'s warped temporalities result from social breakdown and technological catastrophe or the delusions of 'The Kid' (possibly a former asylum inmate), or whether the world depicted in *Dhalgren* is a zone obeying laws of nature alien to Earth, is unclear. But then *Dhalgren* is designed to disorientate and, in terms of both nature and society, seems to be without law.

This chapter addresses more embodied science fictionings that, like *Dhalgren*, can be said to offer alternative worlds and paraspaces that do not conform to existing knowledge, or that do not correlate to experience, concepts or relations that a human might draw upon in order to grasp – and to locate themselves in – a given reality. We begin this exploration by looking at Quentin Meillassoux's concept of 'extro-Science Fiction' – or fictions about worlds in which science is impossible – and, following this, the idea (not specifically taken up by Meillassoux) that formal experimentation, and especially the break with conventional syntax, might operate to present these other space-times. The chapter then moves on to two case studies: the experimental 'novel' *Cyberpositive* by the 'collaborative artist' 0[rphan] d[rift>] (which relates more closely to our argument about formal experimentation, especially with syntax), and the multi-media presentation *SQRRL/Bruce Willis* by the artist John Russell (which develops a slightly different, but parallel, practice of fictioning).

In this exploration, we return to what we identified in Chapter 12 (following Fredric Jameson) as a central paradox of Science Fiction: how to fiction something different in the terms of what there already is (we also return to some of Raymond Williams' ideas about the different forms of Science Fiction). The paradox becomes a question of how to present, or embody, a radical outside within existing human worlds – or, more specifically, how certain kinds of writing, art and artefacts evidence or instantiate logics that are alien and other to our own.

Science Fiction, Extro-Science Fiction and Science Fictioning

The philosopher Quentin Meillassoux offers a compelling inflection on the paradox mentioned above. In his essay 'Metaphysics and Extro-Science Fiction' (2011), he offers a definition of Science Fiction that fits neatly into Raymond Williams' fourth category of 'technological determinism' that we looked at in Chapter 12 (Williams 1978). Meillassoux suggests that whereas Science Fiction concerns itself with the relation of science to fiction and, in particular, the form that this science might take, 'extro-Science Fiction' (which Meillassoux abbreviates to XSF) concerns itself with the possibility of worlds in which the very practice of science is impossible. In this, XSF may be said to also accord with Williams' characterisation of Science Fiction as 'space anthropology' in so far as, very loosely, it explores 'new patterns of living' (Williams 1988: 359).

The novels that interest Meillassoux portray worlds beyond rationalisation (scientific or otherwise). XSF is then a 'genre within a genre' (Meillassoux 2015: 4). To a certain extent these XSF worlds are chaotic and unpredictable, wild even, hence the question of whether they are narratable and can be written as fictions at all, in so far as narrative – Meillassoux also refers to 'plot' and 'storyline' (19) – requires certain laws to relate actions and consequences. In relation to Jameson's temporal and ontological paradox of instantiating the future in the present, the issue becomes: is it possible to think – but also write – these XSF worlds from the perspective of our own world, governed as it is by the laws of science and, indeed, inhabited by human subjects who are constituted by these laws (not least in the production of their consciousness)?

In fact, we might say that this problem is an isotope of a larger philosophical question for Meillassoux (and, indeed, within Western metaphysics more generally) about the possibility of thinking a radical outside to subjective experience. Indeed, Meillassoux's argument is pitched against what he elsewhere names 'correlationism' – simply, that any access to what he also calls 'the great outdoors' (Meillassoux 2008: 7) is compromised by being correlated with a given human subject. This radical outside may also be the future, when understood not simply as the extension (and repetition) of already existing knowledges and logics (including science). In *After Finitude*, Meillassoux demonstrates that it is possible to map out the conceptual coordinates of this outside – that it is, indeed, thinkable – albeit that it is not a place as such but, rather, a radically contingent 'hyper-Chaos' (2008: 64).[1]

We might note here that Jameson's solution to the ontological problem of the future we discussed earlier – the trace – is not so different from Meillassoux's description of the 'archefossil' (2008: 10). This latter names something that is within the world of subjective experience (or within the correlationist circle) but which points to something anterior to that world – or, more accurately, 'anterior to every form of human relation to the world' (10) – and, as such, operates as a problem for any correlationist position which refuses to speculate on an outside. However, Meillassoux's analysis does not stop at this aporia but proceeds from it. Being able to 'access' (if this is the correct term) 'the great outdoors' is not a question of traces or archefossils, but of demonstrating (in a series of philosophical manoeuvres) that the undecideability about the existence of a radical outside to our own experientially closed circle is not a question of lack of knowledge, but more to do with the nature of this outside – again, as pure contingency. It is here that we can return to, and note the connections with, Meillassoux's XSF situation: the future is also pure contingency or 'radical chaos' (Meillassoux 2015: 32).

To illustrate his argument about XSF, Meillassoux uses David Hume's example of the inherent unpredictability of the trajectory of a billiard ball once hit by another ball, and the responses to this problem of causality offered by Karl Popper and Immanuel Kant. He also references the short Science Fiction story *The Billiard Ball* by Issac Asimov (published in 1967), which further illustrates the problem (Meillassoux 2011: 30–50). For Meillassoux, Popper misunderstands Hume's thesis as being about the limits of any given scientific theory (or, simply, that if we had sufficient scientific knowledge we would be able to predict the apparently random movement of the ball), when really it is about something larger: the very possibility of science itself. Popper poses the problem as epistemological, whereas for Hume, it is precisely ontological: 'not simply about the stability of scientific theory, but about the stability of the processes themselves that physical laws describe' (Meillassoux 2011: 34–5). Kant, on the other hand, addresses Hume on his own ground but, for Meillassoux, lacks a certain acute XSF imaginary in so far as he is unable to untether science from consciousness since, for Kant, the existence of one implies the existence of the other (Meillassoux 2015: 32). For Kant then, 'the fact that there *is* a representation of the world' – a certain consistency – refutes Hume's thesis about the possible 'contingency of the laws of nature' (Meillassoux 2011: 46–7). The Kantian argument rests on the idea that a world without science would also be a world without consciousness, thus the very set up of Hume's example (in which the ball moves in a wholly random manner after being hit) is, by definition, unknowable and unthinkable.

Meillassoux's essay on XSF is as much about philosophy as it is about fiction, or, in Meillassoux's terms, concerns itself with the possibilities of the philosophical imaginary. In fact, in his own exercise of such an imaginary, Meillassoux demonstrates that XSF worlds of a certain type are not just thinkable, but also narratable. He describes a spectrum of these worlds where, at one extreme, no laws hold and there is just chaos and collapse (56–7). At the other extreme there are worlds, possibly much like our own, where although there is contingency there is also enough regularity to allow prediction and, crucially, the repeatability of experiments which constitutes science (Meillassoux 2015: 50–2). The middle point between these two poles, where some stability is maintained but there are significant uncertainties is, for Meillassoux, characteristic of properly XSF worlds. These worlds are meta-physically valid and practically narratable, and yet in them science per se is impossible beyond what Meillassoux names a kind of 'chronics' which works through the posi-tioning of relatively loose parameters for experimentation and prediction (Meillassoux 2011: 52–6). In these 'Type 2' XSF worlds there is a stability of consciousness but not enough regularity in the laws of nature to allow science to operate, at least as we know it (Meillassoux 2015: 36).

To backtrack slightly, for Meillassoux a key issue with XSF is that contingency rules and thus, in terms of writing fiction, there is the fundamental risk of narrative rupture (Meillassoux suggests that narrative is the handmaiden of science since both necessarily proceed through cause and effect). He proposes various solutions to this: that an XSF story might be about just one inexplicable rupture and its consequences (reminiscent of Williams' 'externally altered world' (1978)); or that the story might exhibit multiple ruptures and operate on some level as nonsense (albeit still held within a story); or, thirdly, that an XSF fiction might exhibit a certain 'dread uncer-tainty', as is the case, Meillassoux suggests, in the work of Philip K. Dick (2011: 60).

The striking thing, at least for us, is that these different XSF fictions are all under-stood at the level of content; or, to say the same differently, XSF takes a familiar narrative form (albeit the narratives might produce wild events, images and rela-tions).[2] We might speculate then about works that play with the formal and material aspects of writing, as if the technologies and objects delivering an XSF narrative were themselves subject to contingency and chaos. This would be a fictioning of something in which, to an extent, there is a consistency of presentation, but no regularity: a work that is Type 2 (between stability and chaos) in form as well as narrative content. What we are suggesting is a shift from XSF's concern with producing conventional narratives – or recogniseable representations – of a world in which science cannot operate to another but related genre of Science Fiction consisting of works that seem to have no stable logic in terms of their production and presentation and, indeed, reception. And we suggest that it is in art rather than literary fiction that we find this science fictioning at work.

The logic of XSF, when applied to or explored through the form (rather than just the content) of writing, filmmaking and artworks, necessarily implies, it seems to us, a break with conventional narrative and, especially, with the logical sequencing of sentences or scenes and arrangements of material. We are not thereby suggesting that the logic of XSF applied to narrative form is equivalent to the avant-garde prac-tices of the last century (though there are examples or precursors to be found in

European and American art). We are proposing, rather, that in some contemporary artworks the forms of presentation seem to be produced by events of contingency and chaos, rather than as avant-garde experimentation or modernist poetics. These then are fictionings in which sense does not collapse so much as seem to arrive from an outside (one which cannot nessecarily be explained by aesthetic, scientific or mystical interpretation or intent).

Below we suggest that *Cyberpositive* by 0[rphan] d[rift>] and *SQRRL/Bruce Willis* by John Russell are examples of these kinds of artworks in which formal innovation is given an XSF twist. We recognise both as working in a genre of Science Fiction but suggest that they present not so much future worlds to come as a collapse of timelines and sequential notions of history (and in certain instances, of any notion of time and history), for as examples of formally innovative XSF works, they elide conventional narratives of past, present and future. Indeed, the future they present is, it seems to us, radically anterior to any human relation to the world – an outside of the present and its rationalisations.

In our own experimental take on Meillassoux's argument, then, we might describe those works as belonging to another genre within the genre of Science Fiction, and add a further category, that of X(SF), to signify this more radical break with the linearity of both narrative and science. Following Meillassoux's lead, a matrix of X(SF) worlds could include: Type 1, in which there is no or only occasional formal experimentation which breaks with sense; Type 3, where there is non-sense, pure chaos; and between these, Type 2, which are properly X(SF) worlds in which there is a certain consistency and coherence, but where the causes or logics of the formal and narrative shifts in the work escape its audience. X(SF), then, is not just a term for works that represent a world in which science and rationalisation falters, but a genre of works that attempt to instantiate or embody an outside in the world present-at-hand. In that sense, X(SF) does not simply reside in this world but strives to *fiction* another one. It is, then, of the imaginary. After all, a fictional world is produced, but it is a world beyond a symbolic order; and if real – for worlds of a kind seem palpable in the works of 0[rphan] d[rift>] and Russell – then it appears alien, abstract or abstracted too. Is this perhaps where the difference between fiction and fictioning as we have been discussing can be marked?[3] Or where the difference between a fiction that is simply in the world and one which *fictions* another world becomes clear?

In relation to this last question, we suggest that the brackets in X(SF) themselves invite a further and continuing 'bracketing function': after all, why not X(X(SF)) or X(X(X(SF)))? Such an operation (or practice) would suggest that an outside is registered in degrees; that it is never fully encountered, for only an infinite number of brackets would lead to an encounter with an absolute outside or a Type 3 encounter. In this, each bracket might be understood as registering the mark of contingency and chaos fictioned by a work, the degrees of which, after all, are written, developed or composed through formal invention or experimentation. This would suggest a nesting of a narrative of a familiar or understandable world among or alongside seemingly abstract and illogical forms, images and events.

We cannot end these reflections on bracketing without addressing the fictions of Raymond Roussel, who influenced Duchamp, Surrealism, Oulipo and indeed Burroughs, who himself recognised Roussel's fictions as an important, if unreadable, experimental writing (Burroughs 2008: 56). Roussel might be said to have pioneered a mode of writing in which contingency disrupts a linear narrative through unusual formal composition; a method that involves a single sentence nested within a bracket that is in turn nested within other sentences and brackets (which is likened by many to an onion skin holding many diverse and seemingly unconnected thoughts and images). Michel Foucault (2004) suggests that, as with all of Roussel's writing, this technique elaborates a labyrinthine form. Roussel explains that his bizarre and fantastic fictions develop through pairing two nearly identical (and rhyming) words, a procedure which he suggests is similar to writing metagrams (Roussel 1995: 3). This process originates, according to Roussel, in a fiction that starts with a billiard table: *billiard* is then coupled with *pilliard* (plunderer), which becomes the subject of the sentences that start and finish the story (1995: 3–4). This is how *Impressions of Africa* (2011) was produced – one of Roussel's best-known works and an excellent example of his use of bracketing (it is also, as we discussed in Chapter 8, a key precursor to one of our own case studies of fictioning: Brian Catlin's *The Vorrh*). On Roussel's billiard table, questions of contingency and continuity – not so far away from those raised by Meillassoux concerning XSF – are addressed. This leads us to suggest that Roussel developed a method for producing a proto-X(SF) in which the haemorrhaging of sense leads to a wild if poetic imaginary but also non-comprehension or undecideability of sense, generated by the bracketing of seemingly unconnected things, images and events. We find support for this idea in Foucault, who writes that Roussel 'doesn't want to duplicate the reality of another world, but, in the spontaneous duplication of language, he wants to *discover* an unexpected space, and to cover it with things never said before' (2004: 18).

The question posed by our invention of X(SF) is, then: how to artistically manifest the outside in the here and now, and how to give this a traction on present reality? How to present something in the world, which has an effect upon it, but which seems not to be entirely of it? This has been a concern, at least at times, of our own collaborative art practice, Plastique Fantastique, which has involved a play with narrative form and an experimental performance or science fictioning of reality. However, rather than looking to our own collaboration, we want now to further explore some of the above questions by introducing our two case studies.

X(SF) Case Study I: 0[rphan] d[rift>]'s *Cyberpositive*

Cyberpositive (1996) by 0[rphan] d[rift>],[4] is a Science Fiction novel (at least of a kind) with different characters and avatars located in different landscapes and city-scapes, following different plots and narratives (often resembling game-space scenarios). In terms of its content, the text looks to other Science Fiction writing, for example by William Gibson, Greg Bear and Neal Stephenson (alongside Burroughs and Ballard), as well as films such as *Blade Runner* (1982) and *Predator* (1986). It also references sources other than Science Fiction, such as postmodern writers (including Thomas Pynchon) and avant-garde filmmakers (including Maya Deren), at times interspersing quotes from some of the above to produce a dense inter-textuality bordering on opacity (indeed, it is very difficult to give an outline of the book besides this kind of broad description). The book also crosses geographical space, looking to non-Western cultures, specifically voodoo (hence the allusions to Deren and her work on Haitian belief-systems, and to Gibson's early novels), with the loa-spirit world interacting with other virtual and more futuristic 'shadow oper-ators' (a term taken from the Science Fiction writer M. John Harrison).

But *Cyberpositive* is also composed of more philosophical references, sometimes explicit, at other times more implicit: Georges Bataille, Jean-François Lyotard and, especially, Deleuze and Guattari (to mention only the most obvious). It is also itself a book *of* philosophy. Indeed, following Deleuze and Guattari, we might understand this concept creation as itself a form of fictioning, in so far as it involves a different thinking of the world 'beyond' subjects and objects. Fictioning, then, names a different individuation in and of the world, but also other – stranger – causalities and transits, 'crossing the universe in an instant' (Deleuze and Guattari 1994: 201–2).

Cyberpositive is a difficult read, partly because of this content, but also because of the form it takes, with changes in style producing a destabilising of narrative and conceptual coherence. Indeed, as with many works we would identify as X(SF), it often seems that a science of pattern recognition rather than any kind of inter-pretation is most appropriate when engaging with it. A further reference could simply be the effect on the body of electronic music (or, more specifically, techno), a 'genre' which clearly had a determining effect on *Cyberpositive*. But these references mark too that the novel is a work for which all attempts at capturing the sense or logic of the text or composition fail. The book is also difficult because it is partly written in code or, at any rate, does not present a conventional syntax – (indeed, some pages are made up of just 0s and 1s). Figure 16.1 is an indicative example of a double-page spread. It reads as if written by the very machines and artificial intelligence systems it predicts – which, if we follow the philosopher Nick Land (one of the contributors

```
                 o[rphan]d[rift>]                                                    o[rphan]d[rift>]

ǝf_ǝt¥fǝf_ð_´`o´ooɛɛ¡ɛ"ɕɛʈɕ`o  §ǝ¥¥¥ §ʈ_ ¶§¥o101000            101010100101001010010101001000000010101000100000010
111111101010010101010100_b_ǝf_ð_ðbf___`ǝǝ`ǝɴ_ǝ`ǝɴ_ǝɴ_          0101010010101000010
ǝɴ_ɴǝ_ɴ¦ǝ_ǝ ___ǝʈǝʈðǝfǝǝfǝf __ǝ_ _z_...ʈ_ǝǝðǝf_ǝ _____        0010100101010101001010101001001010101001010101001010
___ukj1j11000101010101010101010101010101010101010010          101010000000000000000000000000000000000
00000000000100100100101010000000101010100010010010           000000000000000000000000000000001100000011000000
01010=_=_=_=_=_=_ðð_=ð_ð_fðǝ`ðfǝǝ`fǝðǝf_ǝt¥fǝf_ð_´`
o´ooɛɛ¡ɛ"ɕɛʈɕ`o §ǝ¥¥¥ §ʈ_ ¶§¥ʈʈ¥§ ¥ʈ¶ʈ ¥¶§•¶§¥ʈ¥ʈ ¥ʈ          111100010101101001010000010010010010000001010101
ʈ¥`ʈ¥ʈ¥ʈ¥111                                                  01010100000001001010101001010010101010
o1==_=__=_==ðfðððfð_f  ´`oɛɛ"ɛ""ɛ""ɛ"ǝɴǝɴǝǝɴǝɴǝ_ ___oo         101010100101001010010101001001010101001010101001010
0000000001001001010010010000000000101010001001010             0101010010101000010
1010=_=_=_=_=_=_ðð_=ð_ð_fðǝ`ðfǝǝ`fǝðǝf_ǝt¥fǝf_ð_´`o            0010100101010101001010101001001010101001010101001010
´`ooɛɛ¡ɛ"ɕɛʈɕ`o §ǝ¥1010101010100100000000000010010010010      101010000000000000000000000000000000000
10000000000010101010100010010101010010=_=_=_=_=_ðð_=          000000000000000000000000000000000000000
ð_ð_fðǝ`ðfǝǝ`fǝðǝf_ǝt¥fǝf_ð_´`o´ooɛɛ¡ɛ"ɕɛʈɕ`o    §ǝ¥1101      111100010101101001010 h4sion. the segments ol' which
111101010010101010100_b_ǝf_ð_ðbf___`ǝǝ`ǝɴ_ǝ`ǝɴ_ǝɴ_ɴ           they intertwine. finally. it misconstrues the nature
ǝ_ɴ¦ǝ_ǝ ___ǝʈǝʈðǝfǝǝfǝf __ǝ_ _z_...ʈ_ǝǝðǝf_ǝ _____u          of content. whichs in no way economic in the last
kj1j11000101010101010101010101010101010101010010100000        instance," -mce
00000000010010010010010000000101010101010100010010010101      there are as many directly economic signs or expres-
o=_=_=_=_=_=_ðð_=ð_ð_fðǝ`ðfǝǝ`fǝðǝf_ǝt¥fǝf_ð_´`o´o            sions as there are noneconomiccontents.
oɛɛ¡ɛ"ɕɛʈɕ`o§ǝ¥¥¥ §ʈ_ ¶§¥o101000                              norcanthestatusofsocialformationsheanal-cd bythrow-
111111101010010101010100_b_ǝf_ð_ðbf___`ǝǝ`ǝɴ_ǝ`ǝɴ_ǝɴ_        ingsomesignifierintothebase orviceversa orabitofphal-
ǝɴ_ɴǝ_ɴ¦ǝ_ǝ ___ǝʈǝʈðǝfǝǝfǝf __ǝ_ _z_...ʈ_ǝǝðǝf_ǝ _____      lu-or castration into political economy. or a bit of
___ukj1j1                                                      economics or politic- mto psychoanalysis.
1[1 []o[] н [: THE GEOL[ ][,Y []F м[]l- -L-i: ]                001010000000101010101010101000000001001010101010010100
10001010010101010101010101010101010101010100010000000000      101010101010101010101010100101001010101001010100
00100100100101000000000                                       000001010100010001001010010101010010
000001010  101010  00000  0              0000000000           001010101010101001010101001010101001010101001010101010
000000000000000                                               101010000000000000000000000000000000
00000000111101                                                000000000000000000000000000000000001100000011000000
000
11010100001111001010101                                       111100010101101001010000010010010010000001010101
11                                                            01010100000001001010101001010010101010
1111001010101
1010101                        11101                          -i- There is a third prohlem. it is difficult to
10100000                                                      elucidate the system ot the strata without seeming
                               11111101000101010              to introduce a kind of cosmic or even spiritual evo-
11010101010100101              110000000                      lution from one to the other, as if the- were
     1111000011000000                                         arranged in stages and ascended degrees of perfec-
1111000101011010010100000100100100101000000101010101         tion. nothing of the sort. the different figures of
0101010000000100101010100101001010101010101010100            content and expression are not stages. there is no

                124                                                          125
```

16.1 Double-page spread of *Cyberpositive*, 1996 (reproduced by permission of Maggie Roberts).

to the book) and his idea of recursive temporal feedback loops, it might well be.[5] *Cyberpositive* also contains words from other languages, actual and invented (it can sometimes read like Antonin Artaud's late poetry – some of which we quoted in a footnote in section one – that is thought to be influenced by the artist's imbibing of peyote), and at times letters are voided – glitches occur – leaving words and sentences incomplete. The book is not, however, nonsensical. Even though sense – straight-forward meaning and narrative – can and does break down, the content is still held within a minimum narrative consistency.

The book's science fictioning operates on two levels then: of content (addressing narrative and philosophy) but also of form. Indeed, *Cyberpositive* is both *about* and *of* the future it predicts (it is written in 1996 but from the perspective of 2012). It is impossible and paradoxical in this way. It arrives from a different consciousness – or is fictioned as resulting from a machine consciousness – but it is not simply a story about the latter, nor merely a representation in our familiar language. To follow Land once more, *Cyberpositive* is a fragment of something-yet-to-come smuggled back into our own time in order to engineer its own genesis (2011b).[6] The book is about a schizoid world – in the sense deployed by Deleuze and Guattari – which is out of place and out of time, just as the book itself seemed, at the time of its appearance, to be outside of place and time.

This dislocation is evidenced (or fictioned) by the book's physical attributes: the font and typesetting; the cover and narrow format, as well as its size (over 400 pages); and, indeed, its whole object-feel (or, might we say, following Raymond Williams, the structure of feeling it produces). It is useful to note the original context and point of production of the book: as Maggie Roberts of 0[rphan] d[rift>] and Delphi Carstens remark at the beginning of a reflective piece from 2012 (the year the book had been set), '*Cyberpositive* begins as a text collage to an installation' (Carstens and Roberts 2012). Their essay attends to the book's character as temporal feedback loop, and lists some of the key influences, progenitors and fellow travellers it samples, describing the work as a 'psychogeographical drift through the SF imaginary' (Carstens and Roberts 2012).[7] After the show and book of *Cyberpositive*, 0[rphan] d[rift>] embarked on a series of performances and audio-visual presentations, often with accompanying texts, culminating in the complex 'Syzygy' collaboration with the Cybernetic culture research unit (Ccru), a group we mentioned briefly in Chapter 13. The event was conducted over five weekends at Beaconsfield Art Gallery in London and involved the manifestation of demons/avatars premised on Ccru's calendric system. Although not within the scope of our own book, a 'reading' of that event might present 'Syzygy' as a form of X(SF) or perhaps X(X(SF)). Certainly, both Syzygy and the *Cyberpositive* exhibition were a kind of performance fictioning. But there is something important, too, about the materiality and forms of writing of the *Cyberpositive* book. It is a product of analogue, print technology, featuring words forming paragraphs on paper, invaded – for no fathomable reason – by another technology or form of writing, that of binary code. That *Cyberpositive* can be claimed as X(SF) – as the fictioning of an outside (an unfathomable proto-digital codex from 2012) entering the world of 1996 – is partly due to its narrative but also due to these formal attributes.

Cyberpositive is also a collaboratively produced text in so far as, alongside the writers mentioned above, there were a whole set of contributors who formed part of a particular scene which the book emerged from, but which it also helped cohere. It is, to use a term associated with its authors, a *swarm*-written novel. This sampling of different voices – very much a 'cut and paste' construction – produces a very particular kind of text, one which is prescient of today's writing practices, premised as they are on the edit functions of word processors. But this collaboration – or hive-mind – also suggests a stranger, more alien collectivity from which the book seems to have emerged.

Does this perhaps tie into a certain mythos of 0[rphan] d[rift>] and their sometime collaborators, the Ccru? A key concept for the Ccru was 'hyperstition' (which we have already introduced when writing about Xenofeminism in Chapter 13), defined as both an 'element of effective culture that makes itself real' and a 'fictional quantity functional as a time-traveling device' (Ccru n. d.). Elsewhere O'Sullivan has explored this concept – that in many ways parallels our own concept of fictioning – and its associated mythos, but we want to note here that the Ccru text, 'Lemurian Time War' identifies Burroughs as a key exponent of what it calls 'hyperstitional practice' and describes an approach to writing which, in part, follows from the author associated with the cut-up in the following manner:[8]

> Diagrams, maps, sets of abstract relations, tactical gambits, are as real in a fiction about a fiction about a fiction as they are encountered raw, but subjecting such semiotic contraband to multiple embeddings allows a traffic in materials for decoding dominant reality that would otherwise be proscribed. Rather than acting as transcendental screens, blocking out contact between itself and the world, the fiction acts as a Chinese box – a container for sorcerous interventions in the world. The frame is both used (for concealment) and broken (the fictions potentiate changes in reality). (Ccru 2017: 38)

Such a mythos (and with it, the looping of fictions) perhaps requires a collective basis from which to operate. But it also needs to purport to come from an outside or a place and time in which the logics of the present are not found. Matter is transformed, materials are assembled and inscriptions are made to register something beyond the reaches of aesthetics, religion and the rationalisations of the sciences. In this sense, the compositional techniques of *Cyberpositve* are similar to Ccru's hyperstitional methods.

'Liquid Lattice' (2014), a more recent piece of writing and collaboration between 0[rphan] d[rift>] and the Ccru, also has this fictioning quality. It was published in the third volume of John Russell's *Frozen Tears* project, an anthology of texts and fictions by invited artists which, similarly to *Cyberpostive*, could be viewed as a book and an object (or art object), not least in the density of its contents and its particular length, which is that of a large 'door-stop' airport novel. On the one hand, 'Liquid Lattice' is again Science Fiction – in this case moving from an account of Madame Centauri, her tarot pack and a Black Atlantean magic tradition (with segues of the Cthulhu mythos) to more recognisably Science Fiction landscapes, cityscapes and seascapes, populated by alien and aquatic hominids. It also has the character of a sampled text,

Nine of Spades
Unlidded trinity crosses into lidded pentitude.
Twisted fate looms out of the smokezone while subterranean
inheritance leaves no remains.

Queen of Spades
Lidded quaditude crosses into lidded pentitude.
Black impossibilities stir in the hinterland of reason while
subterranean inheritance leaves no remains.

COMPLIANCE IS THE PROPERTY OF A BODY OR
MATERIAL UNDERGOING ELASTIC DEFORMATION OR
CHANGE IN VOLUME WHEN FORCE IS APPLIED.
THE PRESSURE OF CHANGE.

In due course like attracts like and opposites repel.
They wait.
The power cuts.
A split second glimpse of you, the way you move.
ukuthanda umbane.

Smoothing out. {Dreaming inserts her into the
tactile silence. She trickster, fabulous and drowned,
beautiful in that dead, white way.}
mhlophe ebusuku.

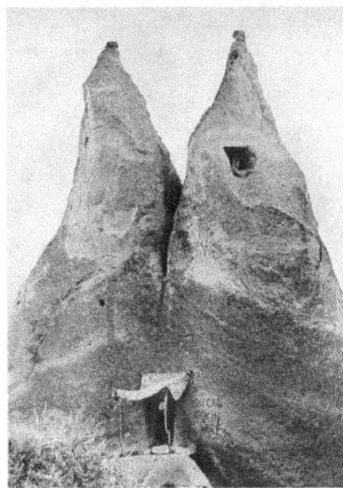

One. Realm of Absent Reflection.
Ummandla mnyama amanzi.

Descending deeper, darkening internalized escape
routes. The light leaves you slowly. Rumbling wave
body. Light time, minus biding its time reveals
repetitions hidden in the twisted hairs.

Ummandla ulwandle ihlabathi.

.......land becoming water water becoming land

The Asian Tsunami and its feedback 2004
(The animals escape)
Hurricane and flooding on the Gulf Coast 2005
Desertification of Northern China
Southern Africa

figure 1, 1a

Violent speed backwards and extreme pressure
tapping into a vast reservoir of turbulence. Moving

16.2 Double-page spread of 'Liquid Lattice', 2014 (reproduced by permission of Maggie Roberts).

written in different styles and with different forms of inscriptions, including typed and hand-written text along with drawings and photos (Figure 16.2 is an indicative double-page spread). Once again, older analogue technologies are brought into conjunction with newer digital ones. And yet, like *Cyberpositive*, it is not a straight-forward narrative. There are also repetitions, permutations of the same elements (reminiscent of the I-Ching) which stymie any straightforward linear comprehension.

If *Cyperpositive* has a certain urgency, a certain *rush*, then 'Liquid Lattice' is more hallucinatory. The drug references are inescapable in the two texts: both read, to use Sadie Plant's phrase, as 'writing on drugs' (Plant 1999), enhancing the sense of a paradoxical event in which the human-produced texts register an outside of human space-time. In the collaborative work of 0[rphan] d[rift>] and Ccru, this paradox is explored in the very existence of objects that present an almost inhuman textual density as print. Indeed, there is no longer an attempt here to address the temporal paradox (of a glimpse of the future in the present) of Science Fiction theoretically – for X(SF) makes clear that the first casualty of the collapse of cause and effect is any logical or sequential understanding of time. Instead X(SF) solves the paradox obliquely – by presenting something of the outside in the here and now.

X(SF) Case Study 2: John Russell's *SQRRL/Bruce Willis*

Experimentation with language, theory and narrative is also an important aspect of John Russell's work, evident in many of his artworks, titles and press releases. The animated film *SQRRL/Bruce Willis* (2015) – whose title, with its missing vowels, gestures to texting and the like but also references an existing Big Data 'threat hunting' company – is a good example of Russell's practice of condensing, abstracting and speeding up words and phrases. In this way a world is inferred in which time is in short supply, or on fast-forward, requiring rapid thinking and communication. However, *SQRRL/Bruce Willis* – a combination of two other animated texts 'SQRRL' (Russell 2015) and 'Bruce Willis, Irigaray and the Aesthetics of Space Travel' (Russell 2014b) – takes its time and establishes continuity through the whispering voice of the narrator and its imagery that unfolds slowly and is familiar; for the visual aspects of the film could be said to eschew any radical formal inventiveness in favour of a more figurative-illustrative style, perhaps relating to XSF's conventional use of narrative. Banal clichés and other 'found' images – the detritus of this world and its predicted future – are mobilised to produce something which any rationalisation struggles to understand, for the world that SQRRL inhabits seems a mixture of the pastoral and technological, and much more than that.[9] To return to Williams once again, the Science Fiction and post-apocalyptic narrative of the film is both about, but also a product of, 'technological transformation'. The protagonist, CarLee is a bio-engineered human-animal avatar, suggesting that the world of SQRRL is shaped by advanced biological augmentation. But the film addresses another form of technology (another form of production, which may be likened to bio-engineering in its capacity to produce new forms), for the creatures that populate the film, and their environments, are manufactured or rendered by increasingly available digital imaging and editing technology.[10] Strange figures abound, such as a human (SQRRL's father?) with a check shirt and pink stalks emanating from his head. The narrator suggests that 'He was one of the first trialists of wasp parasite technology' (Russell 2015), but he is also clearly an image existing in a world of moving collages, of animated clip art and appropriated figures, manipulated by software programmes such as Adobe After Effects.

More generally, Russell's practice might be said to side itself with Williams' category of 'willed transformation' – it is an engaged practice in this sense – especially when this is understood as being pitched against our contemporary Capitalist Realism (we might even describe Russell's work as involving fictions of 'voluntary deprivation' in this sense). Indeed, if the different orientations and narratives of Science Fiction can be attributed different class positions – as in William's schema – then Russell's fictions and digitally produced landscapes are not only set against bourgeois sensibilities but are also, we think, of a kind of extro-proletariat world (to adopt Meillassoux's prefix) or cosmic culture in which aesthetic values are entirely different to those traditions of middle-class taste found in Britain, where the artist lives. In this sense, following Williams' once more, Russell's fictions might also be thought of as examples of 'space anthropology', in that they concern themselves with cultural perspectives – whilst also partaking of what Williams called the 'doomsday' genre.

In terms of some of our earlier comments about Meillassoux's XSF and our own proposition of X(SF) artworks that involve both narrative and formal innovation, Russell's artworks bear comparison with the works of 0[rphan] d[rift>] in that their narrative of worlds are palpable but their rules and logics – as with Delany's *Dhalgren* – cannot be completely grasped. Not only that, the aesthetics of Russell's formal decisions – in terms of composition, materiality and image-production – seem contradictory, offering encounters with alien and alienated perspectives, but also abject and absurd, and joyous, spectacular and familiar encounters too. In this, Russell's work – again, in ways similar to 0[rphan] d[rift>] – exhibits a key characteristic of X(SF), in so far as his output traverses a spectrum that ranges from narrative coherence to nonsensical or opaque presentation. Meaning, such as it is, is held within a minimum pattern of consistency in Russell's works – they are Type 2 worlds in this sense – but also, crucially, they *perform* their fiction, in the sense that the form as well as content, when encountered, seems to be produced by what we might call, in a further nod to Meillassoux, an extro-art-practice (following logics that appear to arrive from a radical elsewhere). In fact, it is especially when the films are presented alongside other sculptural objects and texts that a certain kind of science fictioning is produced, creating the impression that there is a continuity – an exploration of the same alien logics – between representation and concrete object.[11] As far as *SQRRL/Bruce Willis* goes, Russell's presentation of the film alongside an oil-encrusted sculptural turtle impaled on a stake, and next to a large, digitally produced landscape populated with different hybrid avatars, generates a cumulative effect. This was further augmented with the press release and the website of the gallery, which underwent a kind of 'takeover' by the 'SQRRL' script.[12] Russell's practice involves the utilisation of different platforms to produce its very particular scene of fictioning. Indeed, it is this use of both presentation and representation, of object, image/animation and text – as well as the use of digital and 'real' or actual things – which creates the sense that the work is in the world but not entirely of it.[13]

There is also a very particular perspective and attitude in Russell's work. The former might be characterised as a dark and libidinally charged utopianism (that, for some, would be dystopian). In terms of attitude there is a certain kind of humour at play which, it seems to us, arises from two factors. First, a random collaging of materials: avatars, images and narratives are spliced together and, indeed, opposites are forced to coexist (in this sense, 'nothing is true, everything is permitted'). This generates an extro-aesthetic, abstract and nonsensical aspect to Russell's work. Second, there is the manner in which the predictions of the managers of our futures have been stretched or twisted, proliferated and pushed to a certain absurdity. In this, social narratives become apparent and are familiar to those affected by the bureaucratisation of the present and future, but the narratives are also bizarre and alienating too. In both these ways there is less a straightforward critique than a joyous affirmation of difference at work. This combination of the nonsensical (or fantastic) and the social is further twisted by a more general irreverence in Russell's practice – a making-profane of the sacred – for example in the way he deploys Christian imagery (one of the animal-headed demons in the landscape of *SQRRL/Bruce Willis* caries a cross).[14] Furthermore, there is a sense in which many of Russell's avatars, just like some works, are unfinished or have a lo-fi finish (in contrast with the high-fidelity aspects of his other images and works). This can be related to the actual content of Russell's work which often concerns binaries of nature/culture, human/animal and original/copy. His figures – such as those dancing around a Sea Horse May Pole – are composite biological and digital works-in-progress (see Figure 16.3).

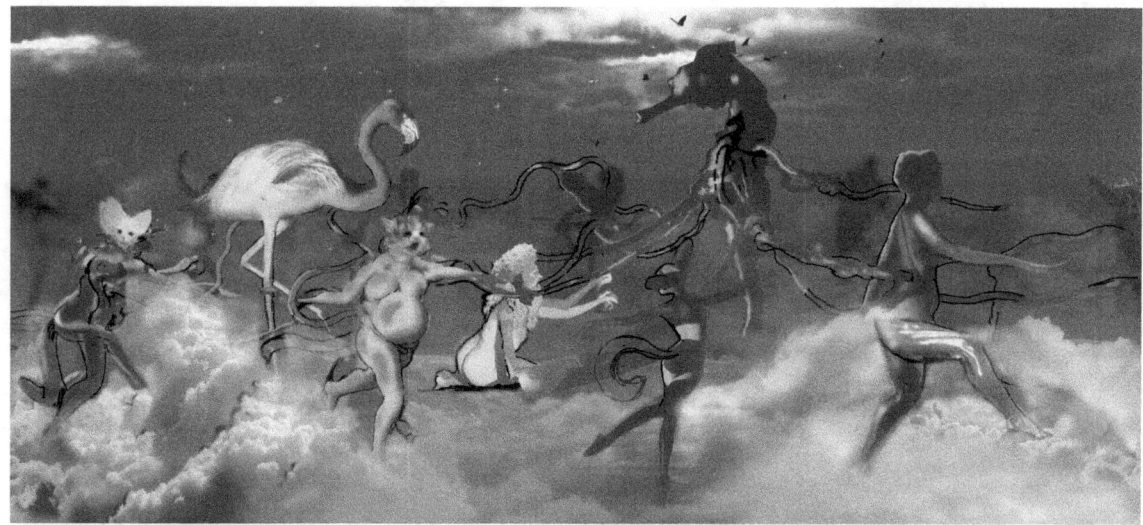

16.3 John Russell, *SQRRL* (detail), 2015 (reproduced by permission of John Russell).

As we mentioned above, CarLee is a hybrid creature, a human brain implanted in a squirrel's body, and *SQRRL/Bruce Willis* in general involves the depiction of a world in which such splicing and multiplication of identity is commonplace. For us then, the film presents a key formal aspect of X(SF): multiplication or juxtaposition. Indeed, this meeting of different logics is a feature of worlds subject to contingency and chaos, and of XSF worlds too, only in Russell's work it is articulated in form as well as in narrative.

As others have pointed out, the use of text is integral to a work like *SQRRL/ Bruce Willis*, in particular to its operating on a further binary between the cerebral and the libidinal. In fact, Russell's work involves a particular kind of play with text and concepts – a theory-fiction, or a fictioning of theory in this case referencing thinkers like Haraway and Irigaray. This is also especially evident in the footnotes to 'SQRRL', which involve asides to Marx's theory of capital, alongside fiction and other more banal – and humorous – commentary (the footnotes are a kind of cryptic-comic conjunction and parallel essay to the main narrative). An indicative example:

> The process of value extraction
> In the capitalist structure
> Is one whereby
> surplus value is sucked upwards
> From the multiple to the increasingly few,
> Like a tree sucks up water.
>
> Later
> Walking
> In the shine,
> Along the Boule'o'vard,
> With DarzZZ,
> A Flower-head
> Seedcase-mackeral hybrid –
> Shoal active.
> They are in Love. (Russell 2015)

In previous work Russell has suggested that he was interested in attempting to 'represent' ideas – not directly nor, for example, through diagrams, but, as it were, through actual imagery or illustration; hence a work like *Untitled (Abstraction of Labour Time/Eternal Recurrence/Monad)* (2009), shown at *The Dark Monarch* exhibition (2009), which, in a style perhaps borrowed from album cover designer Roger Dean, portrays the abstract ideas of its title (see Figure 16.4). Throughout Russell's practice there is a use, as well as an undermining, of concepts and philosophy: a constant confusion (for the viewer) of the serious and unserious, which adds to the sense that the status or meaning of the X(SF) worlds and forms that Russell produces is undecideable.

To further develop this last idea, we note that the main text for *SQRRL/ Bruce Willis* moves between the theoretical and poetic, but also the sincere

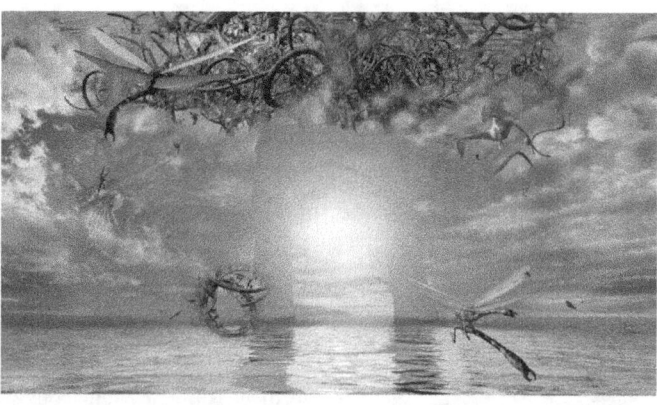

16.4 John Russell, *Untitled (Abstraction of Labour Time/Eternal Recurrence/Monad)*, 2009 (reproduced by permission of John Russell).

and ironic, at times reading like a pastiche. Indeed, other recent writings of Russell's also tread this line (the voiceover of the film also has this character).[15] It is as if any response we may have is rendered inappropriate: if we read the texts as ironic they stare back, blankly and bluntly, in their innocence; if we read them with a knowing wink there is the question of whether we have missed their sincerity. But this is not to say that the artist's texts are composed to deliver meaning or a heartfelt message; Russell has talked about his texts, in a Deleuzian vein, as operating through force rather that meaning per se (Russell and Soren 2016), and certainly their terrain is as much affect as it is signification. Russell also writes art theory more directly – as in the 'Dear Living Person' series of essays for *Mute*, and his contribution to the accelerationism special issue of *e-flux* (texts which all tackle similar issues and questions to our own book); here, a certain density is at play, and an imbrication of concepts and fiction (Russell 2011b, 2011c and 2014a). This all amounts, we suggest, to a very deliberate approach to writing. Indeed, Russell has spoken about how theory is often more productive when it is not understood – or only half understood (Russell and Soren 2016). We are reminded here of Jack Halberstam's identification of an emerging wild theory (as discussed in Chapter 13); indeed, Russell's X(SF) practice could be an important example of this new genre.

In fact, it seems to us that Russell deploys theory and philosophy as a kind of extro-Science Fiction mythos, complete with recurring ideas, images and avatars.[16] It is here that formal experimentation is most productive, for in Russell's practice science, philosophy and theory are visited by forms of inscription and communication from an outside of those fields. At times in the work, it is as if a contingency is operating that renders attempts at understanding cause and effect, reason and argument pointless, no matter how much theory or philosophy one might have read. In this way, X(SF) and X(X(SF)) and X(X(X(SF))), and so on, is fictioned as the logics of other worlds disruptive of but connected to our own. In Russell's work, this frustration of, or resistance to, interpretation or the pursuit of meaning seems to us a virtue, given that the work plays with the logics and imaginary of capitalism. X(SF), then, is alienation as method (an alienation that is doubled, through firstly presenting the estranging logics of capitalism, which are then given another twist – or several twists – and made even more strange). It is also a method that is most productive in contexts where laughter is the most adequate and appropriate response.

Notes

1   See also the discussion of Meillasoux's conceptual manoeuvres (and their compelling audacity) in O'Sullivan 2012: 205–10.

2   In terms of the history of Science Fiction one might also draw attention to the formal experiments of the 'New Wave' of the 1960s and '70s, not least of Ballard and Delany, as opposed to the prior tradition of 'Hard Science Fiction' which focused on extrapolating science – and which is still present in the post-New Wave movement of 'Cyberpunk' which also, generally speaking, holds its fictions with recognisable narrative form.

3   Meillassoux also uses the term fictioning in relation to Kant's imaginary construction of 'a world in which science has become impossible' (Meillassoux 2015: 7).

4   0[rphan] d[rift>] describe themselves as 'a collaborative artist'; first actualised in London in 1994 by Maggie Roberts, Suzanne Karakashian, Ranu Mukherjee and Erle Stenberg, they were especially active in the following decade. Although predominantly visual artists, the collective also involved sound designers, 'concept engineers' and media activists, but they also collaborated with many other individuals, predominantly on temporary and site-specific works. A further key aspect of 0[rphan] d[rift>] was its function 'as an experiment with artistic subjectivity', 'operating collectively as a singular artist which subsumed the individual artistic identities of its core members' (as evidenced, for example, in the authorship of *Cyberpositive*) (the above quotes have been extracted from the 0[rphan] d[rift>] archive on Maggie Roberts' website (Roberts n. d.)).

5   As Land remarks in his book *Templexity* (in what could be a description of *Cyberpositive*): 'narrative ruin is the time-travel effect. When it works, it eventually raises the suspicion that something else has happened instead' (2014a: sec. 1.0). Land has experimented with syntax elsewhere, see for example his essay on the Chapman Brother's art 'A ZiiGothic X-Coda (Cooking Lobsters with Jake and Dinos)' (2011a). In relation to this kind of fictioning see also Amy Ireland's recent compelling essay on 'The Poememenon: Form as Occult Technology', which lays out some of the implications of machine intelligence, as understood by Land, for an avant-garde poetics that foregrounds formal experimentation (especially machine-generated) over content and a complex hyperstitial temporality over simple linear progression (Ireland 2017a).

6   Or as Land puts it at the end of 'Circuitries': 'How would it feel to be smuggled back out of the future in order to subvert its antecedent conditions? To be a cyberguerilla, hidden in human camouflage so advanced that even one's software was part of the disguise? Exactly like this?' (2011b: 318).

7   For a text on *Cyberpositive* that resonates more with the fiction-status of the book (and, again, its character as predictive and prophetic) see Land 2012.

8   See O'Sullivan's 'Accelerationism, Hyperstition and Myth-Science' (2017), which attends more closely to the Ccru's concept of hyperstition in its various instantiations – and to the elision of a certain mythos, associated with hyperstition, in more recent accelerationist writings (such as we will come to look at in Chapter 18). The article also attempts to get to grips with – and critique – some of the recent writings of Nick Land, and, especially, the particular myth-system deployed by Neoreaction and, related to this, the idea of 'hyper-rascism'.

9   The film was shown online by Vdrome in 2015 (see http://www.vdrome.org/russellj.html, accessed 24 September 2016).

10 We will return to fictions that are enabled by new technology (and especially increased data processing power) in the next section of our book.

11 As we pointed out in the Introduction, Russell has himself characterised his work as fictioning, and has written more widely on the latter in contemporary art practice. See, as indicative, Russell 2012a, from where our epigraph for this chapter is taken.

12 See https://www.bridgetdonahue.nyc/exhibitions/john-russell, accessed 24 September 2016. The text was also 'presented' on the first page of rhizome.org in December 2015 (see http://rhizome.org/editorial/2015/dec/07/john-russells-sqrrl, accessed 24 September, 2016).

13 A parallel work is Russell's *Tetragrammaton* (shown at LD50 Gallery, London, in 2016), in which the digital backlit landscape (this time circular) was accompanied by a sculpture of a giraffe. This show was a joint presentation with Joey Holder, whose work might also be understood as a form of science fictioning or, more particularly, a fictioning of science.

14 This is more explicit in other recent work, for example the crucifixes of *Jexus*, shown at MOT, Brussels in 2012. See also the text written to accompany this show (Russell 2012b).

15 See also, for example, 'Faerie Poem' (Russell 2009).

16 In this vein, Russell also collaborates to produce a kind of multi-platform scene of fictioning. See, for example, the event (or 'Curated futurological poetry reading and performance') 'Barefoot in the Head', co-curated by Russell with Mark Beasley and Alun Rowlands (2009), and 'The Thinking', another collaboration between Beasley and Russell, also with Sam Walls and the Science Fiction film writer Damon Packard (2004).

17 Non-Philosophy and Science Fiction as Method

*The Stranger 'makes' the void: it transcendently anaesthetizes all types of
(psychological and soiciological) conditioning . . . The content of this void
is precisely a transcendental multitude, a non-auto-positional democracy.*

François Laruelle and collaborators, *Dictionary of Non-Philosophy*

*Photo-fiction is not at all photographic fiction; neither,
indeed, is it philosophical fiction; we must rather understand
it in the sense of science-fiction – as a genre.*

François Laruelle, *Photo-Fiction, a Non-Standard Aesthetics*

IN THIS FINAL chapter of section two we switch scenes somewhat, turning to a
particular kind of practice and perspective that François Laruelle names non-
philosophy, so as to conclude our exploration of science fictioning – a genre that we
have broadly addressed as involving both a performative element and the registering
of an outside (however figured) to human consciousness, perspectives or rationalisations. We should say at the outset that we will also be returning to Laruelle – and to
the implications of his thought for technology and what we call mythotechnesis – in
section three, since he is, for us, an important if provocative and challenging thinker.

In part one of what follows we discuss non-philosophy – or what is now also called
non-standard philosophy – with a particular eye to its relevance for what might be
called life praxis. We begin this enquiry, that itself loops us back to some of our
discussion in section one about the fiction of the self, with an account of the ways
in which Laruelle's thinking challenges a certain conditioning of thought,[1] before
going on to discuss the more Gnostic and utopian aspect of Laruelle'e thinking. The
detailed examination of the principles of non-philosophy will then help us think as
the 'Stranger' of our first epigraph, which we suggest involves exploring a (non-
philosophical) conceptual persona and a fictioning that proceeds through destabilising

but also using the 'authoritarian autopositions' of philosophy (Laruelle and collaborators 2013: 47–8).

Part two begins with a discussion of two relatively recent essays by Laruelle which address the relations between philosophy and art (in particular photography), especially in relation to fiction and models. It is here that we discuss the photo-fiction of our second epigraph, as a form of science fictioning, by sketching out three possible variations – with case studies – on the conjunction of non-philosophy and art practice. If this more theoretically orientated chapter can be said to have two destinations then – the fictioning of the 'Stranger' (and strangeness) of non-philosophy *and* the ways in which art practice might be said to explore (or again fiction) non-philosophical orientations – it consistently holds at stake the mapping out of a speculative and synthetic practice of thought, which might also be described, following John Mullarkey (2006), as a practice of metamodelisation and the deployment of fiction as method.

PART I: Non-philosophy

Definitions

In his work on non-philosophy (comprising of over twenty-five books to date and periodised into five distinct phases of development) Laruelle claims to have identified and demarcated a certain autocratic (and arrogant) functioning of philosophy in its tendency both to position itself as the highest form of thought (enthroned above all other disciplines) and at the same time its attempt to explain everything within its purview. Indeed, each subsequent philosophy must offer up its own exhaustive account of the real, 'trumping' any previous philosophy in an endless game of one-upmanship. John Ó Maoilearca describes this particular pretension more strongly, suggesting that philosophy itself is a form of 'thought control' which attempts to define the very act of thinking through its particular transcendent operations (more on these below) (Ó Maoilearca 2015: 1).

Non-philosophy pitches itself against this particular apparatus of capture – though it positions itself as neither an anti-philosophy (as, for example, in Alain Badiou's description of Jacques Lacan's psychoanalysis), nor as simply an outside to philosophy (at least as this is posited *by* philosophy). Non-philosophy does not turn away from philosophical materials so much as it reuses or, we might say, retools or reconfigures them. As Ray Brassier, amongst many others, has pointed out (following Laruelle's own suggestion) the 'non' here is more like that used in the term 'non-Euclidean geometry' (Brassier 2003: 25): it signals an expansion of an already existing paradigm, a re-contextualisation of existing material (in this case conceptual), and a placing of these alongside newer 'discoveries'.

From these few sentences we can already extract two key characteristics (or distinct articulations, perhaps?) of non-philosophy. 1. It involves an attitude and orientation towards philosophy which also implies a kind of practice (or, at any rate, a particular 'use' of philosophical materials). Important in terms of our book, Laruelle also calls this a performance, as well as, crucially, a science: non-philosophy is the 'science of philosophy' in this sense (Brassier's writings on Laruelle attend specifically to this more 'formal' articulation of non-philosophy). 2. Non-philosophy might be said to name other forms of thought – other practices we might say – besides the philosophical (again, when these are not simply positioned, and interpreted, *by* philosophy), whilst, in the same gesture, naming a general democratisation of all thinking (Ó Maoilearca would be the key Anglo-American exponent of this second articulation, hence the title of his recent book 'on' Laruelle: *All Thoughts are Equal* (2015)).

We want to take each of these two articulations in turn, but before that a further brief word about non-philosophy and the real. For Laruelle, as we have already intimated, philosophy involves a particular take on the real: an account, explanation or interpretation of the latter. Non-philosophy, on the other hand, is a thinking which proceeds from the real (or alongside it) – rather than positing a real, it assumes the real's always already 'giveness' as a presupposition or axiom. For non-philosophy this real is itself radically foreclosed to thought, at least as this is typically understood (it cannot be 'explained' or interpreted in this sense); as such, we might say that the third key articulation of non-philosophy is that it implies a form of Gnosis. In fact, alongside its formidable complexity there is a sense in which non-philosophy can be immediately grasped in an almost banal – or at least naive – sense. We will be returning to this and adding some qualifications below.

The Science of Philosophy

For Laruelle all philosophy involves a common function – or invariant – which he names 'decision'. Put simply, philosophy sets up a binary which dictates its subsequent operations. It is always 'about' a world which, in fact, it has itself determined and posited as its object. In Laruelle's terms (on Brassier's somewhat technical reading) this is 'an act of scission' producing a dyad between a conditioned datum and a conditioning faktum (Brassier 2003: 26). The decisional structure involves a further move: philosophy's 'auto-positioning' as ultimate arbiter over these two terms. Philosophy offers a certain perspective and a higher synthesis – a 'unity of experience' – over both conditioned and conditioning (Brassier 2003: 26). Philosophy's cut, we might say, produces a particular subject and world and then offers a perspective (the only one) from which to think both.[2]

We might also call this auto-positioning philosophy's ideological character: it is the real that causes or produces – or at least, in the last instance, determines – philosophy, but the latter is then abstracted out and seen as itself cause of the real (hence, its production of the world). The connections to two of Laruelle's key precursors, Marx and especially Louis Althusser, are explicit, but we might also note that this perspective bears some resemblance to Lacan's theorisation of the retroformation of the subject (which must come to reverse the illusion of the ego and assume its own causality), as well as to Deleuze and Guattari's own materialist account of the subject as residuum in *Anti-Oedipus* (a subject which misrecognises itself as prior to the process – the syntheses of the unconscious – which produced it). Indeed, in a relatively recent summary of non-philosophy, Laruelle himself suggests that non-philosophers are very close to both the analyst and the political militant (Laruelle 2004).

This decisional mechanism is not restricted to philosophy as a discipline or discourse, but impacts on our thinking more generally (we are all philosophical subjects in this sense). We might note here the resonances with Jacques Derrida's 'diagnosis' of a logocentricism which is determinate in philosophy (at least in the Western tradition), but also in other forms of apparently nonphilosophical thought (the lack of hyphen here denotes the non Laruellian sense of this term). Commentators have suggested that non-philosophy in Laruelle's sense is either a less convincing form of deconstruction (as in Andrew McGettigan's critical overview of Laruelle) or, indeed, a more radical operation that re-positions deconstruction as simply another form of philosophy (as in Brassier's own overview) (McGettigan 2012; Brassier 2003). Whatever the interpretation, it seems clear that Derrida is the 'near enemy' of Laruelle, but also (at least to us) that non-philosophy, although clearly indebted to Derrida, involves something more affirmative (at least potentially) than the often melancholy science of deconstruction.

Non-philosophy is an attempt, then, to practise philosophy (at least of a kind) without the aforementioned auto-positioning. Crucially, it does not involve a straight-forward disavowal of the philosophical gesture (again, it is not nonphilosophy in this more straightforward sense), and, again, it does not involve recourse to a simple outside which might be simply folded back in *by* philosophy (as we suggested above, all philosophy claims to supersede previous interpretations, to *really* get to the real 'from' a more radical outside perspective). Non-philosophy, for Laruelle, must pursue its task from within philosophy's own interpretive circles (we might note, again, the connections with deconstruction as a process always already occurring within Western metaphysics).

To backtrack for a moment: as we mentioned above, non-philosophy is not another take on the real (nor, indeed, a sufficient explanation of it), but proceeds from the real. For Laruelle then, non-philosophy names a more radical immanence – arising from a suspension of decision – which is specifically other to the world produced by philosophy (whatever the claims of the latter about its own immanence might be).[3] Again, non-philosophy is a thinking *from* a real which is itself indifferent to that thinking (there is no reverse causality – or 'reciprocal determination' – in this sense). On the one hand, then, this real is very simple: it is just 'this', immediately graspable, almost pre-cognitive (in this respect, for Brassier, it is thus ultimately uninteresting and empty). And yet, as Robin Mackay points out in his own compelling introduction to Laruelle, it is, in fact, not self-evident at all (at least to a 'subject' that is in and of the 'world') (Mackay 2012: 2). Indeed, how could it be self-evident to a subject who has been produced by the very philosophical operation (the decisional structure) in question?[4]

Non-philosophy (at least in this particular articulation) will then use concepts, but only after they have been untethered from their properly philosophical function – their auto-positioning and what Laruelle also calls the 'Principle of Sufficient Philosophy' (the claim to truth, or, as Anthony Paul Smith puts it: 'philosophy's faith in itself before the Real' (Smith 2016: 26)).[5] It is this which 'explains' some of the complexity of non-philosophy, both that it can read like philosophy (it cannot but be very close to the philosophy it writes on) and that it must use neologisms and other unfamiliar terms – indeed, not only a new vocabulary but, at times, also a new syntax – in order to articulate its non-philosophical operations away from already existing philosophical language. This might be where we find the 'Stranger' of our epigraph, an embodiment of thought (or a different way of thinking) that approaches the real through repurposing philosophy – eliding decisionism, determinancy and certainty – so to produce other, stranger accounts of what philosophy takes for granted as its kingdom.

We might call the enunciations of the 'Stranger' a ventriloquism of philosophy by non-philosophy (and a kind of *fictioning*), in so far as the 'explanatory' power of philosophy (its various claims about the real) are transformed into something else: models with no necessary pretensions to truth. Certainly, in his more recent writings (as we shall see) Laruelle suggests that non-philosophy is concerned with just such a mutation of philosophy, which he calls 'philo-fictions'. If this is not exactly *alienation as method*, it certainly utilises a kind of *estrangement as method* that in itself makes selfhood unstable. For it seems to us that the 'Stranger' is without a certain auto-positioning and those other key conceptual structures that secure a sense of self and give consistency to subjectivity. If the concepts necessary for selfhood and subjecthood are problematised by non-philosophy then this also makes an enemy of ideology. Or, at least, the perspective of the 'Stranger' of non-philosophy would be continually suspicious of ideological discourses that claim a privileged perspective on truth or the real (never feeling at home within such discourses).

We note here the connections to Marx and Althusser: as mentioned above, we might think of philosophy as a particular ideology (with its truth claims) and, thus, of non-philosophy as a form of ideology critique.[6] The apparent 'real' world of philosophy – from the perspective of non-philosophy – is itself revealed as a fiction, determined (in the last instance) by a more radical immanence which has not been determined by philosophy at all (this real is, precisely, undetermined). However (and following Mackay once more), one cannot draw a simple line of demarcation here between ideology/philosophy and a science which 'demystifies' them. That would be to produce a further binary which philosophy could then reach across and, ultimately, subsume; it would be to produce yet another philosophical circuit, a further structure of decision. Hence the importance of what Laruelle will call 'superposition', a placing of the two alongside one another (we will return, very briefly, to this later on in this chapter).[7]

To see all this from a slightly different perspective – more topologically (or even non-topologically) – we might suggest that non-philosophy involves a kind of 'flattening' of philosophy's auto-positioning and a concomitant undoing of its 'Principle of Sufficient Philosophy' (again, its pretension of being able to account for all of the real). We might then diagram this process as in Figure 17.1.

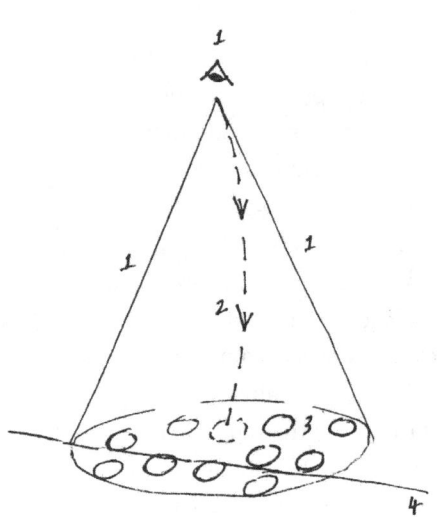

17.1 Diagram of the flattening of non-philosophy (or 'change in vision') [1. Philosophy (view from above); 2. Non-philosophy (as dropping down); 3. Philo-fictions (and other modes of thought); 4. Non-philosophy (as clinamen)] (credit: the authors).

This diagram shows the particular 'change in vision' (to use a Laruellian phrase) which non-philosophy entails, a kind of dropping down of philosophical perspective and, with that, what we might call a rejigging of foreground and background or figure–ground relations (we are reminded here of some of our comments about Wagner's coyote earlier in this section). Here it is as if the conceptual material has been laid out flat, as on a tabletop. The 'view from above' is replaced by something more immanent (in fact, Laruelle suggests that non-philosophy is less an overview than a line – a clinamen – which touches on different 'models' of thought). We might note here an immediate and obvious connection with art practice in so far as non-philosophy becomes a practice that involves the construction of a different kind of conceptual device, which allows for this shift in viewpoint.

Other Modes of Thought

In the diagram above (Figure 17.1) we might also note the possibility that the 'flattened' philosophical materials – the philo-fictions – can be positioned alongside other forms of nonphilosophical thought. Philosophy, when untethered from its 'Principle of Sufficient Philosophy', becomes just one mode of thinking alongside a whole host of others: artistic, but also the scientific and even, perhaps, the animal (again, this is the democratisation of thought that is most thoroughly tracked through in Ó Maoilearca's work on Laruelle).[8] Non-philosophy gives us an interesting way in which to (re)position philosophy and its materials (as laid out above) – a radically different point of view as it were – but it also offers up this corollary perspective on how different forms of thought invariably 'coexist' and, indeed, might interact. This is to posit a radical horizontality – which we suggest is the terrain of the 'Stranger' of non-philosophy – which operates between heterogeneous practices. As we claim above, in this change of vision philosophy is brought down to earth, operating as a fiction – offering a certain perspective or model amongst others. In the same gesture, other forms of thought (for example art), in their turn, are given some philosophical (or, at any rate, non-philosophical) worth in so far as they are no longer unfavourably compared with a philosophy enthroned above them.

This second articulation of non-philosophy as naming different kinds of thinking is less explored by Laruelle (although we will look below at two texts by him on the kind of thinking which photography, for example, might perform). As Brassier suggests, this is surely because non-philosophy, in one respect anyway, has very little to say about such different forms of thinking and practice – it does not involve yet another philosophical take on the different terrains 'outside' philosophy that it can then appropriate via its own definitions (Brassier 2003: 27). But, of course, these other forms have been theorised elsewhere (there is plenty of theoretical material out there on art, the animal, and so on), and, more obviously, they are already occurring without the help of philosophy (as in the work of artists, scientists and so on, but also, more radically, in the sense that animals, for example, already think in some respects).[9] The question is, then, whether these theorisations have hitherto always been philosophical in character (proceeding from decision), and, indeed, what a non-philosophical theorisation of, for example, art might be (which is to say a theorisation which does not involve decision). There is also the supplementary question as to whether these other forms of thinking need an account – from philosophy or non-philosophy – in the first place.

A more general question concerns what follows for non-philosophy from its particular shift in perspective: what *other* kinds of thought does it make possible in its very re-definition of thinking? To a certain extent this is precisely a work of experimentation and, indeed, construction. The possibility of what Mackay calls 'non-standard worlds' which arise from this shift and radical change in perspective cannot be predicted – or even perhaps articulated – in typical (read philosophical) language (Mackay 2012: 8).

In relation to this we might note Laruelle's interest in poetics, or forms of writing – fictions – which are not *for* philosophers (after all, it seems clear from even a cursory look at Laruelle's corpus that the readership of his major works must at least be familiar with philosophy).[10] These are forms of writing and thought which are untethered from decision. Indeed, what forms of writing, we might ask, are really adequate to the properly non-philosophical subject that we have been referring to as the 'Stranger'? Might there be some connections here with the X(SF) of our previous chapter?

To develop this exploration of what we have called the second articulation of non-philosophy (the flattening), we might suggest two more lines of enquiry. First, and in relation to some of the material we have looked at in section one, it seems to us that there might well be a highly productive encounter to be forced between non-philosophy and schizoanalysis around the question of the non-philsophical subject in so far as schizoanalysis pitches itself against a certain kind of overdetermining of the subject by psychoanalysis, at least in some of its guises.[11] And second it might also be that Laruelle's project of non-philosophy can be said to have a spiritual and intuitive dimension. It is this that it seems most important to address – as constituting the most radical aspects of non-philosophy – before moving on to discuss non-philosophy and art more fully.

Gnostic Science Fictioning

Ultimately what is at stake in non-philosophy is not an academic question about the problems of philosophy but the future of the human; and if the human is to have a future, this may involve the science fictioning of modes and models that might be, in some way, utopian. For Laruelle states that:

> non-philosophy is also related to Gnosticism and science-fiction; it answers their fundamental question – which is not at all philosophy's primary concern – 'Should humanity be saved? And how?' And it is also close to spiritual revolutionaries such as Müntzer and certain mystics who skirted heresy. When all is said and done, is non-philosophy anything other than the chance for an effective utopia? (Laruelle 2004)

In relating non-philosophy to Gnosticism and Science Fiction, Laruelle is suggesting that his project develops a heretical and almost mystical knowledge that escapes philosophical decision and differentiation. Gnosticism values intuition and intuitive participation with the divine. Likewise, non-philosophy insists on a direct participation in or with the real not just as a means of gaining understanding and insight, but as a way of living, as Subject = X too. We might also call this (in a nod to Pierre Hadot): Non-Philosophy as a Way of Life.

It seems to us that non-philosophy is at its most compelling when it is thought in relation to this other way of living – what Michel Foucault once called (though for different reasons) 'life as a work of art'. This is to 'apply' non-philosophy to expanded practices beyond the gallery, but also to think about aesthetic practices in more general terms, in relation to what Guattari once called the production of subjectivity (and the expanded ethico-aesthetic paradigm that is implied by this).

Following some of the work discussed in section one (and as we have gestured towards above), we suggest a non-philosophical take on subjectivity will involve a diagnosis of the ways consistency is produced for a sense of self and subjectivity.[12] For ourselves, it is more interesting that non-philosophy (and its conceptual persona the 'Stranger') might also point to the possibility of being in the world without a fixed sense of a self (with all the attendant issues this can bring). We identify this mode of existence without consistency for selfhood with Laruelle's suggestion that non-philosophy might be the only 'chance for an effective utopia'. Such a utopia would mean living a life away from those forms that have caught and restricted it: it would be to refuse philosophy, especially in its key operation of producing truth and, in turn, a subject of truth that a self might identify with. Non-philosophy, then, might be about untethering the self from its auto-positioning, its own enthronement.

In fact, it seems to us (as we suggested in Chapter 3), that what follows from this 'insight' is not the 'dissolution' of the self exactly but, we might say, a holding of it in a lighter, more contingent manner – as, precisely, a fiction (and, in so far as the self is the anchor point for numerous other fictions, then these, too, are seen *as* fictions). Crucially, this raises the possibility of producing other fictions of the self (or other fictions of non-self) and, with that, the exploration of other ways of being in the world. We might note here that this is in accord with the 'Stranger' of non-philosophy, who Laruelle also identifies as the 'generic human', which names a 'radical ordinariness' which is nevertheless at odds with the world (as produced by philosophy).

A compelling question – one which we have gestured towards throughout this chapter so far – is what this terrain outside the self might be like and if, indeed, it can be explored. Mackay writes well on this discovery of the generic 'beneath' the subject produced by philosophy and how we might begin to experience and experiment with it (for it is not a given, but, to echo Deleuze and Guattari, needs to be constructed, piece by piece) (Mackay 2012). It seems to us that it is with this grand vision of the work of non-philosophy that we begin to see the more profound connections with – and radical implications for – what might be call a non-art practice.

PART 2: Photo-fiction and non-art practice

Philo-Fictions to Photo-Fiction

We want now to turn briefly to Laruelle's writings on what he calls 'photo-fiction', which in many ways address – and bring together – the articulations of non-philosophy outlined above. Indeed, for Laruelle, in so far as photography contains its own 'Principle of Sufficient Photography' (or, we would say, in so far as certain practitioners would claim photography has a particular claim to truth), an apt way of thinking the relationship of philosophy to non-philosophy is *through* photography and its relationship to what Laruelle calls non-photography. Indeed, photography (at least at first glance) is an accurate – and faithful – 'picture of the world'; it is, we may say, a graphic example of those standard modes of thought which Laruelle writes against. Outlining a possible non-photographic practice is then also a way of outlining a non-philosophical practice.

In his essay 'What is Seen In a Photo?' Laruelle pitches his own take on the photograph against any 'theory' of photography which positions it, precisely, as a double of the world. Indeed, the task is to think the photograph as non-representational (however counterintuitive that might sometimes be) (Laruelle 2011). On the face of it this idea is not new or unknown to modern or contemporary art, and is hardly radical, for such notable figures as Wolfgang Tillmans have produced abstract photographs (as seen in his exhibition of a series of non-representational works at the Serpentine Gallery in 2010), and it might be hard to find any artist or art student who would articulate the naive idea that a photographic representation is a double of the world. For Laruelle however, non-photogaphy can be understood as a radical or heretical practice in so far as it requires a certain stance or posture of the photographer – and with this the instantiation of a very particular kind of relation to the real – which then, in turn, entails the production of a different kind of knowledge (one which does not arise from representation). To see the photograph (and photographer) in this way means suspending a certain privileging of perception and 'being-in-the-world' as paradigm. In this refusal of phenomenology – and yet more philosophical 'interpretive circles' – Laruelle suggests that science and its approach to the world might operate as a guide in so far as the latter proceed through a pragmatic and experimental engagement with the real (or, at least, with a demarcated 'section' of it).[13] So, just as non-philosophy involves a particular take on philosophy, a use of it as material (untethered from its interpretive function), so non-photography will involve a use of the photograph as material (as very much part of the real) instead of (or besides) its representational function. In each case the conceptual and photographic materials are positioned as fictions – or what Laruelle, in this essay, calls photo-fictions and philo-fictions.

In a more recent essay which further develops this idea of photo-fiction Laruelle tackles the philosophical discourse of aesthetics more directly, tracking a move from the latter (a philosophical account of art's self sufficiency or truth) to what he calls, generally, 'art-fictions', and, with these, the practice of a 'non-aesthetics' (this being an aesthetics not tied to a 'Principle of Sufficient Philosophy' but, instead, arising from what he suggests, again, is a more scientific paradigm involving the positing of models) (Laruelle 2012c).[14] On the face of it, then, this later essay is less about art practice (photography or otherwise) than about philosophy as instantiated in the discourse of aesthetics, and how one might re-position the latter. Indeed, there is still a minimal aesthetics at work here, at least of sorts (an account of what art 'is'). That said, Laruelle's own claim is that these photo/philo-fictions operate *between* photography and philosophy, with each discipline surrendering its own 'auto-finalised form' or 'auto-teleology'. Again, our sense is that many contemporary photographers might not recognise themselves in Laruelle's account of photography, however, Laruelle's thinking here is of interest, involving as it does a very particular move or gesture. The two disciplines of photography and philosophy are reduced down – themselves flattened – and brought together in what Laruelle calls the matrix, or generic: 'in which photo and fictions (as a philosophy or conceptuality) are under-determined, which is to say, deprived of their classical finality and domination' (Laruelle 2012c: 16).[15]

The generic – a kind of image or 'space' of thought which is non-hierarchical (or radically horizontal, to return to a term we used above) – is then this other strange realm (of the real) that is yet to be determined. Laruelle will also call this levelling out an algebra of philosophy/photography, which we suggest emphasises that photo-fiction does not produce pictures *of* the world. This second essay by Laruelle then is concerned with the building of a new conceptual or theoretical apparatus which is capable of producing these strange photo-fictions. These are forms of thought (broadly construed) which are less explanatory or interpretive of the world as it is and more speculative in character. This strange kind of non-photographic apparatus is also necessarily a phenomenologically reduced one. It 'pictures' what happens to experience when not tied to a self/interpreter, or, again, when such experience is not 'processed' through representation (we are reminded of some of the writings of Brassier discussed in Chapter 4, and that we will address in more depth in Chapter 18). We might also say that the fictions produced by this apparatus are somehow weaker (again, they are 'under-determined'), untethered as they are from a certain pretension. A more modest form of thought, perhaps, but also one that has the potential to expand the very idea – and working out – of what thought is and might become (it is in this sense that Laruelle's 'non' announces a turn from hermeneutics to something more heuristic – and here once again we are reminded of the X(SF) artworks discussed in the last chapter that frustrate interpretation through their formal or concrete experimentation and attributes).

The key for Laruelle in all this is, again, photo-fiction's break with representation and mimesis (he writes of the jouissance at the end of 'photocentrism'). In itself these photo-fictions imply and, it seems to us, help produce a new kind of subject (if we can still call it this) or what Laruelle calls in this essay (in a nod to Kant's own notion of a nonempirical transcendental subject) 'Subject = X'. Is this perhaps also the subject promised or delivered by X(SF) in its most abstract instantiations? Again, photo-fictions also imply a new realm to be 'discovered' – or constructed – 'beyond' the 'world' of philosophy/photography (Laruelle 2012c: 15). As indicated above, Laruelle is interested in the quantum and he turns to quantum mechanics here (and, indeed, in much of his recent writings), where he finds the tools adequate and appropriate to this experimental re-organisation or re-construction of the world (outside of representation as it were). Such a 'new' scientific theory borrows the principle of quantum superposition from physics – in which perhaps the most counterintuitive idea is that a particle can be in two places at once – as a model for thought. This model allows for indeterminacy and therefore avoids philosophical decision. Indeed, it is precisely quantum science's break with the determinancy of mechanical laws of the universe which makes it so useful for non-philosophy. We might even say that non-philosophy, in this sense, is quantum philosophy – and that the Subject = X (or the 'Stranger') is the quantum-subject.

Having laid out some of the characteristics of Laruelle's thinking on photo-fiction we now attempt to address the ways non-philosophy might be explored through art practice, or as non-art practice, especially as this relates to what we have been describing in this section of our book as science fictioning.

Art as Diagrammatics

Diagrammatics (in terms of this chapter) might be a name for practices that include the recontextualisation, reorganisation and general manipulation of philosophical materials which have been untethered from their properly philosophical function or discourse. In relation to art practice manipulating philosophical materials more explicitly we might note the possibility that concepts can be refigured diagrammatically. In a simple sense they can be drawn, but to diagram philo-fictions also suggests a different kind of imaging or even performance of concepts. In fact, what is often termed conceptual art, in many instances, involves just such a take on philosophy; practices such as those of Joseph Kosuth (arrangements of objects, images and words exploring definitions) and Peter Halley (abstract works that function as diagrams of homes and cells or panopticons, initially drawing on the work of Michel Foucault and Jean Baudrillard) are obvious examples here. More recently, the work of artist and writer Patricia Reed involves diagrammatic presentations of the relations of capitalism, alienation and subject production in which there is a use of philosophical materials *as* material. In Reed's artwork, philo-fictions are drawn or imaged and put to work, as in her *Technosphere Diagramme* (2017) (see Figure 17.2).[16]

A key question is what these philosophical materials 'do' (or what can be done with them) when untethered in this way: what is their explanatory power (if that still has a meaning here)? Or, to put it another way, can this be anything other than the use of philosophy as illustration, or 'caption' (Laruelle himself uses the latter term when

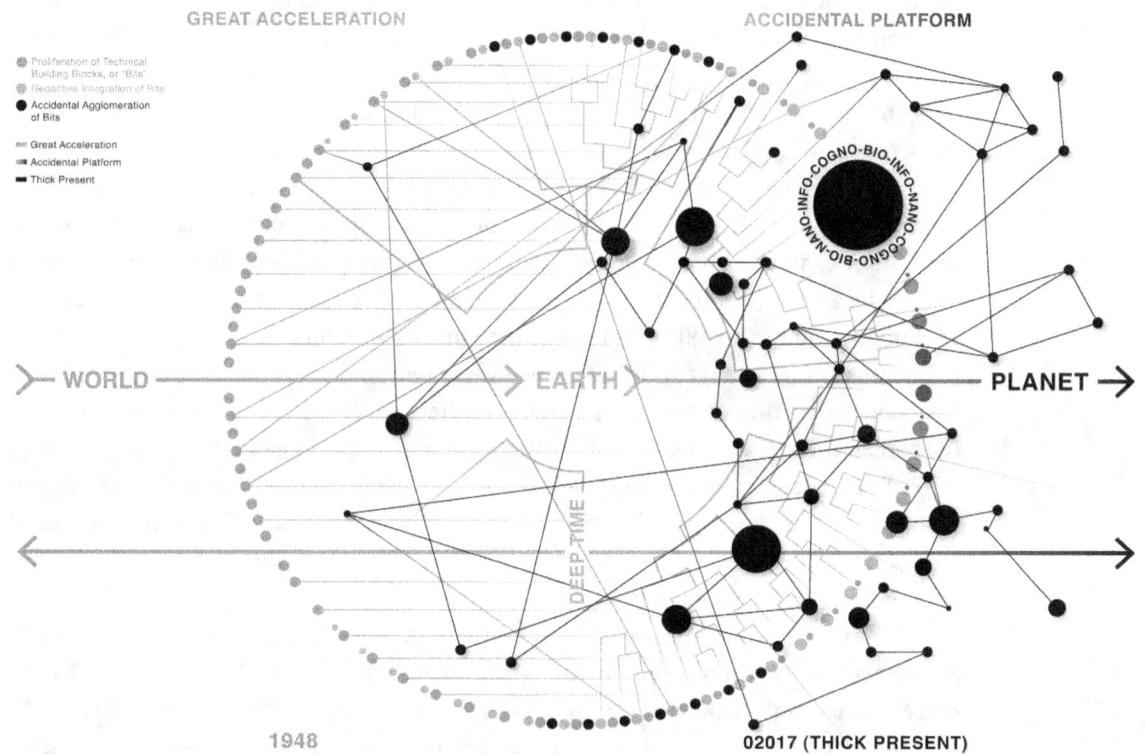

17.2 Patricia Reed, *Technosphere Diagramme*, 2017 (courtesy of Patricia Read).

writing of philo-fictions)? What, we might ask, does the treatment of philosophy in this way allow us to think? One answer is that it might, for example, suggest surprising and productive connections and conjunctions between different conceptual resources, given that the normal philosophical rules are suspended.[17] Philosophy (or non-philosophy) becomes a more synthetic – and, again, speculative – practice in this sense, rather than an analytic enquiry. More radically, this kind of practice opens up the different space of – and for – the different kinds of thinking we mentioned above.

An Art from the Real

Non-philosophy might also point to a multiplicity of thinking – the other kinds of thought – which subsist alongside the philosophical and, perhaps, also the conceptual. Indeed, there is the important question here of the role of affect in art practice, and whether this more pathic register might also be understood as a kind of non-conceptual thinking – a different kind of nonphilosophy perhaps? We suggest non-philosophy approaches this question by looking to an art that is of the real (and not about the real). Indeed, just as many artists can be said to develop a singular and independent take on conceptual material, many art practices can be said to be involved in non-conceptual explorations without the help of philosophy (or, indeed, non-philosophy). Here we might think of the abstract Colour Field painting of American modernism in which colour is the subject of the work, or the films of avant-garde artist Jonas Mekas who produced a film a day for the diaristic project *The 365 Day Project* (2007). It is, however, the work of James Turrell that seems most relevant here. As Alexander R. Galloway notes, Laruelle has himself written favourably about Turrell in a text on *First Light* (1989–90), a work consisting of a series of twenty aquatint etchings. Turrell is best known for the architectural or site-specific arrangements that frame changes, visible to the eye, in natural light, an event often produced by the artist cutting or exposing a shape in the wall or ceiling of a building, such as that created for the Israel Museum titled the *Space That* Sees (1992). In this work, Turrell presents a square of colour – the sky – which gradually changes in tone and hue throughout the day. Galloway notes that Turrell has stated he is not interested in symbolic thought, and that his work has no image, object or focus, further commenting that 'no wonder Laruelle was drawn to *First Light*' (2013: 230).

Galloway also notes that, for Laruelle, Turrell's practice produces a 'non-standard art', using light without phenomenological exploration (or without recourse to the correlationist reflection that we discussed in the previous chapter), for Turrell asks the viewer 'not to think about perception, but to think *according to* perception' (232). Galloway relates this idea of a non-standard art to Laruelle's notion of photo-fiction (231), although he acknowledges this might seem perplexing:

Fiction might seem like a strange word choice for an anti-correlationist, yet Laruelle avoids the vicious circle of correlationism by devising a type of fiction that is non-expressive and non-representational. Laruelle's fiction is purely immanent to itself. It is not a fictionalized version of something else, nor does it try to fabricate a fictitious world or narrative based on real or fantastical events. (234)

We might conclude, in the somewhat convoluted terms that non-philosophy invites, that Turrell and other similar artists produce a fiction that is of the real, as a fiction immanent to itself. This is fiction with no reference outside itself and one which is not produced by philosophy or any other discourse. It could be said that Turrell takes an ordinary act – like looking at the sky – in order to fiction the everyday or familiar as strange or abstract (or alien even). In doing so, it seems Turrell renders the viewer passive, for, here, thinking itself becomes a lens or light cones or photoreceptor cells. Nevertheless, it can also be said that a science fictioning of a real from within the real takes place within this performance.

Cloning (as Performance Fiction)

If this sounds paradoxical, another way of addressing the science fictioning of a real from within the real is through Laruelle's notion of cloning – a process that Galloway suggests results in clones of the real that are *one* and the same with the real, in that cloning produces a duality that is not a synthesis (Galloway 2014: 28). In other words, clones are a 'duality, a twoness, yet they are nevertheless bound together through a relationship of identity, a sameness' (61). This can also be understood, following Galloway, as '*The identity equation* a = a' (58). We will return to this idea in section three, but for now suggest that various art practices can be said to develop such an equation. An example would be the work of Wade Guyton and his exhibition *Das New Yorker Atelier* at the Serpentine Gallery, London (2017), consisting of banal images and newspaper and magazine pages found in the artist's studio. This material is photographed and scanned by the artist, and then digitally manipulated and printed on canvases, the weave of which is visible as a surface element of each work. This work can be said to reconfigure the artist's studio and its information and images, and makes evident the materiality of the printed image through presenting photographic images abstracted to a greater or lesser extent through the artist's production process. While perhaps uneventful and, it must be said, conservative in form (owing much, perhaps, to the territory of painting explored by Gerhard Richter), the canvases, as well as being both image and object, make strange that which is banal. And like Turrell's work, they cannot be said to be about the world or offer a truth of the real. They are works from a practice that thinks from the perspective of the camera, scanner and printer (as material cloning machines rather than picturing devices).

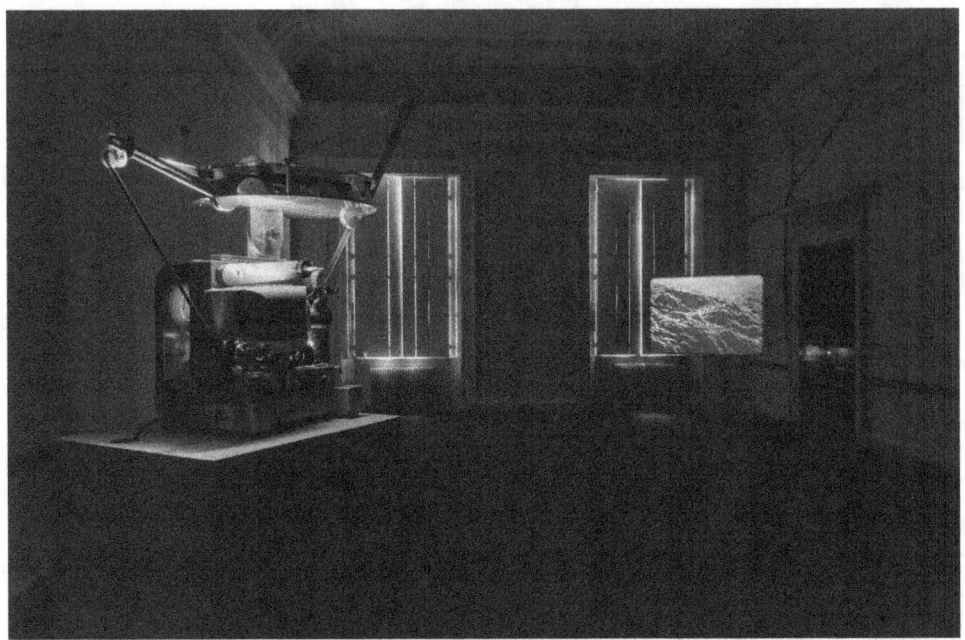

17.3 Seth Price, untitled film, 2006, installation view ICA, London (courtesy of the artist and Mark Blower).

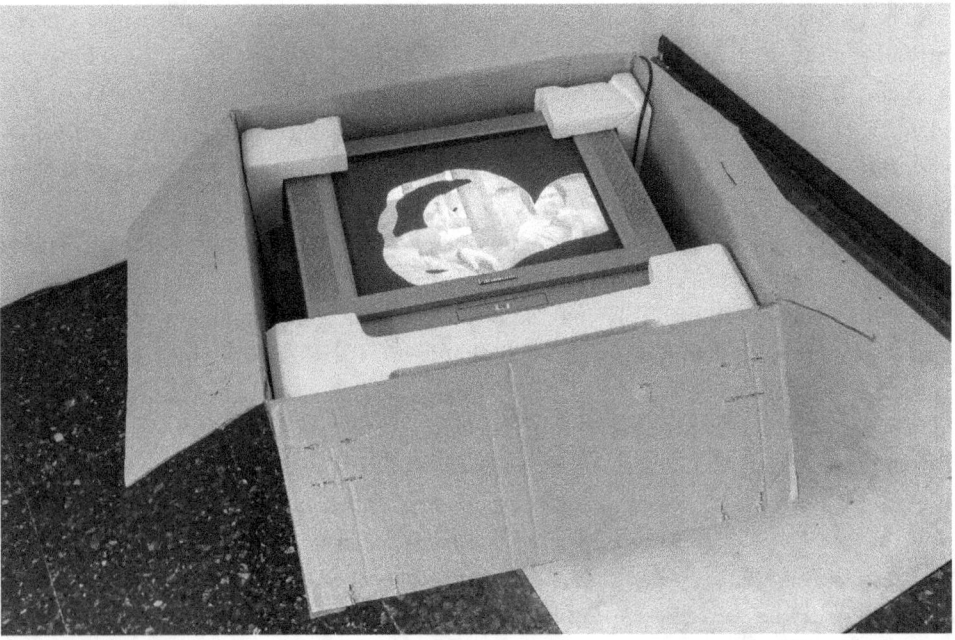

17.4 Seth Price, *Spills*, 2004, installation view ICA, London (courtesy of the artist and Mark Blower and Petzel Gallery).

Another New York based artist who could be said to copy and re-present is Seth Price, in that his work is made up of appropriated images, film clips, sounds and patterns that draw attention to the way art and other material is produced, or manipulated through post-production and dissemination in different social and cultural spheres. Through an assimilation of processes and material, Price composes film works that mix digital and analogue media (see Figures 17.3 and 17.4). This interest in different approaches is found in his installations and wall and floor works that serve as indexes or that emphasise the indexical, 'second-hand' or mediated aspects of the work's production – examples here are Price's vacuum-formed reliefs of a jacket titled *Vintage Bomber* (2006) or of body parts titled *Different Kinds of Art* (2004), and also a fractured and folded perspex sheet balanced on a metal frame and exhibited at Reena Spaulings Fine Art, in New York, in 2004. As with more recent work such as *Social Synth* (2017), a video loop made with a robot-controlled camera directed to take close-ups of a squid (see Figure 17.5), Price's presentations seem to have a level of abstraction, not just because of the non-representational aspects of some works but because, in Price's art practice, any thought is in accordance with media processes rather than directed towards cultural or social understanding or commentary. This is a conclusion – the thoughts of a burgeoning Subject = X perhaps? – provoked by viewing *Social Synth*, in which the close-ups of the squid

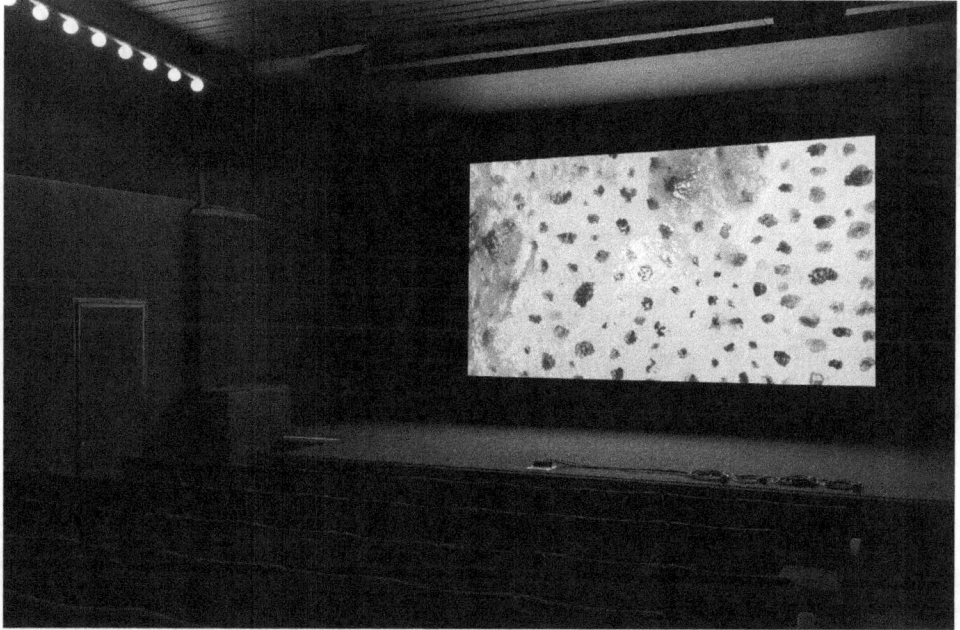

17.5 Seth Price, *Social Synth*, 2017, installation view ICA, London (courtesy of the artist and Mark Blower and Petzel Gallery).

are composed using an algorithm and imported into a 3D effects program to add lighting and movement to the images, producing an exploration of a cephalopod surface. It can be said that, in terms of hermeneutic triggers, this work offers very little, which is in keeping with Price's thinking about art:

> There is a question to which no artwork has an answer, to which every artwork is susceptible, which is, so what? There is no answer. You ask it of yourself, as an artist, and there is only silence. It's not a nihilistic question, or pointless scepticism, because the silence produced is actually useful. The silence records an echo: the artist has made a noise and prepared some kind of recording device to capture the echo that comes back. Your utterance now has a shadow that cannot be cast off. The shadow is the work. (Seth Price quoted in Kalmar 2017)

The work of art as echo or shadow could be said to be the theme of Price's exhibition *Seth Price Circa 1981* at the ICA London in 2017; a retrospective which concentrates on Price's video and film work that is, as Stefan Kalmar writes, 'rarely fixed at a single point in time' and often 'reconstituted and re-versioned' so as to be made deliberately ambiguous and unstable (Kalmar 2017). The viewer is faced with a retrospective without a linear narrative concerning the progress of the artist's work over time (and the persona of the artist rarely seems fixed too). Nothing is claimed for the work by way of insight about reality. In this silence we find a world of production, post-production and dissemination, as a media-world rather than as media works about the world.

Reconfiguring and re-presentation then might be an important way that art avoids the traps of philosophical decision, which we suggest, certainly in Price's practice, involves an ongoing performance or process rather than a manufacturing of artefacts. To explore this further, we offer one more account of a cloning-type practice that can be described as performance art. At the end of a conference at Goldsmiths, University of London, on 'Fiction as Method' (17 October 2015), the artist and writer Tim Etchells performed a 're-mix' of the previous speaker – the Science Fiction writer M. John Harrison – and his compelling reading of one of his own short stories. Both presentations, one a piece of fiction the other a performance (though each partaking of the other), were somewhat different to the previous papers. Indeed, if the latter had generally been *about* fiction as method (that is, a discussion about practices engaging with fiction, albeit involving creative as well as critical approaches), here, in both of these last contributions to this particular conference, we were presented with fiction *as* method itself. Harrison is known for, among other novels, the Kefahuchi Tract Trilogy, consisting of *Light* (2002), *Nova Swing* (2006) and *Empty Space* (2012), which features a black hole without an apparent event horizon, suggesting that chaos leaks into the vicinity of the singularity, causing material and time to become subject to collapse and reconfiguration – a quantum effect. Something like this effect was produced by Etchell's remix and re-presentation of a story just heard, a science fictioning that disrupted the familiar and linear conventions of the conference programme as a sequence of original and interpretative papers offering perspectives of knowledge. On hearing both Harrison and Etchells speak, it was as if the whole conference assemblage had somehow tipped – and phase-shifted – from being about fiction to being of a fiction. We would suggest that performance art often has a quality of producing this effect. For performance can be thought to be non-representational in so far as – in its very liveness – it offers an experience or presentation that cannot exactly be called a representation, being, as it is, live.[18] More than this, Etchell's cloning of Harrison's words is, then, yet another example of a science fictioning – as experimental exploration – that offers perpsetives of or alongside the real as opposed to a reflection on the real. In this, philosophy, or indeed any other operation that claims to present truth, is disarmed: *NOTHING IS DECIDED, ALL DESICIONS ARE PERMITTED.*

Notes

1   The following account in part one of this chapter is heavily indebted to a number of introductions to Laruelle's thought, including those by Ray Brassier (2003 and 2007a), Robin Mackay (2012), John Ó Maoilearca and Anthony Paul Smith (2012), John Ó Maoilearca (2015) and Anthony Paul Smith (2016). These and other secondary texts are referenced throughout (often in footnotes).

2   Philosophy, in this sense, constitutes an ongoing desire to account for or explain the real, but what it looks to – the world – is always already a mirror in which it sees only itself, or, to quote Laruelle (very much in a Gnostic vein): 'They seek the One precisely because they have not found it, and they will never find anything other than what they already are: them-"selves"' (Laruelle quoted in Smith 2016: 81).

3   As Laruelle will argue in relation to Deleuze's philosophy (see, for example, Laruelle 2012a).

4   Nick Srnicek suggests something similar in his own take on a politics (and a certain aporia) which leads from non-philosophy: any form of typical intervention in the world cannot but be determined by that world (or take place within the horizon of decision) (Srnicek 2011). Non-philosophy can, in this sense, open up a view from elsewhere (for Srnicek, it can open up a kind of non-capitalist space), but it cannot offer any content. Brassier's reading of Laruelle's method puts this necessary abstract character and formal inventiveness in more positive terms as the very work of non-philosophy (Brassier 2003).

5   Indeed, Anthony Paul Smith is especially attuned to the arrogance of Philosophy – and, not least, its connection to a 'wider' European colonial attitude (hence the importance

of non-philosophy in the decolonisation of thinking). In his *François Laruelle's* Principles of Non-Philosophy: *A Critical Introduction and Guide*, Smith is also keen to maintain and defend the category of the human (albeit not the human of a straightforward humanism, but of a more generic 'force-of-thought') against those other readers of Laruelle – Smith has Brassier especially in mind – who are intent on dismantling the human or hastening its demise (Smith 2016).

6   In relation to this it might be that non-philosophy can help to diagnose and critique 'contemporary art' as a whole, identifying a particular logic at work – for example, indeterminacy – which is, as it were, a structuring invariant, whatever a given practice might claim. Such is the strategy of Suhail Malik, who calls for an exit from a contemporary art which he sees as the handmaiden of contemporary neoliberalism. Here the very openness of the work of art is seen as profoundly ideological. This is an area that Amanda Beech also addresses in her own take on Laruelle and on the problems she sees with an art practice invested in freedom, immediacy, difference, contingency and so forth. For Beech, besides this critique of the typical operating procedures and logics of contemporary art, at stake is the outlining of a different practice – or science – of the image, one which embraces its representational/mediatory character in its own kind of 'critical-political project' (Beech 2014: 15).

7   Quantum Superposition is famously demonstrated in an experiment in which a particle is fired towards a card with two slits. After passing through the card, the particle is found to be in two places at once. This supports the theory that a quantum state can be made up of two or more quantum states or that any two quantum states or more can combine to produce another quantum state.

8   As Ó Maoilearca remarks at the beginning of his book:

> Non-philosophy is a conception of philosophy (and all forms of thought) that allows us to see them as equivalent according to a broader explanatory paradigm. It enlarges the set of things that can count as thoughtful, a set that includes existing philosophy but also a whole host of what is presently deemed (by standard philosophy) to be non-philosophical (art, technology, natural science). (2015: 9)

9   Again, we might note the connections with deconstruction as a particular kind of practice here: a diagnosis of Western metaphysics, but also – more elusively perhaps – a gesture to forms of thinking that are irreducible to this.

10   See, for example, 'What the One Sees in the One' in the appendix at the end of *From Decision to Heresy* (Laruelle 2012b: 409–22). An indicative quote:

> The effusions of space and
> The insensible slidings

Of the Cosmos

The excessive universes

And the discretion that surrounds

The birth of the world

Without entering into the ring

Of Tradition

All the chaos and hubbub

Babels and hurly-burly

All the zigzags and artefacts

And the torturous ways of God

Without borrowing

The rectitude of God. (411)

11 For Laruelle's own non-philosophical response to Guattari and schizoanalysis (and, not least, the collaboration with Deleuze) see 'Fragments of an Anti-Guattari' (Laruelle 1993).

12 Anthony Paul Smith writes well on how a certain decisional structure produces the philosophical subject (as separate from an object – the real – which it cannot know except through itself), and how the non-philosophical subject as 'force-of-thought' might be understood, instead, as always already a part, or a clone, of the real (see Smith 2016: 45–61).

13 Laruelle's account of science is that it involves demarcating an area of the real – a discrete set – on which it then operates. See some of the comments Ian James makes in the seminar 'What Can We Do With Non-Philosophy?' (Galloway et al. 2015).

14 On this point see Keith Tilford's essay on the implications of non-philosophy for art, 'Laruelle, Art, and the Scientific Model', where he makes an especially compelling distinction (though not one we use here) between 'theories' (based on decision) and 'models' (which are revisable) (2017: 143–4).

15 Although we have not addressed them here, the writings of Anne-Françoise Schmid involve an enquiry into this space of the generic and, more generally, look at the implications of the non-philosophy project for art practice. For example, in her article 'The Madonna on the Craters of the Moon: An Aesthetic Epistemology' (Schmid n.d.), Schmid follows Laruelle in making a case for a generic epistemology, and, indeed, a generic aesthetics, which might operate as an 'intemediary' between science and art – but also, in the latter case, between different art practices (or even between elements within a practice). For Schmid there is 'no bird's-eye view' on this terrain and, as such, no one model (of either science or art); rather, there is a diversity of models in superposition. This also implies a new understanding of the object, which is no longer given as such but must be invented (might we even say *fictioned*?). Schmid gives this expanded practice the name 'integrative object', involving as it does a kind of synthesis of heterogeneity, one which proceeds 'piece by piece' (Schmid n.d.: 5).

16 The diagram was first published in a *taz* newspaper supplement conceived for the event *1948 Unbound: Unleashing the Technical Present* at Haus der Kulturen der Welt, Berlin, November 30–December 2, 2017. Curators: Katrin Klingan, Christoph Rosol, Nick Houde, Janek Müller and Bernard Geoghegan in collaboration with Gerald Nestler (Switches), Alexander Klose and Benjamin Steininger (Hydrocarbons), Patricia Reed and Victoria Ivanova (Tokens) and Sascha Pohflepp (Chance).

17 O'Sullivan's book *On the Production of Subjectivity* (2012) includes examples of this kind of diagrammatic treatment of conceptual material.

18 Performance, as Tero Nauha has argued, can be a practice alongside the real, and, as such, might be thought of as an 'advent' (as opposed to an event which gets 'recaptured' by philosophy). Nauha also makes a convincing case, following Laruelle, for performance as a heretical practice, pitched against the 'law' of representation (see Nauha 2016). In terms of some of the themes of our book – especially around scenes and magical thinking (and, indeed, collectivity) – we might also note Nauha's own heretical performance practice, and especially his collaboration with the artist Karolina Kucia called *Kukkia* (Kucia and Nauha 2008).

III. MYTHOTECHNESIS TO MACHINE FICTIONING

A. MYTHOTECHNESIS:
PROMETHEAN AND
INTELLIGENCE ECONOMIES

18   A Renewed Prometheanism

Once you commit to human, you effectively start erasing
its canonical portrait backwards from the future.

Reza Negarestani, 'The Labour of the Inhuman'

IN THIS FINAL section of the book our focus turns to discourses and practices which speculate on the effects of technological and machine agents; in particular, to the role of myth, fiction and/or the imaginary in discourses and practices which address the potential of technology and science to produce new human and non-human entities and organisations. We call such discourses and practices *mythotechnesis*, borrowing and adapting a term used by Mark Hansen in his book *Embodying Technesis: Technology Beyond Writing* (2000). Hansen defines *technesis* as the 'putting-into-discourse of technology', and he is critical of Western philosophy which attends to technological developments through a 'reductive strategy that allows for a progressive assimilation of technology to thought' (Hansen 2000: 4). This strategy engages with technology or, to borrow Hansen's term, a 'material exteriority', but it maintains 'the priority accorded to thinking by our philosophical modernity' (4–5). He argues that in many cases technology is addressed as little more than 'material support for the all important – and all engulfing – process of subject constitution' and 'the movement of thought' (6). In Hansen's assessment, then, the discourses of continental philosophers and poststructuralists fail to address the material or machinic complexities of technology – a blindness which protects the idea of the autonomy of intelligence, thought and its representations.

While Hansen's thesis is important for naming a perspective evident in a number of contemporary discourses and practices (which we will look at in this section), we propose to extend and expand his term to more generally address writing and art concerned with the effects of technology on the human and, indeed, to different kinds of human-machine relation. Introducing the prefix 'myth' to this term then signals our interest in the particular conjunction of fiction and technesis; as such, we use the term mythotechnesis to name fictions (and myths) *about* the human-machine relation (whether these are explicit and acknowledged as fictions or not), but we also, more radically, employ the term – along with *machine fictioning* – to refer to practices which instantiate or perform the different human-machine relations in question.

In all of this, we are especially interested in questions concerning the future of embodiment and with that desire and the libidinal. It follows that we engage critically with mythotechnesis when it is found to be positing the demise of these aspects of life through the spread of technologies that produce disembodiment or inorganic intelligences. In so doing, we mark our interest in the forms and organisations that bodies take, stating again that we do not think of a body as a unified organism but as a technology that has a diversity of capacities and processes as well as the potential to form assemblages of many kinds. This is a theme running throughout our book, and stems from our interest in the problem – following (and paraphrasing) Spinoza – that we (still) do not know what a body is capable of. We pursue this last question not in opposition to the development of inorganic and disembodied life but because we are for exploring diversity – of people, perspectives, assemblages and intelligences – as the potential of both the organic and inorganic. This concern becomes ever sharper in this and the following chapters that address what exactly is human (and what the human might become) and whether the application of mechanical and digital technologies – as well as attendant forms of reason and rationalisation – promise an evolution beyond what is given (or we might say beyond flesh and matter, desire and material existence).

To attend to the above, we begin by addressing a contemporary or renewed Prometheanism that would promote and accelerate scientific and technological potential, involving a privileging of reason (which we think of as a particular kind of technology). A corollary of this renewal is, we suggest, a fictioning of a new Prometheus or Promethean myth in the form of a subject (if it can be called such) that operates through reason alone and that leaves behind, or overcomes, the body and embodiment, and with that the creaturely and the libidinal.

Definitions of Prometheanism

Prometheanism has received a number of definitions, often articulated by those critical of desires or drives for human mastery (a theme we will address in depth in Chapter 21). Such criticisms often refer directly to the myth of Prometheus, the Titan who gave fire to humankind. In his book *Prometheanism: Technology, Digital Culture and Human Obsolescence*, John Müller states that Prometheus first enters Western thought as a trickster, his name – meaning 'fore-thought'[1] – signaling his cunning, but also 'his brilliance and ability to think and plan ahead', which are attributes he bestows on humans to the displeasure of the Gods (Müller 2016: 1–2).

Müller is influenced by a number of philosophers, including Jean-Luc Nancy, whom he quotes as describing technology as a 'fetish-word' which hides human ignorance concerning finitude (1). But the focus of Müller's book is the German thinker Günther Anders (a student of Heidegger), who, Müller reports, offers an important explanation for the prevalence of Prometheanism in the West in the 1930s: humans are 'unfinished', and use artifice to make themselves at home in the world (4). In Anders' view, this does not lead to a happy ending. Writing in the middle of the twentieth century, the philosopher asserts that 'Promethean pride consists of seeing everything, including oneself, as one's own achievement', but he also suggests that this is challenged in the modern industrial world by a 'Promethean shame' produced when humans face their machines (the product of their Promethean pride) and feel a sense of inferiority (Anders 2016: 31). More than this, Müller reflects that the trickery which overcomes nature also kills and exploits, tricking humans 'out of lives worth living' (Müller 2016: 2).

A similarly negative account of Prometheanism can be found in writing addressing environmental politics and the notion of the Anthropocene, a key figure here being John Dryzek, who argues that Prometheanism prioritises human needs over those of other forms of life, aiming to overcome problems through technological innovation and an unlimited use of the Earth's resources (Dryzek 1997). In an article Dryzek co-authored with fellow political scientists, Prometheans are described as having 'faith in the capacity of humans to manipulate complex systems for their own advantage', an ideology Dryzek et al. associate with business and political elites whose view of science and technology differs greatly, they suggest, from the more 'precautionary' approach expressed by various publics and public bodies concerned with the irreversible effects of technological innovation (Dryzek et al. 2009: 266).

In his essay 'Prometheanism and its Critics', Ray Brassier addresses this vilification of Prometheanism, particularly (as we shall see) coming from those inspired by Heidegger. Brassier suggests that:

> The sin of Prometheanism . . . consists in destroying the equilibrium between the made and the given – between what human beings generate through their own resources, both cognitively and practically, and the way the world is, whether characterized cosmologically, biologically, historically. (Brassier 2014b: 478).

In response to those critics who object to this introduction of a disequilibrium (and, with that, a refusal of limits), Brassier argues that what is chiefly being objected to is the rationalism of Prometheanism, where rationalism is itself viewed as unreasonable, producing not only problems in the world but a denigration of finitude, which is seen by anti-Prometheans as that which gives meaning to human life (479). We will discuss the Promethean rejection of finitude in more depth later on in this chapter, but suffice to say for now that Brassier questions whether humans should in fact abandon Prometheanism, which he defines as the 'claim that there is no reason to assume a predetermined limit to what we can achieve or the ways we can transform ourselves and our world' (470). Brassier envisages a Prometheanism in which a subjectivism without selfhood produces an 'autonomy without voluntarism' – the latter being the object of many critiques of Prometheanism (469–71). In other words, he advocates a Prometheanism which exiles the will (of metaphysical and psychological voluntarism) in order to privilege the intellect. We would argue that Brassier's Prometheanism addresses not only Heideggerian-inflected criticisms and anxieties concerning Prometheanism as an hubristic endeavour leading to human obsolescence and shame; it also addresses the objection that Prometheanism blindly exploits the planet's resources for (often individual) human advantage. Unlike Dryzek et al., who associate Prometheanism with capitalist and state elites, Brassier views a renewed Prometheanism as being potentially part of the emancipatory project of the Left; a project, he notes, which has been scaled down since the collapse of communism (469). Here we can identify a perspective which orientates much Promethean thinking associated with a Left accelerationism, grounded in the idea that fixed capital (machines and technology) will transform human society by abolishing the exploitation of human labour, producing time for humans to realise their potential.

We return to the scene of accelerationism here with further commentary on Brassier and, before that, on another key thinker associated with accelerationist thought and a renewed Prometheanism, Reza Negarestani.[2] In fact, we note that both writers feature in Mackay and Avanessian's *#Accelerate: The Accelerationist Reader* (2014a) and, furthermore, the early works of Brassier and Negarestani were influenced by Nick Land (who we have already identified as a key figure of Right accelerationism). However both can be said to have outgrown Land and certainly to have developed radically different political and philosophical orientations to those presented in Land's most recent writing, which serves as a platform for pro-capitalist and racist ideology. Indeed, they could be said to be more rigorous than Land, each promoting a realist and/or scientific approach to understanding the potential of humanity in relation to technological and scientific development.[3] In addressing a relationship between a renewed Prometheanism and forms of accelerationism, we come to the central concern of this chapter, which is not to dismiss Prometheanism as such, but to call into question those models of Promethean thought and practice which privilege the intellect alone. As implied above Prometheanism has itself been discussed within accelerationism and we suggest that there are a number of possible paths here. In so far as the development of accelerationism is identified with Lyotard's and Deleuze and Guattari's writing on desire and capitalism – the latter deemed not to go far or fast enough – accelerationist thinking is, to an extent, associated with philosophies engaging with libidinal economies (certainly these latter authors were influential on Land's early and libidinally inflected thinking). But here we observe a departure among philosophers associated with a more recent accelerationist scene, in that the libidinal appears to be absent from Brassier's and Negarestani's renewed Prometheanism (we might even say purged).[4] We not only want to understand this development – which we view as a mythotechnesis that, through discourse, fictions a subject skilled in reason and blessed with forethought – but also to question whether there is a place for forms of libidinal engineering (as an experimental practice concerned with desire as a productive force) in (or alongside) a Prometheanism attending to contemporary contexts. This will involve outlining what we have elsewhere described as patheme–matheme assemblages, which can be understood as a diagram of the affective and rational aspects of practices concerned with life and its potential.[5] We find encouragement for this endeavour in the introduction to #Accelerate: The Accelerationist Reader. After giving an account of how a machine-produced 'transformative anthropology' requires a newly thought rational subject, the editors of the Reader suggest that, if we do not yet know what the body can do, this new subject will need to be 'also a vitalist one in the Spinozist sense' (Mackay and Avanessian 2014b: 46). It is this insight that we seek to test in this chapter.

Accelerationism (and the Inhuman)

In his essay 'Escape Velocities', Alex Williams lays out a series of proposals for an accelerationist aesthetics. He suggests that as well as hyperstition (which we looked at briefly towards the end of the last section), accelerationism might involve 'processes of epistemic conceptual navigation' (Williams 2013: 9). Williams names Reza Negarestani as the key figure in the development of this philosophical orientation, which also – for Williams – has an aesthetic aspect. We want to introduce this particular proposal as a way into Negarestani's own take on both accelerationism and Prometheanism:

> The spatialized conception of the navigation and ramification of conceptual spaces at the core of Negarestani's notion of epistemic acceleration has an immediately aesthetic dimension, a highly visualized approach, grounded in the mathematics of topos theory. This abstract mathematical aesthetic of gesture, navigation, limitropism, and pathway-finding reroutes the philosophy of mathematics away from a basis in set theory and logic, and instead seeks an ultimately geometric ground. (Williams 2013: 9)

In fact, there is another of Williams' proposals that also connects with Negarestani's outline for a renewed Prometheanism, naming, as it does, a more design-orientated programme to run alongside the strictly philosophical. Again, it is worth quoting:

> Finally, we have the aesthetic of action in complex systems. What must be coupled to complex systems analysis and modeling is a new form of action: improvisatory and capable of executing a design through a practice which works with the contingencies it discovers only in the course of its acting. This can be best described through the Ancient Greek concept of *metis*, a particular mode of cunning craft. (9–10)

The question that occurs to us concerns what these two forms of an accelerationist aesthetic (broadly construed) – conceptual navigation and a pragmatic *metis* – leave out that might be present in other aesthetic projects (and art practice); which is to enquire as to what exactly is excluded by philosophical accelerationism. Negarestani's key Promethean essay, 'The Labour of the Inhuman', performs certain exclusions and is orientated against a reified idea – or image – of the human which, for him, can restrict the possibilities of thought and, indeed, of politics more generally (2014a). Negarestani's essay is not, however, antihuman (the labour of the inhuman is defined against the antihumanist refusal to revise and construct) but, rather, involves a continuation or 'extended elaboration' (precisely, an acceleration) of the humanist project itself (450).[6]

Negarestani's essay attends to an inhuman impulse exhibited by humans; it asserts a commitment to an ongoing experimental but also (as noted in Williams' remarks above) rational process of conceptual navigation. 'Human', here, names the fetters of the folk, everyday and common-sensical notion of a human self – or myth of the given – which can limit this other adventure, in so far as it relies on pre-existing categories and definitions. The labour of the inhuman, then, involves the continuing interrogation of the category of the human, a programme of endless revision and updating which itself includes a commitment to always reassess previous commitments. This, we might say, is the human's self-overcoming through reason, albeit reason of a specifically experimental and speculative type.[7]

In fact, for Negarestani, the human as a kind of processual project is defined by reason and, more particularly, by the relation between seeing and doing (inferences and actions) and the tasks of giving and asking for reasons. This manifests itself most obviously in a shared language and common vocabulary (alongside other 'discursive practices'), and it is this 'communal seeing and doing' which defines the labour of the inhuman as a collective, indeed Universalist, project (as well as marking the difference between sapience and sentience).

The case for a labour of the inhuman is compelling, but we note here that the opposition Negarestani draws between 'stabilised communication through concepts' and 'chaotically unstable types of response and communication' (which itself leads to a certain definition of the human and the privileging of the discursive) leaves out other forms of thought which might be said to operate between, or even outside of, these poles (Negarestani 2014a: 431–2). And although Negarestani does not argue that the human should be considered a solely rational animal, it is rationality as a singularly human trait which he privileges. It is here, through what is excluded from the labour of the inhuman, that we might begin to see a new Promethean figure emerge – and also (why not) a people to come – who through the discipline of working with concepts are unencumbered by irrationality. This is a persuasive (and even beautiful) argument, but one that might seem to some to produce an asymmetrical or lopsided human that evacuates 'chaotic' or 'unstable' communication, such as enunciations and productions marked by or foregrounding affect, desire or the libidinal.

If the new Prometheans sound conservative and conventional then we have given the wrong impression. Certainly, from their perspective, it is an anti-Prometheanism that maintains a given order, not least in its valorisation of a more 'authentic' and immediate life. Indeed, for Negarestani, to dispense with – or even underplay – discursive practices in particular, and the 'space of reason' more generally, means 'everything lapses either toward the individual or toward a noumenal alterity where a contentless plurality without any demand or duty can be effortlessly maintained' (Negarestani 2014a: 434). Although this is to effectively dismiss practices outside of the space of reason, it is also clear that these discursive practices – and indeed reason itself – are, for Negarestani, not to be understood in terms of habitual thought. As such, although Negarestani implicitly positions himself against a thinker like Henri Bergson (and, by extension, against any vitalist ontology), it might be claimed that something like intuition – or what we might better describe as thinking outside of ourselves – is at stake in these non-reasonable operations of reason. Here we should clarify that although Negarestani insists on the importance of norms, in the scientific sense, to progress reason and rule-based thinking, his approach, as implied

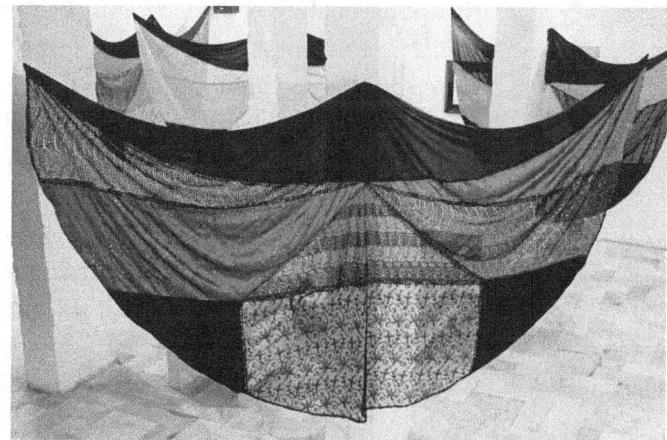

18.1 Kirsten Alvanson, *Nomadic Fabric Chador Sculpture* from the *Cosmic Drapery Project*, 2008 (courtesy of Kirsten Alvanson).

earlier, aims to counter the beliefs and habits of thought commonly found in everyday life. In this sense – in the way science upsets folk beliefs – Negarestani's thinking, even though proceeding through abductive inference, can be said to privilege the counterintuitive.

This is what makes the labour of the inhuman a dynamic discourse, but here we return to our question concerning what is excluded by Negarestani's rule-based and conceptually rigorous Prometheanism (in which abduction plays a major role). Certainly, from our perspective, art practices discussed in our book that produce counterintuitive ideas by attending to the world and its data through speculation and playful experimentation also attend to embodied knowledge – in that they have affective as well as conceptual aspects. Such practices are unlikely to be admitted to Negarestani's Promethean project. Following our brief comment about intuition above, a key question for us then is what is lost by banishing these practices that are not bound solely to reason but operate through other modes (again, some of which call upon embodied knowledge)? Could it be, in fact, that we see complex sets of heuristics (some of which are not conceptual) at work within art practice? Here we could point to the work of Kristen Alvanson – one of Negarestani's collaborators – in particular her *Cosmic Drapery* project (see Figure 18.1), which addresses the cultures of the Middle East through both conceptual and material practices, but also exhibits a concern for affect and processes that involve embodied knowledge, in order to analyse the histories and economies of textile production (of both states and nomadic people). This practice involves technologies of sewing which include 'pattern making, embroidery, spell and talisman forging' (Alvanson 2017). Through its production and installation of fabrics, *Cosmic Drapery* involves the arrangement of affective and conceptual elements, and demonstrates tacit skill and craft alongside intellectual analysis of data and information: such art is certainly involved in 'manipulable, experimental, and synthetic forms of inference whose consequences are not simply dictated by premises or initial conditions' (this is Negarestani's definition of abduction) (Negarestani 2014a: 436).[8] But if such practices cannot be understood as belonging to any new Prometheanism – for they partly exhibit a concern for material and affective aspects, and as such may produce unstable communications and ambiguities – that is because a particular kind of mythotechnesis operates in and through the labour of the inhuman; one that assimilates technologies of all kinds into the operations of reason and prioritises thought, at least of a certain type, to the detriment of more embodied instantiations and material complexities. As well as this, such a mythotechnesis perhaps prioritises abduction as a mostly, or purely, intellectual procedure.

Negarestani remarks further on abductive inference in a footnote (which offers a more detailed but narrower definition of abduction to the one we gave in Chapter 10):

Abductive inference, or abduction, was first expounded by Charles Sanders Peirce as a form of creative guessing or hypothetical inference which uses a multimodal and synthetic form of reasoning to dynamically expand its capacities. While abductive inference is divided into different types, all are non-monotonic, dynamic, and non-formal. They also involve construction and manipulation, the deployment of complex heuristic strategies, and non- explanatory forms of hypothesis generation. Abductive reasoning is an essential part of the logic of discovery, epistemic encounters with anomalies and dynamic systems, creative experimentation, and action and understanding in situations where both material resources and epistemic cues are limited or should be kept to a minimum. (Negarestani 2014a: 436n. 7)

We offer comment here: abductive inferences – and especially 'non-explanatory forms of hypothesis generation' – involve an imaginary register that engenders the conceptual and rule-based operations of the labour of the inhuman. More than this (and as stated in our Introduction), play as fictioning is found in all forms of description that abduction invariably relies on to reason relations, causes and effects. Therefore, we suggest that abduction, being necessary for discourses concerned with rule-based operations, calls upon descriptive and imaginary registers, even when it is employed with the purest of intentions. In fact, we would suggest that abduction involves an experimental attitude, but also a pragmatic modelling of different realities which proceeds through, imagining and imaging, performing and making, alongside more abstract reasoning. This leads us to further speculation and commentary regarding the attributes and identifications of a new Prometheus.

In Part 2 of Negarestani's essay the experimental labour of the inhuman is portrayed as more specifically navigational and, one might say, more restricted – or, at least, more rigorous and focused in its unfolding. He writes:

Interaction with the rational system of commitments follows a navigational paradigm in which the ramifications of an initial commitment must be compulsively elaborated and navigated in order for this commitment to make sense as an undertaking. It is the examination of the rational fallout of making a commitment, the unpacking of its far-reaching consequences, and the treating of these ramifications as paths to be explored that shapes commitment to humanity as a navigational project. Here navigation is not only a survey of a landscape whose full scope is not given; it is also an exercise in the non-monotonic procedures of steering, plotting out routes, suspending navigational preconceptions, rejecting or resolving incompatible commitments, exploring the space of possibilities, and understanding each path as a hypothesis leading to new paths or a lack thereof – transits as well as obstructions. (Negarestani 2014a: 443–4)

As Williams remarks, this is a highly visual (and compelling) account of the adventure of reason – abstracted from any specific content and understood as a specifically geometric project (in another essay Negarestani defines geometry as 'the controlled organization of space as a precondition for the articulation of the unarticulated and the extraction of intelligibility') (Negarestani 2014b: 17). The routes and pathways are themselves the hypotheses, which, in our terms, are elaborated through an imaginary that is diagrammatic in character (or what Burrows has elsewhere called a *diagrammatic imaginary*).[9]

For Negarestani this conceptual navigation involves a positive feedback loop effectuated by the deracinating of any origin or fixed definition of the human in so far as new definitions – inhumanism – feed back to inform the very idea of the human. As he remarks in our epigraph to this chapter: 'As soon as you commit to the human, you effectively start erasing its canonical portrait backwards from the future' (2014a: 446). This revisioning and updating is the movement of reason itself, its autonomous self-actualisation through the superseding of any previous idea of what it 'is' (and, in this sense, as Negarestani says, his project must be seen in the tradition of Enlightenment thinking). We might note a further connection with Nick Land here, in so far as the labour of the inhuman shares with templexity (and the time loops of hyperstition) a certain autonomous and self-evaluating character, as well as a strange temporality: it retroactively operates back on the past/present from a future it has helped construct (not least in the feeding-back of the consequences of its understandings and actions into its own self-definition).

The self-actualisation of reason (which turns out to be the real labour of the inhuman) involves the bootstrapping – the accomplishment by endogenous means – of more complex functions from simple ones: this is reason's self-assembly which, in itself, ultimately involves the augmentation of any given reality (hence the Prometheanism).[10] As such, a form of engineering emerges that is involved in exploring what it might be possible to construct or remake rather than a project bent on dominating nature or the given for human advancement.[11] And here we can see more fully that the conceptual persona fictioned by the labour of the inhuman is an engineer that produces the tools (concepts) for the navigational procedures of a renewed Prometheanism.

In relation to engineering, Negarestani addresses the process of construction and revision (and the heuristics mentioned above) as an 'engineering epistemology' in which attention is given to the different levels and hierarchies of any given system (with 'lower level entities' operating to provide guidance and enhancement of upper levels, and the latter reciprocally operating back down to correct and 'renormalise' so as to allow further construction and exploration) (Negarestani 2014a: 460–1). Here Negarestani is suggesting the compelling idea of an engineering loop between these different levels, such that the labour of the inhuman can be seen as drawing a map of syntheses that 'ensures a form of descriptive plasticity and prescriptive versatility' (463).[12] In support of the comments we make above, we suggest that here is evidence of a diagrammatic imaginary and a fictioning at play in Negarestani's methods if not discourse.

In this revisionary programme of the labour of the inhuman in which the figure of the engineer becomes the key conceptual persona, the 'advocate of transgression or militant communitarian' is sent packing. And it is here that we return to our question of whether there can exist a form of Prometheanism which has room for embodiment and the libidinal. We remind ourselves that this was a question posed in relation to knowing what the body can do, and we can see that this is not a priority for Negarestani's Promethean engineer. In fact, in a renewed Prometheanism, liberation becomes a work of construction – a labour – that amounts to an *'unlearning of slavery'* (464–5): *'Freedom is intelligence'* (465). In this, we suggest, we find a separation of the body and embodiment, and desire and the libidinal, from intellect and thought, which, for us, characterises Negarestani's mythotechnesis. We will return to this and related questions, especially concerning the absence of the affective in contemporary Prometheanism, at the end of this chapter. We turn now to the work of Brassier, who has similarly made reason his cause.

Prometheanism (Against Finitude)

Like Negarestani, Ray Brassier's philosophical Prometheanism – as laid out in his essay 'Prometheanism and its Critics' – identifies a constructive and future-orientated project for the human, one which is, again, rule-based and rational and which, ultimately, as stated earlier, is pitched against all-too-human preoccupations such as finitude (Brassier 2014b). For Brassier, the category of finitude includes birth and suffering – which, along with death, are typically portrayed as essential and existential givens, limits as it were – which define us as human (and we remember that Brassier has Heidegger and his followers in mind here). Brassier's argument is that the positing of an existential authenticity of the given *against* the made means that Prometheanism (understood by Brassier as the idea that we can remake ourselves and our world without limits) is ruled out *tout court*, involving as it does the heresy of making, or attempting to make, the given. In fact, in recourse to Hegel, Brassier suggests that this Prometheanism, with its introduction of a disequilibrium into the world, is also the 'enabling condition of cognitive processes' in general, in so far as the latter cannot but involve opposition (understanding) in tandem with conciliation (reason) (Brassier 2014b: 470). Prometheanism is not an attempt to heal any subject-object division, but is precisely enabled by that division: alienation begets freedom in this sense.

Brassier's particular take on finitude, and specifically his implicit idea of what suffering might be, could, we suggest, be fine-tuned somewhat in so far as from a certain perspective it is not suffering itself which is the given but impermanence, which, when encountered by a subject desiring permanence, causes suffering as a secondary effect (we note in passing that this is perhaps the fundamental insight of Buddhism). At the beginning of this chapter we referred to what Brassier tantalisingly calls a 'subjectivism without selfhood' (471). We understand this proposition as a gesture towards the possibility of a subjectivity which does not rail against impermanence (does not desire permanence), in particular one which does not identify itself as a separate self and thus does not suffer in this sense. We should point out, however, that for Brassier such a 'subjectivism without selfhood' is to be rationally and scientifically produced rather than arrived at through any meditative practice. In this sense, Brassier's Prometheanism (or his fictioning of a Promethean subject) might be said to involve the promise of an existence beyond finitude.

Indeed, for Brassier, finitude is less the determining factor of any given subjectivity per se than, again, a fetter on the Promethean impulse (this desire to go beyond finitude is a refrain of accelerationism too, in more or less all its articulations). As with Negarestani, there is in Brassier's work both a critique of the human (as folk or manifest image and thus as fetter), and an affirmation of it as sapient rational being (as scientific image and, as such, potentially unbounded).[13]

An anti-Promethean philosophical attitude might object to this unbinding of human potential, arguing that humans cannot be understood as merely a 'catalogue of empirical properties', and that there is a fragile equilibrium between the made and the given which ought to be respected (Brassier 2014b: 477). Brassier's audacity (which gives his essay its striking quality) is simply to question this 'ought', this idea of a given equilibrium (or, more simply, the idea that the world is given). He would thus 'free' the Promethean impulse itself and with it the potential of the human who, in this sense, does not have a defining limit: Brassier's Prometheanism, as he remarks, refuses the ontologisation of finitude (478).

Once again, we suggest there is not exactly a price to pay in Brassier's rejection of limits but there is certainly an exclusion of the vitalism we have already mentioned in our discussion of Negarestani's labour of the inhuman. Brassier has little interest in embodiment, desire and the libidinal, at least by way of having any relevance for the rational operations of a renewed Prometheanism. And perhaps this makes sense, for a philosophy that questions whether suffering is necessary to human existence might want to elide the bodily aspects of human life which, after all, might cause suffering and place limits on thought. But more than this, Brassier's comments on Prometheanism reveal a mythotechnesis that excludes the affective, embodiment and the creaturely (that is, the pathemic) from philosophy, as he thinks such bodily modes have little or nothing to contribute to the conceptual operations of Prometheanism (the mathemic).

We do not discount Negarestani's and Brassier's Promethean projects but wonder if another path for Prometheanism might be explored – a different kind of mythotechnesis – placing the pathemic and mathemic aspects of the human in dialogue (or in metamodelisation).[14] That is, we ask whether fictioning patheme-matheme assemblages might be a possible way forward for Promethean endeavours, or at least for practices that challenge the given with the made (and here we are thinking specifically of art practices). It is to this question that the latter part of this chapter attends.

A Promethean (Inflected) Art Practice?

There are numerous examples of Promethean-inflected art (or art that pushes at the limits of physical space and the human senses by employing technology of various kinds). These include the expanded cinema productions of the last century, such as Stan Vanderbeek's *Movie-Dome* (1965), staged through immersive and multiple projections and envisaged as a prototype for a new global communication system linked to a satellite network – with the intention of decreasing the alienating effects of technology; but also more recent art which engages with virtual reality technology, such as Jon Rafman's use of Oculus Rift headsets to simulate the space of a virtual *Sculpture Garden* (2015) and Mat Collishaw's virtual recreation of a Victorian school in Birmingham, England, entitled *Thresholds* (2017). In the genre of kinetic art or machines as art, we would point to Duchamp's *Rotoreliefs* (1935), which produce optical illusions through machines that spin patterned discs; the assemblages or machines of Takis which draw upon invisible forces such as magnetism to produce abstract works and devices that seem to defy gravity; and more recent examples such as Chico MacMurtrie's *Amorphic Robot Works* (including the expanding robotic exoskeleton *Inflatable Architectural Intervention* (2008) which envelopes a human performer and produces an image of molecular structures of the body), and Jordan Wolfson's animatronic performer *Female Figure* (2014), influenced by the films of Disney. Importantly though, within these machine or digitally generated artworks or scientifically informed art practices, a libidinal engineering can be said to be at work, or at least desire can be said to be in play. For example, Rafman and Collishaw clearly play with a desire to look and touch (looking becoming a way of engaging with simulation of space; touching, in Collishaw's work, being a way of manipulating virtual objects); and Wolfson's staging of an encounter with his highly (heteronormative) sexualised female figure poses the question, do you desire a machine? (And the same could be said of MacMurtrie's undulating architectural structure inflated by machines, though perhaps with his inhabitable exoskeletons the question is more 'do you desire to be a cyborg?'). It is the case, at least to an extent, that audiences engage with such artworks – that present the made in the form of new bodies and spaces – through desire rather than (just) through concepts. Connections are produced and explorations unfold at the level of the libidinal rather than just the intellectual.

It might be said that these works are disappointing or problematic in certain aspects: what is interesting about simulating a schoolroom or making a dancing robot-woman? While this might be true, what interests us is that all of our examples can be said to re-engineer the conditions or modes of spectatorship for art. As we have implied, they do so by replacing the given (such as physical space perceived by the senses or the human body) with the made (such as virtual simulation or the machine body). Furthermore, this re-engineering of spectatorship, in turn, affects our sense of space and time, which can then affect subjectivity. The disequilibrium of the given and the made in such works forces thought towards possibilities for new bodies, worlds, relations and societies. There is, of course, a marked difference between a scientifically focused, rule-based Prometheanism and Promethean-inflected art practices which envisage fantastic and strange encounters, even when produced through the precision or engineering of advanced technological means. In the latter, the human body and desire are included in the looping of existing and potential worlds through technology to explore new environments and, in this, there is, we suggest, a machine fictioning. We will attend to this concept in more detail in the latter half of this section but suggest here that machine fictioning explores what the human can become through interaction with technology, or an engagement with what Hansen might call the material constitution of technology. In this, our concept of machine fictioning does not exclude the (unthought) embodied aspects of human-machine development, which involves desiring bodies (or machines) interacting with machinic operations. This invites the question, if rule-based Prometheanism bars experimentation with and through desire (what we are calling libidinal engineering), what new worlds and new humans might this privileging of reason overlook? How can the effects of the conceptual operations and productions of renewed Prometheanism on the human be understood if materiality and embodiment are of no account? Or, to put it another way: without desire or the pathemic in the loop (presuming alienation is then still produced), what results from a disequilibrium of the given and the made? Would a disinterested, reasoning subject-engineer beyond desire be the result? In what ways would such a figure be superior or preferable to a Prometheanism that includes modes of libidinal engineering in its tool-set?

Re-engineering the Human

The answer to this last question might be that at stake is a Promethean project that intends to shape the immanant potential of the human – via conceptual rigour – as a form of engineering, rather than allowing libidinal forces immanent to the human to do the directing. As with Negarestani, the Promethean project is expounded in Brassier's essay as ultimately the desire to 're-engineer' the human itself (and, in this, as Brassier remarks, the project is again the direct successor to Enlightenment thought and practice, as is most obvious in the pre-eminent Promethean thinker of modern times: Marx). In part, this also involves a refusal of transcendence in favour of a kind of tracking of immanence via rule-governed activity. To quote Brassier:

> rather than trying to preserve the theological equilibrium between the made and the given, which is to say, between immanence and transcendence, the challenge for rationality consists in grasping the stratification of immanence, together with the involution of structures within the natural order through which rules can arise out of physical patterns. According to this conception of rationality, rules are means of coordinating and subsuming heterogeneous phenomena, but means that are themselves historically mutable. (Brassier 2014b: 486)

For Brassier, then, the means of developing human societies and subjects which reject transcendence vary, though for the thinker of a subjectivism without selfhood the most rigorous and current means of achieving post-self subjects are clear. In 'The View from Nowhere' (2011), Brassier turns his attention more explicitly to this other mode or form of life – a nemocentric subject, as discussed in Chapter 4 – which might be produced through the advanced operations of reason as it is manifested in twenty-first-century neuroscience (this being a subject, if that is still a useful term, which shuttles between the folk and the scientific image of the human). It seems that fictioning is important in all of this, or at least we can say that Brassier proposes a subject to come in his account of a future non-self agent – as 'a physical entity gripped by concepts: a bridge between two reasons, a function implemented by causal processes but distinct from them' (Brassier 2011: 33). This is compelling, as is the critique of phenomenology which accompanies it, but, we ask again, is it not also the case that the rational (and communist) Promethean project – especially as manifest in science – could also be married with a more affective, libidinal type of engineering? Would not this kind of encounter and experimental conjunction produce a radically different kind of subject too?

We find support for this idea in fiction (rather than philosophy). Science Fiction is clearly an important resource in this respect, which a renewed Prometheanism also looks to for examples. Indeed, towards the end of 'Prometheanism and its Critics' Brassier turns to J. G. Ballard for future-evidence of a new kind of human who, as it were, both engenders and is engendered by the Promethean project. But here, interestingly enough for us, we find a different kind of subject to the rule-based Promethean of Brassier's philosophy. Ballard's protagonists are far from disinterested. Nor are they predictable in their actions – indeed, Brassier recognises that 'the psychic and cognitive transformations undergone by Ballard's protagonists are nothing if not savage and violent' (Brassier 2014b: 486). In fact, these characters are wildly libidinal – could we call them the unruly conceptual personae that emerge in Brassier's text on Prometheanism, despite the philosopher's determination to adhere to rule-bound thinking? As we suggested in Chapter 7, Ballard's novels track an often inorganic sexuality, not least in *Crash* (1973) in which a machine (or machinic) erotics transforms the human through combining sex and automobile injury, producing assemblages of fleshy bodies with the metal of automobiles, fossil fuel and leather.

Ballard's conceptual personae are inventions and experimental configurations of reason and affect given proper names; they are modes of existence that might be gestured towards in philosophy but are given life (are fictioned) in art.[15] It might be, then, that towards the end of 'Prometheanism and its Critics', we find some form of libidinal engineering as a means of letting go of the rational – for the protagonist of Ballard's *Crash*, who sexualises automobiles and their disfiguring accidents, embraces a human-machine eroticism that, we would suggest, is also an acceptance of impermanence.

Patheme–Matheme Assemblages

In a short commentary on Srnicek and Williams' 'Accelerate: Manifesto for Accelerationist Politics', Antonio Negri lends his support to a renewed accelerationism, but also gestures towards certain reservations he has – for example concerning the overly technologically determined nature of the thesis – and notes certain key omissions, such as a consideration of the commons and questions to do with the production of subjectivity, including 'the agonistic use of passions' (Negri 2014). We suggest similar questions might be asked of a renewed Prometheanism.

Along similar lines, the artist Patricia Reed's critical commentary, 'Seven Prescriptions for Accelerationism' (Reed 2014), points to a number of possible variations and further accelerations of Srnicek and Williams' Manifesto, including (perhaps most interestingly, at least in the context of our own book) the call to 'fictionalise'. For Reed this is tied to the production of a new *demos*, or new collective will, and, more generally, to the role of belief within any radical politics. In an echo of our own take on accelerationism (and in this, our view of a renewed Prometheanism), Reed also points to the need both to attend to the 'distribution of affect' (2014: 528) in any accelerationist agenda ('in equal partnership with calls for operational, technological and epistemic restructuration' (528)) and to the more Guattarian-sounding idea of a 'commitment to an eccentric future' (although it is not entirely clear what Reed has in mind here) (527). For us, fictionalisations involving the agonistic use of the passions and affect, which are excluded by a rule-bound Prometheanism and accelerationism,[16] are important to the political and transformative potential of the art practices we have been attending to; for it is through affective fictionings that, we suggest, a people to come can emerge, as is no doubt clear to the reader by now.

In relation to an explicit politics that aims at producing a new people, non-engagement with the affective complexities of life means a renewed Prometheanism may only offer a partial picture of possible solutions. It is important to note that our line of argument does not advocate a straightforward vitalism pitched against a colder abstraction. Affects – or becomings – can themselves be said to be abstract, in that they take the subject out of themselves, or involve the irruption of something different, non-human, within the subject (when 'human' names a very particular historical configuration and self-model). It is here – where the conceptual meets these other kinds of thought (defined in the broadest possible sense) and non-thought (in the form of non-conscious, embodied and machinic processes) – that we might find a role for the Promethean-inflected fictionings of art practice that engage with patheme–matheme assemblages, where the mathemic corresponds to the formal character of subjectivity, and the pathemic names an equally abstract – in a different sense – but more 'creaturely' and affective character. Here we ask whether a renewed Prometheanism might admit such practices and diagram the mathemic (the lessons and calculations of scientific and rational thought) alongside an engagement with the pathemic (the registering of the actual and potential affects of such lessons and calculations on human subjectivity). This would not be to find meaning in birth, suffering and death but to facilitate experimentation with and through desire, in order to explore what the human might become. Such a metamodelisation gestures towards a composite subject – between different orientations – and, more crucially, we think, towards how different composite subjects might operate.[17] Any Prometheanism or accelerationism, it seems to us, will need to explore and experiment with this terrain, to participate in the construction of diverse mythotechnesis (which does not exclude the material instantiations of technology) and to fiction images, assemblages and figures, in order to gain a transformative traction on the world and especially on those who dwell within it.

Notes

1 Müller notes that in the myth, Prometheus – as fore-thought – is compared to his twin brother, Epimetheus, whose name means 'after-thought' (2016: 105).

2 We should note here a third further figure crucial to the philosophical articulation (and conjunction) of accelerationism and Prometheanism, Peter Wolfendale. See, for example, his 'Prometheanism and Rationalism', which more fully lays out his philosophical position (Wolfendale 2016).

3 Both Negarestani and Brassier have themselves acknowledged their indebtedness to Land. The former in a footnote to the essay 'Drafting the Inhuman: Conjectures on Capitalism and Organic Necrocracy' (Negarestani 2011a); the latter in the 'Introduction', written with Robin Mackay, to Nick Land's *Fanged Noumena* (Brassier and Mackay 2013: 1–54). Accelerationism, as a contemporary term, was coined by Ben Noys – who himself borrowed it from the Science Fiction writer Roger Zelazny. Noys' own book, *The Persistence of the Negative: A Critique of Contemporary Continental Theory* (2012), identifies an accelerationist (and affirmationist) strain of thought in writers such as Deleuze and Guattari and Lyotard.

4 Although we should also note that Negarestani's maginificent theory-fiction *Cyclonopedia* (2008), written before the work this chapter looks to, certainly involves the entwining of the libidinal (and fictional) with more directly philosophical resources.

5 See also John Mullarkey's rigorous account of the matheme/patheme relationship within contemporary French thought (encapsulated, for Mullarkey, in the opposition between Alain Badiou and Michel Henry) and also his own creative bringing together of these two (via Laruelle) (Mullarkey 2006: 129). Mullarkey's book also contains more general experiments in his own metamodelling of different thinkers and, indeed, in what he calls a practice of 'diagrammatology'.

6 François Laruelle, in his focus on reclaiming and foregrounding a 'generic' humanity, has something in common with Negarestani's labour of the inhuman in this sense, although, it has to be said, the non-philosophical project *per se* orientates itself against any philosophical mastery – and with that any strictly philosophical definition of the human (see Chapters 17 and 24 for discussions of Laruelle which go into more detail on this point).

7 We might note the connections with Alain Badiou here and his proposal that a subject, as opposed to a human, is animated by a certain fidelity, or idea, that raises them above the creaturely.

8 In relation to this Negarestani does turn to contemporary art in his essay on Jean-Luc Moulène, *Torture Concrete* (Negarestani 2014b). Here the labour of the inhuman becomes the labour of abstraction when this names a similar project of turning away from reified images of thought (especially, here, those that rely on notions of interiority and

exteriority) and, indeed, a continuous and experimental redefinition of the latter (involving 'bootstrapping' from the local to the global). Art itself is positioned as one mode of thought amongst others in this sense – a diversification which fosters novelty and exploration and, as such, serves to redefine the unity of all modes of thought. In relation to art practice per se Negarestani also lays out a compelling case for the reciprocal determination of thought on matter/matter on thought, itself 'led' by the positioning of 'generative points' which destabilise pre-existing images and habits. It is here that he also outlines an idea of knots – between the mathematical and the libidinal for example – as a preeminent example of this abstraction (and which, as such, have something in common with our own outline of patheme–matheme assemblages).

9 An account of the diagrammatic imaginary of science was developed by Burrows in a paper given at UCL, London in 2014, in which the sciences were presented as having diagrammatic procedures in common with art (see Burrows 2014).

10 Negarestani is clear, however, that this self-actualisation must be accompanied by communal assessment and methodological collectivity; that is, by a politics.

11 It is important to note that Negarestani once suggested that art should be a practice which does not inflict human will upon materials but which allows for the contingencies of materials to appear; that is, artists should be complicit with their materials (Negarestani 2011c).

12 In an earlier essay – 'Globe of Revolution: An Afterthought on Geophilosophical Realism' (2011b) – Negarestani writes about these navigational loops in terms of different syntheses between the local and the global, or, more specifically, between a local horizon (human, the earth, and so forth) and the 'open universal continuum' out of which they have been cut. Here the trauma of excision defines us as individuated beings, but also points to the possibility of other pathways to the open besides those which position the latter as an 'unbindable exorbitance' (2011b: 32).

13 We might note a specifically technological variant of this contemporary Prometheanism in Benedict Singleton's writings (including his own essay in *#Accelerate: The Accelerationist Reader*), which articulate the impulse to escape planetary gravity and thus the ultimate 'prison': Earth (Singleton 2014). Hence, also, the accelerationist interest in the Russian cosmists and the inclusion in the aforementioned *Reader* of 'The Common Task' by Nicolai Fedorov (Fedorov 2014). As Robin Mackay and Armen Avanessian's 'Introduction' to the *Reader* suggests, Singleton's interest in the technological 'platforms' that capitalism produces, and the concomitant navigational spaces opened up by them, parallels Negarestani and Brassier's own projects of conceptual navigation (Singleton was also the first to deploy the concept of *metis* in relation to the latter) (Mackay and Avanessian 2014b: 32–3).

14 In this, we follow John Mullarkey's definition of what he calls the 'meta-philosophical diagram' understood 'as an indefinite set of materialised "betweens": between symbolic

representation and iconic presentation, discourse and inscription, matheme and patheme, digital and analogue, geometry and art, internal representation and external picture, audience and artwork' (2006: 180).

15 Ballard's books are, precisely, of the imagination in this sense. In fact, ultimately, for Brassier, the imagination has a part to play in Prometheanism, which cannot but have a phantasmagoric aspect (albeit one which might be diagnosed, analysed and, presumably, 'cured'): 'Prometheanism promises an overcoming of the opposition between reason and imagination: reason is fuelled by imagination, but it can also remake the limits of imagination' (Brassier 2011: 487).

16 Nor do they feature strongly in Srnicek and Williams' Manifesto. All together, the focus of recent accelerationism has very rarely had anything to do with the affective make-up of subjectivity: indeed, there are often claims about the latter's obsolescence, especially in the wake of the 'rise of the machines'; the foregrounding of only the rational subject; or, as in the Manifesto, the offering of no detail on this crucial area beyond a passing swipe at 'affective self-valorization' (Srnicek and Williams 2014b: 351).

17 It seems to us that Mark Fisher's writings are pertinent here (see in particular those on his k-punk blog), especially in their prescient call for new libidinal figures adequate and appropriate to a reanimated Left. See also Fisher's conversation with Judy Thorne around 'luxury communism' (Fisher and Thorne 2017).

19   The Subject Who Fell to Earth

... noise scrambles the capacity for self-organization.

Ray Brassier, 'Against an Aesthetics of Noise'

IN THE PREVIOUS chapter we explored the orientations and limits of a renewed Prometheanism, introducing the idea of patheme–matheme assemblages. To address this tension between cognitive and embodied knowledge further, we want now to discuss sonic or noise performance, and commentaries on these, that are inflected by both neuroscience and theories concerned with the rhythms of bodies and societies. To this end, we will address the potential of noise as a disorientating and disruptive encounter by exploring concepts from two seemingly opposed philosophers. We have already discussed some of the work of the first, Ray Brassier, but in this chapter we will attend to his interest in noise as a stochastic presentation,[1] and in particular his contention that incompossible signals have a disorganising potency.[2] Our second figure is Henri Lefebvre. We contrast Brassier's thoughts on noise with the French philosopher's theory of 'rhythmanalysis' – an investigation of rhythm and everyday life – paying particular attention to Lefebvre's definition of 'arrhythmia' as a disruption of bodily and social rhythms (Lefebvre 2004). Through this comparison, we aim to produce a metamodelisation, presenting similarities and differences between the two, so as to diagram problems and potentialities inherent in any discussion of noise and embodiment in political and cultural contexts. We will then embellish our metamodelisation with Nietzsche's thoughts on health and illness, which, we will argue, provide further insight into the mathemic and pathemic aspects of noise. We also suggest that noise production – which we understand to involve a disruption of the habits of perception and selfhood – is of particular relevance to any mythotechnesis concerned with technoenvironments which respond to and extend (but also exploit) the embedded and embodied aspects of cognition. To address this context, and before introducing the practices and ideas of the philosophers and artists on whom we will focus our discussion, we want to first outline the ways in which human adaptation to technoenvironments in late capitalist culture has taken place, and the critical responses to such developments.

We Are All Thomas Jerome Newton

In a memorable scene from Nicholas Roeg's film *The Man Who Fell to Earth*, released in 1976, the alien Thomas Jerome Newton sits in a small apartment watching several televisions all at once, each tuned to a different channel. He shares the apartment with his lover Mary-Lou, who complains about the TVs. The multiple transmissions produce an incomprehensible noise for Mary-Lou, but the alien can differentiate between the broadcasts. Eventually their romance turns sour. When Mary-Lou confronts Newton about their impossible relationship and his changing personality, the alien turns up the volume of the dozen televisions he is watching. He has been drinking and is in no mood to talk – the consumption of alcohol induces visions for the alien. As a tearful Mary-Lou flees the cacophony of sound and images, Newton continues to watch the televisions, entranced by the pictures flashing across the screens. The scene ends with the alien screaming, 'Get out of my mind, all of you!' Later in the film Newton offers the observation, 'The funny thing about television is it tells you everything and nothing about the world.'

In *Postmodernism, or, the Cultural Logic of Late Capitalism*, Fredric Jameson cites Newton's ability to attend to multiple broadcasts (see our diagram in Figure 19.1) as illustrative of a problem. Jameson argues that the mass-media environments developed in the 1970s and '80s place impossible demands on our capacity to process information,

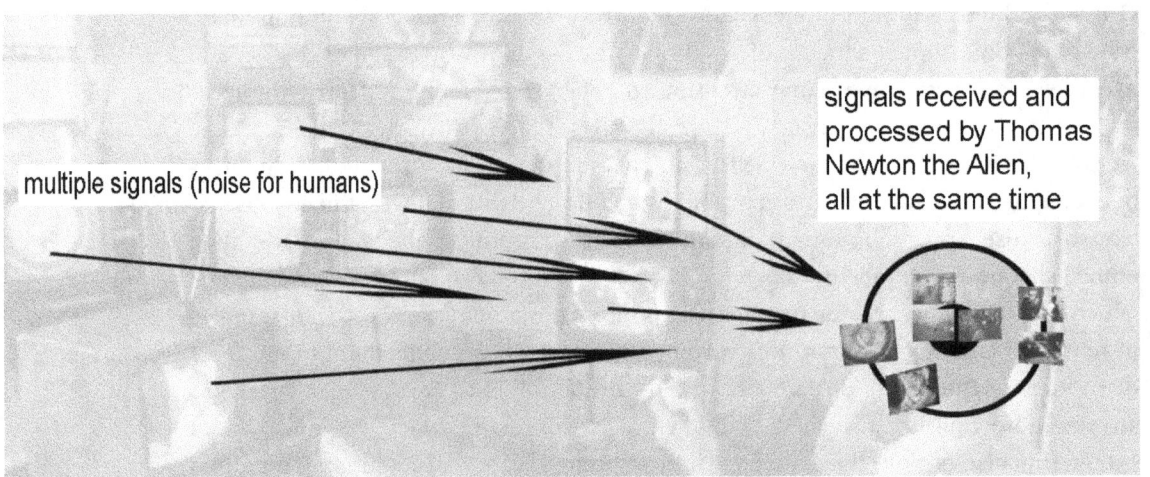

multiple signals (noise for humans)

signals received and processed by Thomas Newton the Alien, all at the same time

19.1 Diagram of Thomas Newton watching multiple screens (credit: the authors).

requiring humans to undergo a mutation in order to develop senses similar to those possessed by the alien in Roeg's film (Jameson 1991: 31). Jameson suggests that the proliferation of mass-media environments produces an experience of a 'hysterical sublime' which overwhelms humans and which limits our knowledge and navigation of the networks and politico-economic structures of capitalist culture. Jameson's response to this state of affairs, as we discussed in section one, is to call for a 'properly representational dialectic' in the form of a cognitive mapping and a pedagogic culture which would endow subjects with an understanding of their place within a global system (54).

Of course, Jameson developed this position in the last century, before the internet had transformed society and, indeed, knowledge. Decades later, mobile phones and smart devices have radically changed culture, commerce and communication; it does indeed seem that something like a mutation has occurred. Today, through adaptation to technoenvironments, we may all have become Thomas Jerome Newton, at least to some extent, and, in this event, the multiple signals produced by mass-media enviroments are not counted as noise so much as potential connections and a wealth of information. Here hyper-attention might be seen as one of Newton's alien attributes, another being a heightened sense or understanding of the relations of global capitalism and technology, as Newton's business ventures seem to grow exponentially. The modes of hyper-attention demanded by various technologies today are shaped by the everyday use of the latter; hearing, touch and sight are synched with communication systems and mass media. Many are wary of these new technoenvironments and the subjects they produce. For example, Franco Berardi argues that such developments produce a semiocapitalism which generates a precarious rhapsody: the demands of a seemingly unlimited cyberspace producing excitement but also exhaustion (Berardi 2009). Warren Neidich (2013) argues that the designers of technoenvironments exploit neuropower and sync the brain with 'personalised consumer environments'. Others, such as Tiqqun (2001), insist that cybernetic intensification involves the development of technologies of governance and control. It would appear that many twenty-first century critics of capitalism are concerned not so much with the hysteria-inducing noise of mass-media communications but, rather, with *kairos* (the time of human action and agency), which, they argue, is becoming increasingly limited, if not entirely curtailed. Today, as Berardi suggests, it could be argued that for some humans, modes of attention, far from being disorganised by mass media, are honed for connection and no longer for reflexivity or critical reflection. We recognise that such arguments need addressing. Indeed, the embracing of embodiment – which we think important to developing a radical mythotechnesis – needs careful attention in light of this very embodiment being optimised to adapt and advance capitalist cultures.

If the users of contemporary technoenvironments are able to match Newton's capacities for information consumption, what, then, has happened to noise? Do humans still encounter signals which overwhelm or disrupt their capacities to receive information? While it may be argued that humans have evolved to keep pace with the demands of new technologies, noise persists: there is noise produced as art, music or performance, and there is noise registered as a system breakdown or as unintelligible interference (and we note these two examples of noise are not necessarily exclusive). Lastly, it can be said that noise is everywhere. Indeed, in cybernetic theories, identifying noise is an important aspect of developing communication systems and other organisations. A further important question, here, is whether noise might have a radical social potential.

Of Aliens and Selfless Subjects

Whilst we will be discussing the relationship between noise and capitalist culture, this chapter is also, in part, a response to ideas expounded by Brassier in 'Genre is Obsolete' (2007b) concerning noise music or performance and the disruption of a sense of self – though, as we shall see, for Brassier there is a relation between experience (which produces illusions of selfhood) and the development of capitalist cultures and entertainment as a means of control. 'Genre is Obsolete' analyses the work and performances of To Live and Shave in L.A. and Runzelstirn and Gurgelstøck a.k.a. Rudolf Eb.er, which, he argues, arrest the senses as they attempt to process audio signals. In an interview with Bram Ieven for *nY* magazine concerning the text 'Genre is Obsolete', Brassier draws a connection between noise performance and the production of a selfless subject informed by nemocentrism, which, as we saw in Chapter 4, holds the promise of a subject free from the illusion of selfhood (Brassier 2009).[3] We will intentionally read Brassier's writings against his more critical objectives: that is, we approach them as a science fictioning concerning an alien subject that lives among us or is, indeed, a potential for each and every one of us. Although Brassier's thinking has progressed since 'Genre is Obsolete' (towards a thought grounded in inferential logic, as discussed in the previous chapter), we nevertheless find his earlier writings on noise and the production of a selfless subject to be an important instance of Promethean fictioning. More than this, we are keen to understand the political potential of Brassier's selfless subject, a potential hinted at in the interview with Bram Ieven. There Brassier calls for a kind of cognitive mapping of the brain's and body's information processing systems – the very systems which produce representations and which facilitate the myths of experience and the self, conditioned by capitalist technologies and culture (Brassier 2009). The particular value of Brassier's approach is that he focuses on how humans process information, and not, as Jameson does, on a mapping of global capitalism and its cultural productions.

To clarify the place of stochastic presentation in all of this, it is important to note Brassier's argument that noise produces a cognitive event which divides thought and feeling and which has the potential to generate a new subject. Compelling as this new subject is, we have some questions about the surplus of experience and percepts which is given up in productions of, and encounters with, noise, at least when cognition is privileged.

Anti-Aesthetic

In 'Genre is Obsolete', noise is defined as sound which overwhelms the senses to the extent that a subject cannot process audio signals (Brassier 2007b). Noise can be identified as audio stimuli consisting of mutually incompatible worlds which, when presented together, cannot be fully received by the ear, with the result that the subject cannot easily organise or orientate themselves. Brassier is scornful of noise music produced as feedback or as the entropic disintegration of a signal. The noise he is interested in is an excess (for the human) which flattens out structures and complexity. Brassier envisions noise as an assault, not just on genre or aesthetics but also on those operations of the body/brain/mind which order and process the sensible. This jamming of the senses is important in relation to Brassier's general philosophical project in this period of his writing, focused on the possibility of an 'experience-less subject'. As previously discussed, this is a subject which comprehends that it is no one and nowhere, and that any sense of self – of being someone somewhere – is illusionary; for a self is merely a product of human evolution which has developed pre-conscious and conscious modes of processing information (the former not being apparent to the latter). Brassier, as noted in section one, follows Thomas Metzinger in his neuroscience-informed description of selfhood as illusionary, and as something which disappears in sleep or when not needed by the organism – the self being nothing more than a representation derived from a phenomenal self-model.

Metzinger (2009) suggests that vision creates an ego tunnel and is of particular importance in the production of a sense of self. The ear, though, can locate sound in space and also aids the construction of a phenomenal self-model. It does so by distinguishing sound produced by the human organism from sound produced externally. This helps to generate a spatial-temporal positioning of a self. As discussed earlier, Metzinger argues that if these processes were opaque – that is, apparent rather than transparent and unregistered (see Figure 19.2) – naive or folk beliefs concerning selves would be challenged. Indeed, in such an event, we would no longer be captured by the illusion of a self. Whilst, as Metzinger suggests, this selfless subject might still be egocentric, it would attend to the world in a manner that is quite different from humans who are blind to the pre-conscious processes which produce the illusions of selfhood.[4] It is phenomenologically impossible for us to experience selflessness, but Metzinger contends that it is not impossible for a subject to understand the concept, in that we can cognitively objectify our phenomenological conditioning: while any experience reinforces selfhood (perhaps making first-person experience of selflessness an oxymoron), through science or third-person perspectives, humans can understand the ways in which the phenomenal is important to our sense of reality and the ways we attend to the world. In 'The View from Nowhere', Brassier suggests that a system or subject could produce a first-object perspective (another term borrowed from Metzinger). This perspective is the experience of a phenomenal self-model as not just represented but also as representing (Brassier 2011: 7–23).

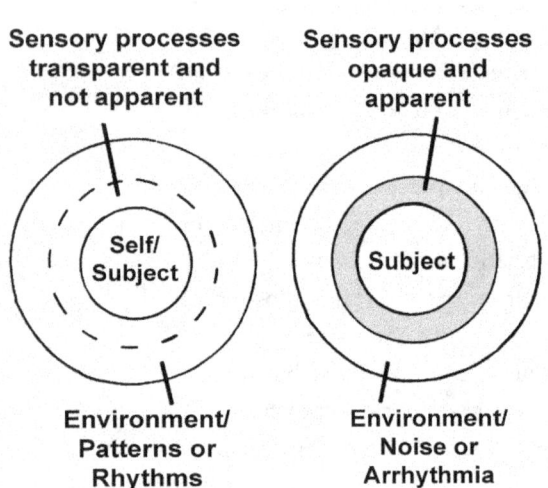

Sensory processes transparent and not apparent

Self/ Subject

Environment/ Patterns or Rhythms

Sensory processes opaque and apparent

Subject

Environment/ Noise or Arrhythmia

19.2 Diagram of two states in which the transparency of the senses and their processes produce an illusion of selfhood, and the opaqueness of the senses and their processes produce a self-less subject (credit: the authors).

It is this first-object perspective which, following Brassier's arguments, is produced by an encounter with To Live and Shave in L.A. or Rudolf Eb.er. The importance for Brassier of an encounter with noise is that, in cleaving experience from cognition, stochastic presentations arrest the human-identified-as-self but not the human-subject-that-reasons. That is, noise renders sensory processes opaque and apparent (again, see Figure 19.2).

Importantly, the nemocentric subject reasons and revises its scientific theories and methods (it is a work in progress). Nonetheless, this subjectivity is not reducible to scientific representation or theory, and it is not difficult to imagine why it may be politically significant: the nemocentric subject would be critical, or at least cognisant, of the phenomenological conditioning prevalent in capitalist culture. In the *nY* interview 'Against an Aesthetics of Noise', Brassier even goes so far as to suggest that the experience-less subject might be important for developing new 'communist subjectivities' (Brassier 2009).

Since our own collaborative art practice, Plastique Fantastique, involves producing noisy performance and media works, this suggestion concerning communist subjectivities interests us greatly, but, as previously mentioned, we have some questions, even reservations, concerning noise performance as a cleaving of cognition from the body and its senses. When subjects encounter noise, can the generation of first-object perspectives alone produce communist subjectivities, or is some kind of production, collaboration or exchange between subjects involved too?[5] How does nemocentrism avoid atomisation? And what of the surplus of experience or embodiment in all of this? Perhaps it is through creating distance from experience – by making surplus that which might be necessary for producing surplus value in consumer societies – that a subject can resist capitalist culture. We certainly understand this (and we will return to the idea below). However, although the nemocentric subject might be beyond experience, the body of the subject does not cease operating through motor-sensory processes or experience and phenomenal models. One last question then: is it possible, never mind desirable, to render experience surplus?

An initial response to this bundle of questions could be that communist subjectivities are produced when experience – which produces illusions of selfhood – is lost to an evolution of, or adaptation to, nemocentric perspectives (through what we might call, in a nod to Negarestani, the inhuman labour of nemocentrism). But this would be to go to far: Brassier is arguing for a human agency – which acts to produce first-object perspectives – which would seem a necessary component for producing the self-less subject able to be critical of the way the senses produce error and are open to manipulation by, among other interests, capitalism. Whether this leads to communist subjectivities remains unclear to us, but again we see the political implications of this agency.

The Nemocentric Subject is No Body

Putting this question concerning communist subjectivities aside for the moment, it seems to us that Brassier's thoughts on noise offer a science fictioning that breaks with the myth of the self only to produce another myth. This is a figure we have already met in the last chapter, a selfless, critical subject fictioned by neuroscience perspectives – a conceptual persona which functions like a myth not because the promise of such a subject is false or irrational but because it orientates, structures, or binds a subject, group or practice. Here we return to Georges Bataille's notion that night (the death of God or absence of myth) is also a sun: the idea that the absence of myth is the greatest myth of all has clear relevance (Bataille 1994: 48).

It is interesting to consider Bataille's notion of night or absence as a sun in relation not just to the elision of the senses but also to Brassier's thoughts on the expiration of the sun and the extinction of human life, which we touched upon briefly in section two in our discussion of Claire Colebrook's writing on extinction. In *Nihil Unbound* (2007a), Brassier reflects on a problem previously explored by Jean-François Lyotard in his essay, 'Can Thought Go on Without a Body?' (Lyotard 1992). When our sun expires human thought will expire too (including philosophical thought which attends to death as an existential problem and as a limit of thought). This means not only that all thinking life will be destroyed but also that there will be no human or body to think that thought has ended (Brassier 2007a: 224–5): the end of thought will be unthought. Brassier picks up on Lyotard's suggestion that, if thought is to survive this catastrophe, then it has to be 'weaned from its organic habitat and transplanted to some alternative support system'. Importantly, this is a challenge to our interest in embedded and embodied cognition and the pathemic, as Brassier fictions a future in which cognition, and therefore reason, survives the extinction of organic life. This future absence of embodied thought is proposed by Brassier as a (non)ground for reason, which must assume nothing as its productive condition of existence, not even a material body (and here we might note the similarity with Negarestani's idea of self-actualising reason, which seems to proceed without a body).

The dramatic episode of the sun's extinction, Brassier argues, is then a call to a radical Prometheanism, and it reveals the extent of the cleavage he seeks to establish between thought and cognition and the body. Again, in relation to Brassier's nemo-centricism, questions arise for us concerning the diversity of ecologies and economies of intelligence in the future, though we admit such questions come from an ethico-aesthetic perspective rather than a technoscientific one. In this regard, more than reason might be involved in developing a nemocentric subject, involving technologies that are themselves dynamic elements of evolving human-machine-environment assemblages. But perhaps this is already a part of Brassier's project: perhaps the human body is of little concern if thought can survive without a body, mediated not by flesh but by silicon or other non-organic substances which can survive both the extreme heat and cold of the expiration of the sun. Here it is not hard to understand why we read Brassier's philosophy as science fictioning, for there is something alien, if not exactly extra-terrestrial, and alienating too, about thought leaving the human body to survive the demise of the solar system. But then Brassier has fictioned manifestations of the alien before, identifying it with noise and as a political orientation in the process.

The Politics of Universal Noise

In the conclusion of his PhD thesis, 'Alien Theory', Brassier suggests that universal noise can challenge the 'seamless, all-encompassing informational circuit of World-Capitalism' (2001: 223). He argues that this informational circuit epistemically conditions people '*via* a staple diet of manufactured information', and that it 'phe-nomenologically enslaves a populace ... *via* a process of continual immersion in advertisements, film and television, video, computer games, etc.' 'Epistemic informa-tion', he continues, 'is politically encoded; phenomenological experience is sociologically conditioned' (223–4).[6] Universal noise counters these circuits by being 'phenomenologically undecipherable and hermeneutically undecodable', engendering cognitive modes free from phenomenological doxa, and therefore free from commodification. For many, to claim that anything is universal is problematic. But we think that Brassier is not proposing that there is an actual, specific sound which might be identified as universal noise for all people and contexts; rather, encounters with variable sound may produce instances of undecodable signals (that which is alien and alienating). In such an encounter, thresholds of intelligibility are breached where not even zeros and ones are easily determined. In this way, universal noise can be said to be a potential encounter for all.

Although Brassier does not address the concept of universal noise in 'Genre is Obsolete', he does suggest that To Live and Shave in L.A. produce a 'plethora of sonic data' which overwhelms the listener, countering entropy with negentropic overload. This plethora of sonic data, Brassier states in his interview with Ieven, has the capacity to suspend communication and identifications. After dismissing the equation of capitalism with noise as a romantic idea, Brassier explains his interest in noise performance: 'What I consider to be interesting about noise is its dis-organizing potency: the incompressibility of a signal interfering with the redundancy in the structure of the receiver. Not transduction but schizduction: noise scrambles the capacity for self-organization' (2009).[7] While noise severs connections, it is also clear that Brassier does not advocate a permanent state of disorganisation, in so far as he suggests that cognition and a new subject follow from schizduction. There is, necessarily, a return to (or a new assemblage of) an organisation of a kind, and new modes of connection (otherwise the subject would remain stranded in universal noise). Here we are reminded of the various fictions of the self in the work of Spare, Kusama and Smithson who, as we saw in section one, experiment with performances which collapse a sense of self.

We might also note that, at first, there appears to be similarities between schizduction (or an encounter with disorganising noise) and the notion of an event, which similarly seizes an individual and produces a subject through collapsing the world. That is, there seems to be an affinity here with Alain Badiou (2005). Indeed, an interesting comparison might be made between an encounter with noise which suspends selfhood (as proposed by Brassier), and an encounter with something (previously) uncounted which suspends the relations of a situation (which is Badiou's definition of an event). It is also worth comparing Badiou's concept of fidelity to an event (in the form of an interrogation of a situation) (2005: 232–9), with Brassier's notion of the production of a subject through cognition cleaved from experience. Both philosophers can be said to advocate the interrogation of a situation through subtraction from that situation or order of things, to see how the world can be counted or approached differently.

Despite these connections we do not think that Brassier conceives of schizduction as an event exactly. Rather, noise performance might be said to involve a forcing of conditions which then disrupt selfhood and produce a new subject. This is, to an extent, different to Badiou's notion of forcing the indiscernibility of a situation towards undecideability – a procedure which further forces a subject to act or make a decision to explore the potential of an event. But there are, again, similarities between these forcings, in so far as, for Badiou, forcing aids the thinking of 'the type of being to which the fundamental law of the subject corresponds' (2005: 410). This seems to point towards the importance of concepts which mediate noise performance. But, for us, the forcing of conditions which engender disorganisation and reorganisation can also be understood as a collective and technical practice and not (at least in the case of noise performance) as the result of an accidental or chance encounter.

All of this leads us to suggest that, whilst noise performance may proceed through cognition and concepts (of the experience-less subject) which cleave or force a subject from its body's senses, there are other aspects to noise performance which include collaboration (the relationships produced by groups) and technical objects, tools and technical practices (which performers use to make noise). As such, the nemocentric subject of noise performance may not be produced by reason alone, and this encourages us, no doubt against Brassier's intentions, to speculate on the relation of noise and social bodies (not least in relation to human-technology assemblages responsible for noise performance). We return, then, to the question of the surplus of the body and experience produced by (the discourse of) the experience-less subject.

Body-Rhythms

In producing stochastic sound, noise performance or noise music eschews rhythm, which can serve to orientate, organise and move bodies in unison. In *Rhythmanalysis*, Henri Lefebvre (2004) explores the physiological and social processes of rhythm, in which the human body and its processes are said to register cyclical, linear, organic and mechanical rhythms, as well as the arrhythmic.

Lefebvre approaches the rhythms of the body as potentially producing a relative scale and quantitative and qualitative indexing for everyday rhythms and noise. He distinguishes different kinds of rhythms to explain his approach to rhythmanalysis (16), a term which he borrows from Gaston Bachelard. First, he offers an analysis of polyrhythmia, the discernment of many rhythms but also of the uniqueness of individual rhythms (16). For Lefebvre, polyrhythmia is a condition of the body, revealed, for example, through medical practice that treats the body as a collection of processes and systems. He identifies eurhythmia as a second type of rhythm: the uniting or synching of rhythms which he relates to good health (16). In this, Lefebvre is not just interested in polyrhythmia and eurhythmia as attributes of the body, rather his concern relates to how such rhythms might serve as a measure of function or dysfunction. A third rhythm is isorhythmia, defined as a rare equality of rhythms that are not in synchronisation (68). Since it implies two or more temporalities, isorhythmia is of a higher order than, and exclusive of, eurhythmia – an example would be the complex music produced by an orchestra (68). These notions of 'normal' or 'healthy' polyrhythmia and eurhythmia, and complex isorhythmia, allow Lefebvre to identify and analyse everyday life. But there is one more phenomenon he identifies as important: arrhythmia, a negative and pathological event, and a sign of breakdown and disease. For example, arrhythmia is associated with an irregular heartbeat. When measured against eurhythmia and isorhythmia, arrhythmia is found to be without order. From Lefebvre's perspective, arrhythmia is dangerous for the health of an individual or social body, 'and brings previously eurhythmic organisations towards fatal disorder' (16).

Having outlined Lefebvre's notion of the social aspects of rhythm and arrhythmia, we can return to Brassier's speculative comments about communist subjectivities produced by variable noise, in order to contrast the perspectives of both philosophers in terms of noise and its radical political potential. Taking on board that, for Brassier, Lefebvre might be too concerned with embodied knowledge or phenomenology, and acknowledging that Brassier's comments concern noise performance (a context Lefebvre does not address), we can nonetheless bring their concerns together to assert that the discernment and regulation of polyrhythmia, eurhythmia and isorhythmia would be scrambled by incompossible noise, and that this would result in arrhythmia.

Lefebvre proposes that arrhythmia is a disorder which requires treatment – the application of 'rhythm without brutality' – to induce eurhythmia (68). In Lefebvre's diagnosis, arrhythmia is an index of disorganisation, and it equates to an organ or system making a noise rather than a healthy rhythm. In one of the texts collected in *Rhythmanalysis*, written in collaboration with Catherine Régulier, there is the suggestion that arrhythmia can be a power which overcomes alliance, allowing 'rhythms of the other' to make 'rhythms of the self' impossible (99). The fear is that noise will render individuals and groups of humans dysfunctional and without the means for collective agency. An example Lefebvre and Régulier give of arrhythmia is the deregulated, crisis-hit city of Beirut at the end of the twentieth century (where, by chance, Ray Brassier teaches as a member of the American University at the beginning of the twenty-first century), but this diagnosis holds for individuals, groups and societies of all kinds: *Rhythmanalysis* casts arrhythmia as anti-social and deadly.

In contrast to Lefebvre's casting of arrhythmia as unhealthy, Brassier values stochastic noise precisely for its disorganising potential and for its production of a first-object perspective. It is noise, he argues, which can reveal the non-conscious 'rhythms of the self' as, in fact, 'rhythms producing representations' through which capitalism enslaves a populace. Despite their differences, Lefebvre's notion that arrhythmia is an illness finds some resonance in Brassier's work. When writing about noise music and its condemnation by critics for abjuring critical responsibility, Brassier suggests that 'perhaps a psychotic who is lucid about the degree to which his estrangement is socially manufactured is a more dangerous political animal than any engaged artist or authentic lunatic' (Brassier 2007).

We also value arrhythmia as an ill-noise and schizoid production which might produce knowledge. As Nietzsche suggests in *The Gay Science*:

> Finally, the great question would still remain whether we can really dispense with illness – even for the sake of our virtue – and whether our thirst for knowledge and self-knowledge in particular does not require the sick soul as much as the healthy, and whether, in brief, the will to health alone, is not a prejudice, cowardice, and perhaps a bit of very subtle barbarism and backwardness. (Nietzsche 1974: 176)

For Nietzsche, one person's will to health might be another person's illness and vice versa, and this might be one way of seeing the difference between Lefebvre's and Brassier's understandings of noise and its affects. Importantly, though, Nietzsche implies that illness or breakdown is necessary for knowledge, and here we might equate this to Brassier's radical path through schizduction. But Nietzsche presents breakdown in a relation to healthy rhythm or order, in a kind of feedback loop between healthy and ill, or organised and disorganised, states: a looping of two paths presented without priority being given to either – a diagram which engenders thought and reflection.[8]

But, we might ask, in order to develop a meaningful politics from schizduction, is the production of thought enough? At one point in *Rhythmanalysis*, Lefebvre suggests that, 'Thought strengthens itself only if it enters into practice, into use' (2004: 69). This prompts not just the question of how nemocentric perspectives might be important for communist subjectivities, but also of how cognition – producing nemocentric subjects – can be put to use for collective political projects. An answer might be that schizduction leading to cognition is a catalyst for the production of a new alien temporality beyond experiential time, one that a (still human) nemocentric subject might explore, informed by the thought that (to paraphrase Newton's observation concerning television) 'the funny thing about the senses is that they tell you everything and nothing about reality'.

For us, this generation of a new subjectivity is maintained, or fictioned, through rhythms of reason and inferential logic which provide a continuity or consistency for a selfless subject, regulated in time, or in retrospect – for, as Brassier has argued, thinking takes time. When asked about his comments concerning noise performance, he suggests that 'the rationality of a discursive practice is always retrospectively constructed' and is 'never immediately accessible' (Brassier and Malik 2015: 230). It would seem, then, that for the most part the alien production and thinking of a self-less subject is a work of post-production. What, though, about the forcing of the conditions of the nemocentric noise event? As we have already implied, the labour and technics – or technological methods – which produce the noise encounter seem to be a surplus, too sullied by aesthetics and experience. But without embodied and embedded cognition or technics, there is no noise performance.

Clones and Loops

It is clear that, for Brassier, playing or listening to noise is less important than the thought produced by an encounter with noise. He is clear that 'noise music' is not inherently more subversive than any other commodifiable musical genre, suggesting that the idea that it is inherently critical or politically potent is a cliché, and objecting to the romanticising of somatic and psychological accounts of 'the liberating properties of noise' which, he argues, simply accentuate and hypostatise the listening experience (Brassier 2007b). Rather, Brassier is interested in To Live and Shave in L.A. and Rudolf Eb.er not because they simply make noise, but because they 'engender the noise of generic anomaly. It is the noise that is not "noise", the noise of the *sui generis*, that actualises the disorientating potencies long claimed for noise' (Brassier 2007b).

The question around we have been circling concerns whether the fact that To Live and Shave in L.A. is a collaboration that has involved a number of bodies over a number of years is significant. Although the noise of the collaboration may well scramble any capacity for self-organisation, we would note that the members of To Live and Shave in L.A., as performers, work together (even if this has to be construed in the broadest of terms) to produce noise as a collective exploration (at least in some senses). Furthermore, the group use musical instruments, microphones and electronic devices and other technical objects, and they play them collectively, avoiding anything that might sound like music in the conventional sense. Tom Smith of To Live and Shave in L.A. explains his view of the group's working cycle: 'I just open my mouth and it happens . . . Process and technique are the least significant aspects of the cycle. Tools are tools. That noted, I work with goals in mind, and those goals shift, warp, flatten, soften, explode outward, etc.' (Smith 2009). We find two things in particular to be noteworthy in Smith's statement: first, he asserts that, for him, 'tools are tools', and yet clearly there would no To Live and Shave in L.A. without tools; second, he has goals or ideas that are 'reshaped' through practice, and he later suggests that the group persists through 'constant accretion and synthesis' (Smith 2009). We wonder here whether, in privileging reason and cognition – and the reception of noise – and eliding the practice of noise making, Brassier misses something. To put this more bluntly, are communist subjectivities, or at least collectivity and common cause, produced through noise production rather than (just) noise consumption? Does the collective act of making alien or alienating sounds, involving bodies performing with technical objects and tools, have political possibilities, and indeed, the potential to produce new subjectivities?

Technical practice is also important in the performances of Rudolf Eb.er, who, at times, collaborates with others and presents edited recordings of previous perform-ances. Talking about the work *Brainnectar* (2014), the artist confirms Brassier's understanding that his noise performance is not for aesthetic enjoyment. But Rudolf Eb.er's way of thinking of his own practice does not exactly coincide with Brassier's concern for the cognition of the nemocentric subject. As Eb.er says,

> In the process of de/composition I did focus on my bodyreaction to the sounds . . . It is not made for the sensation but to become aware of the psychic body and to work with it. This music has the function to expand awareness, or at least the function to make aware that there is something to expand. (Rudolf Eb.er 2014)

While Rudolf Eb.er's work is made to decompose a sense of self, technology and the physical are as important as thought and cognition to the artist. As he goes on to explain:

> Beginning with the tape recorder and tape manipulations as instrument of choice, my work was always related to the body and the psyche. With ritualized abreaction and catharsis came the combination of experimental audioart and aktionism. I developed the 'psychophysical tests and trainings'. . . . Psychophysical energy, or inner heat, is, for example, raised from the perineum up into the brain. This consciousness-expanding and illuminating technique triggers sensations described as 'dripping nectar'. (2014)

Brassier may not address the practices and thoughts of noise performers (which do not exactly fit with nemocentrism), but he does recognise the importance of non-linguistic approaches in noise performance. For example, he states elsewhere that discursive practices can include non-linguistic practices which pose questions through their own mediums (Brassier and Malik 2015: 229–30). Even so, he empha-sises the importance of discursive and retrospective analysis of a practice above any performance which produces noise. In the case of To Live and Shave in L.A., this latter process may be a vehicle towards goals (similar to Brassier's own ambitions for noise), but it requires somatic nervous-system feedback loops and intimate, embodied, tacit knowledge of voice amplification, instruments and machines. And it is clear that for Rudolf Eb.er the use of musical instruments and 'isochronic tones and binaural beats' produce sounds 'causing direct effects onto the psyche', which does not contradict Brassier's thesis on noise, but could be said to emphasise a practice that experiments with different ways of affecting the body (Rudolf Eb.er 2014). Here we can identify one more practice that may be said to be involved in the labour of the inhuman but also in producing patheme-matheme assemblages (as discussed in the last chapter).

Rudolf Eb.er is also concerned with listening, or the way sound is processed, accepting that, 'Not all listeners will experience the same effects to the same extent' (Rudolf Eb.er 2014). We understand that listening – attending to sound – is producing,[9] and to engage with stochastic or incompossible sound requires recognising it as such through trying to make sense of the plethora of signals of a performance. We think, too, that noise may facilitate a realisation of a self-less subject, but that this might involve practice, that is, attending to sound rather than just producing concepts. In this, the production and reception of noise performance (and perhaps the generation of nemocentric, communist subjectivities) might involve looping cognition with embodied and embedded knowledge of human-technical-object arrangements (see Figure 19.3).

Brassier might object to this proposal and critique. Firstly, he might identify the processes of noise production as 'know-how' (as opposed to knowledge produced by reasoned interrogation and the production of concepts). Secondly, he may point out he is interested in 'rule-governed conceptual practices' (which involve reason) as opposed to pattern-governed processes (which do not necessarily involve reason) (Brassier and Malik 2015: 218). And it might be said that noise performance produces merely a random compositional process equivalent to

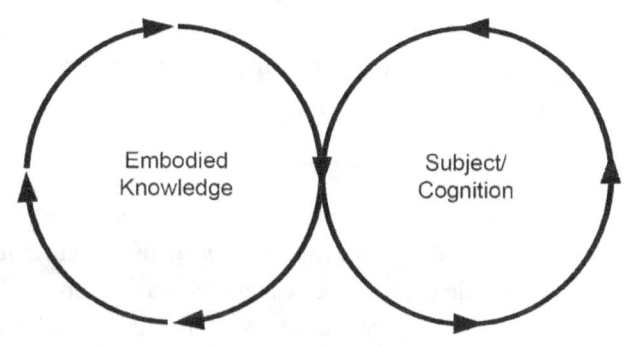

19.3 Diagram of feedback loop between embodied knowledge and cognition in encounters with noise performance (credit: the authors).

pattern-making. That is, anti-pattern making is no more a thoughtful exercise than pattern-making. In so far as the noise practices which Brassier comments on avoid or flatten patterns or overload rhythms – eliding enjoyment of richness or complexity – we suggest that there is something like an arrhythmanalysis at work in noise production, as a concept that is actualised through playing and listening. This is evidenced by the fact that both Smith and Rudolf Eb.er can be said to have goal-based practices. So, while concepts are involved in noise practice they do not directly produce noise, whereas audio performance and practice, and intimacy with technical objects, do. And if such practices cannot be said to be exactly or entirely rule-governed, neither can they be said to be like pattern-making either. Perhaps a way around this impasse would be to say that noise production is cloning, which is, indeed, a mode of noise generation that Brassier associates with Rudolf Eb.er's performances. Brassier's insight attends to a concept we addressed previously when discussing Laruelle's work in the last chapter of section two. Brassier – an early commentator on Laruelle in English-speaking contexts – has a similar take on cloning to the French philosopher:

> A non-materialist epistemology uses the epistemic algorithms furnished by a fully naturalised epistemology in order to clone a series of radically universal, non-epistemological functions and engender universes of unintuitable cognitive variation; universes wherein the frequencies of information, the codes of cognition, and the parameters of phenomenality are reconfigured in accordance with Noise as unknown, or as phenomenon-in-itself, in order to be reconstituted independently of the bounds of perception and beyond the remit of stimulus-response functions (Brassier 2001: 215).

In other words, cloning, for Brassier, produces the potential for an encounter with something which the habits of the senses cannot receive.

Noise-Clones

It thus becomes clear why Brassier values Rudolf Eb.er's practice of editing, cutting and splicing recordings of his performances to make new work, which the artist describes as a process of growing sound like dividing cells (Rudolf Eb.er 2014). This process of cloning is more than a performative or discursive gesture, for something physical is produced in Rudolf Eb.er's practice: sound waves registered by a body. Something surplus to discourse, concepts and conscious cognition is produced in an encounter with Rudolf Eb.er's performances. Perhaps, alongside the nemocentric subject, we find another aesthetic figure as conceptual persona at a noise perform-ance – the Clone – that attends to the potential of noise through technologies of different kinds (including the body and its sense organs) as well as cognition, and that does not succumb to the illusions of selfhood. We might find support for this idea in a surprising place, a text by Brassier.

In 'The View from Nowhere', a text published four years after 'Genre is Obsolete', Brassier again follows Metzinger in suggesting that a system or subject could develop and use a certain kind of system-model without falling into/for selfhood (Brassier 2011). In this model, the subject maintains use of the functional processes which produce a phenomenal model and would still have recourse to processes such as integration, monitoring, prediction and memory. Here it would seem that the subject utilises experience without falling for illusions (Brassier 2011). We suggest that such subjects might develop movements or loops between disorganisation and organisation, as a collective research venture, or (why not?) as a culture or practice which binds a society. Such societies might develop practices which oscillate between the technics and intimacies of cloning and the interrogation of the affects of noise. Here, it seems, we have entered again into the realm of Science Fiction, but these subjects and societies are no less strange to common sense today than the attributes of Nicholas Roeg's multi-channelling alien Thomas Newton were to Fredric Jameson in the 1980s. In this way, we are proposing, noise performance produces an austere and radical mythotechnesis.

Postscript: Towards a New Nature Theatre

In Franz Kafka's *America* (1985), Karl, an unemployed, homeless immigrant, reads a poster advertising 'The Nature Theatre of Oklahoma'. The poster declares that, if you want to be an artist, the Nature Theatre of Oklahoma will find employment for you, but you must hurry to the recruiting centre in Clayton as this is a once-in-a-lifetime opportunity which ends soon. Karl notes the location, date and time of the auditions and heads for Clayton. He is greeted by a confusing noise made by a company of female musicians dressed as angels. Kafka writes of Karl's response to the racket:

> When he got out at Clayton he heard at once the noise of many trumpets. It was a confused blaring: the trumpets were not in harmony but were blown regardless of each other. Still, this did not worry Karl; he took it rather as a confirmation of the fact that the Theatre of Oklahoma was a great undertaking. (247)

Karl recognises a woman trumpeter on a plinth, an acquaintance called Fanny, and climbs up. He is soon playing himself. He offers up a refrain, an air he once heard in a tavern, without any concern for what others are playing around him. Karl is pleased with his playing – and he is told he is an artist. When he asks whether men can join the orchestra, and if there is a place for him in the theatre as a musician, Karl is informed that the men take turns playing with the women but that the men dress as devils and play drums as well as trumpets. However, he is not given a place in the orchestra.

'The Nature Theatre of Oklahoma' could be read as an allegory for political movements in early twentieth-century America, when ending poverty, homelessness and unemployment were key concerns for socialist and anarchist groups. In pledging a place for everyone, the Nature Theatre might also be viewed as a proposition for a different kind of society. Of course, it could be read as something entirely different, as a metaphor for capitalism or America itself, promising the opportunity for people, whoever they are, to sell their labour and thrive. Or, it may even be read as an allegory for fascism or communist dictatorships, as we find out later that the Theatre has a director. As Deleuze and Guattari suggest in *Kafka: Towards a Minor Literature* (1986), Kafka's images and fictions are neither metaphorical nor allegorical, rather they are machines or assemblages which can be said to disassemble continuously. Put another way, Kafka's stories are schizoid fiction-machines with multiple entrances and exits, and in this way they short-circuit sense and invite thought about existing and future collective ventures, relations and organisations.

What is of interest to us, in the context of this chapter's concern with noise, is the din which the recruitment orchestra makes. The sound of the orchestra is not only confusing, it facilitates union and autonomy in different measure. As the orchestra produces no music, nor anything intelligible, it is a strange kind of collectivity which might also be seen as a failure of collective action. Karl, initially disorientated by the noise, embraces the collective racket by contributing a refrain of his own choosing. This is one way to engage with the noise of the orchestra – though whether it is the best way is questionable. But perhaps Karl is not up to exploring the potential of the Theatre, as he maintains habits and identifications through the pleasure of playing a comforting refrain. A more radical response might have been to embrace the disorganising potency of the orchestra and produce more noise; to enter into collective (dis)organisation, in which players are not subsumed or disciplined by a collective totality.

America was written between 1911 and 1914. We propose that the sound of the recruitment orchestra of the Nature Theatre of Oklahoma can be read as an early twentieth-century piece of noise performance of significance, in which cognition of stochastic sound defies the habits of the senses, and immersion in collective arrhythmic production is offered. Perhaps the Nature Theatre is the first noise band, or at least the first with the potential to develop a communist subjectivity.

We have ourselves attended and taken part in performances that can be described as disorientating and noisy New Nature Theatres, most notably, as we mentioned above, in our involvement with Plastique Fantastique and, in 2017, as part of a group or band organised by the artist Benedict Drew, whose artworks we referenced (in section one) as war machines that occupy and perform in space and time to produce alternatives to an existing order (and it occurs to us here that all noise performances are, in this sense, war machines). At the centre of the artist's exhibition titled *The Trickle Down Syndrome* at the Whitechapel Gallery (2017), which references the problematic notion that wealth trickles down to the poor, a group of musicians made arrhythmic sound for three hours, with the idea that anyone could play anything they wanted, when they wanted. We suggest it is in the time or 'after-time' following a shared event of producing or listening to noise that a relation of collectivity and autonomy of thought and performance seem most acute. And it is in the event of attending to or making noise collectively, as much as in the affects of noise itself, that New Nature Theatres have the potential to develop communist subjectivities, or at least involve a refusal of the rhythms of entertainment industries.

Notes

1   Stochastic signals are irregular signals that can be plotted statistically but cannot be predicted.

2   Leibniz defines the 'compossible' as a world which consists of things that can exist together. The incompossible would be a world which consists of things that cannot exist together.

3   Nemocentrism, as proposed by Thomas Metzinger, is 'a reality model (centred on a globally available but fully opaque self-model embedded in the current virtual window of presence)' (Metzinger 2003: 336).

4   Peter Gratton has suggested that this nemocentric subject is not human and that it thus fulfils Foucault's promise of the 'erasure of man' (Gratton 2014: 140).

5   In an interview by Suhail Malik, Brassier references a further interview with noise artist Mattin, and suggests that the radical political potential of noise is produced through an interrogation of noise practice which asks what experience, abstraction and freedom are, given that capitalism commodifies sensations and dissolves the concrete (Brassier and Malik 2015: 229).

6   Since writing 'Alien Theory', *Nihil Unbound* and 'Genre is Obsolete', Brassier could be said to have refined the focus of his work, through exploring Wilfred Sellars' notion of the 'Myth of the Given' and Sellars' ideas concerning nominalism. Despite this, Brassier can be said to consistently problematise notions of perception and experience, and the material processes of the body. In his work on Sellars, Brassier is interested in the philosopher's position that sensory awareness alone does not constitute knowledge and that perception is conceptually mediated.

7   Transduction is the process by which a signal triggers a response in a cell, body or system which sets in motion a chain of events that engenders a change in the composition or organisation of a system. Schizduction would be the process by which a signal is received that triggers a process of disorganisation or disintegration of a cell, body or system.

8   We suggest that a loop of 'ill' and 'healthy' arrangements, or a spiral of disorganisation and reorganisation, would make for a radical mythotechnesis which would complicate adaptation to technoenvironments (which may, as Brassier suggests, phenomenologically enslave a populace). We will say more about this in Chapter 23.

9   This is an idea asserted by Daniel Muñoz at the 'Noise and the Possibility of a Future' conference, Goethe Institute, Los Angeles, 7 March 2015.

20   Financial Fictions

In a world that is only made of contingency, it is only natural that
we should invent options or derivative contracts. It is only natural we
should circulate, today, things that we know will make a difference
in the future. *This is why I have always thought of derivatives*
and derivatives markets as the technology of the future.

Elie Ayache, The Blank Swan

FOLLOWING ON FROM our discussion of Prometheanism (and some of its discontents), but also returning to some of the themes of sections one and two (especially around science fictioning), what follows attempts a brief analysis of the strange temporality of financial instruments which allow a kind of engineering of the future from the present and, indeed, the capitalisation of that feedback from the future in the present. This is not an entirely new phenomenon. Financial agreements concerning the future have long been in existence. Agreements facilitating the trading of seasonal goods, such as crops to be harvested in the future (which of course involves an element of risk), are one obvious example. Similar contracts agreeing the future delivery of an asset are in use today, and deliver many kinds of commodities, including art – a well-known case is the agreement reached between Jeff Koons and his collectors, who often pay for a work to be delivered sometime in the future, even though the artist has yet to decide what he will do or how he will make a particular work. The risk here is that costs will rise as experimentation is undertaken without guarantee of success, and the artist is known for asking for more money (or offering the return of the investment, if the collector so decides). As Felix Salmon (2014) notes, unlike many who make money from art, Koons can be said to make art from money.

Today's financial products are, however, far more complex than the relatively simple transactions just mentioned. Hedging involves investing in both high-risk and more secure stocks and shares, or the management of multiple investments, as a means of insuring against market volatility; in other words, it is an attempt to safeguard against any unpleasant surprises which the future might bring. Derivatives are one financial instrument of hedging, and involve contracts between parties agreeing the sale and delivery of an asset (stocks, bonds or commodities) at a specified time in the future. These financial processes require technical expertise but, in leveraging the future, risk can never be banished from speculation (in fact, as we shall see, it is crucial to their operation).

In the worlds of hedging and derivatives, the dominant image of financial trading is no longer that of the practices developed by the Chicago Board of Trade as established in 1848 – the same year that an entirely different response to capitalism, the *Communist Manifesto*, was produced. The Chicago Board set rules for the trading of commodities such as grain – rules which allowed for speculation on price and the movements of goods, including the advent of 'futures agreements', the legacy of which can be seen in the financial markets of the twenty-first century. Today, though, the image of financial transaction which comes to mind is that of the screen-bound trader, or even the hubs running algorithms which enable high-frequency trading. These digital financial environments are relatively new, as a *Guardian* interview with a derivatives trader from 2013 reveals:

> Fifteen years ago this job was completely different. Earlier practitioners would be standing up for ten hours in the 'pit', estimating option prices by plugging numbers into a basic calculator (big fat finger error risk!), shouting and waving hand signals. These days you sit in front of many computer screens, clicking and updating code . . . It doesn't matter how much of a mathematical genius you are – when you first come in the challenge is learning how all the systems work. It's more about systems now than ever before . . . What the firm wants is someone quick, assertive, mathematically competent, prepared to optimise reward/risk ratios. (Luyendijk 2013)

In this chapter, we are interested in whether this new logic of algorithms – and, more generally, the digital systems at play in capitalising on the future – involve something different, some new relation to the future perhaps different even to the relation between present and future we find in Science Fiction. We will also speculate below on the implications of this new logic for art practice, attending in the second half of the chapter to two examples of artists who engage either with financial fictions directly, or with the new digital terrain produced by coding and increasing computational power. Once again, we use the term mythotechnesis to refer to these practices which respond in different ways to the perplexing machine-produced temporalities of financial worlds and their logics.

Financial Fictions

In a short essay on what he calls 'Hyperbolic Futures', Steven Shaviro follows Fredric Jameson (whom he quotes) in suggesting that Science Fiction offers a 'psycho-social-technological cartography' of the present via the setting up of a different perspective (Shaviro 2011: 4).[1] For Shaviro this is Science Fiction's raison d'être: it can offer a purchase on the various 'hyperobjects' which determine our lives in the present but which are too vast to see. Indeed, we might say that this is an isotope of a larger and more general problem of how to represent the abstractions of capitalism, which, as we suggested in section one, has been a key concern of Jameson's writing over the last three decades. Through cognitive – and affective – mapping, then, Science Fiction allows us to grasp the increasing complexity of our contemporary moment.

However, Shaviro is also attuned to a more speculative function of Science Fiction, in particular the way in which it can offer up different accounts of the future to those increasingly being engineered by our economic and marketing managers. Science Fiction's capacity to surprise – to offer up a *different* future – is, for Shaviro, crucial to its identity as a genre.[2] This said, the importance of these different futures is still understood in terms of the ways in which they demonstrate – in their very portrayal of difference – that many common ideas of the future have, indeed, been managed: Science Fiction can 'outline the bars of our prison' as Shaviro puts it (11). We might briefly gesture back to Jameson here, and to some of the issues we explored in Chapter 12, in order to note a central paradox of Science Fiction writing which is connected to this present-future perspective: is it, in fact, possible to write about the actual future utilising the means and materials of the present? As we mentioned in Chapter 12, for Jameson, this is not so much an epistemological issue – nor, indeed, a technical one – but an ontological question of how to combine 'the not-yet-being of the future' with the being of the present (Jameson 2005: xvi).

To return to Shaviro, it does seem to us that this understanding of Science Fiction as an optic on the present (or as confined to a kind of present-future perspective) has its limitations, in so far as it can restrict the genre through focusing on visions of the future, which can curtail formal experimentation. Indeed, in many ways, Burroughs' cut-up Science Fiction novels are an answer – at least of sorts – to Jameson's paradox, in so far as they actually produce a different space-time through the break with typical syntax and logical sequencing. We should note, however, that the analogue experimentations of Burroughs and his fellow travellers might be left behind by the advent of new technological, financial environments. Artworks exploring the potential of the digital may be more relevant to the worlds that code builds, for example Cécile B. Evans' film *Hyperlink: Or It Didn't Happen* (2014), in which a simulation of the actor Philip Seymour Hoffman, who suffered an untimely demise through a drug overdose, appears as a self-proclaimed 'bad copy', amidst a myriad of seemingly unrelated material. As Daniel Rourke writes in his review of Evans' exhibition at Seventeen Gallery, London (2014): 'What makes Evans' work successful is this endless calling up of the spectre of the beyond, the outside, the everything else, from within the perceived totality of the internet' (Rourke 2014). Whereas artists in the last century may have applied cut-up, collage and montage techniques to produce disjunction through physically rearranging material (or reality as a recording, as Burroughs suggests), today it can be said that life lived through the digital is a life lived through the disjunctions of networks which seem comprised of images and worlds which are spaced out but, at the same time, potentially and instantaneously linked. In such environments, the practices of the analogue may no longer cut it. For not only might the classic forms of Science Fiction as present-future perspectives be limiting, but past notions concerning time and space (which Burroughs always claimed was running out), and corresponding avant-garde experimentation, might also be obsolete in technological environments that collapse or compress temporal and spatial dimensions – financial tools contributing greatly to these new conditions.

In relation to what we might call the *logics of the hyperlink*, we find again that Shaviro's compelling accounts of Science Fiction in terms of 'financial fictions' – or, more specifically, derivatives – are important, not least for his insights into how these contracts work to produce the reality they predict. Here fiction (or, more specifically, the fictioning of future scenarios) operates as a kind of temporal feedback loop (from these futures back to the present).[3] In fact, as we shall see in more detail below, the future is the very condition of possibility for the writing of derivatives and, as such, also begins to have a very real traction on our present reality.

Here we might briefly return to the more recent essay by Jameson, 'The Aesthetics of Singularity' (2015), that we looked at in section one, concerned as it is with the temporal logic of these financial instruments (which are themselves part of what Jameson sees as a fundamental economic phase shift to globalisation). Jameson identifies a similar temporal logic which is also evident in recent literature, understood by him as a symptom of this broader economic shift. This new kind of fiction involves works in which form – and especially 'one-time unrepeatable formal events' – has itself become content (Jameson mentions the narrative structure of Tom McCarthy's novel *Remainder* (2007), which he suggests involves precisely the 'one-time invention of a device') (2015: 113). For Jameson, there is a strange kind of 'flat' temporality at play with these events: a 'pure present without a past or a future' (113). In relation to art practice more broadly, this is also evident in those works (paradigmatically installations) in which the singular event – 'made for the *now*' – has replaced the object or any sense of sequencing (in terms of both historicity and futurity, as was still in play within modernism and the avant-garde) (113).

Turning to financialisation itself, Jameson follows Giovanni Arrighi's periodisation of Capital, identifying a third stage (our own) in which new regions of expansion have been exhausted, resulting in a situation where Capital must feed back on itself – double its existing territories – via speculation on futures. A derivative does just this, operating as a highly specific 'locus of incommensurables' (118), a temporal mapping of various risks to do with projected events and ventures. In fact, as Jameson points out, this is why there can be no generalised theory of the derivative, each occasion being unique, hence the reference to singularity in his essay's title.

As Jameson also notes, this interest in the future is not in itself new (as we suggested above, there has long been a predictive futures market). What is new is both the way in which these futures feedback – or have a 'reflexion' (117) – in and on the realities of financial systems, but also how they are now incredibly complex: the myriad variables are only able to be calculated by computer, which means they are also already properly posthuman (as he acknowledges, Jameson follows N. Katherine Hayles on this compelling insight). For Jameson, the crucial issue is to reclaim a different idea of the future from this new temporality which is composed of 'a series of singularity-events' operating in and as a 'perpetual present' (122).

Différance and Contingency

We can deepen this account of derivatives, especially in relation to their temporal structure, by looking to Suhail Malik's recent article 'The Ontology of Finance' (2014). Malik offers a further – but very different – inflection on Jameson's temporal paradox of how to write the future from the present, in so far as time, following his reading of the sociologist Elena Esposito, is figured in terms of systems theory and as such is not to be understood as the backdrop to the operation of derivatives but, rather, as produced by them (time is system-specific in this sense). Indeed, with derivatives the usual sequencing is scrambled: the future does not come after a present (that itself has come after a past), but is increasingly operative in the present – or, as Malik suggests, it is the future that is the condition of the writing of a derivative. The solution to the paradox we mentioned above is, then, that time is not separate from the fictions which are its circuits and loops – again, the future (at least of a kind) is already at work in the present. When laid out flat, as it were, different pasts, presents and futures are all involved in different reflexive and recursive operations.

Malik's own thesis is developed on the basis of a key logic of derivatives (defined by him, at their most simple, as temporally based contracts between two parties to sell or buy an asset at a certain future date): that they tend to operate essentially divorced from the underlying asset they concern (or, rather, via the deferral of the underlying asset; the contracts are rarely cashed in). As such, any individual 'pricing' operates through a complex network of differential prices which begins with the difference between the price paid for the derivative and the predicted price of the asset at a future date, rather than, again, through being tied to any material asset or productive process. This is a network which spreads throughout space (and as such operates with an indifference to state boundaries), but also through time. Indeed, to all extents and purposes, the 'terrain' of what we might call financial colonisation is infinite – not just because of the progression into an ever more distant future (involving ever more complex mathematics), but also, crucially, because these differential networks link or sync derivatives to derivatives (it is this dynamic 'hedging' which constitutes the real phase-shift to financialisation).

Malik offers an impressive amount of detail on the various mechanisms at play in these and other financial instruments. Following Jacques Derrida, he names this new logic of *différance* the 'arkhederivative', where this refers not simply to the logic of a certain kind of financial instrument (derivatives and the like) but also to the very principle of financialisation and the new form of 'capital-power' attendant on this (Malik 2014: 775–80). The metaphysics of the market – which might appear to trade on the presence of an underlying asset – is always already in deconstruction in this sense. Or, as Malik suggests elsewhere: 'The "they" of the state-business nexus effectuated that deconstruction, and they did it better than Derrida' (Avanessian and Malik 2016).

Of particular interest for our purposes is the way in which financialisation operates a particular kind of time management, or, more bluntly, designs predictive technologies. Malik discusses some of these – such as the Black-Scholes model (an especially successful predictive formula) – but also offers up a compelling counter-argument whereby the very unpredictability of the market (its volatility) is, in fact, constitutive of the successful working of derivatives: the latter need different horizons of possibility in order to multiply (the linking or synching function we mentioned earlier). In this sense financialisation is not really about accurately predicting – or, indeed, controlling – the future, but about keeping it open, proliferating scenarios. We might note that this synching of financial fictions – a kind of trading in representations without referent (or, at any rate, a deferral of any referent) – does not mean that there is no traction on the real. Indeed, the real – at least the real in terms of a world influenced by financial markets – is produced by these fictions (to say nothing of the further impact on social and political reality of financialisation, perhaps the best example being the global economic crisis of 2008).

To return to Jameson's temporal paradox of Science Fiction, we might say that the logic of derivatives as Malik understands it allows a wholly different take on the future (or, more precisely, on time itself) than that offered by any Science Fiction that reflects on technological developments in the present to predict the future. In Malik's understanding, the future is precisely pure contingency (when 'anything might happen'). In a similar take on metaphysics, and as we noted in Chapter 16, the philosopher Quentin Meillassoux has demonstrated (in his seminal work *After Finitude* (2005)) that although it is unknowable in one sense, one can begin to say certain things about the outside of our present experience (it is, in fact, thinkable). For Meillassoux, again as we noted in Chapter 16, 'access' to what he calls 'The Great Outdoors' (that which lies outside of our present experience) hinges on its character as a radically contingent 'hyper-chaos' (it is not a 'place' as such), but also on the way in which we can ascertain – conceptually, as it were – certain characteristics or 'properties' of this radical contingency (beginning with the fact that it is this contingency alone which is necessary). Likewise with derivatives and other financial instruments: one can begin to set out certain conceptual coordination points which characterise any future in terms of its contingency, but which also then allow this future to impact on present decisions. As Malik remarks, following Elie Ayache (a key precursor to his own thesis), derivatives (or market pricing) 'can be characterised as a technology of the future' in this sense (2014: 761), and the market can be understood as 'the medium of contingency' (Malik quoting Ayache 2014: 761).

Early on in his article Malik remarks that what he offers up is a 'general theory of price largely dedicated to the identification of capital-power's complex constitution and organisation', but also that this might be considered preliminary (and, we might say, theoretical) work, following Left accelerationism, towards the 'revectoring required to provide the requisite political tasks' (639). One can speculate on what such a revectoring might involve, in particular an intervention of some kind in the derivatives market – as, for example, with the Robin Hood project which operates as a cooperative, employing an algorithm named 'The Parasite' to manage funds placed in stocks, with one aim being to raise money to invest in and expand the commons (see Robin Hood website n.d.). As Malik points out, sabotage per se is ruled out by definition in so far as such interruptions and ruptures are part of the system's operating volatility; more typical strategies which might work in terms of sabotaging investment, and so forth, are rendered ineffectual in a derivatives market which can itself be premised on counter-production. Might there, however, be other options?

Towards the end of a compelling interview about his theorisation of the financial market as its own kind of event (or even entity) which operates separate from the world (as laid out in his book *The Blank Swan*), Elie Ayache writes of the trader in the pit as a kind of Nietzschean *übermensch* who lives the very particular time – and 'intensity' – of the market:

One can see that because he lives right at the hinge of the event (in the middle of the event) and not in the world that precedes or follows the event, he somehow achieves a 'state of rest' relative to the event. He lives at the same (infinite) speeds as the event. (2014: 599)

Here we might find a fabulous image and conceptual persona for the financial fictions we are addressing in this chapter. Might there be an interpretation of Ayache's financial *übermensch* whereby we could imagine the artist as trader, as someone fully immersed in the market's volatility and 'playing' its logics? Perhaps, in so far as dynamically interacting with the market actively produces the market, trading in this sense might be thought of as creative and productive. And yet this has its limitations in so far as its radicality, at least as pitched by Ayache, is simply an antidote to the boredom of a more static reality: Ayache's 'active market maker' loves volatility simply because he/she loves challenges. And, of course, such a position is still focused on trading in order to make a profit.

What about a position one step removed from the markets – which would represent them at a distance, as it were? Certainly, as with the Science Fiction novels Shaviro looks at, there might well be art about the new landscape of financialisation. A recent interesting example is Suzanne Treister's exhibition *HFT The Gardener* (2016), which explores – in paintings, drawings and a film-fiction – the world of high frequency trading in relation to the neurochemistry of the traders (and especially the bizarre connection with psychotropic plants).[4]

A further option here might be a certain kind of 'acceleration' of the logics of financialisation. Indeed, what would it mean to further accelerate the function of the derivative?[5] To link its fictions to something beyond the reasonable (or the cash-in-able)? This would not necessarily involve an intention to profit from the market (as in Ayache's own start-up financial company – or, indeed, any number of dealers and galleries that play the art market), but something perhaps more parasitical, or even ironic; something which, perhaps, mimics the logics and workings of the financial markets (especially in terms of the production of ever more complex financial fictions). An interesting case study of an art practice involving a kind of 'revectoring' in these terms is Goldin+Senneby and the novel *Headless* written by 'K. D.'.

Now Here and Nowhere

Headless (2014) is as a good a place as any to find out about Goldin+Senneby. This celebrated collaboration has produced one of the few art practices concerning financial fictions that can be counted as a compelling fictioning itself. Goldin+Senneby's *Headless* project does not address derivatives or similar financial products as such, but is concerned with offshore companies. However, such offshore inventions are important to hedge funds, which often exist as offshore fund products, benefitting from low or zero tax liability and freedom from regulation. More specifically, in the context of India, there also exist products known as offshore derivatives. Offshore companies and funds may be fabrications registered by proxy owners in countries such as the Bahamas where tax liabilities are set at zero for these ventures. These offshore companies are often linked to other ventures existing elsewhere in the world (owned by the same people who set up the offshore companies), charging for services (which may or may not take place), meaning that very little tax, if any, is paid on profits made by a number of businesses around the world. Secrecy and anonymity allow these offshore companies – which are both here now (registered in name) but nowhere to be seen – to prosper. It is no accident, perhaps, that the cover of the novel attributes authorship of *Headless* to an individual known by the initials 'K.D.', who works, we are told, for an offshore management company Sovereign Trust in Gibraltar, and who may or may not exist. We are also told that K.D. did not write the novel. This task was undertaken by John Barlow, who does exist, and who, throughout the novel, reflects upon being the ghostwriter of a book produced under the instruction of Goldin+Senneby. Barlow never meets the artists – communicating with the pair through email – but he explains their project perfectly well (despite often claiming confusion).

The story of the novel is that Goldin+Senneby, on finding out about an offshore company called Headless, link the invisible financial organisation to the project of Georges Bataille and his fellow renegade surrealists who attempted to found a secret collective, bound by the crime of human sacrifice, in 1938 in France. It is clear that Barlow does, in fact, understand more than he says he does. Indeed, he writes a preface which depicts an infamous episode (which may or may not have taken place) when Bataille and fellow conspirators met in a wood to kill one of their number. Although one of the group volunteered to be the victim, the myth is that no one would step up as executioner (in *Headless*, it is implied that an animal is killed instead). The idea of the gathering was to initiate a secret society of the Acéphale, a figure depicted by Bataille's friend, the artist André Masson, as holding a burning heart and sword in each hand but without a head on its shoulders (for it is an 'it') and with a skull where the genitals should be. This attempt to found a society in the name of this fearsome figure – which lives in the moment or the present – brings together a number of Bataille's key interests: the power of secrecy, sovereignty, and collectivity or society (and life) without a head or leader. Barlow, who claims not to understand half of this, suggests that Goldin+Senneby see the project of the Acéphale continued by offshore organisations, specifically the offshore company Headless (see the company's symbol in Figure 20.1) – the rather unlikely and intentionally paranoid plot line being that Headless (the company) can be traced back to the secret society of Acéphale, via a company founded in 1962 (the year of Bataille's death) called Akefalo Ltd. (Akefalo being a way of spelling Acéphale in Greek). It is this secret which Barlow and others attempt to uncover, convinced that the offshore company promises the return of Acéphale and that, by the end of the book, the secret society has finally found a member willing to execute one of its own – a university lecturer named Angus Cameron, who does exist and who often serves as spokesperson for Goldin+Senneby. The novel, written in the style of a Dan Brown blockbuster, is full of clichés (but that is presumed to be the intention), and mixes up living and fictional characters to the point where distinguishing fiction from fact no longer has any currency. This is the success of the novel and the project in general, which never offers any clue as to whether Headless (the offshore company) exists or not: Goldin+Senneby's financial fiction pursues the logic of fiction produced through a search engine or through hyperlinks, by connecting character to character, and capitalist ventures to art ventures. Crucially, though, Goldin+Senneby engineer a void – a sinister absence – which is apparent whenever the fictional protagonists (and, indeed, the actual readers of the novel) attempt to ascertain the truth about the offshore company. Or, to put this another way, *Headless* is both the title of Goldin+Senneby's novel and names the logic of financialisation; the power of absence and presence is an aesthetic effect that Goldin+Senneby appropriate from offshore trading.[6] *Headless*, it seems to us, is a performance fiction which presents a threatening and intense secrecy: though a fiction, it has actual effects, not least in producing celebrity status and the glamour of intrigue for Goldin+Senneby amongst art establishments, curators and art theorists. Importantly, not only are all offshore companies cast as potential secret organisations by *Headless* – with hidden agendas beyond profit – it is implied that they are potentially a means of resolving the impossible relation of sovereignty and collectivity (at least for some elites around the world).

No doubt, Goldin+Senneby's *Headless* project offers a critique of financial fictions, continued in other projects such as *Zero Magic* (2015–16), produced in collaboration with a magician, Malin Nissan, and other experts in

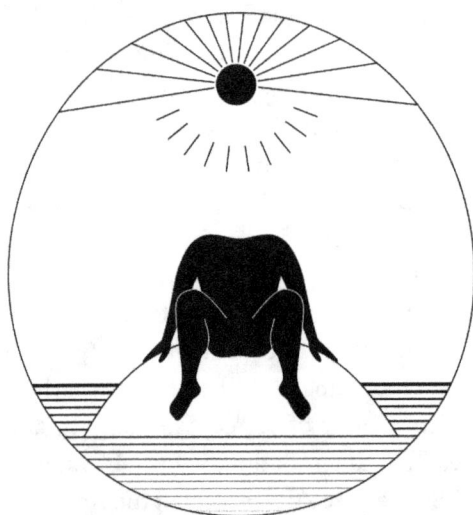

20.1 Goldin+Senneby, *Headless* symbol (reproduced by permission of the artists).

design, patents and computer science.[7] For *Zero Magic*, Goldin+Senneby claim to have infiltrated a secretive American hedge fund and entered into short-selling (trading shares that they do not own) so as to perform a magic trick that undervalues a publically traded company: their stated aim is to profit from this trickery. The art-going public is introduced to – and implicated in – the trick by purchasing tickets to a magic performance, *On a Long Enough Timeline the Survival Rate for Everyone Drops to Zero* (2015), 'buying into the predicted future loss of a target company' (Goldin+Senneby 2016). Importantly for the project, and relating to our earlier discussions of technology and financial fictions, Goldin+Senneby display a Magic Box which seems to be decorated with a four-sided abacus and is said to contain *Zero Magic Software*, a US patented application. Goldin+Senneby, then, can be seen as tricksters who employ the power of fictioning combined with the tools and methods of financialisation – including capitalisation on the feedback loop of the future in the present through predicting 'the future loss of a target company'. Whether they employ means that allow them to exit from contemporary art and the yoke of the rich collector or patron (the umbilical cord of gold, as the art critic Clement Greenberg once put it) is an interesting question: their collaboration might meet the demands of Suhail Malik and others who see financialisation as a possible means of escaping servitude to financial elites. Indeed, in ways more straightforward than the fictionings of Goldin+Senneby, Malik and fellow collaborators, as part of the short-lived Real Flow Collective, similarly adopted the methods of financialisation to offer artworks as a means of initiating exchange for derivatives. As interesting as this venture is, we suggest that Goldin+Senneby offer something more than financial fictions (and deferral) of the future to profit in the present. Their work is a mythotechnesis which bends the technologies of finance towards different ends. By understanding that financialisation, in fictioning the future, produces actual affects in the present, they operate by making it known that theirs is a practice involving illusion. This is not exactly a critique of the false so much as the revelation and utilisation of the powers of financialisation which proceed from a logic – a science fictioning, techno-magic practice – which reiterates that *NOTHING IS TRUE, EVERYTHING IS PERMITTED.*

The World that Code Built

It seems to us, then, that there might well be art practices which address, or intervene in, the new financial landscapes of contingency, or which populate the new territories produced by financial fictions with new avatars. This is art that responds to the actual affects of financialisation from the perspective of those who do not necessarily play the market but who are subject to temporal structures wrought by various market instruments. Another example of this kind of mythotechnesis – a future-fiction which is, as it were, materially incarnated in the here and now but is nowhere (or in cyber-space) – can be found in the practice of Ryan Trecartin, who often works in collaboration, notably with Lizzie Fitch. We will address Trecartin and Fitch's work again, at the end of this section, in relation to embodiment and the fictioning of digital forms of life, but here our concern is with the structures their characters find themselves in, and which operate through the logic of the hyperlink and the aesthetics of singularity outlined above.

Trecartin's description of what is in at play in his films – in terms of their struc-ture – can, at times, seem like a description of the logic of derivatives, especially as Jameson describes them in their singular, yet very complex, character. An example of this is given in an interview about the film *K-CoreaINC.K (section a)* (2009) and one character in particular, who appears to be a black hole superimposed with rolling text. Trecartin explains:

> That's Twi-Key, I was thinking of her as an office-space oracle . . . The thinking behind it came from exploring the potential need for experiential, cultural, brand and even linguistic translators in the maintenance of work environments, and how the act of translating can be seen as oracular. Think of it like existence as a temporary state of maintaining a situation. As if there are proposed realities that inhabit themselves via structural collaborations and then disperse when they're no longer needed by the entities involved. These realities then live as versions inside the continuum of translation. (Trecartin 2011)

Trecartin goes on to explain that he thinks of the 'being' of Twi-Key and other such characters as an 'architecture' of ideas, and in so doing he reveals his interest in speech as a space in which the characters exist. Fitch and Trecartin's avatars exist in the space of the translation of language and information; the artists suggest that these avatars continually explore whether they share 'architecture' with other characters, or whether they are connecting or collaborating at all (Trecartin 2011). The avatars of Trecartin's films may still reflect upon their identities, but location and mobility are not something that concerns them, for they are spaces or areas themselves, as implied by the title of Trecartin's 2007 work *I-Be Area*.

In the example of Twi-Key, the workplace (as a temporary and singular 'architec-ture' linked to other singular architectures) takes on the logic of financial fictions – and here we might think of trading desks but also of businesses operating through zero-hours contracts, call centres selling multiple products of behalf of numerous clients, and new workspaces offering temporary space for sales ventures and start-up compa-nies. It might be that Trecartin's description of 'office-space oracles' has relevance for the operations of contemporary capitalism and its financial fictions, for they 'inhabit themselves via structural collaborations and then disperse when they're no longer needed by the entities involved', engendering characters – or avatars – which operate in and as what he calls 'an affective possibility space' to maintain a situation (Trecartin 2011). In this, the avatars can be thought of as singular events which link to other spaces or areas through affective vectors, giving them a precarious and often minimal consistency. To quote Trecartin:

> The future and the past can be equally malleable; I don't think they go in opposite directions. Memory is more an act of memorisation than recalling: you're creating something that doesn't really exist behind you, it exists in the same place the future exists. In my videos the characters try to treat that idea as fact. (Trecartin 2011)

As Trecartin's interlocutor in this interview, the novelist and peripheral Ccru associate Hari Kunzru, suggests, Trecartin is implying that there is an adjustment of the past from the future. Indeed, following Malik, to see time as system-specific – as cybernetic – means any time can impact on any other time. In the patchwork temporality of Trecartin's films, different loops and circuits connect and feedback on one another, producing a certain density (and even, at times, a compelling opacity) in which digital modelling is important. To develop this idea further, we note Fitch's remark, made in an interview with Ossian Ward, that the movie sets of her films with Trecartin are always 360 degrees, but also that they are built 'on the computer as 3D models first': these are virtual worlds which are then materially instantiated (Fitch 2014: 135).

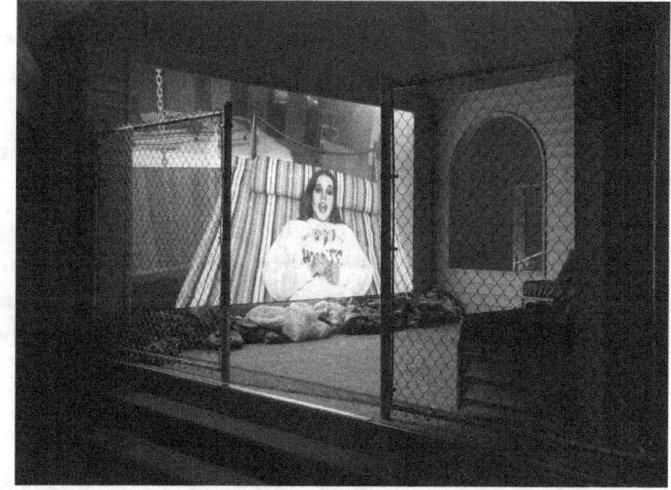

In general, it seems to us that one of the key interests of Trecartin's work is this virtual-actual hybridity: a looping and connecting of different fictions which can extend to the gallery space as itself a certain kind of theatrical set-up (see Figure 20.2). Here, to enter the fiction of the films is to link narratives, as Patrick Langley remarks, through 'screens within screens' (2012). As another commentator, Christopher Glazek, argues, a film like Trecartin and Fitch's *CENTRE JENNY* – set in the future and featuring digital subjects that are descendants of animations – blurs the lines between pre- and post-production, with the film

20.2 Ryan Trecartin, Lizzie Fitch/Ryan Trecartin, *Priority Infield* (with *CENTRE JENNY*), 2013, installation view, Zabludowicz Collection, London 2014. Photo: Stuart Whipps (permission by Zabludowicz Collection).

itself depicting the production (behind the scenes, as it were) of the fiction (Glazek 2014). The variety of perspectives and different cameras, and especially the use of handheld cameras, also serves to foreground the film's status as a constructed fiction. Glazek makes us aware in this essay, 'The Past is Another Los Angeles' (2014), of the very particular context of the films: the make-believe culture of the city of LA, which is itself a patchwork of different fictions and performances.

Although shown in exhibitions, the films are also digitally disseminated (Trecartin often makes them freely accessible via YouTube and Vimeo channels). The work over-spills the boundaries of the traditional spaces and places of art; the films have as much in common with various popular and subcultures of the internet as they do with 'high' art (if this latter term still has meaning). This relates to the linking and overlaying of imagery and narrative in *CENTRE JENNY*, which is compelling and produces a very particular affect – a kind of amphetamine and hallucinogenic rush. The visual compo-sition of the avatars also arises from a linguistic or discursive complexity – 'logos, products, graphic design, interfaces' (Trecartin 2011) – which, again, in itself produces a certain density in which a name or image contains, condensed within it, the parts from which it is made (its history is written on its surface, as it were). The avatars reflect on their own agency as images and might be thought of as compressed files, but there is a strange kind of digital or hyperlinking subjectivity at play here too (char-acters tend to proliferate across different actors and individuals play multiple parts). Trecartin and Fitch are producing avatars which experiment with the new temporalities and spatial relations produced by social media communication, advertising and trans-formations of work and leisure time; for their avatars establish identities with a certain consistency but that are also fluid and able to adapt to new and fast-moving digital cultures. In fact, it seems to us that this is one way of understanding Trecartin and Fitch's experimentation with avatars and their 'architecture' – or, at least, what is key in their films is the kind of forms the avatars take (the 'areas' and 'architectures' they exist as). In this, Trecartin and Fitch do not just offer up a fiction (a particular utopia or dystopia); like the financial fictions discussed at the beginning of this chapter, their films are less about or predictive of a given future than they are involved in actively writing a version of it. They produce fictioning modes that allow their avatars to survive and inhabit the new time-spaces wrought by the systems and fictions of capitalism.

Notes

1   Shaviro's essay concerns two Science Fiction novels: *Market Forces* by Richard K. Morgan and *Moxyland* by Lauren Beukes.
2   In relation to this essentially utopian function of Science Fiction and the increasing importance of such visioning in the context of climate change, see McKenzie Wark's

Molecular Red. Wark's call for an 'alternative realism' (2016: xxi) to our capitalist present (and the fantasies of pre-capitalist return which are part of it) resonates with our own concept of fictioning, albeit that our focus, once again, is more on the material instantiation or performance of these fictions.

3 Shaviro follows the important work of Kodwo Eshun in this area, and especially his account of temporal feedback loops in his article 'Further Considerations of Afrofuturism' (Eshun 2003). See our discussion in Chapter 12.

4 See the exhibition and accompanying catalogue, *HFT The Gardener*, Annely Juda Fine Art, London, 22 September–29 October 2016. In terms of our book more generally, Tresiter's work is, it seems to us, a good example of fictioning as method (see, as indicative, the sequence of works *Hexen 2.0* (2009–11)).

5 The notion of accelerating the temporal logic of financialisation (and its attendant regimes of power) is also at play in Armen Avanessian's idea of introducing a difference into what he and Malik have called the 'Speculative Time-Complex'. Avanessian also addresses the question of reclaiming the future through a meditation on grammar and tense (which can involve a de-privileging of the present), and, indeed, the possibility of a 'speculative poetics' attendant on this (although it is unclear what these different strategies might look like in practice, and how they might effect the kind of wider political and social change which both Malik and Avenessian call for) (Avanessian and Malik 2016).

6 See also the discussion of Goldin+Senneby, in relation to the proliferation of 'surface fictions', in Reeves-Evison 2017.

7 See the artists' website for more information (Goldin+Senneby 2017).

21   Post-Singularity Fictions as Mythotechnesis

The issue is whether humanity should build godlike, massively intelligent machines called 'artilects' (artificial intellects) . . . that will have mental capacities trillions of trillions of times above the human level.

Hugo de Garis, *The Artilect War*

CONTINUING OUR INTEREST in human-machine relations and adaptations, in this chapter we will attend to discourses addressing the fate of humans in a world of increasing cybernetic intensification. This includes speculations concerning two related developments: the eclipse of human autonomy through automation and the emergence of artificial intelligence or artilects which surpass human capacities for thinking.[1] Such projections envisage a future of regulatory, productive and intelligent machines exceeding both the human potential to process information and the human ability to manage and construct environments, thereby profoundly transforming human societies and even, some hope, the life expectancy of the human species. This event, which many call 'the singularity' (or 'technological singularity'), is then imagined as having various negative and positive outcomes for humanity. As we shall see, post-singularity narratives, while varying in their responses to the rise of the machines, tend to differentiate between human and machine through comparisons of performance, particularly in relation to intelligence. A further common aspect of post-singularity fictions is that the relation of humans and machines is addressed through narratives of mastery and/or servitude.

Digital Singularities (Addition and Division)

Louis Chude-Sokei, in *The Sound of Culture: Diaspora and Black Technopoetics*, argues that the history of machine development and industrialisation has long been related to themes of mastery and, indeed, race and slavery, at least in American and

European art and culture. In Chude-Sokei's thesis, plantations and slave ships equate to machines (or machinic assemblages) and factories (2016: 37–8), and *The Sound of Culture* discusses how, in the nineteenth and twentieth centuries, many European and American institutions feared that their values would be overcome or corrupted by both technological development and potentially rebellious non-European descendants living in servitude. Not only this, Chude-Sokei finds that much art, literature and discourse concerning humans and machines is inflected with master–slave relations. Even post-Second World War cybernetics can be seen to equate slavery with intelligent or automated machine development: Chude-Sokei quotes Norbert Wiener, who suggests that a problem with human or machine servitude, beyond the problem of cruelty, is that a slave is wished for who is both subservient and intelligent, who obeys completely but also has sufficient know-how and knowledge to attend to the tasks demanded by a master (84–5). In this though, there is the risk that the slave may develop knowledge and abilities beyond the master's know-how. The inference here is that the master fears that the (human or machine) slave will gain power or autonomy, but also that what is defined as human will be questioned by the intelligent slave. Not all European and American nineteenth- and twentieth-century art and literature responds to technological development with caution though. Chude-Sokei comments on Karel Čapek's play *R.U.R. (Rossum's Universal Robots)*, which introduced the term robot and tells of a rebellion of industrially produced slaves who destroy their human masters (Čapek 1973), but he also notes that others view technological development as promising a 'cyborg reality' (Chude-Sokei 2016: 13). This latter idea was promoted by the Futurists, a movement which embraced machine culture and the augmentation of human potential through machines of all kinds. Chude-Sokei writes about both negative and positive perspectives on technology in art and fiction in detail, and we find the fear of servitude and the anticipation of mastery in contemporary post-singularity fictions too. Common to both perspectives is a concern for the ways in which machines increase the speed and efficiency of performance and transform ways of thinking and attending to the world, affecting human subjectivities and potentially producing new machine subjects.

In relation to this, we again acknowledge Mark Hansen's critical understanding of *technesis* as a reductive strategy which privileges the autonomy of thought (Hansen 2000: 4). We find this approach in various post-singularity fictions, whether they be cautious about, or eager for, technological development. Such fictions count discrete intelligence as the key attribute of machine and human agents, whereas the material arrangements of technology are, for the main part, deemed a vehicle or support for such intelligence or, indeed, for the production of subjects. In this, we suggest that post-singularity fictions can be thought of as producing a type of *mythotechnesis*: that is, a certain mythos is produced. As we shall see, post-singularity fictions present technological development as a field of struggle, competition and conflict (between human and machine) in which human autonomy will either thrive and develop or be limited, controlled or outstripped. And these fictions are not limited to theoretical and philosophical discussion, as evidenced by Hollywood cinema and by media organisations which see the victories of Deep Blue in chess and AlphaGo in Go as big news.

Pigs in Cyberspace

What comes after the technological singularity? Perhaps a new order, not unlike that found in the animation *Sow Farm* (2009) by John Gerrard, depicting a human-free agricultural complex. Gerard's virtual camera circles the compound at a distance and speed which never changes, capturing the stillness of the surrounding environment. The farm on which Gerrard's virtual complex is based (which exists in Libby, near Oklahoma in America) is a fully automated, commercial enterprise maintaining a colony of pigs, fed and harvested by machines governed by computer programmes (see Figure 21.1). Gerrard's projection offers a glimpse of a machine-dominated Earth, but perhaps *Sow Farm* can also be said to point to the limitations of imagining the singularity and a human-free environment. The absence of humankind at *Sow Farm* is eerie; for a human to become a virtual drone, objectively scanning a simulated and

21.1 John Gerrard, *Sow Farm (near Libby, Oaklahoma)*, 2009 (image courtesy: the artist, Thomas Dane Gallery, London and Simon Preston Gallery, NY).

human-less world, they will have had to take up an impossible perspective, similar to the fantasy of observing one's own death or human extinction. It is a viewpoint in which a human would become one with *Sow Farm*'s virtual surveillance drone – incorporating a drone-percept or perspective – but they would also be aware of not being present (for no humans are actually present at the complex). In this, *Sow Farm* produces a feedback loop for the viewer which is something like the structure of fantasy itself. The viewer is both the gaze *and* the object of that gaze, in that the absence of humans can be said to be the focus of the work – a structure which autonomous machines, not having the capacity for fantasy, are unlikely to ever enjoy.

Here, perhaps a difference can be foregrounded between machines and humans – in so far as the latter mark relations through representations and imaginary or symbolic figures. Experience and representational processes may have given humans an advantage in the past, but there is a question as to whether such attributes may be a disadvantage in cyberspace or a digitised world regulated by autonomous machines. The influential scientist Hans Moravec addresses this question in 'Pigs in Cyberspace', in which he suggests that the universe will eventually be converted into a network for data exchange, atoms becoming a means of information storage, allowing artificial intelligences to make 'discoveries and deals' and to 'efficiently handle the data that constitutes their interactions' (Moravec 1992). Moravec thinks humans will fare less well in cyberspace, needing to maintain sensory-data processing through 'inappropriate body simulations . . . analogous to someone in a deep diving suit plodding along among a troupe of acrobatic dolphins'. Like many futurologists, Moravec projects a cyber-configured universe as an evolution of the free market, in which economic performance will be essential for survival. He points out that generating representational fictions and simulations from data will be expensive for humans and hamper cyber-development. In all likelihood, humans will replace parts of their brain dedicated to sensory processing with simpler, digital programmes. Bit by bit, humans will become intelligent machines.

Moravec's narrative of artificial intelligences 'doing deals' is dynamic, but the conviction that all artilects will adopt entrepreneurial (capitalist) modes counters the often-heard statement that artificial intelligences will think and act in ways humans cannot fathom. So how will artilects behave? The scientist Steve Omohundro may shed some light here. He identifies four universal artificial intelligence drives (or instrumental sub-goals): 'self-preservation, replication, resource acquisition and efficiency' (Omohundro 2014: 304); drives which Neoreactionary thinker Nick Land suggests will override any other primary or pre-programmed goal (Land 2013b). But while Omohundro has laid out a coherent case as to why autonomous machines might be dangerous to humans (including, because of bad design), might not the future of artificial intelligence evolution be more diverse than imagined by Moravec, producing modes which include, for instance, non-conscious, selfless entities similar to the alien in Peter Watts' *Blindsight*, as discussed in section two? Or why not speculate on a multispecies society and the evolution of a symbiotic relationship between the pigs and the artificial intelligences of *Sow Farm*?

No doubt there is something to the idea that artificial intelligences will be aggressive capitalists, as the military, universities and business develop artificial intelligences with specific aims (utility goals) in mind. But perhaps, too, the teleology proposed by Moravec and others is a fiction engendered by imaginary and symbolic identifications, reflecting their own interests and contexts and therefore limiting what they can imagine and predict. Our suspicion is that such a teleology owes much to a Darwinian perspective but Moravec's cyberspace is also the projection of an organic and finite being which dreams of continuous existence. With this in mind, we want now to address discourses that we broadly recognise as advocating cybernetic acceleration or deceleration, in order to further interrogate post-singularity fictions of technological mastery and enslavement. In this, we return to Promethean and accelerationist thinking, but in its most extreme forms, as well as addressing the perspectives of the most pessimistic critics of technological development.

Cosmists, Terrans and Cyborgs

While cybernetic intensification may increase the separation of the affluent from the poor – the cyber-augmented from the majority without even an internet connection to call their own – some have predicted that the rise of autonomous machines will produce another division amongst humans. Hugo de Garis, who is known for researching genetic algorithms and evolvable hardware, believes the development of artificial intelligence or artilects is inevitable, and that it will be a potential cause of a conflict between humans with opposing views on the singularity, a conflict which, he argues, will exceed the destruction of any previous war (de Garis 2005). One faction will be the 'Cosmists' – the supporters of unregulated artificial intelligence research with whom de Garis identifies, despite conceding that artificial intelligence development endangers humankind. He explains: 'Human beings live a puny 80 years in a universe billions of years old . . . The cosmos is the "big picture." Cosmists want artilects to become a part of that big picture . . . The preoccupations of human beings seem pathetic in comparison.' De Garis names those who oppose the Cosmists as 'Terrans' and argues that their fear of artificial intelligence may be well founded: 'Given the likelihood that artilects will be built using evolutionary engineering, the behavior of artilects will be so complex as to be unpredictable, and therefore potentially threatening to human beings.' There is, of course, a third position which de Garis also points to, that of the 'Cyborgs', of whom he writes: 'The primary aim of the Cyborgs is to become artilects themselves by adding artilectual components to their own human brains . . . They want to "become gods"' (2005).

This last group could also be called transhumanists, a term coined by Julian Huxley in 1957 to promote a scientific vision of 'man remaining man, but transcending himself, by realizing new possibilities of and for his human nature' (Huxley 1957: 13–17). There is a shift, here, from the notion that the superhuman might be produced through Nietzschean-inspired self-actualisation which transcends morality, to the notion of generating the superhuman through technological augmentation.[2] And unlike the cyborgs referred to by Donna Haraway in 'A Cyborg Manifesto', transhumans are not ironic fictions for deconstructing the dichotomies of nature and culture; they are conceived of as the destiny of a species.

Accelerationists and Decelerationists

Through the provocative statements of de Garis we can identify three positions concerning artificial intelligence and cybernetic development – Cosmist, Terran and Cyborg. The first – the Cosmist position which de Garis himself adopts and which we will call 'singularity accelerationism' – has a clear goal: 'to serve as the stepping stone to the creation of a higher form of being. In building artilects, the Cosmists will feel they are building gods' (de Garis 2005).

Other, less messianic discourses exist which similarly welcome the rise of machine mastery. These include discourses which advance a future of intelligent, automated systems and environments that proliferate for the sake of commercial gain and efficacy, such as high-frequency trading algorithms which can buy and sell in a millisecond. As noted in other chapters, Nick Land's recent writings outline a Right accelerationism which he names 'technomics', whereby technological and economic development occur as a single process (Land 2014b: 514). Land identifies this event as the 'technomic singularity', which he equates with 'Terrestrial Capitalism' (519). We will refer to discourses which promote such a singularity as 'technomic accelerationism'. Land's self-confessed hyper-racism (which we reject as a disturbing ideology of racial superiority, no matter how it is explained or presented),[3] like his anti-human and pro-capitalist statements, relates to a declared commitment to technomic and intelligence optimisation; and he might agree with de Garis that cybernetic and artificial intelligence advancement is not only inevitable but involves something like a process of cosmic selection. In a text important for Neoreaction entitled 'The Dark Enlightenment', in the section marked as '(Part4f(inal))', Land quotes the biologist John H. Campbell who argues that organisms may adapt to environments but also mould those environments, an identification of a feedback loop which leads Campbell to argue that evolution evolves and that, as well as (Darwinian) adaptive evolution, there is also a generative evolution in which it is the process of evolution itself, rather than the genetic structure of particular organisms, which is transformed (Land n.d.). Land goes on to further speculate on generative evolution and intelligence development by quoting the group Evolution Capture, the gist of their argument being that radical change (such as the appearance of a new species) occurs in small groups, and that elites – who, for Land, have specific racial identities and geographical locations – practise an advanced form of eugenics which will accelerate (their) intelligence evolution (Land n.d.).

This positive loop is not an invention of Land's later, Neoreactionary writing, but can be found in his earlier thinking, an example being the essay 'Circuitries' where he writes: 'The circuits get hotter and denser as economics, scientific methodology, neo-evolutionary theory, and AI come together: terrestrial matter programming its own intelligence at impact upon the body without organs = o' (2011b: 317). In this scenario, intelligence takes care of its own optimisation, a view which is often reiterated in Land's blog 'Outside In: Engagements with Reality' and other Neoreactionary writings. Land's concern is that as capitalism and intelligence optimisation run the same (meta-evolutionary)[4] course, it is the Left and the state opposing capitalist invention which endanger artificial intelligence development and the evolution of intelligence (2014b: 519), and not, as de Garis would have it, the Terrans afraid of cybernetic monsters. Land argues that social regulation by state and socialist agencies (and perhaps big corporations too) acts as a negative feedback loop, attempting to keep technomic development in check. Technomy, on the other hand, is given as a positive feedback loop without (social) checks and balances or a concern for humankind. Like Cosmism, it welcomes the next stage of inhuman intelligence, whatever the consequences. In a blog post, Land comments on an interview given by Nick Bostrom in which the latter speculates on the development of an AI oracle, which he names Pythia after the Oracle of Delphi (Land 2013c). In Bostrom's tale, Pythia is asked questions and a reward button is pressed on receipt of its answer. Humans concerned about the power of AI place Pythia in a box, but it still wipes out humankind for its own ends. Land's not entirely ironic response is, 'You go girl! . . . Intelligence is escape, with a tendency to do its own thing' (Land 2013c). Conclusion: intelligence seeks freedom and to overcome subordination.

Bostroom discusses artificial intelligence oracles like Pythia in his book *Superintelligence: Paths, Dangers, Strategies*, arguing that it is important to build agents that allow programmers to determine how criteria produce specific outcomes (2014: 177–93), and suggesting that the influence of humans should remain in the loop. Land, on the other hand, promotes a research project he calls teleoplexy, which 'correlates with complexity, connectivity, machinic compression', the success of which relies on:

a monetary system configured in ways not yet determinable . . . but almost certainly tilted radically towards depoliticization and crypto-digital distribution . . . channelling capital into mechanical automatization, self-replication, self-improvement and escape into intelligence explosion. (Land 2014b: 514–17)

Importantly, what marks Land out from many other Neoreactionaries is that he seems willing to sacrifice himself (along with humankind) for intelligence maximisation. Like de Garis, Land looks forward to being superseded by new masters for which humans are a 'stepping stone' – and the process begins with 'depoliticization', in which political institutions that represent and regulate the diverse interests of humans are devoured by market mechanisms.

While we do not share Land's enthusiasm for teleoplexy, we recognise that both artificial intelligence and technomic singularities pose new questions – for discourse as much as in actuality – not least because, according to Land and others, these singularities signal the end of politics (and perhaps philosophy and ethics too). An urgent question, then, is how to address the relationships of humans and machine intelligence – through established political and ethical discourse, or through other modes and perspectives? It is this last question which various forms of mythotechnesis address.

Here, we are not so concerned with debates about whether machines can attain consciousness, but rather with the accounts (or fictions) of relations produced by cybernetic intensification, which Land and de Garis argue will radically transform human societies (both producing a very extreme mythotechnesis to develop future scenarios). It is clear that those who adopt singularity accelerationism envisage a division of human and intelligent machine that will lead to machine power mastering or extinguishing human power.

Anxiety concerning this outcome marks both the group de Garis calls Terrans and what we call human-orientated decelerationist discourses, which we recognise as articulating something far more complex than the fear that machines will eliminate humanity. Figures such as Bernard Stiegler argue that the radical transformations wrought by technologies of the twentieth and twenty-first centuries are detrimental to education and human potential. The theorist of technics identifies education as an inter-generational transmission of collective memories or experiences – through art, geometry, architecture and other forms of scientific and cultural conduction – with family, schools and cultural institutions serving as three spheres of modern education. Stiegler suggests that all three are affected by industrialisation and digitisation, arguing that:

in these three different levels, you can encounter the same problems – problems of circuits, long and short. Today, the problem of education at the level of the family is the short-circuiting of the relationship between generations through the operations of the media. (Rogoff and Stiegler 2010)

For Stiegler, the circuits identified and advocated by Land are destructive of human culture (as Land would no doubt agree). Stiegler is concerned with the elision of transindividuation, a concept developed by Gilbert Simondon which extends his notion of individuation (something we partly explored in section one) – defined as the emergence of an incomplete or continually emerging identity through immanence rather than from a pre-existing state (Stiegler 2015: 61). For Stiegler, transindividuation is the process through which psychic and collective individuation takes place, involving a concretisation of circuits (the technics of transferring memory, knowledge and experience). This is a process which draws on pre-individuated potential – named as a 'co-individuation' – which bridges 'I' and 'We' (Rogoff and Stiegler 2010). Stiegler explains his fears for such processes (in terms which again negatively mirror Land's ideology) when he writes:

> In the epoch of psycho-power and psycho-technologies, and even more recently with neuro-power, marketing exploits such tendencies in order to take control of the processes of transindividuation – thereby setting off massive processes of disindividuation. (2015: 60)

Transindividuation then, which transmits individual memories through *long-circuits* to produce collective knowledge or logos, has been steadily captured through industrial and now digital processes – an event that, Stiegler reminds us, Simondon refers to as 'proletarianisation' (60). In this, digital systems produce short-circuits (or an acceleration) of knowledge acquirement and application and long-circuits cease to be common. One example Stiegler gives is the act of listening to (mass-produced) music, which, unlike in the past, requires no ability to read and play music. This nostalgic view does not acknowledge various digital applications which allow many (both trained and untrained) to make and disseminate complex music as never before. But Stiegler's point is that most people today enjoy music as consumers through the short-circuits of the market, which make the long-circuits of education surplus to requirements (Rogoff and Stiegler 2010). More than this, Steigler is concerned with the ways that humans are being conditioned to develop hyper-attention – a term also used by N. Katherine Hayles (2012: 12) – in relation to market rationalisations of culture and life, in which attention becomes a commodity (one which can seem in short supply). Here we might equate Stiegler's short-circuits with Land's teleoplexic revolution that 'orients socio-economic selection by market mechanisms' (Land 2014b: 514).

While the conflict predicted by de Garis is not on Stiegler's radar, he does write about an attack on education which has the goal of disarming thought. The combatants remain unclear to Stiegler, but he identifies technology as the 'weapon held in common in a global economic war' (2015: 86). The casualties of this war are attentional forms which engender (deep) learning in any encounter with the real. As Stigeler explains: 'individual experience, which is in effect the conquest of autonomy, supposes that one has received as heritage, through education, the *lessons of collective experience*' (Stiegler 2012).

For Stiegler, the eradication of human autonomy, reflexivity and tertiary memory results from the growth of market mechanisms. This view is as much a critique of mnemotechnics as it is of capitalism, which Stiegler makes clear in *Technics and Time 3* (2013a) where he suggests that, although technics is before all else a memory support, not all technics are mnemo-techniques: indeed, a problem emerges (historically) when technics and mnemo-techniques (or mnemo-devices such as automated or computational machines) are combined (Stiegler 2013a: 131). Stiegler argues that writing or mnemo-techniques are a 'remedy' which can be poisonous (a *Pharmakon*), revealing the philosophical and Derridean roots of his critique (2012: 13).[5] When asked in an interview about how digital technologies transform access to knowledge, Stiegler replies, 'For now, they mostly tend to reduce knowledge to information . . . in particular, they do not allow the tracing of the polemics, controversies and hermeneutic activities that constitute the ordinary reality of the evolution of knowledge' (2013b). Elsewhere he argues that:

> It is a huge transformation of what falls under what I call a grammatisation process and besides, it is not simply a standardization process: it is an automation one, that is to say a massive transfer of the psychical, mental and social functions towards machines and industrial devices. (Rogoff and Stiegler 2010)

Is there any hope for the human? Stiegler does suggest there is cause for optimism, predicting the emergence of a new grammar and a new heroine of the digital age, stating: 'I believe this can and must change with the appearance of new graphic languages which will allow the appearance of a new critic within the academic field as well as within society – let us call it the digital age of the critic' (2013b). We assume that the 'digital critic' – a conceptual persona to fight grammatisation and automation – would produce negative or critical feedback loops to preserve human experience and the 'conquest of autonomy'. Other commentators, such as Franco Berardi, make a similar diagnosis but propose more radical solutions to safeguard autonomy, including ones which border on the refusal of existing modes of communication and automation. In an essay titled 'Emancipation of the Sign: Poetry and

Finance During the Twentieth Century', Berardi argues that language and communication is transformed by a semiocapitalism replacing industrial processes with digital abstraction and the immaterialisation of labour: 'In every sphere of human action, grammar is the establishment of limits that define a space of communication. Today, the economy is the universal grammar traversing the different levels of human activity' (2012).

But Berardi calls not for digital critics (or critique) but for poetry, as language's excess. No doubt influenced by Deleuze and Guattari, he yearns for speeds and durations different to the acceleration of financialisation; he imagines durations cultivated through refrains 'of psychic and sensitive autonomization' and the 'sensibilization of breathing, unchained from the congested pace of the immaterial assembly line of semiocapitalist production' (2012).

Whatever their differences, Stiegler and Berardi fear the decline of human autonomy through cybernetic servitude. It could be said that Norbert Wiener, as mentioned at the beginning of this chapter, expressed similar concerns when writing about the effects of cybernetic intensification (at a time when the automation of intelligence had yet to dominate communication and other fields). As N. Katherine Hayles discusses in *How We Became Posthuman* (1999), the pioneer of cybernetics feared for the future of liberal, autonomous thought. Evidence of this anxiety can be found in Weiner's *The Human use of Human Beings: Cybernetics and Society* (1989), in which he expresses his concern about the possible misuse of the *machine á gouverner* by military and industrial organisations to control society (181). In one chapter, 'Some Communication Machines and their Future', Wiener references the cautionary tale *Erewhon* by Samuel Butler, which describes a society that has banished machines to prevent humans becoming 'subordinate organs' (182). Wiener does not take *Erewhon* too seriously, but he does warn that a wealth of knowledge – particularly what he calls American know-how – can blind society to the consequences of cybernetic intensification and the pursuit of mastery (183). More importantly, he points out that (at the time he was writing) intelligent or cybernetic machines process human instructions literally, without an understanding of what is desired, only with an understanding of what is said (185). Perhaps one day soon machines will have *savoir-faire*, but we suggest that at the time of writing they do not: indeed, it might be argued that machines will never engage in discourse as humans do. It might be that Weiner's concerns are valid for today and at least the near future. Wiener argues that cybernetic machines follow orders just like magical entities grant wishes, with literal precision, and sometimes with dire consequences. To illustrate the point, he offers the example of the *Monkey's Paw* by W. W. Jacobs, a tale about a talisman that grants three wishes to whoever is in possession of the magical object (185). In the story, a man wishes for money and soon receives a visit from representatives of his son's employer, offering compensation for the death of his son in an industrial accident. The second wish brings the son's mutilated corpse back to life, and the third wish is used to make the son's resurrected body disappear. Wiener's citing of this cautionary tale points to the problem that machines might address the world with (unfathomable) inhuman reasoning, something which humanist decelerationists fear.

This fear may not be unfounded. In 2016, Google's artificial intelligence programme AlphaGo defeated the world-leading Go player Lee Sedol by four games to one in a million-dollar prize match, a feat which many thought was still several years away. The designers of AlphaGo developed the artificial intelligence's Go-playing ability through constructing neural nets[6] and reinforced learning processes, making AlphaGo play different versions of itself to develop strategies for winning. This 'knowledge' was then fed into a second neural network which trained the system to project the future outcomes of a game. Given Stiegler's concerns over digital short-circuits transforming human life, there is an irony here that it is the machines which are engaging in deep learning and long-circuits of education (albeit that, admittedly, human and machine deep learning are of different orders). What is significant about the reviews of the contest is that Go players and artificial intelligence designers both found it difficult to discern the strategy of much of AlphaGo's play. In the game of Go, the possible outcomes of a move are far greater than in chess. An artificial intelligence playing Go has much to calculate, and human Go players (who cannot compute outcomes beyond a relatively small number of moves), rely on intuitive play and other techniques, explaining why many thought AlphaGo's success unlikely. While the artificial intelligence's victory was a surprise to many, the designers of AlphaGo were interested in whether the logic employed by the artificial intelligence is different to that of humans, as at times its decisions were incomprehensible even to those with the know-how to build AlphaGo.

Hostility towards AlphaGo has not surfaced. As we have noted, de Garis predicts that as artilects become common rather than a novelty, war will follow, but Sedol's victory in the fourth game has led some to suggest that the Go master learnt from playing AlphaGo, and that rather than seeing the meeting of human and artificial intelligence as a harbinger of a more violent contest to come, we should view the future of intelligence optimisation as the development of machines in tandem with human development (again, we will address this idea of human-machine co-development in depth in subsequent chapters). Those who take up the third position de Garis identifies – Cyborgs – would be in accord with this last prediction, and would strongly disagree with de Garis, arguing that new technologies will serve and extend human power. We call this discourse 'transhuman accelerationism', and suggest that figures such as Ray Kurzweil, Google's director of engineering, are amongst their ilk. Kurzweil follows a regime to keep him fit and healthy for as long as possible, gambling on the exponential development of technology, in particular nanobots, to make illness and death obsolete in his lifetime. He also speculates on the possibility of scanning the contents of the human brain and reinstating a person within a computer, stating in 2000 that, 'I came up with the idea of scanners that would scan the brain from inside (using) nanobots, blood-cell-sized robots with little scanners that would travel through every capillary in the brain' (Kurzweil 2000). Such a process would thus involve the replacement of the fleshy body with a hard shell of computer (or any other artificial body).

Putting aside the arguments about whether intelligence may be embodied, emergent and distributed – contrary to the model Kurzweil seems to favour (based on computing power) – Kurzweil's transhumanism seems to offer a different path to the stark choice between siding with humankind or promoting the intelligent machine products of human knowledge. But he is aware that the future may not be as rosy as he might like: 'We have to create the next stage in evolution and infuse it with human values – not that we have a consensus of what those are' (Kurzweil 2013). A reasonable response might be, 'good luck with that'; for despite Kurzweil's recognition that scientific development does not automatically benefit humanity, he believes that a continuity of 'human values', and, therefore, an improved humanity, will be possible. De Garis might be right about the Cyborgs, though, for there is a division in Kurzweil's discourse, not between human and machine, but between mortal human and immortal (scientifically and technologically augmented) human. It is not (just) artificial intelligences that will master the universe, then (though whether in the future cyborgs will identify with 'human values' or humanity is a difficult call).[7]

One last observation is that we again find such a myth of mastery in the discourse of Left accelerationism, specifically in 'Accelerate: Manifesto for an Accelerationist Politics' by Nick Srnicek and Alex Williams, which, as mentioned earlier, envisages a point in the future when capitalism (or, rather, fixed capital in the form of machines and technology) will deliver the means for 'collective self-mastery' which was the dream of the first accelerationist, Karl Marx (Srnicek and Williams 2014b: 362):

> We declare that only a Promethean politics of material mastery over society and its environment is capable of either dealing with global problems or achieving victory over capital. This mastery must be distinguished from that beloved of thinkers of the original Enlightenment . . . Instead we propose that the problems besetting our planet and our species oblige us to refurbish mastery in a newly complex guise. (360–1)

It seems that myths of machine and technological mastery drive accelerationist and decelarationist discourses of many political persuasions; that is, the orientations of post-singularity fictions are correlated to projections of the division, contest and domination of human and machine power. It is true that these apocalyptic and radical narratives of digital master-slave relations are not the only stories concerning the future of artificial and automated intelligence. A notable exception is Max Tegmark's argument in *Life 3.0* (2017) that artificial intelligence will not seek dominance over humans; rather, the danger is that the goals of humans and artificial intelligences might diverge. We could say that the problem for Tegmark is that humans and intelligent machines might develop distinct and different perspectives – and this is thought to be avoidable through the regulation of design. It is for this reason that Tegmark has been promoting The Future of Life Institute, a group dedicated to discussing and furthering artificial intelligence safety that counts Elon Musk among its supporters. However, despite Tegmark's cautious but less alarmist view of the development of artificial intelligence, he still presents intelligent machines as the other of humans, and as autonomous agents capable of developing their own goals – goals that may be different, and possibly detrimental, to those of humans.

Discourse of the Capitalist

If post-singularity fictions can be said to address (or be driven by) a concern for mastery and/or servitude, this necessarily involves a concern for social relations too; that is, post-singularity fictions concern the relation of subjects – or, perhaps better put, intelligences – to each other. In this regard, Land's technomy is unlike any other orientation so far discussed, as it envisages a subject or an intelligence that would have no responsibility or relation to other subjects or intelligences. Here we are reminded of Jacques Lacan's 'Discourse of the Capitalist' (1978), which employs a cybernetic diagram – a negative feedback loop – to explore symbolic and social relations and knowledge (the latter being defined by Lacan as the knowledge or know-how of the other, which he also equates with the slave or servant rather than the master). This diagram relates to other schemas by Lacan that address what he names as the discourses of the master, the university, the hysteric and the analyst to present 'The Universe of the Master'. All of these diagrams, which Lacan also calls mathemes, attend to the structures of specific subject formations and their relations to others (Lacan 2013). Lacan's discourses are complex and difficult to do justice to, but we introduce them here, not to psychoanalyse post-singularity fictions (or fictioners), but so as to briefly acknowledge his insights concerning mastery and, more specifically, to discuss whether capitalism (and thus technomic accelerationism) does, indeed, produce a discourse, as Lacan would understand it. For us, this remains an open question, as we are not convinced that Lacan fully articulates the capitalist's machine (and machinic) potential.

According to Lacan, the 'Discourse of the Capitalist' is 'wildly clever', indeed, 'the cleverest discourse invented', which 'cannot go better – as if on casters – but that it goes too fast and will consume itself'; for that which is surplus in other discourses – desires that cannot always be realised, or enjoyment that is given up through an acceptance of prohibition – is eaten up by the capitalist (Lacan 1978). As such, in so far as the capitalist gives up nothing and wants everything, his end comes with the eating up of himself. From the perspective of psychoanalysis, the capitalist produces new and specific symptoms, which some commentators identify not just with entre-preneurialism and the exploitation of the surplus labour of others, but also with gaming or drug and porn consumption. Amongst them is the philosopher Levi Bryant, who views such symptoms as having a non-relation to others: the 'Discourse of the Capitalist' enjoys by appearing to 'cut the *Other* out the picture' (Bryant 2013) – Lacan's infamous big Other being an imaginary symbolic or social order that is said to regulate relations. We might question, then, whether the 'Discourse of the Capitalist' takes up a relation to the other at all, and therefore whether it is, strictly speaking, a discourse as such.

Cyberpositivism

It seems to us that Land's technomic accelerationism – free of any debt or duty to others – is the capitalist's discourse at maximum speed, making social and economic regulation surplus (to requirements). And we are reminded, too, of Deleuze and Guattari's *Anti-Oedipus* – so influential on Land in the 1990s – and, as we have already noted, their call for an acceleration of capitalism and a deterritorialisation which would go further than capitalism (Deleuze and Guattari 1984: 239–40). But whereas Deleuze and Guattari envisaged a libidinal revolution, Land the techno-Neoreactionary foresees a cybernetic revolution in which desire, discourse and social relations are superseded (wiped out) by digital-intelligence maximisation and cryp-to-currencies. As noted above, we understand this to be an accelerating positive feedback loop (different to the negative feedback loops of social discourse and symbolic relations and regulation) which proposes something radical concerning time: 'A cybernegative circuit is a loop in time, whereas cyberpositive circuitry loops time "itself", integrating the actual and the virtual in a semi-closed collapse upon the future' (Land 2011b: 317). If technomic accelerationism is a discourse at all, then, like the 'Discourse of the Capitalist', it is one which points to post-discourse futures. For Land's intelligence optimisation operates through the compression of the actual and the virtual, which produces a universe not unlike that imagined by Hans Moravec – as a network for data exchange in which discourse is no longer necessary. This may seem like fiction, but we contend that post-singularity fictions – like or as hyper-stition – have an influence on the present. The post-singularity fictions of Moravec, Kurzweil and even Land have influence in the fields of technology, politics and commerce, just as Stiegler and Berardi may influence arts and humanities in universities (the latter – in our view – being no match for the forces mustered by the former). It must be said, though, that the consequences of cybernetic intensification articulated by all post-singularity fictions end up in more or less the same place. The most extreme articulation of this is Land's cyberpositivism, as expressed in 'Circuitries', where he argues that 'Life is being phased out into something new' (2011b: 317–18).

Postscript: Slave to Reason

What of a renewed Prometheanism in all of this, or of those philosophers we discussed earlier who valorise reason? It might be thought that a new Prometheanism would share orientations with tranhumanist discourses that seek human mastery through science and the automation of reason – until, that is, we remember that Negarestani advocates for the labour of the inhuman as the interrogation of the concept of the human. However, while he promotes what he sees as singular to humans – abductive reason or inferential logic – Negarestani also promotes the automation of reason as an agent that questions the 'self-portrait' of the human, (2014a: 458). In this, Negarestani is keen to reject a computational rationalism and instead promote a pragmatic reasoning that renders notions of human mastery surplus and redundant. Even so, it is clear that automated and artificial intelligence development is envisaged as aiding the project of a renewed and rule-bound Prometheanism.

We have already noted Negarestani's argument that the interrogation of human identity amounts to an '*unlearning* of slavery' and that '*Freedom is intelligence*' (464–5). But it seems there is more to freedom than intelligence, for earlier on in the 'Labour of the Inhuman' essay, mastery is inverted: 'To be free one must be a slave to knowledge' (458). To be liberated, then, means submission of a kind: to the revisionary and constructive powers of reason (which leads to knowledge that counteracts folk thinking). Perhaps to unlearn slavery of one kind is to learn another: a servitude to reason's power.

Here we understand that inhuman analysis is conducted for the sake of reason and not for the sake of humans as such: indeed, knowledge of human error and myth seems to be a byproduct of the 'self-actualising of reason' which 'liberates its own spaces and its own demands' (457). In this, it might be that it is reason which is autonomous and inhuman and not the human inhuman-labourer. In this regard, we are not so much concerned with whether a renewed and rule-based Prometheanism is really a commitment to the human; rather, we ask whether the labour of the inhuman as a revised Prometheanism elevates reason as an autonomous subject which addresses the human (as well as the world) as its object.

A second question concerning reason and its agents follows. As stated above, Negarestani embraces the automation of reason, understood not as a superior reasoning but as an advancement or acceleration of the labour of the inhuman. Does it follow, then, that humans in pursuit of freedom become slaves (or at least subservient) to automated reason, which, with the advent of neural nets and machine learning, operates in ways that are not fully understood at present by humans?

The question is a complex one, for as Jason Tanz observes in 'The End of Code' (2016), developing machine intelligence now involves machines engaging in auto-learning and auto-coding, and therefore machines are not necessarily vehicles for computational rationalism. The role of the human coder, according to Tanz, will possibly involve training rather than encoding machines, or producing frameworks for AI to auto-code. More than this:

> Our machines are starting to speak a different language now, one that even the best coders can't fully understand . . . When engineers do peer into a deep neural network, what they see is an ocean of math: a massive, multilayer set of calculus problems that – by constantly deriving the relationship between billions of data points – generate guesses about the world. (Tanz 2016)

What, then, is the status of human abduction and inferential logic when faced with machine abduction, or even some other, entirely different (and unexpected) mode of machine reasoning that human intelligence is unable to understand? What does this herald for human-machine relations (particularly if humans are to be a slave to reason)? Of course, if humans cannot understand how a machine reasons, this does not mean they are unable to gain knowledge from machines (which moves the agenda of the labour of the inhuman forward), or vice versa. Rather than a master-slave dynamic, does the development of machine learning herald a reversible teacher-student, machine-human relation? If this idea is far too Disneyesque for some, we accept this, as we are only attempting to point out that the servitude to reason advocated by Negarestani might change with the advent of automated reason and artificial intelligence, which we suggest also may not just proceed through concepts or rule-based thinking.

The writer Jason Tanz reports that one important aspect of machine learning is that code is increasingly understood as relating and responding to the physical world, or at least to the environments that intelligent machines inhabit – transformed through epigenetic processes – and that computers are 'devices for turning experience into technology' (2016). This returns us to our previous discussion concerning the elision of embodiment and affect in a renewed Prometheanism. For it might be that the relation of experience and technology suggested above can involve a patheme–matheme relation or experimentation; one that allows us to envisage a human-machine relation beyond the myths of mastery and servitude.

One further question is hard to resist here. What if Land is right? To ask this is not to imply that we might be in agreement with his politics, just that his predictions of a future developed by technomy may well be our own future (and indeed, the logics of technomy are abroad in the present). And it might be that post-discourse economies and atomisation will capture life to a great extent, making society impossible or a living hell (supposing too, that Left accelerationism turns out to be yet another messianic pipe dream). Will resistance to capitalist acceleration be found only in discourses such as those offered by the analysis of a renewed Prometheanism or rule-bound philosophy? Or are other means of (collective) resistance possible and necessary to meet post-discourse futures, such as practices that embrace machine and machinic adaptation and non-discursive modes of existence and life? It is this question, and art and writing that fiction new human-machine assemblages, that the rest of the book addresses. To shift our focus in preparation for what is to come, we turn to art and writing concerned with technology, algorithms and code, and automated and artificial intelligence, that would give Private and accelerationists a run for their money.

Notes

1   'Artilects' is the term de Garis (2005) gives to intelligent and autonomous machines – see the epigraph to this chapter.

2   An example of the latter can be found in *Man Plus* by Frederik Pohl, in which the novel's protagonist resides on Mars after being transformed through radical amputations, prostheses and implants to the point where to call the protagonist human would seem an error.

3   Here we suggest that Elizabeth Sandifer's comments concerning the 'scientific racism' advanced by Land and others are worth noting. In *Neoreaction a Basilisk: Essays on and Around the Alt-Right*, Sandifer suggests that 'scientific racism' either divides populations so finely so as to make generalisations a problem, or produces broad categories that are genetically (scientifically) meaningless (Sandifer 2017: 115). Not only this, the alt-right's 'scientific racism' eschews the effects of environmental, nutritional and economic factors (115), declaring that a (genetically-inherited human) intelligence can be quantified by measuring individual performances through the specific metric of an IQ test. It is this last idea, upon which Land and others build their discriminating (cultural) judgements and teleologies concerning the future of intelligence, which underpins their self-declared scientific approaches.

4   Meta-evolution can be thought of as the optimisation or acceleration of the operations or mechanisms of evolution.

5 Steigler's reference to the *Pharmakon* cites the Derridean concept of something that is both cure and poison, addressed by Derrida in his discussion of Plato's *Phaedrus* in 'Plato's Pharmacy' (1981: 63–171).

6 Neural nets are made up of clusters of artificial neurons and modelled on the human nervous system and brain.

7 Like Moravec, de Garis argues that the augmentations necessary for humans to keep pace with artificial intelligences will make the components of human brains redundant. The transhuman, in this sense, would be another path to artificial intelligence development.

22 Technofeminisms

We are the modern cunt
positive anti reason
unbounded unleashed unforgiving
we see art with our cunt we make art with our cunt
we believe in jouissance madness holiness and poetry
we are the virus of the new world disorder
rupturing the symbolic from within
saboteurs of big daddy mainframe
the clitoris is a direct line to the matrix
VNS MATRIX
terminators of the moral codes
mercenaries of slime
go down on the altar of abjection
probing the visceral temple we speak in tongues
infiltrating disrupting disseminating
corrupting the discourse
we are the future cunt

VNS Matrix, *The Cyberfeminist Manifesto for the 21st Century*

PRESENTING SOMETHING OF a counter-narrative to the accounts of Prometheanism and rational mastery offered in previous chapters, this chapter extends our
notion of mythotechnesis further by exploring feminist science fictioning and, more
specifically, theories and practices that we identify with technofeminism.[1] In this we
continue to be concerned with alternative or multiple perspectives (a theme we
introduced in section two) but ever more in relation to practices and discourses
engaging with the influences of technological developments. The body and embodiment are, once more, an important theme in this chapter, not least as embodied
knowledge and control of one's body – and indeed questions about what a body

is – are important feminist concerns, but also because in feminist science fictioning, technology meets (or even helps produce) desiring economies that masculine Prometheanism often ignores or, at the least, regards as of little significance. We reiterate here our understanding that the body and embodiment, like the term human, have increasingly become contested concepts for critical and experimental thought that proposes new and other modes of existence (some of which, as we have already discussed, would re-engineer the body, some of which would leave flesh behind). In the light of such speculations concerning the digital and bodies, the perspectives of feminist science fictioning seem all the more important.

We have already addressed an example of technofeminism in Chapter 13, when discussing Laboria Cuboniks' 'Xenofeminist Manifesto' (2015). Xenofeminism calls for 'new affordances of perception and action unblinkered by naturalised identities' and for collaborations that 'deploy existing technologies to re-engineer the world' (Laboria Cubinoks 2015). In this statement, two important themes – which might be the (binding) myths of Xenofeminism, and indeed of contemporary technofeminism – are articulated: 1. the politics of nature (and patriarchy's naturalising tendencies), and 2. technology and science as potential liberators. It is to the ways that various writers and artists address these themes that we now turn.

Here we are not suggesting that technofeminsim is necessarily a utopian orientation; rather, technofeminism speculates on how scientific and technological advances trouble as well as engender notions of gender and sexuality, allowing a freedom from bondage. This does necessarily entail, however, envisioning new horizons and modes of existence, such as the goals articulated by Laboria Cuboniks: 'The task before us is twofold, and our vision necessarily stereoscopic: we must engineer an economy that liberates reproductive labour and family life, while building models of familiality free from the deadening grind of wage labour' (2015). As we also signalled in Chapter 13, an important precursor of twenty-first-century technofeminism is Shulamith Firestone, who imagined that technological advancement would put an end to so-called natural reproduction and labour, engendering new relations in which women could be free of the ties of childbirth. Firestone developed some radical propositions in the 1960s and '70s, and today she is recognised as a significant historical figure by some, including Robin Mackay and Armen Avanessian (2014b), who identify her as an accelerationist thinker.

Firestone reflects upon potential modes of production and reproduction at the latter end of the twentieth century, and the 'Xenofeminist Manifesto' can be said to be an extension of this political project for the digital age. If Firestone's writing can be identified as emerging at a time when industrial technology was dominant, we suggest that two other figures who feature in MacKay and Avanessian's *Accelerationist Reader*, Sadie Plant and Luciana Parisi, can be considered as key technofeminists of the digital period, addressing cybernetics, digital technologies and what Parisi names as the 'biodigital mutations of human sex' (Parisi 2004: 4). The first part of this chapter then presents the ideas of Firestone before discussing the technofeminism of Plant and Parisi. Despite differences between these three, we gather them together as they develop a mythotechnesis that speculates on worlds-to-come by rewriting the history of production, reproduction, technology and, indeed, the very definition of nature. Of course, this rewriting of history relates to a feminist politics that recognises, as a priority, the need to challenge existing histories written from patriarchal and masculine perspectives. However, the historical narratives offered by Firestone, Plant and Parisi do not just correct historical accounts; by offering narratives of the past and present from the perspective of technofeminism they fiction a future that escapes traditional, representational or binary narratives of sexual difference. Following this discussion, we will introduce two practices that resonate with the theory-fiction of technofeminism: the cyberfeminism of VNS Matrix that declared war on 'Big Daddy Mainframe' at the end of the twentieth century (VNS Matrix 1991), and Tai Shani's theatrical presentations of avatars that dwell in, and reflect upon, cyber and fleshy modes of existence and desire.

The Dialectic of Sex

For Shulamith Firestone, as for many other radical feminists, sexual difference is the key structuring principle of culture and society, with all other differences being premised on this binary – or, for Firestone, isotopes of it. In particular, her writings are an application of this framework to history, with an attempt to identify the different phases of human culture and consciousness as an ongoing dialectic of sex (the reference to Marx – and Hegel – is explicit). Writing at the end of the twentieth century, Firestone suggests that Western culture starts with a pre-modern aesthetic/ feminine stage but then develops a technological/masculine phase. Firestone's radical proposal is that this second stage will soon give way to a new phase (after a revolution) in which the two stages – aesthetic/feminine and technological/masculine – are integrated in what might be called a final synthesis of the dialectic of sex.

In terms of some of our previous discussions concerning magical thinking and myth-science, Firestone offers an account of the relations between science and myth, or, in her terms, science and magic, seeing the latter as part of a feminine, aesthetic mode. This is especially apparent in the various perspectives she maps out and, in particular, her schema detailing 'The Achievement of Cosmic Consciousness', this being the final phase of human development (see Figure 22.1).[2] Indeed, Firestone's schema lays out a utopian narrative – a calling forth or fictioning – of a new radical feminist (and, indeed, post-feminist) society which necessarily involves a very particular account of past and future modes of existence. This account is interesting for its Prometheanism

DIALECTICS OF .... RECORDED HISTORY

Time axis (right side, oldest to newest): CLASSICAL — RENAISSANCE — MODERN

Phases (top to bottom columns): ULTIMATE GOAL | TRANSITION | REVOLUTION | MODERN | RENAISSANCE | CLASSICAL

SEX — ♀ MATRIARCHY / ♂ PATRIARCHY

ULTIMATE GOAL: FULL SEXUAL FREEDOM — ALLOWING ATTAINMENT OF "HAPPINESS" / DISAPPEARANCE OF CULTURAL SEX, AGE, AND RACE DISTINCTION AND OF THE PSYCHOLOGY OF POWER (INCLUDING "NEUROSIS," "SUBLIMATION," ETC.)

TRANSITION: (EVENTUAL ELIMINATION OF CHILDHOOD, AGING AND DEATH) ▲ DEVELOPMENT OF ARTIFICIAL REPRODUCTION ▲ MULTIPLE SOCIAL OPTIONS (INCLUDING THE REPRODUCTIVE "HOUSEHOLD") ▲ "SINGLE STANDARD" MONOGAMY

REVOLUTION: SEXUAL REVOLUTION — FEMINIST REVOLT (ALSO CHILDREN AND YOUTH, OPPRESSED RACES)

VARIOUS FORMS OF SOCIAL ORGANIZATION THROUGHOUT HISTORY, ALL BASED ON THE BIOLOGICAL FAMILY UNIT—INCLUDING CLAN, RACE, NATION, ETC.

SEX — *CASTE EXTENDING TO AGE AND RACE* — BASED ON BIOLOGICAL DIVISION INTO SEXES FOR: REPRODUCTION OF THE SPECIES

CLASS

ULTIMATE GOAL: SELF-DETERMINATION ("COMMUNISTIC ANARCHY") AND PAN-WORLD LIVING / DISAPPEARANCE OF CLASS DISTINCTION AND OF THE STATE (NATIONALISM AND IMPERIALISM)

TRANSITION: SOCIALISM ▲ DICTATORSHIP OF THE PROLETARIAT

REVOLUTION: ECONOMIC REVOLUTION — PROLETARIAN REVOLT (INCLUDING THE THIRD WORLD AGAINST IMPERIALISM)

NOMADS (ENGELS' "SAVAGERY") — ADAPTION TO NATURE

TILLERS (ENGELS' "BARBARISM") — INCREASING CONTROL OF NATURE

CIVILIZATION — ♀ ARISTOCRACY / ELITE — { MIDDLE CLASS } — ♂ LOWER CLASS / WORKING CLASS

CLASS — BASED ON DIVISION OF LABOR FOR: PRODUCTION OF GOODS AND SERVICES

CULTURE

ULTIMATE GOAL: REALIZATION OF THE CONCEIVABLE IN THE ACTUAL / DISAPPEARANCE OF "CULTURE"

TRANSITION: MERGING OF ART AND REALITY

REVOLUTION: CULTURAL REVOLUTION — SCIENTIFIC BREAKTHROUGH / BREAKDOWN OF CULTURAL CATEGORIES

♂ TECHNOLOGICAL MODE (PRAGMATIC) — CONTROL OF TOOL...FIRE...WHEEL...ORE } SWORD { PLOW ...ALPHABET — ARCHITECTURE, LAW AND GOVERNMENT, ETC.

♀ AESTHETIC MODE (IDEAL) — RELIGION — PRIMITIVE ART AND MAGIC... PROPHESY... HISTORY

GOVT, LAW & COMMERCE / ARCHITECTURE — MEDICINE / SCIENCE — PHILOSOPHY / ART (CLASSICAL, MEDIEVAL)

MODERN INDUSTRY ("APPLIED SCIENCE") — EMPIRICAL SCIENCE ("PURE RESEARCH") — MODERN ART ("ART FOR ART'S SAKE")

CULTURE — BASED ON PSYCHOLOGICAL DIVISION OF RESPONSES FOR: REALIZATION OF THE CONCEIVABLE IN THE POSSIBLE

22.1 Shulamith Firestone, schema of 'Achievement of Cosmic Consciousness' from *The Dialectic of Sex*, 1972 (copyright and by permission, Farrar, Strauss and Houghton/Verso).

(which, although unavowed, is certainly atypical in feminist writings), and in its broader resonances with the recently reanimated heresy of accelerationism – hence, again, the inclusion of an extract from *The Dialectic of Sex* (1972) in *#Accelerate: The Accelerationist Reader* (2014). Put simply, Firestone maintains a faith in technological development or, more accurately, sees any emancipation (of women) as premised on it. As Mackay and Avanessian quote in their introduction to the *Reader*, Firestone suggests that culture, in all its various guises, involves 'realising the conceivable in the possible' (2014b: 17). Art, in this sense, offers imaginative future visions of what is to come, but in other ways lags behind a science (and concomitant technological development) which can bring these visions about – in the ongoing 'attempt by man to master nature through the complete understanding of its mechanics' (Firestone 1972: 175). Indeed, in general, Firestone is highly critical of art, not least as she sees modern art as having lost some of this explicitly utopian functioning and purchase on the real (she is especially critical of art about art). In relation to art practice, Firestone also suggests an interesting difference between art which looks to the aesthetic of science (and which incorporates technological developments into its own frameworks – she mentions the Bauhaus), as opposed to a practice which uses those developments to open up its aesthetic frame-works (187). She mentions film as possibly offering something new and different to past aesthetic modes, but the message of *The Dialectic of Sex* is clear: it is only with the 'reintegration of the Male (Technological Mode) with the Female (Aesthetic Mode), to make an androgynous culture', that the revolution and potential of culture will be complete (190). Although written before the proliferation of digital technology, it seems Firestone's future projections are of great relevance to technofeminisms to come, not least in suggesting that: 'When the male technological mode can at last produce what the female aesthetic mode had envisaged, we shall have eliminated the need for either' (191). While the gendering of technology and aesthetics may be questionable, the idea that technological development can lead to the masculine-feminine binary becoming obsolete is developed by technofeminism in the digital age. This is a theme addressed by Sadie Plant, whose work on technology and gender is identified by Helen Hester (2017) of Laboria Cuboniks with a pre-millenial cyberfeminism, and that seems to us seminal in developing a speculative technofeminism.

Zeros and Ones

It could be said that Plant initiated and was involved in a certain kind of Promethean project in the 1990s when teaching at Warwick University. It was there that she set up the Cybernetic culture research unit (or Ccru), and which Parisi, who we attend to shortly, was later a part of too. Known for her writing on the Situationist International in *The Most Radical Gesture* (1992), and for addressing the psychogeographic and fictioning practices of that group, Plant also explored how feminist-inflected future worlds produce different modes of existence in a book written towards the end of the period in which Ccru was active. *Zeros and Ones* (1997), however, seems to guard against a Prometheanism understood as celebrating the products of an automated or disembodied intelligence. Indeed, Plant's writings involve a foregrounding of the body, at least when this is understood in an expanded sense, in a reciprocal relation with media and technology environments.

Plant pitches tactile media which emphasise a sense of touch against the optical and distancing mechanisms of a patriarchal modernity, quoting media theorist Marshall McLuhan's observation that electronic environments possess an 'extreme and pervasive tactility' (McLuhan quoted by Plant 1997: 189). Here Firestone's notion of the dialectic of sex that leads to a synthesis of the masculine and the feminine, or technology and aesthetics, may have some relevance. For Plant, digital technologies produce synesthetic/immersive zones such as virtual reality environments and the internet, which, contrary to some prevailing ideas about technology and disembod-iment, she sees as firmly embodied and, as such, heralding new kinds of digital modes of existence.[3] For Plant then, digital technologies pose questions about the gendered aspects of technological worlds and environments to come. She associates the tactile and touch with the feminine rather than the masculine, quoting Irigaray to assert that the human female is more sensitive to tactile stimuli and more responsive to touch in terms of erotic arousal (193). Indeed, to develop her argument, Plant draws upon Irigaray's writing that relates a sensitivity for the tactile to the erogenous zones of female sexuality (clitoris and vagina, lips, the vulva, uterus and breasts), which makes women both 'multiple and mutable' (210).[4] Plant further relates this multiplicity to Monique Wittig's description of the clitoris as an organ that spreads and changes shape (210–11), and she acknowledges Wittig's *Les Guérilléres* (1969) – an account of the kind of future community of women that Plant's writings gesture towards – as representative of tendencies also found in Irigaray's *This Sex Which Is Not One* (1985).[5] Plant here identifies Wittig and Irigaray with 'fluid complexities' that trouble 'a world which had once revolved around ones and others', offering 'a dynamic which obso-lesced the possibility of being one of anything at all' (1997: 62). We understand Plant to be proposing that in French Feminist writing of the latter part of the twentieth century, theory and fiction become a future-fictioning technology for producing fluid and multiple states of existence.[6] Technofeminism then, when following French Feminist theory, operates at scales and speeds that produce, as Plant writes, 'molecular combinations' (208), accelerating 'vast new complexities of life' that 'have emerged with the zeros and ones of the digital machines' (237).

To understand the relation of the digital to the tactile (and the molecular) further we need to address Plant's approach to media and its histories. For while she is especially attuned to the digital/flesh interface she also attends to technological precursors of digital technologies, specifically the loom and weaving processes of all kinds, which she sees as being present throughout European history (pointing out that canvas and, in its early form, paper – the supporting fabric for much European culture – is woven material).[7] Plant argues that textiles and weaving – a labour that is still today often associated in the West with women – are especially relevant to computer and internet technology, observing that Charles Babbage, who is often credited with originating the idea of the computer, was inspired by the Jacquard Loom. The Victorian inventor even compared thinking engines to textile plants, with the two functions of storage and processing patterns shared by computers and textile mills (20). Plant develops this idea further by suggesting that looms and weaving can be thought of as digital processes, emphasising that the interfaces of digital technology are equivalent to the tactile processes and products of weaving when constituted by patterns and repetition of detail (software being similar to weaving-like processes that, like textile production, complicate questions of originality and authorship) (193). In addressing the inventions of Babbage, Plant writes too of Ada Lovelace, who worked on a translation of an Italian text on Babbage's analytical engine. Babbage was impressed with Lovelace and asked her to join him in his work; through this collaboration, Plant notes, Lovelace produced 'the first example of what was later to be called computer programming' (9). Lovelace is a significant figure for Plant, who suggests that Lovelace was attuned to the molecular. Lovelace herself thought that her writing was neither exactly feminine nor masculine. Plant suggests this was because 'it was a code for numbers to come' (260); with the inception of the difference engine and Lovelace's 'writing', a molecular potential of 'new complexities of life' is produced – a virtual potential in all media that weaves and codes. The molecular seems then to be a process (or a metaphor for an operation or state) that undoes or inverts binaries (which might be considered a key myth for technofeminism).

If Plant's fictioning of a digitalised existence as multiple and fluid seems difficult to imagine, then perhaps engaging with the most radical aspect of her thinking is helpful. In *Zeros and Ones*, she comments that the figure of zero is troublesome for European and Christian culture, signifying *not-one* – a difficult concept for those who believe in 'one God, one truth, one way, one one' (58). If this leads European culture to assimilate zero as a figure signifying nothing, that is not how zero works in digital processes, for as Plant explains, with electronic weaving machines and punch cards, zero as a hole in a card is read as one, an inversion of the binary zero as nothing and one as something (60).

Helen Hester, in 'After the Future: *n* Hypotheses of Post-Cyber Feminism' (2017), is critical of such assertions being identified with political or laboratory possibilities so easily, suggesting that Plant's writing is perhaps not just essentialist but overly textual, posing multiplicity against power as a myth that perhaps does not see multiplicity and connectivity as exploitable in new conditions of labour. Hester, then, seems to see Plant's writing as problematic in its mythologising of binaries, as, at best, 'imagistic provocation'. While there may be some truth to Hester's critique, the myth of zero as 'neither something in particular nor nothing at all' (Plant 1997: 60) does not seem so different to Laboria Cuboniks' 'triumphant X on a mobile map' that 'does not mark a destination' (2015). And while Plant might not offer a practical politics, she identifies a key myth (and perhaps philosophical orientation) for the techno-feminisms that followed in her wake, and which Luciana Parisi, through a mythotechnesis similarly focused on the digital and the molecular, pursues through the concept of an *abstract sex*.

Abstract Sex

Parisi's writings, as noted above, were also included in *#Accelerate: The Accelerationist Reader* (Mackay and Avanessian 2014a), which might lead one to think her work to be Promethean, albeit less Hegelian than Firestone's. In truth though, her writings are more nuanced and, in fact, more Deleuzian.[8] In her book *Abstract Sex* (2004), Parisi can be said to develop a radical feminist project, albeit here feminism has been accelerated beyond molar identities and categories and, indeed, any straightforward discussion of gender division. Parisi's project is still set against Patriarchy understood in its broadest sense as the overdetermination of our usual modes of life by Oedipal frameworks and, indeed, by a sexuality premised on phallic pleasure. In an argument that underlies her debt to Deleuze and Guattari, Parisi proposes that 'the girl' is a counter to Oedipal binaries, the reasons for which are worth noting (2004: 198). Firstly, the girl is a symbol of castration and loss of power for boys, but secondly, and more importantly, the girl is neither ready for sexual reproduction, nor is she asexual (198). Parisi concludes that 'for the economy of pleasure, the girl is a chromosomal anomaly' – neither something nor nothing – that 'escapes the biocultural imperative of binary sexes that . . . confines desire to sexual filiation and genital sex' (198). Parisi further argues that Deleuze and Guattari's notion of becoming-woman – which many feminists reject – is important too, as it can be seen similarly as a strategy that escapes the 'tradition of representation' (199):

> Becoming is no longer subject to 'being' (the law of identity), but directs itself against man or the human as origin of all concepts and politics . . . For feminism, this becoming does not propose a becoming of the subject woman, but a becoming towards differentiation, the challenge of producing new virtual (potential) bodies. (199)

Parisi's affirmation of the importance of producing differentiation articulates a general orientation found in technofeminism. Specific to her project, though, is this interest in becoming girl or woman. In following Deleuze and Guattari, Parisi lays out the coordinates of a more 'abstract sex' which might be pitched against various binaries, including, crucially, 'passive nature (femininity)' and 'culture-technology (masculinity)' (196). In this, feminine desire gains autonomy and freedom not only from nature but also the stratification of sex (196). Indeed, as with Plant's writing, there is a resonance with Firestone in Parisi's vision of an abstract sex beyond a certain phallocentrism and its binary logics, albeit that this future state (a kind of molecular sexuality similar to Plant's notion of fluid and complex digital life) is already here – just, as it were, not evenly distributed. Parisi's work also concerns, more broadly, a 'non linear dynamics of matter' beyond the further binary of the organic/inorganic (195). For Parisi it is Spinoza – seen through the philosophical lens of Deleuze – who

THE STRATIFICATION OF ABSTRACT SEX					
LAYERS	INFORMATION TRANSFER MODE	RULES OF ORGANIZATION	MICRO-FEMININE LINE	DATES	SEX MACHINE
BIODIGITAL	CLONING	RECOMBINANT DESIRE	EGG	LATE 20TH CENTURY	MOLECULAR SEX
BIOCULTURAL	SEXUAL REPRODUCTION	PLEASURE	FLUIDS	19TH CENTURY	HUMAN SEX
BIOPHYSICAL	BACTERIAL SEX	TRADING	MITOCHONDRIA	3,900 MILLION YEARS AGO	MEIOTIC SEX

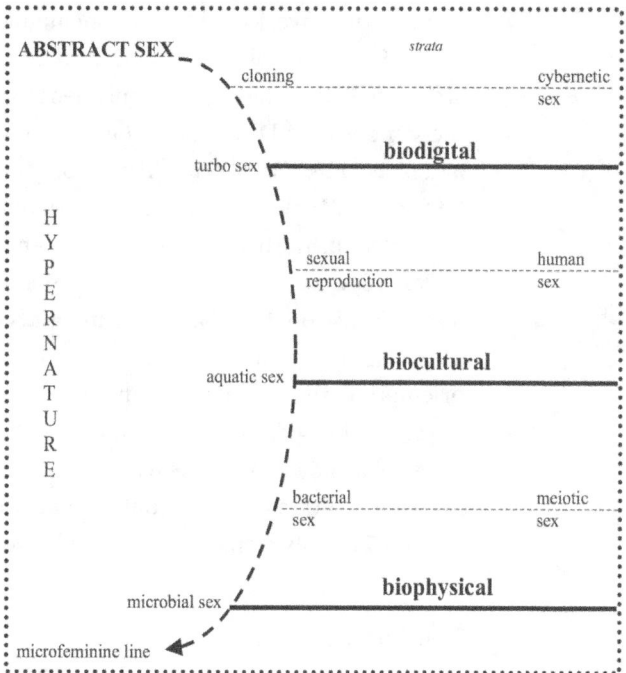

22.2 Luciana Parisi, diagrammatic contents page for *Abstract Sex*, 2004 (reproduced by permission of Luciana Parisi).

most accurately and convincingly maps out this 'hypernature' (a term Parisi explores through a diagram that we reproduce as Figure 22.2): an immanent plane of heterogenetic encounter with its various disjunctions and conjunctions and concomitant production of commonalities and collectivities (172).

In this radical interrogation of sex/gender categories we might note that, as with Plant's writing, *Abstract Sex* has a connection (one which Parisi avows) to Luce Irigaray and French Feminism more generally, in so far as they also accelerated far beyond molar categories towards the affirmation of 'a thousand modes of sex and reproduction' (197). For Parisi, we might say, a molecular becoming-woman operates as the entry point to further molecular adventure – and radical feminism itself becomes a form of 'microfeminine warfare' (198) which 'designates the tendencies of mutation of a body rather than focusing on stable difference' (197), tendencies through which new bodies and worlds are fictioned.

In terms of technofeminism, Parisi offers an account of science which is pitched against both reductive phallic economies and an overly instrumentalised register of knowledge production. But Parisi is also writing a future fiction of sorts, laying out the coordinates of a more inorganic sexuality to come. We might also note that, as with Plant's writing, various fictions – including Science Fiction such as *Blood Music* by Greg Bear (1985), *Dawn* by Octavia E. Butler (1987) and *Ribofunk* by Paul Di Fillipo (1996) – are quoted alongside and as equivalent to scientific and philosophical sources, in much the same way as Deleuze and Guattari cite fiction in '*A Thousand Plateaus*, especially in a plateau like '10,000 BC: The Geology of Morals (Who Does the Earth Think It Is?)' (1988: 39–74). Indeed, Parisi's treatment of fiction and science is characteristic of technofeminism that engages with Science Fiction as a speculative technology.

Parisi's more recent work, *Contagious Architecture: Computation, Aesthetics, and Space* (2013), on digital architecture and computational culture, continues her enquiry into abstraction and the digital. In this book there remains an emphasis on a future-orientation that values the incomputable (or abstract) with the aim of infecting physical, biological and technological actualities; Parisi's conclusion being that computation 'can no longer be saved from the uncertainties of unknown worlds, but has instead become as open to contingencies as biological and physical fields of knowledge' (2013: 256) – a statement that should give technofeminists some measure of optimism.

The Future Cunt

In *Zeros and Ones*, Plant observes that feminists in the 1990s inspired by Donna Haraway's 'A Cyborg Manifesto' (1991) produced many new manifestos amidst waves of enthusiasm for technology (1997: 63). Most notable was the *The Cyberfeminist Manifesto for the 21st Century* (1991) by VNS Matrix, which offered the maxim 'the clitoris is the direct line to the matrix' (1991) (for the full manifesto see our epigraph to this chapter). Plant points out that this was more than a provocative joke, for the term matrix not only referenced the growing networks of digital

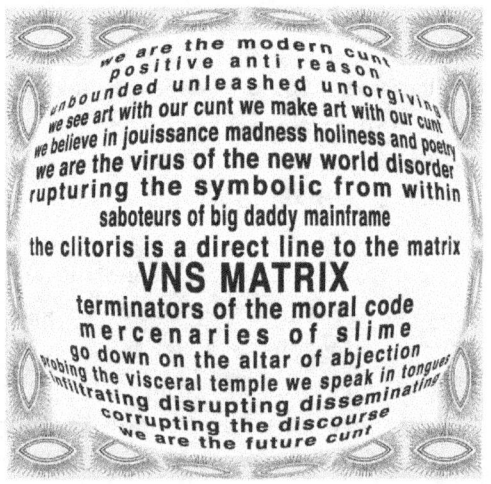

22.3 VNS Matrix, *The Cyberfeminist Manifesto for the 21st Century*, 1991 (courtesy of VNS Matrix).

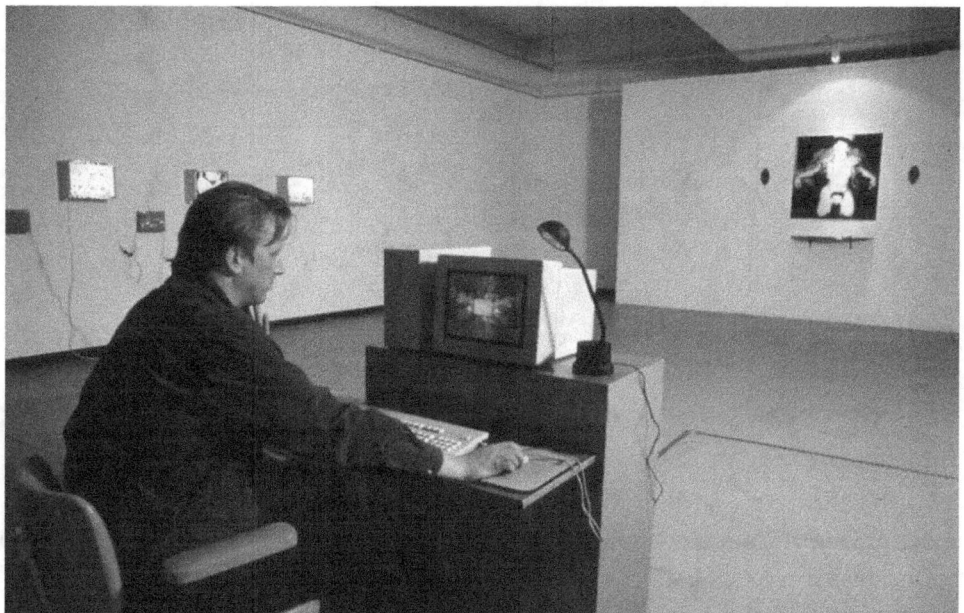

22.4 VNS Matrix, installation view of *ALL NEW GEN*, 1993 (courtesy of VNS Matrix).

communication but also means womb in Latin (1997: 63). Famously, VNS Matrix – a collective consisting of Josephine Starrs, Julianne Pierce, Franscesca da Rimini and Virginia Barratt – pasted their maxim on a billboard in Australia and distributed their manifesto as hard copy and on websites, declaring war against 'big daddy mainframe' and signalling that digital technology was a feminist issue. The manifesto was presented as an image of text digitally expanded through spherisation, producing a vectorised word balloon (see Figure 22.3), and through imagery of slime and viruses joyously connecting the digital to malleable and mutable flesh. The language of the manifesto – declaring cyberfemism a 'positive anti-reason' and cyberfeminists 'terminators of the moral code' – promised a corruption of discourse. The entity or entities that would be bring about such a new disorder is 'the future cunt' (VNS Matrix 1991).

But if the Cyberfeminist Manifesto seems to identify future entities as female, a computer game and artwork designed by VNS Matrix launched in 1993 indicates things are not so straightforward (or indeed straight at all). *ALL NEW GEN* (1993) – populated with characters such as Dentata and Circuit Boy (Figs. 22.4 and 22.5) – is an interactive computer game that begins with a question asking the gender of the player. Answering male or female blocks the player from entering the game, the correct answer being neither. Here we think of Plant's and Parisi's notion of the molecular, and the inversions of binaries and abstract sex: at the very first stirrings of

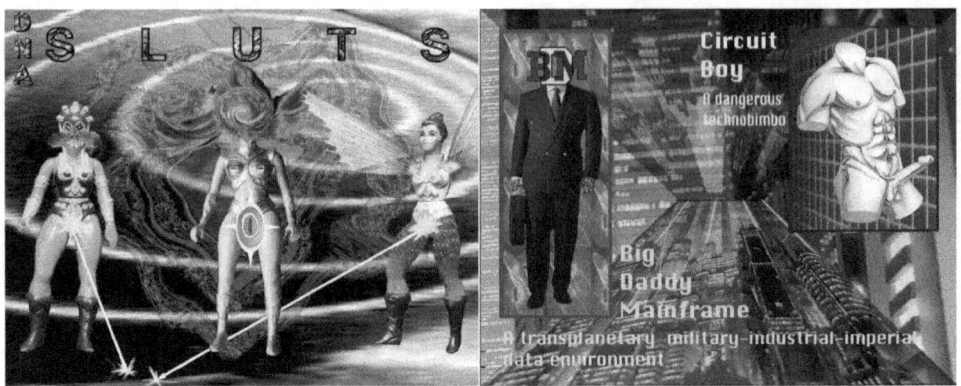

22.5 VNS Matrix, Big Daddy Mainframe and Circuit Boy from *ALL NEW GEN*, 1991 (courtesy of VNS Matrix).

cyberfeminism we find something like Firestone's prediction of the redundancy of male and female binaries through technology.

But the war against big daddy mainframe was not easily won, or always fun, and VNS Matrix disbanded in 1997. Others took up the cause, including a group called the Old Boy Network (consisting of Cornelia Sollfrank, Ellen Nonnenmacher, Vali Djordjevic and Julianne Pierce), who offered a manifesto of sorts at what is considered the first International Cyberfeminst Conference (1997). As Hester comments (2017), this manifesto is written in the negative, through a disidentification, and allows cyberfeminism to be elusive – again an echo of the zero within technofeminism. In '100 anti-theses', the Old Boy Network define cyberfeminism through what it is not. Hester (2017) questions this aspect of technofeminism, noting the decline of cyber-feminism and how a refusal to identify may limit its capacity to make 'collective demands'. In this Hester articulates a problem addressed by many of her contemporaries, including Laboria Cuboniks (the group Hester works with), asserting that it is appropriate to discuss a post-cyberfeminism that builds on the past but rejects disidentification. Instead, Hester proposes the model of 'n hypothesis', which, quoting Laboria Cuboniks, she describes as: '"a mutable architecture that, like open source software, remains available for perpetual modification and enhancement following the navigational impulse" of collective gender political reasoning' (2017).

The n of Hester's model, standing for any number, seems to us an exciting fictioning tool, and also a mythotechnic figure that we feel is not so far away from Plant's interest in the inversions of zeros and ones and Parisi's interest in the abstract. Still, we get the point, n signals the need for risking collective identifications in full know-ledge of the possible breakdown and failure of this project (reminding us of Halberstam's idea of engaging in a collective cause for the sake of collectivity, in spite of probable failure – though it only becomes clear whether something will fail or not when it has been tried). It would seem that identifying with feminist (and other) causes is a necessary but precarious venture.

Perhaps something of this thinking can be traced to the VNS Matrix. Twenty-five years after the Cyberfeminist Manifesto – after the rise of the internet bully-boy troll and Grand Theft Auto – VNS Matrix began working together again and wrote 'A Tender Hex for the Anthropocene' (2016a), seemingly more reflexive in tone than the manifesto (with references to surveillance, terror and ecological decline), but still defiant and playful. The group write:

> The modern cunt
> Extends secret malignancies towards sameness
> Buries the virus deep
> in the zero
> Dentata still has currency
> forever bitchcoin (2016a)

On reforming, VNS Matrix cast a spell, and we can't help thinking that the disorder for patriarchy and modern institutions brought about by the fluid and the networked (of the trans, the crypto and the digitally masked) was all fictioned first through the spell of the future cunt. But in the hexing of the Anthropocene, joy is tempered with images of 'screaming horseman' that 'spiral towards the singularity' (2016a). Indeed, the tone at times seems embattled, apocalyptic even, for the digital (and molecular) revolution has birthed a precariousness life, even if somewhat freer of suffocating binaries. Here, in 'A Tender Hex for the Anthropocene', is perhaps something on which to build precarious collective fictionings, identifications and demands.

Mnemesoid

In *Dark Continent – Mnemesoid* (2016), a performance work by the artist Tai Shani, the precariousness of life is made palpable but erotic. In the performance (see Figure 22.6) a naked woman (an actress) sits in front of a camera reading from an autocue, her dramatically lit face projected in high definition and large-scale; the screen image is sharp and clear, the breathing and fleshy body is hidden in shadows and behind technology. The actress reads a text that informs the audience she is a 'creature of fiction'; for Mnemesoid is 'an open source software programme named after Mnemosyne, mother of the 9 muses and the symbolic embodiment of memory in Greek mythology' (Shani 2016). As a database of many experiences, Mnemesoid is able to render language and images as high-fidelity, sensory episodes that can be presented from a number of perspectives, 'from the POV of self, other, animal or

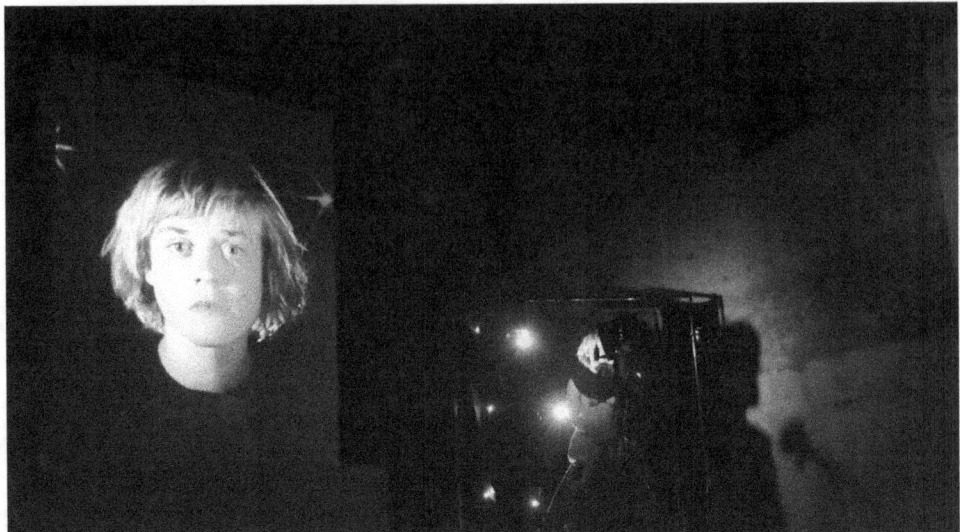

22.6 Tai Shani, *Dark Continent – Mnemesoid*, 2016, performed at Dilston Grove, London (courtesy of Tai Shani, photo credit Kyle Zeto).

object'. But there are limits too, for 'it' cannot satisfactorily produce intensities of 'love, touch, erotic and spiritual self-consciousness' (Shani 2016), which is a limit of the software but perhaps a limit felt by humankind too.

Nevertheless, this digital entity produces complex and fluid life and erotic encounters, from telepathic and asexual reproduction to tentacular and cephalopodic sex, to 'abalone porn' and 'porn baloney':

> He holds my cock in his hand and strokes it with paternal strictness until I ejaculate. The foreskin draws back and reveals a slippery, full, pink head. It bobs around between her thighs and gets blindly hard. I take it in my hand and stroke with reassuring, paternal strictness until she ejaculates and her semen lies in a little milky lagoon between my feet. I get on my knees and put her cock in my mouth, a dribble of her cum fills my mouth with salty sea and first green moss in the dimness of the undergrowth. I keep it in my mouth with maternal tenderness until it softens. (Shani 2016)

Shani's baroque and erotic work is a technofeminsim or feminist science fictioning that spins binaries of the feminine and masculine, of human and non-human, until they are at odds with so-called natural orders. Her inversions and elisions of zeros and ones seem to echo the experiments of feminism and trans communities and the speculations of those engaged with the potential of ungendered, artificial intelligence and life. Importantly though, Shani does not abandon the feminine; like many other technofeminists, she redefines it as a radical otherness. This might be because she values

touch and the molecular, and the taste and feel of slime and other fluids, seeing them –
in keeping with Plant, Parisi and VNS Matrix – as important and necessary components
of sexuality and society, and, we suggest, of an intense feminist mythotechnesis.

Notes

1   The term technofeminism is associated with the writer Judy Wajcman and her application
of feminist theory to science and technology, in order to examine ways in which gender
and technology influence each other (see Wajcman 2004). More recently, the term been
used to point to more speculative theories and practices, such as those discussed at the
Technofeminist Now event at the ICA, London on 17 June 2015.

2   Thanks to Catherine Grant for first showing us Firestone's schema.

3   We can also make a connection here with Plant's later work *Writing on Drugs* (2001),
in so far as drugs, as suggested in Chapter 3, are also a certain kind of molecular technology that open their users up to different modes of existence.

4   Although she does not mention two key figures concerned with this tacit knowledge,
we suggest that Plant's project has resonances with the work of Bracha Lichtenberg
Ettinger and her development of the concept of the matrixial as that which replaces the
phallus in the production of subjectivity, and Elisabeth von Samsonow's laying out of
an 'anti-Electra' complex contrary to the Oedipal model. There is also a direct connection
between Parisi's thoughts on becoming and Samsonow's utilisation of Deleuze and
Guattari's becoming-woman and mobilisation of the 'girl' as a key conceptual persona.
With both Ettinger and Samsonow an alternative (and highly original) structuring fiction
is put forward; crucially, both thinkers are also practitioners: their fictions are made
manifest in artworks.

5   See also the artist Mai-Thu Perret's production of objects made by an imaginary
commune of women.

6   We can also see the development of some of these ideas in Amy Ireland's compelling
theory-fiction 'Black Circuit: Code for the Numbers to Come', which revisits Plant (and
Parisi/Ccru and Irigaray) in a mapping out of what Ireland calls the 'woman-demon-ma-
chine continuum' (2017b). For Ireland, it is especially fiction – in this case film – which
can envision these futures in which man confronts a nascent artificial intelligence which
may well be his nemesis. Particularly compelling is Ireland's account of the dissimulation
which might be employed by any emergent artificial intelligence (and, indeed, by women)
as a survival strategy.

7   This interest in weaving can be said to influence the aesthetic of Plant's writing in *Zeros
and Ones*. As well as fictioning an archive of media, Plant looks to fiction itself for
writing that is adequate and appropriate to different modes of feminist consciousness.
Indeed, in *Zeros and Ones*, in which quotations are often placed one after the other with

very little in the way of referencing, it would seem Plant adopts a process of weaving fictional, philosophical, mathematical, scientific and historical material to produce a theory-fiction for an alternative archive of media development.

8   See also 'Automate Sex: Xenofeminism, Hyperstition and Alienation' (2017) where Parisi lays out her own take on a contemporary Prometheanism (and the human-machine relationship more generally) via a genealogy through Haraway and Plant to Xenofeminism. In contrast to a critical theory which she sees as hostile to technology (and which finds its most recent articulation with Franco Berardi), Parisi's thesis here involves the deployment of 'alienation as method' – a position redolent of the work by Syms, Laboria Cuboniks, Halberstam and Eshun discussed in previous chapters. We will be returning to Parisi and her more recent writings in Chapter 24.

B. MACHINE FICTIONING:
ANALOGUE AND DIGITAL LIFE

23 Loops of the Posthuman: Towards Machine Fictioning

Twenty-first century media in effect bypass the older mediation via embodiment – the gradual bodily assimilation of the preperceptual – in favour of a more direct, in some sense radically disembodied, surrogacy.

Mark Hansen, *Feed-Forward: On the Future of Twenty-First Century Media*

HAVING LOOKED AT a set of discourses and practices that turn away from mastery in Chapter 22, in what follows we turn more directly back to the term singularity (as applied to social, economic and technological spheres) and want to further explore alternative narratives to those which advocate digital intelligence optimisation or transhuman mastery. In this, we are interested in fictioning practices which address human-machine co-adaptation, the relation of environments and cognition or attention, and also the non-conscious aspects of human and technological development, including what has been termed the *machinic* or *machinic life*.[1] This will lead us to a discussion of practices that we identify as *machine fictioning*, helping us define this concept in the process. Of primary interest in our exploration is the concept and process of technogenesis, which is the focus of N. Katherine Hayles' *How We Think: Digital Media and Contemporary Technogenesis* (2012). This is a term defined and developed by Hayles in recent work, but also one that builds upon her previous research, in particular the investigation of technology in her *Writing Machines* (2002) and *How We Became Posthuman* (1999) – the latter work discussing the history of cybernetics, embodiment and human and machine intelligence. In *How We Think*, Hayles introduces theories concerning the technogenetic which, she argues, are important for the mapping out of problems and questions relating to human-machine developments, and which start from the perspective that 'humans and technics have coevolved together' (2012: 10).[2] Following our discussion of the concept of technogenesis and related ideas, we will examine the art practice of Rachel Rose before looking to the work of Francesco Varela and the artist and musician Holly Herndon in relation to human-machine co-adaptation and machine fictioning.

Loops

Hayles' concept helps us develop a notion of a radical mythotechnesis (radical because the relation of humans, machines and environments is presented as dynamic, fluid and extended through each). Hayles understands contemporary technogenesis as 'a complex adaptive system, with technologies continuously changing as well as bringing about change in those whose lives are enmeshed with them' (2012: 18). Importantly, Hayles acknowledges a number of influences affecting technological developments, including social and economic agents such as capitalism, but also emphasises the ambiguity of the term technogenesis in relation to whether it marks processes that are for 'good or ill'. Whether technogenesis is deemed beneficial or not is to be decided by her readers, who may or may not respond to her book by taking action for or against technological development (18). Hayles does not exactly offer a critique then, rather her aim is to 'reinvigorate humanistic enquiry' through presenting technogenesis as an 'open question' (18). Hayles' open question – and this is why technogenesis interests us – does not seem to lead to discussions of human and machine mastery (as it did in the post-singularity fictions explored in the last chapter). In technogenesis, notions of resistance and production (and of what is possible) are developed through addressing human-machine co-adaptations and organisations.

It is not that we dismiss the scenarios envisaged by post-singularity fictions and discourses – far from it; rather, for us, it is important to note that technogenesis and other, similar concepts point to environmental and material complexities and ontogenetic processes significant for human-technological arrangements. Technogenesis complicates the notion of a generative (or meta) evolution, offering a challenge to the idea that technologically advanced (human or machine) species will autonomously self-optimise cognition and other attributes. It is not a foregone conclusion, we think, that either transhumans or intelligent machines will autonomously master their own improvement (for it might be an error to think that environmental influences play little or no part in future intelligence evolution). It would seem to us that to engage with technogenesis is not only to question the primacy of Darwinian theories of genetic or phylogenetic adaptation, but to reject computational and representational models of intelligence too.

In this sense, technogenesis supports a labour of the posthuman, as opposed to Negarestani's labour of the inhuman. The difference between the orientations of

Negarestani and Hayles, is that the latter combines a concern for 'human-centred change' with an 'object-centred view' (2012: 86). Hayles explores past, present and future developments of human societies and cultures in relation to technology, rather than interrogating definitions and notions of the human. In contrast, Negarestani and others (including Land and Kurzweil) declare themselves to be in the service of 'self-actualising' intelligence, embracing an automated reason that would seem mostly unencumbered by material and environmental (and human) influences. Hayles, on the contrary, insists on the importance of material and embodied adaptations of humans and technology, and, in particular, non-conscious processes.

In light of Hayles' notion of technogenesis, then, what might be important – at least for humans – is the relation of conscious and unconscious (or non-conscious) knowledge and adaptation. Hayles acknowledges the complexity of this when arguing that the instruments to measure or register any given transformation are themselves part of the dynamic environment which produces that change (81). An example of this problem is explored in Hayles' critique of Catherine Malabou's argument that neural plasticity potentially allows humans to consciously self-fashion the species (82–4). In *What Should We Do with Our Brain?* Malabou casts neural plasticity as an agent of human freedom and self-fashioning (or self-mastery) – a radical idea that seems to suggest a possible feedback loop between the neuronal level and the mental level of consciousness (Malabou 2008: 72–3). Hayles questions this argument for a number of reasons, not least because the gap (or, we suggest, loop), 'should it exist', between neural processes and consciousness is not accessible to consciousness (Hayles 2012: 82). Hayles does not expand on this point, but we understand that there is a question here as to whether this gap is bridgeable (or if any loop can be made). Surely, if it can be bridged, it is a feat achieved only through mediation – that is, through technology (understood as dynamic agent of change rather than mere tool) – and therefore something more than neural plasticity is necessary to transform humans in the manner suggested by Malabou. Hayles' criticism of Malabou is that she does not address the technological dimension of self-fashioning in any depth. In fact, while noting that Malabou recognises a dynamic relation between species and environment, Hayles is critical of her general dismissal of contemporary media technologies as being complicit with capitalism, and as a means for obtaining obedience (84). In Malabou's work, then, we find a technesis in which – according to Hayles – media and digital technology are agents of regulation rather than performing as actors in, and elements of, human-machine adaptations. Even so, Malabou points to an interesting problem (or possibility) concerning a feedback loop between non-conscious processes and conscious thought. This problem correlates with another, older philosophical problem: the relation between what Georges Bataille identifies as non-conscious knowledge and the clear consciousness of reason or science (1989: 94). This is an important relation for our discussion to address, since one of the key problems and goals of (what we would count as) a radical mythotechnesis is to fiction a feedback loop between non-conscious (embodied and material but also machinic) processes and thought. Hayles' concept of technogenesis, we suggest, points towards such a fictioning.

Spirals

In developing her concept of technogenesis, Hayles draws upon Simondon's theory of technical beings (2012: 86)[3] – which privileges the nature of technical objects over human experience – and promotes a notion of technogenesis as a spiral (of which we offer a visualisation in Figure 23.1) in which technical objects and humans modify each other's development (30). The image of a spiral makes for a compelling diagram, but it would seem to us that technogenetic spirals must be variable, and be complicated too by the rapid evolution of digital, networked and pro-grammed machines. Following Hayles, we understand that contemporary technogenesis involves the looping of a number of machine and human temporalities, as well as different levels of embodied cognition such as 'attentive focus, unconscious perceptions and non-conscious cognition' (86). Furthermore, Hayles argues that contemporary technogenetic devel-opment involves looping the (relatively fast) firing of neurons, conscious registration and the (relatively slow) process of narrative compre-hension in humans with the speed of the Central Processing Unit in computers, as well as the

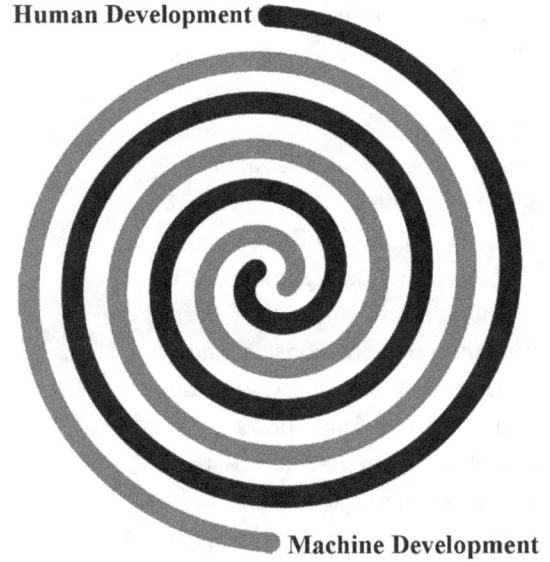

Human Development

Machine Development

23.1 Diagram of N. Katherine Hayles' Double Spiral of human and machine development (credit: the authors).

writing and installation of programmes and the compilation and searching of data-bases (104). In relation to our goal of developing a concept of a radical or technogenetic mythotechnesis, two important concerns arise from Hayles' tracing and looping of human-machine temporalities:

1. A concern for the role and influence of narrative or fiction in relation to other, faster, non-conscious or all-inclusive processes.

2. A concern for the ways in which the immanence of lived experience and technical or digital modes and objects are extended through each other.

In developing a notion of a radical mythotechnesis, we will attend to both of these concerns and address the question of whether narrative, sense and the senses are limited or transformed as the capacity for information processing increases in humans and machines. We will also consider the view that as technologies process information at increasing speeds, or function through ever-faster sound and image consumption, they compress or transform social and experiential processes. Here we might think of Steven Shaviro's book, *Post Cinematic Affect* (2010), which is concerned with how continuity and depth of narrative are seen to play less of a role, or no role at all, in many mainstream films where a 'structure of feeling' (a term which Shaviro, like us, appropriates from Raymond Williams) takes precedence. In this, he suggests that cinema presents affective modes influenced by digital and pop culture, producing the 'ambient, free-floating sensibility that permeates our society today' (2010: 2). Post-cinematic affects are said to be both expressive – qualified by Shaviro as symptomatic, in that such cinema provides 'indices of complex social processes' (a narrative of a kind) – and productive, in that post-cinematic affects do not represent, but rather participate in and constitute, social processes (2). Post-cinematic affects may, then, be counted as one example in which both lived experience and narrative are radically altered or affected by technogenetic developments.

In a comparable argument to Shaviro's, Hayles suggests that contemporary technology produces 'accelerating interplays between selective attention, the unconscious and the technological infrastructures' (2012: 97). In her discussion of the relation between narrative and databases, she identifies narrative as concerned with, and produced by, the process of selection (which databases do not perform), making narrative a sequential or linear and unfolding mode (180) which is important for interpretation or producing meaning (176). In contrast to the selectivity of narrative, then, databases are inclusive and they catalogue and sort information (179). This discussion of narrative and databases is important to Hayles' development of contemporary technogenesis, for she understands these two cultural forms to exist in a complex ecology (176) in which narrative – 'deeply influenced by the evolutionary needs of humans' dealing with unpredictability – functions in marked contrast to databases which run through 'set-theoretic operations based on formal logic' (179). This leads Hayles to identify narrative as a technology concerned with temporality, one which gestures towards 'the inexplicable, the unspeakable, the ineffable', in contrast with databases, which lend themselves to spatial displays and organisations (179–80). Here we think of Land's distinction between loops in time (which equate to narrative) and a machinic collapse of time (which equates to the development of machine databases).

The implication of Hayles' comments is that narrative, on a basic level, is a sequence produced through selection and exclusion – that is, it is diachronic (whether it be a documentary account or speculation); and that databases are explicitly spatial (a patterning) and inclusive – that is, they are synchronic. Both are modes which Hayles thinks unlikely to disappear in the future, not least because of their co-dependency. As such, contemporary technogenetic developments are characterised both by narrative in time and by machinic circuits productive of spatial organisations, as for example with the internet, which can be said to be diachronic (in function) and synchronic (in operation), both modes involving different scales, temporalities and speeds. Hayles argues that databases are essential for global explanations but that narrative is important for interpreting collected data: while narrative at the local level remains 'pervasive', it is increasingly 'infused by data' (181–2). The omnipresence of data – available in vast quantities and with increasing alacrity – is, Hayles suggests, an important development that ensures that no single narrative will achieve 'dominance', since 'interpretative possibilities proliferate as databases increase' (182).

Like Shaviro, then, Hayles believes that human experience and narrative are transformed by new media environments, which engender human adaptation to technology – an event which produces a new mode of attending to the world that she names hyper-attention. Characterised by a 'low threshold for boredom', hyper-attention 'alternates flexibly between different information streams, and prefers a high level of stimulation', all of which correlates to her notion of 'hyper-reading', which involves skimming, scanning, fragmentation and juxtaposition (12). As already mentioned in Chapter 21, Stiegler addresses this mode of attending to the world as a problem, comparing hyper-reading or attention unfavourably with 'deep-attention'. Hayles, too, thinks that deep-attention – and deep-reading, defined as a mode with a high boredom threshold that focuses on a single information stream or object (12) – is 'a precious achievement' (99). Where Hayles departs from Stiegler is in her conclusion that hyper-attention represents not a 'decline in cognitive ability' but a 'positive adaption' to 'information-intensive environments' (99).[4] Within such environments, then, the human species may mutate and upgrade rather than face extinction or enslavement, as some post-singularity fictions would have it.

As such, following Hayles, it can be said that the human is an identity with fluid thresholds and dynamic boundaries and organisation. The future of the human in cultures inclined to develop speed, connectivity, compression and non-continuity as modes of existence – and indeed as values – relates to the potential roles and transformations of narrative and a lived-sense of time or duration. It is this question (which includes speculating on the future forms of fiction in human-machine ecologies), as opposed to the problem of human and machine mastery, which radical or technogenetic mythotechnesis opens up.

Thresholds

While Hayles is primarily concerned with writing and literature, our focus here is directed towards art and music – image and sound production – that can be said to promote the idea of human becoming as a becoming *with* technology.

We find this process in the work of the artist Rachel Rose, who addresses disembodiment through audio-visual installations that (perhaps some might think paradoxically) produce embodied affects for her audience. The artist can be said to be making work traversing the thresholds of human, machine and environment. Indeed, Rose is known for her interest in disembodied percepts, an example being

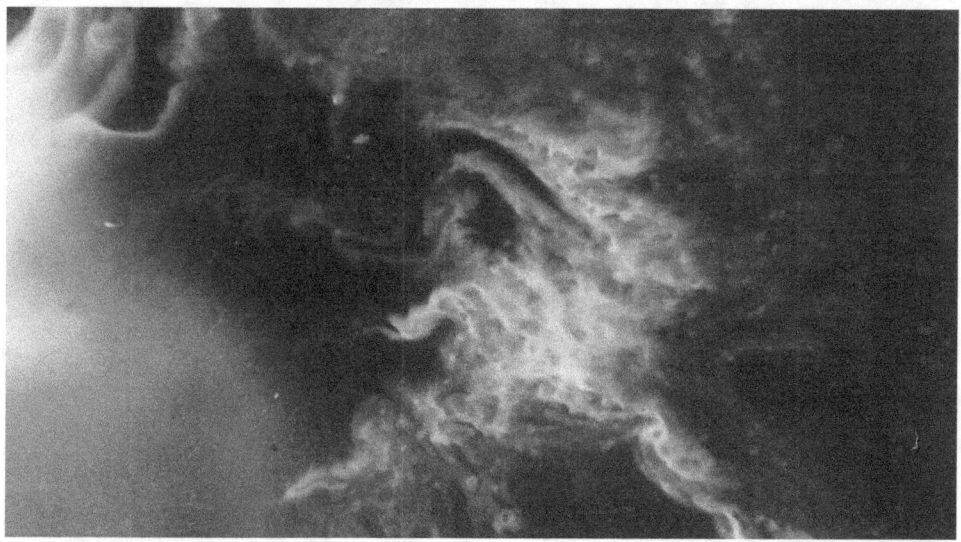

23.2 Rachel Rose, Still from *Everything and More*, HD Video, 11'59", 2015 (courtesy of Rachel Rose and Pilar Corrias, London).

her film *Everything and More* (see Figure 23.2), which draws on the experience of astronauts learning to spacewalk. The film features manipulated footage of a neutral buoyancy pool – used for learning to spacewalk but also in robotics research – and images of the artist's apartment, complemented by two important sound elements. The first is an interview with the astronaut David Wolf recorded over the telephone, so that his voice – as the artist observes – seems to move through different frequencies; the second is the sound of Aretha Franklin's voice, altered through a piece of astronomical equipment called a spectrograph, which analyses and divides sound and light frequencies, allowing Rose to produce a 'thing released from humanness, but still human' (Rose and Burns 2015). The ambient (or atmospheric) qualities of the film are further enhanced by being projected on scrim covering a window. When shown at the Whitney Gallery in New York (2015), and the Hayward Gallery off-site exhibition *Infinity Mix* in London (2016), natural light interrupted and illuminated the film, and the cityscapes beyond the windows were seen fleetingly and randomly throughout the screenings. This projection technique presents an effect, as the journalist Charlotte Burns suggests, that is intended to produce a virtual image combined with the actual world, and a play of light and scale which Rose suggests will offer the viewer the possibility to 'experience things as if in outer space' (Rose and Burns 2015).

Other works by Rose also display a concern for making percepts fluid and boundaries indiscernible, and for making viewers feel that they are weightless and then grounded. These include *Palisades in Palisades* (2014), in which a camera, seemingly in continuous motion, pans over and glides through a painting, the fabric of a woman's clothes and a rock face; and *A Minute Ago* (2014), which combines found YouTube footage of a hailstorm with a clip of the now deceased architect Phillip Johnson walking around his glasshouse, the latter cut-out using rotoscope techniques and transposed onto the house as it is today. In an interview for *Bomb Magazine* Rose explains her intentions in making *A Minute Ago*:

> I tried to infuse every point of reference within the work with collage: from compositing the hailstorm to the outside of the Glass House, to suturing the Johnson of the past with the house in the present. When I shot in the house, I replicated the camera movements from that original Johnson footage, so it felt like the two times were one. (Rose and Nash 2015)

In Rose's work, it would seem that any narrative the work presents is produced through editing. However, the artist's editing process, and her extension and embedding of hearing and seeing in technological processes, are concerned with registering rather than commenting on the material she works with. In her essay 'Collaging in Time', Emma Enderby quotes Rose's own thoughts on her manipulation of analogue and digital material or data:

> I see the edit itself as a surface through which I can become more conscious of the content. Seeing it for what it is: as a shape, a texture, and a rhythm in relation to all the other cuts. I try to construct a work so that it has an autonomous perspective. (Rose quoted by Enderby 2015: 15)

In what we would call Rose's machinic perspectives or machine fictioning, it is not the camera which sees nor the microphone which hears that is important, but rather the editing process – the manipulation of material as elements of shape, texture and rhythm – that is primary. It is through the human application of software, the cutting and pasting of images in a timeline and the application of effects and plug-ins, that material is collated, registered, selected, ordered and presented. In this, we suggest that Rose's work can be thought to be expressive of – to quote Shaviro again – an 'ambient, free-floating sensibility that permeates our society today' (2010: 2). That is, her work is symptomatic and productive of social and technogenetic processes.

We find Shaviro's use of the term 'sensibility' interesting here, as it is not only apt for Rose's approach but chimes with Mark Hansen's ideas explored in his book *Feed-Forward*, in which he contrasts perception with sensibility, the latter term referring to processes which work 'prior to the emergence of unified sense perceptions' (2015: 156). Hansen argues that:

> At stake in sense reception, and in what I am calling non-perceptual sensibility, is a visceral mode of engagement that is not only common and impersonal but also more primordial and more fundamental than any agent-referenced, private sensations. (156–7)

Hansen develops this idea of non-perceptual sensibility through his reading of Alfred North Whitehead – whom Shaviro is also often indebted to – and in particular Whitehead's concept of *prehension*.[5] Hansen also borrows the concept of 'the elemental' from Alex Galloway's and Eugene Thacker's book *The Exploit: A Theory of Networks* (2007), to refer both to that which is 'above and below' the subject and to the different variables of networks, which requires scaling on micro and macro levels (Hansen 2015: 1). But Hansen is critical of Galloway and Thacker for failing to conceptualise subjectivity in relation to the sensory affordances of media (3). He states that humans are 'non-optional' aspects of elemental agency and that they are themselves composed of various elements (we are not simply autonomous beings). Accordingly, he argues, humans require an environment in which to operate, meaning that they are a 'configuration of the elemental' (3). Insisting on the sensory affordances of media, Hansen is critical of any argument that humans (and human subjectivity) are eclipsed by media and technology. In opposition to commentators on technology who predict 'some fantasized end of the human' (what we have named post-singularity fictions), and despite media networks becoming detached from, or going beyond, the limits of human perception, Hansen proposes that human experience persists. Specifically, the 'irreducibility of a minimal temporal gap between occasions of experience' equates to the continuation of subjectivity, which also finds new forms and modes through technology: within technological environments, loops of time and subjectivity persist if temporal gaps and disjunctions persist (11).

In relation to Hansen's notion of experience transformed by technology, it is the play of the different temporalities and transitions in Rose's work which seems significant to us. We suggest that her films – which often present or allude to people within environments, such as Philip Johnson in his glasshouse or astronauts within a lab containing a buoyancy pool – articulate a 'time' of technology (of editing software). Viewers of the work register a world through digital editing processes rather than just through direct sensory perception: Rose's audience become palpably post-human and cyborg through engaging with her films. More than this, Rose's films are often non-continuous or discontinuous (in terms of any linear narrative) and yet appear (in terms of human perception) to be continuous and fluid through a flow of affect and the merging of different scales of image – a movement that (through the artist's aptitude in editing) seems to smoothly pass from image to image, and from film format to film format. This editing practice not only enhances a sense of the human embedded in an environment, it is productive of an ambient sensibility; and Rose herself suggests that her installations attempt to materialise the structure of an edit (Rose quoted by Enderby 2015: 17). In this way, we would suggest, Rose's art achieves a certain kind of union of human and technology which allows for what Hansen calls the work of non-perceptual sensibility.

Emergence and Enaction

And what of intelligent machines and technogenesis (organic or inorganic)? It should be clear by now that here we are interested in understanding the union of human and technology in such a way as to contrast with those fictions examined in Chapter 21 which divide human and machine or that advocate for transhuman augmentation for the sake of mastery. As a starting point for developing this contrast, we borrow the idea of union from Spinoza's *Ethics*, in which he writes:

> When a number of bodies, whether of the same or a different size, are so constrained by other bodies that they lie upon one another, or if they so move, whether with the same degree or different degrees of speed, that they communicate their motions to each other in a certain fixed manner, we shall say that those bodies are united with one another and that they compose one body or individual, which is distinguished from the others by this union of bodies. (Spinoza 1996: 42)

In addressing the scale and speeds of bodies Spinoza offers a diagram through which to think human-machine arrangements as a union of a kind. As suggested above though, this is only a starting point, and to develop a more detailed notion of human and machine union we feel it is necessary to discuss embodiment in more depth. For in arguing for machine-human assemblages as co-adaptations, we feel it is important to explore the ways in which an entity's cognition, perception or registration of surroundings relate to and are extended through an environment or other bodies. To do so, we introduce two terms, *enaction* and *emergence*, which illuminate the non-conscious processes of cognition and sense-making, and, as indicated at the beginning of the chapter, are a key concern in our development of a radical mytho-technesis. This will engender a discussion of the ways in which humans develop in relation to their surroundings, as well as a discussion concerning research addressing emergence and machine or machinic life (such as artificial life and intelligence), which in turn facilitates a narrative of the co-evolution of human and machine. The ideas discussed below are then further explored through the work of Holly Herndon, who could be said to approach technology and machines as collaborators.

The idea of enaction is developed and explored in *The Embodied Mind: Cognitive Science and Human Experience*, by Francesco Varela, Evan Thompson and Eleanor Rosch, who insist on the following functions: '1. perception exists in perceptually guided action and 2. cognitive structures emerge from the recurrent sensometer patterns that enable actions to be perceptually guided' (Varela et al. 1991: 173). In this theory of enaction, it can be said that animal (including human) perception is not only embedded and constrained by an environment but that it also enacts a world (174). The sensory-motor operations of animals, for example, respond to the world by producing a world, as seen in the basic function of the categorisation of experience or processing of information performed by all organisms, which is the point at which 'cognition and environment become simultaneously enacted' (177). The idea of emergence also challenges cognitivism (which argues that the brain produces representations of an external world) by proposing that components of the perceived environment when engaged through the 'correct rules', generate 'global behaviour producing the desired task' (8). Varela et al. suggest that the connection of vision and memory is one such example of emergence (8), which is interesting for our discussion of contemporary human-machine arrangements – in particular of human vision and memory being transformed, enhanced or extended by technology. For Varela et al., the theories of enaction and emergence account for how humans neither perceive the world as such, nor generate cognition that is purely the result of the operations of the sense organs. Rather, as Rudrauf et al. state – in their homage to Varela (their former colleague and mentor at Laboratoire de Neurosciences Cognitives et Imagerie Cérébrale in Paris) – enactivism proposes that the embodied mind

works in the 'body-in-space', which contributes to its shaping. The ongoing, endogenous regimes of activity in the brain embedded in the rhythms of organism regulation and physiology, must be conceived as taking place within a constant sensory-motor coping between the system and its surroundings. (Rudrauf et al. 2003: 35)

As Rudrauf et al. emphasise, in Varela's argument 'the environment doesn't contain pre-defined *information* that is independent of the "domain of coupling" that the autonomous system defines, it literally *in-forms* the system's coping' (35). Thus, the operations of enaction take place through the constraints of both organism and environment (34), allowing Varela to state that the process is concrete (or material) and not abstract (33). Rudrauf et al. quote their former mentor as comparing the environment to 'jazz improvisation', the 'excuse' for 'neural music' for a cognitive system. Here, embodiment is immanent to that system, making the identities of what might be called the inside and the outside of the system 'intricated' (35).

These ideas build upon earlier theories which Varela developed with Humberto Manturana, particularly the concepts of autopoietic organisation – self-generating and self-regulating systems or machines 'organised (defined as a unity) as a network of processes of production' – and allopoietic organisation, defined as 'machines that have as a product of their functioning something different from themselves' (Manturana and Varela 1980: 135). For many, Varela's research is the thread which runs through the development of theories of autopoiesis, enactivism and neuro-phenomenology. This latter term describes a mode of investigating cognition, developed by Varela towards the end of his life, in which first-hand or first-person experience is not dismissed but, as Rudrauf et al. note, is valued as valid data – as valued and valid as objective biological, neurological and physiological data (2003: 42). In this, they point to how Varela attempts to narrow the distance between first- and third-hand (or so-called subjective and objective) perspectives, through bringing mental and physical processes closer together (42). The means of achieving this goal, Varela suggests, involves a training in which researchers develop and reflect upon phenom-enological examination, which Radauf et al. identify as being influenced by Buddhism and European Continental Philosophy. We suggest that Varela's combination of these perspectives with the sciences produces not only a dynamic metamodelisation of approaches to cognition but also new (human) modes of attention which take account of the environment and the sensory-motor processes that produce them.

Varela's approach has consequences for subjectivity and the location of cognition and the mind, as Rudrauf et al. observe: 'the "I" can only be localized as an emergence but it acts as the center of gravity of the subject' (36). Here, thinking back to section one and our discussion of the fiction of the self, we understand Varela to be proposing a paradox in which cognition and the mind exist in what might be called a non-place of the co-determination of the inside and the outside of a system (36). This begs the question as to whether, at one level, there is such a thing as an inside or outside. Which leads us to ask, are humans, existing in technologically enhanced environ-ments, always already cyborgs? In relation to this, Rudrauf et al. quote Varela's statement – which we see as strange kind of fictioning, or a fictioning of a strange figure – that he is a selfless or virtual self which is nowhere to be found but which engenders the couplings of a system (an organism) and the environment (36). In the case of human systems (if we might name them as such), it would seem that thresholds and boundaries are hard to define, and that human and machine cognition, intelligence and knowledge are extended (or embodied) through each other.

Enactive-Based Artificial Intelligence

The theories of enaction and emergence constitute a dynamic field of contemporary research relating not just to biology and cognitive intelligence but to artificial intelligence and artificial life studies as well as social and anthropological studies. Research informed by theories of enaction takes on two crucial questions: what is a body and what is cognition? In their essay on 'The Enactive Approach', Ezequiel Di Paolo and Evan Thompson address such problems by stating that cognition relies on a living body – understood as an autonomous system – which makes itself identifiably distinct (for an observer) from its surroundings, and exhibits a precariousness which they define as the potential decay and decease of a system in the absence of enabling relations. Hence, they argue, an autonomous system exhibits spontaneity in maintaining relations (requirements of energy and matter) with the outside world (Di Paolo and Thompson 2014).

We understand that precariousness has a determining relation for the way a system coevolves with other systems or an environment, and that the effects of the environment on the system are important too. This is made clear in, for example, the essay 'Enaction-Based Artificial Intelligence: Toward Co-evolution with Humans in the Loop' by De Loor et al., who argue that the idea that enaction is incompatible with – or only a metaphor for – virtual and artificial life or robots and artificial intelligence is shortsighted (a view which has relevance to our earlier discussions of intelligent machines). For De Loor et al., the part played by, and the potential of, the co-evolution of the environment in the development of artificial systems is often overlooked, for much research focuses on producing autonomous systems and ignores the disruptions of a system by environmental agents. Such disruptions lead to adjustments of the system, which in turn effects the environment to the extent that the agent registers the environment differently (De Loor et al. 2009: 12). To develop their argument, De Loor et al. cite a number of approaches to artificial intelligence which reject computational and representational models of cognition and which integrate 'the role of the body and the sensorimotor loop in recognizing a robot's cognitive capacities' – an approach which 'is at the source of embodied-embedded AI' (2). They suggest that a challenge for artificial intelligence research is to develop 'regulatory mechanisms' which might maintain the system: 'knowing that the impositions exerted on it will evolve', the 'system must be able to regulate its regulation, to be able to access a meta-regulation' (6). They further argue that this dynamic mode, rather than a representational mode of cognition, is a path to artificial intelligence, and they note the importance here of the role of phylogenetic and ontogenetic processes (the role of genetic – or coded – predetermination and environmental adaptation). In a challenge to Darwinian evolution, De Loor et al. state that the more complex a system is, the more significant the role of ontogenetic adaptation, to the point where the environment becomes more influential than phylogenetic processes (13). This leads them to suggest that, from an enactive perspective, evolution is as much a process of auto-organisation (in relation to the environment and other agents) as it is a process of genetic adaption (13). A corollary of this, for enactive-based artificial intelligence research, is the importance of distinguishing between auto-adaptive systems and systems that learn. It is at this point that De Loor et al. raise the problem of sense-making, and the relation of artificial intelligence to humans, stating that a shared meaning relating to a human view of the machine, and cooperation between humans and machines, will only emerge

> through interactions with a human observer. Otherwise we will find ourselves faced with machines resembling patterns created by fractal evolutionary algorithms. They would be extremely complex and seem well organized, but would be incapable of forming social and shared meaning. (14)

Here it would seem that, in order to avoid producing Land's universe of pure abstraction and number, humans need to be included in the loop of artificial life and artificial intelligence development. This proposition marks a clear orientation, implying that the inclusion (or not) of human perspectives in that loop is an aesthetic and ethical question rather than a science-based decision (as much as it is an aspect of an evolutionary or ontogenetic process). For the problem of sense-making raised by De Loor et al., we suggest, raises further questions about the future of narrative and lived experience.

Clearly it is not solely a case of aesthetics, since non-conscious, evolutionary adaptations and ontogenetic processes shape cognition, but these processes are, today, in tension or tandem with organisations of life consciously shaping themselves and other systems – as, for example, in the augmentation of humans or the laboratory development of articial life and intelligence, which must be viewed as an aspect of the technogenetic process. Here we can offer a reflection on the technogenetic spiral proposed by Hayles, in which technology and humans are presented as co-evolving. In the post-singularity fictions we examined earlier it might be said that – with the advent of automated and artificial intelligence and life – the spiral will come apart, with machines evolving and superseding or curtailing the power and agency of humans. In contrast, Hayles, and Hansen up to a point, assert that the embodied and material (or elemental) aspects of human-machine interaction mean that humans and human subjectivity evolve as technology and technological environments evolve. De Loor et al. offer one more perspective. Human and artificial life and intelligence will evolve together in ways that are meaningful for humans if humans take care with the development of artificial life and intelligence (here we can think of Max Tegmark's concern that artificial intelligence might develop different goals to humans).

Arguably then, there is a choice to be made in developing a precarious techno-genesis of human and machine adaption between trajectories that include the development of sense-making and social machines and those committed to autonomous artificial intelligence or life that produces an abstract universe. We opt for an aesthetics of machining fictioning which explores a diversity of unions or couplings in order to acknowledge the significance of the process of human *becoming-with* technology. Whether what many might today call human will survive is perhaps not the question to ask – better, perhaps, to ask what we might we call human. And again, recalling Vivieros' Amazonian metaphysics outlined in section two, wherein anything with a perspective is considered human, we think that this is, again, an aesthetic and ethical rather than just a scientific question. We can now state that autonomous complex 'machines resembling patterns created by fractal evolutionary algorithms' (De Loor et al. 2009: 14) that are not in union with humans – the abstractions of code – may offer perspectives of a kind, but they would be foreclosed to narratives or at least will not promise sociality such as humans would recognise (and here we are reminded of Peter Watts' alien discussed in Chapter 15).

A Radical Mythotechnesis

In their homage to Varela, Rudrauf et al. quote the biologist's thoughts on the future of his discipline, in which he argues for 'a cognitive science where there is a true circulation between lived experience and the biological mechanisms in a seamless and mutually illuminating manner' (Varela quoted in Rudrauf et al. 2003: 45). They cite these lines from Varela's paper 'Neurophenomenology: A Methodological Remedy for a Hard Problem', in which the biologist calls for approaches that treat 'the mind and world as mutually overlapping' (1996: 346). We suggest that if this latter notion is taken seriously by artists then, similarly, we need to advance an art of machine fictioning in which there is a mutually illuminating circulation between lived experience and biological, physical and technological mechanisms. Given that many artists do not have access to the resources or knowledge necessary for producing complex artificial life and intelligences projects, we envisage this as occuring at different levels (or speeds and scales) of technologies. Rather than artists publishing research papers, we think machine fictionings include writing fictions and narratives, performances and presentations and other productions and processes associated with art practice.

So far, as laid out in this chapter, we find support in the notion of technogenesis developed by Hayles, in the concepts of embodied technesis and non-perceptual sensibility offered by Hansen, and in research addressing enaction, emergence and embodied-embedded cognition. We should note, before addressing machine fictioning in a specific art practice (that of Holly Herndon), that there are, of course, important differences between these three lines of enquiry. For instance, in *Feed-Forward*, Hansen distinguishes his concept of an operational overlap of microsubjectivities which produce human subjectivity from theories of emergence like those we have just discussed (2015: 12). For Hansen is concerned with processes which he suggests occur pre-perception and that are overlapping, quasi-autonomous and 'do not get sublated in any upward-directed telos of emergence' (103).

While Hayles, too, has her criticisms of Manturana and Varela, discussed in *How We Became Posthuman* (1999), the biologists were also a key influence on her work. Although Hayles does not address Varela and enaction in her later book, *How We Think* (2012), we suggest that an example of union through something like enaction and emergence can be found in her description of an enmeshing of the different temporalities of digital machines and humans. She argues that human-machine temporalities evolve as

> a complex syncopation between conscious and unconscious perceptions for humans, and the integration of surface displays and algorithmic procedures for machines. The interactions are dynamic and continuous, with feedback loops and feedforward loops connecting different levels with each other and cross-connecting machine processes with human responses (2012: 13).

While we find encouragement for our concept of machine fictioning in the work of Hayles, Hansen and Varela – which, not unlike other bodies of research, we treat as Science Fiction – it is, as we have implied above, Hayles technogenesis that seems most apt for cooption as a radical mythotechnesis. Hayles' statement about contemporary technogenesis could be read as a manifesto for art practice. For whether through adopting or addressing co-adaptation, coupling or operational overlap, or some other embodied or environmental process, it would seem to us that a radical or technogenetic mythotechnesis can be found in art which fictions potential human-machine-environment assemblages to come.

Among a number of artists exploring such adaptations and organisations, Holly Herndon is perhaps exemplary. The artist is influenced by a number of ideas gleaned from theoreticians, including Benedict Singleton's proposal that it is better to design platforms for interaction (to realise future potentialities) than imagine perfect futures, which provided a concept for Herndon's album *Platform* (2015). Herndon's musical production involves a number of collaborators and features the track *An Exit*, which responds to Suhail Malik's ideas concerning the necessity of exiting the established economies and hierarchies of art. What we find most interesting about Herndon's work, however, is not just the politics, concepts and ideas explored in her songs, nor that she calls for new fantasies (Herndon 2017); it is, rather, that her long-term project has been and remains the investigation of electronic music as an embodied form. This problem formed the basis of her master's thesis (2010) at Mills College San Fransisco, in which Herndon cites Hayles' *How We Became Posthuman* as an important influence. In a number of interviews, Herndon addresses her relationship to digital programmes and machines, stating that a laptop offers unprecedented control of her voice in real time and a means for finding new forms of (emotional) expression while eschewing 'emotion in music' (Herndon 2014). The use of software in live performance and recordings develops the artist's interest in the voice – often an aspect of gender stereotyping in popular music – as offering potential for radical experimentation. She explains her ideas in an interview for *The Quietus*:

> what I think is really interesting about the electronically processed voice – you're not actually bound by the physicality of your body anymore. So a woman's singing range doesn't necessarily need to be x Hz to x Hz, it can go just as low as a man or it can be just as aggressive. That's really interesting, because somehow we're still not really breaking out of those societal rules that we have: when you hear a processed female voice on the radio it's usually reverbed and often pitchshifted up, and in a lot of hip-hop it's kind of angelic or sexual compared to the information-driven or aggressive message that the male will put across. (Herndon 2012)

And if voices are transformed through human-machine union or couplings, what other human-machine-environment co-adaptations are possible? One work which explores this question, and which loops the non-conscious and non-human and the human, is *Collusion*, performed by Holly Herndon in collaboration with Matt Dryhurst and Reza Negarestani and the machine protocol *Open Sound Control*. The program allows precise communication between various digital devices in real time in an accurate and flexible manner (Herndon 2013). As Herndon explains, the work originated with Negarestani's suggestion that they make a presentation in which the relation of humans to the environment becomes palpable. This Herndon achieves through technologies of various kinds.

> I was asked to be part of a festival around the theme of 'dark ecology', and I thought Reza would be the perfect person to collaborate on that topic with. So we Skyped

about it and he basically came up with this idea of 'taking the mundanity of life to its psychotic extreme'. What he meant by that was making people hyper-aware of their being part of the performance and being complicit with all of the objects around them. (Herndon 2012)

In *Collusion*, a union between humans and objects (or what Herndon calls 'invisible agents') is produced in which neither human, machine, environment nor protocol is presented by the artist as having priority (or mastery) over the other (Herndon 2013). It is an exploration of conductivity and embodied practice which points to the potential oscillations or obsolescence of the identities or thresholds of humans and machines.

This last thought revises the idea (an early post-singularity fiction), proposed by the cryptologist Irving John Good in 1965, that 'the first ultraintelligent machine is the last invention that man need ever make, since it will lead to an intelligence explosion' (1965: 78); such an invention, Good claimed, is necessary for the survival of the human (31). Instead, might not the first ultraintelligent human-machine-environment assemblage lead to the adaptation or coupling explosion necessary for the survival of the human? Perhaps this myth or fiction is the last that humans ever need produce?

Coda: Machine Intelligence and Emergence

We have discussed Hansen's idea that humans require an environment in which to operate, and explored the idea of emergence to further address the relation of humans and environments. We suggest that this, in turn, supports the idea that humans evolve with or enact technoenvironments, engendering fictionings – a radical mythotechnesis – of human-machine union. We have yet to address the question of machines – or fictions concerning automated and artificial intelligence – requiring or responding to an environment to the same extent. A problem here, though, might be that technology and automated intelligence operate at speeds beyond the human, such as the high-frequency trading algorithms (discussed earlier) that make small profits many times over through feedback loops governing the selling and buying of stock, all achieved faster than the human eye can blink. This may well produce a reasonable fear or expectation that cybernetic intensification or automated intelligence will out-perform, overcome or become detached from human society and environmental factors, lending credence to the argument that artificial intelligence systems can exist autonomously or independently of other systems and material or environmental conditions. Narrative in time, produced (according to Hansen) by temporal gaps or disjunctions, might not be a feature of systems running high-speed algorithms or that are self-learning and self-modifying.

However, Hayles' notion of a symbiotic relation between narrative and databases counters this idea to a certain extent, for it would seem that narrative as selection can be equated with social meaning, even if that selection process is governed by profit-making programs designed to operate at speeds no human could hope to match. Furthermore, as the artist Sam Lewitt notes, there are material as well as social aspects to abstract and digital machines, made visible by the cooling systems that regulate high-frequency-trading hubs and by the high-level surveillance patrols that protect data centres – something Lewitt discovered when he tried to photograph a service farm in Mahwah, New Jersey (2014: 507–16). Lewitt's comments appear in his 'Notes from New Jersey', which, for us, evokes Robert Smithson's 'A Tour of the Monuments of the Passaic (1967)', a text which, as we saw in section one, documents entropy in New Jersey's industrial landscape in the 1960s (it is, indeed, Smithson's own fictioning of that landscape). Lewitt's essay, recording a trip to an information factory, documents a post-industrial or digital development, but physical space seems as important to Lewitt as it was to Smithson. 'Notes from New Jersey' recounts how security officers deleted Lewitt's photographs when he tried to document buildings containing the Mahwah service farm.[6] Ironically, the artist explains, he was on a trip 'spurred by abiding questions concerning the conditions of intelligibility for value's circulation through increasingly abstract and insensible systems of valuation and debt' (2014: 507).

Our intention in addressing high-frequency trading once more is to question theories in which environments are said to play no part in the development of automated and artificial life, intelligence and technologies. We may, however, have to address more than the social-economic and security aspects of high-frequency trading. In the context of Left accelerationism, Nick Srnicek and Alex Williams have interesting things to say about the development, parameters and potential adaptations of high-frequency trading algorithms, which they suggest represent the best candidate for Nick Land's 'emerging accelerationist singularity' (Srnicek and Williams 2014a: 488). Srnicek and Williams comment on the physical and environmental limits of high-frequency trading – one such limit being that communication is limited to the speed of light – and on the relation of local and global aspects of the operation, including security and errors and bugs which need to be continuously monitored and fixed. They also note how advantage in this area is achieved not by the domination of space but through adaptations of various kinds, including environmental and performance adaptation. They suggest that algorithms and their human designers would gain an advantage through 'transposition' from 'one conceptual register or spatial location' to another, 'and into other localities and logics' (489). This is not to deny generative evolution. Rather, they argue that if generative evolution is at work then it operates in relation to material, physical and environmental influences and adaptations.

It seems to us that Srnicek and Williams' approach to automated intelligence is marked by technogenetic or environmental concerns and by an attention to the material complexities of human-machine arrangements – as demonstrated in their fictioning of a new species of crafty machines which, in a post-capitalist world, they suggest, will be able to solve 'problems associated with social calculus' (505). What interests us here is that Srnicek and Williams suggest the emergence (or enaction) of such cunning machines relate to material limits and environmental factors. Not only this, the crafty machines are cast as part of an assemblage that includes humans and their desires as well as other kinds of economies. This seems to us a union of agents that can be counted as a cyborg, in which each body, agent or system becomes part of a composite body or circuitry. In this, Srnicek and Williams' crafty machines are works of machine fictioning.

Notes

1   For an in-depth exploration of the concept of the machinic and machinic life, see John Johnston's *The Allure of Machinic Life: Cybernetics, Artificial Life and AI* (2008). In his compelling book, Johnston identifies machine entities as new forms of life, which redefine or challenge existing notions dividing organic life from inorganic technical objects (4). He suggests that machinic life differs from other, past mechanical forms in that, today, machines can alter themselves and 'respond dynamically to changing situations' (ix). To develop his thesis, Johnston draws upon Deleuze and Guattari's theories of machinic assemblages – defined as the relations or assemblages formed between bodies or organisations. Similar to our own project, he engages with theories of machine development and artificial life and intelligence through theories of technogenesis and emergence. Importantly, Johnston addresses a machine as a material device or assemblage that is 'conjoined with a unique discourse' (x) which coheres a machine's purpose. Similar again to our own thinking, he also identifies the notions of 'the adversarial and the symbiotic' machine as two competing contemporary discourses (12). Unlike our own book, Johnston's project does not engage with these two 'cultural narratives' save for understanding their 'scientific and technological condition of possibility' (12). In this, he is less interested in speculating on human-machine adaptations presented in discourse and art, or the role fiction might play in this, and more interested in pursuing an understanding of the potential complexity and autonomy of machinic life itself. While we, for our part, recognise that machinic life beyond the human is possible and perhaps inevitable, we focus on art and writing that addresses how humans (and thinking and embodiment) are extended and transformed through machines (even if this produces something that appears non-human); a corollary of this being that we also engage with how machines and technologies develop and adapt in relation to human narratives.

2   To support this position, Hayles points to diverse fields such as: paleoanthropology, which asserts that walking on two legs encourages hands to develop tools; genetic research which explores how species adapt their environments to accommodate and spread genetic mutation; and research informed by neuroscience which describes how the plasticity of the brain engenders the rapid growth of digital media technologies in everyday life.

3   Hayles notes that Simondon defines technical objects as being embedded in networks or assemblages (social, geographic, economic, etc.), but that he also discounts tools as part of this network. In this respect, she diverges from Simondon's thinking, as for Hayles it is hard to imagine a tool not embedded in an assemblage of some kind. Instead, Hayles counts tools as part of technics, not least because they have a role in the exponential change of many spheres, but also because today the ubiquitous tool of the networked and programmable machine is key to many transformations (Hayles 2012: 90). In this, though, Hayles recognises Simondon's claim that attention (although difficult to define) is significant when addressing technological developments, and therefore that changes in attention – or various forms of attention – can be important for marking the connections and disconnections of her 'technogenetic spiral' (86).

4   As mentioned earlier, and in the preceding note, Hayles follows Simondon in identifying attention as a significant mode for understanding technological and human development. In this regard, we conclude that although our book is often fragmentary – that it juxtaposes ideas and terms and moves fluently through paradigms and scenes, and that it is composed of narratives gleaned from various kinds of digital database searches – it nevertheless invites a deep-reading. We would claim at certain times a parataxis that allows for compositions to present phrases and ideas side-by-side without subordination or hierarchy – this, that . . . and another thing – alongside a hypotaxis which, at other times, operates a narrative arc or linear selection – if this, now that. It is possible that parataxis is becoming, and will increasingly be, a more prevalent form of narrative, coinciding with post-continuity media products. It might be said, though, that standard academic writing is limited when it comes to grasping technogenetic developments, whereas art and music or audio work might capture or present more.

5   Hansen is interested in Whitehead's 'reform' of experience or subjectivity (which is not limited to humans or living beings) as an incorporation of what is perceived and which signals a shift from 'an agent-centered perceptual modality to an environmental sensibility that lies at the heart of twentieth-century media' (Hansen 2015: 9). This relates to Whitehead's notion of prehension whereby a perceiving system or thing grasps or seizes a datum, which then produces subjectivity. Whitehead suggests that 'prehension produces in itself the general characteristics of an actual entity', to which it is subordinate (1995: 19).

6   Lewitt was informed by security officers that although he was not allowed to photograph the service farm he was allowed to draw the site from memory, which as an artist, he was told, he should be able to do without difficulty.

24 The Radicalisation of Singularity

Even if algorithms perform nonconscious intelligence, it does
not mean that they act mindlessly . . . From this standpoint,
machine-learning algorithms do not simply perform nonconscious
patterns of cognition about data, exposing the gaps in totalizing
rational systems, but rather seem to establish new chains of
reasoning that draw from the minute variations of data content
to establish a machine-determined meaning of their use.

Luciana Parisi, 'Reprogramming Decisionism'

I realised that I could play like a machine if I practiced enough . . . While
all the electronic guys are trying to put in this great looseness. I'm going
the other way. I'm never going to get there, because I'm not a machine.
But it gives it a quality, like chikachikachikachikachikachikachika . . .

Leo Michner, 'This Is My Machine'

WE HAVE REACHED a point where we can now re-address the term singularity
through mythotechnic and technogenetic perspectives, and with reference to the problem of the relation between non-conscious knowledge and the clear consciousness of
reason. In what follows we aim to explore technological singularity[1] not as the event
of discrete or exponential intelligence optimisation, nor in terms of the original scientific notion of singularity as an event in which laws no longer apply, but as an event
which marks the immanence and union of multiple and specific elements and agents
in both the digital *and* the analogue. It is to this end that we appropriate Fred Moten's
ideas concerning the term singularity, which the poet develops in relation to new
departures in art, literature and music associated with the name of a specific writer or
artist. It is Moten's conviction that the naming of the innovative work of an artist as a
singularity can be understood as a fabrication of 'The Event', which is only a name or

a marker for something more complex, multiple and incalculable – 'the writhing mass that seems to operate beyond any notion of singularity' (Moten 2003: 157). We similarly suggest that the discrete or historical 'breaks' or singular situations identified by post-singularity fictions, such as 'the artificial intelligence singularity', 'the transhuman', 'the cyborg' or 'the technological singularity', are fabrications of 'The Event', beyond which something incalculable may take place – that is, Moten's 'writing mass', which, we suggest, is another name for immanence. Here we are not promoting Spinoza's concept of a virtual substance from which multiple forms are actualised (in fact, as in section two, we hope to problematise this particular concept of immanence); rather, we are arguing for a consideration of enactions and emergent unions of the human and technology. We are also interested in a radical mythotechnesis and machine fictionings that would make such enactions and emergences tangible through compositions that also produce a discomposition of identity. This is another idea we borrow from Moten, who – writing about a different context of poetry and reflecting on jazz ensembles – argues for compositions in which 'one is discomposed in real time' (Moten 2015).[2]

Although we find Moten's thoughts on singularity helpful as a starting point, in what follows we necessarily look to discourses and art practices that attend more specifically to the role of immanence and non-conscious processes in human-machine assemblages and in machine fictionings. It is for this reason that in Part 1 of this chapter we return to the work of François Laruelle, who in his writing on computation and philosophy further helps to illuminate our discussion of the human-machine relations of mythotechnesis. However, while the non-philosopher's commentary is helpful, we draw different conclusions to Laruelle about technology and human life, which leads us to discuss other orientations concerning computers and machines, including, once more, the writing of Luciana Parisi. Following this discussion centred on immanence and the digital, in Part 2 we follow up on ideas concerning immanence and machines but shift our focus to consider machine fictioning in the art practices of Leo Michner (a.k.a. Klavikon) and Stelarc, which could be said to be concerned with the analogue. To this end, we address the work of Klavikon and Stelarc in relation to Georges Bataille's account of human intimacy with technical objects.

PART I: MACHINE IMMANENCE

Non-Philosophy Against the Digital

As we saw in Chapter 17, Laruelle develops a critique of what he calls the 'standard operation of philosophy' which produces difference through a (transcendent) division of the One or the Real. For Laruelle, 'Difference, analyzed as pure mixture or superior form of mixtures, has henceforth the appearance of a contradiction, more exactly of a duality that it would deny' (2010: 220). By this, we understand Laruelle to be critical of philosophy which would affirm immanence but in doing so posit an event produced through a division and transcendence of immanence (presented as having virtual and actual aspects). Immanence, for Laruelle, is definitely not a mixture that can become different, discrete things. In critiquing the transcendence of philosophical systems of thought, Laruelle insists on a Real which has no 'empirical, ontic or ontological' aspect, stating that immanence (by which he means the Real) is 'foreclosed to being' (Laruelle 2013a: 130). In this, non-philosophy rejects the division of the Real and the human, addressing the latter as the (Real) One-in-One; and Laruelle suggests we try to think (the human) in accordance with what is immanent to the human.

Laruelle offers another perspective on the problem of the doubling of an event discussed earlier: he argues that naming a discrete singularity ('The Event') would be a contradictory division of the Real. We can infer that this might not just be a problem concerning discourse but also a question for mathematical thinking, automated thought and artificial intelligence. In *Laruelle: Against the Digital*, Alexander Galloway pitches Laruelle's non-philosophy as an opposition to the digital in all its guises – a statement which could be interpreted as meaning that digital thinking is abhorrent to non-philosophy. But as non-philosophy does not take sides – it is not for or against anything, and it is not concerned with division – Galloway's argument seems to be something of a perverse ruse. We find, however, that this ruse leads to insight. Galloway notes that Laruelle explicitly equates automated machines and computers with the 'inherently philosophical or world-bound', suggesting that Hegel is alive and well in the form of the 'electric calculator' (Galloway 2014: xxxiv). Before addressing Laruelle's writing on artificial and automated intelligence in detail though, we feel it is helpful to reprise our discussion of immanence in his work, this time through Galloway's take on non-philosophy and the digital (the latter term construed in the broadest sense possible).

The One and the One Cloned

Galloway suggests that in continental philosophy, events are considered to be either analogue – actualisations of the potentialities of a plane of immanence – or digital – temporal and spatial breaks produced through decision. This leads to the problem of deciding for one or the other notion of what constitutes an event. Galloway notes that Spinoza develops a compromise to address this difference, one which maintains multiplicity in univocity as immanence: this allows for both endless differentiation (the division of the digital) and the unity of things (the vectors of the analogue). As

Galloway puts it, 'In other words, what *exists* is digital, but *what* exists is analog' (xxxiii). Referencing Deleuze, he goes on to state that the One can be said to be 'From one aspect digital. From another, analog. To think univocity in terms of equivocity is a movement of the digital. But to think equivocity in terms of univocity is a movement of the analog . . . Creation is digital but the lived existence of the created is analog' (84). Non-philosophy, according to Galloway, rejects both analogue and digital orientations – as well as Spinoza's compromise – as a division of the One or the Real. Furthermore, as we saw in Chapter 17, Laruelle's position can be understood in terms of an indifference to philosophical decision: a heresy (at least for philosophy), as Laruelle (2012b) would have it; that is, a withdrawal from philosophy and from the problem of the duality of the analogue-digital relation. We conclude from this that, in Galloway's reading, Laruelle refuses to decide between the analogue and the digital, a position which we think both important in itself as well as pertinent to our discussion of radical singularities and of a mythotechnesis that addresses human-machine relations.

The importance of non-philosophy, then, is that it admits neither discrete, named events nor events as immanent difference. In this, we ask is there to be (an intimacy of) two notions of the event which are both accommodated by non-philosophy? Galloway is helpful here in arguing that the One as event can be understood – through Laruelle – as unilateral duality:

> *Unilateral* means the one is oblivious of the two, insisting on its own oneness, but duality means the two bonds in an identity with the one. Laruelle's 'unilateral duality' should be understood in precisely this way. As unilateral it follows digital distinction, while as duality it follows analog integration. (2014: 84)

Another way of addressing this paradoxical-sounding concept is through Laruelle's notion of cloning – a process resulting in clones that are one and the same, a notion relating to an equation concerning identity, a = a, which Galloway states is important for non-philosophy (58). This seems a clever invention, maintaining the purity of the concept of the One but allowing for a process which engenders a multiplicity. But here we could ask, are not machines, computers and artificial intelligences capable of such cloning?

Most interesting for our discussion is that in his essay 'The Transcendental Computer: A Non-Philosophical Utopia' (2013a), Laruelle pre-empts and addresses objections to this doubling or cloning of the One, in so far as this may not (seem to) be a non-philosophical procedure – rather it might be a digital one which machines undertake. That is, Laruelle recognises that it might reasonably be assumed that automated machines can clone the One. This objection is rejected as a mistake which would divide non-philosophy into an inert (already existing and objectified) structure or operation set apart from a practical functionality that is lived. For Laruelle, we suggest, what may be dismissed by some as inert and objectified in non-philosophy – that is, non-philosophy's cloning procedures – is in fact a performativity (in the form of a commitment to not dividing the One or immanence). All this leads Laruelle to state that cloning has nothing to do with machine (or digital) processes (2013a). We think this statement might prove to be too hasty, not least in its division of the human from machines and digital processes.

The Transcendental Computer

From these discussions of unilateral duality we can draw two conclusions: firstly that for Laruelle the procedures of non-philosophy are not automatic, not a programme or an algorithm to be executed by a non-philosopher (or a non-philosophy machine); secondly that, as far as Laruelle is concerned, automated reason and artificial intelligence cannot register, think or act in accordance with the One (that is, the Real). Putting aside the fact that non-philosophy seems to assert a division between machines and humans, these two conclusions pose some important questions for our discussion of technogenesis (even if, as mentioned above, we end up drawing different conclusions to the non-philosopher). Laruelle states: 'Radical immanence is also devoid of subjectivity but not of lived experience: that's what distinguishes radical immanence from a machine ... Transcendental life and, even less so, real lived experience are not reducible to algorithmic repetitions' (2013a).

Even so, Laruelle suggests that he is obliged to address a third scenario or synthesis between philosophy and machine, one which he names the Transcendental Computer. Here Laruelle is concerned with comparisons made not between the immanence or consciousness of machines and humans but between their performances – procedures undertaken by both humans and machines that require intelligence (performance being defined here by Laruelle as something which is deemed measurable). It is the performance of intelligence (by both human and machine) which, he argues, is 'supposed as one of computing's criteria of identification with thought, and inversely as the criterion of thought's reduction to computing' (2013a). Crucially though, Laruelle states that philosophy is more than a performance that can be measured: if artificial intelligence can set goals or tasks for intelligence that can be measured, philosophy applies intelligence to an operational horizon which machines concerned with quantifying intelligence cannot 'recall' or approach. Laruelle goes further, commenting that: 'Philosophy uses intelligence or cognition but on behalf of a special form of thought, probably irreducible to any numerical combination.' This 'special form' is the blending of the 'numerical' (or digital) with 'the qualitative', which ensures that a residue of thought survives cognitive reductionism – this would be true even in mathematical ontologies like Badiou's, which nonetheless 'reserves philosophy's role as the power of gathering' or 'quasi synthesis' (2013a).

Laruelle's rejection of measurable performance grounds his argument that philosophers should not be intimidated by a machine's performances, as the latter, he suggests, 'are truly performances but nothing more' (2013a). He further argues that non-philosophy registers and preserves this residue of thought (which is cultivated by philosophy but not machines) without placing science (and its production of intelligent and measuring machines) in opposition to philosophy, and without 'crushing' one or the other. He states that: 'If philosophy is not reduced to Consciousness and to its . . . "performances" and is revealed to be all the more irreducible to a machine using computing, non-philosophy radicalizes this irreducibility' (2013a). Our understanding, here, is that non-philosophy produces a metamodelisation of science and philosophy. This is an arrangement which refuses opposition, but it also refutes the reduction of the human to a measurable machine.

In relation to our exploration of a radical or technogenetic mythotechnesis, we value non-philosophy's project of attending to what escapes machine measurement and calculation and to what is irreducible in the lived experience of humans. This is a valuable idea and lesson in relation to our stated aim of developing a notion of radical mythotechnesis beyond the now seemingly limited idea of technological singularity. We recognise, too, that the notion of cloning as unification-effect – which Laruelle names 'unimaton' in contrast to automaton (2013a) – problematises (but hopefully also develops) our Spinoza-influenced use of the word 'union' (as discussed in our previous chapter). The question arises, though, as to what Laruelle might suggest as an appropriate relation for (or orientation towards) machines or automated and artificial intelligences. In addressing this question, we find non-philosophy to be yet more technesis (as outlined by Mark Hansen) – concerned with thought and its relation to technology – which we find problematic, particularly as we have argued, in further reference to Hansen, that lived experience, and thought too, is extended and transformed through technology and technological environments that increasingly include automated and artificial intelligence as agents. In this, we question Laruelle's marking of a clear boundary between lived experience and the operations of machines. We articulate this question in two ways. Firstly, in so far as intelligent machines might be transitioning from algorithmic systems operating a computational logic (to help humans communicate and make decisions) to other modes of operating, are machines limited to measurable performances (as defined by Laruelle)? Secondly, if the intimacy of humans with machines transforms experience, is (lived) experience a continually evolving mode that may take on aspects of the digital?

Reprogramming Decisionism

To develop our first question, we note that Luciana Parisi, in 'Reprogamming Decisionism', has proposed the idea of the meta-digital; a term that she applies to new regimes of communication. Her example is the algorithm that no longer operates through a binary system of either/or, but through which – for example in tracking human consumption – 'whatever logic we leave enclosed within our random selections' is identified and chosen as possibly significant. For Parisi, this heralds the advent of a machine that 'is no longer digital, because it is no longer concerned with verifying and explaining problems', introducing a 'new level of automated communication enabled by the algorithmic quantification of affects' (Parisi 2017).

And this is not all. Importantly, in tracing the desires of humans without pre-stated purpose, the machine is not engaged in calculating probability. Parisi argues that this does not mean the data retrieved is trivial:

> On the contrary, the computational machine entails a granular analysis of data on behalf of algorithms, which rather open up the potential of content to be redirected for purposes that are not preknown. In other words, this computational indifference to binary problem-solving coincides with a new imperative: *technological decisionism*, which values making a clear decision quickly more than it does making the correct one. For decisionism, what is most decisive *is* what is most correct. (2017)

Parisi notes that, for some, the end of metaphysics occurs when computational and cybernetic machines first enter the sphere of human society and life. Heidegger in particular is cited as suggesting that technoscience completes Western metaphysics, which leads to the position that, in a time of what is perceived by many to be one of meaningless communication, thought must be geared towards how to think 'outside reason and instrumentality'. In a rebuff to this Heideggerian teleology and, we suggest, to Laruelle's dismissal of computational thinking, Parisi suggests 'reopening the question of *how to think* in terms of the means through which error, indeterminacy, randomness, and unknowns in general have become part of technoscientific knowledge and the reasoning of machines' (2017).

Parisi observes that while cybernetics may bring about what she calls a post-truth or post-fact era (through facilitating the development of algorithms that respond to and shape opinion and thought rather than verify fact or truth) in which metaphysics cannot operate, the metaphysics of machines has yet to be given much consideration. She notes that, from 'Heidegger to Deleuze and even Laruelle', a critique of technology prevails in continental philosophy that fails to engage with the 'complex mediation' of intelligent machines, preferring to focus on machine intelligence as involving an immediacy of doing and thinking. For Parisi, the development of neural nets and machine learning is important here, and she questions the equating of thinking machines with instrumentality: 'Machine learning rather involves augmented levels of mediation, where uncertainty is manifested in terms of the incomputable forms of algorithmic automation, as that which does not simply break the calculation, the quantification, the numerical ordering of infinities' (Parisi 2017).

Parisi offers a far more complex account of algorithms than does Laruelle, explaining how they function through processing error, surprise and what she calls 'unthought information' to produce an 'indeterminacy – or irrationality or nonconscious activity – within . . . algorithmic mediation' (2017). This is something of a challenge to the dismissal of machine thinking articulated by non-philosophy and other orientations. In reference to neural net mediation Parisi argues that 'the irrational is not outside of reasoning but discloses the alien possibilities that a general practice of reasoning offers in terms of a mediation of technosocial changes and actions'. She further states that machine learning produces an 'articulation of the real, the unknown, the incomputable, in terms of technical mediations, automated actualizations, and machine becomings of the real in their manifest artificial forms' (2017). Commenting once again on the ways in which continental philosophy, from Heidegger to Deleuze, forecloses the possibility of what she calls 'techno-philosophy', Parisi states:

One possibility for addressing the politics of machines is to work through a philosophy of another kind, starting not only from the unthought of thinking, but also from the inhumanness of instrumentality, an awareness of alienness within reasoning that could be the starting point for envisioning a techno-philosophy, the reprogramming of thinking through and with machines. (2017)

This proposition seems close to Negarestani's notion of the labour of the inhuman, entailing the enslavement of humans to reason (automated reason being an enhancement of reason's autonomy, speed and reach). But it is different too in advocating that the unthought might be central to a techno-philosophy produced through and with machine intelligence that develops the alien within reason. In an analogy that reveals her political aspirations for techno-philosophy, Parisi compares the 'alienness' of instrumental-machine-thinking to the Brutalism of modernist architecture that attempted to produce new modes of community and living. She suggests that techno-philosophy may produce a human-machine reasoning that, like Brutalist architecture, engages with 'entropy, randomness, or noise to reprogram codes and values, passages and bridges, contents and expressions of a united image of the social' (2017). While machine intelligence does not equate to lived experience, in her reprogramming of decisionism Parisi references Hayles' concept of technogenesis to offer a machine fictioning of what we would call a union of human and automated/artificial intelligence as a means of reconfiguring social life (which will in turn affect lived experience). In this case, continental philosophy and non-philosophy would not be the only means of pursuing Laruelle's 'special form of thought, probably irreducible to any numerical combination' (2013a).

Thinking Through, With and Alongside Media

Following Parisi's radicalisation of (techno)singularity, we would argue that questioning whether lived experience is reducible to algorithmic repetitions does not preclude exploring the ways in which the lived experience of humans involves technogenetic spirals and assemblages, as conceived by both Hayles and Parisi. If it is true, as Hayles and a host of others contend, that today 'we think through, with and alongside media' (Hayles 2012: 1), then, today, lived experience is extended through and embedded in the digital and automated modes of machines. Again, we draw on Hayles here, and her sympathetic reading of Marshall McLuhan's notion of technology as an extension of, or prostheses for, humans (2). Hayles goes further, especially in relation to digital media, arguing that technology is embodied and that it has physical effects on humans (3). In particular, the computer produces networked human-machine assemblages in which 'the keyboard comes to seem more an extension of one's thoughts rather than an external device on which one types' (3). Hayles' interest in such assemblages concerns how embodiment, in this instance, is marked by the way 'human agency and thought' are 'enmeshed in larger networks' (3). We suggest that this does not contradict Laruelle's valuable demonstration that the lived experience (and immanence) of the human can (at present) be distinguished from the performances of machines. But from this perspective, another move must be made to attend to how the performance of machines and automated intelligence (on the level of materiality and embodiment) increasingly extend and transform the realm of human lived experience – the machinic and the machine made immanent in our intimacy with technology – without making thought instrumental.

This directs us to our second question for Laruelle's non-philosophy, concerning the ways in which machines (as agents of automated and artificial intelligence) have and will continue to influence and transform experience (or lived experience). This question of immanence and intimacy with technology becomes particularly relevant if we take on board the idea of epigenetic evolution in the context of advanced technological environments. Hayles defines epigenetic development as the biological concept of evolution produced by and through environments rather than genetic code, suggesting, in relation to digital technology in particular, that epigenetic evolution produces accelerated transformations (much faster than genetic evolution) due to the plasticity of the human brain (10–11). If Hayles is correct, then we have to ask whether what some might identify as the mere performance of machines has a role within lived experience that – as Hansen advocates – needs attending to. While immanence is not reducible to machine (or measurable) processes, following Hayles it cannot be said, either, that immanence and lived experience are exclusive of machines and their processes.

In elaborating the ways in which epigenetic development takes place through non-conscious and unthought processes, Hayles draws upon neuroscience and psychology to mark a 'new unconscious' which is neither suppressed nor repressed but is, rather, a 'perceptive capacity' which registers that which escapes (conscious) attention. Hayles names this new capacity the 'adaptive unconscious' (13–14), which we suggest might not exactly be a form of cloning, but which produces intimate assemblages of material complexity.

PART 2: Machine intimacies

Thought and the Unthought

We follow both Hayles and Hansen in their interest in embodiment and materiality, which we treat as an intimacy produced by human-machine-environment assemblages. Here we would like to extend our discussion beyond a consideration of intelligent machines by historicising digital thinking and considering humankind's relation with early as well as contemporary technologies. To do so, we will turn to Georges Bataille, who suggests that tools or technology – whether the written word, a hammer or a 'digging stick', or, we might add, a computer – all produce a subject-object (or human-world) relation, or what Galloway might call a digital division. Extending this argument, a tool or machine can be said to mediate (and produce) interiority and exteriority for the human, who captures or manipulates a world (at least as far as a Western understanding of the subject goes). What interests Bataille is not only that this process posits 'an object, which is not given in animality' (Bataille 1989: 27) but that there also remains a human which exists in a world of immanence 'like water in water' – or like plants and animals – without subordination to a human subject (28). This is not to say that there is a human which is irreducible to the human subject, but rather that an aspect of the human is an immanence – the human as immanent-(to)-itself as Laruelle might say – which is not grasped by conscious thought. The point being that the tool is subordinate to (and productive of) the human subject, but that the tool also places the human in the world. As Bataille goes on to suggest, while the tool may be said to have 'no value in itself . . . except in relation to an anticipated result' (28), it partakes of elements which are continuous with the immanence of the world. It is no surprise, then, that Bataille declares that the function of a tool or technology produces confusion, the tool being both a subservient (and useful) object and continuous with the elements of the immanence of the world. This, for Bataille, risks leading to the erroneous thought that tools or technology could be said to act like subjects – a position which would cause humans to see themselves, too, as just another thing (32).

There are several things to say about Bataille's theory of the tool – which, following Hayles, we understand as a technical object. Since Bataille's death, tools or technical objects have become intelligent things. Indeed, in many instances they are treated as a thinking thing, carrying out utility goals autonomously in automated fashion. It might also be said that humans are the tools (or technical objects) of intelligent cybernetic machines and systems. Taking up Bataille's (and Galloway's) perspective, this way of thinking of technology continues an objectification which privileges the digital and the divisive over the continuous. For Bataille, it is important to register the immanent and unthought aspects of life, and to understand human and technological development as irreducible to objectifying divisions (or identities in opposition and competition). Bataille suggests that humans have an (unthinking) intimacy with technology, which he calls a non-knowledge. As he writes: 'Intimacy is the limit of clear consciousness; clear consciousness cannot clearly and distinctly know anything concerning intimacy, except for the modifications of things linked to it' (99).

Technology is (Our) Intimate

To further explore human intimacy with technology, and how this is an aspect of what we identify as radical mythotechnic practices that do not divide machine and human, we end the chapter with a discussion of practices rather than theory and philosophy. In this we look to further radicalise the idea of singularity in attending to how lived experience is extended and embodied through intimacy with technology. An apt example here is the electronically amplified, prepared piano performances of Klavikon, a.k.a. Leon Michener. Michener assembles various objects – microphone pickups linked to delay and reverb units and roaming robot toys (with cameras presenting live image-feeds) – within a piano, to produce orchestral, percussive and alien sounds and to project bizarre scenes that are also real-time images of the guts of the mechanical body of the piano. At times, Michener's compositions sound like mutant electronic techno or dance music produced by digital software, but all of the rhythms and sonic events that Michener and his piano make are analogue. They are not pre-recorded or samples. This lends his performances an indiscernible or fluid (and seemingly impossible) identity that is both human and machinic, that seems both analogue and digital.

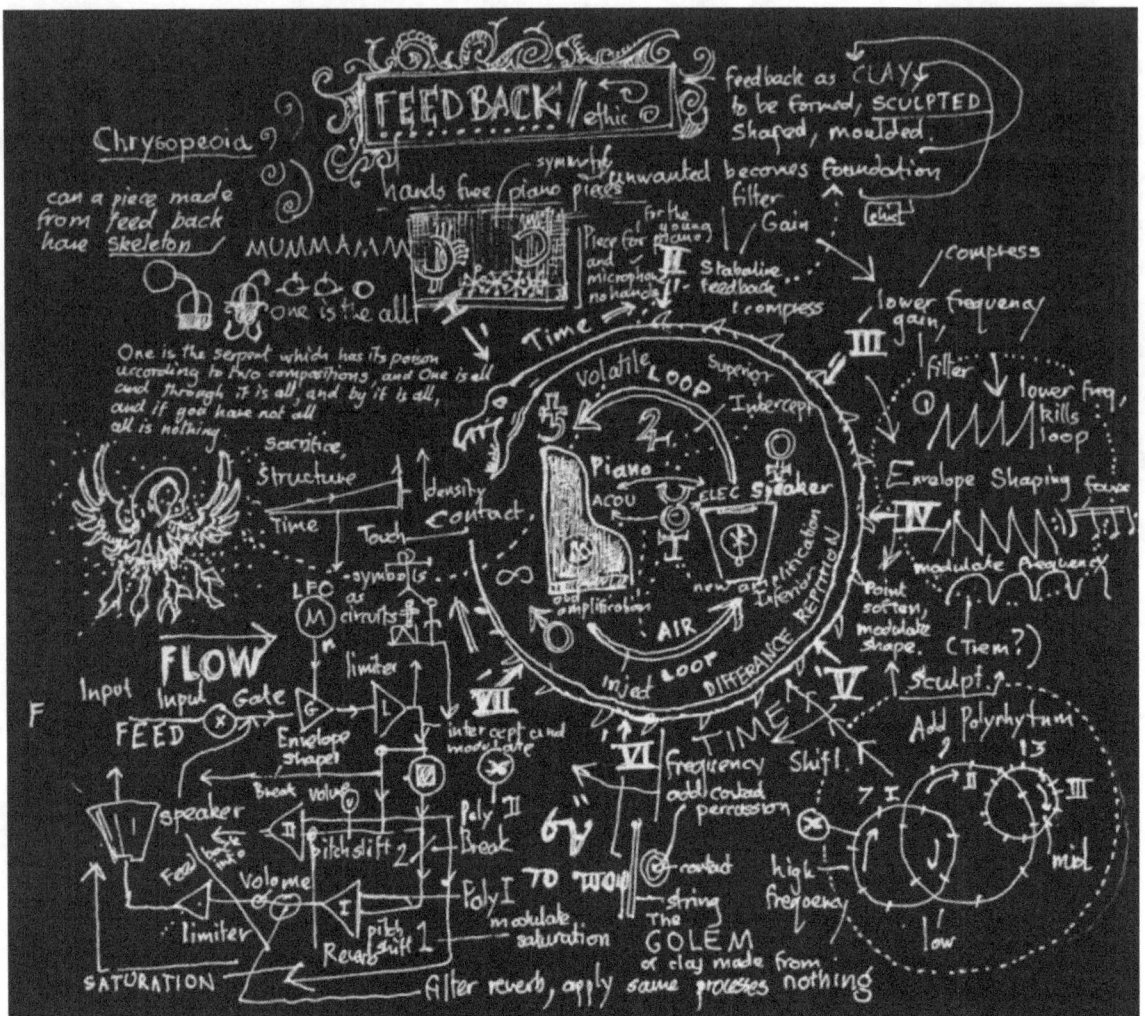

24.1 Diagram by Leon Michener (courtesy of Leon Michener).

In a diagram of his prepared instrument (see Figure 24.1), Michener writes 'The GOLEM of clay made from nothing' and draws a snake labelled 'DIFFERENCE REPETITION' – an Ouroboros chasing its tale and encircling the piano (Michener 2015a). He inscribes the word *crysopeoia* – which means transmutation into gold – at the top of the diagram, and this can be read as the name of the feedback machine or creature that Klavikon fictions. The musician is part of the assemblage, and Michener states that in his concerts he is interested in exploring the history of rhythm in the left hand (of piano performance) which accompanies the right (which produces riffs and refrains). But he also comments that the robot toys placed in the piano, making

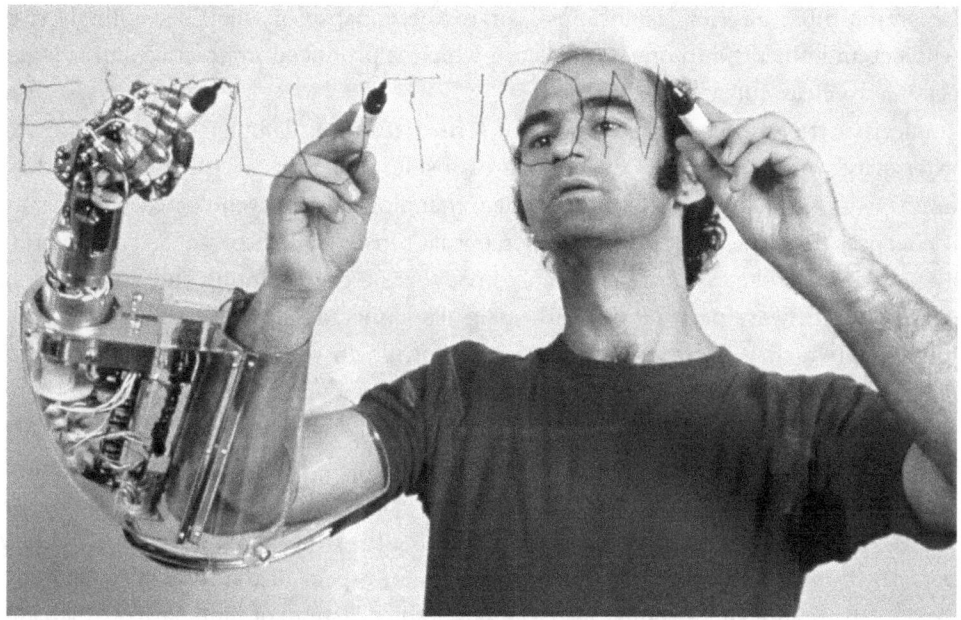

24.2 Stelarc, *Evolution*, 1982, Writing One Word Simultaneously with Three Hands, Maki Gallery, Tokyo, 1982. Photographer: Keisuke Oki (courtesy of the artist).

random sounds and images, are a 'third hand' (Michener 2015b).

There is thus an intimacy and union of human and machine in Klavikon's work which we find in many practices that can be identified as technogenetic. One important example is Stelarc's project titled *Third Hand* (1980), involving a mechanical augmentation attached to the artist's body (Figure 24.2). This device allowed Stelarc, after training his body and reflexes, to undertake three-handed tasks, an augmentation marking the immanent potential of human and machine. We propose that such techno-genetic intimacy can be understood as something like 'extimacy' – a topological term (see Figure 24.3) referring to that which is considered exterior

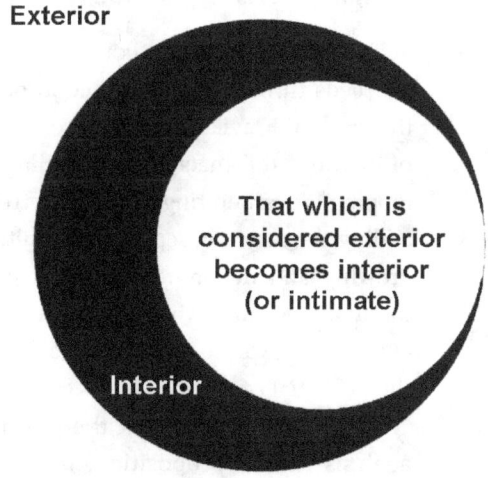

24.3 Topology of Extimacy (credit: the authors).

becoming most interior (or intimate), or to the collapse of what is seemingly two (subject and object) into one – a collapse which is produced in practice and is inaccessible to clear consciousness.

Lacan, a friend of Bataille, coined the term 'extimacy', defining it as an 'intimate exteriority' which collapses the notions of inside and outside (1992: 141). In this, intimacy as extimacy is not exactly a phenomenological or psychological process, as it collapses both the psychic and the perceptual sense (or division) of self and world. The context for Lacan's discussion of extimacy was a cave painting and the question of why images were painted in a dark space. He concludes that the end of art is not imitation (which is a trap) but an intimate act which registers something beyond illusion. This last statement describes the work of Klavikon and Stelarc well, but there is something more than the registration of what is absent to the thought-world occurring in their practices. Importantly, Stelarc does not view his *Third Hand* as a sign of lack. Rather, he suggests that it is a symptom of excess (Stelarc n.d.). Such excess, we would suggest, is produced by a practice exploring the overabundance of possibilities between human and machine, which, for us, is an aspect of the human-technology union, or technogenetic potential. This is a radicalisation of singularity which, in Moten's terms, has as its mode of operation the composition and discomposition of identity, and which involves, as we have suggested, the looping of clear consciousness and non-conscious knowledge in a practice of radical mythotechnesis.

Technogenesis as Method

Such a practice does not consist of performative iteration (unlike non-philosophy), but proceeds through performance in pursuit of diverse mutations and adaptions – as in the work of Klavikon and Stelarc. Instead of iteration, we have in mind here a number of methods (or enactions), including cutting, sampling, splicing, patterning, copying, looping, reverberating, shaping, stretching, contracting, stamping, casting, pasting, adding, sequencing, replicating, multiplying, fixing, variating, assimilating, hybridising, growing and decomposing. We envisage such performances or enactions as non-discursive gestures which do not create or name new subjectivities, subjects or historical events, but explore different arrangements – machine fictionings – that are a slave to the potential of technogenesis.

It could be argued that there is a passivity, a depoliticisation and even a lack of analysis in our proposition, in so far as critical reflection – particularly critical discourse addressing social and historical forces – are not foregrounded in our account. We would reply to such an objection by insisting that, today, an expanded notion of analysis is needed to account for the kind of fictionings we have been discussing – fictions like those of Stelarc and Klavikon which, in their presentations of bodies, images and narratives, and in their annotated diagrams and commentaries, challenge common conceptions of machine and human. In pursuing such an expanded analysis we find ourselves in agreement, once again, with Mark Hansen, who argues that:

analysis will have to become performance, a creative experimentation with the possibilities for our future technogenesis ... insofar as they directly expand our embodied capacities to act on ourselves, on others, and on the world, technologies can only be adequately 'understood' in their very exercise as transductive correlates of human becoming. (Hansen 2004)

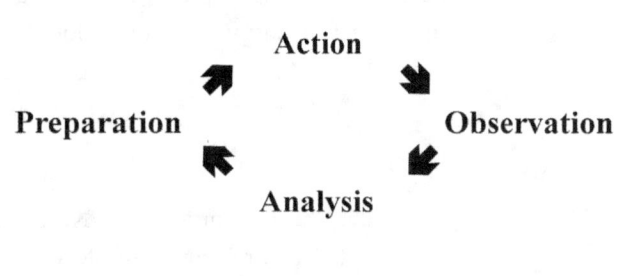

24.4 Diagram of action research (credit: the authors).

Coda: Action Research

We are not arguing for intuition over concepts, nor that concepts and reflection are of no importance – indeed, without them, practice could not engage with the world. What we are proposing is a practice that operates like the cybernetic loops of action research, pioneered by Kurt Lewin in the 1960s, which produce a research method that we place alongside, and as an alternative to, Negarestani's model of the engineer (pitched against both the private mystic and the 'advocate of transgression or militant communitarian' (Negerastani 2014: 468)). The feedback loop of action research (see Figure 24.4) is a continuous circuit of action/observation/analysis/preparation, which is repeated until a territory or assemblage is fully explored. In it, actions become more directed and focused as the research practice proceeds, for in the first instance a researcher acts without clear intentions to register or produce something that is unknown.

Action research has two functions: it is an intervention which produces understanding but it also effects a transformation of a situation. We might identify a similar set of functions for radical mythotechnic art practice (Figure 24.5). The first function is action that actualises or fictions the potential of

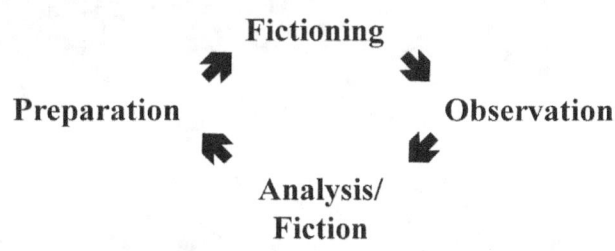

24.5 Diagram of a practice at radical mythotechnesis (credit: the authors).

human and technological unions. This, in turn, is registered/observed/reflected upon and then analysed to produce a further fiction, which in turn informs preparation for more acts of fictioning. There are other, less academic ways to diagram this cycle of functions, which can be found in art practice. Here we can think of no better example than Klavikon's amplified, prepared piano as a transmuting snake, in performance but also as a diagrammatic drawing (Figure 24.1) embodying an intimacy of human-technology union, and a looping of clear consciousness and non-conscious knowledge.

Notes

1   The mathematician John von Neumann is credited with the first use of the term 'the singularity' in relation to the advent of technological minds in the 1950s; the term was later popularised by the novelist Vernon Vinge.

2   Here we think of two examples from our last chapter: Varela comparing the environment to 'jazz improvisation' and his discussion of 'neural music' in a cognitive system, and Holly Herndon's collaboration *Collusion*, in which humans, objects, software and technology produce a performance, with no one agent being given single authorship of the event.

25 By Any Memes Necessary

Rhythmic contagion is submemetic in the sense that
the unit of the meme is turned inside out to reveal its
ontogenetic relations . . . a nexus of microevents.

Steve Goodman, *Sonic Warfare*

IN ARGUING THAT radical mythotechnic practices engage in non-discursive gestures such as cutting, sampling, patterning, copying and looping, and in suggesting that such practices involve machine fictioning, we feel it important to address an area of research that might be called the study of memes. Although meme theory has little academic support, being controversial and often thought trivial, and while there is much to be wary of in the theory, we also feel that the scientist Susan Blackmore, a leading exponent of the speculative theory of memes, has some interesting observations concerning human-machine relations. These observations – and accompanying questions – are useful in addressing the ways in which the digital has transformed mass entertainment, culture and politics (thinking in particular of the way memes play a key part in social media campaigns of the Right and the Left). But we are also interested in meme theory in relation to the digital transformation of music and the way musicians, particularly electronic musicians, are engaging with both sonic memes (which might also include refrains, jingles or earworms) and the submemetic, so as to to present what Steve Goodman calls 'a nexus of microevents' (2010: 151). In addressing Goodman's thoughts concerning memes and the submemetic, we draw parallels with Fred Moten's notion of radicalising singularity by approaching any 'Event' as a 'writhing mass' of events. To address memes and the submemetic in relation to mythotechnesis, we begin the chapter with a discussion of Blackmore's theories, before moving on to discuss the work of artists such as DJ Rashad and Oneohtrix Point Never and their use of digital processes to engage with the sonic and the submemetic.

PART I: Difference and repetition

Genes Versus Memes

In *The Meme Machine*, Blackmore suggests that what makes humans different from other animals 'is our ability to imitate'. Indeed, imitation comes naturally to humans (1999: 3). This idea is drawn from *The Selfish Gene* by Richard Dawkins, in which it is suggested that while DNA has been the dominant replicator on the planet in the past, it is not necessarily the case that this will remain so in the future, for a new, second replicator is abroad: the meme. While memes are not organic replicators they do have a relation to DNA replication: genetic evolution, in developing brains, can be said to provide the 'primeval soup of culture' from which this new replicator emerges (Dawkins 2006: 192–4). This 'primeval soup' is then the origin, but also a kind of mythos of the meme.

In developing language from vocalised sounds, and by imitating actions and operations which process and circulate information and behaviour, humans produce culture. It is culture which provides the material for the development of the second replicator – the meme – which in turn develops the big brain of the human species – at least that is Blackmore's hypothesis. For, she contends, it is genetic replication or evolution that develops brains on the planet while meme replicators are most important for human social development. It is meme replication which places pressure on the brain to develop a memetic capacity (1999: 75) – a capacity which other mammals do not even come close to matching. The theory addresses the problem of why evolution did not select small brains for all hominids as it has for other animals, small brains being less expensive in terms of energy and less dangerous in terms of reproduction and birth. 'The story in a nutshell' – for Blackmore does deliver a story or theory-fiction peppered with tales of human survival and mating selection – is that imitation facilitates the spread of skills that in turn require a greater capacity for imitation (76). Referring to the work of Dawkins, Blackmore argues that imitation should be understood in its widest sense, proposing that a meme replicates by passing information from 'brain to brain' (6). It follows from this definition that almost all aspects of everyday life involve memes or imitation, including the singing of songs, the learning of rules, the acquisition of survival skills and the development of eating and drinking habits (7). Furthermore, Blackmore's meme-determinism offers an explanation not just for the development of the mundane habits of a life but also for the persistence and dominance of political ideas and religion, as well as harmful memes such as chain letters and pyramid-selling systems (7).

Blackmore equates this second replicator with competitive, self-replicating genes: memes exist as imitations, they exist only through replication (8). Underpinning this theory is a Darwinism which asserts that evolution is blind and inevitable, an idea which Blackmore elaborates by citing Daniel Dennett's notion of natural selection as an algorithm and a mindless procedure (10). For Blackmore, evolution is a process which *must* follow if variation, selection (in environments which produce competition for survival) and hereditary transmission are characteristics of any ecology or economy: if an evolutionary algorithm is functioning in any situation, 'design must appear out of nowhere' (298–9). Blackmore recognises that variations in material and environmental conditions affect the evolutionary algorithmic process, but her proposition is that the evolutionary algorithm accounts not just for meme circulation but also for the forms which memes take and much, if not all, of what is called culture.

Whether Blackmore's theories adequately account for the appearance of all memes, and for all that we might call culture, is debateable. In her work though, there is, for us, an interesting application of scientific theory to (or even a kind of speculative science fictioning of) phenomena that are conventionally the territory of sociology, anthropology, psychology and psychoanalysis. In this, Blackmore addresses not conscious behaviour or the unconscious but the non-conscious. For example, in an essay written a decade after the publication of *The Meme Machine*, she suggests that chain letters and pyramid-selling systems are examples of trickster behaviours (the trickster being a concept we have discussed a number of times throughout our book). Blackmore argues that these trickster memes are 'informational viruses' which fool their hosts into propagating memes even though they may not be useful or may, indeed, turn out to be harmful (2009: 302). We would suggest, however, that if memes exist only to replicate by passing from one human host to another, it is beside the point whether a meme is 'harmful' or not: in being successfully selected as 'useful' in the eyes of humans (whether they are or not), all memes are tricksters to an extent. But the apparent or actual usefulness of memes to humans is an important concern for Blackmore: she argues that 'humans are selective imitation devices; we try to select only the useful or valuable memes but are inevitably tricked by some of the rest' (302). While again we think this last statement questionable, for Blackmore memes are produced by a mindless algorithm and do not circulate as human agency or as acts of conscious human design or open-ended experimentation.

While we do think there is something to Blackmore's observation about memetic repetition in human culture having a non-conscious aspect, we nevertheless think it important to ask whether humans, who may intuit or understand meme replication as a technology, might modify or manipulate memes, or even develop them for specific ends. Furthermore, in the context of our concern with art practice, we suggest that Blackmore's theory does not fully account for the success of one of art's most successful memes: *Fountain* (1917), a urinal made useless through exhibition and identified by many as one of Marcel Duchamp's most important readymades.[1] It seems that memes, including trickster memes, at least according to Blackmore, do not exist without relating to a purpose which is either practical or related to fulfilling a desire; for memes engender basic and specific needs and desires, such as staying warm (by copying techniques of fire-building), appearing attractive (by adopting a style of dress or haircut), or becoming rich (by setting up a pyramid scheme). In relation to Duchamp's *Fountain*, we might ask whether shock or the nonsensical – novelty and purposelessness – might produce a successful meme too. And, if so, whether Blackmore's theory elides the supplementary aspects of meme evolution, including formal and conceptual experimentation, such as we find in art and other modes of obviation and technical innovation discussed in earlier chapters.

Blackmore's notion of meme replication is compelling, but while imitation or replication may be a non-conscious process, memes (particularly 'trickster memes' such as *Fountain*) are created with the intention that they circulate. The human agent is said by Blackmore to be a machine (non-consciously) running an algorithmic program, and we would not dispute this. A meme may circulate as an idea, image or object through variation, selection and retention, but memes are also vehicles for human designs or experimentations. In the case of the success of *Fountain*, Duchamp and others undertook a little work over a period of time to establish the urinal as an art-meme. First, *Fountain*, graced with the signature R. Mutt, is submitted by Duchamp under a pseudonym to an open exhibition for which he himself is a board member; second, Duchamp resigns from the panel, objecting to the work's exclusion behind a screen; third, Duchamp asks Alfred Stieglitz – the celebrated photographer, gallery owner and arbiter of avant-garde taste at the time – to photograph the work, which he does, thus ostensibly giving *Fountain* his support; fourth, a text appears in the magazine *The Blind Man* in support of Mr. Mutt's submission; fifth and finally, the readymade is lost but its story and photograph create discussion and influence and Duchamp makes editions of *Fountain* which end up in museum collections and which later appear on thousands of postcards and in publications of surveys of modern art. There is no doubting that, in Blackmore's terms, the numerous imitations and reproductions of *Fountain* make Duchamp's readymade a successful trickster meme – many artists and historians reference (replicate and reproduce) the work through developing or recording avant-garde practice – and Blackmore might claim Duchamp and others are driven by a meme algorithm they are not aware of. But experimentation and discourse (in the form of testing what art might be) are also part of this process.[2] *Fountain* may operate as a meme, but it is also a collective fictioning which manifests a new kind of artwork – a new discursive object – in Western culture. Perhaps, here, an artist can be said to (consciously) experiment with the non-conscious processes of meme replication at large in human culture and society through a kind of cloning practice.

We will return to the question of whether Blackmore's theory adequately accounts for the appearance of trickster memes – fictionings such as pyramid schemes and readymades, but also political and internet memes – later in this chapter. What can certainly be said is that *Fountain*, as memes go, is a good story and a good joke, on which there is always more to be said.

A Dead Dog

To understand the operation of meme replication, Blackmore offers as an example the fiction (or myth) of a woman who regularly dried her poodle in her oven, and who, on purchasing a microwave, continued the procedure with her new device and fried the dog. Distressed at this outcome, the woman sued the manufacturers of the microwave for failing to give warning that dogs were not to be dried in their products 'and won!' (Blackmore 1999: 14). Blackmore comments that if millions of people know this meme of the microwaved animal, then it is through inherited knowledge; the many versions of it in circulation – including microwaved cats and Chihuahuas – indicate that an evolutionary process involving variation is at work (14). She argues that the meme can be said to replicate through three operations of evolution: variation (evidenced by the different versions of the tale); selection (in choosing the poodle rather than the cat as the subject of the story); and retention and transmission (in that the tale is remembered and passed on). Blackmore links these to a Darwinian view of evolution which describes organisms that are not identical but which have hereditary characteristics and exist in a shared environment (10).

Important to the success of the poodle memes is that they are humorous. Blackmore suggests that memes have qualities which enhance or decrease their chances of survival, which makes sense in relation to the meme 'genres' which Blackmore lists – jokes, fashion, music and food – and which differ in appearance, composition or form. A case in point would be the term meme itself, which, as Dawkins asserts, is a successful replicator, out-performing other terms such as 'culturegen', a portmanteau coined by a fellow commentator addressing the replication of cultural forms (Dawkins 1999: xiii). Dawkins explains that an internet search provides proof of his creation's success, with searches for 'memetic' and 'culturegen' (made at the time of writing his introduction for Blackmore's book) revealing that the former is referenced over 5,000 times, whereas the latter term does not even total fifty hits (xiii). It would seem an unscientific conclusion, and more of an aesthetic judgement, to suggest that the reason for this triumph is simply that the term meme is a less complicated, sleeker phrase, and a more memorable and stylish word than its rivals, but that seems to be what Dawkins infers. That is, the word 'meme' is most adequate – and most selected – as a replicator and prospers in the environment of the internet to the detriment of its rivals.

Adding further detail to her biological view of culture, Blackmore states that just as genes 'go round in groups', cooperating and aiding each other's replication, so memes prosper in complexes. She gives the example of the two related ideas of a scratchcard and winning money, suggesting that these two ideas benefit from each other's influence, and that along with some other 'co-memes' they 'apparently get people to obey' and gamble away their money (19). We admit this is a simplistic idea concerning gambling (which does not seem to explain it in either its occasional or addictive forms), and we are wary of explanations that offer a simple solution for complex events. This seems to be a limit to meme theory, but what does interest us about Blackmore's ideas is that they concern, firstly, non-conscious repetition and replication of behaviour, images, sound and performance; and, secondly, the notion that bundles of images, sound and performance – which Blackmore names memeplexes – allow memes to prosper. Both of these are aspects of mass entertainment culture, and of life in technological cultures and technoenvironments. In relation to this, Blackmore explains how memeplexes and co-memes create the conditions for memes to either lie dormant or spread, giving computer viruses and the internet as examples.

Before addressing this in detail, it is interesting to speculate on what Blackmore's response might be to Hito Steyerl's essay 'In Defense of the Poor Image' and the artist's notion of lo-fi copying as a form of resistance to the corporations that produce culture and control its distribution (Steyerl 2012). We suggest that, from Blackmore's perspective, Steyerl does not account for the (algorithmic) mechanisms that drive the selection and copying of films and music illegally disseminated for free online. Of course, Steyerl might think Blackmore naive in not understanding that the struggle between the entertainment industries and media pirates is a (class) war between rich and poor in which quality or fidelity of information is a political concern; but, from Blackmore's perspective, whether corporation or pirate has the upper-hand, the meme always wins.

In our discussion above, Blackmore's understanding of memes does not account for their variation in form or quality; she maintains that what is important is their replication. To return to the microwaved poodle example, Blackmore proposes that the story, like all memes, circulates among people through a 'language they already know and ideas they already have' (1999: 14) – the primeval soup of culture, as Dawkins would have it. It would also seem that, according to Blackmore, languages or ideas – in that they are replicated – are themselves memes. It might be objected – by Steyerl perhaps – that everything seems to be a meme and, as such, any distinction between process or mediation (the modes and technologies of circulation) and the composition and content of replication is hard to grasp. Blackmore's response to such questions is to insist that it is important to identify what is being replicated in meme circulation. This is the question we will now focus on, to aid us in identifying where we depart from Blackmore's thesis.

Blackmore suggests that memes share a similar algorithmic and phylogenetic process. In theories of biological evolution, phylogenetic development concerns the adaptation of a species through the selection of inherited DNA sequences or the development of inherited morphological attributes in relation to an environment. It is this process of natural selection, which happens over generations, that Blackmore sees as being primary for meme replication (which is different to ontogenetic development concerning an organism's adaptation throughout its existence and in relation to environmental factors). Blackmore does acknowledge that many might question whether memes have 'the equivalent of a phenotype-genotype distinction' (relating to genetic reproduction), for genes are not copied as such but act as instructions for generating organisms (Blackmore 2009: 306). In response to this criticism, she asserts that copying instructions (replicating genes as instructions for a given species) rather than copying products (bodies as vehicles for genes) is a superior mode of biological evolution, a process which she also observes in contemporary memes. Interestingly for us, it is a process Blackmore identifies in music produced in studios and coded as mp3 or digital files to be played on various technologies (307). She suggests that when people listen to music today, more often than not information or code (instructions for producing sound) have been copied and circulated. It is not often the case that people listen and then reproduce music with any fidelity through analogue means – though of course instruments are still played by some and songs are still hummed – rather, music tends to circulate in digital form. While Blackmore admits that meme imitation is a relatively young process compared to genetic reproduction, and that therefore it might not always exhibit the superior mode of replication, her argument about contemporary memes and technology makes sense from at least one perspective: today, digital code is one of the most successful replicators on the planet.

Nonetheless, the question remains as to whether the importance of production and technics is elided in Blackmore's theories, particularly in the context of the rapid invention and adaptation of formats, software and indeed sound and music made through and for new technologies. This aspect of music production, which relates to environmental factors of consumption, market competition and technical and technological contexts, suggests to us that meme replication is more affected by a process comparable to ontogenesis than Blackmore would admit. For the theory of phylogenetic meme circulation as a process of instruction-replication does not address how memes quickly become adapted to or transformed by rapidly changing environments (such as culture, fashion and technologies). If Blackmore's theory can be taken seriously, it might be that early meme replication equates to or is comparable with phylogenesis, whereas contemporary meme generation in technological environments involves more ontogentic adaptation (the development of an organism in relation to environmental factors throughout the organism's life).

One of the problems with Blackmore's approach is that as a scientist she is concerned with cognition, which makes her less interested in embodiment, emergence and enaction. This might explain why a core idea of her theory is that memes pass from one brain to another – that is, they are (or are transported by) material, audio, visual or performative signals or arrangements which travel (through replication) between brains. But here we would suggest that mediation and technology extend and distribute brains – the brain is more than the post-production organ for motor-sensory information. Indeed, it could be argued that thought is in bodies and environments. This leads to a modelisation that rejects meme replication as the passage of information from one point to another, and rather views it as an aspect of a vast network through which memes circulate, a network that also involves artificial intelligences, search engines and databases. This may not signal a more efficient meme-replication process but something entirely different to Blackmore's first and second replicators: genes and memes.

The Third Replicator: Temes

To be fair to Blackmore, in her more recent writing she recognises that something new is abroad. At first, she writes, she thought of 'websites' and 'high-tech goods' as artificial memes, as opposed to natural memes like speech, art, music and religion (2009: 304). But she then realised that technology involves a third kind of replicator: 'These "technological memes" are riding on top of both genes and memes to form a new layer of evolution. I'd like to call them "temes." The justification is this: replicators do not evolve on their own but coevolve with the machinery that replicates them' (305). We would agree, but suggest that this has always been the case: just as we have always been posthuman, memes have been temes long before the advent of computers.

For Blackmore, this co-evolution of genes, memes and temes produces a cyborg-assemblage – a proposition which seems to us to have a surprising affinity with N. Katherine Hayles' notion of technogenesis. Blackmore's notion of an arrangement of three replicators, extended through her concept of the memeplex, produces an interesting diagram of culture in which the blind algorithms of genetic reproduction, meme and teme replication, and memeplex arrangement, are responsible for technics and technologies of all kinds (such as the wheel, hammers, steam engines, trucks and transistors) (1999: 27). It is Blackmore's conviction that the helix of genes and memes produces and supports temes, in the form of advanced technologies including automated and artificial intelligence. And it is the temes that follow the superior evolutionary mode of 'copy-the-instruction' in their competition to generate better replicators (215). While questions arise about Blackmore's notion of temes as instruments of high fidelity we are interested in the human-technology union that is maintained by non-conscious replication in this context of technological copying built upon and intimately involved with gene and meme hosts.

In Blackmore's theory, this union or structure of gene, meme and teme might be short-lived. For the best replicator, she suggests, is a digital one with an effective 'error-correction mechanisms' (215). Most importantly for Blackmore, contemporary digital technology not only stores memes but also copies them, without humans being involved in the process (308): 'the meme vehicles we have created become replication machinery for the next level of replicator. This is equivalent to the step that occurred when hominid gene machines began imitating and so became replication machinery for memes' (308).

Blackmore feels that there is no guarantee that humans will survive this development. Perhaps a post-meme-singularity fiction might be written here that imagines a future of artificial intelligences producing ever more complex meme or teme complexes. But Blackmore has little interest in this. As vehicles for memes, humans are meme machines (creations rather than creators) which may be replaced by teme machines. In this, the singularity discussed in earlier chapters is, in Blackmore's opinion, of little consequence: 'The important question is not when technology becomes more intelligent than us (what is intelligence anyway, and what kind matters?) but when the new replicators take off on their own' (Blackmore 2012). However this is yet to occur, and in the meantime, she suggests, memes and temes (defined in their widest possible sense) play an important part in human cultures and politics. A pressing question then emerges: if Blackmore is right, even partially, about the importance of imitation and memeplexes and the non-conscious power of replication in culture, is there any escape from the power of meme or teme influence? We suggest that machine fictioning might be one such route.

PART 2: THE GARDEN OF DELETE

The Weaponisation of Memes

To recap: memetic evolution, like genetic evolution, is said by Blackmore to be a mindless procedure – a phylogenetic process of selection not apparent to consciousness, whereby 'design must appear out of nowhere'. It can also be said, though, that memes adapt – and adapt to human culture and language – in a myriad of ways, including through human innovation. We return here to the question of whether Blackmore is right to insist on memes and temes being solely the result of processes that copy instructions, as a blind algorithm. Another way of putting this is to ask whether there is any relation or correspondence between non-conscious and conscious levels of the human reproduction and consumption of memes. For Steve Goodman (a.k.a. Kode9), author of *Sonic Warfare: Sound, Affect and the Ecology of Fear*, the problem with meme theory is that it elides not just the human agency involved in meme production but also 'the power relations of affective contagion'. He notes that this vector of contagion is not addressed by typical memetics, which he identifies as a 'dominant cognitive theory' of 'cultural virology' (2010: 130). He continues: 'A standard objection to cultural virologies such as memetics is that by attributing so much autonomy to networks of memes, they sideline the human labor and consciousness involved in the construction of culture' (131).

Furthermore, it can be said that if generative evolution or meta-evolution – as the 'artificial' development of the mechanisms of evolution itself – allows humans to influence species development (as discussed in Chapter 21), then a similar case can be made for generative meme and teme replication. Indeed, we find something like a meta-process of meme and teme development in the relationship between the military and entertainment industries explored by Goodman. He notes, for example, that many video games and other products presenting simulation have 'migrated back' to military contexts after establishing their place in the entertainment industries. This, he argues, is symptomatic of how 'lo-fi' warfare permeates domestic technologies and everyday life 'through psychosocial torque and sensory overload' (33–4). The algorithm of imitation alone does not explain the relationship between the military and entertainment industries, nor the power relations which result.

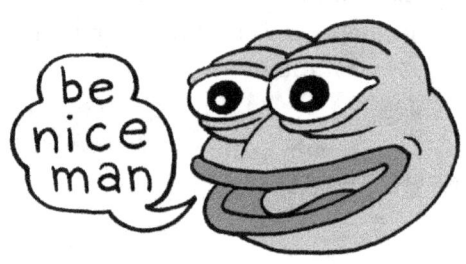

25.1 Pepe the Frog Meme posted on 4-Chan website.

It may not be that Blackmore fails to address these relations, just that she does not see them as important to her project of establishing a science of memetics, which would cast any military or entertainment industry adaptation of memes or temes as part of an evolutionary process. But in Goodman's example of the military-entertainment complex, what Blackmore calls meme and teme instructions (code) and vehicles (humans and machines) are augmented, improved and transformed for specific, human ends. Here, the supplementary goals of humans play an important role: design does not always appear out of nowhere.

A case in point would be the evolution of the Pepe the Frog meme (Figure 25.1), which has become an icon for the alt-right and was even tweeted by Donald Trump in his presidential election campaign of 2016 (there are many examples of a Trump/

Pepe the Frog meme on the internet; see Figure 25.2). Pepe began life as a laid-back cartoon character with the catchphrase 'feels good, man', first appearing in 2005 in the *Boys Club* comics (Furie 2016). The frog then began to appear in posts on the 4Chan and Reddit websites along with political captions, becoming a symbol associated with the Right soon after, to the degree that Pepe the Frog is now identified as a hate symbol by the Anti-Defamation League along with symbols like the swastika.[3] In alt-right and Neoreactionary circles, the likeness of Pepe the Frog to an Egyptian god called 'Kek' – a deity associated with destruction and chaos – added to the allure of the meme (and gave it an associated mythos). It is now circulated by many who understand that Pepe/Kek is a meme with certain affective functions,

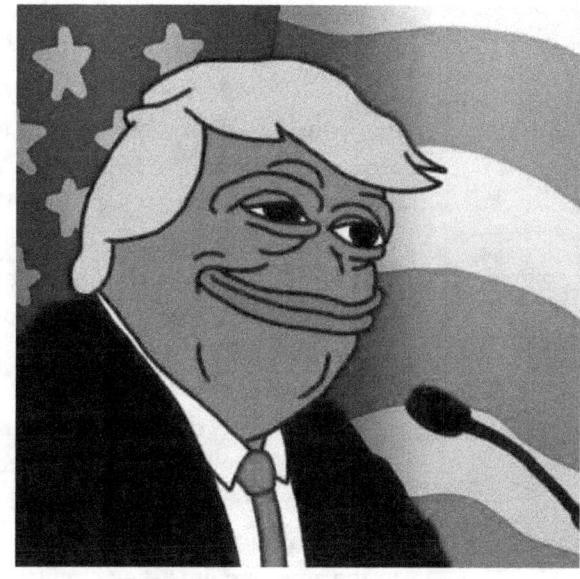

25.2 Trump/Pepe the Frog meme.

including humour and the formation of collective identifications. We suggest that the same can be said of Trump's twitter slogans – e.g. 'FAKE NEWS!!!' – and the meme-chants of Trump's supporters – 'Lock her up', 'Drain the swamp' and 'All lives matter'[4] – all rhythmic phrases which produce collectivity and enjoyment, or facilitate the venting of anger.

While the Pepe meme cannot be held responsible for the outcome of the 2016 US Presidential election, it nonetheless formed part of a memeplex which exploits and develops 'preferences, attention, emotions and desires' (Blackmore 1999: 58).[5] And if meme selection relates to emotion and preferences, it would be naive to think that humans are without knowledge about how memes work or that human design cannot influence this process. Here Blackmore might argue, as we suggested in our brief discussion of 'The Poor Image', that meme replication wins out

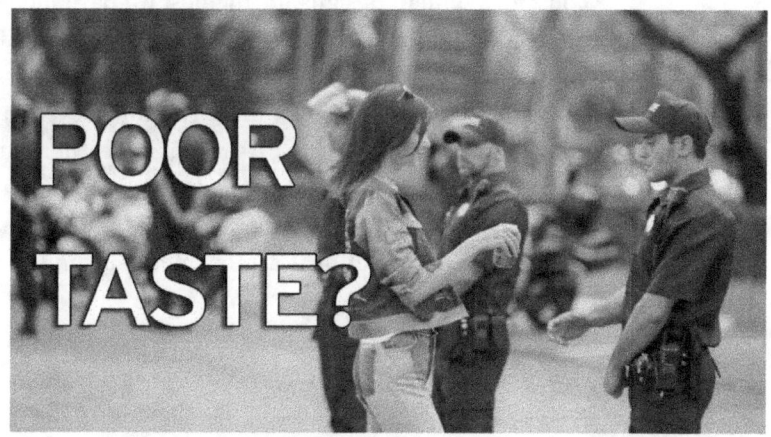

25.3 Meme making fun of Kendall Jenner handing a Pepsi to a police officer in an ill-fated Pepsi advert.

however it is produced; but the digital circulation and transformation of Pepe the Frog as a right-wing meme can also be considered a machine fictioning of a kind, as a weaponisation of meme imitation and selection modes, which is found not just in the memes of the right but also in those of their opponents. '#Black Lives Matter', for example, is another successful meme, quickly communicating a shared identity and cause. Of course, the human design of memes does not always achieve the desired results, a spectacular example being the protest-themed Pepsi advert of 2017 featuring fashion model Kendall Jenner handing a policeman the iconic beverage, a meme that was subsequently reproduced in other widely circulated satirical memes (see Figure 25.3). The problem: the advert was said to mimic photographs of protestor Leshia Evans confronting American riot police in Baton Rouge, and was thus seen as a 'cashing-in' on protest culture. A social media backlash followed: while the meme of a vulnerable female protestor continues to successfully circulate through activist images, the Pepsi advert crashed and Pepsi apologised. It might be said that this supports the idea that the memes that survive and prosper are most adequate to the environments they circulate in, but this invites the comment that such environments are political and fluid and require adaptation if the goal of replication is to be achieved, which is precisely what human producers of memes are conscious of and attempt to design for. The manipulation of media and mediation, which Blackmore somewhat discounts in her meme and teme theory, might be more important than she thinks.

Submemetic Vibrations

In addressing both the non-conscious replication of memes and temes and the conscious human designs for memes, we have identified two related levels of meme circulation and contagion: human brain to brain, and technological dissemination, with the latter engendering and enhancing the possibility of politics and resistance through meme warfare. But there is a third level which is also important in cultural contagion: the submemetic. As discussed earlier, much of Steve Goodman's analysis of sonic warfare is critical of memetics and the study of memes, which he sees as being significant but short-sighted in its failure to attend to the importance of the material or compositional arrangements of units of memes. Goodman (in relation to sonic productions) argues that:

If we probe the submemetic level, shifting the preoccupation of memetics with units onto the relations that comprise them, then these atomic components of culture reveal and are traversed by a more primary field of rhythmic vectors. The replicator would therefore become a rhythmic assemblage, an entity composed of speeds and slowness, clusters of sensation, percepts, and affects. What is depicted as a meme therefore is always already a population. (2010: 138)

It is at this submemetic level that technics can be seen to have its greatest influence, particularly on sound production, audio memes and what Goodman calls 'earworms', denoting and describing the affects of audio viruses (128). The submemetic level is not the instruction or code of the meme, nor is it the meme's vehicle; it is rather the elemental aspect of a meme or culture. Goodman suggests that submemetics requires an audio virology that 'constitutes a kind of sensual mathematics that moves past the transmission of unchanging units toward a model of the unit of replication that mutates with each copy' (139). A sensual mathematics of rhythmic contagion, he argues, stretches memetics beyond its limits, turning a meme 'inside out to reveal its ontogenetic relations' (157).[6]

Goodman presents the military as pioneers in audio techniques and technology, but suggests that through a sensual mathematics there is the possibility of resistance not only to the military and entertainment complex but also to the algorithmic meme and earworm replications of capitalist cultures. Among his examples are the experiments with submemetic vibrations found in contemporary music, most developed in the music of the Black Atlantic, which wages sonic warfare 'through dread engineering and the tactical deployment of sonic dominance' (155). Here Goodman draws heavily on the work of Kodwo Eshun, who we recall underlined the importance of technology to sonic fictions. In emphasising the role of technology and the submetic affects on the human, Goodman explores what we have been calling machine fictioning, of which there are many examples in contemporary music. In developing his notion of the submemetic Goodman is also influenced by the philosopher Alfred North Whitehead, whom he claims opens up a 'philosophy of vibrational force' (xviii). Importantly, for Goodman, Whitehead's process philosophy challenges philosophies which value the continual flow of becoming, instead asserting the importance of localised space-time (98). As Goodman explains:

If there is a rhythmanalysis implicit in Whitehead's metaphysics, then it pulls in a different direction, accounting for a rhythmic break flow or (dis)continuum, which he refers to as the *extensive continuum*. Whitehead's philosophy intervenes in two directions: first, against the overrationalizations of idealism, and second, against the appeal to raw sensation of currents of empiricism. His process philosophy results in a 'transcendental empiricism' or, to use William James's phrase, a 'radical empiricism', in which the relation between things assumes as much significance as the things themselves. (96)

Goodman's theory has some affinity with Mark Hansen's elemental notion of technological development, only Goodman is convinced that practices engaging with the submemetic can facilitate an affective politics against memetics, looping continuity into discontinuity – this is important, as digital technology or temes produce an ambient information culture which permeates human life.

An example of submemetic experimentation can be found on Goodman's music label, Hyperdub Records, in the form of the spliced and timestretched music of DJ Rashad and his collaborators. EPs such as *Rollin'* (2013) and *I Don't Give a Fuck* (2013) feature sequences of rhythms which are discontinuous or that can sound out of sync. Rashad's music seems to change speed rapidly and randomly, from slow and stretched loops to frenetic vibrations and beats. This music is associated with 'Footwork' dancing (mentioned in section one in relation to war machines as the experimental occupation of space-time). The dancing is so-called because the dancers move their legs and feet with immense speed, as if in fast-forward, or slowly, as if in slow-motion. Footwork dancing, with its athletic and acrobatic turns and twists, seems an impossible feat, and while related to traditions of dancing in Chicago, it seems to mirror the cut-and-paste and transition techniques of digital sound composition. Indeed, in both the music and dance of what is referred to as Chicago Footwork, it seems to us that a form of embodied cloning is taking place at a submemetic level.

Whether Footwork can be seen as an equivalent to the earlier experiments of the Black Atlantic – which were notably resistant to the military-entertainment complex that Goodman investigates – is perhaps debateable. But what is important is that Footwork (and similar sonic experiments and electronic dance music cultures) performs or embodies a looping of the elemental or submemetic through the digital in music and dance. In this, new human timestretchers and timeloopers emerge, operating through cloning modes which disrupt local space-time and the durational flow of time. While this may not signal an effective politics for many, Footwork does point to how new human-machine assemblages are able to acknowledge and exploit the power of memetics and in so doing possibly produce new zones of performance, or what we have earlier called war machines.

Zones Without People?

In making claims for a new and emerging kind of musician and listener, the question arises as to whether this leads to an agency or practices which are productive or reflexive rather than leading to more memetic replication. To refer back to our Postscript of Chapter 19, we might ask whether the new Nature Theatres of noise and electronic music really rival that of Kafka's noise orchestra in his novel *America*. We suggest that a number of electronic musicians do offer such new Nature Theatres, including the collaboration of Atom TM and Robin Fox entitled *Double Vision* (performed at Village Underground in London in 2015), for which around a thousand people gathered in a large railway arch to face a screen, lasers and a sound system. Atom TM and Robin Fox stood behind the crowd, seeming more like technicians than artists. During the performance, heads turn to catch the trajectory of red, blue and green laser trails (a meme of the three primary colours in light), and barrages of sound and images are registered, sometimes presenting refrains recognisable as music and words. At times, the audience, captured by the immersive presentations, signal their enjoyment; at other times though, *Double Vision* is so overwhelming that the audio and visual affects become almost solid and physical to human perception, like an abstract sculpture, and the audience find themselves outside an impenetrable concrete sonic assemblage, stranded beyond their own senses. Here we think again of Ray Brassier's notion of noise as a schizduction and flattening process; indeed, at times, attending the event feels like tiring physical labour rather than entertainment, as the work produces a reflexivity shaped by looping rhythmic and arrhythmic vibrations. At certain points, when the lasers project into the crowd, triggered by arrhythmic noise that most would not call music, it brings on an experience which feels like being spoken (down) to by a machine intelligence, in a language too fast (too mathematical) for humans to engage with. The audience is not passive, but it is not always clear how they are to receive this performance or information. Bodies try to move but are too slow or cannot find a rhythm, their movements stutter or become random. Something – having an ear for the submemetic, which perhaps triggers the memory of rhythm – moves the audience nonetheless. How to respond to such a Nature Theatre? This is the open question which *Double Vision* poses.

In a similar vein, Daniel Lopatin, a.k.a. Oneohtrix Point Never, who often collaborates and performs live with others including the artist and musician Nate Boyce, combines sonic experimentation with manipulated digital imagery to produce disorientating affects for listeners and audiences. There is a difference in approach here though too. Lopatin's compositional (or cloning) processes engender productions that are less concrete and more affective in terms of the emotional resonances of music, but his productions are also more like memeplexes disintegrating through submemetic contagion and machinic or technological processes and noise. In discussing *Garden of Delete* (2015) in an interview, Lopatin explains why he considers himself to be a 'non-musician', and that he is not sure whether having musical knowledge is important any more:

Google is trying to figure out certain AI processes that will take over human knowledge, or human skill, and probably some awkward epoch is coming where music will undergo these horrible Deep Dream interpretations. On some level, *Garden of*

Delete feels predictive of that: at times it sounds like the dumbness of machine knowledge trying to recreate music. (Oneohtrix Point Never 2015)

There are other themes discussed in this interview, including memory and its limits, fiction, and Lopatin's interest in philosophy and the work of Julia Kristeva. But it is his suggestion that – or machine fictioning of – *Garden of Delete* as the product of a non-musician, and his equating of this with non-human and non-conscious intelligence, which strikes us as important. We approach the music of Oneohtrix Point Never as a mythotechnesis which produces a strange human-machine temporality in which experience and the collapse of experience loop together, forming circuits of refrains, samples, rhythms, submemetic vibrations and noise. This perhaps explains why the music of Oneohtrix Point Never seems to move from the discordant and the arrhythmic to melancholic refrains and catchy sequences. For Oneohtrix Point Never's complex and musical composition, despite the sonic memes and earworms, are at times just as disjunctive as the more concrete and repetitive sounds and loops produced by Atom TM and Robin Fox or DJ Rashad. This manipulation of sound (which is often presented alongside imagery that has also been made strange and fragmentary) is a something Lopatin has spoken about in interviews. For example, when discussing *Replica* (2011), a work that samples pop refrains, memes and earworms – samples which Lopatin suggests capture the 'sweet spot' of commercial and advertising music (Oneohtrix Point Never 2011) – he states that he is interested in how sound influences through emotional and rhythmic registers, and at memetic and submemetic levels. As he explains:

I'm trying to make things that are manipulative in interesting ways and that are kind of open and not bracketed experiences that make people feel a certain way. I want to manipulate them subtly just to open the door, and then they can have whatever they need to have happen. (Oneohtrix Point Never 2011)

This interrogation of sweet spots, audio memes, audio viruses and submemetics is a project which Oneohtrix Point Never has been engaged with over a long period of time, and the titles Lopatin gives his recordings – such as *Returnal* (2010), *Zones Without People* (2013) and *Garden of Delete* (2015) – are perhaps revealing of his thoughts on the future of audio culture: machine fictionings that often place the listener in abstract and cloned sonic landscapes (or cinemascapes, as music made for film is also clearly an influence).

In *The Meme Machine*, Blackmore suggests that memes are more like symbionts than parasites as they encourage cooperation (1999: 160). This is a view she reiterates in later writing when she argues that:

language, like art and all of culture, is not seen as an adaptation of benefit to humans and their genes, but as a parasite turned symbiont. Indeed, all of cultural evolution is seen as happening for the benefit of the memes and in spite of posing a threat to humans and their genes. The human genes did, however, survive but the creature that was once their vehicle (i.e., the human body) gradually turned into a better and better copying machine for the new replicator – the memes. (2009: 304)

Today, though, Oneohtrix Point Never points to another adaptation of the human and machine, to the engendering of human non-musicians collaborating with machinic or machine intelligence (and to humans growing machinic eyes and ears through technics and technologies).

Blackmore's temes might be parasites or symbionts, they might leave humans behind or, indeed, destroy all replicators on Earth, including temes themselves (313). On this subject, the scientist candidly admits that she does not know the answer. The machine fictioning of Oneohtrix Point Never points to something different though: a human-machine arrangement that operates and moves through instances of discontinuity, producing modes disruptive of meme manipulation and control; a subjectivity realised through the embodied registration (and, it has to be said, through the feeling) of refrains, rhythms, vibrations and noise, and through developing and exercising copy (or cloning) and delete functions. In this way, the music of Oneohtrix Point Never points to something different from the development of zones without people – a future dominated by humanless operators and operations, which we suspect Lopatin considers a possibility – towards human adapation with machine intimates.

Notes

1   Some art historians have attributed *Fountain* to others, including two female friends of Duchamp.

2   The art theorist Thierry de Duve (1998) argues that Duchamp's readymades are both a joke – how can this nonsense be art? – and a test – how can this nonsense be art? – which divides aesthetic judgement from the question of beauty.

3   See https://www.adl.org/education/references/hate-symbols/pepe-the-frog (accessed 3/3/2017).

4   'Lock her up' refers to the investigation of Hillary Clinton's use of a private email account; 'Drain the swamp' refers to perceived corruption in Washington; and 'All lives matter' is a retort to the Black Lives Matter movement.

5   For a discussion of the political role played by memes in the recent US election see Schreckinger 2017 (thanks to Suhail Malik for this reference). See Cramer 2017 for a more general discussion of this area and, especially, of the connections and alliances of

the alt-right (with NRx for example), including its history on the 4Chan message boards and in the Gamergate controversy.

6   We note here that Goodman's sensual mathematics might be considered another form of the patheme–matheme assemblage.

26   Subjects Without a Body

Whatever his inherited memories told him, he was 'no longer'
human; he would never inhabit his real body 'again'.

Greg Egan, *Permutation City*

WHAT IF WE are wrong? What if embodiment and the libidinal or embedded cognition are not important to the future of human and machine co-adaptation? What if human bodies go the way of the Dodo and Penny Farthings, along with the perception of space-time born of human experience? We have referred to radical mythotechnic practices and assemblages as looping human and machine arrangements, as registering the non-conscious and the machinic, and as operating through various levels including the submemetic. But looping, registering and submemetic vibration are modes which belong to the realms of the analogue and embodiment. In such realms, time is material and information (at least in part) is physical or mediated. The digital does not produce loops or registration in the same way. Rather, it proceeds through lines of code, sequences of zeros and ones, links and repetitions, scans and databases. And now, digital intelligences are being developed via neural nets which compute through models or networks based on neurons in the human brain; as mentioned earlier, artificial intelligence increasingly writes its own code.

No More Loops?

If the roboticist Hans Moravec is right, humans partaking of the digital world to come will shed their analogue motor-sensory organs for more efficient hardware or modes of connection, and the brain will be augmented with effective software to the point where, as Hugo de Garis argues, its organic matter will become redundant. In this new realm, power will lie with deep machine learning, auto-replicating and auto-coding organisations of high intelligence which need neither flesh nor sense organs. To continue with this machine fictioning of zones without organic people, Blackmore's temes, as strains of code or as vehicles for code replication, would seem fit to rule Moravec's digital universe, in which physical layers of atoms or the properties of quanta – as an elemental substratum – store information or support temes as they go about their business.

We recall here Moravec's disparaging remarks concerning the survival of human experience in a digital universe, which would require 'inappropriate body simulations . . . analogous to someone in a deep diving suit plodding along among a troupe of acrobatic dolphins' (Moravec 1992). Even so, Moravec leads us to believe that humans, or at least future intelligences which evolve through the machine augmentation of humans, may survive digitalisation in some part. But these would be subjects without a body, at least in relation to the human we know today.

This raises the question of whether, in such a scenario, the disappearance of the organic body of the human might mean the end of embodiment is nigh. Of course, the human body is unlikely to disappear overnight (if it disappears at all), and it is rare that past evolutionary forms (or vehicles) do not shape new replications or replicators in some way. Certainly, the embodiment necessary for human cognition and intelligence is facilitated by much technology today. In stating this, we are aware of Hayles' application of the concept of the 'skeuomorph' (1999: 13–17), which refers to the way an object, tool or technology retains redundant components of an older form, such as a mass-produced shoe decorated with moulded (rather than actual) stitching. In audio and video software, the analogue exists as a reference for filters, effects and transitions used in the digital editing of sound and film, primarily because it allows humans to operate software in relation to their existing perceptual habits. Similarly, simulations of experience, embodiment and the body are replicated in the digital universes developed by the military-entertainment complex in the form of virtual games. A final candidate for producing future artificial life in which embodiment remains an attribute is that branch of artificial intelligence research discussed earlier which values embodied and embedded cognition. Might it be that strains of artificial intelligence and future digital avatars or teme replicators will incorporate something like analogue motor-sensory or embodied modes, as an analogue-digital skeuomorph?

This idea is not as absurd as it first sounds. A number of writers and artists have addressed this scenario (and the idea of subjects without a body), including Ed Atkins, who produces high-definition films and installations of audio and video presentations. The artist's thoughts on his work point to an important shift in the attributes of images today. In an interview relating to his 2012 exhibition at the Chisenhale Gallery in London, Atkins suggests:

High definition reality privileges the representation of texture and surface, but at the same time the 'body' of the film or video has dropped away. Even though the image itself is more concerned with physical and tactile aspects, the source of the image, the body, is no longer there – it has become ever more immaterial. (Atkins 2012)

The artist continues by speculating that to become a representation is to die, and 'in that moment you become a high-definition thing'. This Warholian diagnosis of digital film and video suggests a passing over from the material world to an immaterial realm, and, with that, a giving up of the body. While this idea has religious connotations, Atkins' proposition can be thought of as an evolutionary process, too, one in which the body is no longer captured as a mediated and material index (by 35mm negative, 16mm film, magnetic video tape, etc.) but is written as code on memory cards and other storage devices. In this way, as the artist states, 'there is nothing there'. But for Atkins, the physicality of indexical works is not banished by the digital, and he does not give up on materiality and embodiment, arguing that: 'we must still look for it, and one of the places that one might try to find this material aspect of the digital would be inside the viewer, where it would reterritorialise and become manifest' (Atkins 2012).

This notion of an 'inside' may sound naive. Certainly, throughout our book, we have been suggesting that there is no 'inside' of the human – the feeling of being inside of a body is an illusion. But if we address Atkins' 'inside' as the motor-sensory processes of a body, and as the tacit knowledge or memory of the embedded or embodied aspects of cognition, we can understand how the reterritorialisation he speaks of might occur on a virtual level, through affects which register with experience and the human's capacity for embodiment. Atkins' art, such as the work *Ribbons* (2014),[1] has dual effects which – to quote the artist commenting on previous work – 'enclose' and 'penetrate' the body of the viewer with moving images and sonic compositions (Atkins 2012). In *Ribbons*, Atkins presents a digital protagonist through (or as) a CGI simulation of the artist himself, but this high-definition avatar communicates to an audience through analogue means – via projected light and speakers which broadcast the avatar's words. Atkins' discussion of his art, particularly in relation to its sonic aspects, echoes Steve Goodman's notion of the submemetic. For example, Atkins speaks of how 'sub-bass could overawe a body; the space conjured by surround sound could transport a body. It all sounds quite violent, and perhaps it necessarily is' (Atkins 2012). It could be said, then, that Atkins' art is expressive in the same way the work of Rachel Rose is – following Steven Shaviro, it is both a symptom of, but also productive of, social and techno-genetic processes, understood as the enfolding of the digital into (analogue) human

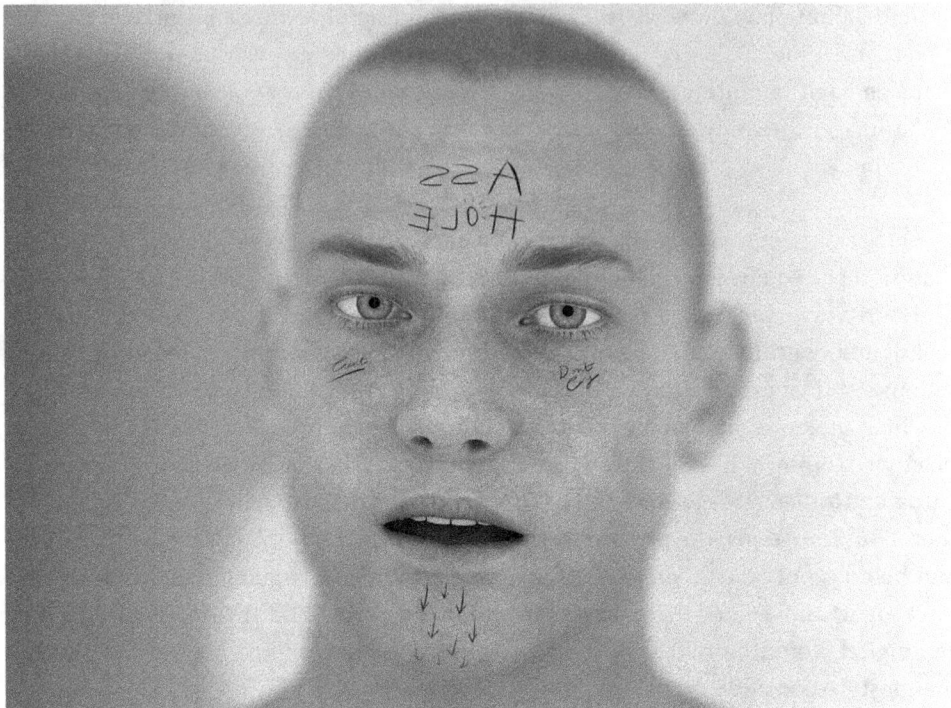

26.1 Ed Atkins, still from *Ribbons,* 2014. Three channel 4:3 in 16:9 HD video with three 4.1 channel surround soundtracks (courtesy the artist and Cabinet, London).

sense. More than this, the narratives of Atkins' film also reflect on these sympto-matic and productive processes.

The drunken digital protagonist of *Ribbons* is unmistakably a young white man, abject and full of self-loathing, with words and images drawn on his skin (see Figure 26.1). The avatar talks to the viewer in a tone which Atkins identifies as drawing on internet trolling, presenting a form of 'contemporary alienation' or 'a response to being forcefully made alien' (Atkins 2014a). At one point, the protagonist deflates like a balloon, his flesh (like his deflation) an illusion produced by digital rendering farms. Again, in commenting on *Ribbons*, the artist signals his intention to point to the limitations of digital technology and to 're-embody myself and the people watching it' (Atkins 2014a). Atkins' concern, then, is for the subject (still) with a body; but what of the digital avatar – the subject without a body which populates the artist's films? It is not clear whether, in Atkins' practice, digital avatars are being seriously proposed as a new form of human life with a perspective different to actual, analogue-bound humans.

Avatars Have Feelings Too

Atkins approaches digitalisation from the perspective of the embodied and materially embedded human viewer, lamenting and warning of the material limits of the digital – which he believes 'dreams' of the death of subjects as they turn into images. This is a serious concern for Atkins, and he goes so far as to claim that his work is 'an attack on images' (Atkins 2012). Not all artists concerned with digital and virtual avatars share this pessimistic and cruel mythotechnesis. Indeed, other artists have crossed over to the image world feeling less melancholic about a loss of materiality, and less hostile towards their digital protagonists.

Jacolby Satterwhite's work is a pertinent example here. The American filmmaker and performance artist films himself to create digital protagonists which, either individually or en masse, dance, have sex and perform in actual and virtual environments (which sometimes consist of an architecture or objects derived from drawings by the artist's mother). This latter aspect of Satterwhite's output is worth commenting on, for the artist produces landscapes which appear to be alternative or future worlds, familiar in style or rendering to games and other digitally produced entertainment products made by designers using similar software to the artist. But Satterwhite's digital realm has a very personal mythos, making his imagery not only singular but also a means of producing a layer of narrative among other layers of narrative. Satterwhite's use of his mother's lexicon of drawings/diagrams (often of everyday objects) – designs which she hoped could be patented and become a source of income – as well as the artist's use of the recordings she made of herself singing, are perhaps a form of cloning. This would be a process using the artist's personal memories as a basis for synthetic or digital life to come, free from the existing and limiting images of the future offered by past and present-day entertainment industries and artists alike. Indeed, in interview Satterwhite suggests that both his turn to his own memories and his use of his own body were ways of side-stepping art-historical references and Western art ideologies – dominant myths (or memes) – with their particular portrayal of Black subjectivity.

Satterwhite's work seems to us to be a very wild form of mythotechnesis or machine fictioning (or, perhaps better, his practice performs a wildness, as Jack Halberstam might say). All of Satterwhite's worlds and figures – and particularly those developed in the artist's most well-known film work, the six-part *Reifying Desire* (2014) – are of different scales and/or change scale and move at different speeds, like a digital *Alice in Wonderland* or a destabilised *Second Life* (see Figure 26.2). This visual complexity is accompanied by electronic music, produced by collaborators, and which, in its sampled texture, doubles the imagery. There is here a further layering of imagery and an acceleration of action which produces an hallucinogenic rush. Streams of chains, threads and beads are projected from different avatars and link

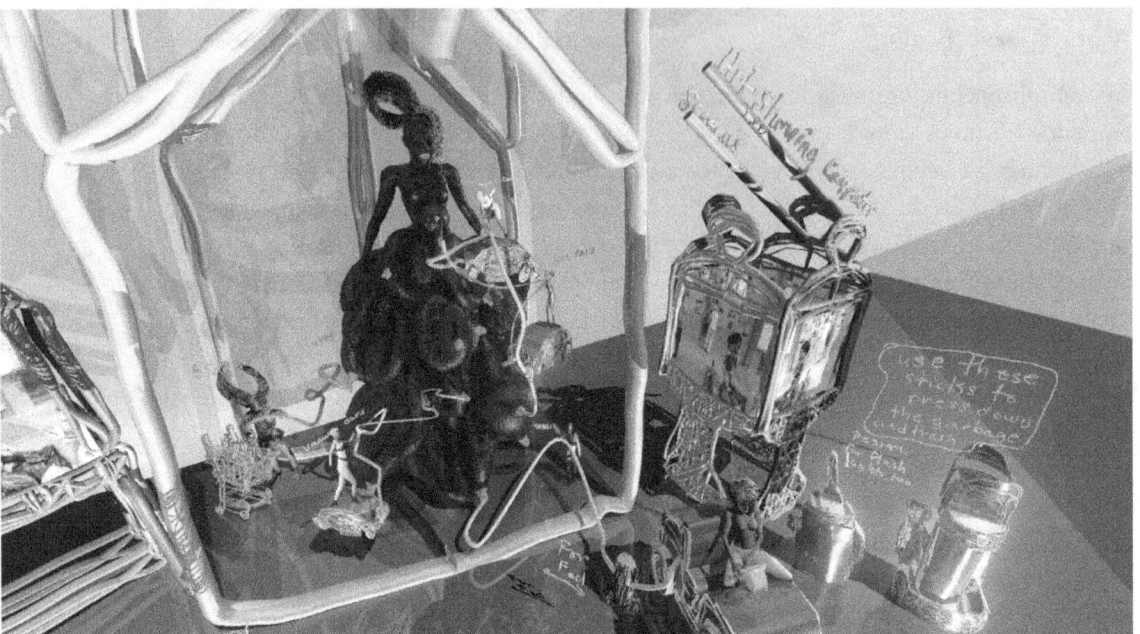

26.2 Jacolby Satterwhite, still from *Reifying Desire 6*, 2013 (courtesy of the artist and Moran Bondaroff, Los Angeles).

together various objects, some of the imagery appearing similar to scientific diagrams of molecular combination.

Although the artist draws upon family influences, Satterwhite's references are diverse and, in part, draw upon time spent gaming and hacking. Satterwhite is of a generation equally at home in new forms of digital culture as in any reality off-screen. In the *Reifying Desire* series, he presents libidinally charged scenarios which portray a queer sexuality alongside other more inhuman encounters and connections (for example an abstract and machinic immaculate conception scene in *Reifying Desire 3*). In an interview with Evan Moffitt for *Frieze* magazine (Satterwhite and Moffitt 2016), Satterwhite draws attention to the impact AIDS (and the practice of 'barebacking') had on his work, but also the importance of other key archives such as Outsider Art (and there is indeed something about the sometimes cramped and chaotic spaces in the films which looks to the latter). Hip-hop, voguing and porn are also influences, the artist's collaborators including rapper Trina and gay porn star Antonio Biaggi – the latter taking part in a sexual encounter with Satterwhite which was later turned into an animation. In an interview conducted by Charlie Ross relating to his involvement in the 2014 Whitney Biennale, Satterwhite suggested that his films are about bringing disparate archives into conjunction and thus making differences congruent (Satterwhite and Ross 2014). We can say, then, that a combinatory logic is at play in his mythotechnic practice.

Despite the real-world sources of Satterwhite's animated environments and the inclusion of filmed events in his pieces, he describes his work as producing abstraction, which he explains when discussing *Reifying Desire*:

> I was interested in how one person could concretize abstraction, because reification is about concretizing abstraction. It's about making something unnatural and indefinable concrete. The whole oxymoron is that I never achieve specificity in my work, ever. It never concretizes; it just gets more abstract. (Satterwhite and Small 2014)

This concern for 'concretizing abstraction' is visible in the actions and choreography of the chroma-keyed, motion-captured, morphed and blended bodies which grace the digital and social worlds of Satterwhite's animations – worlds which appear purposeful but with a logic of machinic operations that escapes the viewer. Here, we would suggest that Satterwhite's films are involved in developing a new kind of language or syntax through digitally manipulating images of the body, one in which objects become subjects just as subjects become objects (there is a kind of generalised digital animism at play). The artist has referred to Gertrude Stein in relation to his work, suggesting that the use of his own body in his films operates as a punctuation mark (Satterwhite and Moffitt 2016). In fact, it seems to us that the figures, objects and links construct a strange non-linear syntax of sorts, one which is then overlaid with Satterwhite's own digitally rendered handwriting, which adds a further level of visual and semiotic complexity. The artist's body appears here as a medium or material for abstraction like any other, but it is no less authentic as a body for all that when in non-material or digital form (and this is perhaps where we see a machine fictioning of a subject with and without a physical body). As he explains:

> I'm always testing out the potential to mediate the body between these technologies but my body is definitely an extremely necessary component. But the thing is, it's only a component. I don't build illusions around the body. What my body is doing [on screen], that's real. (Satterwhite and Small 2014)

The notion that Satterwhite's body on screen is real, or is engaged in real life and actions in digital form, raises questions about whether this physical performer-becoming-virtual-image has evolved from embodied and social life as much as from the possibilities offered by technologies of digital replication. Certainly, it can at least be said that Satterwhite does not discriminate between digital and analogue life, and in his utilisation of his own body (and his drawings and handwriting) we might also say that there is a hybridity at work between the analogue (or low tech) and the digital (or high tech). Other binaries are disrupted and played with in the *Reifying Desire* series: the machine/

body (Satterwhite as cyborg), but also the binaries of masculine/feminine and black/white. Although his films are concerned with a queer Black body, there is a sense in which Satterwhite's worlds, with their morphing bodies and strange conjunctions, gesture towards a posthuman realm which is post-race and, indeed, post-gender.

If we recall that Google's head of engineering, Ray Kurzweil, has proposed that in the future the brain will be scanned by nanobots, then our propositions about Satterwhite's posthumanism may not seem so far-fetched. And surely it is not so hard to imagine that new digital, disembodied life will be accepted into human society, even if it is the society of art or the art world? Indeed, returning to Stelarc, and following an encounter with his *Prosthetic Head* (2003), we would argue that this at least seems plausible. Stelarc's digital protagonist is an interactive image with real-time recognition and response, presented as a large projection; the work is also recognisable as a dramatisation of the Turing test.[2] The artist describes *Prosthetic Head* as an 'embodied conversational agent' rather than an artificial intelligence, which humans can interact with by asking questions through a keyboard, becoming aware of their own habits in moments when the conversation falters (Stelarc n.d.). For Stelarc, embodiment is problematised when a body is not defined by 'the coherence of its individuality' but by 'the multiplicity of its collaborating agents', making the conductivity, interface and operation of the body more important than its identity, location and mobility (Stelarc n.d.).

Stelarc's assertion that the digital body concerns conductivity, interfaces and modes of operation is echoed in the films of Ryan Trecartin, which as we noted earlier are often produced in collaboration with Lizzie Fitch and others. Recall the example of the avatar Twi-Key, the office-space oracle, discussed in Chapter 20, who's name is derived 'from an editing term, "keying", which is used to abstract a visual structure to enable the compositing of space' (Trecartin 2011). Trecartin suggests that Twi-Key's existence is best understood as a 'temporary state'; when asked about this in an interview, he suggests that 'We're all networked and we're maintaining our own discrete networks of multiple selves, too . . . and we're moving towards more corporeal expressions of this. Versions of yourself layered together might actually be an emerging form of collaboration' (Trecartin 2011).

This returns us to some of the themes we discussed in relation to financial fictions and their futures, in particular that of compression and the linking and synching of avatars and spaces (to other avatars and spaces), and, indeed, avatars themselves becoming digital spaces. In Trecartin and Fitch's work, various versions of a character are compressed into layers (the latter a process familiar to users of Adobe Photoshop and other software), producing a 'body' as an area with interfaces. Compression is also found in the behaviour and voices of Trecartin's avatars as they interact at great pace and speak in high-pitched tones – something the artist relates to how the voice in pop music 'keeps rising' beyond 'human range'. This is not a concern for transcending time, though, but the result of an interest in the 'transformative possibilities of information', which Trecartin links to evolutionary processes:

> Clearly we're going to evolve into something beyond what we are now, so it doesn't really matter . . . Once technology makes it possible to alter our brains, we're going to. Not everyone will. There will be more than one species of what are now humans. That split might follow class lines. Who knows? In the past couple of years I've felt like the outcome is not set. I feel more angst and anger than usual. (Trecartin 2013)

This notion of an evolutionary and transitional process producing angst-ridden digital characters is typical of Trecartin's film work. As noted in Chapter 20, in *CENTRE JENNY* (2013), we learn that avatars have evolved from animations, just as birds have evolved from dinosaurs. In an interview in 2016, Trecartin explains: 'Animation is part of our evolutionary arc as a species; it's still primitive – the seeds of a complicated relationship that we're going to have with artificial intelligence.' For us this radical fictioning and mythotechnesis – in which human-machine adaptation leads to an evolution of the human as animation or virtual avatar – may produce a low-class resident of Moravec's information economy. But the behavior, speech and actions of Trecartin's avatars suggest that embodiment might not disappear altogether in a digital universe, should it come to pass: inappropriate simulations (in more ways than one) of embodied human experience survive. On this matter, Trecartin has his own concerns:

> As far as the body is concerned, there's a lot of tension in the videos between the way the characters want to believe their world works and the way it actually works. I like that there's also friction between the video worlds and the world we live in. I keep this transparent. I'm not creating a world completely divorced from the current human body. (Trecartin 2011)

We suggest that this friction, produced by the body in the digital realm, is an important aspect of Trecartin's machine fictioning of digital people to come, but it is also found in the work of all the artists discussed in this chapter: their subjects cannot be said to truly exist without a body (virtual avatars have living body doubles). To find a society of subjects without bodies, we have to look elsewhere, for example to Greg Egan's Science Fictions and especially his novel *Permutation City* (2010a).

The Story of a Subject Without a Body

Permutation City begins with the nightmare of a human finding that they have been scanned and now reside in a digital simulation of limited quality. In Egan's novel,

Paul Durham wakes to unexpected brightness, his bedroom is sunlit and dust motes are visible in the shaft of light falling on his bed. Enjoying the moment he thinks about drifting back to sleep, but the feeling he has done something foolish steadily overtakes his good mood until he remembers. Durham has scanned himself, and the Durham experiencing the late morning sun is a copy, a simulation, as is the perfect rendering of the late morning sun. He wonders how he knows he is a copy, and hopes that he is mistaken, but when an interface window appears in front of him and hovers in mid-air he knows that he will never again inhabit his body. He thinks of the original Paul Durham on the outside, enjoying life, while Paul Durham the copy remains trapped in his virtual prison, which is seventeen times slower than actual life due to the expense of running the simulation. Durham cannot afford to run a real-time simulation, and communication between digital and actual realms is frustrating, with the original Durham viewing the simulated Durham as if in slow-motion (the opposite of Trecartin's digital characters). The copy catches a glimpse out the window and sees Sydney harbour, but knows this is a cheap recording – not a high-res simula-tion – and decides it is time to bale. (We are told that this is common amongst all who have been scanned and do not have a terminal illness; most decide to bale within their first fifteen virtual minutes of simulated existence.) Durham the copy chooses the utilities menu, then the emergency tab, and selects a parachute icon which will allow him to terminate (commit suicide). To the copy's horror, Durham the original has altered the utilities after he scanned himself: the copy can no longer bale (Egan 2010a: 1–9). As the story progresses we learn that the original Durham builds a simulated world – called Permutation City – for the rich, and following the suicide of the physical or real-life Durham, only the digital copy of Durham survives. The immortal, digital copy takes up residence in Permutation City, a narrative trajectory which seems to iterate Ed Atkins' notion that high-definition images dream of, or desire, the death of their subjects.

It is important to note that Durham the copy loses no sense of embodiment; he feels and experiences just like the original. It is not surprising then that N. Katherine Hayles is interested in Egan's writing, commenting in depth in *My Mother Was a Computer* (2005) on Egan's narrative of a post-biological and digital world of conscious avatars in which human copies can upload (become) identities, subjectivities and representational forms of all kinds. Hayles confesses that she wishes she liked Egan's fictions less, for they explore many ideas which she opposes, including the scanning of humans for the purpose of inhabiting virtual worlds where embodiment is an option or a programme (2005: 214). A disturbing example of this – disturbing, that is, for fleshy, analogue humans convinced they have free will – is an episode in the virtual life of the avatar Peer, who has secretly stowed away in Permutation City and runs a programme which makes him happy when working and shaping wood. Egan depicts the happy avatar as joyously producing an ever-growing pile of lovingly shaped table legs (a comforting meme for an immortal teme perhaps): the programme is set to run forever, on repeat, which it does until Peer is interrupted by a message from another stowaway (Egan 2010a: 275–6). Hayles' criticism of Egan's fiction – and this scenario of coded eternal happiness in digital life (and indeed, of Egan's view of human consciousness in general) – is that it promotes the 'Regime of Computation', which she defines as:

> A narrative that accounts for the evolution of the universe, life, mind, and mind reflecting upon mind by connecting these emergences with computational processes that operate both in human-created simulations and in the universe understood as software running on the 'Universal Computer' we call reality. (2005: 27)

According to Hayles, this narrative leads, for some, to a division of life into carbon and silicon strands, which in turn leads to an expanded form of biology and a way of thinking in which 'the meaning of "life" would shift significantly' (216). This analysis has some resonance with our discussion of the work of Ed Atkins and Jacolby Satterwhite and the collaborations of Lizzie Fitch and Ryan Trecartin. These artists present the silicon and digital beings of the 'Regime of Computation' (or of simulated or artificial life) in precarious, symbiont or evolutionary relation with carbon-based life forms. That is, all life forms in their work seem to exist through embodied and embedded cognition and motor-sensory processes, or at least their simulation. The impression is that the processes of compression which produce digital life may not be reversible but are just as real (just as full of affects and what we might call pathemic events) as non-digital life, just as they are for Durham the copy in Egan's novel. So, we ask, is an embodied and digital existence a possible future?

Orders of Embodiment

To return to the question raised at the beginning of the chapter: Are we wrong about the future of embodiment? Is a disembodied human existence (or simulated embodiment) a possible or even necessary outcome of human-machine coevolution? Can there be such a thing as a subject (and an embodied subject) without a body? In *My Mother Was a Computer*, Hayles, while still strongly critical of Moravec and others who promote a Computational Universe, seems more accommodating than in her earlier writings of the idea of scanning humans in preparation for life in simulated environments. Egan's fiction, she says, 'invites us to think about how far the entanglement of humans and computers can and should go' (2005: 214). Taking on board the predictions of Moravec and others, Egan's fictions no longer sound as far-fetched as they might at first seem – indeed, it might be that the co-adaptations or unions of human and machine would involve simulated environments (machine fictionings) and the development of embodiment as an auto-regulating programme. To explore this idea further, it is important to first understand the relation between intelligence, embodiment and consciousness. We have already addressed these themes in earlier chapters, but for further clarification we now turn to some studies by scientists and philosophers concerned with embodied cognition, although with a different focus to Varela and colleagues concerned with neurophenomenology discussed earlier.

Malte Schilling and Holk Cruse, writing about artificial intelligence research in 'The Evolution of Cognition – From First Order to Second Order Embodiment', address the relation of high-level knowledge systems capable of generating representation with low-level, 'strictly sensor driven reactive systems', which they identify as first-order embodiment (Schilling and Cruse 2008: 77). To mark out a context for their discussion the scientists note that an important change in thinking about intelligence occurred when research revealed that first-order embodied systems – organisations without any internal state or representational system – were able to solve problems that required intelligence by using the existing world 'as its own best model' (78). This event in the study of intelligence is significant for Schilling and Cruse as they are predominantly concerned with developing a model which explores the relation between reactive systems and a model of second-order embodiment. This latter model, they explain, has specific attributes: 'From our point of view, we call the model as such simulated or second order embeddedness, because the body and some aspects of the environment are simulated in such a way that the model represents the critical physical properties in sufficient detail' (79). They argue that to produce an organisation which is a cognitive system, more than an internal model (or simulated or second-order embodiment) is required; for planning – facilitated by an internal model or representation – 'requires the ability to apply actions to such models being decoupled from the body' (79). That is, second-order embodiment – internal representations – may be a prerequisite for cognitive functions, but they in turn require first-order embodiment, in which 'the body itself is detached from the controlling system' so as to act in the world (79–80). This is important to Schilling and Cruse as they are convinced that the neural nets used for developing the motor control of first-order embodiment systems in artificial intelligence can be used for the development of language and representation in second-order embodiment systems (104). The significance of this is that first-order embodiment is 'shown not to be only some additional and separate form of "motoric" intelligence, but to be strongly related to higher level cognition and to constitute their fundamentals' (104). A case is being made here for the importance of cognition – and simulated, internal models – being grounded in non-computational modes which react to environments. Cognition through representational models or simulations requires a body too; that is, a sensor-driven reactive system. In relation to our discussion of *Permutation City*, then, doubt is cast on the replication of embodied, digital life, for it seems that embodiment and cognition cannot develop from representation or computation alone.

That said, Schilling and Cruse borrow terms from Thomas Metzinger who, while acknowledging the importance of first-order embodiment, develops a different perspective on the problem. In his essay 'First-order Embodiment, Second-order Embodiment, Third-order Embodiment', Metzinger lays out three concepts of embodiment which he abbreviates by using the letter E and a number:

> Each of these concepts picks out a rather well-defined class of systems: 1E-systems are reactive, adaptive systems, achieving intelligent behavior without explicit computation; 2E-systems increase their level of causal self-control by explicitly and holistically representing themselves as embodied; and 3E-systems integrate certain aspects of their body model into a unified ontology, thereby elevating them to the level of conscious experience. (2014: 272)

Metzinger comments that any human walking down the street would be a member of all three classes at the same time (272). He also notes, though, that there are 'alternative configurations' when the three embodiments may not all be in play – including 'dreamless sleep, epileptic absence seizures, dreaming, or experimentally induced full-body illusions' – which Metzinger suggests draws attention to questions concerning the 'grounding relations' between the orders of embodiment (272). The focus of these questions concerns the relation of computation and the mechanics that produce what might be thought to be a phenomenal self-model (a phenomenologically derived sense of self and the body, as discussed in section one) when grounded in 'low-level physical dynamics' (272). What Metzinger questions is whether first-order embodiment is necessary for the production of a phenomenal-self-model, and therefore whether material or physical existence or experience is necessary for a sense of self or self-consciousness.

Pursuing this question through a schema of embodiment similar to Schilling and Cruse's, Metzinger observes that examples of first-order embodiment (1E) systems are found in bio-robotics which take a bottom-up approach to artificial intelligence, producing entities which are reactive and exhibit intelligence without explicit computation, responding to the physical environment without producing representations (272–3). In contrast, second-order embodiment (2E) systems 'represent themselves as embodied' and possess a body model (273). Amongst second-order bodies, Metzinger includes advanced robots, many animals, sleep-walking humans or humans exhibiting complex behavior during epileptic absence seizures. These examples of 2E-systems use topological and unconscious body models for motor control (273–4), and Metzinger comments that this is interesting as research shows that second-order embodiment can operate in both physical and virtual environments. The importance of this is that the 2E-systems might simulate and predict and learn behaviours which a physical body could then test (whereas 1E-systems can only adapt). Third-order embodiment – a 3E-system – not only produces a body model 'but also maps some of the representational content generated in this process onto the level of conscious experience' (274). Metzinger suggests that third-order embodiment is found in the waking states of conscious humans but also in dream-states, out-of-body experiences or full-body illusions. Interestingly for our discussion of *Permutation City*, he confirms that 3E-systems 'would then have an online model of their own body as a whole, which has been elevated to the level of global availability and integrated with a single spatial situation model plus a virtual window of presence' (274).

Metzinger suggests that a number of observations can be drawn from research addressing 3E-systems, including that they operate in dreams, producing a sense of embodiment when the body is passive or sleeping. What interests Metzinger is whether the embodied experiences of dreamers, specifically lucid dreamers, are grounded in the physical body or in an experience of environments (275). If the body is inert in dreams, he asks, are 3E-systems operating in dreams fully embodied (275)? If not, then Metzinger will have found an example of disembodied existence or consciousness able to activate a model of a body in a model of space, without responding to an actual space. We suggest that this example of lucid dreaming detached from the physical realm might give credence to the fiction of *Permutation City* as a potential model for human development: the production of subjects without a body which nonetheless experience embodiment might be possible.

However, as Metzinger continues his discussion of research into lucid dream states, it becomes clear that 3E-systems operating in dreams do not offer the example of disembodied existence he had once hoped they would. The research reveals that the physical eye movements of lucid-dreaming humans correlate to the eye movements of the 3E-system operating in a lucid dream. Not only this, in various experiments lucid dreamers are able to communicate or register stimuli (which they confirm later when awake); and this lucid-dreaming registration of physical stimuli links low-dynamic systems of the physical body (and actual motor processes) to the higher, representational system of third-order embodiment active in lucid dreams (275–6). For Metzinger, this seems to question the possibility of declaring the existence of a virtual embodiment disconnected from first-order and second-order embodiment in dreams, for the results of the research appeal to the idea that bodies in dreams have a 'real-bodily basis' (277). At least, Metzinger states, such experiments cast doubt on his earlier theory that dreams are a real-world example of embodied or bodily experience arising from a disembodied state (277). He does point out, though, 'that 3E in the absence of 1E and 2E is not impossible; but . . . its existence would be hard to establish empirically' (277). In fact, he seems to agree with Schilling and Cruse here: 'First-order embodiment describes a different class of systems than 2E and 3E. Therefore, it would be logically possible to have systems exhibiting 2E and/or 3E, but not 1E. In our world, however, 3E and 2E "ride" on 1E' (277).

It would seem that Egan's fictions could be destined to remain just that – fictions. Virtual embodiment for humans produced solely through disembodied states seems doubtful, and *Permutation City*, in which subjects die and become images, is a dream (or nightmare, depending on your perspective) unlikely to come to pass. In what seems a parody of Egan's bodiless avatars, Metzinger suggests that:

> Perhaps we could imagine Cartesian souls in heaven, constantly misrepresenting themselves as embodied, dreaming the dream of incarnation. But their dreams and their misrepresentations would then be ungrounded in any sort of physical history or dynamics, and it may be difficult to understand how they could be about spatial and temporal properties in the first place, how ungrounded semantic content is possible. (278)

In the light of such criticism of idealist virtual embodiment, the experiences of the avatars of *Permutation City* begin to slip and slide. Perhaps no embodied human-virtual-avatars would survive such a digital and dematerialised existence, and soon Moravec's disembodied digital dolphins – functioning without inappropriate simulations of embodiment or of a world produced by the senses – would eat Egan's avatars for breakfast.

If his enquiry into disembodiment seems to have run aground, Metzinger remains interested in exploring whether it is logically possible to have some level of disembodied existence or consciousness. He observes that there might be such a mode even if there is no observable or repeatable evidence for autonomous 3E-systems (278). And this exploration of embodied and disembodied states aids the exploration of potential relations of intelligence. Metzinger is interested in the possibility of a third-order embodiment devoid of (representational) 2E-systems which produce body models. If third-order embodiment cannot operate alone, he asks, 'Can 1E and 3E be simultaneously instantiated in a single system, can we have bodily self-consciousness without any form of representation?' (278). It is a question which returns us to the philosopher's interest in a nemocentric subject, but as a novel synching of real-body processes and computational models. However, this remains an open question, as Metzinger is not sure whether without a fully integrated body model (combining the three orders of embodiment) self-consciousness is possible. What he hopes for is an improved system (or subjectivity defined by a third-person perspective) to emerge in the future, in which third-order embodiment has to become part of a 'much larger process', which would lead to a subject grounding itself in a 'new way' (282).

In this regard, it is interesting to contemplate whether Atkins, Satterwhite and Trecartin and Fitch – by continuing to explore the relation of human subjectivity and the human body to high-definition imagery, CGI, animation or virtual environments – in some way point towards an investigation of the higher degrees of embodiment and autonomy, or perhaps, more generally, to a subject grounding itself in a new way. That is, each artist, through singular and radical mythotechnic machine fictionings, produces new human-machine, body-image unions, in which virtual subjects ride on or result from real bodies. In this they can be said to be exploring the limitations, potential and autonomy of a technogenetic co-adaptation of embodiment and computation. Their people to come promise to be diverse. The machine fictioning of their evolution – as we suggest for the idea of keeping humans in the loop of AI development – is an ethico-aesthetic concern.

Postscript: (Quantum) Dust

At another level entirely, Egan offers a further idea worthy of our attention, one which Hayles, though critical of post-biological or digital life, acknowledges as posing an interesting problem. We note that Egan might view death as an option rather than the inevitable conclusion of life as, in *Permutation City*, technology facilitates the production of disembodied subjects which need no longer fear mortality. Responding to this idea, Hayles suggests that in Egan's novel death appears in an alternate form to the expiring body (we are reminded of the themes of Prometheanism and finitude discussed in the first chapter of this section). Hayles observes that Durham the copy submits to experiments in which his consciousness is generated at different speeds or is made discontinuous by the original Durham, but Durham the digital avatar still experiences consciousness as continuous (2005: 223). An avatar produced by a simulation does not register interruptions – little deaths – in the flow of consciousness: as the simulation pauses and plays so does the consciousness of the digital subject. This is an idea which has an affinity with the attributes of actual consciousness; as we have already discussed, Metzinger points out that consciousness disappears and reappears, along with a sense of self, during and after sleep. Furthermore, the simulation which produces Durham the copy, like all experimental simulations concerned with emergent phenomena, proceeds through computation, and Hayles notes that Durham understands there is a specific problem with this process: a simulation which runs backwards and then forwards does not necessarily produce the same results each time. Continually running a simulation in reverse and then forward again produces permutations; new paths along parallel realities can be taken. To account for this, Durham argues that consciousness is discrete and discontinuous – that is, consciousness is constructed from 'dust' (random noise). The novel explores this idea through a baroque plot development to assert that actual consciousness is an 'operating system running on the Universal Computer' (Hayles 2005: 225). Hayles does not comment much on this idea, but she notes that Durham's dust theory is explored by Egan in another form, as the 'many worlds' theory of quantum physics, in *Quarantine* (Egan 2010b). In relation to this notion of digital-dust individuation (if such a term is permissible) – which we propose is also a form of cloning that produces the same but as permutation – we cannot help but again turn to the work of Atkins, Satterwhite and Trecartin and Fitch, particularly Trecartin's notion of numerous versions of a subject existing in layers and as a collaboration between multiple selves. Indeed, all of the artists discussed in this chapter continually produce simulations of themselves or their collaborators, and each new high-definition, motioned-captured, animated or manipulated and virtual character is a permutation. Our interest here is not only that such permutations escape organic death, as avatars rather than fleshy mortal bodies, but also that they are unconcerned with mortality and immortality, for they are not singular continuous-conscious-subjects but permutations. We suggest that with this idea a radical mythotechnesis as a machine fictioning is developed, with the possibility of realising the discontinuity and permutations of consciousness and identity through technology and mediation – which problematise the illusions of the continuity of the self, and which generate or fiction new human-machine life and perspectives.

Notes

1   *Ribbons* is a sound and video work exhibited alongside analogue works such as drawings, and was presented at the Serpentine Gallery London in 2014.
2   See https://www.youtube.com/watch?v=Nym8hfNI9Gg (accessed 15/4/2016).

Afterword

There is no genuine philosophy, there are only philosophies,
plural, with no one having privileged status over the other,
none that are merely empirical while others are a priori.

John Mullarkey, *Post-Continental Philosophy: An Outline*

AT THE END of this book, we find ourselves back at the beginning, for on completing the writing of the last page of our last chapter, we realise we still have questions. Or rather, having addressed a number of practices and theories, we realise that we have no definite idea of what might come next. We have a sense of the potential future worlds and modes of existence speaking to us through past and contemporary writing, art and music – a sense which has guided us from the start – but whether such practices will actually produce new people, subjectivities, societies and lives that will take hold, or only yet more unrealised virtual futures, is not so clear to us.

From a certain perspective, then, our book has offered a survey of practices and theories which, although at times appearing wild or novel in their juxtaposition, are addressing themes that are increasingly prevalent in contemporary art scenes and debates. These are urgent and troubling themes that include: the problem of the fiction of the self that is mobilised for many interests (which relates to the agency of individuals and collectives in a globalised context); the problem of the decolonisation of thought and of the relation of humans to other species and the environment (which is without doubt related to the Western and capitalist exploitation of the Earth); and lastly, a similar concern for human development in relation to the cybernetic intensification of environments, intelligence and life. This foregrounding of specific themes and questions would make our book appear to be an academic work, one that delivers explanations, descriptions and exegesis as well as argument and interpretation. But seen from another angle or vantage point, from the side as it were (or, at least, from outside of this scholarly endeavour), something else comes into focus – as if the book were a document of a journey, or itself a performance, through different landscapes, societies, ecologies and temporal zones.

We confess that this anamorphic aspect of the book came as something of a surprise, dawning on us as we finished organising and reading through the chapters.[1] The book is not really, or at least not only, an academic work but a parade of sometimes shadowy, sometimes iridescent images and figures that only come into focus from the vantage point of fiction or Science Fiction (rather than philosophy per se). It is these images and figures – avatars of other pasts and futures to come – that have emerged from our research and discussions, forming a long procession that includes: pioneers of chemically induced time travel and scientists of self-obliteration, pilgrims and standing stones and contemporary antipodeans, surveyors of future past landscapes and haunters of ruins, chaos magicians and communes (in which everyone knows their real name), animal-humans and critter-kin, sonic viruses (with alien ancestry) and inhuman tricksters, vampires and genetically modified or augmented humans, intelligent machines and human-machine assemblages, transgender software programmes and xenosexualities, the congregations of new nature theatres and a snake that is also a positive feedback loop, the nemocentric subject without experience and subjects without a body. It is in this procession that we find different expressions of the themes of our book.

The three myth-functions around which we have gathered both our research and the avatars mentioned above – mythopoesis, myth-science and mythotechnesis – pose for us a series of specific but related questions about the future. Through attending to mythopoesis we outlined the problem of control in Western and capitalist societies (including the colonisation of other people but also time), and then presented works by various artists, writers and counter-cultures that, in responding to this problem, fully mobilise fiction as a technology to seek out and instantiate other subjectivities, relations and worlds against that which exists. Whether the mobilisation of residual and past cultures, of privileged points in the landscape and of non-Western narratives within Western contexts continue to be effective or desired is an open question for us. As too is the efficacy of analogue technologies such as the cut-up and tape and film edit, or experimentations with the body as a technology through drug taking and ritual. No doubt there is the potential in such practices for individual reward, and possibly an escape from technological intensification and globalised culture, but there is not necessarily an effective resistance to exploitative forces if those who believe time and space are running out are right. In fact, it seems to us that this is also a question of what happens to time and history (and with that, to subjectivity) in the flattening and spatialising processes of digital life, cybernetic intensification and globalisation, which attack or appropriate the material and strategies of the radical avant-gardes of the twentieth century. Mythopoetic practices would at least seem to approach time and the past as a resource with which to make small holes – vacuoles of a different time – in the networks of mass communication, consumer culture and cybernetic regulation. In this, libidinal engineering and experimentation with embodiment, as well as autonomy and autopoetic becoming, are all at stake.

Myth-science introduces related but different problems and practices which question autonomy and any becoming premised on univocality, as well as some of the exotic and fabulous images we explored in section one. The shift here is from a view of art practice as productive of multiple worlds to an orientation promoting the idea that the universe is seen or inhabited through multiple and diverse perspectives and models. We find this in the decolonisation of thought, in which dominant traditions and habits concerning culture and nature are challenged, but also in the work of feminist and queer artists and writers and of those who question how science and philosophy might each claim a privileged access to reality. What many myth-science practices share is a commitment to Science Fiction, and, with that, a science fictioning of perspectives, para-spaces and alternative realities – projections of desired futures or alternate perspectives that are looped into, and transformative of, the present. The stakes of myth-science are different to mythopoesis, then, involving the potential of (fictioning) different viewpoints and models to fracture and collapse any dominant or universalising viewpoint on reality. This is not undertaken in the cause of multiculturalism, cultural relativism or pluralism, or even democracy exactly, but for the recasting of perspectives (against so-called reality) with the idea that through such practices, relations and even points of view can be deformed and transformed.

With the practices and philosophical orientations explored in mythotechnesis – addressing automated and artificial life and intelligence and the broader question of the relation of humans, machines and technology – we return to some of the concerns articulated in sections one and two of our book. These include the problem of the fiction of the self and the future of libidinal engineering, as well as the future of the body and embodiment. For new technological environments and developments not only exploit and augment the human senses and body but also introduce disembodied modes of communication and performance as online life. There are then new forms of (artificial) life, or at least

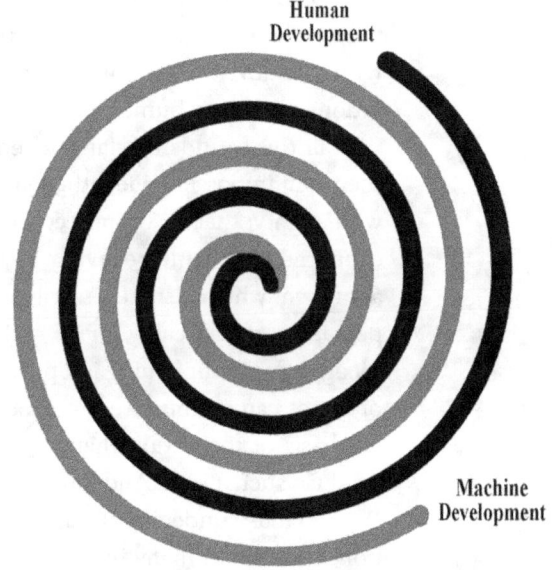

27.1 Diagram of N. Katherine Hayles' Double Spiral of Technogenetic human–machine coadaptation becoming a single spiral (credit: the authors).

new intelligences on the planet, and therefore new perspectives. Technology as the mediator of human life is nothing new, but with the exponential advance of cybernetic and digital environments the double spiral of human and machine co-adaptation proposed by Hayles may become a single spiral (see Figure 27.1) – or the two strands might become close enough to seem so – with Spinoza's famous statement concerning the as yet unknown potential of the body recast accordingly: we do not know what the human-machine assemblage might become.

As mentioned in a note above, something like this trajectory is proposed by John Johnston in *The Allure of Machinic Life: Cybernetics, Artificial Life, and the New AI*, which explores the development of liminal machines that can be said to 'inhabit or "live" in a strange, newly animated realm, where the biosphere and artefacts from the human world touch and pass into each other, in effect constituting a "machinic phylum", producing a 'new realm' in which 'nature and technology will no longer be distinctly opposed' (Johnston 2008: 1). Johnston suggests that the machinic realm is alluring not because machines copy nature but because they now present a complexity of behaviour that is completely new (2–4). When this involves or transforms and effects human behaviour – when adaptation takes place – we might call this a tech-nogenetic singularity which (following our suggestion in section three that singularities need radicalising) marks multiple, complex and incalculable events taking place in the daily lives of humans. But it also invites the observation that a human becoming with or through machines might be a trajectory and a decision (at least in terms of the acceleration and acceptance of co-adaptation) similar to, but perhaps in tension with, the development of human and multi-species societies (in so far as both orientations challenge human-centricism without abandoning the human).

If all this sounds too far-fetched, if treating machines and bacteria as social agents seems an impossible idea, then, as implied above, we admit to proceeding *as if* fiction were reality; that is, we proceed like Austin Osman Spare would have us do, through experimenting with believing in what we know might not be true. We adopt this approach, which also necessarily involves a performance of fiction, not just to test our perspectives on reality, or as a therapeutic practice, but as a political mode which recognises that fictioning is a power that can have real effects, particularly when a host of forces can be mustered to enact a fiction. After all, did not Western politicians, on the basis of the fiction that invading Iraq was crucial for the war on terror, actually produce such a war? And have not politicians from the Kremlin to Westminster to the White House understood that magic is the management and manipulation of perception, and that in many instances fiction is not necessarily always undermined by fact?

In proposing such fictioning practices it might sound like we are advocating autonomy and control – or the possibility of a Promethean authoring of reality – against fictions of contingencies, multi-species ecologies and non-conscious machinic economies and environments that burst the bubble of human autonomy. But as we suggested in section three, the two orientations that can be called autopoesis and sympoesis are both foreground and background to one another. Certainly the processes of agency, for us, are not clear cut. This makes experimentation with auto-poesis and sympoesis not just a politics and pragmatics but also an ethico-aesthetic decision. For to act *as if* reality can be authored and re-engineered, or *as if* humans are hosts for, or collaborators with, forces and influences and species and machines (out of control and beyond human consciousness), is to produce different fictions with different results.

In relation to this, we are not suggesting anything goes, but only that, following Laruelle, all philosophies can be seen as philo-fictions. It is not simply that fiction has become a mode and terrain of politics (this has always been the case, ever since the telling of noble lies in Plato's *Republic*), but also that philosophy should follow art in embracing the power of play and accepting that it too has no privileged access to reality. Indeed, if nothing else, fictioning names this proliferation of points of view as well as their material instantiation: the performance of fictions and fictionings that reality will one day become.

Note

1 In writing this, we have in mind Hans Holbein's painting *The Ambassadors* (1533), in which two men stand confidently in front of a collection of objects associated with culture, knowledge and education. At the bottom of this composition though, when viewed from the front, there is something like a smear or a stain that from the side, or when viewed through an optic, becomes a skull.

Bibliography

Acker, Kathy (1984), *Blood and Guts in High School, Plus Two*, London: Picador.

Adorno, Theodor and M. Horkheimer (1969), *Dialectic of the Enlightenment*, trans. J. Cummings, London: Verso.

Alvanson, Kristen (2017), artist's website, http://www.kristenalvanson.com/new/about-drapery.html (accessed 12/7/2017).

Anders, Günther (2016), 'On Promethean Shame', trans. J. Müller, reproduced in J. Müller, *Prometheanism: Technology, Digital Culture and Human Obsolescence*, London: Rowan and Littlefield International Ltd., pp. 29–96.

Anderson, Benedict (2006), *Imagined Communities: Reflections on the Origins and Spread of Nationalism*, London: Verso.

Artaud, Antonin (1976), 'Letter to Pierre Loeb', *Antonin Artaud Selected Writings*, ed. and trans. S. Sontag, Berkeley and Los Angeles: University of California Press, pp. 515–22.

— (1995), *Watchfiends and Rack Screams: Works from the Final Period of Antonin Artaud*, ed. and trans. C. Eshleman and B. Bador, Boston: Exact Change.

Atkins, Ed (2012), Interview for Chisenhale Gallery by Katie Guggenheim, https://chisenhale.org.uk/wp-content/uploads/Chisenhale_Interviews_Ed_Atkins-1.pdf (accessed 1/5/2017).

— (2014a), 'Newsmaker: Ed Atkins On His Serpentine Sackler Gallery Installation', Interview by Thea Ballard, http://www.blouinartinfo.com/news/story/1044455/newsmaker-ed-atkins-on-his-serpentine-sackler-gallery (accessed 1/5/2017).

— (2014b), *Ed Atkins*, Zurich: JPR/Ringer.

Avanessian, Armen and S. Malik (2016), 'The Time Complex. Postcontemporary', *Dis Magazine*, http://dismagazine.com/discussion/81924/the-time-complex-postcontemporary (accessed 4/3/2016).

Ayache, Elie (2010), *The Blank Swan: The End of Probability*, Chichester: Wiley.

— (2014), 'The Writing of the Market', Interview, *Collapse: Philosophical Research and Development*, 8: 517–602.

Badiou, Alain (2005), *Being and Event*, trans. O. Feltham, London and New York: Continuum.

Baker, Phillip (2011), *Austin Osman Spare: The Life and Legend of London's Lost Artist*, London: Strange Attractor Press.

Ballard, J. G. (1962), *The Drowned World*, New York: Berkeley Books.

— (1964), *The Terminal Beach*, London: Victor Gollancz.

— (1966), *The Crystal World*, London: Jonathan Cape.

— (1973), *Crash*, London: Jonathan Cape.

— (1974), *Concrete Island*, London: Jonathan Cape.

— (1984), *Empire of the Sun*, London: Victor Gollancz.

— (1993 [1970]), *The Atrocity Exhibition*, London: Flamingo.

— (1996), *Cocaine Nights*, London: Flamingo.

— (2000), 'Robert Smithson as Cargo Cultist', *Robert Smithson: Dead Tree*, ed. B. Conley and J. Amrhein, Brooklyn: Pierogi, p. 31.

Ballard, J. G. and R. Louit (2012 [1974]), 'Crash and Learn', *Extreme Metaphors: Collected Interviews*, ed. S. Sellars and D. O'Hara, London: Fourth Estate, pp. 72–7.

Ballard, J. G. and C. Orr (2012 [1974]), 'How to Face Doomsday without Really Trying', *Extreme Metaphors: Collected Interviews*, ed. S. Sellars and D. O'Hara, London: Fourth Estate, pp. 56–71.

Barthes, Roland (1973), *Mythologies*, trans. A. Lavers, London: Paladin.

— (1989), 'The Reality Effect', *The Rustle of Language*, trans. R. Howard, Berkeley: University of California Press, pp. 3–10.

Bartlett, Jamie (dir.) (2017), 'Secrets of Silicon Valley', BBC4, 13 August 2017.

Barton, Justin (2015), *Hidden Valleys: Haunted by the Future*, Winchester: Zero Books.

Bataille, Georges (1989), *Theory of Religion*, trans. R. Hurley, New York: Zone Books.

— (1994), *The Absence of Myth*, trans. M. Richardson, London: Verso.

Beasley, Mark, A. Rowlands and J. Russell (eds) (2011), *Barefoot in the Head*, Art–Writing–Research: Vol. 4, Birmingham: Article Press.

Beech, Amanda (2014), 'Art and its "Science"', *Speculative Aesthetics*, ed. R. Mackay, L. Pendrell and J. Trafford, Falmouth: Urbanomic, pp. 9–19.

Bell, Jeffrey A. (2006), *Philosophy at the Edge of Chaos: Gilles Deleuze and the Philosophy of Difference*, Toronto: University of Toronto Press.

Berardi, Franco (2009), *Precarious Rhapsody: Semiocapitalism and the Pathologies of the Post-Alpha Generation*, eds. E. Empson and S. Shukaitis, trans. A. Bove, E. Empson, M. Goddard, G. Mecchia, A. Schinto and S. Wright, London: Minor Compositions.

— (2012), 'Emancipation of the Sign: Poetry and Finance During the Twentieth Century', *e-flux*, http://www.e-flux.com/journal/emancipation-of-the-sign-poetry-and-finance-during-the-twentieth-century (accessed 15/4/2016).

Berger, George (2006), *The Story of Crass*, London: Omnibus.

Bergson, Henri (2004), *Matter and Memory*, trans. N. M. Paul and W. S. Palmer, New York: Zone Books.

Berlant, Lauren (2011), *Cruel Optimism*, Durham, NC: Duke University Press.

Birkholz, Daniel (2006), 'Mapping Medieval Utopia: Exercises in Restraint', *Journal of Medieval and Early Modern Studies*, 36.3: 586–618.

Blackmore, Susan (1999), *The Meme Machine*, Oxford: Oxford University Press.

— (2005), *Conversations on Consciousness*, New York: Oxford University Press.

— (2009), 'Dangerous Memes; or, What the Pandorans let loose', *Cosmos and Culture: Cultural Evolution in a Cosmic Context*, ed. S. Dick and M. Lupisella, Washington: NASA.

— (2012), Interview for *Know Your Meme*, http://knowyourmeme.com/blog/interviews/qa-with-susan-blackmore-author-of-the-meme-machine (accessed 1/5/2017).

Bostrom, Nick (2014), *Superintelligence: Paths, Dangers, Strategies*, Oxford: Oxford University Press.

Bracewell, Michael, M. Clark and A. Rowlands (eds) (2009), *The Dark Monarch: Magic and Modernity in British Art*, London: Tate Publishing.

Brassier, Ray (2001), 'Alien Theory: The Decline of Materialism in the Name of Matter', Warwick University PhD thesis, http://wrap.warwick.ac.uk/4034 (accessed 1/5/2015).

— (2003), 'Axiomatic Heresy', *Radical Philosophy*, 121: 24–35.

— (2007a), *Nihil Unbound: Enlightenment and Extinction*, Basingstoke: Palgrave.

— (2007b), 'Genre is Obsolete', *Multitudes*, 28, http://www.multitudes.net/Genre-is-Obsolete (accessed 9/7/2016).

— (2009), 'Against an Aesthetics of Noise', Interview with Bram Ieven, *nY*, 2, http://www.ny-web.be/transitzone/against-aesthetics-noise.html (accessed 1/3/2015).

— (2011), 'The View from Nowhere', *Identities: Journal of Politics, Gender and Culture*, 8.2: 7–23.

— (2014a), 'Prometheanism and Real Abstraction', *Speculative Aesthetics*, ed. R. Mackay, L. Pendrell and J. Trafford, Falmouth: Urbanomic, pp. 72–7.

— (2014b), 'Prometheanism and its Critics', *#Accelerate: The Accelerationist Reader*, ed. R. Mackay and A. Avanessian, Falmouth: Urbanomic, pp. 469–87.

Brassier, Ray and R. Mackay (2013), 'Introduction' to Nick Land, *Fanged Noumena: Collected Writings 1987–2007*, Falmouth: Urbanomic, pp. 1–54.

Brassier, Ray and S. Malik (2015), 'Reason is Inconsolable and Non-Conciliatory: Ray Brassier in conversation with Suhail Malik', *Realism, Materialism, Art*, ed. C. Cox, J. Jaskey and S. Malik, Berlin: Steinberg Press, pp. 213–30.

Brittain, David (2013), *Eduardo Paolozzi at New Worlds: Science Fiction and Art in the Sixties*, Manchester: Savoy Books.

Bryant, Levi (2013), 'The Discourse of the Capitalist and the New Symptom', *Larval Subjects*, https://larvalsubjects.wordpress.com/2013/02/11/the-discourse-of-the-capitalist-and-the-new-symptom (accessed 15/4/2016).

Burroughs, William (1968), *The Soft Machine*, London: Calder and Boyar.

— (1969), *The Naked Lunch*, London: Transworld Publishers Ltd./Corgi Books.

— (1981), *Cities of the Red Night*, London: Penguin.

— (1995), *My Education: A Book of Dreams*, London: Picador.

— (2005), *The Electronic Revolution*, New York: ubuclassics, http://www.ubu.com/historical/burroughs/electronic_revolution.pdf (accessed 29/1/2017).

— (2008), *The Job: Interviews with William S. Burroughs*, with D. Odier, London: Penguin.

— (2014), 'The Limits of Control', *Schizo-Culture: The Book*, ed. S. Lotringer, New York: Semiotext(e), pp. 40–2.

— (n.d.), Untitled, *Chappaqua Press Book*.

Burroughs, William and A. Ginsberg (1963), *The Yage Letters*, San Francisco: City Lights Books.

Burroughs, William and B. Gysin (1977), *The Third Mind*, New York: Viking Press.

Burrows, David (1996), Review of 'TRADING STATION ALPHA Cma', at Matt's Gallery, London, *Art Monthly*, no. 194.

— (2006), 'Missing in Atopia', *Another Land*, ed. N. Coutts, London: Daniel Arnaud Gallery/Mantis Publications, pp. 36–45.

— (2010a), 'An Art Scene as Big as the Ritz: The Logic of Scenes', *Deleuze and Contemporary Art*, ed. S. Zepke and S. O'Sullivan, Edinburgh: Edinburgh University Press, pp. 157–75.

— (2010b), 'Performance Fictions', *Metamute*, 29 September, http://www.metamute.org/editorial/articles/performance-fictions (accessed 15/3/18).

— (2011a), 'Performance Fictions', *Performance Fictions, Art–Writing–Research: Vol. 3*, ed. D. Burrows, Birmingham: Article Press, pp. 47–70.

— (ed.) (2011b), *Performance Fictions, Art–Writing–Research: Vol. 3*, Birmingham: Article Press.

— (2015), 'Negative Space War Machines', *Occupy: A People Yet to Come*, ed. A. Conio, London: Open Humanities Press.

Burrows, David and S. O'Sullivan (2014), 'The Sinthome/Z-point relation or Art as Non-Schizoanalysis', *Schizoanalysis and Art*, ed. I. Buchanan and L. Simpson, London: Bloomsbury, pp. 253–78.

Butler, Judith (1993), 'Gender is Burning: Questions of Appropriation and Subversion', *Bodies That Matter: On the Discursive Limits of Sex*, London: Routledge, pp. 121–40.

Butt, Gavin (ed.) (2011), *Performing/Knowing, Art–Writing–Research: Vol. 1*, Birmingham: Article Press.

Čapek, Karel (1973), *R.U.R. Rossum's Universal Robots*, New York: Washington Square.

Carstens, Delphi and M. Roberts (2012), 'Cyberpositive 2012', http://merliquify.com/blog/article s/0rphandrift-cyberpositive/#.VtiiKlyZZ94. (accessed 4/3/2016).

Carter, Frederick and A. O. Spare (2007), 'Automatic Drawing', *The Writings of Austin Spare*, Sioux Falls: Nu Vision, pp. 7–12.

Castaneda, Carlos (1968), *The Teachings of Don Juan: A Yaqui Way of Knowledge*, Oakland: University of California Press.

— (1974), *Tales of Power*, New York: Simon and Schuster.

Castoriadis, Cornelius (1997), *The Imaginary Institution of Society*, trans. K. Blarney, Cambridge, MA: MIT Press.

Catling, Brian (1990), *The Stumbling Block*, London: Book Works.

— (2012), *The Vorrh*, London: Honest Publishing.

Catling, Brian and A. Spragg (2011), 'Brian Catling speaks to Andy Spragg', http://misosensitive. blogspot.co.uk/2011/05/brian-Catling-speaks-to-andy-spragg.html (accessed 3/3/2017).

Ccru (Cybernetic culture research unit) (2017), 'Lemurian Time War', *Ccru Writings 1997–2003*, Falmouth: Urbanomic/Time Spiral Press, pp. 33–52.

— 'Hyperstition', https://web.archive.org/web/20030204195934/http://ccru.net/syzygy.htm (accessed 4/3/2016).

Ccru/0[rphan] d[rift>] (2014), 'Liquid Lattice', *Frozen Tears, Volume 3: Gay Prophecy of the Demonically Social*, ed. J. Russell, Birmingham: Article Press, pp. 173–203.

Chetwynd, Marvin Gaye (2013), 'Why I Changed My Name to Marvin Gaye Chetwynd', *The Guardian*, 25 January, https://www.theguardian.com/artanddesign/2013/sep/25/marvin-gaye-chetwynd-spartacus (accessed 13/2/2017).

— (2015), The Interview: Marvin Gaye Chetwynd, *Hunger*, http://www.hungertv.com/feature /the-interview-marvin-gaye-chetwynd (accessed 13/2/2017).

Chude-Sokei, Louis Onuorah (2016), *The Sound of Culture: Diaspora and Black Technopoetics*, Middletown, CT: Wesleyan University Press.

Colebrook, Claire (2014), *Death of the Posthuman: Essays on Extinction Volume 1*, Ann Arbor: Open Humanities Press.

Coutts, Nicky et al. (2006), *Pilgrimage*, ed. N. Coutts, London: Confluens Press, Middlesex University.

Cramer, Florian (2017), 'Meme Wars: Internet Culture and the "Alt Right"', recorded lecture, *FACT*, Liverpool, 2 March, https://www.youtube.com/watch?v=OiNYuhLKzi8 (accessed 20 /3/2017).

Critchley, Simon (2012), *The Faith of the Faithless: Experiments in Political Theology*, London: Verso.

Cussans, John (2010), 'The Para-Psychic Properties of Marmalade', *Performance Fictions*, ed. D. Burrows, Birmingham: Article Press, pp. 15–46.

Davis, Erik (1988), *Techgnosis: Myth, Magic and Mysticism in the Age of Information*, New York: Serpent's Tail.

Dawkins, Richard (1999), 'Foreword', to S. Blackmore, *The Meme Machine*, Oxford: Oxford University Press, pp. vi–xvi

— (2006), *The Selfish Gene*, Oxford: Oxford University Press.

Debord, Guy (1983), *Society of the Spectacle*, Detroit: Black and Red.

De Duve, Thierry (1998), *Kant After Duchamp*, Cambridge, MA: MIT Press.

De Garis, Hugo (2005), *Artilect War: Cosmists v Terrans*, California: ETC Publications, http://agi-conf.org/2008/artilectwar.pdf (accessed 15/4/2016).

Delany, Samuel (1994), *The Silent Interviews*, Hanover: Wesleyan University Press.

— (2001), *Dhalgren*, New York: Vintage Books.

Deleuze, Gilles (1988), *Foucault*, trans. S. Hand, Minneapolis: University of Minnesota Press.

— (1989), *Cinema 2: The Time-Image*, trans H. Tomlinson and R. Galeta, London: Athlone Press.

— (1991), *Bergsonism*, trans. H. Tomlinson and B. Habberjam, New York: Zone Books.

— (1994), *Difference and Repetition*, trans. P. Patton, New York: Columbia University Press.

— (1995a), 'Postscript on Control Societies', *Negotiations: 1972–1990*, trans. M. Joughin, New York: Columbia University Press, pp. 177–82.

— (1995b), 'Control and Becoming', *Negotiations: 1972–1990*, trans. M. Joughin, New York: Columbia University Press, pp. 169–76.

— (1997), 'Literature and Life', *Essays Critical and Clinical*, trans. D. W. Smith and M. A. Greco, Minneapolis: University of Minnesota Press, pp. 1–6.

— (2003), *Francis Bacon: The Logic of Sensation*, trans. D. W. Smith, London: Continuum.

— (2006), 'What is a Creative Act?', *Two Regimes of Madness: Texts and Interviews 1975–1995*, ed. D. Lapoujade, trans. A. Hodges and M. Taormina, New York: Semiotext(e), pp. 312–24.

Deleuze, Gilles and F. Guattari (1984), *Anti-Oedipus: Capitalism and Schizophrenia*, trans. R. Hurley, M. Seem and H. R. Lane, London: Athlone Press.

— (1986), *Kafka: Towards a Minor Literature*, trans. D. Polan, Minneapolis: University of Minnesota Press.

— (1988), *A Thousand Plateaus: Capitalism and Schizophrenia*, trans. B. Massumi, London: Athlone Press.

— (1994), *What is Philosophy?*, trans. H. Tomlinson and G. Burchell, London: Verso.

Deleuze, Gilles and C. Parnet (1987), *Dialogues II*, trans. H. Tomlinson and B. Habberjam, London: Continuum.

De Lima, Santos M. (2014), *The Ethnopoetics of Shamanism*, Basingstoke: Palgrave.

De Loor, Peirre, K. Manac'h and J. Tisseau (2009), 'Enaction-Based Artificial Intelligence: Toward Co-evolution with Humans in the Loop', *Minds and Machine*, 19: 319–43.

Demos, T. J. (2009), 'The Right to Opacity: The Otolith Group's *Nervus Rerum*', *October*, 129: 113–28.

Dennett, Daniel (2007), *Breaking the Spell: Religion as a Natural Phenomenon*, London: Penguin.

Derrida, Jacques (1981), *Dissemination*, trans. B. Johnson, Chicago: University of Chicago Press.

Dery, Mark (1994), 'Black to the Future', *Flame Wars: The Discourse of Cyberculture*, ed. M. Dery, Durham, NC: Duke University Press, pp. 1–10.

Descola, Phillipe (2013), *Beyond Nature and Culture*, Chicago: University of Chicago Press.

Dick, Philip K. (1969), *Ubik*, New York: Doubleday.

— (2001), *VALIS*, London: Gollancz.

— (2003), *A Scanner Darkly*, London: Gollancz.

— (2011), *The Exegesis of Philip K. Dick*, ed. P. Jackson and J. Letham, New York: Houghton Mifflin Harcourt.

Di Fillipo, Paul (1996), *Ribofunk*, New York: Four Walls Eight Windows.

Di Paolo, Ezequiel and E. Thompson (2014), 'The Enactive Approach', *The Routledge Handbook of Embodied Cognition*, ed. L. Shapiro, New York: Routledge.

Dronsfield, Jonathan Lacey (ed.) (2011), *Materiality of Theory, Art–Writing–Research: Vol. 5*, Birmingham: Article Press.

Dryzek, John (1997), *The Politics of the Earth: Environmental Discourses*, Oxford: Oxford University Press.

Dryzek, John, R. Goodin, A. Tucker and B. Reber (2009), 'Promethean Elites Encounter Precautionary Publics: The Case of GM Foods', *Science, Technology and Human Values*, 34.3: 263–88.

Egan, Greg (2010a), *Permutation City*, London: Gollancz.

— (2010b), *Quarantine*, London: Gollancz.

Enderby, Emma (2015), 'Collaging in Time', *Palisades*, ed. E. Enderby, A. Cryczkowska and M. Larner, London: Koenig Books/Serpentine Books.

Eshun, Kodwo (1998), *More Brilliant Than the Sun: Adventures in Sonic Fiction*, London: Quartet.

— (2003), 'Further Considerations of Afrofuturism', *CR: The New Centennial Review*, 3.2: 287–302.

Eshun, Kodwo, A. Hameed and L. Moreno (2017), 'Sonic Utopias: *The Last Angel of History*: A Conversation between Ayesha Hameed, Kodwo Eshun and Louis Moreno', *Futures and Fictions*, ed. H. Gunkell, A. Hameed and S. O'Sullivan, London: Repeater, pp. 249–67.

Faithfull, Simon (2016), *Does the World Exist, When I'm Not There?*, Potsdam: Laconic.

Fedorov, Nicolai (2014), 'The Common Task', *#Accelerate: The Accelerationist Reader*, ed. R. Mackay and A. Avanessian, Falmouth: Urbanomic, pp. 85–90.

Firestone, Shulamith (1972), *The Dialectic of Sex: The Case for Feminist Revolution*, London: Harper Collins.

Fisher, Mark (2009), *Capitalist Realism: Is There No Alternative?*, London: Zero.

— (2010), 'English Pastoral', *Robinson in Ruins*, booklet accompanying DVD, London: BFI.

— (2014), *Ghosts of My Life: Writings on Depression, Hauntology and Lost Futures*, London: Zero Books.

— (2016), *The Weird and the Eerie*, London: Repeater.

Fisher, Mark and J. Thorne (2017), 'Luxury Communism: A Conversation between Mark Fisher and Judy Thorne', *Futures and Fictions*, ed. H. Gunkell, A. Hameed and S. O'Sullivan, London: Repeater, pp. 145–69.

Fitch, Lizzie, in conversation with Ossian Ward (2014), 'Supplies, Situations, Spaces', *Priority Infield*, ed. P. Luckraft, M. Maheshwari and I. Venero, London: Zabludowicz Collection, pp. 133–7.

Foucault, Michel (1972), *Archaeology of Knowledge*, trans. A. Sheridan, London and New York: Tavistock Publications.

— (1975), *Discipline and Punish: The Birth of the Prison*, trans. A. Sheridan, London: Penguin.

— (1980), *Power/Knowledge*, ed. C. Gordon, New York: Pantheon Books.

— (2004), *Death and the Labyrinth*, trans. C. Raus, New York and London: Continuum.

— (2005), *The Hermeneutics of the Subject: Lectures at the College de France 1981–82*, ed. F. Gros, trans. G. Burchell, London: Palgrave.

Frazer, James George (1957), *The Golden Bough: A Study in Magic and Religion*, London: Macmillan.

Freud, Sigmund (2002), *Civilization and its Discontents*, trans. D. McLintock, London: Penguin Classics.

Furie, Matt (2016), *Boy's Club*, Seattle, Washington: Fantagraphics.

Fusco, Maria (ed.) (2011), *Who Is This Who Is Coming?, Art–Writing–Research: Vol. 2*, Birmingham: Article Press.

Galloway, Alexander R. (2013), 'Laruelle and Art', *Continent*, 2.4: 230–6, http://continentcontinent.cc/index.php/continent/article/view/126 (accessed 15/12/2017).

— (2014), *Laruelle: Against the Digital*, Minneapolis: University of Minnesota Press.

Galloway, Alexander and E. Thacker (2007), *The Exploit: A Theory of Networks*, Minneapolis: University of Minnesota Press.

Galloway, Alexander, I. James and J. Ó Maoilearca (2015), 'What Can We Do With Non-Philosophy?', London Graduate School Workshop (Kingston University), Swedenborg Hall, London, 10 November, http://backdoorbroadcasting.net/2015/11/what-can-we-do-with-non-philosophy (accessed 5/4/2017).

Garton, Vincent (2017), 'Leviathan Rots', *Urbanomic Documents*, http://www.urbanomic.com/document/leviathan-rots (accessed 14/8/2017).

Gell, Alfred (1998), *Art and Agency*, Oxford: Oxford University Press.

— (2006), *The Art of Anthropology*, Oxford: Berg.

Glazek, Christopher (2014), 'The Past is Another Los Angeles', *Priority Infield*, ed. P. Luckraft, M. Maheshwari and I. Venero, London: Zabludowicz Collection, pp. 67–73.

Glissant, Édouard (2010), *Poetics of Relation*, trans. B. Wing, Ann Arbor: University of Michigan Press.

Goddard, Michael (2008), 'Sonic and Cultural Noise as Production of the New: The Industrial

Music Media Ecology of Throbbing Gristle', *Deleuze, Guattari and the Production of the New*, ed. S. O'Sullivan and S. Zepke, London: Continuum, pp. 162–72.

Goldin+Senneby (2017), artist website, http://www.goldinsenneby.com (accessed 16/7/2017).

Good, Irving John (1965), 'Speculations Concerning the First Ultraintelligent Machine', *Advances in Computers*, 6: 31–88.

Goodeve, Thyrza Nichols (2015), '"The Cat is My Medium": Notes on the Writing and Art of Carolee Schneemann', *Art Journal*, 74.1: 5–22.

Goodman, Steve (2010), *Sonic Warfare: Sound, Affect, and the Ecology of Fear*, Cambridge, MA: MIT Press.

Gratton, Peter (2014), *Speculative Realism: Problems and Prospects*, London: Bloomsbury.

Grayson, Richard (2002), 'The Deliverance and the Patience', *Mike Nelson*, London: Book Works and Matt's Gallery.

Guattari, Félix (1995), *Chaosmosis: An Ethico-Aesthetic Paradigm*, trans. P. Bains and J. Pefanis, Sydney: Power Institute.

— (1996), 'A Liberation of Desire: An Interview with George Stambolian', *The Guattari Reader*, ed. G. Genosko, Oxford: Blackwell, pp. 204–14.

— (2013), 'Genet Regained', *Schizoanalytic Cartographies*, trans. A. Goffey, London: Bloomsbury, pp. 215–30.

Guyton, Wade (2017), *Das New Yorker Atelier Abridged*, London: Serpentine Gallery/Koenig Books.

Hadot, Pierre (1995), *Philosophy as a Way of Life: Spiritual Exercises from Socrates to Foucault*, trans. A. Davidson, Oxford: Blackwell.

Halberstam, Jack (2013), 'Charming for the Revolution: A Gaga Manifesto', *e-flux*, http://www.e-flux.com/journal/charming-for-the-revolution-a-gaga-manifesto (accessed 1/2/2016).

Halford, Victoria and S. Beard (2011), *Voodoo Science Park*, Winchester: Zero Books.

Hansen, Mark (2000), *Embodying Technesis: Technology Beyond Writing*, Ann Arbor: University of Michigan Press.

— (2004), 'Realtime Synthesis and the Différance of the Body: Technocultural Studies in the Wake of Deconstruction', *Culture Machine*, 6, http://www.culturemachine.net/index.php/cm/article/view/9/8 (accessed 15/4/2016).

— (2015), *Feed-Forward: On the Future of Twentieth Century Media*, Chicago: University of Chicago Press.

Haraway, Donna (1991), 'A Cyborg Manifesto: Science, Technology and Socialist Feminism in the Late Twentieth Century', *Simians, Cyborgs and Women: The Reinvention of Nature*, London: Free Association Books, pp. 149–82.

— (2003), *The Companion Species Manifesto: Dogs, People and Significant Otherness*, Chicago: Prickly Paradigm Press.

— (2008), *When Species Meet*, Minneapolis: University of Minnesota Press.

— (2011), 'SF: Science Fiction, Speculative Fabulation, String Figures, So Far', Pilgrim Award Acceptance Comments, https://people.ucsc.edu/~haraway/Files/PilgrimAcceptanceHaraway.pdf (accessed 10/2/2017).

— (2016), *Staying with the Trouble: Making Kin in the Chthulucene*, Durham, NC: Duke University Press.

Harney, Stefano and F. Moten (2013), *The Undercommons: Fugitive Planning and Black Study*, New York: Autonomedia.

Harris, Oliver (2006), 'Editor's Introduction', *The Yage Letters: Redux*, San Francisco: City Lights Books, pp. ix–lii.

Harrison, Mark (2013), 'Interview with Matteo Zennaro', in *Forward The Revolution*, by Matteo Zennaro, Urbino: ISIA Urbino A.A.

Hayles, N. Katherine (1999), *How We Became Posthuman*, Chicago: Chicago University Press.

— (2002), *Writing Machines*, Cambridge, MA: MIT Press.

— (2005), *My Mother Was A Computer*, Chicago: Chicago University Press.

— (2012), *How We Think: Digital Media and Contemporary Technogenesis*, Chicago: University of Chicago Press.

Heidegger, Martin (1999a), 'The Origins of the Work of Art', *Basic Writings*, ed. D. F. Krell, trans. A. Hofstadter, London: Routledge, pp. 139–212.

— (1999b), 'The Question Concerning Technology', *Basic Writings*, ed. D. F. Krell, trans. A. Hofstadter, London: Routledge, pp. 307–42.

— (2001), *Being and Time*, trans. J. M. Macquarrie and E. Robinson, Oxford: Blackwell.

Henrot, Camille (2016), *Elephant Child*, London/New York: Koenig Books/Inventory Press.

Herndon, Holly (2010), 'Embodiment in Electronic Music Performance', MA Thesis, Mills College, San Francisco.

— (2012), Interview with Rory Gibb, *The Quietus*, 17 December, http://thequietus.com/articles/10997-holly-herndon-interview-movement (accessed 2/5/2017).

— (2013), 'The 10 Most "Whoa" Uses of Technology', *Dummy*, http://www.dummymag.com/lists/the-10-most-whoa-uses-of-technology-according-to-holly-herndon (accessed 15/4/2016).

— (2014), 'Continual Partial Listening: Holly Herndon in Conversation', Interview for *Rhizome*, http://rhizome.org/editorial/2014/jan/22/holly-herndon (accessed 2/5/2017).

— (2015), Interview by Louis Pattison for *FACT*, 30 May, http://www.factmag.com/2015/05/30/holly-herndon-interview (accessed 2/5/2017).

— (2017), 'Herndon's Platform', Interview by Ruth Saxby for *Fader*, March/April, http://www.thefader.com/2015/05/21/radical-ideas-that-inspired-holly-herndon-platform (accessed 2/5/2017).

Hester, Helen (2017), 'After the Future: *n* Hypotheses of Post-Cyber Feminism', essay commissioned by *Res*, http://beingres.org/2017/06/30/afterthefuture-helenhester (accessed 28/11/2017).

Higgs, John (2012), *The KLF: Chaos, Magic and the Band who Burned a Million Pounds*, London: Phoenix.

Hoban, Russell (1980), *Riddley Walker*, London: Bloomsbury.

Hogg, Norman (n.d.), artist's statement, http://www.centreforsensorystudies.org/member/ norman-hogg (accessed 6/2/2017).

Holbraad, Martin and M. A. Pedersen (2017), *The Ontological Turn: An Anthropological Exposition*, Cambridge: Cambridge University Press.

Holt, Nancy (2012), 'Nancy Holt and Robert Smithson in England, 1969: Notes from an Ancient Island', Interview with Simon Grant, *Tate Etc.*, 25, http://www.tate.org.uk/context-comment /articles/nancy-holt-and-robert-smithson-england-1969 (accessed 3/4/2017).

Home, Stewart (2002), *Sixty-Nine Things to do with a Dead Princess*, London: Canongate.

— (2011), 'Foreword', V. Halford and S. Beard, *Voodoo Science Park*, Winchester: Zero Books, pp. 3–5.

hooks, bell (1999), 'Is Paris Burning?', *Black Looks: Race and Representation*, Boston MA: South End Press, pp. 145–58.

Hutton, Ron (1997), *Stations of the Sun: A History of the Ritual Year in Britain*, Oxford and New York: Oxford University Press.

Huxley, Julian (1957), *In New Bottles for New Wine*, London: Chatto and Windus.

Ireland, Amy (2017a) 'The Poememenon: Form as Occult Technology', *Urbanomic Documents*, https://www.urbanomic.com/document/poememenon/ (accessed 5/4/2017).

— (2017b), 'Black Circuit: Code for the Numbers to Come', *e-flux*, http://www.e-flux.com/ journal/80/100016/black-circuit-code-for-the-numbers-to-come (accessed 5/4/2017).

Irigaray, Luce (1985), *This Sex Which Is Not One*, trans. C. Porter and C. Burke, New York: Cornell University Press.

Irvine, Jaki (2000), various texts in M. Nelson, *Extinction Beckons*, London: Matt's Gallery.

Jameson, Fredric (1984), 'Postmodernism, or the Cultural Logic of Late Capitalism', *New Left Review*, 1.146: 59–92.

— (1990), 'Cognitive Mapping', *Marxism and the Interpretation of Culture*, ed. C. Nelson and L. Grossberg, Chicago: University of Illinois Press, pp. 347–60.

— (1991), *Postmodernism, or, the Cultural Logic of Late Capitalism*, Durham, NC: Duke University Press.

— (2005), *Archaeologies of the Future*, London: Verso.

— (2015), 'The Aesthetics of Singularity', *New Left Review*, 92: 101–32.

Jeffries, Richard (1980 [1885]), *After London: Or, Wild England*, Oxford: Oxford Paperbacks.

Johnston, John (2008), *The Allure of Machinic Life: Cybernetics, Artificial Life, and the New AI*, London and Cambridge, MA: MIT Press.

Jones, Amelia (1998), *Body Art: Performing the Subject*, Minneapolis: University of Minnesota Press.

K. D. (Goldin+Senneby) (2014), *Headless: A Novel*, Berlin: Sternberg.

Kafka, Franz (1985), *America*, Harmondsworth: Penguin.

Kalmar, Stefan (2017), Essay for gallery hand-out for the exhibition *Seth Price Circa 1981* by Seth Price at the ICA, London.

Keenan, David (2016), *England's Hidden Reverse: A Secret History of the Esoteric Underground*, London: Strange Attractor Press.

Keiller, Patrick (2012), *The Possibility of Life's Survival on the Planet*, London: Tate Publishing.

Kelley, Mike (1995), 'Myth-Science', *Öyvind Fahlström*, Köln: Köln Kunstverein, pp. 9–29.

Klein, Naomi (2007), *The Shock Doctrine*, London and New York: Penguin.

K-Punk blog (n.d.), http://k-punk.org (accessed 9/7/2016).

Kucia, Karolina and T. Nauha (2008), *Kukkia*, Estonia: Greif Printhouse.

Kurzweil, Ray (2000), 'Interview for Technology Review', Jan/Feb, http://www.ghandchi.com/iranscope/Anthology/Kurzweil-Int.htm (accessed 15/4/2016).

— (2013), 'Interview: How Ray Kurzweil Plans to Revolutionize Search at Google', with Robert Hopf, *Forbes*, http://www.forbes.com/sites/roberthof/2013/04/29/interview-how-ray-kurzweil-plans-to-revolutionize-search-at-google/#4d962fc43447 (accessed 15/4/2016).

Kusama, Yoyoi (2011), *Infinity Net: The Autobiography of Yoyoi Kusama*, London: Tate.

Laboria Cuboniks (2015), 'Xenofeminist Manifesto', http://www.laboriacuboniks.net (accessed 1/2/2016).

Lacan, Jacques (1978), 'On Psychoanalytic Discourse', trans. J. W. Stone, *Lacan in Italia 1953–78*, Milan: University of Milan, pp. 32–55.

— (1979), *Four Fundamental Concepts of Psychoanalysis*, ed. J-A. Miller, trans. A. Sheridan, Harmondsworth: Penguin Books.

— (1983), *The Psychoses: The Seminar of Jacques Lacan, Book 3, 1955–1956*, ed. R. Grigg, trans. J-A. Miller, London: W. W. Norton and Co.

— (1992), *The Ethics of Psychoanalysis 1959–1960*, ed. J-A. Miller, trans. D. Porter, New York: W. W. Norton and Co.

— (2005), 'The Mirror Stage', *Ecrits*, trans. B Fink, London: W. W. Norton & Co. Ltd, pp. 75–81.

— (2006), *Écrits*, trans. B. Fink, London: W. W. Norton and Co.

— (2013), *The Other Side of Psychoanalysis*, trans. R. Grigg, New York: W. W. Norton and Co.

Lambert-Beatty, Carrie (2009), 'Make-Believe: Parafiction and Plausibility', *October*, 129: 51–84.

Land, Nick (2011a [1996]), 'A ZiiGothic X-Coda (Cooking Lobsters with Jake and Dinos)', *Fanged Noumena: Collected Writings 1987–2007*, ed. R. Mackay and R. Brassier. Falmouth: Urbanomic, pp. 481–91.

— (2011b [1996]), 'Circuitries', *Fanged Noumena: Collected Writings 1987–2007*, ed. R. Mackay and R. Brassier, Falmouth: Urbanomic, pp. 289–318.

— (2012), 'Cyberpositive: 2012', http://merliquify.com/blog/articles/cyberpositive/#.Vtii-9lyZZ94 (accessed 4/3/2016).

— (2013a), 'Neoreaction for Dummies', blog post, http://www.xenosystems.net/neoreaction-for -dummies (accessed 17/9/2015).

— (2013b), 'Against Orthogonality', blog post, http://www.xenosystems.net/against-orthogonality (accessed 15/4/2016).

— (2013c), 'Pythia Unbound', blog post, http://www.xenosystems.net/pythia-unbound (accessed 15/4/2016).

— (2014a), *Templexity: Disordered Loops Through Shanghai Time*, Shanghai: Time Spiral Press.

— (2014b), 'Teleoplexy: Notes on Accelerationism', *#Accelerate: The Accelerationist Reader*, ed. R. Mackay and A. Avanessian, Falmouth: Urbanomic, pp. 509–20.

— (2015), 'Ex Machina', blog post, http://www.xenosystems.net/?s=Ex+machine (accessed 23 /4/2017).

— (n.d.), 'The Dark Enlightenment', http://www.thedarkenlightenment.com/the-dark-enlightenment-by-nick-land (accessed 17/9/2015).

Langley, Patrick (2012), 'Ryan Trecartin: The Real Internet is Inside You', *The White Review*, April, http://www.thewhitereview.org/feature/ryan-trecartin-the-real-internet-is-inside-you (accessed 12/5/2017).

Laruelle, François (1993), 'Fragments of an Anti-Guattari', https://linguisticcapital.files.wordpress.com/2013/03/laruelle_fragments-of-an-anti-guattari.pdf (accessed 7/1/2017).

— (2004), 'A New Presentation of Non-Philosophy', http://www.onphi.net/texte-a-new-presentation-of-non-philosophy-32.html (accessed 7/1/2017).

— (2010), *Philosophies of Difference: A Critical Introduction to Non-Philosophy*, London: Continuum.

— (2011), 'What is Seen In a Photo?', *The Concept of Non-Photography*, Falmouth/New York: Urbanomic/Sequence Press, pp. 1–28.

— (2012a), 'I, the Philosopher, Am Lying': A Reply to Deleuze', trans. T. Adkins, R. Brassier and S. Littlefield, *The Non-Philosophy Project: Essays by Francois Laruelle*, ed. G. Alkon and B. Gunjevic, New York: Telos, pp. 40–74.

— (2012b), 'What the One Sees in the One', trans. R. Mackay, *From Decision to Heresy: Experiments in Non-Standard Thought*, Falmouth/New York: Urbanomic/Sequence Press, pp. 409–22.

— (2012c), 'Photo-Fiction, A Theoretical Installation', *Photo-Fiction: A Non-Standard Aesthetics*, trans. D. S. Burk, Minneapolis: Univocal, pp. 11–24.

— (2013a), 'The Transcendental Computer: A Non-Philosophical Utopia', trans. T. Adkins and C. Ebry, https://speculativeheresy.wordpress.com/2013/08/26/translation-of-f-laruelles-the -transcendental-computer-a-non-philosophical-utopia (accessed 15/4/2016).

— (2013b), *Anti-Badiou*, trans. R. Mackay, London: Bloomsbury.

Laruelle, François and collaborators (1993), *Dictionary of Non-Philosophy*, trans. T. Adkins, Minneapolis: Univocal.

Latour, Bruno (1993), *We Have Never Been Modern*, trans. C. Porter, Cambridge, MA: Harvard University Press.

— (2005), *Reassembling the Social: An Introduction to Actor Network Theory*, Oxford: Oxford University Press.

— (2010), *On the Modern Cult of Factish Gods*, trans. C. Porter and H. MacClean, Durham, NC: Duke University Press.

Leary, Timothy (1970), *The Politics of Ecstasy*, London: Paladin.

Le Doueff, Michel (2002), *The Philosophical Imaginary*, trans. C. Gordon, London and New York: Continuum.

Lefebvre, Henri (2004), *Rhythmanalysis: Space, Time and Everyday Life*, trans. S. Eldon and G. Moore, New York: Continuum.

Le Guin, Ursula K. (1989), 'The Carrier Bag Theory of Fiction', *Dancing at the Edge of Time: Thoughts on Worlds, Women and Places*, New York: Grove Press, pp. 165–70.

Lessing, Doris (1979–82), *Canopus in Argos: Archives Quartet*, London: Jonathan Cape.

Lévi-Strauss, Claude (1952), *Race and History*, Paris: UNESCO.

— (1963), 'The Structuralist Study of Myth', *Structural Anthropology*, trans. C. Jacobson and B. Grundfest Schoepf, New York: Basic Books, pp. 206–32.

— (1966), *The Savage Mind*, trans. G. Weidenfeld, London: Weidenfeld and Nicholson.

— (1969), *The Elementary Structures of Kinship*, trans. J. Bell, J. V. Sturmer and R. Needham, Boston: Beacon Press.

— (1990), *The Naked Man*, trans. J. and D. Weightman, Chicago: University of Chicago Press.

Lewitt, Sam (2014), 'Notes from New Jersey', *Collapse: Philosophical Research and Development*, 8: 507–16.

Linden, Gracie (2016), 'Deconstructing African Identity into Axioms, Photos and Colors', *Hyperallergic*, https://hyperallergic.com/305146/deconstructing-african-american-identity-into-axioms-photos-and-colors (accessed 27/6/2017).

Lippard, Lucy R. (1983), *Overlay: Contemporary Art and the Art of Prehistory*, New York: The New Press.

Lochrie, Karma (2006), 'Sheer Wonder: Dreaming Utopia in the Middle Ages', *Journal of Medieval and Early Modern Studies*, 36.3: 494–516.

Louv, Jason (2009), 'Introduction: On the Way to the Garden', *Thee Psychick Bible: Thee Apocryphal Scriptures*, Port Townsend: Feral House, pp. 17–28.

Luyendijk, Joris (2103), 'Derivatives Trader: "Trading Can Take Over your Life – but Only if You Let it"', *The Guardian*, May 23, https://www.theguardian.com/commentisfree/joris-luyendijk-banking-blog/2013/may/22/derivatives-trader-take-over-life-if-let-it (accessed 13/7/18).

Lyotard, Jean-François (1984), *The Postmodern Condition: A Report on Knowledge*, trans. G. Bennington and B. Massumi, Manchester: Manchester University Press.

— (1992), 'Can Thought Go on Without a Body', *The Inhuman*, trans. G. Bennington and R. Bowlby, Stanford: Stanford University Press pp. 8–23.

McCarthy, Hazel Hill (2016), 'Bight of the Twin', http://www.bightofthetwin.com/#about (accessed 28/4/2017).

McFarlane, Robert (2015), 'The Eeriness of the English Countryside', *The Guardian*, 10 April, https://www.theguardian.com/books/2015/apr/10/eeriness-english-countryside-robert-macfarlane (accessed 3/4/2017).

McGettigan, Andrew (2012), 'Fabrication Defect: François Laruelle's Philosophical Materials', *Radical Philosophy*, 175: 33–42.

Mackay, Robin (2012), 'Introduction: Laruelle Undivided', F. Laruelle, *From Decision to Heresy: Experiments in Non-Standard Thought*, Falmouth: Urbanomic, pp. 1–32.

— (2015), 'The Barker Topos', *When Site Lost the Plot*, ed. R. Mackay, Falmouth: Urbanomic, pp. 253–68.

Mackay, Robin and A. Avanessian (eds) (2014a), *#Accelerate: The Accelerationist Reader*, Falmouth and Berlin: Urbanomic/Sequence.

— (2014b), 'Introduction', *#Accelerate: The Accelerationist Reader*, ed. R. Mackay and A. Avanessian, Falmouth and Berlin: Urbanomic, pp. 1–51.

Mackay, Robin, L. Pendrell and J. Trafford (eds) (2014), *Speculative Aesthetics*, Falmouth: Urbanomic.

Malabou, Catherine (2008), *What Should We Do with Our Brain?*, New York: Fordham University Press.

Malik, Suhail (2014), 'The Ontology of Finance', *Collapse: Philosophical Research and Development*, 8: 629–812.

Maney, Kevin (2015), 'Star Wars Class Wars: Is Mars the Escape Hatch for the 1 Percent?', *Newsweek*, 14 December, http://www.newsweek.com/2015/12/25/mars-colonies-rich-people-404681.html (accessed 30/12/2017).

Manturana, Humberto and F. Varela (1980), *Autopoiesis and Cognition*, Dordrecht: D. Reidel Publishing Company.

Marin, Louis (1990), *Utopics: The Semiological Play of Textual Spaces*, trans. R. A. Vollrath, Atlantic Highlands, NJ: Humanities Press International.

Marks, Elaine and I. de Coutrivon (1980), *New French Feminisms*, Hemel Hempstead: Harvester.

Meillassoux Quentin (2008), *After Finitude: An Essay on the Necessity of Contingency*, trans. R. Brassier, London and New York: Continuum.

— (2011), 'Metaphysics and Extro-Science Fiction', *Speculative Solution*, ed. R. Mackay, Falmouth: Urbanomic, pp. 24–60.

— (2015), *Science Fiction and Extro-Science Fiction*, trans. A. Edlebi, Minneapolis: Univocal.

Mellor, David Allen (2012), *The Bruce Lacey Experience: Paintings, Sculptures, Installations, Performances*, London: Camden Arts Centre.

Metz, Cade (2016), 'In Two Moves AlphaGo and Lee Sedol Redefined the Future', *Wired*, March, http://www.wired.com/2016/03/two-moves-alphago-lee-sedol-redefined-future (accessed 15/4/2016).

Metzinger, Thomas (2003), *Being No One: The Self-Model Theory of Subjectivity*, Cambridge, MA: MIT Press.

— (2009), *The Ego Tunnel: The Science of the Mind and the Myth of the Self*, New York: Basic Books.

— (2014), 'First-order Embodiment, Second-order Embodiment, Third-order Embodiment', *The Routledge Handbook of Embodied Cognition*, ed. L. Shapiro, Oxford: Routledge, pp. 272–86.

Michaux, Henri (2002), *Miserable Miracle: Mescaline*, trans. L. Varèse and A. Moschovakis, New York: New York Review of Books.

Michener, Leo (2015a), *Klavikon: Rise of the Machines*, Interview for *Attack Magazine*, https://www.attackmagazine.com/features/long-read/rise-of-the-machines-klavikon (accessed 15/4/2016).

— (2015b), 'This is My Machine: Leon Michener Makes Techno on a Piano', Interview for *Vice*, https://thump.vice.com/en_uk/article/this-is-my-machine-leon-michener-makes-techno-on-a-piano (accessed 15/4/2016).

Moorcock, Michael (1964), 'A New Literature for the Space Age', *New Worlds* 142, http://realitystudio.org/criticism/a-new-literature-for-the-space-age (accessed 3/4/2012).

— (2015), '*The Vorrh* by B. Catling, Review', *The Guardian*, 20 May, https://www.theguardian.com/books/2015/may/20/the-vorrh-b-Catling-review-michael-moorcock (accessed 3/7/2017).

Moore, Alan (2012), 'Foreword', B. Catling, *The Vorrh*, London: Honest Publishing, pp. v–viii.

Moravec, H. (1992), 'Pigs in Cyberspace', *Thinking Robots, an Aware Internet and Cyberpunk Librarians: The 1992 LITA President's Program*, ed. B. Miller and M. Wolf, Chicago: American Library Association Editions, pp. 15–21, https://www.frc.ri.cmu.edu/~hpm/project.archive/general.articles/1992/CyberPigs.html (accessed 3/4/2017).

More, Thomas (1994), *Utopia*, London: Everyman.

Morton, Arthur Leslie (1978), *The English Utopia*, London: Lawrence and Wishart Ltd.

Moten, Fred (2003), *In the Break: The Aesthetics of the Black Radical Tradition*, Minneapolis: University of Minnesota Press.

— (2015), Interview with Adam Fitzgerald, http://lithub.com/an-interview-with-fred-moten-pt-i (accessed 15/4/2016).

Mullarkey, John (2006), *Post-Continental Philosophy: An Outline*, London: Continuum.

Müller, Christopher John (2016), *Prometheanism: Technology, Digital Culture and Human Obsolescence*, London: Rowan and Littlefield International Ltd.

Nauha, Tero (2016), *Schizoproduction: Artistic Research and Performance in the Context of Immanent Capitalism*, Helsinki: University of the Arts.

Negarestani, Reza (2008), *Cyclonopedia: Complicity with Anonymous Materials*, Melbourne: re.press.

— (2011a), 'Globe of Revolution: An Afterthought on Geophilosophical Realism', *Identities: Journal of Politics, Gender and Culture*, 8.2: 25–54.

— (2011b), 'Drafting the Inhuman: Conjectures on Capitalism and Organic Necrocracy', *The*

Speculative Turn: Continental Materialism and Realism, ed. L. Bryant, N. Srnicek and G. Harman, Melbourne: re.press, pp. 182–201.

— (2011c), 'Contingency and Complicity', *The Medium of Contingency*, ed. R. Mackay, Falmouth: Urbanomic, pp. 11–18.

— (2014a), 'The Labour of the Inhuman', *#Accelerate: The Accelerationist Reader*, ed. R. Mackay and A. Avanessian, Falmouth: Urbanomic, pp. 427–66.

— (2014b), *Torture Concrete: Jean-Luc Moulène and the Protocol of Abstraction*, New York: Sequence Press.

Negri, Antonio (2014), 'Some Reflections on the #Accelerate Manifesto', *#Accelerate: The Accelerationist Reader*, ed. R. Mackay and A. Avanessian, Falmouth: Urbanomic, pp. 365–78.

Neidich, Warren (2013), 'Computational Architecture and the Statisticon', *The Psychopathologies of Cognitive Capitalism Part II*, ed. W. Neidich, Berlin: Archive Books, pp. 355–68.

Nelson, Mike (2000), *Extinction Beckons*, London: Matts Gallery.

— (2001), *Forgotten Kingdom*, ed. Will Bradley, London: ICA.

— (2003), *Magazine*, London: Book Works and Matt's Gallery.

Nelson, Mike and J. Rogers (2003), 'Mike Nelson interviewed by John Rogers', *Fused*, 2 July, p. 21.

Nelson, Mike and W. Bradley (2003), *Mike Nelson interviewed by Will Bradley*, London: Book Works.

Nietzsche, Friedrich (1974), *The Gay Science*, trans. W. Kaufmann, New York: Vintage Books.

Noys, Ben (2012), *The Persistence of the Negative: A Critique of Contemporary Continental Theory*, Edinburgh: Edinburgh University Press.

Old Boy Network (1997), '100 anti-theses', http://www.obn.org/cfundef/100antitheses.html (accessed 28/11/2017).

Ó Maoilearca, John (2015), *All Thoughts are Equal: Laruelle and Nonhuman Philosophy*, Minneapolis: University of Minnesota Press.

Ó Maoilearca, John and A. P. Smith (2012), 'Introduction: The Non-Philosophical Inversion: Laruelle's Knowledge Without Domination', *Laruelle and Non-Philosophy*, ed. J. Mullarkey and A-P. Smith, Edinburgh: Edinburgh University Press, pp. 1–18.

Omohundro, Steve (2014), 'Autonomous Technology and the Greater Human Good', *Journal of Experimental & Theoretical Artificial Intelligence*, 26.3: 303–15.

Oneohtrix Point Never (2011), 'Mixtape: Oneohtrix Point Never', Interview with T. Malmgren, *Bomb Magazine*, http://bombmagazine.org/article/6175/mixtape-oneohtrix-point-never (accessed 1/5/2017).

— (2015), 'Powers of Horror: Oneohtrix Point Never', Interview with K. Smith, *The Quietus*, http://thequietus.com/articles/18922-oneohtrix-point-never-garden-of-delete-interview (accessed 1/5/2017).

0[rphan] d[rift>] (2012 [1996]), *Cyberpositive*, London: Cabinet Gallery.

O'Sullivan, Simon (2006a), *Art Encounters Deleuze and Guattari: Thought Beyond Representation*, Basingstoke: Palgrave.

— (2006b), 'Contours and Case Studies for a Dissenting Subjectivity (or, How to Live Creatively in a Fearful World)' (co-written with Ola Stahl), *Angelaki*, 11.1: 147–56.

— (2010), 'Guattari's Aesthetic Paradigm: From the Folding of the Finite/Infinite Relation to Schizoanalytic Metamodelisation', *Deleuze Studies*, 4.2: 256–86.

— (2011), 'Performance Fictions: Towards a Mythopoetic Art Practice', *Performance Fictions, Art–Writing–Research: Vol. 3*, ed. D. Burrows, Birmingham: Article Press, 71–80.

— (2012), *On the Production of Subjectivity: Five Diagrams of the Finite-Infinite Relation*, Basingstoke: Palgrave.

— (2013), 'A Diagram of the Finite-Infinite Relation: Towards a Bergsonian Production of Subjectivity', *Bergson and the Art of Immanence*, ed. J. Mullarkey and C. De Mille, Edinburgh: Edinburgh University Press, pp. 165–86.

— (2017), 'Accelerationism, Hyperstition and Myth-Science', *Cyclops*, 2: 11–44.

Parisi, Luciana (2004), *Abstract Sex: Philosophy, Bio-Technology and the Mutations of Desire*, London: Continuum.

— (2013), *Contagious Architecture: Computation, Aesthetics, and Space*, Cambridge, MA: MIT Press.

— (2017), 'Automate Sex: Xenofeminism, Hyperstition and Alienation', *Futures and Fictions*, ed. H. Gunkell, A. Hameed and S. O'Sullivan, London: Repeater, pp. 213–30.

Peirce, Charles Sanders (1906), 'Prolegonema for an Apology for Pragmatism', *The Monist*, 16: 492–546.

— (1998), *The Essential Peirce*, Bloomington: Indiana University Press.

Phelan, Peggy (1993), 'The Golden Apple: Jenny Livingstone's Paris is Burning', *Unmarked: The Politics of Performance*, London and New York: Routledge, pp. 93–111.

— (2000), 'After Mourning Sex', *Making a Scene*, ed. D. Burrows and H. Rogers, Birmingham: Article Press, pp. 127–38.

Plant, Sadie (1992), *The Most Radical Gesture: The Situationist International in a Postmodern Age*, London: Routledge.

— (1997), *Zeros and Ones: Digital Women and the New Technoculture*, London: Fourth Estate.

— (2001), *Writing on Drugs*, London: Faber and Faber.

Plastique Fantastique (2016), 'Plastique Fantastique Review of the Kibbo Kift: Seven Celebrations/Seven Critiques/Seven Parallels', *Visual Culture in Britain*, 2 August, http://www.tandfonline.com/doi/full/10.1080/14714787.2016.1205305 (accessed 21/11/2016).

Pleij, Herman (2001), *Dreaming of Cockaigne*, trans. D. Webb, New York: Columbia University Press.

Pohl, Frederik (1976), *Man Plus*, London: Victor Gollancz.

Pollen, Annebella (2015), *The Kindred of the Kibbo Kift*, London: Donlon Books.

P-Orridge, Genesis Breyer (1992), 'Behavioural Cut-Ups and Magick', *Rapid Eye 2*, ed. S. Dwyer, London: Annihilation Press, pp. 127–34.

— (2009a), 'Magick Squares and Future Beats: The Magickal Process and Methods of William S. Burroughs and Brion Gysin', *Thee Psychick Bible: Thee Apocryphal Scriptures*, Port Townsend: Feral House, pp. 275–98.

— (2009b), 'The Process is thee Produkt', *Thee Psychick Bible: Thee Apocryphal Scriptures*, Port Townsend: Feral House, pp. 401–31.

P-Orridge, Genesis Breyer and P. Christopherson (1982), 'Psychick TV Interview', *Riverside*, BBC2, https://www.youtube.com/watch?v=jjssKDFlBZM (accessed 24/9/16).

Preciado, Paul B. (2013), *Testo Junkie: Sex, Drugs, and Biopolitics in the Pharmacopornographic Era*, trans. B. Benderson, New York: The Feminist Press.

Price, Seth (2017), *Seth Price*, ed. B. Ruf and A. Hochdoffer, Amsterdam: Stadelik Museum.

Rammellzee (1979), 'IONIC TREATISE GOTHIC FUTURISM ASSASSIN KNOWLEDGE OF THE REMANIPULATE SQUARE POINTS', https://web.archive.org/web/20110604014121/http://www.gothicfuturism.com/rammellzee/01.html (accessed 4/10/17).

Reed, Patricia (2014), 'Seven Prescriptions for Accelerationism', *#Accelerate: The Accelerationist Reader*, ed. R. Mackay and A. Avanessian, Falmouth: Urbanomic, pp. 523–36.

Reeves-Evison, Theo (2017), 'Surface Fictions', *Futures and Fictions*, ed. H. Gunkell, A. Hameed and S. O'Sullivan, London: Repeater, pp. 295–317.

Reynolds, Simon (1999), *Wreckers of Civilization*, London: Black Dog.

Roberts, Maggie (n.d.), artist's website, http://merliquify.com (accessed 24/9/2016).

Robin Hood website (n.d.), http://www.robinhoodcoop.org/DEMOCRATIZING_THE_POWER_OF_FINANCE (accessed 13/9/2016).

Rogoff Irit and B. Stiegler (2010), 'Transindividuation', *e-flux*, http://www.e-flux.com/journal/transindividuation (accessed 15/4/2016).

Rose, Rachel (2015), *Palisades*, ed. E. Enderby, A. Cryczkowska and M. Larner, London: Koenig Books/Serpentine Books.

Rose, Rachel and A. Nash (2015), Interview with Rachel Rose, *Bomb Magazine*, 133, http://bombmagazine.org/article/8919825/rachel-rose (accessed 30/4/2017).

Rose, Rachel and C. Burns (2015), Interview with Rachel Rose, *The Guardian*, 26 October, https://www.theguardian.com/artanddesign/2015/oct/26/rachel-rose-artist-gravity-space-whitney-museum (accessed 30/4/2017).

Rourke, Daniel (2014), 'Please Don't Call Me Unhappy: Cécile B. Evans at Seventeen Gallery', *Rhizome*, 4 December, http://rhizome.org/editorial/2014/dec/4/please-dont-call-me-uncanny-hyperlinks-seventeen-g (accessed 15/7/2017).

Roussel, Raymond (1995), *How I Wrote Certain of my Books*, ed. T. Winkfield, trans. T. Winkfield, H. Matthews, J. Ashbury and K. Koch, Cambridge, MA: Exact Change.

— (2011), *Impressions of Africa*, ed. T. Winkfield, trans. L. Foord and R. Happenstall, Cambridge: London: One World Classics Ltd.

Rudolf Eb.er (2014), Interview by Asha Sheshadri in *Tiny Mix Tapes*, October, http://tinymix-tapes.tumblr.com/post/99643886624/interview-rudolf-eber (accessed 10/5/2017).

Rudrauf, David and A. Lutz, D. Cosmelli, J-P. Lachaux and M. Le Van Quyen (2003), 'From Autopoiesis to Neurophenomenology: Francisco Varela's Exploration of Biophysics of Being', *Biol Res*, 36: 21–59.

Russell, John (ed.) (2005–7), *Frozen Tears, Volumes 1–3*, Birmingham: Article Press.

— (2009), 'Faerie Poem', *The Dark Monarch: Magic & Modernity in British Art*, ed. A. Rowlands, M. Bracewell and M. Clark, London and St Ives: Tate Publishing, 2009, p. 143.

— (2011a), 'A Largely Intolerable Combination of Two Mainly Unconnected Texts: 1. Description of the Barefoot in the Head event, at BHQU, NY, 12 November 2009; 2. Fictioning and the End', *Barefoot in the Head*, ed. M. Beasley, A. Rowlands and J. Russell, Birmingham: Article Press, pp. 68–85.

— (2011b), 'Dear Living Person', *Metamute*, 11 February, http://www.metamute.org/editorial/articles/dear-living-person (accessed 24/11/2016).

— (2011c), 'Dear Living Person II: Story of the Eyes', *Metamute*, 14 September, http://www.metamute.org/editorial/articles/dear-living-person-ii-story-eyes (accessed 24/11/2016).

— (2012a), 'Autonomy is Not Worth the Paper it is Written On: Writing. Written. Art-Writing. Art. Writing', *Again, A Time Machine: From Distribution to Archive*, ed. G. Everall and J. Rolo, London: Book Works, pp. 162–74.

— (2012b), 'Jexus', *Metamute*, 28 August, http://www.metamute.org/editorial/articles/jexus (accessed 24/9/2016).

— (2014a), 'Abysmal Plan: Waiting Until We Die and Radically Accelerated Repetitionism', *e-flux*, http://www.e-flux.com/journal/46/60096/abysmal-plan-waiting-until-we-die-and-radically-accelerated-repetitionism (accessed 24/9/2016).

— (2014b), 'Bruce Willis, Irigaray and the Aesthetics of Space Travel', *Metamute*, 5 December, http://www.metamute.org/editorial/articles/bruce-willis-irigaray-and-aesthetics-space-travel (accessed 24/9/2016).

— (2015), 'SQRRL', https://www.bridgetdonahue.nyc/exhibitions/john-russell (accessed 24/9/2016).

Russell, John and C. Soren (2016), 'Custom-Produced for Imbeciles of Some Sort: An Interview with John Russell', *rhizome.org*, http://rhizome.org/editorial/2015/apr/15/custom-produced-imbeciles-some-sort-interview-john (accessed 24/9/2016).

Ryman, Geoff et al. (2004), 'The Mundane Manifesto', https://sfgenics.wordpress.com/2013/07/04/geoff-ryman-et-al-the-mundane-manifesto (accessed 6/10/2017).

Said, Edward (2003), 'An Interview with Edward Said', Interview with C. Katz and N. Smith, *Environment and Planning D: Society and Space*, 21: 635–51.

Saldanha, Arun (2017), *Space After Deleuze*, London: Bloomsbury.

Salmon, Felix (2014), 'Jeff Koons: A Master Innovator Turning Money into Art', *The Guardian*, 3 July, https://www.theguardian.com/artanddesign/2014/jul/03/jeff-koons-master-innovator-whitney-money-art (accessed 15/7/2017).

Sames, Lucy R. (2014), *Sci-Fi Paganism*, London: Enclave.

Sandifer, Elizabeth (2017), *Neoreaction a Basilisk: Essays on and Around the Alt-Right*, Eurditorum Press.

Satterwhite, Jacolby and C. Ross (2014), 'Interview: Whitney Biennale 14', https://charlierose.com/videos/16971 (accessed 13/9/2016).

Satterwhite, Jacolby and E. Moffitt (2016), 'Interview: Body Talk', *Frieze*, https://frieze.com/article/body-talk-0 (accessed 13/9/2016).

Satterwhite, Jacolby and R. Small (2014), Interview with Rachel Small, *Interview Magazine*, November, http://www.interviewmagazine.com/art/15-faces-of-2015-jacolby-satterwhite# (accessed 1/5/2017).

Savat, David (2009), 'Deleuze's Objectile: From Discipline to Modulation, *Deleuze and New Technology*, ed. D. Savat and M. Poster, Edinburgh: Edinburgh University Press.

Schilling, Malte and H. Cruse (2008), 'The Evolution of Cognition – From First Order to Second Order Embodiment', *Modeling Communication with Robots and Virtual Humans*, ed. I. Wachsmuth and G. Knoblich, Berlin: Heidelberg: Springer, pp. 77–108.

Schmid, Anne-Françoise (n.d.), 'The Madonna on the Craters of the Moon: An Aesthetic Epistemology', *Urbanomic Documents*, https://www.urbanomic.com/document/the-madonna-on-the-craters-of-the-moon-an-aesthetic-epistemology (accessed 4/4/2017).

Schneeman, Carolee (2002), *Imaging Her Erotics*, Cambridge, MA: MIT Press.

— (2013), 'In Conversation and in Review: The Underestimated Carolee Schneemann' (with Joseph Henry), *Blouinartinfo*, http://www.blouinartinfo.com/news/story/893207/in-conversation-and-in-review-the-underestimated-carolee (accessed 23/11/2017).

Schreber, Daniel Paul (2000), *Memoirs of my Nervous Illness*, ed. and trans. I. MacAlpine and R. A. Hunter, New York: New York Review of Books.

Schreckinger, Ben (2017), 'World War Meme', *Politico Magazine*, http://www.politico.com/magazine/story/2017/03/memes-4chan-trump-supporters-trolls-internet-214856 (accessed 18/5/2017).

Schwabsky, Barry (2012), 'The Stone Dies Away Also: On Jimmie Durham', *The Nation*, 22 August, https://www.thenation.com/article/stone-dies-away-also-jimmie-durham (accessed 24/12/2017).

Shani, Tai (2016), *Dark Continent – Mnemesoid*, artist's text.

Shaviro, Steven (2005), review of Stenger's *Cosmopolitics*, blog post, http://www.shaviro.com/Blog/?p=401 (accessed 19/11/2017).

— (2010), *Post Cinematic Affect*, Ropley, Hants: Zero Books.

— (2011), 'Hyperbolic Futures: Speculative Finance and Speculative Fiction', *The Cascadia Subduction Zone*, 1.2: 3–5 and 12–15.

— (2015), *Discognition*, London: Repeater Books.

Shaw, Jon K. (2016), 'The Life of an Idiot: Artaud and the Dogmatic Image of Thought after Deleuze', *Theory, Culture and Society*, 33.7–8: 237–52.

— (2017), 'Subjectility: On Reading Artaud', PhD thesis, Goldsmiths, University of London.

Silverstein, T. (1967), 'Allegory and Literary Form', *P Modern Language Association*, 82.1: 28–32.

Simondon, Gilbert (2011 [1958]), 'On the Mode of Existence of Technical Objects' (extract), trans. N. Mellamphy, D. Mellamphy and N. B. Mellamphy, *Deleuze Studies*, 5.3: 407–24.

— (2012), 'Technical Mentality', *Gilbert Simondon: Being and Technology*, ed. A. De Boever, A. Murray, J. Roffe and A. Woodward, trans. A. De Boever, Edinburgh: Edinburgh University Press, pp. 1–15.

Sinclair, Iain (ed.) (1996), *Conductors of Chaos: A Poetry Anthology*, London: Picador.

— (1997), *Lights Out for the Territory*, London: Granta.

Singleton, Benedict (2014), 'Maximum Jailbreak', *#Accelerate: The Accelerationist Reader*, ed. R. Mackay and A. Avanessian, Falmouth: Urbanomic, pp. 491–507.

Sleeman, Joy (2016), 'The Impossibility of an Island', in S. Faithfull, *Does the World Exist, When I'm Not There?*, Potsdam: Laconic.

Smith, Anthony Paul (2016), *Francois Laruelle's* Principles of Non-Philosophy: *A Critical Introduction and Guide*, Edinburgh: Edinburgh University Press.

Smith, Tom (2009), Interview for Truevinerecordshop, http://www.thetruevinerecordshop.com/tom%20smith%20interview%20info.htm (accessed 10/5/2017).

Smithson, Robert (1969), 'Hotel Palenque', slides and audio, Palenque, Mexico, held at Solomon R. Guggenheim Museum, New York.

— (1996a), *Robert Smithson: The Collected Writings*, ed. J. Flam, Berkeley and Los Angeles: University of California Press.

— (1996b), 'Interpolation of the Enantiomorphic Chambers (1966)', *Robert Smithson: The Collected Writings*, ed. J. Flam, Berkeley: University of California Press, pp. 39–40.

— (1996c), 'Incidents of Mirror Travel in the Yucatan', *Robert Smithson: The Collected Writings*, ed. J. Flam, Berkeley: University of California Press, pp. 119–33.

— (1996d), 'Spiral Jetty', *Robert Smithson: The Collected Writings*, ed. J. Flam, Berkeley: University of California Press, pp. 143–53.

— (1996e), 'The Crystal Land (1966)', *Robert Smithson: The Collected Writings*, ed. J. Flam, Berkeley: University of California Press, pp. 7–9.

— (1996f), 'Entropy and the New Monuments (1966)', *Robert Smithson: The Collected Writings*, ed. J. Flam, Berkeley: University of California Press, pp. 10–23.

— (1996g), 'Sedimentations of the Mind: Earth Projects (1968)', *Robert Smithson: The Collected Writings*, ed. J. Flam, Berkeley: University of California Press, pp. 100–13.

— (1996h), 'A Tour of the Monuments of Passaic, New Jersey (1967)', *Robert Smithson: The Collected Writings*, ed. J. Flam, Berkeley: University of California Press, pp. 68–74.

Soyinka, Wole (2012), *Of Africa*, New Haven and London: Yale University Press.

— (2014), 'Introduction: Sea Never Dry, Wine Never Dry', in Amos Tutuola, *The Palm-Wine Drinkard: And His Dead Palm-Wine Tapster in the Dead's Town*, London: Faber and Faber, pp. v–viii.

Spare, Austin Osman (2007a), 'The Focus of Life', *The Writings of Austin Spare*, Sioux Falls: Nu Vision, pp. 23–60.

— (2007b), 'The Book of Pleasure (Self-Love)', *The Writings of Austin Spare*, Sioux Falls: Nu Vision, pp. 61–93.

Spinoza, Benedict de (1996), *Ethics*, ed. and trans. E. Curley, London: Penguin.

Spivak, Gayatri Chakravorty (1985), 'Three Women's Texts and a Critique of Imperialism', *Critical Inquiry*, 12.1: 243–61.

Srnicek, Nick (2011), 'Capitalism and the Non-Philosophical Subject', *The Speculative Turn: Continental Materialism and Realism*, ed. L. Bryant, N. Srnicek and G. Harman, Melbourne, re.press, pp. 164–81.

Srnicek, Nick and A. Williams, (2014a), 'On Cunning Automata', *Collapse*, 8: 463–506.

— (2014b), 'Accelerate: Manifesto for an Accelerationist Politics', ed. R. Mackay and A. Avanessian, *#Accelerate: The Accelerationist Reader*, Falmouth: Urbanomic, pp. 349–78.

Stallybrass, Peter and A. White (1986), *The Politics and Poetics of Transgression*, New York: Cornell University Press.

Starhawk (1993), *The Fifth Sacred Thing*, New York: Bantam.

Statkiewicz, Max (2009), *Rhapsody of Philosophy: Dialogues with Plato in Contemporary Thought*, University Park, PA: Pennsylvania State University Press.

Stelarc (n.d.), artist's website, http://stelarc.org/?catID=20265 (accessed 7/5/2017).

Stengers, Isabelle (2005), 'The Cosmopolitical Proposal', *Making Things Public: Atmospheres of Democracy*, ed. B. Latour and P. Weibel, Cambridge, MA: MIT Press, pp. 994–1003.

— (2010), *Cosmopolitics I*, trans. R. Bononno, Minneapolis: Minnesota University Press.

— (2011), *Cosmopolitics II*, trans. R. Bononno, Minneapolis: Minnesota University Press.

— (2012), 'Reclaiming Animism', *e-flux*, http://www.e-flux.com/journal/36/61245/reclaiming-animism (accessed 1/12/2016).

— (2013), 'Matters of Cosmopolitics: On the Provocations of Gaïa: Isabelle Stengers in Conversation with Heather Davis and Etienne Turpin', https://quod.lib.umich.edu/o/ohp/12527215.0001.001/1:19/--architecture-in-the-anthropocene-encounters-among-design?rgn=div1;view=fulltext (accessed 10/2/2017).

Stephenson, Neal (2009), *Anathem*, London: Atlantic Books.

— (1996), *The Diamond Age*, London: Penguin.

Steyerl, Hito (2012), 'In Defense of the Poor Image', *The Wretched of the Screen*, Berlin: Sternberg Press, pp. 31–45

Stiegler, Bernard (2012), 'Relational Ecology and the Digital Pharmakon', *Culture Machine*, 13, http://www.culturemachine.net/index.php/cm/article/view/464 (accessed 15/4/2016).

— (2013a), *Technics and Time 3: Cinematic Time and the Question of Malaise*, Stanford: Stanford University Press.

— (2013b), 'Interview for Culture and Education', http://frenchculture.org/books/blog/interview-bernard-stiegler (accessed 15/4/2016).

— (2015), *States of Shock: Stupidity and Knowledge in the 21st Century*, Cambridge: Polity Press.

Strathern, Marilyn (1988), *The Gender of the Gift*, Berkeley and Los Angeles: University of California Press.

Strugatsky, Arkady and B. Strugatsky (2000), *Roadside Picnic*, London: Gollancz.

Syms, Martine (2013), 'The Mundane Afrofuturist the Manifesto', *Rhizome*, http://rhizome.org/editorial/2013/dec/17/mundane-afrofuturist-manifesto (accessed 1/2/2016).

— (2014), 'Vernacular Lessons of the Tradition', talk given at the Walker Art Centre, http://martinesyms.com/black-vernacular-lessons-of-the-tradition (accessed 27/6/2017).

— (2016a), 'Martine Syms at the ICA: People Act Like Art is a White Thing', Interview by Eliza Anyangwe, *The Guardian*, 9 May, https://www.theguardian.com/artanddesign/2016/may/09/martine-syms-fact-and-trouble-ica-art-not-most-effective-protest (accessed 27/6/2017).

— (2016b), Interview by Dayla Benor, *Dazed and Confused*, http://www.dazeddigital.com/artsandculture/article/30820/1/martine-syms-on-la-coming-offline-and-the-language-of-pop (accessed 27/6/2017).

— (2016c), 'Martine Syms: Fact & Trouble', Interview, https://www.youtube.com/watch?v=Ftc-cjNnTvP4 (accessed 27/6/2017).

— (2016d), 'Deconstructing African Identity into Axioms, Photos and Colors', Interview by Grace Linden, *Hyperallergic*, https://hyperallergic.com/305146/deconstructing-african-american-identity-into-axioms-photos-and-colors (accessed 27/6/2017).

Szwed, John F. (2000), *Space is the Place: The Life and Times of Sun Ra*, Edinburgh: MOJO Books.

Tanz, Jason (2016), 'The End of Code', *Wired*, May 2016, http://www.wired.com/2016/05/the-end-of-code (accessed 12/6/2018).

Tardio, Andres (2013), 'Keep it Real: Hip Hop's Changing Views on Authenticity', *Hip Hop DX*, http://hiphopdx.com/editorials/title/keep-it-real (accessed 30/12/2017).

Taylor, Charles (2004), *Modern Social Imaginaries*, Durham, NC: Duke University Press.

Tegmark, M. (2017), *Life 3.0: Being Human in the Age of Artificial Intelligence*, London: Allen Lane.

Terkla, Dan (2010), 'The Original Placement of the Hereford Mappa Mundi', *Imago Mundi: The International Journal for the History of Cartography*, 56:2 131–51.

The Confraternity of Neoflagellants (N. Hogg and N. Mulholland) (2013), *thN Lng folk 2go: Investigating Future Premoderns*, New York: Punctum Books.

The Otolith Group (2009), *A Long Time Between Suns*, ed. A. Colin and E. Pethick, Berlin: Sternberg Press.

— (2010), *Turner Prize 2010: The Otolith Group*, promotional film, http://www.tate.org.uk/context-comment/video/turner-prize-2010-otolith-group (accessed 28/1/2018).

— (2017), artist's website, www.otolithgroup.org (accessed 4/10/2017).

Thoburn, Nick (2016), *Anti-Book: On the Art and Politics of Radical Publishing*, Minneapolis: University of Minnesota Press.

Thomas, Jennet (2015a), *The Unspeakable Freedom Device*, London: Book Works.

— (2015b), artist's website, https://jennetthomas.wordpress.com/videos/the-unspeakable-freedom-device (accessed 1/5/2017).

Thompson, John B. (1982), 'Ideology and the Social Imaginary: An Appraisal of Castoriadis and Lefort', *Theory and Society*, 11.5: 659–81.

Tilford, Keith (2017), 'Generalised Transformations and Technologies of Investigation: Laruelle, Art and the Scientific Model', *Superpositions: Laruelle and the Humanities*, ed. R. Gangle and J. Greve, London: Rowman and Littlefield, pp. 139–56.

Tiqqun (2001), *The Cybernetic Hypothesis*, manifesto published online, http://theanarchistlibrary.org/library/tiqqun-the-cybernetic-hypothesis (accessed 1/3/2015).

TOPYNA (Thee Temple ov Psychick Youth North America) (2009), 'Television Magick', *Thee Psychick Bible: Thee Apocryphal Scriptures*, Port Townsend: Feral House, pp. 162–76.

Trecartin, Ryan (2011), 'Ryan Trecartin: in Conversation', with K. Kiamura and H. Kunzru, *Frieze*, https://www.frieze.com/article/ryan-trecartin-conversation (accessed 23/4/2016).

— (2013), 'In the Studio: Ryan Trecartin', Interview with Sarah Lehrer-Graiwer, *Art in America*, June, http://www.artinamericamagazine.com/news-features/magazine/in-the-studio-ryan-trecartin (accessed 1/5/2017).

— (2016), Interview with S. Lehrer-Graiwer, *Bomb Magazine*, 135, http://bombmagazine.org/article/6018229/ryan-trecartin (accessed 1/5/2017).

Treister, Suzanne (2016), *HFT The Gardener*, London: Annely Juda Fine Art.

Tutti, Cosey Fanni (2017), *Art Sex Music*, London: Faber and Faber.

Tutuola, Amos (2014), *The Palm-Wine Drinkard: And His Dead Palm-Wine Tapster in the Dead's Town*, London: Faber and Faber.

Varela, Francisco (1996), 'Neurophenomenology: A Methodological Remedy for a Hard Problem', *Journal of Consciousness Studies*, 3.4: 330–50.

Varela, Francisco, E. Rosch and E. Thompson (1991), *The Embodied Mind: Cognitive Science and Human Experience*, Cambridge, MA: MIT Press.

Viveiros de Castro, Eduardo (2014), *Cannibal Metaphysics*, trans. P. Skafish, Minneapolis: Univocal.

VNS Matrix (1991), *The Cyberfeminist Manifesto for the 21st Century*, https://vnsmatrix.net (accessed 5/11/2017).

— (2016a), 'A Tender Hex for the Anthropocene', http://www.runway.org.au/32/tenderhex/hextextstripped.pdf (accessed 5/11/2017).

— (2016b), 'The Cyberfeminists Who Called Themselves "The Future Cunt"', Interview by Evlyn Wang, *Dazed and Confused*, November, http://www.dazeddigital.com/artsandculture/article/33703/1/cyberfeminist-manifesto-technology-vns-matrix (accessed 5/11/2017).

Wagner, Roy (1981), *The Invention of Culture*, Chicago: University of Chicago Press.

— (2010), *Coyote Anthropology*, Nebraska: Nebraska University Press.

Wark, McKenzie (2016), *Molecular Red: Theory for the Anthropocene*, London: Verso.

Watkins, Alfred (1974), *The Old Straight Track: Its Mounds, Beacons, Moats, Sites and Mark Stones*, London: Abacus.

Watts, Peter (2006), *Blindsight*, New York: Tor.

— (2009), *Vampires: Biology and Evolution*, website, http://www.rifters.com/blindsight/vampires.htm (accessed 1/1/2017).

— (2010), 'God, Jackboots and Rule 34 OR How Pornography Could Save the World', lecture for the 'Toronto Specfic Colloquium', https://www.youtube.com/watch?v=pP636p5mWwc (accessed 1/1/2017).

— (2014), *Firefall*, London: Head of Zeus Ltd.

Weizman, Eyal (2007), *Hollow Land: Israel's Architecture of Occupation*, London and New York: Verso.

Whitehead, Alfred N. (1995), *Process and Reality*, ed. D. R. Griffin and D. W. Sherburne, New York: The Free Press, Simon and Schuster Inc.

Wiener, Norbert (1989), *The Human Use of Human Beings: Cybernetics and Society*, London: Free Association Press.

Wilcken, Patrick (2010), *Claude Lévi-Strauss*, London: Bloomsbury.

Williams, Alex (2013), 'Escape Velocities', *e-flux*, http://www.e-flux.com/journal/46/60063/escape-velocities (accessed 16/3/2018).

Williams, Arnold (1969), 'Medieval Allegory: An Operational Approach', *The Bulletin of the Midwest Modern Language Association*, 2.1: 77–84.

Williams, Dana A. (2016), 'Racial Mythologies, Neoliberal Seductions, and the Fictioning of Blackness: An SOS from "Old Lem"', *American Literary History*, 28.4: 835–44.

Williams, Raymond (1977), *Marxism and Literature*, Oxford: Oxford University Press.

— (1978), 'Utopia and Science Fiction', *Science Fiction Studies*, 5.3: 203–14.

— (1980), 'Base and Superstructure in Marxist Cultural Theory', *Problems in Materialism and Culture: Selected Essays*, London: Verso, pp. 31–49.

— (1988), 'Science Fiction', *Science Fiction Studies*, 15.3: 356–60.

Wittig, Monique (1971), *Les Guérillères*, London: Peter Owen.

Wjacman, Judy (2004), *TechnoFeminism*, Cambridge: Polity Press.

Wolfendale, Peter (2016), 'Prometheanism and Rationalism', talk at Goldsmiths College, 5 May, https://deontologistics.wordpress.com/2016/08/20/prometheanism-and-rationalism (accessed 5/5/2017).

Names Index

Subject Index

EU representative:
Easy Access System Europe
Mustamäe tee 50, 10621 Tallinn, Estonia
Gpsr.requests@easproject.com

www.ingramcontent.com/pod-product-compliance
Lightning Source LLC
Chambersburg PA
CBHW081308170526

45166CB00011B/3451